ERMENGARD
OF NARBONNE
AND THE WORLD OF THE
TROUBADOURS

A VOLUME IN THE SERIES
Conjunctions of Religion and Power in the Medieval Past
Edited by Barbara H. Rosenwein

A full list of titles in the series appears at the end of the book.

ERMENGARD
OF NARBONNE
AND THE WORLD OF THE
TROUBADOURS

FREDRIC L. CHEYETTE

Cornell University Press
Ithaca and London

First published 2001 by Cornell University Press
First printing, Cornell Paperbacks, 2004

Printed in the United States of America

Library of Congress Cataloging-in-Publication Data

Cheyette, Fredric L.
    Ermengard of Narbonne and the world of the troubadours / Fredric L. Cheyette.
        p. cm. — (Conjunctions of religion & power in the medieval past)
    Includes bibliographical references and index.
    ISBN 0-8014-3952-3 (cloth : alk. paper)
    ISBN 0-8014-8925-3 (pbk. : alk. paper)
    1. Ermengarde, vicomtesse de Narbonne, 1127?–1196? 2. Narbonne (France)—Kings and rulers—Biography. 3. Narbonne (France)—History. 4. Troubadours—France—Narbonne.   I. Title. II. Series.
    DC611.N219 C48 2001
    944'.87—dc21

2001002626

Cornell University Press strives to use environmentally responsible suppliers and materials to the fullest extent possible in the publishing of its books. Such materials include vegetable-based, low-VOC inks and acid-free papers that are recycled, totally chlorine-free, or partly composed of nonwood fibers. Books that bear the logo of the FSC (Forest Stewardship Council) use paper taken from forests that have been inspected and certified as meeting the highest standards for environmental and social responsibility. For further information, visit our website at www.cornellpress.cornell.edu.

Cloth printing   10 9 8 7 6 5 4 3 2 1
Paperback printing   10 9 8 7 6 5 4 3 2 1

CONTENTS

Maps *ix*
Genealogies *x*
Preface *xi*
A Note on Money, Weights, and Measures *xv*

Introduction *1*
Chapter 1. The Viscountess Comes of Age *14*

ERMENGARD'S CITY

Preface *39*
Chapter 2. Names and Titles, Histories and Myths *41*
Chapter 3. The Urban Marketplace *54*
Chapter 4. City and Countryside *66*
Chapter 5. Cities of Mammon, Cities of Mars *80*
Chapter 6. The Bishop in the City *103*

THE SINEWS OF POWER: LORDSHIP AND SERFDOM

Preface *127*
Chapter 7. Lordship *129*
Chapter 8. Serfdom and the Dues of Domination *149*
Chapter 9. Ermengard's Entourage *168*

THE SINEWS OF POWER: THE CULTURE OF FIDELITY

Chapter 10. Oaths and Oath Takers *187*
Chapter 11. Anger, Conflict, and Reconciliation *199*
Chapter 12. Giving and Taking *220*
Chapter 13. Love and Fidelity *233*

DYNASTIC POLITICS: 1162–1196

Preface *251*
Chapter 14. Raymond V Builds His Empire *253*
Chapter 15. The Ravaging of Occitania *274*
Chapter 16. Sowing the Seeds of Crusade *286*
Chapter 17. A War Like an Omen *308*
Chapter 18. Impatient Heirs *331*

EPILOGUE

Chapter 19. The Undoing of Occitania *347*

Abbreviations *363*
Notes *365*
Bibliography *441*
Index *463*

MAPS

Occitania   2
Narbonne in Ermengard's time   46
Environs of Narbonne   68
Mill sites   71
Viscounty north of Narbonne   74
Viscounty south of Narbonne   75
Archbishop's castles   112
Castles of William of Alaigne and Raymond of Niort   196
Cathar hierarchy in the early thirteenth century   328

GENEALOGIES

Viscounts of Narbonne   15
Counts of Toulouse   18
Counts of Barcelona and Provence and kings of Aragon   20
Trencavel family   26

PREFACE

During the academic year 1982–83, Margaret Switten, Howell Chickering, and I were assembling materials for a summer institute on Teaching Medieval Civilization, sponsored by the National Endowment for the Humanities. One midwinter day, Margaret called to ask me to put together some translated documents that would illuminate the lives of twelfth-century Occitan women. At her suggestion, I included a few letters that Ermengard of Narbonne addressed to King Louis VII of France and one famous letter he addressed to her. Thus began what would become this book. When the institute was over, I started to enlarge and annotate the collection with a view to publication. I realized that it would need an introduction setting the historical context in which the women acted, and each document would need some notes to explain exactly what it was about. Bit by bit the introduction grew, more documents were added, and the annotations became more elaborate. Slowly, a picture of the society in which these women lived began to emerge from the archival trove I had been collecting since the 1960s. Slowly, Ermengard emerged from the group of women as a subject in her own right.

I began this book as a collection of documents for use in college classes, prepared for teachers in a variety of academic disciplines. The general reader has remained my imagined audience. It has long disturbed me that for the public at large—despite the enormous progress medieval scholarship has made in the twentieth century—the period continues to be summed up in a few general ideas propagated a hundred years or more ago: "a world lit only by fire," suitable for children's stories and fantasy novels, perhaps, but an exotic taste, at best. The point is brought home to me every time I make a new acquaintance. When asked, "What do you do?" I reply, "I'm a medieval historian," and watch the topic of conversation quickly change. The fault, I'm convinced, lies with myself and my colleagues, who have too long addressed our writing only to each other. In this book I try to do otherwise, to share with fellow historians some things I believe may interest them, while at the same time making the period accessible and, I hope, interesting and enjoyable to a larger public. Specialists may wonder why, at certain points, I retell stories that are well known. My response can only be, "Be patient. For some readers these stories are not well known." All of us, in one field of scholarship or another, are general readers.

This book is meant to be read, not consulted. But for those who wish only to see what I have to say about economic and commercial development, those topics (among others) are considered in chapters 3–5; the Gregorian Reform is touched on in chapter 6; my take on the hoary topic of feudalism can be found in chapters 7, 8, and 10–13; troubadour poetry, while cited throughout, I consider in greater detail in chapter 13, the Cathars and the Albigensian Crusades will be found in chapters 16, 17, and 19.

I have made no effort to avoid the magisterial voice that has long been the rhetorical trademark of the historian. I have taught historiography too long, however, to take that voice seriously. On my own behalf I can only quote the words with which the nineteenth-century historian Jacob Burckhardt prefaced his *Civilization of the Renaissance in Italy*, "The same studies which have served for this work might easily, in other hands, not only receive a wholly different treatment, but lead also to essentially different conclusions." On many of the issues treated in this book, other scholars have already reached different conclusions. As much as possible, I have refrained from carrying on controversy with them either in the text or the footnotes. Specialists will immediately recognize where and with whom I disagree. I hope the texts I cite in the footnotes will provide them with sufficient materials to understand why I disagree. Other readers probably will not care.

Over the years I have spent on research and writing I have been favored with the help and kindness of many people—archivists and librarians in Carcassonne, Montpellier, Toulouse, Albi, Nîmes, Perpignan, Marseille, Barcelona, and Paris, many of whom extended me exceptional privileges to expedite my work. Among them I want to recognize Robert Debant in particular, whose care, during many weeks in Carcassonne, included the loan of his substantial collection of *série noire* novels to help me get through long evenings away from my family. The late Jean Claparède, then president of the Société Archéologique de Montpellier allowed me to spend a month reading the Trencavel Cartulary under very favorable conditions. I owe much to many colleagues as well. Jacqueline Caille spent eighteen months negotiating my access to the Trencavel Cartulary. Over many years she has faithfully shared with me her exacting scholarship on the history of Narbonne. Chapter 18, in particular, emerged during a memorable dinner conversation with her in Kalamazoo, Michigan. The footnotes in this book are testimony to my indebtedness to her. Claudie Duhamel-Amado and Monique Zerner extended their friendship and hospitality during my year teaching in Aix-en-Provence. The former kindly sent me her massive manuscript thesis on the aristocratic families of the region of Béziers; the latter has shared with me her writings, both published and unpublished, on the origins of the Albigensian Crusades. It was thanks to my dear friends Noël and Henriette Sautereau of St.-Marcel-sur-Aude that I first went to Narbonne; they have been unstinting in their hospitality during my many trips to the region since then. I owe my knowledge of Old Provencal to the instruction of

Margaret Switten, who also read and commented on early drafts of several chapters of the book and saved me from numerous errors. Many of the translations of troubadour lyrics in the book are hers, done for a course we jointly taught. My thanks, as well, to the readers whose annotations likewise saved me from errors and helped me improve the text: Stephen D. White, Barbara Rosenwein, Dean MacLaughlin, several anonymous readers, and, above all, my Amherst colleague Howell D. Chickering Jr., who commented on everything from the book's architecture to my "Gibbonian sentences" and unwitting gallicisms. Trips to European archives and libraries have been subsidized over the years by grants from the Social Science Research Council, the American Council of Learned Societies, and the National Endowment for the Humanities. During the research trips my then young children put up with my absence more than they should have been required to. In the final stages of assembling the manuscript, Rhea Cabin has been an able, willing, and cheerful assistant. Ellen Baker has kept me smiling. My thanks to them all.

The maps in this book are mine (with the help of the computer wizards at Amherst College Information Technology), as are the photographs not otherwise attributed. Unless otherwise noted, the poetry translations are either by Margaret Switten or myself.

The lithographs from Charles Nodier, Isidor Taylor, and Alphonse de Cailleux, *Voyages pittoresques et romantiques dans l'ancienne France. Languedoc,* (Paris: P. Didot l'aîné: 1833–37) are reproduced here with the kind permission of Houghton Library, Harvard University. The documents from the Archivo de la Corona de Aragón are reproduced here with the kind permission of the Ministerio de Educación y Cultura, Archivo de la Corona de Aragón. The documents from the Archives Municipales de Narbonne are reproduced here with the kind permission of that archive. The photographs of the seals of Constance, Duchess of Narbonne, and of William VIII, lord of Montpellier, are reproduced with the kind permission of the Centre Historiques des Archives Nationales de France. The photograph of the ruins of le Mas-Deu was taken with the kind permission of Michel and Jacqueline Baylion, the owners of the property. Simon Doubleday graciously provided me with a copy of his thesis on the Lara family. Stephen D. White provided me with copies of his many unpublished manuscripts. The music of the Contessa de Dia included in chapter 13 was transcribed by Margaret Switten. Portions of this book have appeared previously in Theodore Evergates, *Aristocratic Women in Medieval France* (Philadelphia: University of Pennsylvania Press, 1999).

This book is dedicated to my late wife, who lived with this project through all our years of marriage. The argument in chapter 13 slowly took form during our many dinner-table poetry seminars. My greatest regret is that she did not live to see it in print.

Fredric L. Cheyette

Leverett, Massachusetts

A NOTE ON MONEY, WEIGHTS, AND MEASURES

The medieval monetary system was based on the penny (denarius, abbreviated as d.). Twelve pennies made up a solidus (abbreviated as sol.). Twenty solidi made up a pound (libra, abbreviated as liv.). In the twelfth century, the penny was the only silver coin circulating in Occitania. Each mint produced coins with a particular weight and fineness, and these varied with time. The most commonly used coin in the region in the twelfth century was the one produced by the mint at Mauguio (abbreviated as Melg.), which was under the control of the lords of Montpellier. It is the most frequently mentioned coin in this book, usually in the form "sol. Melg." There were also mints in Toulouse (abbreviated as Tol.), in Narbonne (abbreviated as Narb.), and in Carcassonne (called Ugonencus and abbreviated as Ugon.). The exchange rates among these coins fluctuated markedly during the twelfth century. After the absorption of Occitania into the French kingdom in the thirteenth century, the monarchy imposed a monopoly of its own coins, those of Paris (abbreviated Par.) and those of Tours (abbreviated Tourn.). Gold coins from Moslem al-Andalus and North Africa also circulated in the region. They were most commonly called morabitani, a name derived from the Almoravids who for a while ruled much of that area.

For weights and measures there were many different terms. Their contents varied widely from city to city and region to region. Their metric equivalents are known only as they existed in the eighteenth century. (These have been canvassed by Zupko, *French Weights and Measures before the Revolution*.) The one most commonly mentioned in the text is the sétier (Latin *sestarius*), a measure of capacity for wine or grain. For most dry products, the sétier contained two émines. Twelve sétiers of grain made a muid. From this measure was derived a measure of land, the sesterée (Latin *sexterada*), which was either the amount of land that could be sown with a sétier of grain or the amount of land that could produce a sétier.

ERMENGARD

OF NARBONNE

AND THE WORLD OF THE

TROUBADOURS

INTRODUCTION

E rmengard of Narbonne. Even to specialists in the history of the Middle Ages her name is hardly known. Eleanor of Aquitaine, who was wife to two kings and the mother of three more? Yes, there is a name—and a story—to conjure with. Countess Marie of Champagne, Eleanor's daughter by King Louis VII of France, patron of Chrétien de Troyes, the poet who invented the Arthurian romance? She too is better known, if only because of the writers who thronged to her court. If we know anything about the Middle Ages we have at least heard of King Richard the Lionheart and his brother King John, who was forced to grant the Magna Carta at Runnymede, both of them sons of Queen Eleanor. We have also surely heard of the mythical King Arthur and his Round Table, of Lancelot and Guinevere, of the quest for the Holy Grail, all of them largely the creation of Chrétien. Ermengard, however, has fallen off the historical map.

And yet in her own time—in the second half of the twelfth century, when Eleanor was marrying her kings and seeing to the education of those who would be kings, when Marie was hearing the freshly minted stories of Erec and Cligès and Perceval—Ermengard was at least as well known. When the author we know as Andrew the Chaplain wrote his dialogues *On Love* for Marie, the arbiters he chose for his imagined courts of love were Marie, Eleanor, and Ermengard. At about the same time, when another singer of tales needed names for the parents of his hero William of Orange, he chose for his hero's father Aymeri of Narbonne (one of the paladins of the Charlemagne of the epic tradition, and as it happened, the name of Ermengard's father and grandfather) and for his hero's mother, Ermengard. In one scene the poet even imagines a speech for her that could have come from the real Ermengard of Narbonne. Failing in her plea to the do-nothing King Louis to come to the aid of her son whose castle is besieged by the Saracens, she declares:

> I myself will ride there
> wearing my coat of mail, my shining helmet laced on,
> shield at my neck, sword at my side,

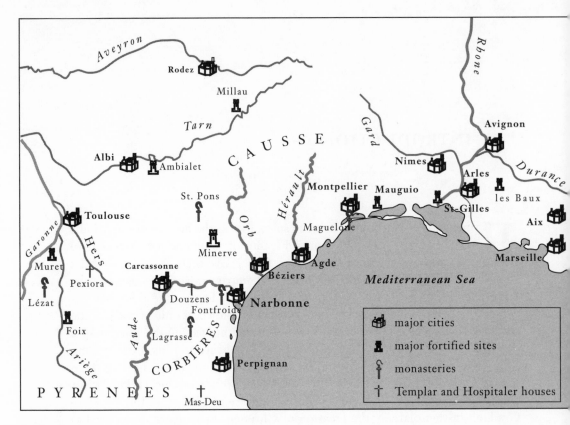

Occitania

lance in hand, ahead of all others.
Though my hair is grey and white,
my heart is bold and thirsts for war.[1]

Even far away in the lands of the Norsemen, on the Orkney Islands north of
Scotland, Ermengard's name was known. There, around 1200, a poet retelling
the stories of his islands' rulers sang of the sea voyage of Earl Rognvaldr to the
Holy Land. Stopping at a sea town called Nerbon (which the poet mistakenly
locates on the shores of the Atlantic), the earl is invited to a feast given in his
honor by the town's queen, a legendary beauty by the name of Ermingerda:

> The queen came into the hall escorted by a group of ladies and carrying a serv-
> ing-bowl of gold. She was in her finest clothes, with her hair falling loose as is
> customary with virgins and a golden tiara upon her forehead. . . . The Earl took
> her hand . . . and sat her on his knee. . . . Then the Earl made a verse:

> I'll swear, clever sweetheart,
> you're a slender delight

to grasp and to cuddle,
my golden-locked girl.
Ravenous the hawk, crimson-
clawed, flesh-crammed,
but now heavily hangs
the silken hair.

And thanks to the distant renown she gained from the poet's song, Ermengard gave her name to generations of Norse girls.[2]

It was among the poets and songsmiths of her own lands that Ermengard was best known, among the troubadours. It was above all thanks to them that her fame as "she who protects joy and youth," who gives "joy and merit," spread to the far reaches of the Latin world. Although they composed in a language that has left only one still-thriving descendant in Europe—Catalan—in the Middle Ages, their lyrics and tunes were known wherever in Europe that men and women sang of love. Their songs served as models for trouvères in northern France and Minnesingers in Germany, for Dante, Petrarch, and many other poets in Italy. The forms they invented continue to inspire the poetic imagination eight hundred years later. From Hollywood to blues singers, their themes are still with us.

Ermengard's city of Narbonne lies just a few miles up the ancient channel of the Aude River from the Mediterranean in the region of southern France now called Languedoc. The region's name refers to a characteristic of the language its people once spoke. Where the French to the north said *oïl* (which became *oui*, meaning "yes") and the Italians to the east said *si*, those who lived here said *oc*: they spoke the *langue d'oc*. This name is, of course, a creation of outsiders. To those who spoke it, their language was simply the *lenga romana*, the vernacular, in contrast to Latin, the language of clerics. But twelve years after Ermengard's death, northern armies—inspired by religion and greed for land—swept across the region in response to the impassioned call of Pope Innocent III. Heresy had taken root in its cities and villages, he said, and it should be destroyed with fire and sword. After a long and bloody war, the region was conquered, and when the Capetians absorbed it into their kingdom, the name for the language became the name for the land: *patria linguae occitanae, pays de languedoc*.[3]

That great war, known to historians as the Albigensian Crusades, casts a long shadow backward over the story I will be telling. The conquerors—nobles, clergy, and above all kings—not only reshaped the culture and rituals of power, they rewrote history to defend and justify what they had done. Their rewriting, in large part unrecognized for what it is, has endured to the present day.[4] Because our story takes place on the other side of that terrible divide, because I attempt to present Ermengard and her contemporaries in terms of their own age rather than as a later age remade them, I adopt the term of other recent historians and call the region between the Rhone and the Pyrenees "Occitania." It is a coinage with but the smallest grain of historical justification and for that very reason has a paramount claim to favor; it avoids all traces of the political anachronism implied by "southern France" and recognizes that before the thirteenth century, in the days when Ermengard ruled Narbonne, this region had not yet been tagged with an alien name.

In the twelfth century, a handful of great aristocratic families attempted to assert their dominance over this region. The counts of Barcelona gained the title of count of Carcassonne by purchase in 1067–68; they became counts of Provence by marriage in 1113 and kings of Aragon, again by marriage, in 1150; for a hundred years, from the early twelfth century until the Albigensian Crusades in the early thirteenth, they maintained a tight alliance with the most important lordly families of the Occitan coastal plain: the viscounts of Narbonne (of whom Ermengard was the heiress), the lords of Montpellier, and the family we know as the Trencavels, viscounts of the cities of Albi, Béziers, Agde, and Nîmes and effective rulers of Carcassonne and the mountainous region called the Razès to its south. The counts of Toulouse, who were popularly known as the counts of Saint-Gilles, after their castle in the important port and pilgrimage center at the mouth of the Rhone River, also claimed rights to Provence through their marriage into its comital house in the early eleventh century; from the days of the great crusader Count Raymond IV, they asserted their dominance through the entire region by taking the title "count of Toulouse, duke of Narbonne, marquis of Provence." Yet for all these vast claims, they were not fully secure even in their home city of Toulouse. The counts of Poitiers, hundreds of kilometers to the north, laid claim to the county of Toulouse through the marriage of Count William VII of Poitou (better known as the troubadour Duke William IX of Aquitaine) with Philippa, the daughter of Count William IV of Toulouse. She and not Count Raymond IV, they asserted, inherited the county in 1094 on the death of her father. Philippa's claim passed to her son, Duke William X, and from him to his elder daughter Eleanor of Aquitaine. In Eleanor's name the claim to Toulouse was reasserted by her two royal husbands, Louis VII of France and Henry II of England.

Members of all these families were patrons of the troubadours. Indeed the first known troubadour was Philippa's husband, William IX, who, although Occitan was probably not his native tongue, chose that language for his songs. Ermengard of Narbonne, two sons of King Henry II of England—the young Henry and his brother Richard the Lionheart—as well as Raymond V and Raymond VI of Toulouse, Eleanor of Aquitaine, various Trencavels, various Williams of Montpellier and their brothers and cousins, the kings of Aragon and Castile, and lesser lords of Occitania, Provence, and northern Italy, all appear under their real names or pseudonyms in the dedications of the songs or in the *vidas*, the largely fictional lives of the troubadours. Theirs is the historical world that welcomed the imagined world of the troubadour lyric. They were the people for whom the poets created their game of love.

Eight hundred years and more have passed since these people walked the earth, since Ermengard proudly called herself viscountess of Narbonne. After all that time, what can we possibly know about them and about her? The usual sources for biographers are closed to us, forever silenced: there are no people we can interview who knew Ermengard or those around her; no diaries, for that genre of writing was still hundreds of years in the future when Ermengard died; the few letters that remain are not personal letters but highly charged political documents, and they are not really from her hand but from a scribe well schooled in Latin epistolary rhetoric. There are not even traces of her in monastic chronicles, for that kind of writing flourished only in northern Europe, and stories of far-away rulers who brought no gifts to the monastery's doors rarely intruded on the chronicler's thick tapestry of the saintly deaths of brethren, the doings of royal patrons, or his house's bitter fights with the local bishop. What we have instead is a thin and tattered fabric of documents, originals or copies, recording her benefactions, a marriage contract, two oaths of fidelity, a last testament, a mention now and then of her presence among the arbiters attempting to settle some dispute, her name among the witnesses to some political transactions, and similar flotsam from what once must have been a substantial archive.

In archives and libraries from Barcelona to Paris, I have discovered sixty-four archival documents that bear Ermengard's name. For a twelfth-century individual who is not a king, pope, emperor, or clerical author, it is a respectable number, even when compared with the 158 extant for her exact contemporary, Count Raymond V of Toulouse; for Raymond exercised power in a far larger region, with many more ecclesiastical foundations to record his benefactions, and his family's archives were eventually absorbed into those of the king. In contrast, almost all of Ermengard's surely numerous benefactions are lost.[5] What percentage do these sixty-four represent of all the documents that once bore her name? There is no way to tell, but it would be surprising if it were more than one-tenth of one percent. Only two of the hundreds of oaths of fidelity that once were sworn to her have survived (although they were both recorded individually and eventually copied into a "Book of Fiefs"); for our purposes, that is surely the greatest loss.[6] And of what was probably never recorded, how dearly we would like to have her dinner invitations, the seating charts of her table, transcriptions of her conversations.

That so much has disappeared is not the consequence of some cultural prejudice against women of power. The archives of the viscounts of Narbonne were eventually deposited in the royal Court of Accounts of Montpellier, and that deposit went up in flames in the great revolutionary bonfire of August 10, 1793.[7] That we know far more about the Trencavels is due to the fortunate eighteenth-century theft of one of their cartularies from the castle of Foix (where the family archives found refuge during the Albigensian Crusades), before that archive too went up in flames in 1803. After wandering through several collections, their cartulary found a home at the Société Archéologique de Montpellier and remained out of the reach of scholars until I was allowed to consult it in 1969.[8] The number of documents bearing Ermengard's name that we do have to work with, a little more than one per year of her effective rule, gives a sense of the uncertainty that attends our vision of her life.

Many more such parchments once piled up in the wooden chests into which her notaries packed them away for safekeeping. But even had most of them not disappeared, not been scraped clean for reuse by later scribes, not been eaten by rats, not gone up in flames during the French Revolution, and most of what remained not been stolen by souvenir hunters, lovers of antiquities, or self-styled scholars, to end up eventually as lamp shades or book bindings, or tossed out with old papers and tattered furniture, or still today be hidden away unrecorded, unannounced, in some private library,[9] even had all those documents survived we would not be any closer to what usually interests a modern reader of biographies: the subject's character, her passions—especially her sexual passions, her secret dreams and demons, the anecdotes of daily life that would help us imagine her as a figure in a novel or a movie. Ermengard will resolutely not stand before us. She is protected by more than what Arthur Koestler once called "the arrogance of the dead,"[10] the way they forever take with them into the grave all the complexities and ambiguities of their lived presence, to leave behind as surrogates only a collection of stories more or less embellished by those who tell them, the contradictory memories of those whom the dead loved or hated and who loved or hated in return, and the datebooks, checkbook stubs, and other dead matter of their lived lives.[11] With the passage of time, her presence, which once doubtless left a thousand anecdotes in the memories of those who knew her and a thousand contradictory judgments in the minds of those who were her friends and enemies, is now little more than a faint ghost, and it is that ghost we must try as best we can to make speak.

It is commonly assumed that Ermengard appears under coded names—my lady of Narbonne, my "You are wrong" (Tort n'avetz)—in the songs of at least five troubadours: Bernart de Ventadorn, Peire d'Alvernhe, Azalais de Porcairagues, Giraut de Bornelh, and Peire Rogier.[12] At first glance their lyrics seem to open a window, however small, on the passionate life of our viscountess and those who entered her charmed circle. They seem to whisper in our ear, "This is the real person who hides behind the name that scribes have written at the bottom of their parchments." And for centuries, historians and literary commentators assumed that these songs and the biographical stories that eventually accompanied them let us hear her voice, however distantly.

Here is one such story that minstrels carried from court to court about a century after her death.

Peire Rogier was from Auvergne and was a canon [i.e., one of the cathedral clergy] of Clermont. He was a noble man, handsome and charming, well versed in letters; he had a natural wit, and he was good at composing and singing verses. He left his canonry and became a minstrel and went from court to court. Everywhere his songs were praised. One day he came to Narbonne, to the court of Lady Ermengard, who was known in those days as a woman of great worth and merit. She welcomed him warmly and showed him great favor. He fell in love with her and composed songs about her; and she welcomed them. He called her "Tort-n'avez" ["You are wrong"]. For a long time he remained at her court. And the people of the region believed that he received the pleasures of love from her, for which they blamed her. And so, for fear of what people were saying, she told him to leave. Sad and thoughtful, troubled and downcast, he departed and went to the court of Raymond, lord of Orange. . . . There he stayed a long time. Afterwards he was in Spain with the good King Alfonso of Castile and the good King Alfonso of Aragon, and then with the good Count Raymond of Toulouse. He had great honor in the world as long as he stayed in it. At last he entered the order of Grandmont, and there he died.[13]

We might imagine this story being told by a performer at a court in northern Italy, where this text and others like it first appear. Clearing his throat, he would then begin one of the songs that Peire dedicated to his lady of Narbonne, perhaps "Tant ai mon cor en joy assis":

Tant ai mon cor en joy assis,	My heart is so fixed on joy
per que no puesc mudar no'n chan,	that I cannot help but sing,
que joys m'a noirit pauc e gran;	for as a child and an adult, joy has nourished me.
e ses luy non seria res,	Without it, I'd be nothing.
qu'assatz vey que tot l'als qu'om fay	I see that everything else that people do
abaiss' e sordey' e dechai,	degrades, dishonors, and defames
mas so qu'amors e joys soste.	if love and joy do not sustain it.
. . . .	. . . .
Mon Tort-n'avetz en Narbones	To my Tort-n'avetz in Narbonne
man salutz, si tot luenh s'estai,	I send greetings, though she is far away,
e sapcha qu'em-breu la veyray,	and may she know that I'll soon see her
si trop grans afars no'm rete.	if great matters don't keep me away.
Lo senher, que fetz tot quant es,	May the Lord who made all that is
guart lo cors de lieys cumsi's fay,	keep her body as he does,
qu'ilh mante pretz e joy veray,	that she maintain worth and true joy
quan tot' autra gens s'en recre.[14]	when all others abandon it.

Or "Ges non puesc en bon vers fallir":

Ges non puesc en bon vers fallir	I will never fail to make a good verse
nulh'hora qu'ieu de midons chan;	when I sing of my lady;
cosi poiri'ieu ren mal dir?	for how can I say ill of her?
Qu'om non es ta mal essenhatz,	Not even a churl is so badly taught
si parl'ab lieys un mot o dos,	that, if he speak with her a word or two,
que totz vilas non torn cortes;	he will not become courtly;
per que sapchatz be que vers es,	so understand this truth:

que'l ben qu'ieu dic tot ai de liey.	whatever I say well I owe to her.
. . . .	. . . .
Mon Tort-n'avetz mant, s'a lieys platz,	I send to my Tort-n'avetz, if it please her,
qu'aprenda lo vers, s'el es bos;	that she learn my song, if it be good;
e puois vol que sia trames	and then I wish that it be sent
mon dreit-n'avetz lai en Saves:	to my "dreit-n'avetz" there in the Savès:
Dieus sal e guart lo cors de liey.[15]	may God protect and guard her body.

We all recognize the plot of the minstrel's tale and how, like the dialogue of a modern musical comedy, it leads directly to the songs: boy meets girl, boy loves girl, boy loses girl; in the closing scene he walks down the road, rejected, heartbroken, and alone, toward a distant horizon. In this version of the tale, however (as in so many film biographies from the 1930s and 1940s), the boy and girl are not entirely fictional. One is a great poet and composer of songs and the other one of the great aristocrats of her age. But what do the tale and the songs represent? What, if anything, do they and the many other songs and tales like them tell us about Ermengard and other twelfth-century aristocratic women or about the world in which they lived? Behind all these questions looms the modern concept of medieval "courtly love" and the relation of literature to life.

Twelfth-century lyric poets and singers spread before us a brilliant spectacle of erotic relations between a lyric "I" and his lady (or ladies), most often a woman of high station. The tone of their poetry covers the gamut from bawdy to tearful, high serious to satiric. Some, like William IX, boast of their sexual exploits in ways that smell of the warrior's campfire (or, as we would say, of the locker room); others, like Marcabru, castigate or mock the lasciviousness of the knightly world; yet others present love as a school of virtue. Some speak of rules of love and debate questions such as whether lovers should treat each other as equals or whether the man should always be subservient to his lady. Others put an ironic twist on the debates and rules and appear to call into question the very assumptions on which they are built. In this game of love, serious and comic, issues of power—especially the power of women—are rarely far beneath the surface.

The voice in these songs always sings in the first-person singular, and a long tradition going back to thirteenth-century Italy, if not before, makes that voice the voice of the poet/composer/performer himself (or herself, since there were also women poets and performers). The apparent sincerity of some poets, such as Bernart de Ventadorn, strongly reinforces our desire to follow that tradition, to make the "I" of the poem the real person of flesh and blood who composed it, and its sentiments a literal account of that person's feelings. Identifying the voice in the poem with the poet's own voice appeals to our own post-Romantic sensibilities as well; for even if we do not hear the personal voice of Irving Berlin in every performance of "White Christmas" or of Cole Porter in "Begin the Beguine," even if we are not likely to confuse the real personalities of our favorite movie stars with the characters they play on the screen, serious lyric poetry is different: the words claim to speak from the heart, and that is the way we have learned to hear them.[16]

If it is the real poet who speaks, if it is the real authorial voice we hear, it is then but a small step to say that the world evoked by that voice, a world of amorous dalliance and jealous husbands, of scandalmongers and deceivers, of knights who desire to learn virtue and ladies who are ready to teach them, was the real world in which they lived. Such was already the way in the later thirteenth century that the writers of the so-called biographies of the troubadours (such as that of Peire Rogier) and "explanations" of their songs—what are known to students of this Occitan literature as *vidas* and *razos*—heard the songs or wanted them to be heard. Such is the way they have frequently been read ever since.

It is impossible to know how much of the story of Peire and Ermengard is true and how much is fiction: there is no other evidence on which to rely, nothing more than whatever conviction the story itself will bear. The "lives" of the troubadours give each of them a kind of identity badge, a specific place of origin and social rank; they tell us that one is from the Auvergne, another from Gascony, a third from the Gevaudan; one is a noble baron, another a poor knight, a monk, a minstrel, or a son of a baker. And often some of the details in these "lives" can be confirmed by other documents, especially when the poets were landed noblemen or clerics whose activities were recorded by chroniclers and whose pious donations were preserved in church archives. It would be easy to convince ourselves that other, unconfirmed details also have some reason to be there, that they were not invented. Although the biographies were written down a century or more after the deaths of their subjects, they could very well represent an oral tradition that went back to the days of the poets themselves, information they gave out themselves or what their contemporaries knew about them. Did Peire in fact spend time at the court of Ermengard of Narbonne? It would be surprising if he did not, for she was one of the great patrons of her age.

The story of the love affair, however, is the common matter of many of the troubadour biographies. Its substance appears to have been drawn from the songs themselves (with the aid of much imagination), giving real names to the mysterious ladies and coded names (known generically as *senhals*) that they use in their songs; thus Tort-n'avetz, "You-are-wrong," became Ermengard of Narbonne. (If the identification was accurate, was this name a private joke? a thrust of ill humor? a reference to a debate he once had with the viscountess? As usual, there is no way to know.) To accept these romances as true history requires us to make a special leap of faith, to imagine the songs to be entries in private diaries or fragments of confessional literature. The very conventionality of the tales and the public nature of the songs make that a doubtful proposition. The lyrics, after all, are not texts found under beds or in secret drawers after the poets die; they are songs their authors sang to make a living as they traveled from court to court or in some cases, such as those of Duke William IX or the Countess of Die, songs that great lords and ladies sang to entertain their companions after dinner or to lighten the arduous marches of their military campaigns.[17] The "I" of the poems claims to be discreet about his love affair, but that discretion is publicly broadcast; he claims to hide his true feelings from his lady, but if this were true, she would be the only one left in the dark. The poet claims sincerity to give literary force to his lyrics, but the claim does not guarantee the lyrics' historical veracity.

For the audience that first heard the "life" of Peire Rogier, his songs and those of his fellow troubadours were already part of an old, we might even say a classical, tradition; to that audience, the events of his life were as far away as the events of the nineteenth century are to us, and hearing about them would have been something like our listening to an aging blues singer tell stories he has heard from his teacher about his teacher's teacher. Both the poets and the minstrels who a century later sang their songs were professional entertainers; they told stories their audiences wanted to hear and in response to a smile or a laugh were always ready to elaborate.

Nevertheless, that imaginary love affair between Peire and Ermengard, and the many others like it, cannot be ignored. The poetry that gave rise to such stories is there, and it is overwhelmingly preoccupied with matters of the heart. Occasionally it exudes a strong whiff of imagined adultery, as when the woman poet we know only as the Comtessa de Dia sings to her "good friend,"

cora'us tenrai en mon poder,	when will I have you in my power,
e que iagues ab vos un ser,	lie with you one night,
e qu'us des un bais amoros?	and give you a loving kiss?
Sapchatz, gran talan n'auria	Be sure, I'd have a great desire
qu'us tengues en luoc del marit.[18]	to hold you in place of my husband.

Even when the lyrics are not so overt, they find a place for the *lauzengier*, the liar and scandalmonger, among their characters.

More often their theme is of love abused or deceived, leaving clothed in ambiguity the exact relation of the poetic "I" to his or her beloved: it is distant, both socially and physically, a space that translates the distance of emotional longing, as when Jaufré Rudel sings in one of his most famous songs,

Rembra'm d'un' amor de loing;	I remember a love from afar;
vauc de talan enbroncs e clis,	I go sad and bent with desire
si que chans ni flors d'albespis	so that neither song nor hawthorn flower
no'm platz plus que l'inverns gelatz.[19]	pleases me more than icy winter.

It is easy enough to see how such songs could give rise to stories like that of Peire and Ermengard.

And so we must ask again, What do their love stories represent? What should we read into them? Within a real world of the twelfth century, they created an imagined world. Was that imagined world an exact replica of the real one? An exaggeration? A fantasy of the taboo and forbidden? A form of wish fulfillment? These are but a small number of the possibilities that critics and historians have suggested. The answer cannot be simple, for the power and richness of poetry depend on the way it plays with the many valences of language. We can begin to comprehend the play of troubadour lyrics only when we understand the many meanings that simple words such as *love* and *joy*, *anger* and *harm*, and more complicated words such as *my lady* and *my lord*, *honor*, *faith*, and *deceit* had in the society in which the troubadours composed their songs. We must be prepared to leave our own world and enter another, the one in which Ermengard and her poets lived.

No ship will let us disembark on that shore. No native guide will welcome us. We must find our way there document by document. Ermengard herself will at first be nothing more than one name among others on a sheet of parchment, and read raw, without a knowledge of contexts, they will tell us little of her passions, her problems, her ambitions, her life.[20] Each one is like an isolated tessera in a pile that once formed a mosaic, or a random piece of a picture puzzle. They are, furthermore, eight centuries old; many of them are missing, and the cover of the box has long since been lost. We cannot assume we know in advance what the completed picture will be. Yet if each document is considered not a set of statements but a set of questions to be answered, the many contexts that gave meaning to each of them will gradually allow Ermengard to emerge. The puzzle, the mosaic, of which each document is a piece, has many layers. As we question each document, it assumes a place in many different contexts, no single one of which gives its full meaning. Each document turns into a well-cut gemstone that, turned under the light, shows a multitude of hues, each of which adds its particular coloration to the portrait of the viscountess. But we must be prepared for the foreignness of the image that will take shape.

The biographer of someone recently alive can assume that her readers share much of the world in which her subject lived. There is no need to create the stage set, to do more than sketch the framework for thought and action; the language of motivation as well as of gesture and expectation is part of a shared conspiracy among author, character, and reader. As we go back in time, however, that shared conspiracy evaporates. Every reader of Flaubert or Hardy knows how the unabridged dictionary must be kept close at hand to decipher the names of articles of clothing, types of horse-drawn vehicles, items of household furnishings. As we go further back, not only the material world but the social and even the psychological world elude our common understanding. Even the commonplace boundaries between the personal and the public, between inner experience and outer performance—the very things that make the dailiness of our daily lives—must be called into question.

For the biographer, that fact of historical distance poses another serious problem. We commonly expect the biographer of one of our contemporaries or near-contemporaries to present us with an individual we might imagine knowing personally. We expect to be told not only how she looked but also the shape of her character, the inner springs of her actions. We expect a portrait of the subject in the intimacy of her private world. Putting aside for the moment the problem of documenting in that manner an individual who lived eight hundred years ago, we must first ask whether a woman of Ermengard's time and place and status had a private life, an inner life distinct from her public life.

For a generation or more, historians and literary critics have urged us to think of the twelfth century, Ermengard's century, as the age that "discovered the individual."[21] The troubadours as well as monks and theologians have been enlisted to bear witness to that supposed discovery. As the American historian Caroline Bynum has pointed out, however, whatever the individuality discovered in that century may have been, it was not our modern individuality—the unique self, the self that is peculiar and unlike any other, the trait that is often taken to be the essence of modernity. It was an individuality, a selfhood, shaped by a community. It is only in this sense that we can understand the troubadours, who on the one hand seem each to be unique, especially in the particulars of their poetic prowess, and yet, on the other, whose phrases and sentiments so often seem to be formulaic, who consciously imitate each other, play their own words and music against those of their predecessors and contemporaries, who so often, to our modern ears, seem like peas from the same pod.

And so it is with Ermengard. She was born into a world of politics and warfare, and the earliest passions she may have learned were the passions for power and for the friendship and loyalty needed to sustain that power. Even more intensely than many of our contemporary politicians, she most likely lived her private life on the public stage. Would she have had any choice if she wished to survive in the world of cunning and blind ambition that was her lot? That public life is documented, however fragmentarily. That is the life this book seeks to reconstruct.

I first ran into Ermengard many years ago when researching another topic in the archives of Narbonne and Carcassonne. The documents among which I discovered her soon set me on a different path from the one I had intended to follow. I had already been teaching medieval history for several years and was no novice to archival research. But what my eyes encountered in those archives was often mystifying. What people seemed to be doing matched little I had been taught about medieval society and little I had ever read. As the documents revealed them, their actions called into question many of the generalizations I had learned in graduate school and repeated to my students. Here were ambitious serfs, one of them called to witness an act of no less a person than Ermengard herself. Here were moneylenders, not just in the city but in the countryside as well. Some of them were great lords. And some of them were women. Women (apart from queens) had figured little in the medieval history I had learned. Every book I had read suggested (if only by their absence) that women were historically invisible, unknowable. Yet here in the documents there were women everywhere—making their own marriage contracts, serving as executors for their husbands' estates, commanding castles. There were even women warriors such as Rixendis de Parez, who early in the twelfth century joined a posse of village lords to attack some mills that she and her fellows claimed were theirs, or the wife of Bernard of Nissan who took revenge on her husband's enemy when the two men were fighting over a jointly held castle.[22] And there were the great women who boasted titles of countess and viscountess, rulers of cities and castles, who roamed the land receiving oaths of fidelity, negotiated treaties, settled disputes among the lords of the land, and who occasionally were to be found with their armies at an important siege. They did not match the tinted Victorian image of the mysterious, retiring lady in the castle, nor did they match anything I had read in books on "feudal society." Among them was Ermengard of Narbonne. This book is in many ways the story of my quest to get to know her.

Ermengard acted on a vast stage for over half a century. Her deeds, however, are unintelligible without their contexts. To understand her we must first comprehend the structure and furnishings of her stage and the instruments through which she acted. Without society there can be no individual.

CHAPTER ONE
THE VISCOUNTESS COMES OF AGE

In the name of God. Be it known to all present and future that I, Ermengard, viscountess of Narbonne, wishing to have you Alphonse, count, as my husband, give myself to you as wife. And by this same donation I give you Narbonne with all that belongs to it, entirely and without fraud, and everything I have there or can have there in any way whatever. I give this under the following conditions, that we have, hold, and possess it together during our lifetimes, and that after our deaths it shall remain to the children we have procreated, if they survive us. And if we have none who survive us and you Alphonse, count, my husband, survive me, you shall have and possess the said city of Narbonne with all that belongs to it as long as you live. And after your death the said city of Narbonne with all that belongs to it will return to my nearest relatives.

This document was written on the twelfth of the Kalends of November [October 21] in the year of Our Lord 1142, in the reign of King Louis.

The sign + of Ermengard, vicountess of Narbonne, who ordered this to be written and who signed it and asked the witnesses to sign it.

Sign + of Peter of Minerve	Sign + of Bernard son of Peter
Sign + of Peter of Montbrun	Sign + of Peter the mint-master (*Monetarius*)
Signs + of Berenger and his son Peter	Sign + of Bardine Saptis
Sign + of Bernard of Carcassonne	Sign + of Peter Belhomme

Peter wrote this[1]

With this marriage contract, we hear Ermengard's voice for the first time in the historical record. We may think of it as the first tessera in the mosaic we are attempting to reconstruct, the first piece of the picture puzzle to come out of the box. Where do we place it? Behind each of its assertions, even behind the list of names at the end, there are questions hiding, questions we must answer before this document begins to speak. Who is Alphonse? Who are the witnesses, and should we pay any attention to them? How did Ermengard come to contract her own marriage rather than have a parent contract it for her? What does her gift

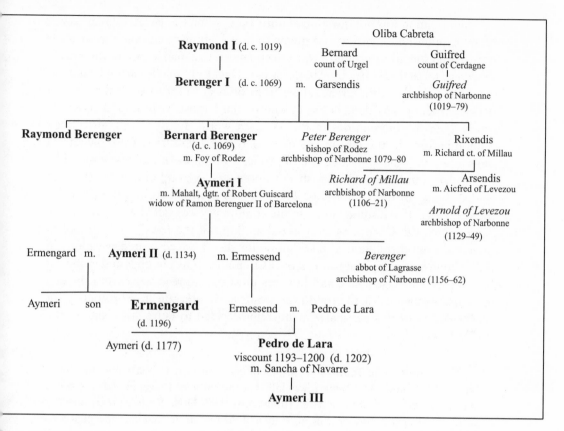

Viscounts of Narbonne

of Narbonne as dowry to her husband really signify? Is this marriage contract only a collection of formalities, or somewhere in it can we hear Ermengard's personal voice? For a girl of Ermengard's status, marriage was necessarily a political act, so the answers to these questions lead us immediately into the political world that she was destined to inhabit. They introduce us to the friends who would become her life-long allies and to the enemies with whom she would have to contend—chief among them the man whom she was marrying.

For early historians of Occitania, most notably Claude Devic and Joseph Vaissete, the learned eighteenth-century Benedictine authors of the *Histoire générale de Languedoc* (whose massive collection of documents is the foundation on which much of this book is built), the identity of Count Alphonse was a mystery. The name itself was not a common one among the regional dynasties with whose members a woman of Ermengard's station might be expected to contract a marriage. The mystery is compounded by the fact that no later document mentions an Alphonse as Ermengard's husband. There were, however, many kings of Castile and Aragon who bore that name (usually modernized as Alfonso or Alfons). Devic and Vaissete therefore concluded that he was a Spanish count.[2]

Their opinion was not questioned until 1966, when the Israeli scholar Aryeh Graboïs published a curious fragment from a Hebrew medieval chronicle. It was written sometime around 1160 and appended to a manuscript of the *Book of Traditions* (*Sefer hakabala*) by Abraham ben David of Toledo, a book that recounts the deeds of the great rabbis from biblical times to the author's own days. Narbonne was then home to one of the largest, richest, and most respected Jewish communities in the Western world. Its members, already an economic force in the city in the ninth and tenth centuries, were owners of mills under the Roman bridge and of property in the surrounding countryside. In the late tenth century, Jewish entrepreneurs even administered the vast landed estates of the archbishop. Their houses crowded around the palace of the viscounts. The leading family in the community was called by the honorific *Nassi* (which the Christians interpreted as "king of the Jews") as a symbol of their authority throughout the Diaspora, for they were consulted as experts in the Talmud by the faithful from all over Occitania.[3] The comings and goings of Jewish merchants, scholars, and litigants must have spread news from the city to people of their faith all around the western Mediterranean. Fortunately for us, the owner of this particular manuscript decided to write down one of the stories he heard:

The days of Rabbi Todros were a time of great calamity in Narbonne, for the lord of Narbonne, Don Aymeri, was killed at the battle of Fraga. He left no son and the government of the city fell to his third child, Doña Esmeneras [Ermengard], who was still a minor. The great men of the region coveted her inheritance, for it was vast and rich, and they bent all their efforts to persuade her to marry the lord of Toulouse, Don Alphonse. But the count of Barcelona, Ramon Berenguer, was the enemy of Don Alphonse, and he urged Doña Esmeneras to refuse the hand of Don Alphonse, and because the count of Barcelona was her blood relative she listened to him and married Don Bernard of Anduze. Then a war began, and the city divided into two factions. Half the city supported the viscountess and her councilors, while the other half declared for the count of Toulouse. Before these events happened, there was a large Jewish community in Narbonne, counting about two thousand persons and including several great men and scholars whose reputation spread throughout the world. But as a result of these troubles, they fled to Anjou, Poitou, and France, for a heavy tax was demanded from the community. The *nassi'im*—Rabbi Todros, his sons, and the members of his family— made great efforts to defend the rights of the community and by their gifts helped its members; in order to guarantee the payment of the tax, they even gave their sons and daughters to the Christians.[4]

The Count Alphonse whom Ermengard married on that October day was Alphonse Jordan, count of Toulouse, son of Raymond IV. Raymond was the first of his lineage to invent for himself the title duke of Narbonne. Now his son, by clasping the hand of the heiress Ermengard in marriage, was turning that title into legitimate control of the city.[5]

Alphonse Jordan had in fact taken over the city at least three years earlier. The witnesses to the marriage contract were most likely the leaders of the city faction that supported him. A few of them we can identify. Bardine Saptis was a consul of the city. As representative of the archbishop and viscount, he had negotiated a treaty with the city of Genoa in 1132. Peter the mint-master and Bernard of Carcassonne had been with Alphonse at least since 1139; Peter had been well compensated for his support by a gift of mills just upstream from the city (with Bernard among the witnesses to the transaction). Peter of Minerve, lord of a fortified town in the wild mountains north of the city, belonged to a family that a century earlier was already at the center of city politics; Peter himself had served Ermengard's father.[6] The people whom Ermengard saw standing around her as the marriage blessings were recited were in themselves an education in politics for the young girl: the new aristocracy of city wealth represented by the mint-master and his friends, and the old political elite represented by Peter of Minerve.

One person is not mentioned in the document, although doubtless he was equally vital to Alphonse's coup and may possibly have officiated at the wedding—the archbishop of Narbonne, Arnold of Levezou. He was represented among the witnesses by Peter of Montbrun, a known figure in the entourages of the archbishop and the abbot of Saint-Paul.[7] Archbishop Arnold's devotion to the house of Toulouse was already evident when he was bishop of Béziers. In 1120, although preoccupied with the work of church reform as papal legate, he found the time to hold Toulouse for Alphonse Jordan during the critical years after the agents of Alphonse's cousin Philippa and her husband Duke William IX had been expelled from the city and before Alphonse's own victorious arrival in the company of the city's militia. He was rewarded for his help in 1142 with a gift of the fortified village of Conilhac not far from Narbonne.[8]

All of these details had been forgotten as the story of the events passed by word of mouth to end up in the Hebrew manuscript in Spain. The tellers of the tale, however, had kept the essential. Ermengard was her father's third child, but her two older brothers had predeceased their father. She was therefore heiress to the city. And her marriage reopened the long-standing conflict between the counts of Toulouse and the counts of Barcelona, the conflict that formed the most basic theme of Ermengard's political life. That conflict had begun in 1113, when Count Ramon Berenguer III of Barcelona married Douce, the heiress to the county of Provence, and received as a gift the lands of both her mother and father. The counts of Toulouse where already entrenched in the Rhone valley, and Alphonse's father, Raymond IV, had also added marquis of Provence to his title. Despite repeated treaties that divided Provence between the two claimants, with Barcelona taking the lands south of the Du-

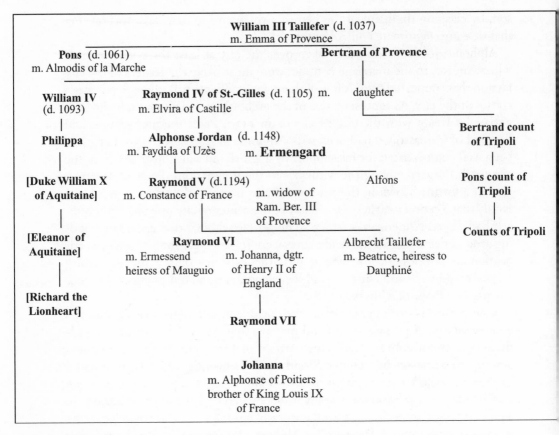

William III Taillefer (d. 1037)
m. Emma of Provence

Pons (d. 1061)
m. Almodis of la Marche

Bertrand of Provence

William IV
(d. 1093)

Raymond IV of St.-Gilles (d. 1105) m.   daughter
m. Elvira of Castille

**Bertrand count
of Tripoli**

Philippa

Alphonse Jordan (d. 1148)
m. Faydida of Uzès   m. **Ermengard**

[Duke William X
of Aquitaine]

Raymond V (d.1194)
m. Constance of France   m. widow of
Ram. Ber. III
of Provence

Alfons

**Pons count of
Tripoli**

[Eleanor of
Aquitaine]

Counts of Tripoli

Raymond VI
m. Ermessend
heiress of Mauguio

m. Johanna, dgtr.
of Henry II of
England

Albrecht Taillefer
m. Beatrice, heiress to
Dauphiné

[Richard the
Lionheart]

Raymond VII

Johanna
m. Alphonse of Poitiers
brother of King Louis IX
of France

Counts of Toulouse

rance River and Toulouse those to the north, hostilities were almost an annual event, and little excuse was needed for them to break out once again. Alphonse's marriage to Ermengard was more than an excuse; it was a major cause for war.

Ranged against Alphonse Jordan on this occasion were the Trencavel brothers as well as William lord of Montpellier and the count of Rodez, the anchors of the Barcelonese alliance in Occitania. Each had his own particular reasons to fear or hate the count of Toulouse and especially to fear the count's control of Ermengard's city.

Although the count had sworn oaths of fidelity with them in 1138 and made a treaty with Roger earlier in 1142, the Trencavel brothers—Roger of Béziers, Raymond Trencavel, and Bernard Ato—had many reasons not to trust Alphonse. Their father had been one of the major Occitan supporters of Philippa and William IX in their effort to take control of Toulouse. They were, in addition, lords over two large blocks of territories whose connections were threatened by Alphonse's presence in Narbonne. One stretched from Albi and the upper Tarn River valley south into the Corbières (the region known as the county of Razès); it lay between Narbonne and Toulouse. The other major block, consisting of the viscounties of Béziers, Agde, and Nîmes, lay between Narbonne and Alphonse's possessions in the Rhone valley. Roads linked these two areas through the mountains; others led along the southern edge of the Montagne Noire from Carcassonne to Béziers. Castles sworn to Trencavel fidelity commanded all these roads. But the major road, lowland all the way, was the old Roman road. It ran directly through Narbonne, over its bridge on the Aude, and through the gate beneath the vicecomital palace. Despite the Trencavels' extensive landholdings and their hundreds of castles in the area, Narbonne was a critical node. In Alphonse's hands it could threaten the unity that their grandmother and their father had labored so long and with such difficulty to create. Alphonse, in any event, had already shown his hand by suborning castellans in the vicinity of Bernard Ato's city of Nîmes. And Narbonne, added to Saint-Gilles, would give him two ports on the Mediterranean, with all that meant in terms of money, ships, and sailors. The challenge was obvious. Although their family had never been traditional allies of the viscounts of Narbonne—in the previous decades, in fact, they had been enemies as often as friends—the Trencavels had to save Ermengard's independence and that of her city.[9]

William of Montpellier likewise had good reason to fear and hate Alphonse Jordan. Only a decade earlier, William had taken advantage of his guardianship of Beatrice, the young heiress to the county of Mauguio, just east of his city, to block Alphonse's attempt to take control of her and her county. As soon as the ink was dry on the treaty that ended this conflict, William negated it by marrying the young heiress to the chosen heir to the Barcelonese county of Provence, thus giving Alphonse's major rival a foothold on the right as well as the left bank of the Rhone, a bridgehead against Saint-Gilles and Alphonse's other castles in the Rhone delta. Alphonse took his revenge shortly before he married Ermengard, when he supported an urban revolt in Montpellier that ousted William from the city. In the back of his mind, the coup in Narbonne may have been an even sweeter revenge.[10]

The connections of the lords of Montpellier with the counts of Barcelona went back at least a century. The count of Rodez also had long-established family connections with Narbonne and Barcelona. One of his ancestors was the sister of Ermengard's great-grandfather. Another had married into the house of the counts of Provence; his daughter was Douce, the girl who married the count of Barcelona and brought the rivalry between Barcelona and Toulouse into being.[11]

It was the Barcelonese connection that brought them all together to free Ermengard from Alphonse Jordan, for among the friends of the counts of Barcelona, Ermengard had inherited a place of honor, summed up in the remark of the Jewish chronicler that she was the blood relative of the count. Marriage connections between the dynasty of Narbonne and that of Barcelona went back to the early tenth century, when Viscount Odo of Narbonne married a daughter of Count Guifred Borrell of Barcelona. In the middle of the eleventh century, Ermengard's great-great-grandfather Berenger found his wife in the house of Besalú-Cerdagne, cousins of the counts of Barcelona; her grandfather married the widow of Count Ramon Berenguer II; in 1130 Count Ramon Berenguer III named Ermengard's father—his own half brother—an executor of his will. Over the centuries, companionship in arms and grants of land on both sides of the Pyrenees reinforced the familial alliance. In the language of the age, the two dynasties were indeed cousins; it would only be natural decades later, in 1156, for Ermengard, when she was in great financial need (probably to pay her troops), to turn to the count of Barcelona for a loan of five thousand marks of silver, giving her city itself as security.[12]

Hardly a month after Ermengard's wedding, these enemies of Alphonse Jordan were swearing oaths of alliance. Warfare quickly followed, with skirmishes all over the region. Castles between Albi and Toulouse were besieged and cap-

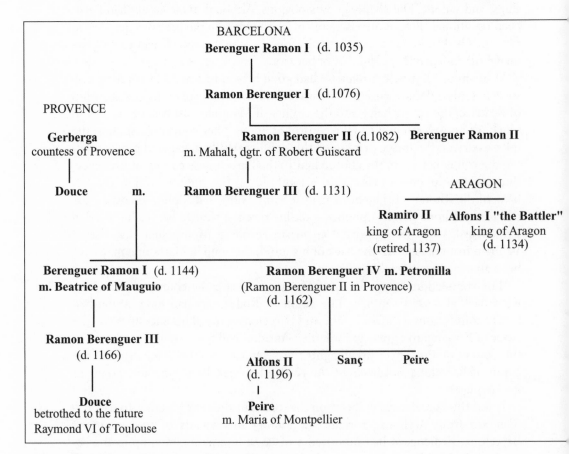

Counts of Barcelona and Provence and kings of Aragon

tured, and within a year after his marriage to Ermengard, Alphonse, defeated and imprisoned, was forced to settle the future of Narbonne to his enemies' satisfaction. The count was forced to promise to

> return Narbonne to Lady Ermengard and release the men of Narbonne and its region from the oaths [of fidelity] which they gave to him concerning Narbonne and the lands belonging to it. He must also return the written records of those oaths to them. . . . The count is to remain in the guard of Bernard of Canet [one of the most important men in the Trencavel entourage] until he has surrendered Narbonne.[13]

Ermengard and forty knights of Narbonne swore to uphold the treaty. So did her principal allies—Roger of Béziers with knights from Carcassonne and the Razès, Raymond Trencavel with knights from Béziers and Agde, and Peter and William of Minerve with their knights. As for Alphonse, he also had to swear to uphold it, along with his chief western ally, Sicard of Lautrec. All the military power of the region had come together to settle the future of Ermengard and her city.

Without further ado, the marriage was likewise dissolved. The victorious allies set their minds to finding Ermengard a new husband. They soon settled on one of their own, Bernard of Anduze, head of a noble family that lorded it over the dry and wild hills north of Nîmes, cousin of the lords of Montpellier, colleague of Ermengard's father, and close ally of the Trencavels. To seal Alphonse's defeat, Peter of Anduze, Bernard's brother, replaced Archbishop Arnold when he died in 1149.[14]

Through all these events, Ermengard appears to be only a puppet in the hands of others. And it is no wonder. She was only four or five on the day in July 1134 when her father, Viscount Aymeri II, was killed before the walls of Fraga in the Ebro valley, fighting the Moslems in the forces of the king of Aragon, Alfons the Battler. She was therefore only twelve or thirteen when she married Alphonse.[15] Had she remained married to him, she might have vanished into the mists of those who are little recorded, like Alphonse's first wife, Faydida of Uzès (who was nevertheless important enough to be named as participant in the first major treaty dividing Provence between Alphonse and Ramon Berenguer of Barcelona[16]—a reminder that one who is little recorded is not necessarily one who has little importance). But those who mobilized to spring her city from Alphonse's grasp and herself from Alphonse's bed had no intention of keeping her a puppet. Their choice of second husband for the viscountess is the demonstration.

Bernard of Anduze—by one very hypothetical reconstruction of his genealogy, Ermengard's first cousin—was probably about forty years of age. He already had several children by his first marriage.[17] And no sooner had he married Ermengard and received the customary oaths of fidelity from the great men of Narbonne than he vanished from the city and from Ermengard's life. None of the records of the city and its countryside ever mentions him again. Even the oaths of fidelity sworn to him assert by implication that in the event of Ermengard's death without heirs, it would be her half sister Ermessend, and not Bernard, who would inherit the viscounty.[18] Not once in all the years that follow does Bernard appear with Ermengard. We can, however, easily follow him and his descendants (none of them, as far as we know, the offspring of Ermengard) in the company of the lords of Montpellier and the Trencavels, participating in many of the most important political events of eastern Occitania. There is more than a suspicion here of a marriage of convenience with an older man who already had a son and successor. Safely married to such a man, Ermengard would be out of the way of fortune hunters, especially neighboring counts. No longer available, she would be more securely in control of her city and a more dependable ally to those who had just freed her.[19]

Sometime during the decade following Ermengard's liberation from Alphonse, her half sister Ermessend was married to the distant Castilian count Manrique de Lara.[20] Was this another step in the same plan? The marriage was a brilliant one, but it does not at all conform to the usual careful political plotting of medieval dynastic unions. At the time of the marriage, the Laras were the most powerful aristocratic lineage in the kingdom of Castile, apart from the monarchs themselves. Manrique was the son of Pedro Gonzalez, who for many years had been the lover of Queen Urraca of Castile and virtual ruler of the kingdom. Although the family fell from favor with the accession of Alfonso VII, they returned in force in the 1130s. Both Manrique and his brother were prominent in the royal court (at this time the prime source of wealth and power in the kingdom). During that decade, Manrique at one point even held Toledo as a tenant of the king. His successes against the Moslems on the Andalusian frontier led a contemporary poet to worshipful heights: "sarracenis fulgeret, christicolisque" (he shone among both Saracens and Christians), he boasted. The connection between the house of Narbonne and the Laras was most likely first made at the court of Alphons the Battler, for Pedro Gonzalez favored a rapprochement between Castile and Aragon, and according to a contemporary chronicle, in 1127 even refused to fight for his own king, the Castilian Alfonso, against Alfons of Aragon. Ermengard's allies may have had another reason as well to look with favor on Manrique de Lara. If a story in that same Castilian chronicle is to be believed, his father, Pedro Gonzalez, was killed in single combat with Alphonse Jordan of Toulouse during Alfons of Aragon's siege of Bayonne in 1130, sufficient reason for Manrique to harbor an implacable hatred for the count of Toulouse.

As brilliant as the marriage was and as strong as the shared enmity for the count of Toulouse may have been, it is hard to see what positive benefits either Ermengard or her dynasty or her allies gained from it. The seat of Lara wealth and power was hundreds of kilometers distant from Narbonne, on the far side of the Pyrenees and Cantabrian mountains, and that power was dependent on the family members' presence in the royal court. Was this itself the advantage—distance? So far away and preoccupied with Castilian court politics, Manrique de Lara would pose no threat to Ermengard's rule in Narbonne. As it turned out, the distant couple eventually provided an unforseen gift to Ermengard and her allies: a successor, indeed a succession of successors. Ermengard had no children. By 1163 she had called one of her sister's sons to be trained at her court—Aymeri, named for his maternal grandfather and obviously destined for the succession. When he died in 1177, he was followed at Ermengard's side by his brother Pedro, the man who would eventually betray her to grab the title to her city and immediately hand it over to his own son, yet another Aymeri of Narbonne.

The name Aymeri, which Ermengard's grandfather, father, brother, nephew, and grandnephew proudly bore, shows the power that poetry had already gained to shape reality early in the twelfth century. Other Aymeris had appeared in the family before this, notably an archbishop who held the see of Narbonne for an astonishing fifty years, from 927 to 977; but until the end of the eleventh century, the viscounts were more likely to be named Raymond or Berenger or Bernard, names they shared with the houses of Toulouse and Barcelona, in whose orbits they themselves had risen to prominence.[21] A legendary Aymeri of Narbonne, however, appeared as one of the emperor's paladins in a cycle of epic poems devoted to the deeds of Charlemagne, poems known all over Europe. He would himself be the principal figure in one of these poems (with a wife named Ermengard).[22] It would not be surprising if the ruling family of the city firmly believed that this epic Aymeri was their own ancestor, for even Occitan monks—men who in their prayers and liturgy preserved the memories of the great families who were their patrons—firmly believed that the legendary Charlemagne had founded their houses, often against the evidence of the parchments in their own treasuries. And so, from the last decades of the eleventh century, Aymeri—a name that shone with far more glorious honor and valorous deeds than did the names of the shadowy Franco, Odo, and Matfred, whom modern historians know as the tenth-century founders of the family's fortunes—was the name the viscounts chose for their eldest sons. With the exception of Ermengard, her nephew Pedro de Lara (who briefly succeeded her), and a thirteenth-century Amalric all the rulers of the city from 1094 to 1388 proudly bore it.[23]

Ermengard inherited this epic tradition along with the viscounty. Had her older brothers not died before her father, she might not have been heiress to her family's power. But they had died, and she was heiress.[24] Her actions in the years following 1143 must have quickly demonstrated that she was well trained to take on the task. Within a decade, her place within the alliance of the Trencavels, Barcelona, and Montpellier had become so important that in 1153, when Raymond Trencavel was captured by Alphonse Jordan's son, Raymond V of Toulouse, and feared for his life, he asked the count of Barcelona to act as guardian for his wife and children, but added that his son Roger and his men were to be "in God's custody and in Ermengard's and in her service."[25] That special place, surely, Ermengard herself had earned, and at the time she was still in her twenties.

Married to a husband of convenience, Ermengard became ruler of her city in fact as well as in name. The treaty that ended Alphonse's occupation of Narbonne marked her true coming of age—far more so than her two marriages in three years. For the pubescent girl, the marriage to the count of Toulouse, the war, the dissolution of that marriage, and the quick contracting of another were a political education of far more importance than any sexual or domestic initiation they might have implied. She saw how easily she could become the pawn of powers both inside and outside her city, especially of the men of new money in the burgeoning Narbonne marketplace, who were exemplified by at least three of the men who had witnessed her marriage. She learned who would threaten her independence and who would come to defend it. She probably learned whom in her own entourage she could trust and who were her enemies. With the exception of Peter of Minerve—whose family was too important to ignore—all the witnesses to her marriage to Alphonse disappeared from the records of Ermengard's court. In contrast, the men who witnessed her first independent acts stayed with her into the 1160s and 1170s, and their descendants remained with her to the very end of her reign.[26] The tumults of 1142–43 shaped her political vision as they shaped the political world within which she would navigate for the next half century. They take us straight to the heart of her long public life.

The years 1142–43 were not the last time she would call on her fellow Occitan lords to help defend her city and her lordship from the preying hands of a count of Toulouse. But henceforth she would be a full partner in the alliance, often on the move from Catalonia to Provence, deploying her military and political forces in the interests of herself, her city, and her friends. From adolescence to old age she would hear the summons of armed men and the trumpets of war, as the houses of Toulouse and Barcelona struggled for hegemony over the lands and lords between the Pyrenees and the Alps. In this struggle, Ermengard's allegiance was critical. With only some momentary exceptions, those who restored Ermengard to sole control of her city remained her allies until her very last years.

We can only imagine what strengths of personality she possessed to win the deep affections of her older allies. There are no vignettes, no journals or letters, no medieval equivalent of paparazzi hiding in the archives or the poetry to tell us; parchments in the archives deal in plain facts—Ermengard was here or there, doing this or that with these people or those—whereas the troubadours give us only the most conventional and formulaic portraits of their ladies. Whatever her personal traits may have been, her role as woman ruler of men, as *domina*, was not specially invented for her. The child Ermengard had many examples present and past from whom to learn.

HEIRESSES, WIDOWS, AND MATRIARCHS

Heiresses were always fair game for the powerful, especially child heiresses who could easily be made to follow the desires of their elders. The counts of Toulouse, like their contemporary kings, would add lands upon lands to their lordships by acquiring heiresses for themselves and their sons. The motto applied to the Hapsburgs centuries later, "Others take by force of arms, but you, oh happy Austria, marry," could have been adopted by the Raymonds of Toulouse, the Angevins, and the Capetians. Heiresses, however, had a way of growing up. Sometimes they found a voice of their own. On occasion their husbands departed for distant lands or died and left them behind as regents. Sometimes, though married, they continued to rule as heiresses in their own right. Women who were not heiresses also took power. They married into it and exercised co-lordship with their husbands. They too ruled as regents or widows, and sometimes sons had to wait years for their mothers to die or retire peacefully before the sons could succeed to their father's rule. Sometimes these matriarchs had to be retired by bribery or by force.

By the time Ermengard was born, almost every great Occitan dynasty (and many a castellan family as well) could name the matriarchs of their near or distant past, women whose lives were as charged with intrigue, ceremony, and warfare as those of their male contemporaries. The deeds of mothers and grandmothers were still alive in the minds of those who had known them. They were alive as well in testaments, oaths, and the busywork of estate management, on parchment carefully stored in family archives or brought to court by monks prayerfully requesting the confirmation of ancestral benefactions.[27]

Alphonse Jordan of Toulouse surely remembered (and doubtless to his displeasure) the widowed Gerberga, heiress to one of the many lines of the counts of Provence, who decided in 1112 to marry her daughter Douce to Count Ramon Berenguer III of Barcelona, thus depriving the child Alphonse of his potential claim to become sole count of Provence. He also knew all too well his cousin Philippa, whose occupation of Toulouse along with her husband, Duke William IX, had kept him out of his city until its urban militia rescued him from Orange and brought him home in 1123; her claim, passed on to her son, Duke William X, who on at least one occasion titled himself "he who was born of a mother from Toulouse,"[28] and eventually to her granddaughter, Eleanor of Aquitaine, posed a permanent threat from the north.

The Trencavels were particularly rich in such matriarchs, beginning on one side with Garsend, heiress to the viscounty of Béziers in the late tenth century, who by her marriage to Count Raymond of Carcassonne joined her coastal

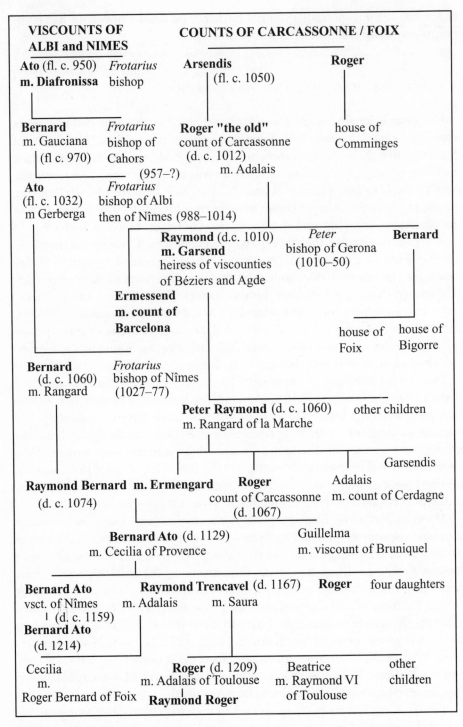

VISCOUNTS OF ALBI and NIMES

COUNTS OF CARCASSONNE / FOIX

Ato (fl. c. 950)   *Frotarius*   **Arsendis**   **Roger**
m. Diafronissa   bishop   (fl. c. 1050)

Bernard   *Frotarius*   **Roger "the old"**   house of
m. Gauciana   bishop of   count of Carcassonne   Comminges
  (fl c. 970)   Cahors   (d. c. 1012)
                     (957–?)   m. Adalais
Ato   *Frotarius*
(fl. c. 1032)   bishop of Albi
m Gerberga   then of Nîmes (988–1014)

                     Raymond (d.c. 1010)   *Peter*   **Bernard**
                     m. Garsend   bishop of Gerona
                     heiress of viscounties   (1010–50)
                     of Béziers and Agde
         Ermessend
         m. count of
         Barcelona
                                                 house of   house of
                                                 Foix   Bigorre

Bernard   *Frotarius*
(d. c. 1060)   bishop of Nîmes
m. Rangard   (1027–77)
                     Peter Raymond (d. c. 1060)   other children
                     m. Rangard of la Marche

                                                             Garsendis
Raymond Bernard m. Ermengard   **Roger**   Adalais
(d. c. 1074)   count of Carcassonne   m. count of Cerdagne
                                      (d. 1067)

         Bernard Ato (d. 1129)   Guillelma
         m. Cecilia of Provence   m. viscount of Bruniquel

Bernard Ato   **Raymond Trencavel** (d. 1167)   **Roger**   four daughters
vsct. of Nîmes   m. Adalais   m. Saura
  (d. c. 1159)
Bernard Ato
(d. 1214)

Cecilia   **Roger** (d. 1209)   Beatrice   other
m.   m. Adalais of Toulouse   m. Raymond VI   children
Roger Bernard of Foix **Raymond Roger**   of Toulouse

Families that became the Trencavels

lands that dominated the land route between the Rhone and the Pyrenees to the interior lands of her husband, which sat athwart the roads from Narbonne and the Massif Central to Toulouse. Their son Peter Raymond married Rangard of La Marche, sister of Almodis (whose three marriages—the second to the count of Toulouse and the third to the count of Barcelona—made her into the stuff of legend in both the Christian and the Islamic world). On her husband's death, Rangard, along with her son, took over the rule of his counties. On her son's death in 1067, she allied herself with the count of Cerdagne (in the Pyrenees, to the south of Carcassonne and Toulouse) in order to stay in power. She was outwitted by her daughter Ermengard and Ermengard's husband, the viscount of Albi and Nîmes, who allied themselves with the count and countess of Barcelona to conquer the lands of the count of Carcassonne with the help of sacks of Moslem gold. This Ermengard was the real creator of the family enterprise that modern historians know as the Trencavels. After her husband's death, she took the reins of power as her mother had done before her, going from castle to castle all the way from Albi in the west to Nîmes in the east and the Razès in the south to collect oaths of fidelity. In the 1080s she repeated the process with her young son Bernard Ato, hoping thus to assure his quiet succession when she passed from the scene. The Trencavels also surely remembered Ermessend, sister of the count of Carcassonne and the bishop of Gerona. As wife and then widow of Count Ramon Borrell of Barcelona, she was twice regent, once for her son and once for her grandson; the latter, along with his wife Almodis of la Marche, had to wage war against her and finally buy out her dowry in order to take personal rule of Catalonia. On the Albigeois side of the family there was Diafronissa, far back in the early tenth century. Clergy bearing an ancient charter could remind them of her, for there she was, listed first in a gift to the canons of Beaumont-d'Aveyron, taking precedence in the document over a son and grandson, both of whom were already viscounts at the time the gift was made, and over another grandson who was bishop. Despite her great age, she had not retired from the concerns of this world.[29]

In a similar way, monks and clerics seeking confirmation of long-ago gifts might have reminded the young Ermengard of Narbonne of her tenth-century ancestor the Viscountess Adalaide, wife of Viscount Matfred, who ruled as widow from her husband's death sometime after 966 until around 990. It was Adalaide and her sister-in-law Garsend, widow of Count Raymond Pons of Toulouse, whom the archbishop of Narbonne and the abbot of Saint-Pons called on to mediate a dispute in 969—the two widows rather than Matfred and Adalaide's two sons, one of whom would eventually become viscount and the other archbishop.[30] Ermengard's grandmother Mahalt would surely have left a much livelier memory around the vicecomital palace. Daughter of the fiery Norman duke of Apulia, Robert Guiscard, she had taken refuge in Rodez immediately after the murder of her husband Count Ramon Berenguer II of Barcelona. There, soon after the birth of the son who would become Count Ramon Berenguer III, she met and married Viscount Aymeri I of Narbonne.[31] When her husband went off crusading in the Holy Land, she stayed behind with her sons, Aymeri, Guiscard, and Bernard, vigorously pursuing her husband's vendetta against Bishop Bertrand of Nîmes, who had been translated to the see of Narbonne in 1097, and finally getting him deposed in 1106.[32]

Although Mahalt remarried, these great aristocratic widows most often did not do so, and surely Mahalt would not have either, had her life and her widow's rights been assured.[33] There were few, after all, who could offer them the status, wealth, and power that their widowhood preserved. All these great women came to power as wives, widows, or heiresses, through the route of inheritance. When Occitan aristocrats made their wills, the only rules that restricted how they could devise their property were the rights of surviving widows to their dowry and marriage gift. Those who gave thought not only to the fate of their soul but to the afterlife of their family and its accumulated wealth and power knew well, however, that their sons would expect to share equally in their father's lands and their daughters would expect to be provided for. When there was no last testament, equality among male heirs was the rule,[34] and fathers would have been foolhardy to ignore it. When Bernard Ato, the Trencavel viscount, made his will in 1118 on the eve of his departure to fight the Moslems in Spain, he left all his lands to the rule of his wife Cecilia for as long as she lived and carefully arranged the division of those lands between his two sons, Roger and Raymond Trencavel, after her death. Eleven years later, he revisited his design on his deathbed, in order to provide for his third son, Bernard Ato. Roger, the eldest, received the western block of Albi, Carcassonne, and the Razès; Raymond, the viscounties of Béziers and Agde; and Bernard, the viscounty of Nîmes. After their father's death, Roger and Raymond confirmed the division, but for greater strength and safety they agreed to hold their lands in common for five years.[35] Despite the French conquest of the region in the Albigensian Crusades, the same expectations of equality remained as late as 1270.[36] Even among the lords of Montpellier, who early showed a decided preference for keeping their lands and powers intact in the hands of their eldest son, there were special provisions for younger sons; as William VI put it when providing for his third son, Bernard William, in his testament of 1146, "It is not fitting that a noble man should have a mean inheritance."[37]

This Occitan preference for equality or near equality did not necessarily extend to daughters. When provided for in testaments, daughters usually took less than their brothers. If they were married and had therefore received a portion of their family's wealth as a dowry, it was commonly expected that they would make no further claim. The earliest Occitan customal, from Saint-Antonin in the Rouergue, excludes such dowried daughters by rule, and eventually that became the custom throughout the region. "Let her be satisfied with this," a testator might say—perhaps with more hope than assurance—when he specified his daughter's inheritance or the sum reserved for her future dowry.[38] But daughters were not always excluded; preference for sons was an option, not a rule. Nor were daughters always so easily satisfied or willing as mature women to accept what they had received as young brides. The Trencavel viscount Bernard Ato had four daughters as well as three sons. Three of these daughters were married in his lifetime, and in his testament he specified only that his eldest son Roger attend to the marriage of the fourth, Pagana, providing her with a suitable husband and a dowry. The other daughters he does not even mention. Yet twenty-three years later in 1152, after Roger's death, his brothers Raymond and Bernard took the precaution to have at least two of their sisters, Pagana and Metilina (had the other two died, or have the documents simply disappeared?), renounce all their rights in their father's inheritance.[39] Clearly, one could never be too sure, and time was no bar to reviving a daughter's long-dormant claim. In later years, Viscountess Ermengard occasionally found herself adjudicating petitions by sisters for their share of paternal or maternal lands, and we should not be surprised to discover lords and ladies of modest rank bequeathing their property, including castles, equally to daughters and sons or nieces and nephews.[40]

Among those of both great and modest rank, however, the most common pattern of substitution when both sons and daughters survived was to require the women to wait their turn, until their brothers died without heirs. Despite appearances, there was nothing strictly misogynist about this practice, no assumption that women were by nature incapable of holding property or playing a proper lordly role. We need only look at a Catalan divorce case of the 1130s that must have set tongues wagging all the way to the Alps. The principals were William Raymond and his wife Beatrice. William, by his rank of seneschal or *dapifer*, was one of the most powerful individuals in the entourage of Count Ramon Berenguer IV and in control of many castles. The property division, negotiated by friends, divided these castles equally between husband and ex-wife; each was to hold all the castles six months of the year, and those who manned the castles were to swear explicitly in their oaths of fidelity to defend Beatrice's rights against her ex-husband. (A few months later, the count of Barcelona gave Beatrice in marriage to another powerful baron, William of Sant Martì, with the honor of Montcada as her marriage gift.)[41]

The practice of making women wait their turn seems designed to limit the possibility that their husbands and husbands' kinfolk (other than a couple's children) might eventually make claims on a family's lands, leading to further conflict or to the dispersion of the sources of wealth and status outside the lineage; it responded to the same anxieties that led fathers increasingly to assign dowries in cash, which the new couple could use to acquire new lands and lordships.[42] Wives, however, were part of the lineage, and men, when faced with death, were quite ready to leave their estates to their widows as long as they did not remarry—we have just seen a striking example in Viscount Bernard Ato's first testament of 1118. If the testators were unmarried, their mothers might become their heirs.[43] Inevitably, in some families, sons would die without heirs, or the roll of the reproductive dice would produce only daughters. Then, after the widow, would come the heiresses.

In the game of succession, heiresses were not always satisfied with playing pawn to male knights, castles, and kings. Women sometimes seized the chance to impose through diplomacy and war their own conceptions of dynastic duty. Far to the north, the "Empress" Matilda, daughter of King Henry I of England, was following a distinguished tradition when she fought to win a kingdom for her son, the future Henry II. Matilda was a generation older than Ermengard of Narbonne. News of her wars against King Stephen may very well have reached the Mediterranean via northern merchants just when Ermengard was gaining her freedom from Alphonse Jordan. But Ermengard did not have to look so far away to learn the rules of the game of lineage. If her stepmother and her father's advisors did not instruct her while she was still a child, if she was not brought up on memories of the great deeds done by the great women in her own family's past, she had striking examples only slightly older than herself right in the neighborhood.

Beatrice of Mauguio, whose marriage to Berenguer Ramon, the count of Provence, spawned the bitter conflict between William of Montpellier and Alphonse Jordan, found herself a young widow when her husband was killed in a skirmish with the Genoese before the walls of her castle in 1143, the most prominent casualty of the war to free Ermengard. The couple already had a son, who would eventually become count of Provence. In the documents that issued from her chancery, however, she was henceforth "Beatrice, countess of Mauguio, daughter of Guilelma and of Bernard, count of Mauguio of happy memory." When she remarried, her husband was merely "count, husband of the aforesaid Beatrice."[44] The son by Berenguer Ramon had no claim to her county. Decades later, when the son by her second marriage contested Beatrice's primacy, she responded with a powerful demonstration that she still controlled her county. But that is a story for later.

The most striking models of powerful lady lords, however, were Stephania of les Baux, against whom Ermengard would actively campaign, and Eleanor of Aquitaine, whose claim to Toulouse was a byword for invading armies. From the 1130s to the 1160s, the inheritances of these women dominated Occitan politics. In the heat of the wars they spawned, the young Ermengard of Narbonne quickly grew to political adulthood.

STEPHANIA AND ELEANOR

On its perch high on the southern rim of a hill range known as the Alpilles, east of Arles in Provence, the castle of les Baux stands sentinel over what was

The twelfth-century village and castle at les Baux. Author photograph.

once the vast stony floodplain of the lower Durance River. The hills have been immortalized in Vincent van Gogh's *Starry Night*, painted while the artist was hospitalized at Saint-Rémy, on the plain just to the north. The castle has given its name to bauxite, the ore from which aluminum is made. In the twelfth century, les Baux was principally known for the powerful family who ruled from its stone keep. Along with the viscounts of Marseille and the lords of Fos, they thought of themselves as the heads of the region's aristocracy, second only to the Barcelonese count of Provence and the Toulousain marquis.

Their prominence was recognized when sometime before 1113, Raymond of les Baux married Stephania, the younger daughter of Gerberga, countess of Provence, and sister of the Douce who took the county with her when she married Count Ramon Berengur of Barcelona. Stephania was dowered and excluded from further rights to the family's inheritance—at least this is what she was later required to confess.[45] This early exclusion (if indeed it happened) did not deter her and her husband from suddenly advancing their own claims to the county in 1144, after decades of loyal service in the entourage of Alphonse Jordan. They had long contemplated the move and had well prepared the ground.

From the ninth to the early eleventh century, a kingdom of Burgundy stretched down the left bank of the Saone and the Rhone Rivers from the Jura Mountains to the Mediterranean, incorporating within its spread the area that became the county of Provence. Conrad II annexed this kingdom to the Empire in 1034, and although it mostly went its own way in the late eleventh century, its status as land of the Empire was not forgotten. Even the hapless Emperor Conrad III tried to keep imperial prerogatives alive in the region. Recognizing a possible ally, Stephania and her husband Raymond of les Baux dispatched one of their children to Conrad's court to cultivate the patronage of those near the throne. Their care paid off. In 1143 or 1144, while the Barcelonese and their allies were distracted by their war to free Ermengard and her city, they petitioned the emperor to recognize Stephania's inheritance. From Conrad's court came a diploma sealed with gold. It declared that they held directly of the Imperial Crown not only the traditional lands of the family of les Baux but all the lands and rights of Stephania's mother and father—by implication their rights to the county, the very rights exercised for thirty-two years by the Barcelonese dynasty. For good measure it also granted them the regalian rights to coin money at Aix or Arles, or at their castle at Trinquetaille on the Rhone.[46] It was a declaration of war.

With the Trencavels, William of Montpellier, and the count of Barcelona recovering from their efforts on the other side of the Rhone and the Barcelonese count of Provence dead on the battlefield, the les Baux and their friends from Lambesc and Fos quickly dominated the western half of Provence. For three years the les Baux were able to parade themselves as countess and count of Provence, until the count of Barcelona mustered his forces at Tarascon and marched them into the heart of his enemies' lands, forcing or inducing those who had succumbed to the temptations of rebellion to come once again to order. Raymond of les Baux went to Barcelona to sue for peace. Stephania and her four sons, however, did not take their oaths of peace and fidelity until 1150, and her son Hugh reopened the conflict in 1156 with a new diploma from Conrad's successor, Frederick I. It was not until 1162 that a Catalan army, supported by the Trencavels and Ermengard of Narbonne at the head of their troops, besieged and captured les Baux itself and finally squelched the family's pretensions.[47]

Meanwhile, the claims of Eleanor of Aquitaine to the city of Toulouse had inflamed western Occitania as Stephania's had inflamed Provence.

The connections of Toulouse to the dynasty of the dukes of Aquitaine, of whom Eleanor was the heiress, were typical of the semimythical historical memories and complex embranglement of familial fortunes that lay behind much twelfth-century state building. To onlookers contemplating the mysteries of the divine plan or barons looking for reasons to take to the field, they must have provided a wealth of material.

Far back in the distant past, Toulouse had been the capital of a Gothic kingdom. Memories of it filtered through the name *Gothia*, which ninth- and tenth-century scribes applied to the whole region from Toulouse to the Rhone. The kingdom of Aquitaine, re-created by Charlemagne in 781 for his infant son Louis, encompassed the city, and as Charlemagne's empire fragmented in the late ninth century, the counts of Toulouse warred with the counts of Poitiers for some kind of hegemony over the region. The counts of Toulouse eventually turned their attention toward the Rhone valley, leaving the title of duke of Aquitaine to their old rivals while keeping Toulouse for themselves. But the memories of rival claims to that city lingered on. When the young Philippa, orphaned daughter of Count William IV of Toulouse, lost her first husband, King Sancho Ramiro of Aragon, she wasted no time in mourning but quickly married Duke William IX of Aquitaine to help her reassert her title to her father's inheritance. Those ancient memories immediately took on new life.

Philippa—her father's only surviving child—had been pushed aside by her paternal uncle, Raymond IV (the man known to crusading chroniclers as Raymond of Saint-Gilles). But when Raymond heeded the call of adventure and salvation and departed armed for the Holy Land in 1096, his son Bertrand, to whom he left his lands in the west, soon found himself battling his disinherited cousin as Philippa and William IX quickly invested and took the city.[48]

The stakes were wealth as well as title. Toulouse was a hub of the old Roman road system. Here the routes leading south from the Loire via Poitiers and Limoges met those coming west from Lyons and Narbonne, east from Bordeaux, and north from the passes of the Pyrenees. Goods passing up the Garonne River had to be unloaded at Toulouse to go by mule across the "continental divide" near Castelnaudary to reach the Mediterranean at Narbonne. Goods coming from La Rochelle or the Loire valley had to go by way of Cahors—also in the hands of the counts of Toulouse—before choosing the mountain road toward the Hérault River and Agde or Montpellier or joining the more southerly route at Toulouse. Commerce meant tolls and easy wealth for those who levied them. But for those without political control, that commerce always lay under a threat: it could always be stopped, and merchants and their goods, in effect, held for ransom. "Without [Toulouse]," writes the British historian W. L. Warren, "the Poitevin lordship of Aquitaine was both incomplete and fatally weakened."[49]

Although Alphonse Jordan eventually gained control of Toulouse, in the house of Poitiers, resentments as well as the ambitions they fed lingered on. Eleanor of Aquitaine brought them with her when she married King Louis VII of France. It was probably to realize those ambitions at her instigation that he marched on Toulouse in 1141, a raid that came to naught. In 1159, it would be the turn of her second husband, King Henry II. By then, as we shall see, Occitania had become the playground of the crowned heads of Europe. Two marriages—Eleanor of Aquitaine and Henry of Anjou in 1152, and Count Raymond V (the son of Alphonse Jordan) and Constance, the sister of King Louis VII, in 1154—made Toulouse the new frontier in the long-standing Angevin–Capetian rivalry.

In 1157, Ermengard met her old allies—Raymond Trencavel, William of Montpellier, and the count of Barcelona—at Montpellier and declared war on Raymond V.[50] Soon envoys were hastening back and forth between them and King Henry II to plan a joint attack. In midsummer 1159, Henry assembled an army at Poitiers and marched on Toulouse. Raymond V immediately called on his brother-in-law to come to his aid. For the space of a few weeks, the two kings faced each other across the walls of Toulouse. Then Henry, announcing he would not fight his own lord, decamped. The incident ended in May 1160 when the two kings made peace. But Henry was making threatening gestures again in 1162 and 1164.[51]

⋅⟞⟝⊃

Ermengard was a young teenager when these wars began. By the time she was in her twenties she was already a full partner in their prosecution. In Philippa as well as in Philippa's granddaughter Eleanor, in the women of Ermengard's own dynasty as well as in those of her friends the Trencavels, and in her enemy Stephania of les Baux, there were many powerful examples of how women could bear the burdens of dynasty as easily as men, how they could carry those burdens into marriage without loss, could spur on their husbands when necessary, and train their sons or daughters to carry their claims into the next generation. But there is no reason to think that the youthful Ermengard needed guides or models. The frequency and ease with which heiresses and widows moved into positions of power can only mean that they were trained from an early age to the demands and responsibilities of their eventual place in society.

And so we find Ermengard with her army aiding the count of Barcelona at the siege of Tortosa in 1148 and again at the siege of les Baux in 1162–63. She joined the alliance against Raymond V in 1157, and she took part in negotiating the peace treaty between Raymond Trencavel and Count Raymond at Homps, near Carcassonne, in 1163. For a brief moment she switched sides, supporting the alliance of the count of Toulouse and the count of Foix against Trencavel's son Roger; then she brought the two sides together when Roger married Raymond's daughter Adalais.[52] During the half century of her rule, she was a full partner in all the region's alliances, sieges, battles, truces, and treaties and in what must have been the constant, tangled negotiations as well that ordered this quadrille of shifting aristocratic friendships. Like other great ladies of her age, she was often courted, but no longer for her hand in marriage. The real prize was power, and especially the strength in men, money, and history of her city, Narbonne.

ERMENGARD'S CITY

PREFACE

To the visitor passing through Narbonne on the way to or from the beaches of the Spanish coast, the importance during medieval times of this sleepy town on its nearly stagnant canal is far from evident. Nothing remains of its once formidable late Antique walls or of the vicecomital palace, long since replaced by a modest department store. The river that brought commerce to its markets has long since moved its waters elsewhere. All but one arch of the medieval bridge that spanned the river where the Roman bridge once stood now lie buried, serving as basements for shops. Only the remnants of the medieval archepiscopal palace (restored in his own manner by Violet le Duc in the nineteenth century) and the partially completed Gothic cathedral, its construction stopped by the city wall and the beginning of what would turn into the Hundred Years War, give some sense of the resources that the city's clergy and great aristocrats could mobilize. Visiting the city in 1838, Stendhal found it "as gay as Carcassonne is sad"; yet it was worth barely twenty-four hours of his time, sufficient to visit the cathedral and look at the city walls but not enough even to complain, as he did elsewhere, about the vileness of the coffee, the rudeness of the servants, or the ugliness of the inhabitants.[1]

To understand Ermengard, however, we must first get to know her city, and the countryside from which it lived, as it was in the twelfth century. Power then relied on the loyalty of men and women whose status and resources made them likewise people of power—*potentes* in the language of the age. To gain and keep that loyalty required display and open-handedness, and that required wealth in money and land and the services and dues of those who worked the land and traded in the market. There were also rivals for wealth and power within the city—the merchant elite and, above all, the archbishop. The threat was therefore ever present of rivals within and without the city joining forces. The lessons were ready to hand: in the cities of her friends the Trencavels and the lords of Montpellier, such combinations led to revolts and even assassinations. Her own career as well would be marked by coups in which such rivals united to oust her from her city. Managing the growing economy and the ambitions it spawned was therefore one of her primary concerns.

It was Ermengard's city and the countryside of her viscounty that made her an object of desire, that made Count Raymond IV of Toulouse devise for himself the title duke of Narbonne and his son to attempt to turn that title into the reality of rule. The time has come to start our visit.

CHAPTER TWO
NAMES AND TITLES,
HISTORIES AND MYTHS

In the Middle Ages, as in our own time, to name was to claim. Over Ermengard's Occitania, claims abounded. The greatest aristocrats adopted cities as their titles: Ermengard was viscountess of Narbonne; the members of the Trencavel clan were viscounts of Albi, Béziers, Agde, and Nîmes; Beatrice was countess of Mauguio; the successive Williams who ruled Montpellier turned the modest title lord of Montpellier into a badge of pride. People of more modest estate were known simply by their village, their castle, or their lord; they were not French or Occitans but lord of Thézan or Aumelas, citizens or burgesses of Narbonne or Toulouse or Montpellier, men and women of this or that count or viscountess or village lord. In the geographical and political language of Ermengard's day, Narbonne's region was an agglomeration of cities and their territories. Before the Crusaders taught its inhabitants their solidarity in butchery and defeat, the region as a whole had no name by which to know itself.[1]

The unity it possessed came from its language and the habits and assumptions of its urbane, aristocratic way of life. That, doubtless, is why outsiders, and especially northerners, chose the language to be the region's name. For although that language included many dialects—Gascon to the west, Limousin and Auvergnat to the north, the dialect of the coastal plain from Toulouse to Marseille and beyond—these were not so far apart that a merchant from Bordeaux could not easily conduct business in Arles or Toulon, or even in Barcelona—for Catalan too was closely related. The language of the troubadours was itself a kind of literary dialect that people shared from as far north as Poitiers to northern Italy and Spain. The first known troubadour was Duke William IX of Aquitaine, count of Poitiers (and husband of Philippa of Toulouse); Dante and Petrarch eventually inherited the tradition that he began. Language and the poets who shaped it could not give the region a political identity, but they did create a powerful sense of shared culture.[2]

"France" for these people was the region now called the Ile-de-France, the Paris basin and its extensions reaching eastward toward Champagne and south across the Loire to Bourges. This was the area in which the Capetians had their crown lands, the area in which during the eleventh century and the early decades of the twelfth they exercised effective control. Although Occitan notaries in accordance with centuries-old formulae dated their documents according to the regnal dates of the French kings, and although counts, viscounts, and bishops recognized the Capetian king as the legitimate successor to the Carolingians and thus in some vague way as their lord, France was an alien country, far away. Counts and viscounts held their title not by the king's grace but, as they had their scribes sometimes write in the introductions to their charters, "by the grace of God."[3]

That sense of estrangement was shared in reverse by the people of the north. In the minds of northern knights, the Mediterranean world suggested marvels and mysteries akin to those of magic castles in chivalric romances; for the poets who on a winter's night entertained bored fighting men around the castle hearth, the oath "not for all the gold in Montpellier" was as strong in the negative as "by the body of Saint Amand" was positive.[4] Northern clergy, less awestruck, reacted with overt xenophobia. In 1181, Abbot Stephen of Saint-Germain-des-Prés, who had just finished a mission through the area, congratulated a colleague promoted to the primacy of Lyon rather than Narbonne for escaping "the barbarity of the Goths, the flightiness of the Gascons, the cruel and savage habits of Septimania."[5]

Septimania, on Stephen's tongue, was an archaic affectation. The name had been invented by the late Antique poet Sidonius Apollinaris and picked up by the sixth-century bishop Gregory of Tours; adopted by the clerks of the Carolingian chancery as a name for the region, it survived as a literary conceit at monastic writing desks but otherwise gradually faded from common use. Gothia, another Carolingian name, was sometimes invoked by writers who were proud of their Latinity. It summoned up the shades of the Visigoths, who before the Frankish conquest had ruled Occitania and Spain from their capital in Toulouse. Even the name Aquitania sometimes served monastic writers to designate all the lands between the Atlantic and the Rhone, although it more properly specified the region to the west of Toulouse, the old Roman province whose boundaries had been inherited by the archdiocese of Bordeaux.[6]

All these names, however, were far too learned to catch the fancy of a larger public. Gothia and Aquitania, furthermore, came with political liabilities attached, were a ruling family in the region brash enough to adopt either as its title. The resonance of the name Gothia only too clearly extended southward over the Pyrenees into Catalonia, Aragon, and Castile, whose rulers each in their own way were laying claim to a Gothic past. And the name Aquitania had already been appropriated in the tenth century, first by the counts of Auvergne and then by the counts of Poitou, to assert their high lordship in the lands between the Massif Central and the Atlantic.[7]

Consequently, when shortly before he left on the first Crusade, Raymond IV of Toulouse—best known to crusading historians as Raymond of Saint-

Gilles—the father of Alphonse Jordan, decided to claim hegemony between the Pyrenees and the Alps, there was nothing ready at hand to give expression to this grandiose dream. Distant cousins in the mountain city of Rodez, however, had maintained the shadowy title of count of Narbonne; its memory was given what substance it had by property in the city and by the claim to share in the profits from selling the archbishopric. When Bertha, the last heiress to that line, died without direct heirs of her own, Raymond of Saint-Gilles fought her husband for her succession and won. The prize was not her impoverished lands on the fringe of the Massif Central, however, for within a few decades the title and powers of the count of Rodez were sold to the viscounts of Milau. The prize was the title to Narbonne.[8] Through his father and grandmother, Raymond of Saint-Gilles already had a claim to title himself count of Provence. He could now add that of count of Narbonne. Yet rather than simply titling himself in one way here and another there, or piling titles one upon the other as a verbal layer cake—as his ancestors had sometimes done—he reached much further back, to fantasies of the Roman past, as they were filtered through late Carolingian traditions. He called himself count of Toulouse, duke of Narbonne, and marquis of Provence—the first title for his city on the Garonne, the second for all the regions between the Rhone and Roussillon, the Roman Provincia Narbonensis Prima, and the third for the Imperial lands to the east, the Roman Provincia Viennensis.[9] Although the Capetians pointedly ignored this newly coined title (even when Count Raymond V became the king's brother-in-law), and the troubadours knew the counts of Toulouse as the counts of Saint-Gilles, the title that Raymond IV invented became the title his descendants regularly employed until the house went down in bitter defeat during the Albigensian Crusades.

What strength was in the name Narbonne? At one time or another, Raymond's predecessors had fashioned a comital title for themselves over nearly every city from Toulouse to the Rhone. What memories, what powers of wealth or enchantment made the city on the Aude worth asserting the title of duke?

THE LEGACIES OF ANTIQUITY

Here on the shores of the Mediterranean, the Greeks and Romans of antiquity had planted cities in whose ports their merchants could take refuge from tempests and profit from trade with the natives; they had planted cities inland as well, along the track that since time immemorial linked the passes of the Alps with the narrow gate of L'Ecluse through the Pyrenees. Between the Rhone and the Pyrenees, this road eventually bore the name of the Roman proconsul Cn. Domitius Ahenobarbus; it was the via Domitia. When the ancient traveler crossed the river heading west, he would find cities less than twenty-five miles apart, an easy day's stage in good weather. (In 1838, over roads surely no better and traveling by commercial coach, Stendhal was able to go from Carcassonne to Narbonne in five and a half hours and from Narbonne to Montpellier in a little over twelve.)[10] In the eyes of the first-century writer Pomponius Mela, the cities of the plain were "urbes opulentissimae," cities as wealthy as could be imagined. Even the lesser settlements along the way provided such urban amenities as temples and public baths along with their taverns, hostelries, brothels, and thieves.[11] Although two millennia have buried Greek and Roman stones deep under medieval and modern layers, there is hardly a major town in the region that does not to this day boast its ancient monument; and there is much more just under the surface. Use a backhoe to lay a sewer line or dig a foundation and you uncover an antique wall or street, the remains of a bath, or skeletons from an ancient or medieval cemetery.

In the Middle Ages, many more of these ancient monuments stood their ground than now greet the eye of the roving tourist. Antiquity and all that shared its mythical prestige was still a powerful living presence. Knights and merchants trod the roads that ancient Roman surveyors had laid out, measured their passage by Roman milestones, crossed streams and swamps on Roman bridges and causeways. The sight of ancient city walls told travelers they were nearing their destination. Ancient gates marked their entry onto city streets. The markets where they gathered to buy and sell were the *fora* where Roman merchants had gathered a millennium before. Along the way they might admire a mighty fortress whose filled archways or brick fabric bore mute testimony to what once had been its antique splendor. The most important barons of Nîmes were those of the Arena, whose fortifications occupied the ancient amphitheater. In Toulouse the count's vicar held his court in what was called the Narbonne Castle, a fortified gate of the old Roman wall. Ancient churches still served the faithful; the builders of the eleventh and twelfth centuries incorporated those walls or entire buildings into many a new-style Romanesque structure.[12] The names on the land, even the soil itself, continued to bear antiquity's heavy imprint, not just in names such as Lezignan (from Licinianum, "Licinius's place") or Aureilhan (from Aurelianum, "Aurelius's place"), and many others like them, all of whose Roman roots were probably forgotten, but more a propos in place-names such as Aquaductum, mentioned by chance in a tenth-century document, a reference to an aqueduct that had once supplied a first-century pottery manufacturer. Was water still flowing in that ancient man-made channel? And how many other such names have been lost to memory?[13] Although ancient roofs collapsed and walls were quarried for building stone (much as medieval buildings were still being quarried early in this century), enough survived to attract the wonder and emulation of Ermengard's contemporaries.

In this world, Narbonne occupied a special place, its old stones long since overlaid with fantasy. Travelers' tales had carried the city's fame across the

Mediterranean and eastward to Damascus and beyond. Its story reached so far back in time that by the twelfth century, neither Christian cleric, nor Jewish rabbi, nor Moslem scholar could any longer distinguish history from myth.

According to twelfth-century Jewish legend, it was Charlemagne himself who asked the king of Babylon to send a rabbi from the house of David to found a Talmudic school in Narbonne; that, so the story went, was the origin of the *nassi'im*, the Jewish leaders of the city. The story was picked up by a monk of the abbey of Lagrasse in the Corbières. It was the Jews, he claimed, who in the eighth century betrayed the city's Moslem rulers and delivered the city to Charlemagne; the emperor in gratitude shared the conquest between the Jews, the archbishop, and the viscount.[14] That, said yet another legend, was but a continuation of a far more ancient friendship; the story was important enough for an official notary to record it, early in the thirteenth century, in one of Narbonne's great record books: "In the days of King David the city of Narbonne was surrounded with a wall, and in those days King David sent two knights to Narbonne to make an alliance with the city. So it has been found in the Jewish archives in Avignon."[15]

The geographers of the Islamic world likewise made the city a place of legend as well as circumstantial report. It was "the farthest conquest of Islam in the land of the Franks." And there, so one of them said, stood a statue bearing this inscription: "Turn back, oh sons of Ishmael! You shall go no further. If you ask me why I will say to you, if you do not turn back you will fight each other until the Last Judgment."[16] This was a sober warning, binding the fate of the Arabs to that of this now alien city.

⋆⟾

The Romans first built on the site of Narbonne in 118 B.C.E. For their new foundation they borrowed the name of an Iron Age fort that dominated the mouth of the Aude from a nearby hill and added the name of their own god Mars: the city became Colonia Narbo Martius. Just downstream from the colony their ships could lie at anchor in a great bay, protected by the hills of the nearby Corbières from the northern winds and by islands and a line of sand bars from the often perilous Mediterranean Sea storms. For hundreds of years already this bay had served Iberian, Phoenician, Carthaginian, and Greek sailors as a major haven along the shallow, shoal-studded shoreline between the Rhone delta and the Pyrenees. It continued to serve the Romans for half a millennium. As Rome's first colony beyond the Alps, Narbonne became the administrative capital of its new possessions; then as Rome's conquests extended north and west, it became the chief city and name giver to a province.

The via Domitia formed the principal street of the colony, exiting across the Aude on a seven-arched bridge, then branching south to Spain and east to Toulouse, Aquitaine, and the Atlantic. In the forum of Narbo Martius, mer-

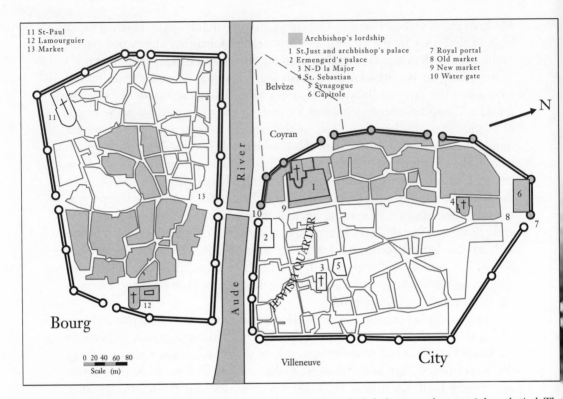

Narbonne in Ermengard's time. Except for the three towers near the cathedral, the tower placement is hypothetical. The archbishop's lordship in the City is based on the rather vague formulations in twelfth-century documents; that in the Bourg is based on thirteenth-century documents. *Source*: Caille, "Origine et développement de la seigneurie temporelle de l'archevêque."

chants who came by sea to the lagoon at the mouth of the Aude or by land from Spain or from the ore-rich hills of the city's hinterland met others who—like their prehistoric forebears—brought precious tin and copper from Britain via the Atlantic, the Garonne, and the road from Toulouse. Over a millennium later, a Moslem geographer would still mention this trade and the ships that took the valued metals from Narbonne to Alexandria. As long as merchants plied these routes along the coast and into the interior, Narbonne's prosperity and its fame were assured.[17]

In Ermengard's time, the remains of this ancient glory were everywhere present. The massive wall that protected the city was a veritable museum of ancient sculpture and inscriptions, for it had been thrown up hastily in the middle of the third century, using stones cannibalized from the mausoleums and monuments that had adorned the city in its golden age. (Rebuilt numerous times afterward and much enlarged by Kings Louis XII and Francis I, it was finally dismantled in 1868; its inscriptions and works of art have found their final resting place in the deconsecrated church of Lamourguier; an attentive eye can spot other monumental remains in the sea walls and railroad fill along the coast to

The Royal Gate of Narbonne. From Charles Nodier et al., *Voyages pittoresques et romantiques dans l'ancienne France. Languedoc.* By permission of the Houghton Library, Harvard University.

Fragment of Roman building material from the old wall of Narbonne, reused as a sea wall south of Narbonne. Author photograph.

the south.) By the northern wall, where the via Domitia entered the city through the imposing Royal Gate, stood an ancient basilica, the Capitole. It had been converted into a palace by the Visigothic kings who made Narbonne their residence in the sixth century, then into a fortress; it gave its name to one of the city's noble families. Below it, a market still gathered on the site of the ancient forum. Just beyond the southern gate, or the Water Gate as it was known in the Middle Ages, the Roman bridge still spanned the Aude. East of the ancient wall the amphitheater, still recognizable, slowly crumbled to dust, its usable stones long since quarried for other construction.[18]

Christian Rome was everywhere as well. The cathedral that squeezed in between the episcopal palace and the city wall had been built by Bishop Rusticus in the fifth century; he was honored in a lintel inscription that told not only of the pious bishop and his faithful priest Ursus and deacon Hermes, but of the many faithful, both lay and clergy, who contributed their gold to pay for its construction. Rusticus was a name that Ermengard's contemporaries would have recognized from another inscription in the ancient funerary chapel of Saint-Vincent, southeast of the city near the river: "Pray for me, your dear Rusticus." In ruins after the Frankish conquest at the end of the eighth century, the cathedral was restored by the ninth-century archbishops Theodard and his successor Arnust, who replaced its eastern apse with the far larger one that the liturgy of the time demanded. (The walls of the chapel of the Annunciation in Narbonne's gothic cathedral stand on the foundations of the tenth-century choir.)[19] By Ermengard's time, the church had long since been dedicated to two Spanish martyrs whose relics, so it was told, Charlemagne had intended to bring back from Saragossa but had lost in his tragic retreat across the mountains, a retreat immortalized in the *Song of Roland*. Indeed, Ermengard's contemporaries commonly attributed the church's construction to Charlemagne (as they did the liberation of the city from the Moslems), a figure looming far away through a thick glowing fog of myth. For Ermengard's great-grandfather Berenger, Charlemagne's refoundation was as essential to the church's fame as were the treasures it enclosed.

> In the days when my uncle Ermengaud was archbishop [Berenger proclaimed in a long diatribe against Archbishop Guifred in 1059] this bishopric was one of the greatest between Rome and the boundaries of Moslem Spain. It was rich in castles and towns, opulent in fields and alods. The church was full of books, gold-plated altars, chests, and crosses; crowns glistened with gold and precious stones. The voices of the cathedral canons could be heard singing regular hours and saying prayers; good works came from their hands. The castles, towns, fields, and possessions of that church were not exploited by lay people; they were in the hands of those consecrated to God. Many years ago, the pious king Charles built this church and had it consecrated in honor of Saints Justus and Pastor and endowed it with famous castles, towns, and lands, as the traditions of our forefathers relate and as can be read in the royal diplomas in the church's treasury.[20]

Around the middle of the twelfth century, the cathedral canons decided to celebrate this (mythical) refounder in the new cloister that abutted the ancient cathedral on its northern side. They set up a sculpted image of the emperor, seated tautly on his throne, his left hand clutching the strap of his cloak, his scepter tensed like a sword of justice, crusader's cross on his breast. He was joined there by the Virgin and the two saints whose relics the cathedral now protected; Archbishop Guifred, whatever his sins both political and religious, had miraculously discovered them in Spain in 1058. This Charlemagne was regal but not remote (unlike the Virgin, enthroned exactly like him, but distant, her frowning stare—accentuated by the statue's now ruined state—seemingly meant to strike terror rather than compassion in the onlooker), ready to punish any who might wrong the church he had planted on this spot.[21]

Across the river Aude was the church of Saint-Paul, surrounded by its ancient cemetery and a rapidly growing settlement. The clergy of Narbonne firmly believed that the third-century missionary to whom it was dedicated— by tradition the first bishop of Narbonne—was none other than Paulus Sergius, the proconsul of Cyprus whose conversion at Paphos by Saint Paul the Evangelist is described in the Acts of the Apostles.[22] His cult, celebrated over his tomb, put worshipers in the presence of the apostles themselves. There were other ancient churches in and near the city as well: Notre-Dame la Major, part of the ancient episcopal group turned parish church (where Rusticus had also placed an inscription) and Saint-Felix just north of the city walls, near the Jewish cemetery. Rusticus had also left his name in village churches in the countryside, most notably on the altar of Minerve, where for centuries afterward pious pilgrims used their knives to add their own names to his.[23]

THE ARCHBISHOPRIC AS REALITY AND AS TYPE

As Viscount Berenger proclaimed, Narbonne's bishopric was part of the city's glory: Paulus Sergius, dispatched there by the Evangelist himself, the saintly Rusticus and his companion, the saintly Theodard. That dignity had been enhanced by Charlemagne himself, and not just in myth and legend. When Charlemagne conquered the Spanish March, he made the archbishop of Narbonne the metropolitan over the newly reestablished bishoprics south of the Pyrenees, because the ancient metropolitan see, Tarragona, was in a kind of no-man's-land still under Moslem control. Elne, Urgell, Ausona-Vic, Gerona, Roda de Ribagorça, and Barcelona thus became Narbonne's suffragans. Charlemagne's decision was dictated by his determination to keep the newly conquered territory firmly attached to the kingdom of the Franks and stifle any separatism that might breed in the ancient Gothic religious and political centers, such as Toledo. Such concerns were reinforced by the spread of the Christological heresy known as Adoptionism out of Toledo in the 780s, a heresy solemnly condemned at a council in Frankfort in 794.

Gothic memories might go underground, but they could not be suppressed, and over the following centuries they periodically erupted. Tarragona remained the focus of Christian desires. In 956, the abbot of the Catalan monastery of Montserrat had himself consecrated archbishop of Tarragona by the archbishop of Lugo and the bishop of Compostela. In 970, the count of Barcelona traveled to Rome to persuade Pope John XIII to transfer the archbishopric to Vic (to which the see of the ruined city of Ausona had been moved). Episcopal resistance in the first case and the assassination of the new archbishop in the second brought these ventures to naught.[24] A century later, however, the moment came. The prelates of the Catalan church, impelled both by the movement of reform emanating from Rome and by a sudden and radical shift in the familial politics within their own group, shook hard on the reins that attached them to Narbonne, and this time they broke. This was just the moment when Count Raymond IV was dreaming of a title that would claim superiority over all of coastal Occitania (and perhaps beyond as well), over all the city territories in which the archbishop claimed primacy. Both count and archbishop realized the congruence of their ambitions, and sometime in the late 1060s or 1070s, Raymond swore to aid the archbishop against "all those bishops who are consecrated without [the archbishop's] agreement and against all those who consecrate them," that is, against all those prelates and their supporters who might be seduced into going their own way.[25]

The archbishop when the battle began, the one to whom Raymond IV swore his aid, was Guifred of Cerdagne, the subject of Viscount Berenger's diatribe. He was a prelate of the old school, an implacable warrior and a toughened politician. He was named archbishop at age ten when his father bought the see for him for a sum of money that became the stuff of fable and a textbook case of simony—the sin of buying the Holy Spirit, the sin of Simon Magus,[26] which the reformers around Pope Gregory VII made into a heresy and the chief object of their campaign to purify the Church. Guifred was struck at least twice with papal excommunications, but to no avail, and when "his" bishops met at Gerona in 1077 to see to the reform of their dioceses, he led an armed troop against them. During the following two years, he was twice deposed by Roman councils. Reconvened at Besalú, the gathering of Guifred's suffragans did not call directly for the reestablishment of the see of Tarragona and its metropolitan privileges, but the issue was joined. A little more than a decade later, in 1091, Pope Urban II declared Tarragona the metropolitan of all the sees south of the Pyrenees that had been subjects of Narbonne.[27] He consoled the defeated archbishop by reaffirming his primacy over his rival, the archbishop of Arles, attempting to resolve a dispute that had raged off and on since the fifth century.[28] It was not much of a consolation.

The fight over the restoration of Tarragona, like the contemporaneous attempt to restore the primacy of Toledo over the bishoprics of Christian "Spain and Gaul," resurrected memories of the old Gothic kingdom. For it was to this "early state," this "authority of yesteryear," that Catalans, Castilians, and ultimately Pope Urban II appealed in their declarations: to the church that preceded the Moslem conquest, whose traditions remained alive in the canons of the Gothic councils. Toledo claimed its rank as capital of the Gothic kingdom, Tarragona its rank as a Gothic metropolitan bishop.[29]

The see of Narbonne, now ruled by Archbishop Dalmacius, fought back with the Carolingian tradition of Saint Theodard, carefully fortified with a fresh *vita*, some newly minted forgeries of eighth- and ninth-century councils and popes, and a greatly elaborated history of the see's apostolic founder, Saint Paulus Sergius, "metropolitan bishop of all the Gauls." The cathedral scribes had already practiced their hands at pious frauds under Guifred's tutelage. Dalmacius had been abbot of Lagrasse in the heart of the Corbière hills, and he brought with him the considerable experience of his abbey's workshop at creatively enlarging and improving its own collection of Carolingian documents. Out of the archiepiscopal scriptorium came a text they must have considered a masterpiece—a bull attributed to a Pope Stephen (presumably Stephen V, 885–891) addressed to three bishops of the Spanish March, condemning them for their craven insolence and presumptuous arrogance, their shame of shames, at rebelling against the eternal decree of almighty God by usurping the see of Tarragona, whose rights belong to Narbonne. The justification of those rights, said the pseudo-bull, lay in the origins of the see of Narbonne and the Christianization of Spain: it was the Apostle Paul himself who brought Trophimus of Ephesus and Paulus Sergius with him, establishing the former as bishop of Arles and taking the latter with him to evangelize Hispania. On their return, the Apostle left Paulus Sergius in Narbonne, giving him the office of apostle throughout the region, consecrating him bishop and metropolitan of Gaul. To go against that disposition was to violate the will of the Apostles and therefore of God Himself, because it was Paulus Sergius who first taught the Christian faith to Spain.[30]

This was mythmaking of the highest order. And although it did not impress Pope Urban II or his legate at the time, it came, with other forgeries (as well as genuine texts), to form the jewel in Narbonne's self-made crown of privileges, still trotted out in the seventeenth century when the extent of the archbishop's metropolitan rights were called into question.[31] To combat the memories of the Gothic kingdom, enshrined in ancient episcopal lists and the prestigious church councils of Gothic Toledo, the Narbonnese called ancient Rome and the Apostles themselves to their defense. Few episcopal sees could declare their apostolicity with such distinguished and enterprising panache.[32]

In 1089, with the impending decision on the restoration of Tarragona the chief order of business, Raymond of Saint-Gilles and Viscount Aymeri I accompanied Archbishop Dalmacius to Rome. The battle also raged at a provincial council in Toulouse itself. The count was fully aware of the weight of Narbonne's name when he took the title duke of Narbonne in 1088.[33]

·——◉

Narbonne's name allowed the new duke to bask in borrowed glory. It did not, however, give him either added power or added wealth, for those required real control of the city, and that the counts of Toulouse did not have. Yet the invention was too good to be abandoned for so slight a difficulty. After all, a claim repeated was one that someone some day might recognize, a hope, a threat, a vision that could become a policy. For Raymond's son, Alphonse Jordan, and his grandson, Raymond V, the title became a possible political prize. Momentarily realized between 1136 and 1143, the ambitions of the counts of Toulouse in Narbonne would remain a constant threat for Ermengard.

There was more to be prized in Narbonne than its name, its history, and its myths. There were also its industry and commerce, the producers of cash to fill aristocratic treasure chests, without which titles were but empty words. And there were its army and its fleet of ships. It was in the cities that counts and viscounts had their palaces; there rural castellans were required to do castle guard; there counts and viscounts collected their most important revenues.[34]

Since the nineteenth century and the invention of the "rise of the bour-geoisie" so dear to the hearts of generations of textbook writers, we have all been taught that the medieval nobility lived by exploiting the countryside, lived by extracting what they could from their subject peasants, and that cities with their merchants, their profit seeking, and their freedoms were antithetical to everything that gave the nobility their place in the world. In a sense, of course, at least part of this has to be true. In any pre-industrial agricultural society, any-one who does not till the land has to be fed by those who do; the ultimate source of all wealth is the land and those who work it (and remains so wherever such societies still exist). In the minds of the Occitan nobility, however, even in the eleventh century, what nourished their power and gave them their wealth were the cities they controlled, with their churches, their markets, and their military force, and the highways along which taxable goods and merchants moved. The count and countess of Barcelona and the founders of the Trencavel dynasty stated as much in 1068 in their alliance to take over Carcassonne and its lands. In return for their bags of gold, the Barcelonese demanded as their share the episcopal city itself, control of the bishopric and of the region's prin-cipal monasteries with their territorial rights; they wanted control of the city's markets likewise, along with jurisdiction over the most important crimes (and the money and property of those who were hanged), control of the fighting force that guarded the city, and the fidelity of the man who would administer it. With the Trencavels they were willing to share the money that incoming bish-ops would pay for their office, justice in the countryside, and the fidelity of the castellans whose fortified towers controlled the major roads and waterways.[35] We could hardly ask for a more precise or comprehensive statement of the in-gredients of territorial rule two generations before Ermengard was born.

In some ways, this agreement of 1068 marks the end of a long era, for at the very moment it was being negotiated, Pope Gregory VII and his friends were launching a great reform movement in the Church that would forever sweep away the buying of bishoprics and lay control of church lands and abbeys. By 1100 it would be impossible even to imagine the claims that the parties to this treaty so nonchalantly included. This ecclesiastical reform made the military, judicial, and economic control of cities even more critical for the high aristoc-racy. And when Ermengard was born, her city was probably the wealthiest of coastal Occitania, seated as it was at the junction of the major trade routes from England and western France with the Mediterranean, the market through which the spices of the East and the gold of al-Andalus spread north, and itself the producer of richly dyed woolen cloth.

CHAPTER THREE
THE URBAN MARKETPLACE

In 1046, Arnold Siguini, lord of Palaja, a little village just visible on the horizon from the walls of Carcassonne, resolved to make a pilgrimage to the Virgin of Le Puy. Although today this would be an easy day's drive across the high, parched tableland of the southern Massif Central, in the eleventh century it was a considered undertaking—not as venturous, to be sure, as a pilgrimage to Compostela, Rome, or Jerusalem from which one might expect never to return, but any long absence from home might bring death from disease, violence, or misadventure. Before departing, a serious soul would think on the afterlife and the eventual distribution of his worldly goods. And so the lord of Palaja dictated his testament. Not far from his village, at a spot where a clear spring ran, was a tiny monastery dedicated to the Holy Sepulcher and to Saint Fulco, the recently deceased bishop of Carcassonne. To this house Arnold Siguini gave a small piece of property. To it as well he gave twenty-nine and a half ounces of gold that were due on loans he had made to other village lords whose lands were scattered from the vicinity of Narbonne to the northern Corbières.[1]

Like a beacon on a fog-bound shore, this chance reference to gold and to loans reveals the outline of a commerce that we can otherwise see only fitfully. Arnold made his loans in weighed metal rather than in counted coin. Others who paid or borrowed gold early in the eleventh century were more specific about its provenance. When the viscountess of Narbonne borrowed two ounces of the metal from the abbey of Saint-Paul in 1023–32, it was of gold, the contract said, of "iafarino obtimo"; so too around 1050, when in return for his fief as the bishop's seneschal, Rainard Salomon paid a fat countergift of twelve ounces of gold to the bishop of Béziers, it was "iafarino bono."[2] *Iafarinus* was the way the Christian world referred to Xafar, the minister of al-Hakim II, caliph of Cordoba, whose name the coins carried on their face. The gold that passed from hand to hand was the "good coin" of al-Andalus, the Spain of Islam, which flowed from the treasuries of tributary Moslem kings to Barcelona and from there trickled into Narbonne and the byways of the interior in the sacks of merchants and the kits of returning fighting men; it early reached as far north as the abbey of Conques deep in the Rouergue.[3]

How extensive this commerce may have been, how many people were caught up in it, directly or indirectly, are questions beyond our ability to answer. Unlike Catalonia, where the golden tribute from the Moslem frontier kingdoms streamed quickly into the local economy and left its traces in the documents that people hoarded in their archives,[4] here in Occitania the local economy remained resolutely silver based. Even after 1067–70, when the Barcelonese money bags opened splendidly to buy alliances north of the Pyrenees and more than three thousand ounces of gold that we know about (and probably considerably more that we don't) changed hands, there is almost no sign of it in the land transactions and testaments that make up almost our entire body of information. It must have been kept for other uses whose records did not have to be preserved for succeeding generations—to acquire luxuries that the local economy could not provide, to finance frontier adventures and eventually that ultimate adventure, a pilgrimage to Santiago, Rome, or the Holy Land.[5] This commerce remains a presence we must acknowledge, a shore we know is there but cannot chart; like the mapmakers of the New World in the early sixteenth century, we can fill its empty spaces only with our imagination.

The flow of gold, in any event, was not the cause of Narbonne's economic growth but one of its many consequences.

The city, a major port of the Roman world, had never entirely ceased to attract commerce from the north and from across the Mediterranean. Even in the darkest centuries after the collapse of Roman power in the west, a trickle of African wares continued to flow onto its wharfs as they did onto the wharfs of Marseille and Fos near the mouth of the Rhone.[6] The Moslem conquest may in fact have fed a brief commercial flowering in the city, with Greeks, Syrians, Jews, Arabs, and Berbers hawking their wares in its forum alongside the native Goths and Romans. If a late copy of an eighth-century Andalusian traveler's tale can be trusted, a substantial suburb sprang up across the river, where Narbonne's Bourg would eventually spread—"the other half of the city," the traveler called it (see map, p. 46).[7] Narbonne survived, even as other Roman cities of southern Gaul disappeared entirely or were reduced to little more than some primitive huts planted in a corner of its ancient ruins; it survived even a destructive Frankish reconquest.[8]

In the first decades of the tenth century we can already spot the fitful glimmers of renewed activity, like distant house lights in a sparsely populated countryside. New energies were reweaving the tattered fabric of economic life. In the countryside, new villages were spreading their spider nets of roads and boundary lines across what had once been the severe grid of the Roman landscape, villages that were already complex places.[9] Churches graced their centers, anchoring the already firmly established parishes; some could even boast their own fortifications.[10] Around these little peasant settlements, the fields were already intensely worked: in the fifty-two boundary descriptions given in a conveyance dating from 911 from the village of Bizanet, not far from Narbonne, fields, vines, gardens, streams, and roads abound, but only six of the descriptions mention the garigue, the bramble- and broom-filled "wasteland" that for nearly two millennia has been the signature of this Mediterranean landscape. There was already a considerable population living off the fruit of peasant sweat and pain: those same boundary descriptions give the names of sixty-one landholders in the village, some of whom, at least, we may be certain never pushed the plow.[11] Along the lanes of villages much like Bizanet, a land market and even moneylenders could thrive.[12]

This rising tide of rural wealth quickly lifted the cities of the coastal plain on its swell. By the turn of the millennium, the bishop and count of Toulouse were sufficiently concerned with the flow of commerce to ask a large assembly of prelates to force the lord of Caraman to give up some of the taxes he was collecting on the markets between his village and Toulouse. By 1050, the suburbs of Béziers were sufficiently built up for one of the city's noblemen to pay the bishop a substantial sum for rent rights there, and a few years later for the bishop to fight the widowed countess and her daughter and son-in-law over their claims to collect bread rent from the householders. At Narbonne, the mills under the old Roman bridge were already a profitable investment in the mid-tenth century as the settlement across the river grew rapidly. By 1080, the commercial relations between Narbonne and Montpellier were significant enough for the rulers of the former to negotiate a treaty with the merchants of the latter regulating the collection duties at the port.[13] Urban development, to be sure, was uneven. In the mid-eleventh century, Nîmes still gave the impression of a farming village inside its vast Roman walls. But Narbonne and Béziers had burst their ancient limits.[14]

The earliest cultivators of this commerce were doubtless the Jews, essential intermediaries in, among other kinds of trade, that of slaves in the centuries when Europe served the Moslem demand for human chattel in the same way that Africa would later serve European demand in the New World. Two Jews, Sabrono and Barala, are the earliest moneylenders we know about in Narbonne; others were prominent tenth-century mill owners on the Aude.[15] By the year 1000, Christians had forcefully moved into the moneylending business as well as into long-distance commerce.[16] What these merchants brought back from their overseas ventures were luxuries, such as the treasured cloth of gold, Spanish leather work, and the cups and goblets and other precious plate that tenth- and eleventh-century clergy listed in their testaments. The most important export product is suggested by the testament of Arnold Siguini with which I began this chapter. After listing the property he was leaving to the churches of the Holy Sepulcher and Saint Fulco, Arnold ordered that the remainder be divided among his wife, his two sons, and his two daughters and their eventual husbands—his castle, his lands scattered in villages along the upper Aude, his securities for yet more loans, and his personal property "in bread and in wine, in wool and in flax, in plate, in large animals and small, in cloth of wool and linen." He most likely made his money by dealing in cloth, the cloth that would in time make Ermengard's Narbonne a major industrial center.[17]

THE MARKETPLACE

North to south, across Narbonne, the "Straight Street," the ancient Roman *cardo maximus*, divided the twelfth-century city in two. To its west was the archbishop's city, to its east Ermengard's. Next to the Water Gate overlooking the bridge, her palace surveyed his across the narrow plaza. The ancient forum, the old market up near the Capitole where the via Domitia entered the city through the Royal Gate, had long since given up trying to contain all the goods that came through the gates on horseback or mule or up the Aude from ships that anchored in the bay. When Ermengard looked out from the windows of her palace to the archbishop's compound and the old cathedral across the way, her gaze fell on the bustling new market in the square below. Across the bridge, in the Bourg, yet another market pushed out from the head of the bridge into the neighboring streets and alleys. As early as 1035 there were markets outside as well as inside the walls.[18]

A tax list of 1153 conjures up the smells and sounds and colors of these markets, bringing to mind the image of a North African souk. There to feed the city's laborers were sacks of wheat, buckwheat, oats, peas, and beans, jars of olive oil, pots of honey, baskets piled with onions and garlic and cabbages, barrels of wine, cheeses fresh and salted, olives, chestnuts, almonds, walnuts, dried prunes and raisins, all fresh from the surrounding countryside. Pigs, goats, sheep, lambs, cows, oxen, hares and rabbits, wild boar, and an occasional bear or deer supplied the butcher stalls. Fish and eels fresh from the bay, the coastal lagoons, and the river filled the baskets of hawkers by the Water Gate. Rarer goods were there as well, enough to satisfy palates enamored of hot and spicy foods and exotic tastes: pepper, ginger, saffron and cloves, rice, dates, figs from the other side or the other end of the Mediterranean. Artisans and dealers gathered there to supply the needs of their trades: iron, tin, copper for the metal workers; for the tanners, sheepskins, lambskins, goat skins, and hides, washed and unwashed, and the mastic, sumac, and sulfur to tan them; for the clothing makers, furry skins of rabbits and squirrels, cats, ermine, and wolves; cordovan leather, linen from Alexandria, silk from Italy and Byzantium. From the city's hinterland came wool from the flocks that wintered in the Corbières nearby and summered in the Pyrenees, and more exotic cotton from Egypt, as well as the necessary alum from Spain and the eastern Mediterranean for the fulling mills, and the herbs, berries, the precious kermes gathered from the oak trees in the garigue outside the city and the equally precious mercury to make the scarlet and vermilion dyes that must have been the pride of the city's cloth and leather makers. Ship outfitters could find wood for masts and steering oars, anchors, hemp, rope, and sails. While lowly weavers could find their scissors and knives, needles, loom weights, brushes, and combs, and ordinary householders their leather harnesses, barrels, pots, jars, pans, and bowls. Even fighting men could outfit themselves in the market or in the shops nearby with hauberks and chain mail, coverings for their horses, swords, shields, daggers, axes, and cross-bows.[19]

The tax list that describes all this is unique in the twelfth century. The rest of our documentation—land transactions, testaments, and occasional disputes—is hardly the stuff of economic statistics. It is only by indirection, by blind touch here and there, that we can hazard a guess at the pace of economic growth. Yet in the brief and fragmentary illumination of what documents there are, we can see the visions that danced before shrewd twelfth-century eyes. It would be more than a century before the poet Peire Cardenal would lament

Li plueia sai es cazeguda
Cobeitatz, e si es venguda
un'erguelhoz' e granz maleza
que tota la gen a perpreza.[20]

The rain has fallen here:
Cupidity; and with it has come
A proud and bloated malevolence
By which all are seized.

But by then cupidity was long fixed in human hearts, and to lament it had become a cliché. As we leaf through our documents we can watch the sacristan of the church of Narbonne buy a house from the archbishop in 1091 for one hundred solidi and almost immediately resell it to two Jews for two hundred. Here in the same decades are the cathedral canons and the abbey of Saint-Paul (the latter apparently only modestly endowed with rural estates) demanding a monopoly of the tithes on the salt flats and the fish caught and marketed in Narbonne and its vicinity.[21] All these were signs enough that the booming real estate market was attracting cagey operators and that the food market was important enough to stoke a thirst for privileged position.

It is the medieval cityscape itself that speaks the loudest of Narbonne's expansion and the passion for gain on which it fed. The old city—the area within the ancient fortifications—covered approximately forty-three acres. Through most of the tenth century, only fields and orchards lay outside the walls, while within a significant portion was occupied by the episcopal complex and the towers and houses of fighting men. By 1032, the little group of houses across the bridge had become known as the Bourg (to distinguish it from the ancient *civitas*); its old rural name was being forgotten. By the end of the century, the Bourg added another thirty-eight acres of urban real estate. Meanwhile, along the river both to the west and east of the old city, other suburbs sprouted, adding perhaps half again to its spread.[22] Was it an intuition of profitable investment that led the viscount and viscountess to spend the substantial sum of a thousand solidi in 1035 for one of the walled settlements that was eventually incorporated into the Bourg?[23] There is no way, of course, to know; but the ease with which those of great status—and before long, those of considerably lesser status—were able to turn land into money and money back into land surely

The Perpignan Gate of Narbonne, from which roads led to Toulouse and to Spain. From Charles Nodier et al., *Voyages pittoresques et romantiques dans l'ancienne France. Languedoc.* By permission of the Houghton Library, Harvard University.

made them aware of the possibility.[24] The great landowners, the clergy of Saint-Just and Saint-Paul, the archbishop, the vicecomital family, and those on whom they bestowed their favors must have been the first to gain.

THE NEW MERCHANT ELITE

By Ermengard's time there were others as well who were profiting from commerce and speculation in land—people of obscure origin, who burst suddenly on the scene out of nowhere, who already when we first discover them are men of considerable wealth and power, with their roots planted solidly in the city. The most astonishing example is that of the Bistani brothers, William and John, somewhat younger contemporaries of the viscountess.

When he died in 1201, William left the immense sum of six thousand solidi in alms, to be assigned on the many mortgages he held—mortgages of houses, fields, gardens, mills, and tithes.[25] The medieval mortgage required that the security be handed over to the creditor; the use or revenue from the property was, in effect, the interest on the money loaned. These revenues were now to be given to churches and other charities. Like all good Christians of his age, William was funding his eternal life with the income from his lifetime investments. Charity was not enough to satisfy his spiritual doubts; another provision hints at how he made the money for those investments. To "the Jews," a number of individuals and "others who shared with me," he asked that restitution be made "for the fraud I believe I evilly committed." The sums to be "restored" to each individual or group—one hundred solidi, fifty solidi, four pounds—suggest a general sense of ill doing rather than a careful search through his account books. The names of the individuals who were to get the money or whose securities he still held suggest the nature of the ventures in which he had been involved, loans or joint enterprises with the archbishop and with men who frequented the courts of the mighty: Berenger of Boutenac, Raymond of Salles, Ermengaud of Fabrezan, people from the families of Pépieux and Raissac—all of them familiars of Ermengard and the archbishop—as well as knights from the entourage of the Trencavels.[26]

William and John Bistani were solid city men. Their father had been buried in the church of Saint-Sebastian,[27] in the northwest part of the old city; it was there that William wished to be buried as well. There the chaplain was to say thirty masses every day for the first ten days after William's death. There, in perpetuity, a priest was to be given his food and clothing to say a mass every day "for my soul and the souls of my parents." All of William's property was in the immediate vicinity of Narbonne, even the property he held as security; nothing was farther away than Cuxac and Coursan, just upstream on the Aude. In his bequests he named nearly all the churches in and around the city, but his money flowed with special concentration to those whose purpose was local charity: 100 solidi to the almoner of the cathedral (and only 100 to the chapter), 50 to the almoner of Saint-Paul, 300 to clothe the poor; in his name a pauper was to be kept in the hospital of Saint-Just, and 750 solidi were provided for that purpose; another 700 he gave to the city lepers' house to support a leper not already part of the community. If his son died before coming of age and his property was divided among William's three brothers, they were to add another 4,000 solidi for charitable works, clothing the poor, ransoming captives, and feeding paupers, widows, and orphans. (To put these numbers in some perspective, here are some twelfth-century prices for things other than land: a horse, 200 solidi in 1110; an ox, 20 solidi in 1138; 30 solidi to build a house in Narbonne around midcentury.)[28] Grandiose as these bequests were, they followed a pattern common to the merchants of other Mediterranean cities and even the village notables of the surrounding countryside.[29] When his moment came to face death, William (like most of us) was utterly conventional; it is exactly this that makes him worth our attention. He made two bequests to churches outside the city's orbit: 200 solidi to the monastery of Cassan—another sign of the way he had inserted himself in the Trencavel network, for Cassan was favored by that dynasty—and 100 solidi to the priory of Espira in Roussillon—the only indication of what might have been a peculiarly personal religious attachment.

William Bistani had good reason for his careful conventionality: the family was among the first of the merchant patriciate to start rubbing shoulders with the military families that had long dominated the city's politics. When we first meet him, witnessing the sale of a mill under the bridge of Narbonne in 1162, he is in the company of artisans—William Ironmonger (Ferrerius), Brunus Silk-Worker (Serierus)—but also of Peter Raymond of the Capitole, from the family of knights who took their name from the old basilica-turned-fortress next to the Royal Gate. When we next see him in 1177 he is again with Peter Raymond. He is part of a small network—his brother-in-law William Minter (Monetarius), Raymond of Saint-George, and Hugh of Plaigne, who seem regularly involved in each other's affairs.[30] About Raymond of Saint-George we know nothing more than that he was a neighbor of Peter Raymond of the Capitole, but the career of Hugh of Plaigne demonstrates how blurred the line between the urban nobility and the new urban wealth had become in the second half of the century. Hugh was already an important member of Ermengard's court in the 1150s, acting as arbiter in a dispute between the viscountess and Raymond, lord of Ouveilhan, who was one of the great landowners of the city. When Hugh made his son a canon of Saint-Paul, the endowment that went with him was the free grinding of the chapter's grain at Hugh's two mills under the bridge.[31]

It was William Bistani's brother John who took the family to the summit of its power. When he first appears in the records in 1193, he is a member of the court of Pedro de Lara, Ermengard's nephew (who, impatient to succeed his aging aunt, had just exiled her). In 1204, when the scions of the old families gathered to witness the oath of fidelity of Dalmace de Creisello for the important castle of Fenouillet in Roussillon, John was there along with William Minter, in the brilliant company of Narbonnese and Catalan knights.[32] John knew even better than his brother how to use money for honor and profit. The previous year, John and a partner had loaned four thousand solidi to the abbot of the ancient monastery of Lagrasse, who was desperately trying to consolidate his abbey's overwhelming debts. As security for their money, the pair received the monastery's rights of lordship in five villages along the lower reaches of the Aude River.[33] A few years later, an even more dramatic opportunity appeared. It was the darkest moment of the Albigensian Crusades, and the armies of the Church were crumbling for lack of recruits and supplies. Amaury de Montfort, the new leader of the crusade, desperate for funds, turned to Arnold Amaury, papal legate and new archbishop of Narbonne; the archbishop in turn sent his men to knock on John Bistani's door. Bistani knew a chance when he saw it, and he drove a hard bargain. In return for a thousand pounds of silver, equivalent to 65,000 sol. Melg., he demanded as security five of the towers on the archbishop's half of the city walls along with the houses belonging to them, the Capitole, and the lordship rights over his own house. Nor would he let himself be cheated of his prize by the Church's mounting campaign against usury. He insisted that the agreement be drafted as a contract of sale, allowing the archbishop the right to repurchase within the year, if he could come up with that thousand pounds. There was no way, of course, for the bishop to raise that money elsewhere and pay off the loan, so Bistani found himself the proud lord of a good portion of the fortifications of the city. In 1224 the archbishop finally had to call for papal aid to force Bistani to return them. That was how one became known in the years around 1200 as a "prudent man" of the city.[34]

When William Bistani died, he left a son under age; John Bistani married his daughter to Peter Margalonis, descendant of a family that had been prominent in city affairs since the eleventh century.[35] Another brother, Raymond Bistani, appears occasionally in the early thirteenth century, and after that the family name disappears. (The Place Bistan, which covers a corner of the ancient Capitole, may harbor the family's memory. Perhaps their house stood near here when the Capitole was razed in the mid-fourteenth century and the quarter was transformed.) No sons, apparently, survived to succeed to the brothers' vast wealth, or like the descendants of modern capitalist robber barons, to carry on the family's public charities.[36] But the will of Peter Margalonis lays out the web of family relations into which the Bistani wove themselves. The sister of Peter Margalonis married into the family of the lords of Bizanet; Peter had served as godfather for a son of Peter of the Capitole; he counted among his cousins men and women with family names of Saint-George (who had also been associates of the Bistani) and Royal Gate (de Porta Regia—an aristocratic family that took its name from the gate and castle next to the Capitole). Knights or merchants, it made no difference; neighborhood, friendship, and family had become all one.

One reason for this easy familiarity was that the Bistanis and their fellow merchants were not the only ones to deal in mortgages and commerce and investments in mills. Already at the beginning of the twelfth century, mortgages seem to have been the instrument of choice for turning land into liquid wealth; because there was no time limit on paying back the lender, one could borrow money yet keep a claim to the land (or tithes or other rights) that could go on forever, needing only payment of the original sum to reclaim what had once been mortgaged.[37] For both creditors and borrowers, mortgage instruments became, in effect, negotiable paper that could be sold, given as a dowry, or bequeathed to a church as alms.

Mortgages appear with increasing frequency after 1100, especially in clerical testaments. Already in 1096, Peter Raymond, sacristan of Saint-Paul, held part of the lordship over a rural quarter of Narbonne as security on a loan. For most of the wealthy clergy, such investments must have been nothing more than a safe haven for the revenues they were drawing from their tithes and benefices, ways to make their profits on the food market fructify in a most traditional way—by putting it into land. And it may have been that more land and revenues were available as security on what were legally only loans (and were therefore not fully alienated) than were available for sale. One testament, however, suggests that some clergy, at least, were far more deeply involved in the market. When Peter of Saint-Hilaire, a later sacristan of Saint-Paul, died in 1148, he left substantial silver plate to his church, as clergy had done since at least the tenth century (for priests went about their ritual duties in luxurious raiment and surroundings rich with burnished gold and silver).[38] Among Peter's various properties was also a 450-solidi loan that he had made on a mill at Bougna, just upstream from the city walls; the mill was one of many pledged securities he distributed to churches and his nearest relations. In addition, his bequests included ten *morabitanos*—almoravid gold dinars, "which Peter de Curtibus and Raymond Catalan stole from me, if they can be recovered." Although Peter used the strongest possible verb, the phrase here points to something other than house breaking or purse cutting, to something not readily justiciable as a criminal act—a commercial confidence game, perhaps, or more simply a commercial venture on which Peter believed he had not received his due return.[39]

Next to Peter of Saint-Hilaire, Archbishop Arnold, who died the following year, looks decidedly old fashioned, with an estate that consists essentially of large quantities of grain and wine stored in his rural castles, farm animals, bed covers, and the rich implements of his chapel.[40] Through the remainder of the century, not only high clergy but rural lords as well left estates that included sizable quantities of "receivables"—silver coins, and occasionally Arab gold, that were out on loan.[41] Six of the nine surviving twelfth-century testaments from the clergy of Narbonne and Béziers mention such investments. Did the clergy's energetic "recovery" of tithes from the hands of laymen early in the century put such plentiful liquid wealth in their hands that they became some of the most important promoters of the city's commercial boom? Would that we still had the notarial minute books from the twelfth century that might tell us. The son of Hugh of Plaigne, who had grown up hearing talk of mills and moneylending, who probably called William and John Bistani and William Minter "uncle," must have felt right at home among the canons of Saint-Paul.

⤙═

The ruling family of Narbonne were no strangers to this prosperity. How could they have been? They shared half and half with the archbishop the taxes on all goods sold in the city, and they collected seven-eighths on what was sold in the bourg across the river.[42] In the old tax table of 1153 we can read exactly how much this was:

Barques with steering oar, if they come from this side of Toulon, 8 d. Melg. to tie up; if they are without a steering oar, 4 d. of Narbonne. Linh [a type of boat] 16 d. Of every ship that is sold, a twentieth of the price. . . .

Scarlet, 5 sol. Melg. the quintal.

Pepper, ginger and spices, 4 d. Melg. the quintal, plus 5 s. 6 d. the load to enter and leave.

Saffron and cloves, 4 d. Melg. the pound. . . .

Silk, 12 d. the quintal, and cotton 8 d. the quintal and another 6 d. if it is taken away by land. . . .

Rice, 8 d. the quintal and another 6 d. if it is taken away by land. . . .

Honey, 2 d. Narb. the quintal.

Oil, 2 d. Narb. the sétier, plus 3 d. Melg. to the viscount if it goes out of the city. . . .

And all these goods pay to the viscount 2 sol. Melg. on each load entering and leaving the city, and if they come in or leave by the Roussillon road they pay 3 sol., 3 d. . . . All [other] loads of plain goods that go or come from Roussillon pay 4 sol. 1. d. Melg. to pass. . . . Improved goods [*avers de creys*] pay 5 sol. 6 d. if they come by the Roussillon road, and otherwise 4 sol. 3 d.; paper pays 1/15th [of its quantity?]; great beasts pay 3 sol. 1. d. if they carry no burden [*se es aze*] and 7 sol. if they have one [*se es grava*]. . . .

Buckwheat, 5 sol. when it is sold, or 3 sol. to pass through; mixed grains [*blat*][43] a half-penny Narb. the sétier, and 2 sol. Melg. if it leaves by sea. . . .

Horses passing through, 3 sol. 1 d. if they leave with their charge; and if they sell, 5 sol. . . .

Merchants who come by the Roussillon road pay 13 d. if they only pass with their pack train [*cavalgadura*], but if they lead mules and sell, they pay 13 d. for each one, and this to the viscount.[44]

The ruling family also knew all about making money by leasing mills on the river and speculating in urban real estate, and, at least according to the archbishop, the road from Roussillon brought Ermengard a fortune; in a complaint of the mid-1150s, he claimed she had taken in more than three hundred thousand solidi from guarding merchants along that road, and he wanted a share.[45] Not that they had turned into what the nineteenth-century would call bourgeois; neither Ermengard nor her ancestors were medieval Louis Napoleons. But their political strength and their military adventures ultimately depended as much on the coin in their treasure chests as it did on the fighting men in their fealty. The ruling family's prosperity depended on the prosperity of its city. Ermengard must have learned this lesson in her childhood. She never forgot it.

CHAPTER FOUR
CITY AND COUNTRYSIDE

Within Narbonne's ancient fortifications, the houses of the city stood wall to wall, with shops at street level, living quarters above; the streets they bordered were barely wide enough for loaded pack animals to pass each other. Although these houses are now a story or two higher (most were rebuilt in the seventeenth and eighteenth centuries), and the gutters no longer run with sewage and the refuse of artisans' shops, the visitor wandering along what is still called the "straight street"—the rue Droite near the unfinished Gothic cathedral—can even today get a fleeting sense of what must have been a crowded, fetid medieval city. It was also a city that was rapidly growing. By 1086, a defensive wall enclosed the Bourg, and by Ermengard's time, Coiran and Belveder, suburbs just west of the archbishop's compound, had likewise been brought inside the walls. Shops squeezed tightly together on the Roman bridge, where butchers discharged the blood and offal of their victims into the river below, right next to the mills that ground the city's grain. In the upper room of her palace over the Water Gate at the end of the bridge, Ermengard must have heard the animals' fearful squeals even as she listened to a troubadour's sweet songs of love or attended to the heated disputes of her nobility.[1] As Johan Huizinga wrote of the fourteenth century, the city and the age "bore the mixed smell of blood and roses."[2]

Although the city was crowded, it still contained pockets of the countryside within its walls. Farm houses with their plow trains, barns, and animals still stood between the Water Gate by the Aude and the Royal Gate with its ancient castle. There were others in the Bourg. Immediately outside the walls spread a thick carpet of gardens and vineyards, copiously fertilized (as was still the case in many European villages well into our own century) by the kitchen wastes and night soil from within. Ermengard's kitchen scullions, like the neighborhood housewives, had only to pass through the gates to gather their cabbages, fava beans, onions, garlic, and pot herbs for dinner.[3]

To the east, the lagoons and marshes that separated the city from the sea were the domains of salt makers and fishermen. For ten kilometers north from the city's port, past the "Jewish village," which lay between the city and the is-

Street scene in Figeac, near Cahors. A street in Narbonne at the time would have looked about the same. From Charles Nodier et al., *Voyages pittoresques et romantiques dans l'ancienne France. Languedoc.* By permission of the Houghton Library, Harvard University.

land of Lec, to the terrain of Saint-Georges near Coursan, the vast expanse of water and marsh grass was cut into a mosaic of temporary walls and laced with drainage ditches and canals to make salt from the seawater that ebbed and flowed across its muddy flats. There were salt pans farther south as well, at Sigean, and farther north in the vast marshland that spread eastward from Ouveilhan and Capestang to the lagoon of Vendres.[4] In the guzzles and drains of this watery world, in the river and its old meanders, fishermen set their nets and weirs for the rich harvest of currents and tide—sea perch, mullet, trout, river bleak, shad, lamprey, and eels to grace the tables of the city as well as their own.[5]

To the west around the church of Saint-Crescentius spread lush grassland; at Cazouls and Champ Redon, on the plain of Narbonne, were heavy bottomlands. Here leper houses, hospitals, and churches nestled among the fields from which Ermengard and her courtiers got the bread for their tables, and the ser-

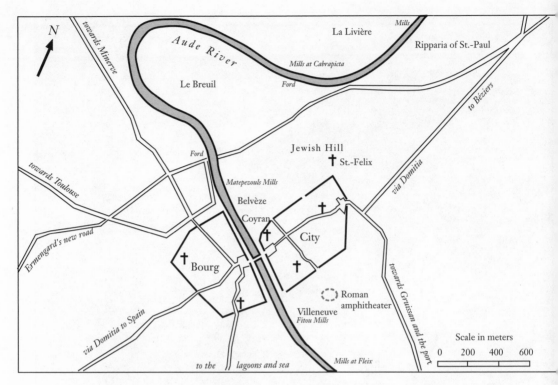

Environs of Narbonne. *Source*: Caille, "Narbonne au moyen âge: Évolution de la topographie."

vants of monks and cathedral canons came at harvest time to collect their tithes.[6]

Beyond this ring lay a world of peasant villages that spread their dense webs of fields across the rich plain of the lower Aude. To the north the plain met the dry, calcareous tableland of the Minervois and the Causses beyond it; to the south were the craggy, steep-sloped hills of the Corbières, whose narrow valleys were watered by streams that often overflowed their banks in winter storms and ran dry in the parched days of summer. Here the peasants tended vines on the terraces they had laboriously built on the hills, or they scratched millet, oats, and chickpeas from fields made rich with alluvium washed down from the slopes, fields that demanded intensive irrigation yet were always in danger of flooding in winter rains. In the large stretches of gorse and broom that separated the tiny Corbières village centers from each other, deer grazed, boars and bears rooted for nuts, and falcons and sparrow hawks cruised for prey; increasingly, however, this garigue was becoming the domain of sheep, which were gradually grazing the wild animals out of their ecological niche.[7]

Much of this peasant landscape has disappeared: the medieval city's own gardens, meadows, and fields, even the names by which they were known, have been swallowed up by nineteenth- and twentieth-century urban sprawl, and the coastal plain by sheets of summer houses and the necessary superhighways to get tourists to them. Yet some of the medieval landscape can still be read in the silty soils of vineyards that were once marshland and salt pans, in the small irregular rectangles of surviving medieval fields (for which medieval notaries could find no term more precise than *pecia terre*, "a piece of land") and the network of field roads that led to them, in the fossilized terraces long abandoned, and here and there in scatterings of pottery shards or the collapsed walls that mark villages deserted in the plague centuries and never reoccupied. They are now no more than ghosts of ghosts, but they can sometimes allow us to set a thousand-year-old transaction in its exact location and, piece by piece, reconstruct the appearance of a long-vanished world.[8]

SALT, SHEEP, AND MILLS

In this world of contrasts, few were as sharp as that between the crowded world of the city, with its stone-gray streets and stone-gray walls, and the open fields and hills of the countryside, where green fields and rust-colored soil were punctuated by the white of limestone *combas* and *serras*, steep-sided valleys and dry plateaus, and here and there the white or sandy-peach walls of a village or rural chapel or isolated castle. Yet for all their differences, the two worlds, urban and rural, were joined by a thousand links.

The ring of fields, vineyards, and gardens that fed the city was defined by the villages that lay just beyond it—Joncquières, Montredon, Moussan, Védillan, Auriac—all about six kilometers from the city's walls.[9] Here, upriver at Matepezouls, Cabrapicta, and Bougna, downriver at le Fitou—all an easy walk from the city gates—were the mills as well on which the city's industrial economy and the wealth of its most powerful people depended.[10]

Here most importantly were the salt pans that produced what must have been the city's most profitable commodity. Already in the late eleventh century (and doubtless much earlier), the rulers of the city placed the control of salt pans and revenues drawn from them—tithes and sales taxes—high on their lists of seignorial rights, along with justice, "services," and those forced and arbitrary payments from their subject peasants that made lordship worth while. Ermengard's father fought with the archbishop over the division of the *tertio salis*, the tax on salt, and the monopoly of salt sales during the month of October— the end of the dry season, when the salt would be collected and prepared for sale to the itinerant merchants who transported it along the "salt roads" deep into the interior. An agreement between the two in 1112 only served as a peg on which later archbishops whittled when the opportunity arose; in the 1150s, Ermengard was fighting to retain her monopoly of salt sales during half of the month of October. Even with her close ally Raymond Trencavel she was forced to engage in a salt-tax war, slapping additional duties on Trencavel subjects in retaliation for duties placed on her own. At the beginning of 1163 they agreed to return to an earlier status quo. Did that settle the problem? We do not know. The salt from the coastal lagoons found customers from Italy to England; the petty details of its trade could even spur a son of the count of Toulouse to write directly to the king of England. How could its profits not be a repeated source of lordly dispute?[11]

As salt drew the countryside and the city together, so too did sheep.

Shepherds and their flocks had been a common sight in the hills of the Mediterranean since prehistory, but before the middle of the twelfth century they had wandered their paths from winter to summer pasture without being noticed by scribes and notaries. In their fragmentary state, the archives of the old Benedictine monasteries—Lagrasse in the heart of the Corbières, Montolieu on the Montagne Noire—say nothing. The administrators of these houses were concerned above all with supplying their own kitchens and wine cellars, and because monks were forbidden by their Rule from eating the flesh of quadrupeds, those who kept the records were little interested in anything beyond the products of grain fields, gardens, fish ponds, and vineyards. Only an occasional dispute over village lordship rights confirms in writing what the landscape itself so loudly announces in the sheep paths hoof-beaten into the hills: that the animals were certainly there and increasingly were bred to serve a commercial market.[12]

Although charters say little about these flocks, there is indirect evidence in plenty. Already in the eleventh century, in the documentation that fitfully illuminates the countryside, we can spot mills planted along Narbonne's major river and the mountain streams that fed it. Around 1050 they are mentioned at Blomac on the Aude about half way between Narbonne and Carcassonne, where by 1150 there was a major industrial center. Early in the twelfth century we find them far up the Aude at Quillan and Esperaza; and not long after that at Villalier, where the Orbiel stream spills out of the Montagne Noire north of Carcassonne; as well as on the tiny Lauquette, at Ferrals on the Orbieu in the northern Corbières, at Douzens on the Aude; and far to the south in the wild highlands around Parahou and at the spot where an underground stream bursts forth from the parched limestone hills north of Salses.[13] Some of these were probably gristmills, but occasionally the scribes are kind enough to tell us that the mills being built or leased or sold were cloth-making mills, *molendini draperii*.[14] And where dams and wheels were numerous, as they were at the major sites along the Aude, or where they were in the midst of pasture land, along the Lauquette and in the southern Corbières, there were surely fulling mills among them to work the wool from the local flocks.

When the Cistercians arrived, just before the middle of the twelfth century, they brought in their baggage an appetite for pastureland and privileges. Ink and parchment followed closely behind. We can begin to map the movements of the ever-growing monastic flocks from the lowland pasture on the Mediter-

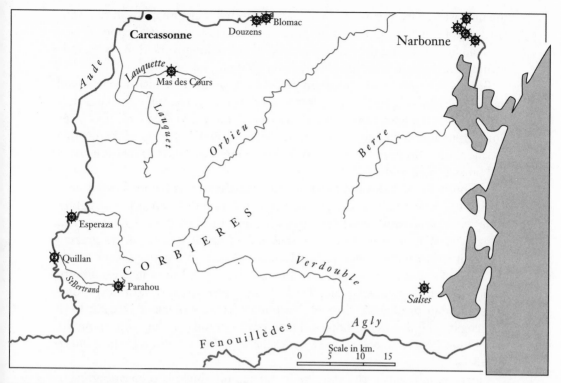

Mill sites mentioned in twelfth-century documents

ranean plain to summer pasture on the Montagne Noire, in the Pyrenees and the Cévennes.[15]

The Cistercian rule required that the White Monks live "far from human society." They were to refuse gifts of churches, altars, burial dues; they were not to live from tithes on the agricultural work of others, nor from the labor of serfs, or rents from land, or income from ovens and mills; they were to eat from the sweat of their brow and the labor of their own hands, from the work of their lay brothers and the produce of their own flocks. From this came the myth, widely propagated by the Cistercian's own writers (and by historians ever since), that they settled in "places of vast and fearful solitude," in the image of the Desert Fathers in the wilderness of ancient Egypt, and transformed forests and the lairs of wild beasts into splendid churches and rural Edens.

Such deserted places would have been hard to find in Occitania (as in much of old Europe), where the countryside was crowded with fields and houses well before the twelfth century. Fontfroide, the major Cistercian monastery in the area of Narbonne, was only ten kilometers, an easy morning walk, from the center of the city. Only a kilometer to its west lay village centers that were already densely occupied in the tenth century; along the eastern boundary of its land ran Ermengard's "new merchant's road" to Roussillon and Catalonia; from the monastery's front gate another road connected it at Ornaisans to the principal road from Narbonne to Toulouse. Unable to find a desert, the monks created one by displacing the peasant families that had long worked the land, welcoming the males as laboring lay brethren on their granges.[16]

Because the production of grain and wine beyond their own needs would have required a substantial labor force and thus meant resettling the land they had emptied, the Cistercians turned to sheep. A few men could look after large flocks, retaining the image of a community far from the society of men, while the monastery profited from its easy access to highways and the thriving shops and ports at their ends.

Although Fontfroide later lived by the myth that it was founded by Ermengard, it had in fact been a major Benedictine abbey with a network of daughter abbeys in Spain before it was incorporated into the Cistercian community in the 1140s. Within twenty years of that conversion it was acquiring grazing rights far away on the slopes of the Montagne Noire, in the high Corbières on the edge of the Roussillon plain, and in Catalonia.[17] Silvanès in the southern Rouergue, with extensive grazing lands in the Cévennes, also most likely commercialized its production through Narbonne, where it obtained free salt from Ermengard and the archbishop, and freedom from tolls on the route along the way. Other Cistercian abbeys were doing the same from the Alps to the western Pyrenees.[18]

Flocks numbered in the thousands. So rapidly did this monastic grazing develop that the monasteries began to quarrel over rights to pasture, with the head of the order called in time and again to arbitrate. The monastery of Aiguebelle in Provence pitted its needs for summer pasture against that of Mazan in the Vivarais and Bonneval in the Rouergue; Grandselve, near Toulouse, quarreled with Belleperche, Gimont, Boulbonne, and the canons of Combelongue over the boundaries of pasture land and rights of passage all the way from Castelsarrazin, near Albi, to the high Pyrenees; fights between the monastery of Silvanès and the Knights Templars and Hospitalers over grazing in the Causses on the southern edge of the Massif Central were so insistent that the Cistercian monastery sought promises from donors not to admit its rivals into parishes in which the Cistercians had rights.[19] By the time Ermengard's reign was over, the hungry maws of sheep had brought the world of urban commerce to the remotest valleys and hillsides of the Occitan world.

ERMENGARD'S RURAL VISCOUNTY

More important still in linking the countryside to the city was the movement of people and, with them, of power. Rural and urban were not separate political worlds; they were the same. All urban lords whether great or petty, men or women, were also lords of peasant villages. Most of them advertised it in the names they took, like the men who surrounded Ermengard: Bages, Capestang, Durban, Fabrezan, Laredorte, Ouveilhan, Saint-Nazaire, Salles—a roll call of villages in the plain of the lower Aude. And even those who did not—such as Peter Raymond of Narbonne, one of Ermengard's closest advisors—were lords of substantial rural property and of the peasants who worked it.[20] Ermengard had hers as well. She was lord of rural castles and rural fighting men; judge of disputes over rights to village towers, fields, and vineyards; arbiter of life and death to village thieves and murderers.

Ermengard's archives must once have contained inventories and account books for these lordships, help for the agents who oversaw her properties and enforced her rights (such men as Peter Raymond of Narbonne, who for a time was her *vicarius*).[21] Fragments of such material survive in other contemporary collections (and we will look at them shortly), but they were not the kind of documents that those entrusted with the safekeeping of records thought required attention or care, once the immediate accounting need was gone: they were not title documents to property and would not count for much in the event that property was in dispute. They could be neglected, scraped and reused if parchment were in short supply, or left for rats and worms to feed on. If they survived the following generation or two, they fell victim to the archivists of the seventeenth and eighteenth centuries, for whom anything not immediately useful for enforcing some "feudal" right or claiming some property was of no interest.[22] Nevertheless, although Ermengard's own account books and inventories have long since disappeared, we can infer the extent of her rural holdings from two precious documents that date from late in the following century.

When Ermengard's great-grandnephew Amalric I died in 1270, he left two sons, Aymeri and Amalric. His testament, if he made one, has not survived. Jointly ruling the viscounty and sharing its income was not the sons' idea. They quickly negotiated a preliminary division. But when complications could not be resolved, they at last put the issues of their father's estate to the arbitration of Guy de Levis, lord of Mirepoix and marshal of King Louis IX.[23]

Amalric the son had from the first agreed to let his brother take sole title to the viscounty and to their father's lordship in the City and Bourg of Narbonne. In return he received 1,000 liv. Tourn. in annual revenue to be assigned on other properties. The division of their father's rural lordships, however, proved intractable; this was what Guy de Levis had to contend with. Thanks to his decision and a recognizance of fief given to the officials of King Louis IX, we have two lists that serve as a quasi-inventory of the viscount's village holdings.[24] They give us the names of 101 villages and castles in which Amalric I had rights of lordship or in which fiefs were held of him.

The contents of great lordships were, of course, subject to constant fluctuations as some lands and rights were acquired and others lost through gifts,

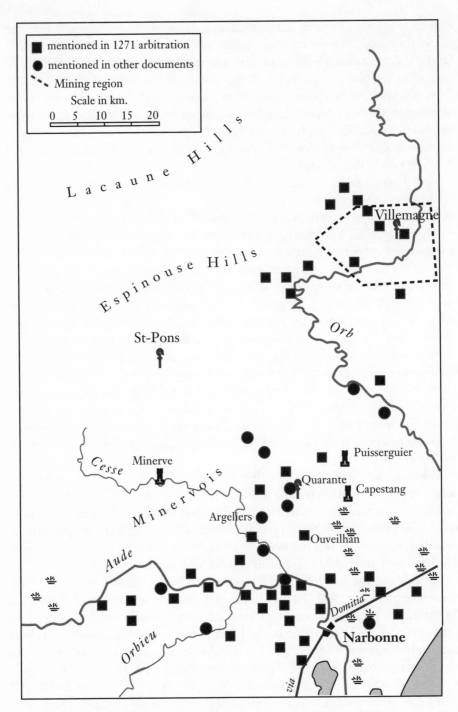

Villages and castles in Ermengard's lordship: the viscounty north of Narbonne

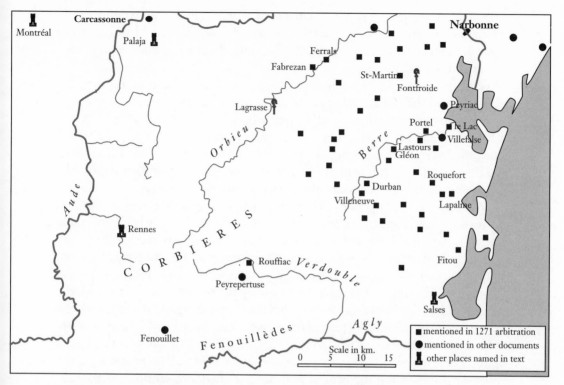

Villages and castles in Ermengard's lordship: the viscounty south of Narbonne

dowries, and disputes with other lords. The agreement between the brothers assumed as a matter of course that there would be some places in which their father had rights that, at the time of his death, for one reason or another, were in someone else's hands. The two lists drawn up in 1271–72 were therefore in all likelihood not exactly the same as an inventory we might have had of Ermengard's rural holdings a century earlier; other documentation from Ermengard's age and the earlier thirteenth century allows us, in fact, to add a handful of villages in the Narbonnais plus some major outlying rights of lordship to those lists.

Despite the distance in time, we can surely take these two mid-thirteenth-century lists as a close approximation of an absent inventory from Ermengard's day. The Albigensian Crusades, which began shortly after Ermengard died, left the viscount of Narbonne unscathed. At the height of his own battle with the archbishop, in fact, Simon of Montfort, the first leader of the Crusade, saw to it that Ermengard's grandnephew Aymeri and his followers were placed under papal protection.[25] There was no thirteenth-century run on the lands of the viscounts of Narbonne as there was on those of the Trencavels. So even if we allow that some villages listed in the documents of 1271–72 may have been acquired by the viscounts only after Ermengard's death, whereas others in which

Ermengard had rights may have been lost or alienated in the intervening three-quarters of a century, we can safely assume that her lands and those of her great-grandnephew were substantially the same, despite the intervening chaos of war and royal conquest.

With the exception of a few outliers, all the villages listed in 1271–72 lay within a band that measured approximately thirty kilometers east to west and seventy kilometers north to south (roughly between 0° 40' and 0° 80' east and 47° 65' and 48° 20' north). They were thickest in a ring around the city and along the lower Aude, thinning out as one moved north toward the Lirou River and the middle Orb. It was most likely from these villages that Ermengard, like her predecessors and successors, drew most of her rural income.

Southwest of the city, her villages and castles formed long fingers through the tortured landscape of the eastern Corbières, occupying nearly all the arable land in the narrow valleys of a countryside otherwise given over to sheep and wild animals. Above all, they sat alongside or astride all the routes that led from Roussillon and the mountainous interior toward the city: Fitou, Lapalme, Roquefort, Villefalse, le Lac, and Peyriac along the old Roman coastal road; the villages and castles between the coast and the Berre along the tracks across the dry tableland of the interior; the extensions beyond Portel and Lastours of Ermengard's "new merchant road to Roussillon"; Gléon, Durban, and Villeneuve up the Berre toward the Peyrepertusès and Fenouillèdes. The routes from the abbey of Lagrasse and the central highlands of the Corbières passed by Fabrezan and Ferrals on the way to join the main road from Narbonne to Carcassonne or by Saint-Martin-de-Tocques on the way directly to the city. Here at the castle of Saint-Martin, Ermengard established a major toll station.[26] Like the familial ties into which Ermengard was born, like the routes her merchants and her army followed, the geography of these Corbières villages and castles points above all toward the Pyrenees and Catalonia.

The vicecomital family did not enjoy exclusive control of the roads into Narbonne. Here and there their control was interrupted by the lordships and castles of the archbishop, especially around the great lagoon that formed Narbonne's harbor, and on the island of Lec that separated the city and its salt pans from the sea. Of these we shall soon see more. But when disputes arose with the archbishop over rural holdings, they involved places in this narrow ring around the city.[27]

In the Corbières, Ermengard's holdings faced those of the abbey of Lagrasse. In two villages at least, the viscountess and the Benedictines both had holdings. There is no trace of conflict, however, or even of much contact; after 966 there are not even traces of donations from the vicecomital house to these monks. Most of the abbey's archives were destroyed in a great auto-da-fé in the market square of Carcassonne during the French Revolution, but the total absence of Ermengard and her ancestors and successors from the documents that remain is remarkable, especially because Ermengard's uncle was abbot of the monastery from 1116 to 1157.[28] The one place at which their claims might have caused problems, at le Lac on the via Domitia, was apparently kept calm by a mortgage in 1114 by which Ermengard's father passed all his rights in the village to the abbey in return for a massive loan of silver and gold.[29]

South of the lands of Lagrasse, the highlands of the Corbières were dominated until the beginning of the twelfth century by the counts of Besalú and their followers. But the viscounts of Narbonne had lands here as well.

Besalú was one of the several Pyrenean ruling families that could trace itself back to Count Guifred the Hairy, who had ruled the entire frontier march of the eastern Pyrenees in the last decades of the ninth century. Tautavel, Vingrau, Queribus, Peyrepertuse, Aguilar—the villages and castles that King Louis IX would refortify in the thirteenth century to mark his freshly established frontier with the kingdom of Aragon—were then the northern reaches of this family's territory, which stretched south across the Pyrenees nearly to the Rio Ter. Like their cousins in Cerdagne and Gerona, these counts were great founders of Benedictine abbeys; Ripoll, Cuxa, Saint-Joan de las Abadessas were the most famous. Lagrasse likewise found at their court a willing ear and an open hand.[30] In 1107, the last count, on the occasion of his betrothal to the daughter of Count Ramon Berenguer III of Barcelona, promised the succession to his father-in-law if he should die without heir, and when he died four years later his lands were absorbed into Catalonia. Not long afterward, perhaps in 1112–13, when Count Ramon Berenguer was seeking allies for his campaign against Viscount Bernard Ato of Béziers, he gave the Fenouillèdes and Peyrepertusès to his half brother, Aymeri II of Narbonne, Ermengard's father.[31] Thereafter, the lords of Fenouillet and Peyrepertuse were firmly in the fidelity of the house of Narbonne. To fix their presence in the region, the viscounts kept control of an important outlier: at the foot of the mountain brooded over by Peyrepertuse, Ermengard and her successors were lords of the village of Rouffiac.[32]

In the lists of villages of 1271–72 there were also outliers to the north. It is here that we can best establish the continuity of the family's rural holdings; here as well that we can see most strikingly the impact of the urban world and its commerce on even the most isolated regions of the countryside.

In a great arc approximately twenty-five kilometers north of Narbonne, the rolling coastal plain quickly gives way to the steep hills and narrow canyons of the southern edge of the Massif Central. The summits, 500 to 800 meters just beyond Minerve and Saint-Chinian, reach 1,100 meters in the Espinouse another ten kilometers to the north. The Orb River and its major tributaries, the Jaur, the Vernazobre, and the smaller streams that feed them, here flow through deep gorges. It is a land of waterfalls, country walks, and distant views, dear to the picturesque heart of the nineteenth century, a favorite for those who took the waters at Lamalou-les-Bains and its neighboring spas. Nineteenth-century laborers armed with explosives and iron tools cut roads into these gorges, plotting the gentlest rise upstream, then winding them up over the passes into the neighboring watershed, roads that could be used by heavily loaded oxen- and horse-drawn wagons, and eventually by motorized trucks and cars. These roads were longer than the old ones, but the teams would survive the haul. They allowed the mountain peasant and the traveling peddler to use that ancient invention, the wheel, and replace his own muscle power with that of animals, before animals were replaced in turn by the internal combustion engine. And they allowed the urban merchant and his wife to escape the grime of the city and enjoy the mountain air. The old roads, by contrast, were shorter but steeper, climbing as quickly as possible up the mountain side; there they would find upland ways that were more direct and less likely to flood or wash out in times of heavy rain. These were the roads La Fontaine was thinking of in his fable of the fly and the coach. In mountain country in France, parts of these old roads are sometimes still followed by *routes départementales*, field roads, and hiking trails, and it is not uncommon when driving or walking them to come upon ancient paving on steep slopes, the vanishing remnants of a Roman camp, or a medieval mill, bridge, or tower. These were roads for pack animals and men on foot, and the communities they served were days away from the commercial centers of the coast.

Yet in the upper reaches of the Orb and along the Jaur, the lists of 1271–72 include fifteen villages and castles in which the viscounts of Narbonne held rights of lordship. One of them, la Voute at the junction of the Jaur and the Orb, the young Amalric had held in fief of his father.[33] It would have been a precious possession. For here, in a roughly pentagonal area carefully mapped out in an agreement of 1164, Ermengard and her Trencavel allies shared the revenues from gold and silver mines. They asserted their rights not only to the revenues from mines on their own lands but to half the revenues of mines that were located in other lordships and to two-thirds of the revenues of those that belonged to the ancient abbey of Villemagne. As early as the tenth century, Ermengard's ancestors had been solidly implanted here, and what we know of the history of Villemagne (whose own archives have completely vanished) consists exclusively of early gifts from the vicecomital family.[34]

The Trencavels likewise had long-standing interests in this area. The castle of Mourcairolles, one of the anchors of the agreement of 1164, had belonged to the ancestors of the Trencavels who were viscounts of Béziers; it was part of the inheritance of Viscountess Garsend, wife of Count Raymond of Carcassonne, in 990. The castle of Boussagues, another anchor of the agreement of 1164, as well as those of Brusque, Boissezon, and Lunas to the north, had been part of the territories of the Trencavel ancestors who were viscounts of Albi and Nîmes.[35] The joining of these two lineages turned this remote plateau into the major crossroads that linked their Mediterranean possessions with those around Albi.[36] At the same time, the mines must have brought in a major portion of the Trencavels' revenues, for in 1189 it was with the income from the mines that Viscount Roger of Béziers guaranteed the payment of the substantial gifts to churches and monasteries in his last testament.[37]

Chateau of Bruniquel. The family of Bruniquel were allies of the Trencavels. From Charles Nodier et al., *Voyages pittoresques et romantiques dans l'ancienne France. Languedoc.* By permission of the Houghton Library, Harvard University.

This region was also home to veins of silver- and gold-bearing lead and copper, of antimony, sulphur, and iron—veins that had been worked in antiquity, perhaps even before the Romans. Some of them were still rich enough to be reworked with industrial methods in the nineteenth century.[38] The agreement between Ermengard and Raymond Trencavel in 1164 suggests a burst of renewed interest in mining these veins and profiting from what they produced. Was it a new discovery that prompted this sudden attention or the demonstration by some local entrepreneur that they could be exploited profitably? No document tells us. But it is the most striking example of the intimate ties of even the distant countryside with the bourgeoning city at the mouth of the Aude.

CHAPTER FIVE
CITIES OF MAMMON, CITIES OF MARS

We must not be misled by all these forceful signs of growth. Twelfth-century Europe—even Mediterranean Europe—still had what we would now consider a third-world economy. It was 80 to 90 percent agricultural; differences between the rich few and the many poor were extreme; population growth was fettered by the high death rate among infants. If good years could sometimes bring the price of grain to such low levels that even monastic chroniclers took the trouble to note it, bad years fed only the profits of hoarders, as the poor tried to fill their stomachs with grass and acorns and soon died of starvation. Even during periods of more or less stable production, the price of wheat could triple from one year to the next.[1] In terms of opportunity—and suffering—Africa or India rather than modern Europe or America is the image we should conjure up, but with one important difference: in the twelfth century there was no "first world" to which to look for technology and capital. Brocades and carpets, indigo and linen, brazilwood and fine ironwork, and above all gold might flow north from Africa and al-Andalus or west from Egypt, India, and beyond, but not engineers or bankers. Even for homegrown financiers the opportunities were limited: real estate speculation, long-distance commerce in luxury goods, cornering the grain market in years of dearth, acquiring privileged monopolies such as bake houses. In the cities as in the villages of the countryside, water mills were the one major investment that increased the productivity of labor. By modern standards, even when cities were booming their rates of economic growth were surely low. Yet city rulers, if they set their minds to it, still had means to boost the source from which their real profit came.

Artisans lived by their trades, investors looked for deals in real estate or sought longer-term gains in mill construction, but the great fortunes in Narbonne as elsewhere were made in long-distance commerce. Both the nature of the goods in the city's markets and the presence of Arab gold in the treasure boxes of laity and clergy point to it. In this trade, the elements on the two sides of the ledger were simple enough. Cost was what you paid for the goods you bought in Italy, or Spain, or Africa, plus the cost of transportation—the price of boat passage, the wages of the muleteers, food and lodging, losses to weather, accidents, pirates and bandits en route, plus the dues and tolls and taxes imposed by the people who controlled the ports, the roads, and the city gates through which you had to pass. Gross income was the amount you made when you sold what was left of your goods in the market. Profits (or losses) were the difference. On the cost of goods, someone in Ermengard's position could have no influence; that was given by the nature of the market. But on transport costs and above all on the myriad tolls and taxes that Narbonnese merchants had to pay abroad she could have some influence, and she knew it. She was not simply a passive exploiter of her city's economy. Almost from the moment she took personal control of the government she attended to what her merchants needed, and that concern continued for decades.

Narbonne's privileged position grew from the confluence of routes by sea and land that met at its gates. All of these had to be maintained both physically and politically.

The land routes were originally of Roman and pre-Roman construction. We should not imagine them as the sumptuous, heavily paved promenades that were the glory of the capital, however. At critical passages, especially in mountainous terrain where they took a steep slope, roads might be paved to prevent erosion during heavy rains (although not as elaborately as the Appian Way); here the local name for these routes is still sometimes *cami ferrat*—literally, "the armored road"—as is the name of the ancient road from Béziers to Cahors after it crosses the Orb and climbs the escarpments of the Espinouse mountain. They were also paved at the approach to major towns—as at the ancient town of Ambrussum along the via Domitia between Nîmes and Montpellier (where the via Domitia has recently been restored). Elsewhere, however, even the major roads were likely to be only beaten earth on a foundation of stones, mortar, and sand—a surface that even in the Roman period was liable to turn to mud in the winter and become impassible during spring floods—and by Ermengard's day they had been used for a millennium and with only a minimum of maintenance.[2] Untended, they were quickly invaded by grass and shrubs, as has happened to many stretches of Roman and medieval roads since they were abandoned in the seventeenth century, some of them now little more than a line of hedges marking the boundary between two villages.

The via Domitia south of Narbonne must have been particularly subject to such ravages, for much of it lay close to the line of seaside lagoons and salt marshes, crossed by innumerable arroyos that can suddenly turn to torrents in the winter rains. For a portion of the year, rain must have slowed or stopped all land traffic to and from Roussillon. One of Ermengard's first projects after she took power was to parallel that road with another that ran farther inland past the monastery of Fontfroide, south to the village of Portel, where it crossed the river Berre on a high-arched bridge and then climbed steeply into the arid eastern Corbières in the direction of Salses, the gateway to Roussillon. It was a

The bridge at Portel built as part of Ermengard's road to Roussillon. Author photograph.

major undertaking and surely an expensive one. Yet as important as this road was, we know about it only by chance, because Ermengard's gift of the land of Fontfroide to the abbey mentions in its boundary description "the new merchant road to Roussillon which was built on my orders."[3] It is one more reminder how limited are our resources for reconstructing Ermengard's impact on the world around her. We are continually at the mercy of documents that were saved mainly by churchmen to defend their property. But once we are told of the road's existence, we can easily follow it on aerial photographs and, thanks to that chance mention, date the first passage of the wagon wheels that eventually wore deep ruts into the stony Corbières hills. Ermengard paid for this project the way that governments have ever since: by charging the people who used it. We have seen those charges in the tariffs of the "old list of tolls" of 1153, in those extra dues of passage on goods and animals going to or coming from Roussillon. Was this her only project, or did she build other roads as well? The documents purse their lips and are silent.[4]

Maintaining trade routes was even more a matter of politics. For trade was not free. To use a road meant to pay a toll and often a protection fee as well. To use a port or even pass along a coast meant likewise to pay a tax. No one sold in a market without first acquiring the right to do so, and that meant getting a privilege. Lower tolls, freedom from tolls, exclusive rights, privileged places—these were the advantages that successful merchants needed, and in the twelfth century they were only given collectively. Such privileges, of course, were not free for the asking. Monks—and especially the Cistercians—eagerly sought to get them as alms so as to gain advantage for their wool in the urban market,[5] but others had to win them either through hard political bargaining or with military force. Here again the fate of urban merchants was intimately tied to the policies of their rulers. But such ties were reciprocal; for here on the shores of the Mediterranean, merchants were sailors, and sailors were warriors, to whom piracy and raiding were sometimes a convenient alternative to more peaceful exchange. The urban militia and its seaborne partner were as essential to a ruler's military force as her knightly host.[6]

THE URBAN MILITIA

We first hear of Narbonne's seaborne militia in 1114 when it joined forces with Montpellier, Pisa, and Barcelona in an attempt to oust the Moslems from Mallorca and Ibiza. Although the expedition was only a temporary success— the Almoravids were back in control the following year, and the islands remained Moslem until 1229—it announced the concatenation of forces to come: Barcelona and the two great powers of the Ligurian–Tuscan coast as allies or (more often) as rivals, with Narbonne and Montpellier sheltering themselves hopefully but warily under their umbrella.[7] In both Occitan cities the call to fight alongside the count of Barcelona would have brought forth pious supplications and dreams of chivalric fame, especially in an expedition graced with crusading privileges by the pope. Yet when next the call was heard, in 1148, the nineteen-year-old Viscountess Ermengard may have found her hopes for her city's profit and her own honor shadowed by the rapid development of the Italian cities, especially Genoa, not just as overweening trade rivals but as exemplars encouraging her own merchant oligarchs to dream dreams of independence.

The target of Christian desires in 1148 was Tortosa, where the Ebro River flows out onto the broad plain of its delta. The city commanded both the coastal route north from the rich Mediterranean cities of al-Andalus and the river route through the sierras to the plain of Saragossa. It was a rich prize. Through much of the eleventh century, much of the golden tribute from the *taifa*, the "party kings" of al-Andalus, that filled the coffers of the counts of Barcelona had flowed through Tortosa, and the city had long gleamed in the counts' acquisitive eyes. Beyond it lay other rich cities: Valencia, Denia, Murcia, and Granada. But first the counts had to grasp the key to the Ebro.[8]

Demands for tribute had not excluded friendship as well from flowing across the confessional divide. In 1058, the king of Denia, ruler of Tortosa and the Balearic Islands, agreed that the Christian churches of his kingdom should be subject to the bishop of Barcelona, in return for the bishop's promise that the

name of the Moslem king would be mentioned in the prayers of the Christian faithful. A copy of this treaty in Latin and Arabic still rests in the Archives of the Crown of Aragon in Barcelona. Almodis, the third wife of Count Ramon Berenguer I, exchanged letters and ambassadors with Ali 'ibn Mochehid of Denia, who addressed her as "glorious queen" and signed himself "your faithful friend." So cordial was this amity that the Moslem chronicler al-Bakhri could imagine the emir of Tortosa lending Count Ramon Berenguer a fleet to spirit the ravishing Almodis away from her jealous husband, the count of Toulouse.[9] And well Ramon Berenguer might have borrowed those ships, for Tortosa was especially known for its shipyards and for the wood, impervious to rot and insects, that came from the neighboring hills.[10] But friendship depended on proper deference, and deference here was measured in counted coin, which was always liable to awaken a greedy desire for more. It also depended on all sides imagining the frontier as a permeable zone, where religion separated but did not divide, where kings, warriors, monks, and merchants could make their careers on both sides of the line (as did El Cid and even King Alfonso VI of Castile himself), where the ideas of holy war and Reconquista had not yet conquered men's minds.[11]

All of these—friendship, frontier ambitions, and the flow of precious metals—rolled on the sea sweep of military power. In 1090, when El Cid became master of Valencia by battering Count Ramon Berenguer II of Barcelona and his army at Tevar, his newly won control of the gold road from the south allowed his coins to chase the gold *mancusos* of Barcelona even from their home market. Ramon Berenguer responded with sieges of Tortosa in 1092, 1095, and 1097, though all in vain. Nor did the death of El Cid immediately improve Barcelonese prospects; on the contrary, it opened the road to the Almoravid conquerors from North Africa, who were only stopped when they were nearly in sight of the gates of Barcelona itself. It was only when this fundamentalist Berber kingdom disintegrated in its turn that Christian thirsts could at last be slaked, thirsts now magnified by the deep spiritual forces of crusade, which gave the warfare a fierceness and a bitterness it had not known for over a century. Four years after the expedition to Mallorca, Saragossa fell to an army of Aragonese and knights from Occitania. Tudela, Tarazona, Calatayud, and Daroca followed soon after, and the broad valley south of the Ebro lay open to conquest.[12] As we have seen, it was while besieging Fraga—with Lerida the only remaining Moslem salient north of the great river—that Ermengard's father, Aymeri II, lost his life in the battle-host of the king of Aragon.

The bonds that joined the ruling house of Narbonne to all these ventures were familial and of long standing. Ramon Berenguer IV, the count of Barcelona who led the siege of Tortosa, was Ermengard's second cousin.[13] Her father Aymeri II had stood at the center of Ramon Berenguer III's network in Occitania, for he was the count's half brother. In 1112, when Ramon Berenguer III assembled a coalition to bring Viscount Bernard Ato of Béziers back into his due fidelity, Aymeri rode by his side, receiving as his reward the lands of the Fenouillèdes and Peyrepertusès with their formidable castles on the northern edge of the Roussillon plain. When the count claimed Provence by his marriage to Douce, the heiress to that county, Aymeri received in fief Beaucaire and rich lands at the mouth of the Rhone. In July 1131 he was called to attend on the count's deathbed to witness his testament and receive the charge of executor.[14]

This brotherhood in arms and piety was cemented by the presence of Narbonne's viscounts in the court of Barcelona on important occasions, by testamentary donations, and by gifts of fief across the Pyrenees, solemn occasions for oaths of fidelity.[15] Of all these gifts, perhaps the most dramatic was the agreement sometime around the middle of the eleventh century in which Ramon Berenguer I and his wife Elisabeth gave the city and county of Tarragona to Viscount Berenger of Narbonne. At the time, Tarragona was still firmly in the hands of the Moslem ruler of Tortosa, and it remained there for over half a century; the agreement came to naught.[16] But a comparison with the parallel grant during the siege of Tortosa reveals the dramatic shifts in military power over the century that separates them; it reveals as well the rapid and forceful entrance of merchant cities into the councils of the mighty.

The agreement of the mid-eleventh century that joined Ramon Berenguer I and Elisabeth to Viscount Berenger of Narbonne spoke of power and the revenues that flowed from power: they were to share in the election of the bishop of Tarragona (and the payment that came from it), in the castle of the city and its lodgings for fighting men, in the profits from coinage, customs dues, ship taxes, and tribute from Moslem kings. Uppermost in the minds of the count and countess were the oaths of fidelity that Berenger and his castellans would make, their presence in the count's camp in time of war, and observation of the peace "when the count and countess wish." This was a military alliance, carefully sharing the profits of power. In contrast, the grant to Narbonne in 1148 while the siege of Tortosa was in progress spoke of a trading settlement and freedom from customs duties, privileges that were close to the heart of merchants rather than fighters, even though it was the city's militia and most likely its merchant ships equipped for war whose fighting won the privileges and who, two months later, would join in celebrating victory over their Moslem enemy, even though the consuls who represented Narbonne spoke not only for their community but its two rulers as well, the archbishop and Lady Ermengard.

The text of the 1148 grant is rich in other implications as well:

> Holy decrees have ordered that those people who fight against the Moors and other barbarians who are enemies of the Catholic faith should be favored with suitable benefits, and those powers who despite danger serve repeatedly and without fear should be duly rewarded, and the names of those who triumph should be enrolled in the censor's list that they may win the perpetual remembrance of fu-

ture generations as well as of the present. For this reason, I, Ramon Berenguer, by the grace of God count of Barcelona and prince of Aragon, with the consent of William Raymond and Bernard of Bel-lloc my counselors, and the permission of the venerable Bernard, archbishop of Tarragona, and the counsel of the worthy consuls of Genoa, Giordano de Porta, Guglielmo Burone, Lanfranco Pevere, and Ogerio Vento, give, concede, and grant to all the people of Narbonne present and future a trading settlement [*fondicum*] in the city of Tortosa. And I command that no duty shall be paid by those who come there from Narbonne by land or sea but that they may freely come and go. This was done in the presence of the venerable Berenger, abbot of Lagrasse, and of the worthy consuls of Narbonne, William Sigerius, William de Volta, Laurent, and Raymond Multone—proctors representing Arnold, archbishop of Narbonne and his successors, the prudent Ermengard, lady of the aforesaid city, and the people of the city—who received possession with hand and heart. And I give them all those rights that by long custom of the city have been possessed by foreign merchants.[17]

To begin with, there is the prominence of the Genoese consuls in this text. Why did the count of Barcelona feel impelled to ask their counsel before granting a trading station and freedom from tolls to the merchants of Narbonne? The answer to this question opens a wide window on the larger world of commerce, adventure, and warfare on the western Mediterranean in the first half of the twelfth century, the world on which Narbonne's economic growth and Ermengard's wealth and power depended.

THE GENOESE

By the time of the siege of Tortosa, the Genoese had been actively engaged in commerce along the Spanish coast for at least three decades; an agreement of 1116–17 with the count and countess of Barcelona allowed the Genoese peaceful passage (on payment of the habitual duties) "to make peace and war on the Saracens as they wish." In 1127 those duties were set at ten *morabitani* (Almoravid gold coins) for all ships engaging in trade with Moslem Spain that touched land "between Nice and the cape of Tortosa," whereas those that took to the high seas to avoid paying this protection money would do so at their own risk.[18] Rivalry on these trade routes could be dangerous; it helped to buy the friendship of those who otherwise could be your enemy. Other risks in these seas required even more powerful patrons. The *Miracles of Saint Gilles*, composed about 1120, tells of a Genoese merchant ship coming from Almeria (then still Moslem) that was saved by the saint from a storm in the straits between the Balearics and Barcelona.[19] Doubtless the saint was also well rewarded for his gracious deed.

The Genoese had thrown themselves first into the Eastern trade, going to the source for the precious "spices" their customers demanded rather than dealing through distant middlemen.[20] The Levant was where the real money was. Alongside merchants from Amalfi and Byzantium, they were already buying dyestuffs and cloth in Alexandria in the 1070s, where cunning local traders spotted them as bumpkins to be easily fleeced. "They don't know the difference between first rate and second rate," wrote one to his associate in Old Cairo, "and pay the same price no matter what the quality." But the Genoese learned fast. By the end of the century there was a resident Genoese colony in Old Cairo itself, whose members were quickly rounded up and imprisoned when their fellow Genoese joined the crusaders to conquer Cesarea, Akko, and Jerusalem.[21]

In the western seas, in contrast, the Genoese were more often raiders than traders, playing a murderous game of prize and reprisal with their Moslem rivals and enemies. Led on by their Pisan neighbors through much of the eleventh century, they had carried their marauding to the islands of the western Mediterranean and the Moslem ports of southern Italy and North Africa: Reggio Calabria and Messina in 1005, Sardinia in 1015–16, Bône (in modern Algeria) in 1034, Palermo in 1062, Mahdia (in modern Tunisia) in 1087—an expedition of three hundred ships under the command of a papal legate—and Tortosa in 1093.[22] Mahdia, so the Hispanic geographer al-Bakri reported, stretched a chain across its port to protect it from raiders from across the sea, and east of Tabarca the local chief built a refuge-castle at Kilâ-Benzert. Indeed, there were *ribats*—fortified camps—all along the North African coast that served to protect the inhabitants of nearby port towns when the Christian pirates appeared. But although the Pisans ousted the Moslems from Sardinia in 1016, the Normans conquered Sicily in the 1070s, and combined Genoese and Pisan forces took over Corsica soon after, Moslem pirate ships could still sail from Tunis and other ports "to carry destruction and devastation to the shores of *Rum*," in the words of al-Bakri.[23] They raided Liguria and the coast of Provence with impunity as late as the beginning of the twelfth century.[24]

At the same time, Pisans and Genoese were afflicting each other with their piratical raids. It was a sign of the possibilities for enrichment that both were beginning to see in the western Mediterranean. Caffaro—the earliest Genoese chronicler and himself frequently a consul of the city and agent to the papal court and elsewhere—says it all in a laconic entry for the year 1119: "There was war with the Pisans, and sixteen Genoese galleys captured Pisans in Gaul with a large quantity of money."[25] The chief prize in this ongoing warfare was control of Corsica, which, to the fury of the Genoese, the pope had placed in the archdiocese of Pisa. It did not solve matters that at a church synod in 1123, the Genoese used large sums of borrowed money to bribe Pope Calixtus II and the College of Cardinals to revoke the Pisan privilege. Ten years later Pope Innocent II mediated a treaty between the two cities which raised the bishop of Genoa to the rank of archbishop and included three Corsican dioceses in his province, but rivalry and desultory warfare between the two cities continued, much of it conducted along the coast of Provence and Occitania as a *basso continuo* to regional politics.[26] Narbonne's position in that rivalry would be one of the many diplomatic and commercial issues that Ermengard would have to negotiate.

In these raids and predations, trade was always the ultimate objective, if it could be had. The raid of 1087 against Mahdia gained substantial booty and ransom—one hundred thousand gold dinars to save the city itself—but Pisans and Genoese insisted before relaxing their siege that they be given commercial access to the entire district of Tunis.[27] A decade later, the experience of the First Crusade only confirmed—if confirmation was needed—that the quickest way to open markets was to cut them open with a sword.

For Caffaro the Crusade was the shaping event in Genoa's history; his first sentence links it directly to the creation of his city's first consulate: "At the time of the capture of Caesaria, a little before, a *compagnia* [association] of three years and six consuls was formed." It is the coronation of Baldwin as king of Jerusalem, Genoese victories over the "arms of Babylon" in the seas off Haïfa, Akko, and Caesarea, and the miracle of the lights in the Church of the Holy Sepulchre on Easter Sunday that together form the first topic of his narrative. "And Caffaro," he assures us, "was there and saw it, and bears witness to it."[28] Victory over the Saracens and the birth of the Genoese polity shared in the same manifestation of God's will.

But God helps those who help themselves. In 1098 the Genoese won a trading house with its own jurisdiction, a medieval version of extraterritoriality, in Antioch.[29] Six years later, their alliance with King Baldwin of Jerusalem promoted them to the status of co-lords in the cities they helped capture. In 1109, their alliance with Bertrand, the son of Raymond of Saint-Gilles who was newly arrived in the east, brought in its wake a first extension of these privileges to the shores of the western Mediterranean. For their help in his siege of Tripoli, Bertrand offered them a third of the city along with the Castle of the Constable. More importantly for their commerce, Bertrand promised them and all the inhabitants of the Genoese riviera freedom from tolls in his lands (*mea terra*), an expression that was surely meant to include his Occitan as well as his oriental possessions. Six weeks later he promised them freedom from tolls and the monopoly of sea trade, as well as one thousand solidi per annum in Saint-Gilles itself, once he recovered possession of that town from his half brother Alfonse Jordan (whom he had left as count of Toulouse). Presumably he expected the Genoese to help him in the west as they had helped him in the east.[30]

It is doubtful that the Genoese were ever able to profit from these privileges in Saint-Gilles, for Bertrand died in Syria in 1112. His son took over his county of Tripoli, but his half brother Alfonse Jordan, firmly established in their father's Occitan lands, had no reason to feel affection for the Ligurian warrior-merchants. The Genoese adventures in the east, in any event, seem to have severely taxed their military and financial resources, and for a number of years after 1110 we hear little of their military activities beyond their own riviera. When the Pisans launched their expedition against Majorca in 1114, they sought allies in Barcelona, Narbonne, and Montpellier and pointedly ignored their one-time allies who were now their rivals.

Although warfare with Pisa preoccupied the Genoese through the following decade and a half, the lessons of the crusade and its profits were not forgotten. When violent fights broke out with Narbonnese merchants around 1130, when Ermengard was an infant, the Genoese applied these lessons with all the force they could manage. Arriving in Genoa to sue for peace in early summer of the following year, the delegation from Narbonne found themselves faced with demands that all commercial disputes between Genoese and Narbonnese be heard in Genoa, that the duties the Genoese normally paid in Narbonne be reduced by a third, and that the Genoese be given a trading station on the banks of the Aude which they could fortify with two towers.[31] Elsewhere they were even more demanding, especially once their war with Pisa had momentarily ended. To protect their North African trade they negotiated a ten-year truce with the Almoravid emir, then systematically reduced the major ports of the Provençal coast—Antibes, Fréjus, Hyères, Marseille, and Fos—to tributary client status. While other Italian cities were gradually making themselves into territorial powers by subjecting the towns and lords of their countryside, their *contado*, to their urban rule, the Genoese were building a *contado* of the sea lanes.[32] They were becoming an Occitan power.

Montpellier and Saint-Gilles were next as the Genoese jumped westward along the coast. When the Montpellerians revolted and expelled their lord in 1142, the Genoese saw their chance; four galleys filled with fighting men were dispatched in 1143 to help William of Montpellier retake his city. William responded with a letter of suitable hyperbole; they were, he told them, "the ministers of God," his city, in gratitude, was their "slave and devoted friend," and he himself "like one of their fellow citizens and perpetually in their service." The gratitude was realized in an astonishing privilege; not only were the Genoese granted the usual freedom from tolls, freedom of passage, freedom from protection money, freedom from depredation in case of shipwreck, and the right to adjudicate all disputed contracts in Genoa; William also promised that Montpellier's merchants would only go east by land as far as Genoa, and if by chance sea winds blew them eastward, they would return to Genoa without trading.[33]

In coming to William's aid the Genoese entered directly into the dynastic politics of the region, joining the allies that at this moment were fighting to free Ermengard from her marriage to Alphonse Jordan and her city from his domination. Forsaking the house of Toulouse/Saint-Gilles, from whom they had profited in the east, they entered the Occitan network of Barcelona.[34] The move was not without its costs, yet it too had its profits. The men of Saint-Gilles in the name of Alphonse Jordan seized ships and goods belonging to the

Italian merchants. Others were probably seized in Narbonne. But with the defeat of the count of Toulouse, the Genoese were well repaid. Although they did not win the same privileges in Saint-Gilles that they had won elsewhere, they received in reparations the enormous sum of two thousand marcs of silver (the equivalent of 96,000 sol. Melg.), a portion of it pledged on the duties charged to ships putting in at the city of Arles.[35]

When three years later the Genoese sent a squadron of twenty-two galleys and six smaller ships for an extended raid on Minorca and Almeria,[36] this foray was not merely a renewal of their predatory practices of a half century earlier and a western prelude to the Second Crusade; it was also both a challenge and an enticement to the count of Barcelona and the king of Castile—in whose prospective spheres of influence these cities lay—to invite the Genoese directly into their clientele. The invitations came almost by return mail.

To both Alfonso VII of Castile and Ramon Berenguer IV of Barcelona (who by then were already plotting their drives into Almoravid lands), the advent of Genoese combat forces along the coast of al-Andalus—bringing with them their own heroic memories of the First Crusade—must have added the final touch to what they and the papacy were now casting as a new crusade.[37] In September 1146, King Alfonso invited the Genoese to join in the siege of Almeria the following spring, in return granting them freedom from maritime taxes and a third of every city and land they jointly conquered—almost exactly the same privileges they had received from crusading leaders nearly a half century before at the other end of the Mediterranean. At the same time and in virtually the same words, they agreed with Count Ramon Berenguer to join in the siege of Tortosa after the conquest of Almeria.[38] With Alfonso they became prospective co-lords of Almeria, the two protagonists bound to each other with pledges of mutual aid and counsel and by the sacred oaths of the greatest lords of Alfonso's court; with Ramon Berenguer they became prospective co-lords of Tortosa, bound by the same sacred oaths and pledges of aid and counsel. That was why, when Ramon Berenguer invited the Narbonnese militia to take part in the siege, he had to ask the Genoese for their consent.

The siege of Tortosa was an extraordinary undertaking even for a lord with the power and wealth of the count of Barcelona. In addition to the third he gave the Genoese, he granted a fifth to the Knights Templars for their support and a third of the rights of lordship in the city to his most important official, his *dapifer* William Raymond, a grant that led to bitter disputes and litigation a decade later.[39] As it turned out, the joint campaigns to take Almeria and Tortosa were too much for the Ligurian commune. They leased their rights in the first to a Genoese merchant and finally sold back to the count of Barcelona their rights in the second.[40] The war, in fact, brought on a fiscal and political crisis in the city itself. We can draw a straight line from this moment to the factional violence that tore the city apart a generation later.[41]

Whatever their fiscal difficulties, however, the Genoese political gains in the western Mediterrean—and more importantly, their social gains—could not be undone. Those gains could only change the way in which the Mediterranean elites viewed the cities they ruled or that they took as allies. The evidence for these social gains may be subtle to our eyes, but to contemporaries it must have marked the difference between success and failure.

When the Genoese first appeared on the military and political scene of the First Crusade, they were recognized as neither a city nor a commune; to others they had no corporate identity. Their identity was that of their patron saint and his cathedral. It was to San Lorenzo of Genoa, patron saint of the city's cathedral, not to the consuls or the people of Genoa, that King Baldwin of Jerusalem gave streets in Jerusalem and Jaffa and a third of Assur and Caesarea and rights in Akko. In 1109 it was likewise to San Lorenzo that Count Bertrand of Toulouse/Saint-Gilles gave a third of Tripoli and the towns in its vicinity, to San Lorenzo that he promised the payment of one thousand solidi per year when (and if) he retook Saint-Gilles.[42] To speak thus was not mere metonymy, not simply an oblique way of referring to the city and its people, as the development we are about to see demonstrates. Gifts gained their meaning in the personal ties of love and obligation they created or affirmed, and the persons thus embraced could as easily be otherworldly as this-worldly. To an eleventh-century nobleman, such gifts to saints would have been part of the normal course of events. King, count, and all their companions had given lavishly to the saints of their native soil before departing on crusade, to win the prayers of their earthly servants and through them to gain heaven's favor for their enterprise. They most likely gave to saints on other momentous occasions in their lives—to thank them for an important victory, a miraculous cure, or the birth of a long-wanted heir, to gain saintly aid in a feud or for the salvation of parents, lords, or other loved ones—and they doubtless planned to give lavishly again in the hour of their death.[43] To give to San Lorenzo brought them military help from his earthly followers but also his otherworldly aid. It demanded no cognitive readjustment in the ordering of the hierarchies of this world or the next. Through their saint, the people of Genoa and their consuls slid easily into categories that had long been firmly established in the proper ordering of God's creation.

At the beginning of the twelfth century, encapsulating Genoa in its patron saint likewise reflected the realities of power within the city, where the bishop still ruled in the emperor's name. The most powerful families of the city, descendents of the city's tenth-century viscounts, formed the bishop's court. It was for this reason that the reach of Pisa's archbishop over the island of Corsica became for Genoese merchant-warriors a *casus belli*.[44] Yet the resolution of that conflict through bribery of pope and cardinals and eventually a military alliance with the pope—all of them undertaken by the consuls and their merchant allies—shows that although the gloved and bejeweled hands of the bishop still held symbolic power, the real center was moving elsewhere.

By the end of the 1130s, this move was being enshrined in pact after pact with the landed aristocrats of the Ligurian hinterland, whose continuing feuds ("Cerberus-like" they have been rightly called)[45] were a constant source of danger to Genoese merchants and merchandise moving across the mountains toward Pavia, the Po valley, and the north. One by one these lords were obliged to take oaths of fidelity to the urban *compagnia* (the sworn association of the merchant elite), to promise to reside in the city for two or three months each year, and in time of war to serve with their armed retinue in the Genoese host. In time they were also allowed to invest in urban commercial partnerships. The oaths they took were nearly identical to those that the holders of Mediterranean castles regularly swore to their overlords, but here they were being sworn to the commune; in effect, the commune was becoming the lord of the lords of its Ligurian countryside. At the same time, in the language of these agreements, those lords became "great and distinguished citizens" of the city. In 1150, even the marquis of Montferrat, the most powerful of all the mountain potentates, submitted.[46] In the mountains that loomed just beyond the city walls and along the Ligurian coast, Genoa was hoisting itself into the highest ranks of lordship.

In the floating diplomatic language of the second quarter of the century, we can see how the larger world responded to this flexing of communal muscle. In 1127 the count of Barcelona still negotiated his agreement to protect Genoese merchants with the city's bishop, who in the text stood first in line, before "the consuls and people of Genoa."[47] In contrast, the settlement between Genoa and Narbonne in 1131 (a text apparently drawn up in Genoa), identified the Narbonnese negotiators as "legates of the archbishop, . . . viscount, other consuls, and all the people," whereas those of the Genoese were simply "the Genoese"; in 1143, the "burgesses" of Saint-Gilles referred simply to "the Genoese and Pisans" with whom they had made peace.[48] By then William of Montpellier had already declared that his treaty of alliance against Alphonse Jordan was made "with the commune of Genoa and its people"; after their resounding victory, his thanks, while giving precedence to Archbishop Syro, addressed equally the "most famous city, most noble consuls and entire people" of Genoa, of which he declared himself a "fellow citizen in perpetuity."[49] This phrase was more than rhetorical hyperbole. It echoed the treaties through which the Genoese were then bringing the lords of their countryside into submission. Three years later, in the alliances the Genoese concluded with Castile and Barcelona, the order of precedence with their saint and bishop was reversed. The king and count addressed "you the Genoese" and—after granting them their thirds of Almeria and Tortosa—seemingly as an afterthought, added, "what your city holds in temporals your church will have in spirituals."[50] Four decades after they first broke out onto the Mediterranean stage, the Genoese were no longer masked by the image of their saint and his church; that church had become but one more manifestation of the city's power.

In these agreements, furthermore, the Genoese engaged themselves as equals: the emperor of Spain (as King Alfonso VII of Castile styled himself after his coronation at León in 1135) and the count of Barcelona spoke of their *pactum et conventio* with the Genoese, using the phrase commonly applied in Occitania and Spain to an alliance of noblemen. It was exactly this view of Genoa's role as equal partner that Count Ramon Berenguer made abundantly clear a decade later in the formal setting of his own judicial court. Sometime in the mid-1150s, the count's dapifer William Raymond complained that he had been deprived of important parts of the profits and income he had been promised in 1146 when the campaign against Tortosa was planned. When he received his share of the conquest, William asserted, the portion promised to the Genoese and Knights Templars had already been distributed; those shares, he said, should have been taken only from the count's portion, and his own portion calculated on the entire city. To this the count replied that "he had given nothing to the Genoese. They themselves conquered their part; therefore he [the count] should not be held accountable for their portion."[51] Under the circumstances, this was a self-serving argument. Yet what an image it was to spread before the comital court: the count not in full control of a conquest he had so long planned.

The official Genoese version of the conquest, once again authored by Caffaro, presents a rather more complex account of the campaign: a carefully debated, cooperative distribution of forces around the walls of the city; the Genoese, the count, and William of Montpellier pitching their tents side by side on the hill called Bagneria overlooking the walls (there where the Narbonnese received their privileges); a sharing of hardships; the labors of all to fill in the deep moat outside the walls. Then, at the critical moment when the siege-castles are attached in place against the city's walls, the main body of the count's forces deserts, angered by a delay in getting their promised pay, leaving the count with the company of only twenty knights and the Genoese. They, however, battle on alone and force the defenders first to sue for a truce and then surrender.[52] Was this the denouement to which the count was referring in his rebuttal of William Raymond? Was he subtly reminding his court of a story of which perhaps they had no reason to be proud? That is quite possible. The most important result, however, was to give full credentials to an image of the Genoese—and thus by extension of all city militias and the communities from which they came—that they themselves were only too anxious to promote: as independent corporate actors in the politics of the Mediterranean, as worthy of being honored as any high-born aristocrat.

What could a maritime city offer to a knightly host to make it so valuable? Its naval force, we would be inclined to reply, and its long experience in piratical ventures and hit-and-run raids on Moslem seaports. That is not, however, what seems to have been uppermost in the minds of the Genoese allies. It was rather the lowly mechanical skills of carpenters and blacksmiths and rope makers that they brought to the bitter business at hand, skills we might imagine noble warriors treating with scorn but that were irreplaceable in the conduct of siege warfare. In the agreement between King Alfonso and the Genoese there was a special provision that the Genoese would receive twenty thousand mora-bitani "for the cost of machinery."[53] And according to Caffaro, it was precisely to fell the wood for the siege-castles and other siege machinery in the hinter-land of Barcelona that the Genoese wintered there after the fall of Almeria, "al-though they had been away from their wives and children and homes for a year." In his account of the siege, it is the maneuvering of siege-castles, the hard labor needed to move them across the moat to the walls, and the battles at their tops that take pride of place. For Caffaro, warfare is a collective enterprise. The Genoese are constantly gathering to talk things over (*parlamentum facere*). As if to emphasize that the Genoese have earned thereby a collective honor, a cor-porate honor—and to distance his account from the standard contemporary tale of warfare composed for aristocratic consumption, tales that boasted the heroic deeds of individual warriors[54]—Caffaro starts his story of the siege by telling how some of the Genoese, eager to push the attack as soon as they landed, rushed the walls of the city "to show the Saracens how worthy they were in arms," only to be quickly reprimanded in conclave for fighting "without the counsel and license of the consuls."[55] Genoese worthiness, Caffaro seems to insist, is in their labor, their collective decisions, and their collective actions: a forceful image to present to a city that clannish factions were about to tear asunder. To the outside world, however, that image was not a mirage or an ex-pression of hope. It represented the hard reality of the city's power. In it lay the city's claim to corporate equality with the great noble houses of the Mediter-ranean.

BOTH ENEMY AND MODEL

Among the first to insinuate itself into this niche that Genoa had opened in the status hierarchy of the Mediterranean world was Narbonne. In 1148, the count's notary opened the grant of privileges in Tortosa to the Narbonnese with the proclamation, "the names of those who triumph should be enrolled in the censor's list that they may win perpetual remembrance." He was not simply showing off his classical erudition with an obscure recollection of the ancient Roman census, the censor's list of those worthy of bearing arms.[56] He chose his reference carefully: it was a reference to republican Rome, a striking choice in the imperial context of the Reconquista. (For even though this privilege was is-sued by the count of Barcelona, not by Alfonso VII, emperor of Spain, the counts likewise had long taken to themselves the historical inheritance of the Visigothic kingdom of Toledo and its tradition of imperial Roman law.)[57] The notary was asked to draft a document that would grant Narbonne some trading privileges. To do so he harkened back to an almost mythical archaic past, when a republican city had ruled the world. He thereby acknowledged the high status Narbonne had won, a status that allowed its consuls to deal with the aristocracy as equals, to represent the city's rulers as well as its people. With this flourish of clerical learning, he came to terms with a strikingly new phenomenon: that a social group as well as an individual, that a merchant city, could claim its place at the table with those whose valor in arms had earned the honors of nobility—and for its share gain the mercantile prizes of freedom from taxes and a privileged trading post.

For the merchants of Narbonne, the phenomenal rise of Genoa thus presented both a model and an opportunity. What their military forces won at Tortosa were exactly the same privileges that Genoese forces had been winning for half a century all around the Mediterranean. Unlike the Genoese, however, they had not won this prize by themselves; their community, although it had its consuls, did not exclude or subsume its aristocratic and ecclesiastical rulers; instead, it formed a joint enterprise with them. The group of noblemen surrounding Count Ramon Berenguer at the time of his concession to Narbonne stood as godfathers to this enterprise. They did not swear to it, as the Genoese had insisted that the great men of the courts of Castile and Barcelona swear to their alliances, but their presence recognized its validity. These witnesses included not only the familiars of the count—the ever-present dapifer William Raymond, Bernard of Bel-lloc (a member of the comital court from at least 1129 into the late 1150s), and the archbishop of Tarragona—but also William of Montpellier and his son (Ermengard's close friends as well as regulars at the court of Barcelona) and Peter Raymond of Narbonne, who would be at Ermengard's side into the early 1180s. The ritual setting for this grant of privilege was as noble as any for which the Narbonnese consuls could wish.[58]

Twelfth-century Occitanian cities would imitate the ways of their north Italian contemporaries, but not entirely. Their scruples—or failure of nerve, if such it was—came mainly from the cozy blending of interests among the merchant community, the local lordly families, and the city rulers. Some other Occitan cities, to be sure, were not as peaceful as Narbonne. In 1142, the merchants of Montpellier tried through armed rebellion to imitate the Genoese only to find the city that was their model arrayed in the forces against them. Toulouse at the end of the century would take advantage of its count's absence to make itself into a commune on the Italian model and use its militia to gain power over the villages and lords of its countryside.[59] For the region as a whole, however, Narbonne was emblematic. It was surely thanks to the century-old familial alliance of the viscounts with Barcelona, thanks to Ermengard's cousinage with Ramon Berenguer IV, that the Narbonnese militia was invited to join in the siege of Tortosa and its merchants graced with privileges. And in this award, neither Ermengard nor the archbishop felt demeaned at being represented by their city's consuls. Even Montpellier learned the lesson and profited mightily in the second half of the century from its overlord's connections to the dynasty of Barcelona. The days when consulates and overlords would be nervous watchdogs jealously surveying the boundaries of their separate rights and privileges were nearly a century in the future; the twelfth century was still, in Occitania, a world of cooperative venture, which first allowed the consuls of Narbonne like those of Genoa to act as fellow players on the stage of the siege of Tortosa.[60]

As much as it was a model and an opportunity for the merchants of Narbonne, however, the presence of the Genoese—and the Pisans—in these western waters was also a threat, one that merchants and their rulers could ignore only at their peril. In 1154, an expansionist group centered around the della Volta family returned to power in Genoa. They immediately repurchased the city revenues that their predecessors had alienated; then they negotiated agreements with the powers at the mouth of the Rhone River to guarantee a special position at that crucial crossroads of European commerce. At the same time they renewed their attention to the city's positions in the eastern Mediterranean (where the della Volta and its allies and clients had strong commercial interests), and in 1156, in return for the city's neutrality in a war with Byzantium, persuaded the king of Sicily to exclude all Occitan merchants from his island.[61] A promise to continue this exclusion was part of the bargain they struck six years later with Emperor Frederick I in return for their support in his war with Pope Alexander III and the king of Sicily. The Genoese, blocked by papal policy from establishing privileged trading stations in North Africa and facing murderous rivalry from Pisans and Venetians in the east, seemed intent on dominating at least the trade of the western Mediterranean. If they could not force all the merchants of the Occitan coast into a strictly tributary relationship, as they had done with Montpellier in the treaty of 1143,[62] they would at least exclude those merchants from their own prized trading grounds in Sicily.

Then came the Pisan slaughter of the Genoese colony in Constantinople and renewed fighting throughout the Mediterranean, and Genoese galleys, now engaged in open war, threatened all merchant ships, whatever their flag and wherever they might be found. These threats intensified once the Genoese entered directly into the Barcelonese–Toulousain conflict in the late 1160s. It was precisely to guarantee the freedom of Narbonne's merchants that Ermengard and the archbishop sent ambassadors in the autumn of 1166 to convince the Genoese not to attack Narbonnese ships as long as they were not carrying Pisans or their goods and to assure that the duties the Genoese charged Narbonnese merchants would stay the same as they had been since the treaty with Aymeri II in 1132. In return the Narbonnese promised to exclude Pisans from their city and to recognize the Genoese monopoly on all pilgrim traffic sailing from Saint-Gilles and Montpellier and the coast of Provence, thus reversing the alliance negotiated only two years before with Pisa.[63]

The agreement of 1166 with Genoa was to last for five years. No sooner did

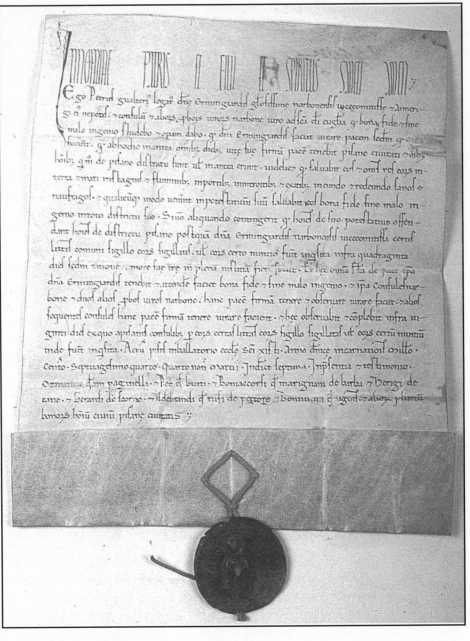

Text of Narbonne's treaty with Pisa, 1174 (AA 199). Copyright © Ville de Narbonne-Archives municipales, photograph by Claude Lebessou. Reproduced by permission.

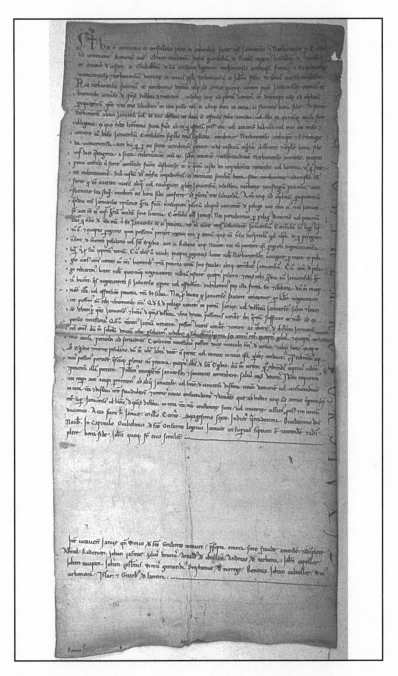

Text of Narbonne's treaty with Genoa, 1166 (AA 202). Copyright © Ville de Narbonne-Archives municipales, photograph by Claude Lebessou. Reproduced by permission.

it expire than the Genoese plunged into the Occitan wars on the side of Count Raymond V of Toulouse.[64] Ermengard responded by renewing her treaty with Pisa in 1174. Some measure of the piracy and reprisals that followed can be taken from the treaty of 1181 that reestablished peace between the two merchant cities. Each pledged to pay the other fifteen hundred Genoese pounds as reparations at the rate of five solidi for every Genoese merchant coming to Narbonne and the same for every Narbonnese merchant coming to Genoa. This time it was Ermengard herself who spoke for her people "in full parlament." It was "on [her] soul" that the oath to observe the agreement was made.[65]

The dangers foreseen in these treaties were immediate and doubtless sometimes tragic. They called for caution and ruse, courage and diplomacy. Would that we had the means to weigh their impact on Narbonne's economy and on the hopes and griefs of individuals; treaties and privileges enshrined in cartularies are but cold substitutes. There were other dangers, as well, that lurked in the Genoese attempt to dominate the western Mediterranean, more subtle and even harder to tease out of the surviving documentation, but doubtless no less demanding of the attention of Ermengard and her entourage.

Ermengard's father had apparently allowed his Narbonnese merchants to follow the Genoese model and form a consulate. He may indeed have encouraged it, for the imperious nature of these Italian inventions had not yet fully displayed itself, and the self-organization of a subject merchant community with its military arm may have appeared to have considerable benefits as long as it could be controlled from the top. But could that control be maintained in the series of crises that Ermengard faced? Or were there temptations in urban self-government that she simply could not risk? She came of age with the war to free herself and her city from Count Alphonse Jordan, who had entered Narbonne with the help of an inside faction, with the help of men whom her father had trusted; the city would be taken over again by Alphonse's son, Raymond V, and Ermengard would be momentarily exiled. Sometime in the course of these battles, the Narbonnese consulate disappeared. Consuls are mentioned in a treaty with Pisa in 1174, and then, despite an increasing quantity of documents in the city's archives, not again until 1205.[66] Ermengard's wariness may have begun earlier: the two ambassadors sent to Genoa in 1166 bear no title other than that of legate of the archbishop, viscountess, and people. More strikingly, Arnold Amalric and Bernard of Quillan, who swore to the treaty of 1181 with Genoa, bore no title at all. Bernard is otherwise undocumented, but when Arnold appears elsewhere in 1177, he and his colleagues are called *probi homines* (prudent men), a title most likely indicating an official role, but one without the heavy Italianate resonance of consul.[67]

A much later document hints at what may have happened. In 1221, when Viscount Aymeri III (Ermengard's grandnephew) confirmed the consuls' right to regulate pasturing in the island of Lec between the city and the sea, he noted

that these rights had originally been granted by Ermengard and later confirmed by Count Raymond of Toulouse.[68] The only point at which Raymond
may have had an interest in doing this (and the consuls in getting him to do it)
was when he briefly ousted Ermengard from the city in 1177.[69] Perhaps there
was complicity with Raymond within the city, and that complicity spelled the
end of an early experiment in city government. It took the growing need for
municipal regulations and the growing emphasis on privilege and particularistic rights in the thirteenth-century world to bring it back.[70]

⊶⟾

Through all these years the character of Ermengard's policy, both with respect to those two combative maritime superpowers, Genoa and Pisa, with
which her city's merchants and fleet constantly had to contend, and with respect to the model of merchant self-government that the two provided to stoke
the ambitions of her subjects, remained the same: caution. Not for her was the
dramatic act that would risk all in a single gesture. Caution and an eye for the
narrow path of independence among contending rivals: we will see this again
and again as we follow her maneuvering among the increasingly numerous
claimants to power in Occitania. Rather than ally herself with one of the Italian
cities, in the same way that the lord of Montpellier had accepted his city's subservience to Genoa in 1143, a position reaffirmed in 1155, she preferred to play
the rivals against each other. She and her merchants did not have the fleet, or,
undoubtedly, the wealth, to go toe to toe with either city. Montpellier prospered mightily as a result of its special ties with Genoa, and it may have surpassed Narbonne by midcentury. Its mint was a powerful pole of attraction; in
the contracts of the Genoese notary Giovanni, the earliest that survive from
that city, the Melgorian penny cedes pride of place among foreign coins only to
those of Byzantium and Sicily.[71] No wonder that in the north, "the gold of
Montpellier" became an expression for wealth beyond imagining.

But Narbonne too would prosper; in the thirteenth century it would acquire
a privileged presence in many Mediterranean markets, not just at Marseille, the
Balearics, and along the Catalan coast, but eventually even in Sicily, North
Africa, and Constantinople itself. One of the treasures of the city's archives
from the late Middle Ages was an imperial diploma bearing the golden seal of
Emperor Andronicus III that allowed the merchants of Narbonne to organize
their own community in the Byzantine capital.[72] Unlike the town of Saint-
Gilles with its famous pilgrimage abbey, its ducal palace, its location on the
Rhone, and its 134 money changers in 1178,[73] Narbonne did not become a
backwater. Ermengard's caution may seem timid and overly prudent when
compared with the behavior of her contemporaries, but in the end it paid off,
and in a later age her memory would be suffused with a roseate glow.

Ermengard had a further reason to be cautious. Power in Narbonne was not just a two-way match between her and her subjects. There was another power center in Narbonne, and the person who governed it had his own agenda and his own means of independent action. He was important enough to be present along with Ermengard's representative and the representatives of the city when Narbonne received its privileges at Tortosa. He was the archbishop.

CHAPTER SIX
THE BISHOP IN THE CITY

I f by some magic of time travel we could walk through the gates of an Occitan city at about the time that Ermengard was born, what would probably
strike us most would be neither the lord's dark and forbidding palace nor
the odorous marketplace but rather the monumental episcopal buildings at the
city's center, and above all the cathedral. Its ancient fabric would doubtless be
covered with scaffolding and besieged by stonecutters and masons and its surroundings littered with carts and workshop debris. For the crowds that pushed
through its doors on holy days demanded space, and the relics that crusaders
brought back from Spain and the East demanded a splendid setting. So did the
newly realized self-importance of the clergy who guarded them. The clergy's
response to their burgeoning flock and their newfound wealth was to build
higher and wider and in the latest Romanesque style. Around this half-en-
closed, half-open structure we would come upon the ancient baptistry and
smaller churches and chapels, many of them marked for absorption into the
new and greatly enlarged cathedral. Nearby, sculptors would be cutting biblical
scenes, allegories, and monstrous heads into the stone capitals for that new invention, the urban cloister, whose quiet enclosure was meant to symbolize the
quasi-monastic life of the cathedral canons—a way of life imposed or eagerly
adopted but a few decades earlier. Elsewhere, masons would be hard at work on
chapter room, refectory, dormitory, and the multitude of service buildings this
community demanded. Across the way, a new wing would be slowly taking
shape on the bishop's palace. Through the dust and the stench of manure and
sweat and open latrines we might be able to detect the scents of herbs and fruit
trees floating over the wall of the bishop's garden. If we rode off into the fields
outside the city walls, we would discover monastic communities competing en-
ergetically with their urban brethren in the elaborateness and sublimity of their
own new churches.[1]

Were we to go to Maguelone on its sandbar across a narrow lagoon from the
village of Lattes, which was then Montpellier's port, we would discover that the
episcopal buildings were about all that remained of the ancient city. In others
places, such as Cavaillon in Provence, they alone would tell us that we were in

The cathedral of Maguelone. From Charles Nodier et al., *Voyages pittoresques et romantiques dans l'ancienne France. Languedoc*. By permission of the Houghton Library, Harvard University.

a city and not a peasant village, for in clerical Latin it was a bishop and his church that made a *civitas*, a city. Twelfth-century Montpellier, that thriving commercial center and principal financial market for the Occitan coast, could not claim to be one because it had no bishop, but lonely Maguelone could. It was a tribute to the last days of ancient Rome, whose administrative map had been taken over by the Church. But it was above all a tribute to the bishops of the obscure centuries between the sixth and the eleventh who had kept alive Rome's memory and the memory of her urban centers. And within the twelfth-century cities of this Mediterranean world, the bishops were, or were becoming, independent powers that city lords had no choice but to contend with.

It was in Ermengard's lifetime that this rivalry reached its apogee in many of the cities of the Occitan shore, although in Narbonne itself the pattern had been set in the days of the viscountess's great-great-grandfather in the middle of the eleventh century. Out of this rivalry sprang the special character of the region's aristocratic courts—and thus both the troubadour poetry they cherished and the attitudes that would in time bait northern clergy to their most spiteful rhetoric. On its outcome hung the fate of those who were closest to the lady of Narbonne. Its culmination would come in the Albigensian Crusades, but of those future events Ermengard had no inkling. For her, the rhythms and perplexities of the persistent battles between these contending urban lordships would have served mainly as continued warning: unless she were vigilant, an enemy outside her city's gates could be abetted by an enemy within.

BISHOPS IN THE FAMILY

Throughout the tenth and eleventh centuries the major dynasties of Occitania had made sure that their own sons or sons of their friends occupied the episcopal sees of the cities in their control. From 927 to 1086, the archbishopric of Narbonne was, with one exception, in the hands of a member of the vicecomital family. The exception, Guifred of Cerdagne, acquired it from Viscount Raymond, his cousin's father-in-law. From the early tenth century to the late eleventh, for four generations, the family that ruled Albi and Nîmes—the ancestors of the Trencavels—had a son in an episcopal see: a Frotarius was bishop (of what city the document does not say) in 942, another Frotarius, probably his nephew, was bishop of Cahors in 957, a third Frotarius was bishop of Albi from around 972 to 975 and then bishop of Nîmes from 988 to 1014, and a fourth Frotarius was bishop of Nîmes from 1027 to 1077. The rights to bishoprics and the profits from conferring them were regularly sold, mortgaged, willed, or even given to brides as their marriage gifts. Every bishopric for which sufficient evidence survives tells the same story.[2]

Historians, at ease in a vocabulary of a later age, have commonly talked about this patrimonial church as a confusion of "secular" and "spiritual," as "the

Church in the power of the laity." But such distinctions—between secular and spiritual, between the Church and the laity—were invented by Church reformers in the eleventh century to radically separate what had once been fused. We adopt their combative vocabulary at our peril; we assume as given the things that were revolutionary for those who lived through their invention. For the great families of the tenth and eleventh centuries, to control the bishoprics of their region was as obvious a necessity as to control the fortifications and the fighting men. Their predecessors had always done so.[3]

In the world of late antiquity and the early Middle Ages, a bishop's office was a culmination to which a great man might aspire. The early medieval clan we can call the Desiderii-Salvii, after the most prominent names in their family tree, provided not only counts and bishops to the region of Albi and Cahors, some of whom dabbled in the most murderous politics of the court of the Merovingian king Chilperic and the queen mother Fredegonde, but also at least four saints: Salvius of Albi, Desiderius of Cahors, Rustica, and Disciola. By the end of the seventh century, not only the most important monastery of Albi but also thirty parishes of the countryside would trust in Saint Salvius's patronage. For a great family, a saint or two in the family tree could add remarkable glitter to the authority of wealth and status. The counts of Mauguio did not forget that Saint Benedict of Aniane had been one of theirs. Saint William of Gellone, Saint Benedict's friend, left numerous progeny well rooted in the soil of Lodève and Béziers. And even the Carolingians found it useful to invent some local saints for their ancestry when they established themselves in the lands that had once been ruled by the Goths. It had been the landed aristocrats of late antiquity who had founded the wealth of the city churches, and their Gothic and Frankish successors (who were perhaps their biological descendants as well) continued in the path they had marked. That wealth had been the strength of the Church. For people of immense generosity, such as Gerald of Aurillac, it could be the high road to sainthood. It is hardly surprising that such families should consider bishoprics and the monasteries they founded and continued to patronize to be extensions of their own wealth and authority.[4]

As for the payments they took for appointments to the bishoprics and abbacies they controlled, those could be viewed—and doubtless were until the reformers came along—as the traditional countergift (the *guerredon* of medieval epic and romance) that acknowledged all great acts of largesse. The reformers may have called those who paid such gifts "simoniacal heretics" (after Simon the Magician who sought to buy the Holy Spirit) and seen the shadow of the devil behind those who received them, but that did not prevent the old-fashioned aristocrats who appointed the bishops and abbots from supporting Church reform in their own manner. It was Count William of Toulouse, the lord who once sold the abbacy of Moissac for thirty thousand solidi, who gave Moissac to reforming monks from Cluny in 1063 and the abbey of Gaillac to reformers from La Chaise Dieu, and later saw to the reform of the abbey of

Saint-Sernin and the cathedral chapter in Toulouse itself. It was the viscounts of Albi who promoted the reform of Saint-Salvi in 1056 and Sainte-Cécile in 1072, Count Roger of Carcassonne who gave Saint-André of Agde to Saint-Victor of Marseille in 1064, and the "simoniac" Bishop Frotarius of Nîmes (albeit under pressure) who gave the abbey of Sorrèze to Saint-Victor in 1062.[5] Monastic reform was clearly one of the responsibilities of power in the mid-eleventh century, if one was careful of her or his immortal soul.

At the time when counts and viscounts regularly installed their younger sons or their friends in bishoprics, the Church was not yet equated with the clergy. Power did not yet fall easily into such neat, abstract categories as Church and State or spiritual and secular. To be sure, power—the simple power to command and be obeyed, to receive deference from inferiors and honor from peers, to collect tolls and tithes and rents, to hang murderers and whip adulterers through the street—was not an undifferentiated mass. But the way it took form in the mind drew more from the sweat of the heavy hand than it did from the dust of the cleric's writing desk. Modest bits and pieces of it were divided up, sold off, given away; but those pieces were as hard as the coin they brought in. *Recepta* (things received), *placita* (pleas, or perhaps things that please?), *forciae* (things for the strong), *acaptae* (things taken), *quistae* (things asked for): these were what gave a sense of one's place in the order of things, the sense that a later age would call "profit and worship." They were carefully guarded and judiciously parceled out.[6] That the person who possessed them might be titled bishop or abbot or count or viscountess or simply *domina* or *dominus*, lady or lord, made no difference. Lordship was lordship. Power was what made great families great and what lesser families aspired to, and it was built up layer by layer, as deposits of symbolic capital.

Power and authority with their privileges and revenues flowed easily back and forth through what a later age would consider an impermeable membrane. Just as counts and viscounts gave bishoprics to members of their family or gave them to their friends and allies, so bishops did the same with the offices at their disposal. Only in 1077, when he placed the cathedral chapter under a rule of common life and allowed its members to freely elect their officers, did Bishop Isarn of Toulouse give up his long-standing practice of granting archdeaconries and archpresbyteries to his military followers.[7] The reform movement of the late eleventh century changed much, but even afterwards, bishops continued to conceive of their positions as great lordships, to infuse their rights with patrimonial passions and their discourse with familial imagery, although now the family was the Church.

What made the bishoprics valuable were, of course, their lands and revenues. In the later tenth century, as the superstructure of the western Carolingian world dissolved, these became yet more valuable. For with the weakening and finally the disappearance of the old royal court with its gifts and favors, these dues and estates securely anchored what the great families now most needed—local power, myriad tolls to tap whatever wealth passed by or through the city's gates, and from those earnings the coin to build castles and towers and pay the armed toughs who would man them. All the more reason, then, for counts to insist on their right to name a bishop to a vacant see when they could, even as viscounts and other lords were appropriating most of the other realities of local control.

By the late eleventh century, rights over the bishops seem to have been all that were left of the powers that the house of Toulouse once exercised in cities in which viscounts now ruled supreme. The vast sum that the viscount of Narbonne accepted to make Guifred of Cerdagne the archbishop of his city around 1019 had to be shared with the count of Rodez, a distant cousin of the count of Toulouse; Guifred later vigorously used his alliance with Count Raymond IV of Toulouse to build his own rival seigniory in Narbonne. At Béziers it was the count of Toulouse and not the local viscount who exercised the traditional right to confiscate the personal property of a deceased bishop and take the episcopal revenues until a new bishop was installed.[8] At Albi the counts of Toulouse and the viscounts long shared the selection of the bishop and its profits. It was probably to affirm these widely dispersed powers that Raymond IV once had himself titled "count of Rodez, Gévaudan, Uzès, Nîmes, Agde, Béziers, and Narbonne."[9] Such elaborate invented titles preserved the strongest memories of the late Carolingian polity. That is why the bishopric and its lands and powers—and even more so, the right to profit from conferring the bishop's powers—figured so importantly in the alliance about 1050 between the count of Barcelona and the viscount of Narbonne to share the conquest of Tarragona, and two decades later in the Barcelonese alliance with the Trencavels to divide up the rights that had belonged to the counts of Carcassonne. Bishoprics were among the most preciously guarded urban rights of the great dynasts.[10]

In the decades before Ermengard was born, however, a slow but inexorable tide of change swept across the land, as the legates dispatched by Pope Gregory VII and his successors railed against the purchase of clerical offices, and the abbots of Saint-Victor of Marseille, Moissac, and even distant Cluny were summoned to bring stringent rule to the lives of monks and cathedral canons. It was no overnight revolution: at Albi, the bishopric was still in the gift of the viscount in 1132,[11] and through much of the twelfth century the archbishops of Narbonne were sometimes still members or friends of the vicecomital family. But by 1100 such cousinage no longer assured control. After the death of Guifred in 1079, the viscounts of Narbonne repeatedly tried to reclaim their prerogatives. In 1096 Viscount Aymeri I appropriated the episcopal lands and refused to let the newly elected archbishop, Bertrand de Montredon, take possession of the see; in 1106 his wife, Viscountess Mahalt, managed to have Bertrand deposed and again laid hold of the property of the see. Richard, the next archbishop, reversed the balance of forces. Although he was the grandson of Viscount Berenger I, he used the resources of Rome to bring his cousin, Viscount Aymeri II (Ermengard's father), to terms. As abbot of Saint-Victor of Marseille (the major reforming monastery of the region) and cardinal, he was well placed to do so; his long career in the papal milieu made him identify his interests with the independence and powers of his see rather than with the family from which he had sprung. Aymeri was forced to swear him fealty and homage, to take some of his rights in the city as fiefs of the archbishop, and to recognize the independent lordship that the archbishops had established.[12] Elsewhere, other bishops were also playing off rival lords and the papacy to gain their "liberty." Gradually the great dynasts who had controlled the bishoprics relinquished their last important rights, the last symbols of the bishops' subjection to their power, their right to take over episcopal property between one bishop's death and the installation of his successor: at Béziers in 1084, at Carcassonne in 1113, at Albi in 1144, and, at long last, at Narbonne in 1155.[13]

The net result of this revolution was not, however, to free the bishops from secular concerns. On the contrary, it turned them—and probably was intended to turn them—into the viscounts' bitter rivals for power. "Reforming" bishops played as aggressive a game as had Archbishop Guifred, their "unreformed" avatar.

ARCHBISHOP GUIFRED

Guifred's father bought the archbishopric of Narbonne for him when Guifred was but ten years old. The young prelate was the cousin of the future viscount's wife, and relations at first seem to have been more than amicable; he promised his patrons that they would receive half the castles of Salses and Castelnau in Roussillon and half of all the other fiefs that Guifred could claim on the death of his uncle, the count of Besalú.[14] But in time he began to show a taste for independence. His father, after all, was a count. Among his uncles, in addition to the count of Besalú, he could number the bishop of Elne and the mighty Oliba, abbot of the Catalan monastery of Ripoll; his sister was countess of Rouergue. He had every reason to think himself the equal, if not the social superior, of his in-laws across the street.

The heartlands of Guifred's family's holdings were the high valleys of the Têt and Segre Rivers, which flow northeast and south out of the Pyrenees. From there his grandfather and father had pushed southward toward Urgell, Besalú, and the lands ruled by the Moslems, northward into the valley of the Ariège, and eastward down the Têt and Agly toward the Mediterranean and the southern Corbières. Conflicts with neighbors (and near or distant cousins) who were equally expansive—the counts of Barcelona and Besalú, the bishop of Urgell, the count of Foix—had given them ample occasions to prove their mettle. Guifred's nephew would eventually parlay a strategic marriage into the guardianship of the infant Count Ramon Berenguer II of Barcelona and, for a brief moment, effective control of the Catalan government.[15] Buying the archbishopric served the family's grand strategy well, for bishoprics and abbeys were as valuable as counties and castles. With their churches' accumulated treasures, the family could fund a series of leveraged buyouts. The money to buy the archbishopric could very well have come from Ripoll and Elne, and it is certainly plausible that (as his enemies later charged) Guifred stripped the assets of his see to buy the see of Urgell for his brother; that bishopric was a long-standing prey of his family's ambitions.

To shore up his personal ambitions at Narbonne, Guifred searched through the chests that held the archiepiscopal archives,[16] and there he found a whole series of Carolingian diplomas dating back to the eighth-century Frankish reconquest of the city from the Moslems. These ordered the return of vast estates in the countryside to the archbishop, gave him a monopoly of justice within those estates, and granted him half of the count's most important fiscal rights— dues on ships coming into port, on merchandise coming through the city, on herds and flocks, and on the produce of the salt works in the marshlands and lagoons that lay between the city and the sea. For the word *count* in these antique documents, Guifred, of course, read *viscount*, for the viscounts had long since appropriated all these dues. And the Carolingian texts with their now obscure words must have seemed marvelously open-ended. The share of fiscal rights they spoke of suggested another share that he could claim in the burgeoning eleventh-century urban world—half of the city of Narbonne itself. That the Carolingian diplomas breathed not a word of such a thing did not trouble him for long. To what end did clerics master the art of writing, after all, if it were not to improve the evidence for what they knew were their rightful claims? The appropriate clauses were inserted into a diploma of Charlemagne's grandson, Charles the Bald, and at the needed time a new, improved "original" came out of the archbishop's scriptorium.[17]

Guifred, like other bishops of his age, also used weapons more forceful than forgery to get his way—at least if we believe the accusations launched in his direction by Viscount Raymond Berenger in 1059.[18]

It had been only a few years since the reform movement had brought its attack on simony to Occitania. A regional council at Toulouse fulminated against the practice in 1056, and similar denunciations were repeated again and again over the following decades.[19] Guifred had already been excommunicated by Pope Victor II when Raymond Berenger strode into a church council at Arles and told the assembled prelates his tale, a tale they doubtless already well knew: how Guifred's father had bought him the archbishopric for vast sums of silver and how Guifred had stripped the cathedral of its altarpieces, crosses, and reliquaries, and pawned its chalices and patens to Jewish moneylenders to buy Urgell for his brother.[20] The viscount knew the prejudices of his audience.

But it was Guifred's military actions in Narbonne itself that brought from the viscount the most finely tuned strains of pathos and affronted faith.

With him seated in the episcopal chair and growing in age and honor [the vis-count said], I trusted that I would find in him a helmsman and a weapon and shield against the darts of my enemies, and that remembering he is a cousin of my wife, and the honors in which I helped to place him, he would help me to defend my own honors as he had sworn to do [a reference to the oath of fidelity Guifred had doubtless sworn but of which no documentary trace remains]. Instead, he rose up like the devil. With haughtiness and rudeness he provoked me to anger. Against me he built castles and raised an immense army, waging a cruel war that cost the lives of nearly a thousand men. From God and His servants he took the castles and villas, the fields and possessions in the lordship of the church, the es-tates and possessions that served the common life of the cathedral canons, and gave them to the devil and his fighting men. . . . He assembled a great council of bishops near Narbonne, and in their presence renounced all arms of war, declar-ing anathema not only himself but all of his bishops who should thereafter take up arms. But a little while afterward, it was he who took up arms like a knight, gird-ing his loins not with a rope but with iron, to make war on me. How many dead, how many wounded, how many who lost their limbs, how many churches burned, how many relics up in flames! Were I to tell you the full story we would be here all day![21]

Whatever the hyperbole in the viscount's broadside, there is no doubt that Guifred had long been busily involved in building castles, and given the costs of such construction in the eleventh century, he would have spent much of his revenue and perhaps sold large amounts of his plate to complete them. We know their names: Capestang, Cruscades, Canet, Villedaigne, Conilhac, Ar-gens, Sijean, Salles, Fontjoncouse, Auriac, and Villerouge, plus a number of sites in the southern Corbières and northern Roussillon.[22]

Guifred did not select the sites for these castles at random. Capestang was probably the most important of them all, for it sat astride the major direct road from Béziers to Carcassonne and Toulouse, overlooking a marsh that stretched all the way to the sea. The most direct route from Béziers to Narbonne, the via Domitia, crossed this marsh on an old Roman causeway called the Pons septi-mus, and during wet winter months it could become unusable, making the de-tour through Capestang the only way from Béziers toward the west and south. It is hardly surprising that one of Archbishop Richard's first tasks was to dispute its possession with the viscount of Béziers. Cruscades sat next to the principal highway from Narbonne to Carcassonne, just where it crossed the Orbieu River.[23] It and three other castles—Villedaigne, Conilhac, and Canet—created a formidable barrier to all communications east–west through the Aude valley. Argens was just across the river on the left bank. Sigean sat next to the major route from Narbonne to Spain and at the same time provided a spot from which to survey traffic in the lagoon that served as Narbonne's port. Salles pro-tected the salt works from which the archbishop drew a portion of his revenues and also the only dry road to the Ile de Lec, where he had many estates. With

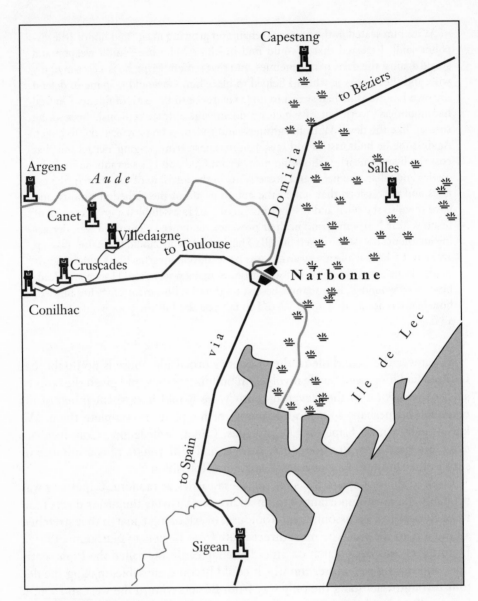

Archbishop's castles around Narbonne

these castles Guifred positioned himself to control all traffic in and out of the city. The remaining castles, in addition to maintaining a presence in the wild southern Corbieres, probably served as way stations on the road to Guifred's portion of his family's lands in Cerdagne, the Fenouillèdes, and Besalú.

Guifred also had his fighting men. For one brief, precious moment we can even see him negotiating with a retainer who has demanded a fief that Guifred was not yet in a position to give. It was with these knights, or the men who had replaced them (sometimes violently), that Archbishop Richard had to negotiate to recover the castles and extract oaths of fidelity in the early years of the twelfth century.[24] While we need not believe Raymond Berenger's "nearly a thousand killed," taken as it is from the rhetorical habits of epic poets, there is every reason to think that the two rivals and their armed men fought it out, for it is hard to imagine Guifred tying this noose of castles around the city without a battle.

In these battles the viscount got the worst of it. Sometime before 1049, he was forced to recognize the archbishop's exclusive rights to part of the city and its fortifications and to guarantee them with an oath of fidelity.[25] Guifred felt confident enough of his own power that after bringing the relics of Saints Just and Pastor out of Spain in 1058 and installing them in the cathedral that bore their names, he almost immediately removed them to a church in the country-side. He was locked in dispute with an archdeacon of the cathedral chapter—possibly, indeed, over who was to pocket the gifts that the faithful left for the saints—and this was the most powerful form of blackmail he had at his disposal. When Viscountess Garsend went to recover the relics and bring them back to Narbonne, Guifred excommunicated the whole family and placed the city and all the viscount's lands under an interdict. By Raymond Berenger's account, this was the last straw. Summoning all his wounded dignity, he asked the papal legates present at the council to lift the family's excommunication and lead Guifred himself in chains to Rome for punishment.

But neither provincial councils nor Rome itself could rein in Guifred. Papal excommunications rolled off without effect. In the late 1060s Guifred presided over a peace council at Toulouges in Roussillon that must have been largely a family gathering; in 1077 he even led an armed band against a provincial council at Gerona, forcing the papal legate and his own suffragans to find refuge in Besalú.[26] When Viscount Raymond Berenger died in 1067, Guifred spied a new opportunity.[27] While the viscount's three sons disputed the succession, Guifred convoked an assembly of his own most powerful supporters—Count Raymond of Toulouse/Saint-Gilles, Count Bernard of Besalú, the bishops of Toulouse, Elne, and Gerona, seconded by some lords of the Narbonne countryside—and presented his case against the young Viscount Bernard Berenger, who he claimed had usurped the archbishop's rights in the city.[28] Raymond of Saint-Gilles hardly needed the invitation. He jumped at the chance to act as Guifred's protector and thereby revive the memory that his distant cousins the counts of Rodez once had power over the archbishopric.[29] He promised not only to support Guifred's fiscal rights and his control over half the city but also gave him the right to open a gate anywhere in his part of the walls—potentially a lethal threat to the viscount's military control. As a direct challenge to the reformers, Count Raymond also promised to combat any bishop within the archdiocese who might have himself consecrated without Guifred's assent. The pressure on the three heirs to the viscounty was overwhelming. Raymond Berenger II surrendered immediately, putting his sign on the oath of Raymond of Saint-Gilles itself. His brother, Peter, bishop of Rodez (who would soon claim Guifred's succession at Narbonne), quickly followed suit; so too did the third brother, Bernard.[30]

Guifred left his successors a powerful and wealthy lordship both inside and outside the city, one they could continue to build on. And build they did. By the middle of the twelfth century, new archiepiscopal castles added to their control of Narbonne's port and dominated the via Domitia at its treacherous crossing of the Capestang swamp, while others controlled the Aude both upstream from Carcassonne and downstream near Narbonne.[31] Guifred also left his successors a plenteous archive. Archbishop Richard, a twelfth-century successor, depended on those documents in the disputes that arose with his castellans and the viscount when he first took power.[32] By the time Ermengard came of age, this rival lordship was firmly anchored in and around her city. It was a fact of life. She would have to deal with it as best she could.

THE CONSEQUENCES OF REFORM

Guifred undertook his swashbuckling enterprise at a time when those with ambition could do wonders, when counts and dukes could dream of becoming kings—like William of Normandy in England or Baldwin of Boulogne in Jerusalem—or of conquering distant principalities—like Raymond of Saint-Gilles in Tripoli, El Cid in Valencia, Ramon Berenguer of Barcelona in Provence, or the epic hero William the Shortnose in his mythical Nîmes. In their shadows, others could savor similar dreams. In this gritty, unrelenting world, the means were simple enough: armed men, sufficient lands and dues to reward their fidelity, and the castles to seal control of the territory once it was conquered.

With Guifred, the world of patrimonial prelacies entered a new era. The familiar style, so well represented at Narbonne for nearly a century, had been to use a bishopric to complete local control, for the ruling dynasty to place its offspring (or its cousins or friends, if no offspring were available) in positions of complementary lordship. Doubtless this is what the future Viscount Raymond Berenger thought he was doing when he urged Guifred on his reluctant father: cousins by marriage or cousins through the female line were familiar, safe candidates for posts of power; they were tied to the family's interests, but they were not in a position to threaten its control. The Cerdagnese, however, had other things in mind. Locked in their impoverished high mountain valley and surrounded by mountain lords of equally hard-nosed ambitions, their solution was to overleap their neighbors, to marry their daughters out and acquire potentially powerful abbacies and bishoprics for their sons, and thus acquire a larger, regional stage on which to play out their dynastic aspirations.

The reform movement spearheaded by Pope Gregory VII in turn replaced this style of patrimonial bishopric with a yet newer one, still patrimonial, but with a difference. Families with ambition might still set their sights on prelacies—that continued to be the case for centuries to come—but the lordships these prelates created, expanded, and protected belonged now not to particular families but to that great universal family, the Church, or as twelfth-century churchmen would have said, to God and His saints, and to their representatives on earth, the clergy. The ambitions to acquire them might be dynastic, but they could no longer be completely absorbed into dynastic patrimonies.

Two striking examples of these new-style prelacies emerged in the mountains to the north of Narbonne, at Rodez and Uzès.

In the late 1060s, Raymond of Saint-Gilles fought and defeated the count of Auvergne for the title and rights of the county of Rodez, to which his distant cousin Bertha had been the last heiress. He soon showed what he really wanted it for. He displayed the title on the coast—as at Narbonne—when he needed to act belligerently as protector of clergy over whom the counts of Rodez had once held proprietary rights. But when he departed on the First Crusade, he was happy to mortgage the heart of the county, Rodez itself, to Viscount Richard of Millau. In 1112–13, Richard bought the county outright from Alphonse Jordan.

Richard belonged to another of those remarkable Mediterranean vicecomital families on the make in the decades around 1100.[33] About the same time he was securing the county of Rodez, his brother Gilbert was taking the title of count of Provence by marrying the heiress to a major branch of that family. Richard, meanwhile, allied himself by marriage to the house of Narbonne, making the bishop of Rodez his brother-in-law. His son by the same name eventually became Narbonne's reforming archbishop.

The core of Richard and Gilbert's domain was east of Rodez, in the dry, impoverished hill country known as the Causses, which stretches from Lodève and Millau to Mende, and around Carlat on the southern edge of the Auvergne. Where they acquired their later wealth is a mystery hidden in a documentary vacuum, but careful placement of their offspring in high ecclesiastical office seems a likely possibility. Bernard of Millau was abbot of Saint-Victor of Marseille from 1064 to 1079, a position to which his brother Richard succeeded. Both were eventually named cardinals. Another brother, Berenger, became abbot of Saint-Amand, the principal urban monastery of Rodez. Richard's son and successor as count styled himself count and abbot of Saint-Amand in 1120. The bishops of Rodez in the early part of the century could have been from the entourage of the Millau family. Yet what had been the usual hierarchy of dominance was now reversed: Bishop Hugh (1165–1211) was the count's brother, but he allied himself with Count Raymond of Toulouse and went to war to force his brother to recognize that he received the county from the bishop and owed him fidelity.[34]

The family of Posquières, lords of Uzès and loyal followers of Raymond V of

Toulouse, also built their power on episcopal offices. Of the six sons of Raymond Decanus, who died in 1138, one became lord of Uzès, another the lord of Posquières; the remaining four became bishops—of Nîmes in the critical years from 1141 to 1180, of Uzès (1150–80), Lodève (1154–61), and Viviers (1158–60). Like the family of Millau, the Posquières came late to the game of building a great lordship, so although they were lords of Uzès, it is not surprising that they should seek to grasp the bishopric as well, for the bishop owned fifteen castles that encircled the city. They also controlled the city's mint and doubtless had no real rival in their tiny mountain diocese.[35]

Although it may appear otherwise, such familial preying on church offices violated neither the letter nor the spirit of Church reform. The reform movement was not meant to be a social revolution; it was meant to reverse the accepted hierarchies of power among those who ruled—exactly as happened at Rodez. As strong as their monastic background may have been, the reformers' ambition was not to flee the world but to dominate it. Their Church, like that of their unreformed predecessors, was aristocratic to the core, as it would be for centuries to come. To the major ideologists of the reform—such men as Cardinal Humbert and Pope Gregory VII—what was vital was to separate the consecrated and sanctified from the unconsecrated and unsanctified, and to recognize in the workaday world the preeminent position of those who had been called to serve the saints and perform the magic of the holy sacraments. This, they firmly believed, could not be assured unless the property of the saints was assured, unless its continuity could be guaranteed from generation to generation. In practical terms, this meant that every bishop and every abbot (and every cathedral chapter, monastery, and collegiate church—for they were less powerful and in consequence had to be more vigilant) had to guard the rights and properties of his office with the same imperious sense of dynastic continuity as aristocratic families had for their lands, rights, and titles.

To defend rights, however, required that they be remembered. How would that be done? To people of the eleventh century the most obvious answer to the problem of continuity was familial memory. That is evident from the penalty clauses inserted into pious donations. "If any abbot or powerful person takes this from the canons, let him pay double or triple, and let my family who are then living have it restored to them by the ruler of Narbonne," declared a simple peasant when he gave his farmhouse and vineyard to the monastery of Saint-Paul outside the walls of Narbonne.[36] "If any bishop or abbot . . . or any power wants to take this property for his own use or to give it as a fief . . . let him incur the wrath of God . . . and let the count of Narbonne who shall be at that time take the property and return it to the community [of Saint-Paul]," Count Hugh of Rodez declared in a donation some decades later.[37] It would be the descendants of the donors who would remember and be vigilant, even when, as in these two examples, the greatest threat to the permanence of their pious gifts came from bishops and abbots themselves (an important sign that the desire for reform had a popular as well as a monastic impetus).

To the question of continuity the reformers gave another, and potentially far more powerful, answer. Memory would be found in documents, in the archives. We can watch the idea burst on the scene in a dispute between the canons of Saint-Nazaire of Béziers and the bishop of Maguelone and his heirs in the late 1050s. When the canons went before a regional council and charged Bishop Arnold with holding a field unjustly, he insisted on seeing their "charter or judgment." Back in Béziers they showed him the charter with which Bishop Stephen had given the canons the field they claimed. "Thereupon," the record of these events says, "his heart was terrified by the great excommunication [in Stephen's donation] and he was silent for a long time." At last, in response to the "humble entreaties" of the canons, he formally renounced his rights.

Laymen, however, were not yet easily cowed by the written word. Bishop Arnold's nephew grabbed the disputed property as soon as Arnold was in his grave. A year of public denunciation got the clergy nowhere. To get the nephew and his family to give up the property took the hand of God himself, who struck the malefactor dead, intestate. Instructed in the moral of this story by the canons, his widow and sons relented. With these laypeople, no one thought once again to dig the parchment out of the clerical treasure chest. Perhaps the canons had learned their lesson eight years earlier when they had pulled out a testament "where Isembertus held the horn and ink" to convince an assembly of laymen that some land should be returned to them, only to be rewarded for their troubles by a judgment stating that they should defend their claim with a trial by battle—and even that possibility got lost in the comings and goings, and the ill will and evil designs of their own Bishop Berenger.[38]

The accounts of these disputes, full of narrative detail, obscure vocabulary, and self-righteous moral posturing, sound all the right preacherly notes: episcopal cupidity, the arbiters' evil hearts and perversion of judgment, and finally the just judgment of God. Their garrulity unveils for once the politics of the occasion, the strong impulses of the reform movement adding their energies to squabbles of clerical self-interest, and the way the canons used the written word to fight the familial memories of their opponents. Teutaldus, the priest who drafted these particular texts, referred to each written text on which the canons based their claims as *iudicium veritatis* (a judgment of truth). These words tell us what he had been reading: not only the charters by which the canons claimed their right but also the judgments of late Carolingian courts, which he had found in the archive, by then a century or more old. These antique but prestigious documents, perhaps dusted off for the first time since they were written, gave him the form of his narrative, with its purported verbatim transcript of what the parties said, and his technical vocabulary, which he significantly misunderstood.[39]

As we have seen, Teutaldus was not alone in reading dusty Carolingian documents. Just down the road in Narbonne, Archbishop Guifred was also reading (and writing) them. When the archbishop won the backing of Count Raymond IV, it was for the archiepiscopal rights "as they sound forth in the precepts of kings."[40] These two, Teutaldus the obscure and Guifred the famous (or infamous), were the prophets of what would soon become a major industry, especially among twelfth-century Occitan prelates—conjuring up the Carolingians. Carolingian grants and immunities, both genuine and improved, were brought out when King Louis VII visited Occitania on his way back from Santiago de Compostela in 1155; during the following decades they were carefully carried north for the king's confirmation. They figured importantly in the construction of every episcopal lordship on the Occitan plain.

THE TWELFTH CENTURY

Ermengard had surely heard of Guifred, for so bitter a dispute over issues so vital to the family's power would not have been easily forgotten; the story would have been passed from generation to generation, warped and reworked in the retelling, slowly altered as memory turned history into myth, but remaining an elemental story of conflict and fidelity betrayed, the stuff of the epic tales that shaped the imagined past.[41] Doubtless whenever conflicts arose with the archbishop about their respective rights in the city, Ermengard would have been shown the Carolingian gifts that Guifred had improved, the old texts perhaps even further improved at the behest of later bishops, for in these repeated disputes she was forced to agree to divisions that retreated from the lines staked out by her father.[42] The rivalry for power within her city's walls would have given her additional reasons to be wary of a developing consulate that might find itself more welcome in the palace that faced hers across the marketplace. Most importantly, she would have witnessed all around her, in the cities of her Occitan allies, the long-term consequences of Guifred's model, as bishop after bishop sought to imitate his conquests in their own cities, establish their own claim to lordship, to the fidelities of castles, the command of armies, and eventually even to vicecomital title, aided and abetted by the counts of Toulouse. Through her entire career, these episcopal appetites formed the constant if often hidden underside of the region's dynastic politics.

The game of episcopal lordship in the twelfth century, however, had become far different from the one in which Guifred had performed his exploits; the hurdles were higher, but at the same time, the chances of reaching the goal were greater. Those who entered the field labored longer; patience had to be their cardinal virtue. Yet they surely found the rewards worth the price. For like the families of Millau and Posquières who gained their fortunes in the mountain bishoprics, the families whose offspring filled the bishoprics of the twelfth-century Occitan plain were also largely newcomers to such high office. As the denunciations of councils and legates forced princely dynasties to abandon the miters and staffs that they had once considered their rightful inheritance, younger sons of castellans and village lords took over.[43] They had strong ties of friendship and deference toward the families whom their families had long served, but the prospect of independent lordship was stronger yet, especially when colored with the hues of ecclesiastical liberty. And the new structure of regional politics and Church politics presented heretofore undreamed-of possibilities. The regional political game was now dominated by the rivalry of Barcelona and Toulouse and the complex play of alliances around it. At the same time, the very success of the reform movement presented both new rivals within the ecclesiastical world and new possibilities for using the ideals they represented.

Cathedral chapters, now more tightly bonded by their communal life, strong in their elected officials, and with finances that were increasingly independent, could give unending trouble to their bishops. A crisis of this sort at Albi in the 1130s was particularly severe. When Innocent II won the support of the canons of Sainte-Cécile, bishop Humbert threw his support to the antipope Anacletus II. The canons succeeded in blocking Humbert from entering his church; excommunicated, he was deposed in 1135. His successor, Hugo, although of the same allegiance as the chapter, fared little better. In the early 1140s, the canons burned down the episcopal palace and camped their armed retainers in the cathedral. Similar disputes wracked the cathedral of Agde. Probably they occurred elsewhere as well.[44]

Monastic orders likewise challenged the authority of the bishops and threatened to turn dioceses into conglomerates of semiautonomous spiritual principalities, in effect replacing the independence of lay church-owners with their own. We can hear that threat in the grant by which Bishop Bremund of Béziers gave the chapel of Saint-Sernin beneath the city walls to the Knights Hospitalers in 1148. "The brothers may reside there and hear the divine office," he allowed, "[but] they may not receive the parishioners of another church, nor create a cemetery, nor impose penance, nor give the body of Christ to themselves or their household, nor baptize, nor perform weddings." The popularity of the new orders, and the willingness of laymen to give the parish churches they owned to monasteries rather than to the bishops, risked creating pockets of exemption into which episcopal discipline—and fiscal demands—could not reach. In the late 1150s, Bishop William of Béziers was forced to go to Rome to get Pope Adrian's help against monks who performed baptisms and the Eucharist, depriving the bishop of his share of tithes and offerings. All through the second half of the century, the archbishop of Narbonne found himself repeatedly forced to appeal to the pope to retain his control over the abbey of Saint-Paul. The violence of monks, who "with the support of secular power" invaded churches they claimed as theirs, was a recurrent nightmare; even the reform of a nunnery could lead to widespread disorders. The popes, meanwhile, confirmed the bishops' rights with one hand while they freely distributed monastic exemptions with the other.[45]

Yet the new religious orders could also provide the bishops with a new weapon in their campaign for independent lordships. Soon after Count Alphonse Jordan was ousted from Narbonne in 1143 and Ermengard was freed of her marriage to him, Archbishop Arnold of Narbonne brought together the principals in the conflict—Alphonse Jordan, Roger of Béziers, and Hugh of Rodez—and had them swear a new peace. It was in many ways an act redolent of an earlier age, when bishops would call together the nobles and clergy of their region and in the magical presence of holy relics enjoin them to swear to "hold God's peace." Such oaths were far more prosaic and more limited than we might imagine: they did not oblige the oath takers to refrain from war but simply to refrain from injuring priests and monks, merchants on the highway, and peasants at their plow. What made Archbishop Arnold's peace unusual and thick with future possibilities were the means the archbishop found to enforce it. The Knights Templars were to put iron into the holy terror of saints' bones, to go after those who violated the peace. To pay for this the owners of every plow in the ecclesiastical province of Narbonne were to give the Templars a sétier of grain per plow per year. The archbishop was to arrange to have "suitable persons" named in each fortified town and village to collect the tax.[46]

As we shall soon see, lordly powers in the twelfth century were not broadly territorial; they were bundles of particulars, defined by specific place and moment.[47] The peace subsidy of the Templars, in radical contrast, overrode those particularistic specificities of lordship. It reached through every doorway in the diocese; wherever someone stabled an ox or a horse, the Templars' agents could demand their sétier of grain. It was truly a territorial power, the image of things to come. And those who could do so did not wait to exploit it.

The Templars' privilege was confirmed repeatedly through the second half of the century. Around 1170 it was extended to the bishopric of Comminges. At the same time, whenever the momentary balance of force provided an opening, both Count Raymond V of Toulouse and a number of bishops turned this new institution to their own advantage. In 1162 or 1163, immediately after the death of Count Ramon Berenguer IV of Barcelona and the temporary collapse of the Catalan alliance in Occitania, Raymond proclaimed a peace in the dioceses of Toulouse and Albi, establishing in the process a claim to jurisdiction over the followers and subjects of his archrivals, Raymond Trencavel and Raymond's son Roger. As the power of Raymond V prospered, some of the bishops protected by its shadow followed his example: Rodez, Béziers, Mende, Uzès. The bishop of Béziers, while confirming the "ox peace" of the Templars, extended his own to clergy, villagers (rustici), fishermen and hunters, ladies and those with them who were unarmed, mourners with the dead, unshod horses, pack horses and merchant-travelers, domestic animals, mills, and olive presses.

Priests were to warn their parishioners to be ready to join the peace militia any time they were called to enforce it. At Rodez and Uzès the bishops imposed a tax on every household to pay for the enforcement. When the bishop of Albi and the count of Toulouse established their peace in Albi late in the century, they also jointly collected a tax on draft animals.[48]

The nature and the timing of each peace show what Occitan bishops most required to build their urban lordship—the support of the count of Toulouse against their shared rivals, who were most often Ermengard's allies—the Trencavel viscounts of Albi, Béziers, Agde, and Nîmes. Although the chronology of episcopal lordship-building in each of these cities is different, the pattern was the same in each. The story at Albi—so important in the history of heresy hunting late in the twelfth century—can stand for them all.

The bishopric of Albi was still in the control of the viscounts of that city in 1132; Bishop Humbert himself witnessed the agreement between Count Alphonse Jordan and Viscount Roger that affirmed it. Humbert was probably encouraged to do so by his own fight with his cathedral chapter. Unable to rule his own clergy, he was not well placed to fight the Trencavels. His successors, however—all of them from the middling lords of the Albigeois (for the cathedral chapter, now fully independent, saw to it that the bishop, if not one of their own, was at least of their own status)—closely controlled the growth of the city, endowing their fighting men with rents and fiscal rights. When the wars between the counts of Toulouse and the Trencavels in alliance with the king of Aragon inflamed the Albigeois in the 1170s and 1180s, they finally had their chance. In 1178, Viscount Roger threw Bishop William III into prison—he was "held captive by the heretics," Roger's enemies cried. William had probably been a little too cozy with Raymond of Toulouse and with Roger's enemies within the city. The next bishop, William Peter, however, at last achieved the dream of recognized lordship. He affirmed his alliance with the city's patriciate, whose spokesmen, the "good men," he admitted to his court in 1188–89, then joined with Count Raymond V to establish their joint peace in the region. Finally, as the fortunes of war continued to shift, he forced the viscount in 1193 or 1194 to recognize that two-thirds of the city's judicial fines and market dues went into the episcopal coffers and to recognize as well that the bishop held lordship over much of the new city that now sprawled below the walls of the ancient redoubt that overlooked the river Tarn. There was, to be sure, a quid pro quo. The bishop on his side had to recognize that the fiefs of his urban knights were held ultimately of the viscount, and that the city's ancient center and most important fortification, as well as its major revenue-producer—the tolls on the bridge over the Tarn—belonged exclusively to his rival.[49]

Where such a local rivalry between the count of Toulouse and the Trencavels did not exist—at Carcassonne and Toulouse—a significant episcopal lordship remained out of reach. In neither of these cities were the bishops able to leverage themselves into even a simulacrum of temporal power. The document in which Pope Pascal II confirmed the possessions of the bishops of Carcassonne in 1115 lists not a single toll or tower or rural castle. And as late as the 1170s the bishop had to ask the viscount's authorization to build a monopoly oven in his suburb of Saint-Vincent.[50] In Toulouse, likewise, when Alphonse Jordan recovered the city from the count of Poitiers in 1114, not a trace remained of what had once been a significant episcopal jurisdiction, and neither Alphonse nor his successors had any desire to promote it in their hometown. Without tolls and justice, without rich tithes, the bishops disappeared from the city's political landscape.[51] William of Puylaurens was probably not exaggerating when he wrote of Fulcrand, bishop at the end of the twelfth century:

> From the little that he earned from his farms and his oven he lived in his house like one of the people of the city. He had no tithes to collect, for those were in the hands of knights and monasteries, and the parish chaplains collected the first fruits . . . [of which] the bishops had no part. When he went to visit his parishes he had to beg the lords through whose lands he passed to give him an armed guard.[52]

For Master William, an official in the triumphal thirteenth-century Church, such modesty was not a sign of piety but of impotence, worthy only of pity or barely hidden contempt. He and his fellow thirteenth-century clergy took more pleasure in contemplating the successes of their predecessors in cities such as Narbonne and Agde, or in the mountain dioceses of Rodez, Uzès, and Mende. Even in the middle of the Albigensian Crusades and the fight against the Cathars and Waldensians, they let themselves be distracted by their appetites for yet vaster lordships.[53] Members of the twelfth-century episcopate bequeathed to those of the thirteenth their thirst for power and wealth, and the rivalry with great lay lords that was its inevitable consequence. Poverty was best left to the friars and humility to monks safely enclosed in their cloisters.

As rivals for urban lordship, the bishops of Occitania were among the major beneficiaries of dynastic politics in the twelfth century. Yet that very rivalry excluded them from the counsels of the great. We search in vain for their names and signs among the witnesses to the quotidian dealings of Ermengard or her princely friends and enemies. Episcopal ambitions could be used, but they could not be trusted. When the archbishop of Narbonne occasionally accompanied Ermengard, it was as fellow and rival lord of her city rather than as advisor or agent. The archbishop negotiated a temporary peace between the count of Barcelona and the Trencavel viscount in 1112, but that was the last time for more than half a century that a prelate joined in a major peacemaking conclave. Not until 1171, when Ermengard helped to arbitrate between Count Raymond V and Roger of Béziers, and then at the great pacification on the island of Jarnègues in 1176, did the archbishop and some of his suffragans appear again among the regional peacemakers.[54] Most of the time, they were notable by their absence. When bishops made war, it was on their own account. If they had views that went beyond what they could see from the bell towers of their cathedrals, we do not know about them. When clergy do at last appear as major actors in regional politics in the last decades of the century, they are clergy from afar, from the north, and they bear the sword rather than the olive branch.

In consequence, although the bishops came to dominate at least part of their cities, although they could claim to be great lords, the true political class of twelfth-century Occitania was resolutely lay. Scribes were often, perhaps always, clergy; they often signed their documents "so-and-so, priest." Notaries, when men begin to take that title after midcentury, may have been clerically trained, but they did not advertise it. And those who acted as vicars and bailiffs for the great, that is, as their administrative help, were, from all we can tell, laymen without exception; a number of them were Jews. The people who accompanied Ermengard, like the people who accompanied the Trencavels or the count of Toulouse, were the men who held urban towers and rural castles, lords themselves, "girded with iron rather than rope." And after midcentury, when men of learning started to appear in Ermengard's and other lordly courts, they were physicians and lawyers, doubtless the products of the newly founded Italian universities. It is possible that these men, who styled themselves "master" or "causidicus" or "jurisperitus," had taken clerical orders, but none thought it worth mentioning, and as far as we can tell, they held no church offices.

In contrast to the royal courts of northern Europe, the great lordly courts of Occitania were exclusively lay courts. It was this that made them the rich soil out of which would grow the first truly secular culture of the European Middle Ages. Doubtless it was also why, when the European clergy at last intervened directly in the dynastic politics of Occitania, they found it such a troubling and frightening world.

THE SINEWS OF POWER

LORDSHIP AND SERFDOM

PREFACE

Contemporary documents often refer to Ermengard as *domina*, the feminine form of *dominus* (lord). For troubadours she was "domna" or "midons de Narbona." What did this term mean? Were the differences between masculine and feminine substantive or merely grammatical? We must, first of all, put out of our minds the idiosyncratic English meaning of "lord" as a select category within the more general class that elsewhere in Europe would be called the nobility. Lordship was far more widespread in Ermengard's world. Nor should we look for a legal definition, a definition that brings to bear special rules or privileges associated with that category, especially rules that could be enforced by court proceedings. There would be no such legal category in Languedoc until the fourteenth century, when noble privileges became worth fighting for in the courts of royal judges. Perhaps it would be best not to think of lordship as a category at all, certainly not a category that was exclusive of others. For, as we shall see, men called lord by some were also called "this man whom I own," that is, serf, by others. "Lord" and "lady" were honorifics; they were forms of address. They expressed a particular relationship of speaker to the person so addressed, a relationship of superiority and subordination, or more indirectly a recognition that the person given that title exercised superiority over others. Such a title was a recognition of power and honor, and of position within a hierarchy of power and honor.

Because there was a hierarchy, all lordships were not alike. There were differences in power and honor, and contemporaries had their own vocabulary to distinguish the powers of those at the top, like Ermengard, from the powers of others who, though lords themselves, still addressed Ermengard and her friends as "my lady" and "my lord." These lords, male and female, were addressed in turn as "my lady" and "my lord" by others. Relative wealth had its role to play in creating this hierarchy. The sums of money and reserves of land at the disposal of Ermengard, the archbishop of Narbonne, the Trencavels, the lords of Montpellier, the counts of Toulouse, and the kings of Aragon were vastly larger than the wealth of their subordinates. The sums of money they lent and borrowed make this clear. But wealth was not identical to lordship. It was possible to be an impoverished lord, whereas the great wealth accumulated by merchants such as the Bistani brothers did not by itself make them lords. And yet, as we shall see, enterprising peasants might cross the boundary into lordship, although they themselves still lived by the sweat of their brow, cutting wood, digging ditches, pushing a plow.

The other side of lordship was serfdom. Not because all those subject to lords were serfs. Far from it. Serfs were a select group of people, and not those we might think of, shaped as our minds are by the terrible histories of modern slavery in the Americas and modern serfdom in Eastern Europe. Serfdom in twelfth-century Occitania, the ownership of men and women by other men and women, reveals by its contours what was at the heart of lordship. It was in many ways the most important act in the theater of lordship, where the arbitrary superiority of one person over another was played out for all to see.

What equally distinguished lords from others and lords among themselves were those whom they could call their friends and the rituals by which that friendship was sealed and regularly demonstrated. Ermengard lived among her friends. They are the people we regularly find accompanying her on her military campaigns, at her side in diplomatic negotiations, joining her when she is required to pacify conflicts between other friends or the friends of other great lords. In many ways, these friends defined Ermengard's place in the world: those with whom she associated as equal to equal, and those who were part of her company. Here too was a theater of lordship, the one that defined what separated those at the top from those who were subject to them.

Among friends, lordship defined a community, one with its special practices and special values, its own particular culture, at whose center was fidelity. This was the culture the troubadours set to rhyme and music. They were its showmen, but even more its scholiasts, commentators, and mystifiers, its masquers and maskers.

CHAPTER SEVEN
LORDSHIP

In 1271, when he divided the estate of Amalric I, viscount of Narbonne, between the viscount's two sons, Guy de Levis specified that each was to have all their father's lordships in the villages they took as their portion. To this he added a breathless list as amplification: "high and low justice, military service, fiefs and the service of fief holders, rights to collect rations for fighting men, taxes, uses, requisitions and demands, agricultural dues, portions of agricultural production, dues from hunting and fishing and the use of pasture, meadows, woodland, riverbanks, quarries, gold and silver mines, the possession of land and vineyards both cultivated and uncultivated, mills, the ownership of ovens and other rights."[1] With one exception, Ermengard would have spoken of her lordships—in the plural rather than the singular—in exactly the same terms. Instead of "high and low justice" (*merum et mixtum imperium*)—a bit of Roman legal jargon that barely begins to creep into local parlance in the early thirteenth century—she would have used the term "justices" in the plural, distinguishing one justice from another by naming the specific crime over which it would be exercised;[2] as late as 1190, notaries were still writing about "justices" in this old-fashioned manner.[3] The remainder of Guy de Levis's vocabulary comes unchanged out of the twelfth century, indeed out of the eleventh, and many elements probably go back even further. It was a rich and ancient lexicon that condensed the exercise of power, expressible in English only by abstract, general phrases ("dues on . . .", "rights of . . ."), into a multitude of lapidary fragments, an assemblage of specific rights, not only over specific places but sometimes even over specific people. "It breaths a vigorous and autocratic spirit," R. W. Southern once wrote about similar language in documents from twelfth-century Anjou, "unencumbered by any feeling after intangible things."[4] In that assemblage, each item stood for a particular place or occasion for demanding goods or coin from subject individuals. Lordship (like the "justices" that were part of it) was multiple and complex.

Modern historians frequently separate these rights of lordship into two groups: those that involve land and buildings, the "agricultural dues and portions, dues from hunting and fishing, etc." of Guy de Levis's list, and the others—justice, military service, and all the rest—which French historians especially are wont to call "banal" lordship (from the medieval Latin word *bannum*, the right to command). Often the former are considered essentially private, whereas the latter are claimed to be of public origin, appearing among the possessions of eleventh- and twelfth-century lords because their predecessors had received them by delegation from the Carolingians or had quietly or violently usurped them.[5]

This comfortable distinction between powers derived from the ownership of land—what we think of specifically as property rights—and other kinds of power goes back in France at least to the decades around 1600, when jurists and historians in the service of Henry IV, Mazarin, and Richelieu strove to delegitimize the levy of customary tallages by lords great and small and the powers of justice that they exercised over subject peasants and townsmen. To the servants of royal Absolutism, such powers could legitimately be exercised only by the State and by the person who embodied it, the king (and by extension, his ministers and servants); property belonged to subjects, but the power to command and to force people to obey, and thus to make and enforce laws, to raise armies, and to collect taxes to support them, could belong only to the king, who represented the public order. This was what made Absolutism absolute; whether Louis XIV ever said it or not, this was the meaning of "L'état, c'est moi." If others who were not the State claimed to exercise such powers, they or their predecessors and ancestors could only have taken them by specific grant from the State; if they could not show such grants, if their only claim to their powers of lordship was custom, then the ultimate origins of such powers could only have been in subterfuge or violence.[6]

When the French Revolution brought down the monarchy, it also completed the monarchy's work in destroying the last vestiges of lordly powers, what the revolutionaries called "the feudal regime"; all that remained as legitimate power was the State as the abstract embodiment of the will of the People. To it and them was sovereignty reserved, whereas property belonged to individuals; protecting those rights in property became one of the State's primary duties. The image of lordship's history, therefore, did not change; if anything, the need to delegitimize lordly power became even stronger. Faced with "feudalism," even the most liberal, the most Republican, and in our own day even the most Marxist historian could be "plus royaliste que le roi." And so, in one form or another, the royalist preconceptions from another age still profoundly shape our image of medieval lordship.[7] (In England we find assertions of an equivalent sort—substituting "king" or "crown" for "state"—as early as the reign of Edward I, but because the distinction did not become a political issue during a revolutionary period, it has marked English historiography much less.)

Ermengard and her contemporaries, however, knew nothing of the State and its unique claims to legitimacy or sovereignty, nor did they have the historical vision of sixteenth-century jurists or twentieth- and twenty-first-century professors. We will look in vain in the twelfth century for the categorical distinctions made so familiar by a later age. Although the various "justices" that lords exercised were distinguished by the crimes they punished or the kinds of disputes they attempted to resolve, no one put the powers they exercised over land into a separate category from those they exercised over people; the latter were as much property as were the fields and vines and mills and the dues and shares of crops that peasants paid. Like fields and vines and shares of crops, people were divided, sold, mortgaged, and given away, and the language the scribes and notaries used to record those actions differed not at all from the language they used to transfer a field of barley.

Each right of lordship could be severed from the others, given away, reserved, disputed, just as we can sever one acre of land from another. This is what lends the sometimes astonishing particularity to twelfth-century conflicts, where rights of lordship are jumbled together with houses and plots of land, such as the dispute that set the archbishop of Narbonne against Ermengard's father in 1112; his claims and protests involved, among other things, the tax on salt, the viscount's monopoly of salt sales during October, the house in which salt was sold, some land called "the woods," some mills that the viscount's men had destroyed, the viscount's claim to levy *beuraticum* (a tax) every six years, jurisdiction over clergy in the city, and jurisdiction over murder and adultery committed by laypersons. Ermengard and the archbishop were still feuding over many of the same issues one-half century later, along with complaints over the removal of stone from the city streets, protection money collected from merchants, a house built in front of the episcopal gate, justice exercised in the fief of Saint-Just, and tolls collected at a rural fortress.[8] There was no reason to distinguish stones or houses from tolls, monopolies, or justices, because they were all pieces of property; their primary reason for being was the coin they brought to lordly purses, the grain they brought to lordly silos, and the satisfaction of lording it over others.

Nevertheless, not all types of lordship were equal, as the 1164 agreement between Ermengard and Raymond Trencavel concerning their shared rights in the gold and silver mines up in the mountains makes clear. The viscountess of Narbonne and the viscount of Béziers were high lords; they lorded it over lords and could in particular cases collect particular revenues, "no matter whose land or lordship it may be."[9] So sure were they of their power, and therefore their right, that they did not even imagine a word of justification. They simply asserted they would do it.

For this kind of lordship there was a special name—*potestativum*. Like *dominatio*, the general word Guy de Levis used to cover all kinds of lordship, this is not a word that appears very often. Ermengard and Raymond Trencavel did not use it in 1164 because they were not describing it, they were exercising it.

A street at Quarante, one of the villages in Ermengard's lordship. Author photograph.

Rarely given away, even to prelates or monasteries, it did not often make the common lists of rights.

On occasion, however, when a donation might seem to threaten that high lordship, Ermengard made sure she carefully reserved it to herself. In 1163, when she approved the gift by Poncia of Coumiac and her husband to the abbey of Quarante of half the castle of Coumiac and its "domination" (*dominatu*), she made clear that this did not include the castle structure itself nor "my potestativum and billeting rights . . . , and justices belonging to the potestativum and military service of the castle and everyone dwelling there." Nineteen years later she granted the monastery "whatever fiefs they might acquire in all my land and potestativum," giving them not only the fiefs but also whatever she had in them "by right of lordship" (*jure dominii*), while once again keeping for herself "the shedding of blood, adultery [that is, the right to punish those crimes], and military service." When in 1215 her grandnephew Aymeri confirmed this grant and at the same time Lady Calva's donation of her part of the castle and village of Argeliers to Quarante, he specified that Lady Calva had held this of him "by right of potestativum, without specified dues, service, or transfer payments" (the kinds of payments that were made for less "honorable" holdings) and so would the monks. In recalling Ermengard's earlier grant, Aymeri clearly meant to assert that he, like his ancestor, intended to keep in his own hands the punishment of crimes of blood and his rights to military service.[10]

In each case, the context shows the term's meaning: it was superior to ordinary rights of lordship—of the same order as demanding military service and exercising justice over crimes of blood, but higher even yet; it was the right from which those who controlled castles derived their domination over those who dwelled within the castle's district; it was the right that along with land defined the extent of Ermengard's power—a lordship over lordships. When in 1176 Ermengard rewarded Archbishop Pons d'Arsac "for his fidelity and service" by giving him the castle of Ferrals "with the potestativum, rights to collect rations for fighting men, military service, justices, oaths and everything whatsoever that ought to belong to the viscount," she was indeed giving up everything.[11]

Potestativum was the top layer of a many-layered cake. It was lordship of the highest sort, fit for the hands of only the highest aristocracy, of Ermengard and those with whom she consorted as equal. Many other layers lay below it, and they, in turn, could be cut in many ways.

LORDSHIP IN THE LANDSCAPE

If we could ask a peasant in one of these twelfth-century villages in Ermengard's potestativum, "Who is lord of this village?" we might very well be met with an uncomprehending stare. For in every village under her potestativum, or the archbishop's or that of other great lords, prelates, and abbeys, there could be many lordships spread unevenly across the landscape. The question, "Who is lord *in* this village?" would in contrast doubtless have elicited a list of names, perhaps even a long list. Poncia and her husband held only half the castle of the village of Coumiac; who held the other half in 1163 we do not know, but a Gausbert of Coumiac held something "in the castle" that he willed to Quarante in 1179; the abbey and Raymond Berenger of Ouveilhan arbitrated their own rights over the castle's fishpond in 1184.[12] Likewise, when Raymond Gaucelin decided to give his half of the tower of Argeliers and "whatever he is seen to hold in lordship there" to Quarante, he ran into trouble with Ermengard, who demanded 1,500 sol. Melg. from the abbey for her approval, even as she expressly reserved her own lordship in the village; a generation later, we find Lady Calva "at the command of my mother Lady Adalais," giving an oath of security for that village's castle to the abbot of Quarante and receiving an identical oath in return (a typical practice among those who shared lordships in a castle).

Over them all, at Argeliers and Coumiac and a hundred other villages, stood Ermengard and her potestativum. She was not a distant lord either, for in her name a local vicar or bailiff took blood for blood (and doubtless goods as well), and each year demanded food and drink for fighting men and their horses and military service from the villagers. And somehow, even when Poncia gave "half the castle" of Coumiac to Quarante, Ermengard kept the castle building itself; Poncia's half must therefore have been rights and revenues she derived from holding the castle rather than the stone and mortar structure itself; at least the two—conceptually and legally—could be divided. Few actions could show more strikingly the difference between medieval ideas of ownership and our own. There was nothing contradictory about Ermengard, Poncia, and the abbey of Quarante all being lords in Coumiac, and it should not surprise us that in the middle of the next century, Argeliers should appear both in a papal confirmation of Quarante's possessions and in the division of village lordships between the heirs of Viscount Amalric I.[13] Nothing, furthermore, even suggests that our reconstruction of lordship in these two villages is complete; we only know about those whose rights in the village and castle were shared with the abbey or eventually came into its hands, for our only sources of information about this village are the few documents remaining from the abbey's archives.

In this handful of documents we nevertheless begin to see the complexities of Occitan lordship. We are far here from the textbook images of life on the medieval manor. There are convolutions here that the scholarly abstractions of banal lordship, household lordship, and landlordship, or all the puzzling over origins that produced these abstractions, cannot easily explain.

⊷⟹

Fragmented into specific rights to specific dues on specific occasions, complex in the way these fragments moved from hand to hand, lordship was also fragmented and complex as it lay in the landscape, on individual houses, fields, vineyards, and gardens. To see in what way, let us follow a village notable across the fields and vineyards that he knew.

Late in the winter of 1158, Pons of Auriac, agent of the abbey of Saint-Pons-de-Thomières, lay near death at his home in the village of Peyriac-Minervois, north of Narbonne. Hearing the news, the abbey's sacristan hurried off to see him, for Pons held in his memory a map of all the monastery's lordship in the village, and the sacristan, as superintendent of the monastery's property, had to make sure that that memory did not die.[14] From the pile of straw on which he lay, Pons let his mind wander across his native landscape as his monastic master and the attendant scribe and witnesses followed closely in his footsteps. In one section of the village lands, we can hear Pons say, there are vineyards, one of which I hold with my brother Sicard; some of the vines in these vineyards are newly planted. Down in the stream is a mill called Saint-Steven's, and just beyond it an olive grove; beyond that are some fields planted with forage crops and many gardens; over there is another vignoble and some grainfields; over beyond that are more fields, gardens, and vines.

For each field, vineyard, olive grove, and garden he lists, Pons also tells the sacristan the amount of the rent it owes to the abbey (or sometimes jointly to the abbey and the viscount of Béziers). Most often the vineyards pay a fourth of the harvest; the grainfields pay a portion known as a *tascha* or half a *tascha*, and sometimes a quantity of malted barley for making beer; the gardens likewise pay a fourth, or a quarter or half a fourth, and sometimes the malt as well; a few tenants owe money for their holdings—three pennies, six pennies, or eleven— or "two pennies worth of olives." As a portion of their rent, four households provide food for one or two men of the abbey twice a day—perhaps these men are the abbey's agents who come to collect the rent, or perhaps they are the laborers who tend the fields and vines whose harvests go entirely into the abbey's granaries, lands that Pons gets to at the end of the account, and which the scribe calls *indominicatus*.[15] In addition, six households hold what Pons calls *mansi*, which we can most likely interpret to mean houses with associated land; these are obliged to billet a few fighting men once a year, providing them and their horses with food and drink.[16]

By Pons's account, the abbey had sixty-nine tenants in Peyriac. Remarkably, however, only a handful of these tenants held more than one piece of agricultural land—a vineyard, a garden, or a grainfield—from their monastic lord. The largest and most complex holding belonged to Arnold of Auriac and his children: a *mansus* (for which they had to give rations to three fighting men), a field of forage crops, vineyards, an olive orchard, and grainfields for which they owed the usual crop shares. No one, not even the other tenants of mansi, held anything approaching this amount or complexity.

How are we to understand this curious fact? Indeed, how are we to understand Pons's account in its entirety, that is, the way what he tells us fits into the geography of lordship in his village? For Saint-Pons-de-Thomières was not the sole lord in Peyriac, just as Quarante and Lady Poncia shared with others the lordship of Coumiac and Lady Calva shared hers at Argeliers. Pons himself tells us that the viscount of Béziers was also lord at Peyriac; other documents speak of the lord of Minerve, the Templars of Douzens, castellans from the Trencavel entourage, and men who did castle-guard all exercising lordship in the village.[17] What does this tell us about the relations of lords to peasants in this village? We cannot ask Pons to tell us more. He appears, says his lines, and is gone.

As in our imagination we reconstruct the landscape of Peyriac around Pons's report, two possibilities present themselves. One is that the sixty-nine tenants held land only of the abbey, that the lands Pons listed were all they had from which to feed themselves. Given their scanty holdings, we would have to imagine them as indigent laborers, eking out their humble sustenance with whatever they might earn from daily wages; for it was surely impossible for a family to survive on the harvest of a garden or a vineyard, even if a portion of the produce was sold; bread land above all was a necessity, and only twenty-one tenants grew grain on the abbey's land. The other possibility is that Pons's account gives us only a fragment of each peasant's total holdings—that they rented their dwellings and other land that sustained them from other lords in the village. In other words, they were tenants not of one lord but of several.

There is no direct way to judge between these two possibilities; no other inventory survives from Peyriac, and no one in twelfth-century Occitania had any reason to produce the village-wide tax rolls, cadasters, and plat books of later ages. It is only by chance that a document tells us of a peasant who holds neighboring plots of land from two different lords.[18] If we assume, however, that the peasants of Peyriac held land of several different lords, we can resolve a number of problems and avoid a maze of perplexities. To begin with, we must ask where the tenants of Saint-Pons-de-Thomières resided. In addition to the six tenants of mansi, only two individuals rented houses from the abbey (for money), and neither of these held any agricultural land from it. Did sixty-one tenants live in hovels in the fields for which they owed no rent and two pay rent without any visible means to feed themselves? One is lost in wonderment. Where are the invisible dwellings, where the invisible assets?

Of all the tenants in Pons's account, Pons himself is the most striking example of the man with invisible assets. As the abbey's on-site agent, the man who knew what every dependent of the abbey owed, Pons must have cut a significant figure in the village; it was surely not to every peasant's deathbed that the sacristan and his scribe would have come running. Yet Pons accounted as his own and his brother's holdings only some vineyards and an olive orchard. For the vineyards he paid the usual fourth as rent; for the olive grove no rent was due. One of the vineyards and the orchard, he reported, he held *in pignore*—technically speaking, as security for two loans, one for three solidi, the other for ten. We have no reason to take this legal terminology literally; we should not imagine the abbey, one of the richest and most powerful of the region, running short of cash and borrowing such paltry sums from one of its dependents.[19] What the abbey seems to have done was to create for this special dependent a special holding, one that also involved the exchange of land for money, but in a form that gave the exchange a higher status. Such "mortgage" contracts were used to affirm alliances and pacify disputes among the most powerful people of the land; in 1067–68 such contracts had even served to structure the alliance that made the Trencavels a regional power and first turned the house of Barcelona toward dreams of Occitan hegemony.[20] Because the mortgage was a mutual exchange—in Pons's case it made the abbey literally the debtor of its dependent—on the scale of subjection it registered as far more honorable than the usual leasehold contract. Pons and his brother were the only peasants in the abbey's lordship here who were so privileged. Yet to engage in such an exchange, Pons and his brother had to have had ready cash. Where did they get it? They held no other land of the abbey in Peyriac. To be sure, it would be easy enough to invent a Horatio Alger story to explain the prominence of a man of so little substance; but it would be easier, and require less suspension of disbelief, to assume that he held other land of other lords, that he was by his holdings as well as his office a village notable.

We can also ask how all the other tenants on Pons's list might have acquired the land they held of the abbey. Many if not most, we may assume, inherited that land from their fathers and mothers. Given what we know of premodern mortality rates, however, it is likely that some, at least, were not the offspring of the previous tenants; at some moment in the past, however many generations back, each family must have been a newcomer to a particular parcel. How would they have acquired it? Already in the tenth century there was a peasant market in arable land.[21] But would a landless, pennyless individual have been able to acquire a tract of land to work? In the tenth or early eleventh century, perhaps. Contracts arranging for the planting of vines are among the earliest documents surviving to indicate how great lords put their property into productive use. Expertise is what they seemed to demand, rather than payment for the privilege of using the land. Although the vinedresser clearly had to draw his sustenance from somewhere, he was usually allowed four years or more before any rent was due.[22] By the mid-twelfth century, however, at least as far as surviving records show, even land deep in the countryside was too valuable to be leased without an entrance fee, without what we might think of as key money. It was by leases with payment up front that the newly founded Templar and Hospitaler houses were putting their land into production by the 1140s.[23] A century earlier, urban landholders were already developing city property in this way; it is hard to believe that the practice had not long since spread through the countryside. No eleventh-century documentation for it survives, but this was not the sort of administrative parchment-work that later copyists would have thought worth including in a cartulary (and—as we shall see—it is possible that the documentation never arrived at the center where it could be copied).[24] The entrance fees were usually small for plots of agricultural land—a few solidi—but that would have been enough to block at the gate those peasants whose only capital consisted of their muscles and strong backs.

The simplest solution to these perplexities is to assume that the tenants of Saint-Pons at Peyriac were also tenants of other lords, in holdings that lay scattered in fields, vineyards, gardens, and orchards across the village's landscape. Because nothing other than the chance survival of this account seems to distinguish Peyriac from other villages, such was most likely also the situation elsewhere, if not indeed everywhere. This, furthermore, is the only assumption that allows us to make sense both of the evidence we have for lordly holdings in individual villages and of some peculiarities of the documentation itself.

Pushed in this way, Pons's deathbed account becomes the Rosetta Stone that allows us to decode the smallest structures of Occitan lordship. Our large-scale map of the vicecomital lordships is only an approximation; adequate to describe the range of Ermengard's potestativum, it is far too generalized to portray the weight of her power as it bore on her subject peasants. For that, an exact map would have to be drawn village territory by village territory, numbering the vineyards and olive orchards, the gardens and grainfields and fields of forage crops, and this we are in no position to do: the documents simply do not exist.

Could Ermengard or members of her court or their underlings themselves have drawn such a map? Pons's account and all our other evidence suggest that they probably could not have.

To begin with, why would the sacristan of Saint-Pons-de-Thomières have come hurrying to Peyriac on hearing that the abbey's village agent was sick unto death, if not that the abbey had no centralized records of its local holdings, that it depended on local records—or more likely, on the memories of its local agents—to maintain its rent collections? To be sure, Saint-Pons-de-Thomières was an old and well-established monastery, founded in 936 by the count and countess of Toulouse. It was perhaps set in its ways, archaic in its administration, not attuned to the new modes of estate record-keeping and administration being developed by the Templars, Hospitalers, and Cistercians.[25] But in this it typified most great lordships in the region.

We can see this as we follow a major gift of land from the hands of Roger of Béziers to the house of the Knights Hospitalers in the village Magrie. In July 1147, about to depart on crusade, Roger presented them with "all he had" in this village on the upper Aude and in the neighboring village of Castelreng, ordering Peter the scribe to record it.[26] Peter knew his craft; the charter of donation he drafted was effusive but unspecific: "all the men and women, lands and vineyards, houses and buildings, gardens big and little, grassland and pasturage, woods and waste, water courses and their banks, rents and uses"—the list followed a formula that went back to the early Middle Ages if not to antiquity. To an untutored modern eye this may seem all-inclusive and may delude the reader into thinking that the viscount had given the Hospitalers the entire village. The Hospitalers, however, knew better.

No sooner did they have the donation in hand than they asked five of the villagers of Magrie—one of them a man called Pons Ministral, perhaps the viscount's agent in the village—to show them exactly what the donation included.[27] And so they did, with the Hospitalers' scribe recording it, plot by plot in thirty-three different sections of the village's territories, two *sestarii* of land here, an *emina* of land there, gardens, vines, fields, meadows, two men who owe an *albergum;* the details are different, but the structure (or lack thereof) looks just like the holdings of the abbey of Saint-Pons in Peyriac—individual plots dispersed over the landscape, some doubtless contiguous, some doubtless mixed among plots that belonged to other lords. It is a map of lordship as land, as Pons's account at Peyriac is a map of lordship as dues; the two could easily be superimposed to imagine the dispersion of the abbey's lands at Peyriac in one case or the dues collected by the Trencavels at Magrie in the other. And as in Peyriac, it seems that the villagers' memory, and especially the memory of his agent, was Viscount Roger's only record.[28]

The Hospitalers, however, took the trouble to put that record in writing, and in several copies. New to the game of lordship and devoted to its strict—one might say its ascetic—exploitation for the furtherance of the business of the Holy Land, in ways that their lay patrons and their contemporary Benedictine monks were not, the Hospitalers saw the need to keep current records of their atomized and widespread holdings. Like so much else in the archives of the military orders, it is a sign of something new and bureaucratic. But only their record keeping was different; their lordship, built up of fragments of their donor-patrons' lordships, was in its structure identical to that of their contemporaries. It was their passion for record keeping that allows us to see it. At the same time, their great patrons could only refer vaguely to "all they had" in a particular place, because their records were not complete enough to list precisely what those holdings were.

THE MULTIPLICITIES OF LORDSHIP

How many lords could there have been in a village, and how many layers of lordship? Once again we have to go wandering into the lands of Ermengard's neighbors: the fullest evidence comes from the village of Pexiora, about thirty kilometers west of Carcassonne, where the Knights of Saint John of Jerusalem (the Hospitalers) were constructing a tidy lordship in the twelfth century.[29] In May 1102, thanks to gifts from a number of local families, the Hospitalers first set up the crosses that marked their protected ground on the top of a little hill in the village. Over the next half century, they slowly accumulated land from twenty-nine different individuals or family groups, most by gift but some by purchase (and most, but not all, within the original boundaries marked by the crosses); fifteen other individuals or family groups contributed tenants with their holdings. These, of course, are what we know about from documents that survive 850 years later; what may have disappeared we cannot even guess.[30] They give us at best a rough approximation of how many landholders there were in the village, but an approximation that other fragmentary evidence suggests is not exceptional (at the very beginning of the tenth century, for example, there were at least sixty landowners in the village of Bizanet, just a few kilometers from Narbonne).[31] At the end of the thirteenth century, Pexiora counted 184 households. There is no way to tell how much it had grown since the Hospitalers were installed there, but a significant percentage of those late-thirteenth-century households had considerable wealth: twenty-four were evaluated at more than 200 liv. Tourn.[32] At the end of the thirteenth as at the beginning of the twelfth, Pexiora was a peasant village, but it would appear that—not counting the Hospitalers themselves—at least 15 or 20 percent of its inhabitants lived partially or entirely from the labor of the remainder.

How many of these individuals and families who sold or gave land and tenants to the Hospitalers should we call lords? Surely those who granted dependent people to the Hospitalers fall into that category. Of those who gave or sold land to the order, some at least specified that what they were conveying were dues from the land. Others gave their share of churches or tithes, unlikely property for peasants to have, or they gave their horse and arms and their bodies for burial, again a sure sign of lordly status. Still others we discover engaging in the mortgage trade for more than modest sums: they at least have wealth if not rank.[33] Several appeared in the entourage of Viscount Bernard Ato.[34] For the rest, the clearest indication that the donors or sellers were at least freeholders is that the conveyances make no mention of any *foriscapium*, the payment for "approval" that weighed on any alienation of dependent land.

Some of these patrons of the Hospitalers, then, were people of substance, especially those who consorted with the viscount; others, however, look as though they were but a step away from the peasants who paid them dues. In 1123 we discover two of the original donors—the brothers Peter Guitard and Miro—selling some uncultivated land in the village to a peasant family to "break and cultivate it," forced to sell, they said, "because of our need and poverty."[35] This land owed no rent in coin or crop share, but three men—Guilabert of Laurac, Peter William, and Bernard of Roquefort—were all paid for approving the sale. What Peter Guitard and Miro sold was dependent land that owed at least this "service" to higher lords.

Although they do not appear in the surviving records as major donors to the Hospitalers at Pexiora, Peter William and Guilabert of Laurac—two of the three who approved that sale—were surely the really big men in the village. Peter William was implicated in the revolt of Carcassonne in 1120 and made his peace with Viscount Bernard Ato in 1125. Guilabert's son was also implicated in the revolt, but Guilabert himself was one of the viscount's closest companions until his death in 1123 and a vital addition to the viscount's entourage, for Laurac was in a strategic border zone where the lands of Carcassonne, Toulouse, and Foix met, and Guilabert had been privy to important acts of both the count of Toulouse and the count of Foix. Sometime after 1112 he swore fidelity to Bernard Ato for the castle of Laurac; he was in his company when the viscount joined Philippa and William IX of Aquitaine in their effort to lay claim to Toulouse; he witnessed the viscount's testament in 1118 and his alliance with the count of Toulouse in 1123. As the local potentate—Pexiora is just a few kilometers north of Laurac—Guilabert must have been instrumental in establishing the Hospitalers there. He witnessed a number of the early donations, and on his death his two surviving sons and thirteen other men, most likely his followers, made donations of land, money, and their horses and arms to the house and asked to be buried in its cemetery. In addition to Bernard Miro, who appears with him on several occasions as witness, a number of the other people whom we see as patrons of the Hospitalers were probably his clients or companions.[36]

The records of Pexiora and other Hospitaler and Templar houses of the region reveal much, when they are pressed. Yet much more of the texture of village lordship must still lie in darkness, not because it was unrecorded but because it involved transactions among laymen whose collections of documents have all but entirely disappeared. There are complex strands to it of which we have only an occasional hint.

Mortgaging was one such complication, as pieces of lordship rights were carved off to serve as pledges for loans. Gifts to Templars and Hospitalers frequently included mortgaged land or even mortgaged tenants.[37] Because the borrower did not give up his or her claim to the property, each such mortgage added one more layer to the structure of lordship, even though to the tenant who actually worked the land such a mortgage only meant paying dues, or a part of them, to another person. And so when mortgaged land was alienated, all the layers of claims to the property had to be recognized or bought out. Occasionally we can even follow the career of someone who uses mortgages to move up the social and economic ladder, starting as a peasant who pays agricultural dues to lords and ending as a person who collects them. Such was Arnold Baldriga, whom we can follow in and around Pexiora in the first decades of the thirteenth century. In 1198 Arnold received as pledge for a loan of one hundred solidi the dues that he and some of his neighbors owed to a local knight; over the next twenty-four years he used the same means to add other dues to his bank of resources. He did not, for all that, cease working the land, for in 1222 he was still leasing land and promising to pay an annual "service" in grain. In fact, at that late date he still owed a service in money and the foriscap or transfer dues for some of the agricultural land he held as pledge for a loan.[38] By 1222 he had still not made it, but he was clearly on his way.

Mortgages could also be used by those at the top of the hierarchy to organize those who were in their fidelity. A century before Arnold played moneylender to grasp at a modest rise in status, Viscount Bernard Ato himself was playing village loan shark. His grants to his loyal retainers after he recovered Carcassonne in 1125 were thick with properties he held as security for mortgages.[39] In the tiny village of Issel, north across the valley from Pexiora, Bernard Ato had picked up property from forty different individuals in this way—revenues of mills, fourths due from vineyards, fifths from the produce of grainfields, portions of rents on houses and gardens, men and women; one mortgage was for the modest sum of two solidi, another was for three, yet others for ten or twenty, or for some measures of wheat, or—in one striking case—for seven ounces of gold. The total valuation of these mortgaged properties came to 688 sol. Tol., 14 sol. Ugon., 19 sétiers of wheat, and the gold. All these he packaged together with one-third of the village castle, fourteen houses beneath its walls, and seven families and their tenancies to give as a life grant to Adalbert "of the little bridge," creating de novo for Adalbert a village lordship whose structure was the same scattering of dues and rights across the landscape that we have already seen at Peyriac and Magrie.[40]

All during the twelfth century and even the eleventh (for evidence of mortgaging land and lordship rights goes back to before the year 1000), men and women in villages all over Occitania were doubtless engaging in enterprises like those of Arnold Baldriga, and great lords in enterprises like those of Viscount Bernard Ato, for again, nothing but the chance survival of documents marks these individuals and these examples as exceptional. As need for coin or the opportunity for a profitable investment arose, or the desire to do a client or dependent a favor, a bit of seignorial revenue here or there was pawned or given, and the map of lordship within a village shifted ever so slightly. It was a remarkably fluid map, well greased by the money that flowed along the commercial highways, out from the urban markets into the deepest countryside.

Along the way, claims to lordship multiplied. We gain a glimpse of how that happened—and the complexity of mutual relationships and varied claims that were built on them—as we watch the Hospitalers of Pexiora attempt to free their donated or purchased land from its duties and obligations to others. Around midcentury, Peter William of Mauremont and his brother gave an "honor" to them (its nature and whereabouts unspecified in the documents that we have). The land was not free of obligations, however, for Bernard of Bigot, both in his own right and in the name of his relatives, Gilbert and William Raymond, had claims there. The documents do not tell us the nature of those claims—perhaps the two brothers of Mauremont had originally received the honor from the family of Bigot—but to the rector of Pexiora it was worth forty solidi to quiet Bernard. The brothers of Mauremont, it then turned out, had granted part of their honor to Arnold of Vilela, who in turn had mortgaged some of that to Bernard Gerardi. On Bernard Gerardi's death, Bernard of Bigot stepped in to defend the rights of Bernard Gerardi's sons. Again the Hospitalers had to satisfy him by giving him a peasant family and their holdings in the village of Saint-Rome.[41]

Attachments and obligations rode along with these fragments of lordship as they passed from hand to hand, most clearly when they were granted to religious institutions; even the dispute between Bernard of Bigot and the Hospitalers was resolved by gifts from Bernard to the knights, gifts for his soul and those of his wife and children as well as those of his relatives, and eventually for the souls of the sons of Bernard Gerardi. From the Hospitalers he received a countergift in money and lordship rights. But although money and rights pass back and forth, the formula is always careful not to make such exchanges a straightforward sale; it is always "I have given you," and "You have given me." Nor should we be quick to translate that exchange into modern commercial language. Was there an assessment of the monetary value of what was being exchanged? There is no sign of it, no clear indication exactly what Bernard of Bigot's interests were in the property. And in any case, what by implication he and his family members and the children of Bernard Gerardi received in return was literally priceless: the prayers of the monk-knights for their souls. Bernard of Bigot was affirming his membership in a community, a sacred community, a social community, a community of lords. The piece of parchment on which the scribe wrote his Latin phrases was only a sign of that repeatedly negotiated membership. Once the mutual gifts were affirmed, there was no need to say anything more. This was one of the many functions of lordship—lordship as a coin of exchange; it would be possible to make the case that it was the most important.

Thus, even a many-hued map would not be adequate to describe the incidence of lordship within a village, even less the complexities of the communities that lordship linked together. From the peasant's point of view there were most likely several lords to whom he paid rents in crop share or money for his land and dwelling, and a map of all of those would show who collected those basic rents. But some of these rent collectors in turn might owe dues to others, payments, for example, when land was sold or mortgaged; some might themselves be peasants owing rents in kind or money for land they worked themselves. Yet other rent collectors would owe service of other kinds, the specific demands of castle guard or military service, or the more general and weightier demands of fidelity and friendship, of sacred patronage or secular clientage. Those too were expressions and consequences of lordship.

JUSTICES

The lordships we have been looking at up to now are only a small portion of the long list in Guy de Levis's division of the properties and rights of the viscounty of Narbonne with which this chapter began. We have looked at the potestativum of the highest lords and at the agricultural dues and the other petty sources of income that could be collected by almost anyone, whether viscountess or cabbage baron, someone little higher than his peasant dependents. In between these two very different levels of lordship were all those other rights and powers that create the peculiar taste of medieval lordship, the powers that Guy de Levis referred to as "high and low justice, military service, fiefs and the service of fief holders, rights to demand rations and quarters for fighting men, taxes, uses, requisitions and demands, . . . mills, ovens and other rights."[42]

Controlling access to land, to the basic source of food and drink, is surely a major exercise of power in any agricultural society; yet rents, even in the form of crop shares, look familiar to us; they have the appearance of a simple exchange—I give you land, you pay me for it. Other forms of medieval lordship seem to our modern eyes, in contrast, to take on the lurid hues of brute force; they lack any quid pro quo; they are untranslatable into the categories of a purely market economy, into a vocabulary of capital, labor, and contract. To a modern sensibility they smack of the neighborhood bully's heavy fist; to many modern commentators, that was their origin. But if such in fact was their origin, it was lost to twelfth-century memories and categories of thought. To Ermengard and her contemporaries they were simply other forms of property, other resources to exploit, to grant to followers or to saints and their servants, to mortgage or sell if necessary, to fight over as they might fight over tolls collected at the city gates or in the marketplace. They were, after all, another source of income.

They were also more than that. They were ways that lords told stories about themselves—stories of status and control, of high and low, of the right to say yes and no. For status and honor, the place one might claim in the hierarchy, was likewise property, a kind of property the West has long since forgotten, as the State absorbed protection, domination, and punishment, and status has been left to the blind operation of the marketplace.

Among these more transparent signs of power, what Ermengard and her fellow lords called justices, in the plural, took pride of place. They were prominent among the powers that the ancestors of the Trencavels shared with the count and countess of Barcelona when they took over Carcassonne in 1067–68; they were likewise on the mind of Archbishop Richard early in the twelfth century when he sought to give meaning to the vast claims his predecessor Guifred had inscribed on parchment.[43]

Guifred, the architect of the archiepiscopal lordship in Narbonne, had concentrated on military control and on the financial resources to support it. Archbishop Richard set out to fix his lordship in the daily life of the city. A series of great arguments punctuated his relations with Ermengard's grandfather and father.[44] Tolls and the salt monopoly were a constant source of friction; that's where the money was. In 1112, however, it was the viscount's exercise of justices that most heated the archbishop's ire and demanded the closest attention of the arbiters who finally made peace between them—justice over clerics and over laymen who lived in property belonging to (or held of) the cathedral or the abbey of Saint-Paul, justice over the members of the bishop's household (his *familia*, in the language of the age) and those of the cathedral canons. Even the justice that the archbishop recognized belonged of right to the viscount— over homicide and adultery—required close regulation; the viscount's men were not to use convictions for such crimes as an excuse to invade or seize property in the archbishop's honor. In the final agreement, the settlement of these issues required as much ink and parchment as the settlement of all the archbishop's other contentions over tolls, salt, mills, towers, and houses.[45]

Nearly twenty years later, Bishop Bremund of Béziers took advantage of the death of Viscount Bernard Ato to establish a separate urban lordship in his city. Fiscal rights were, as usual, at the top of his list: requisitions, taxes on wine and wine pressing, taxes on lime burning (for construction), fees for marriage contracts, the right to take the beds on which people died, the monopoly of selling wine in August—as striking example as we might find of the bizarre specificity of medieval lordships. But the bishop's real ambitions focused on practices far more vital than these. Bernard Ato's two sons had required an oath of fidelity from all the men of the city, even those dwelling in the parts of the city that belonged to the cathedral and the two major urban monasteries. To the bishop the oath implied that these men would be obliged to follow the viscounts even when they warred upon the bishop; even worse, the bishop's men had already refused to follow the bishop when he called out the urban militia. To add to this injury, the Trencavel brothers insisted on their right to demand rations for a hundred fighting men from the bishop. Above all there was the issue of justices; the Trencavels claimed to judge thieves, murderers, and adulterers, even those who dwelled in the bishop's "honor."

As arbiter, Count Alphonse Jordan—quick to support a potential ally in a rival lordship—found in the bishop's favor. On the critical issue of justices, he divided the city "by the street that runs straight from the main gate to the church of Saint-Saturninus," a gesture, Solomonic or not, identical to the one that Guifred in alliance with Alphonse Jordan's father had performed in Narbonne over a half century before. To one side would be the bishop's city, where he alone could make requisitions, demand oath takings, preside over disputes and agreements, have his justices, take guarantees and hostages, and enforce his precious wine-selling monopoly; in it the viscounts would be prohibited from demanding oaths, taxes, and their own justices. Roger and Raymond's claims to collect rations for fighting men and judge thieves, murderers, and adulterers in the bishop's half of the city were taken care of separately. The two young men and their mother, Viscountess Cecilia, agreed to mortgage these rights to the bishop for 5,000 sol. Melg.—a mortgage that was clearly meant to be permanent—and that was the end of it.[46]

The ways that lords collected coin for their treasure chests and foodstuffs for their barns varied from place to place and over time, but justices were essential—especially the punishment of murder and adultery; more than anything else it was justices that separated the greatest lords from the rest. That was why Archbishop Richard and Bishop Bremund fought for their judicial monopoly in their urban lordships. It was why Ermengard specified, "these I keep for myself," when she allowed other powers and rights in a village to be given to a monastery. With justices the greatest lords were freehanded only to those of their own station.[47]

Was this justice more symbolic than utilitarian? How often were people tried and punished? There is no way of knowing; no records survive from this early date to measure criminality or even to know how these justices functioned, except that they resulted in fines, corporal punishment, and the confiscation of property.[48] The viscounts of Narbonne had their gibbet just beyond the city walls on the road to the leper house; it is mentioned already in the late tenth century and repeatedly in the eleventh and twelfth (although only as a place name, ad Furcas). Other cities probably had the same, and by the fourteenth century, villages did as well.[49] Their presence must have "wonderfully concentrated the mind" (to quote Dr. Johnson) of those who passed by, even if ragged, rotting bodies were not swinging from the ropes. But did a spot outside every twelfth-century village look like a scene from Jacques Callot's *Les misères de la guerre*? We may imagine it so or not, as we like.

Judging murder and adultery and sometimes robbery, the crimes that demanded corporal punishment, gave the highest status. Other crimes could be added, but murder and adultery were always included.[50] Justices, though, came in many varieties, and many of them could easily be let slip into lesser hands. It is not unusual to come across grants such as the one that Viscount Bernard Ato conferred on his vicars, Lupetus and Bernard of Béziers in 1114: "One-third of all the perjured and thieving Christians caught between Saint-Julian and the cross of Saint-Affrodisius outside the city and between the leper house of Béziers on the road to Saint-Thibéry and Bagnoles and the French Ford . . . and one-third of all the quarrels of the men and women of Béziers with those outside Béziers, and one-third of the quarrels of those who pass through Béziers and make a claim there, and all the pleas of the Jews," or the one the archbishop of Narbonne conferred on Gerald of Brueil in 1160 to induce him to give up the market tolls and other revenues he collected in the Bourg: "All the justice in the archbishop's part of the Bourg of Narbonne up to the value of 5 sol. and the tenth penny from all other justice there."[51]

Justice marched side by side with all powers to profit from the labor of others. It was part of the common formula—"fields and vines, houses and gardens, fourths, *tascha*, requisitions, usages, services, justices, men and women"—that scribes used to express the generality of rural lordships. Justice went with mines, with weights and measures, with markets.[52] It also went with people. And there its role as a sign of hierarchy was most overt. That was where it spoke most loudly and most personally of dominion and subjection.

Soon after Raymond Trencavel succeeded his brother as viscount of Albi and Béziers and lord of Carcassonne, he found himself in a dispute with the Escafredi, a clan whose members had served Raymond's family loyally since at least the early eleventh century and who had profited enormously.[53] Loyalty demanded repeated renegotiation in a world in which rights pushed their roots deeply into the soil of selfhood, and times of succession were just such moments. Raymond had decided to add to the defenses of the village of Alzonne (which lies a few miles east of Carcassonne) by digging a moat outside the walls; Ugo Escafredi and his brothers objected that the moat cut through their lands. Raymond seems to have found the money for his project by expanding the exercise of his justice in the village and found the laborers by requisitioning men. The Escafredi claimed that both the justice and the men were theirs. Rancor and arguments quickly escalated to involve rights that Raymond and Ugo and his brothers shared elsewhere.

The status of the arbiters who were finally summoned to settle the dispute— the bishop of Toulouse (here making a rare appearance in the affairs of the Trencavels)[54] and some of the most important of Raymond's companions—testifies both to the importance of the Escafredi and the stakes for which they were playing. The care with which the arbiters cast their decision suggests they were laying out general statements of practice. The moat should stay, they ordered, "because it was made for the common good."[55] Was this an early sign of the influence of people who had studied Roman law in the schoolrooms of Montpellier? It seems likely. On the question of justice the arbiters were especially fastidious. Raymond, they declared, had justice in all cases of "theft, murder, sacrilege, perjury, spilling blood, casting spells, adultery, breaking the peace on the public way." For such crimes he could judge not only his own men but all the village's inhabitants. The Escafredi and other village lords, they decided, may on their side judge those who are their *proprii iuris* or their fighting men when there are disputes over lands, vines, debts, or other goods—disputes in which no one will be subject to corporal punishement. In these cases, they said, Raymond ought not claim to do justice.[56] Here too the arbiters went beyond the specifics of the disagreement. They were voicing the belief that this was how justices were divided—or should be—everywhere. Without the terminology of high and low justice, *merum et mixtum imperium*, the distinction that would be summarized by those terms was already in their minds: great lords may inflict capital punishment, but all lords, great and small, have the right to judge disputes over land and debt in which the accused are fighting men in their household or their *proprii iuris*.

What did this last term mean? Who were these men who were *proprii iuris?* It is at this point that the story of Occitan lordship leads into the story of Occitan serfdom.

CHAPTER EIGHT
SERFDOM AND THE DUES
OF DOMINATION

Who are these men and women who are *proprii iuris*? An approximate translation of the Latin would be those "who belong [to someone] by right." The phrase implies that an individual or a family is someone else's property. Other phrases ring the same sound: claims to be someone's "natural lord" or, even more exactingly, his "bodily lord"; mentions of people who are *indominicatus*, just like fields and vineyards; and especially the hundreds of charters in which men and women, whole families and their progeny in perpetuity, are given or sold, using the same formulaic words that were used for grain land or pasture or mills—"We give to you [the Knights Templars] Bernard Modul . . . our man who did our will"; "I give a man of mine, William the cloth-maker and all his posterity and all his property, for you to have and hold to do all your will as your own alod in full right in perpetual possession"; "I Bernard Modul [the same Bernard Modul, in fact] and my wife Ermessend . . . sell you a man and his wife and children . . . and transfer him from our power to your power"; "We give you these two men and this woman and transfer them from our right to your lordship [or proprietary right] to have and possess." Occasionally, individuals are manumitted, using formulae that look very Roman, as if this were an ancient slaveholding society. The other side of lordship in this society was clearly serfdom, and given the number of documents that attest to it, serfdom was widespread.[1]

But what was this serfdom? What did it mean to say, "This person is mine, to do my will"? The long and tragic history of slavery in the modern world raises harsh images of pitiless overseers and downtrodden workers getting by on gruel and roots. Is this what twelfth-century serfdom should conjure in our minds? What was the connection between serfdom and the way that peasants got land to plow and vines to tend? What was the connection between serfdom and the numerous rights of lordship that scribes delighted to set marching across their parchments? No answers taken from elsewhere will do, for scholars have long since abandoned any attempt to find a unitary definition for medieval serfdom. It was too variable from place to place and from one century to the next; Catalan serfdom was not English serfdom, and both were very different in the eleventh or twelfth century from what they became in the fourteenth.[2] These questions must therefore be answered for this time and place, for twelfth-century Occitania.

Part of the problem in doing so is the way twelfth-century people talked about serfdom; the words they used and the contexts of ideas and law that gave those words meaning were themselves an exercise in symbol mongering. Whereas to us serfdom is a form of economic exploitation, to the people of Occitania the symbols of subjection spoke rather of power; the words that named lordly exactions did so most explicitly—"forcibles" (*forcia*), "requisitions" (*quista*), "takings" (*tolta*)—and the scribal vocabulary of gift and sale hardly less. Power, these words seem to say, is an end in itself, property with its own value, not just a way to get bread or meat or coin.

Yet as forceful and as striking as this language is, it does not tell us some important things. Who were serfs? What did "serf" mean as a social category? For all the talk of *homo proprius*, the word *servus*, the most common term for serf in medieval Latin (it is the Latin word from which ours comes), rarely appears in Occitan documents;[3] as for the word *servitium*, it manages to encompass peasant dues at one end of the spectrum and the obligations of people who held castles, even the obligations of the viscount of Béziers to the archbishop of Narbonne, at the other; and *servitus*, on the rare occasions it appears, is an obvious importation from learned Roman law.[4]

HOW TO RECOGNIZE A SERF

Let us begin with a simple question: How did people in the twelfth century know whether someone "belonged to" lady A or lord B, or perhaps to no one but himself? This would not have been an unlikely question in the twelfth century, for as people and families were given or sold just like fields and vineyards, so the rights to them would on occasion have been disputed. In the case of disputes over fields and vineyards, the neighbors could see who was plowing and who was trimming the vines, who was coming to collect the share that belonged to the lord and whose barn or winepress it was taken to; those were the tangible signs of possession and right, and sometimes, in fact, when possession or right changed hands there was a little ceremony when the new landholder put her hand to the plow. But fields and vineyards stand still. People have legs. What tagged them?

That very question came up in the dispute at Alzonne we witnessed at the end of the last chapter, for among the properties the viscount and the Escafredi argued about were rights to some men whom both claimed were their own *homines proprii*. The arbiters called for witnesses to settle the question, and not just to swear that one side or the other was in the right but to tell how they knew. Those who testified that the men belonged to Raymond Trencavel claimed that Raymond's father, mother, and brother had levied requisitions and collected provisions (*alberga*) from those men. The witnesses for the Escafredi asserted no less for their side. Faced with a dead heat, the arbiters put off their decision until an oath-taking match could be arranged,[5] but the reported testimony tells us clearly what they—both witnesses and arbiters—thought marked a man as being someone else's "by right": being subject to the *queste* and the *albergum*.

About twenty years later a similar kind of dispute broke out in the little village of Raissac just south of Toulouse. In this case it was not two lords fighting over who owned a man, it was a cleric arguing that he owned three brothers and the three brothers arguing that they were not owned by anyone.[6]

The claimant was the prior of Saint-Antoine of Toulouse, a church that was subject to the abbey of Lézat. The three brothers, he charged, "belong to the abbot of Lézat and the priory of Saint-Antoine . . . and are obliged to provide provisions at the will of the abbot and prior and serve them with money and grain, bread, meat and wine, wood, straw and chaff, lambs and milk-fed pigs, chickens, and leeks and do all the other services that men ought to do for their natural lords." This exquisite attention to the table was perhaps the reason why the prior chose to call himself their *dominus carnalis*—"bodily lord" or "lord of the flesh." The brothers, of course, denied every word of it, even the charter the prior waved at the judges to prove his case. Once again, witnesses were assembled. Some, like the priest Raymond Xatbertus, simply asserted that they had seen the brothers serve the prior in the way he described. Others were more explicit. But let them speak for themselves.

Amelius of Bordes, priest and monk: When I lived in the house of Saint-Antoine in Toulouse I saw Amelius of Bordes the prior [obviously another man with the same name—most likely a relative] send his messenger to Peter of Raissac and his brothers [the defendants] to come and bring provisions [*ut venirent . . . et facerent sibi albergum*]. They came with four or five loads of wood, with cakes and meat, chickens and leeks, bringing provisions at his order and domination [*per mandatum et per dominationem*]. And I saw Peter and his brothers hold Amelius the prior as their lord and he possessed them as his men, and they served him doing all his will.

William of Firminum: When I was living with Amelius of Bordes the prior at Saint-Antoine he sent me to Peter of Raissac and his brothers . . . to order them to bring provisions to Toulouse where he was going to be with the abbot of Lézat. . . . And they came bringing wood and bread and meat and wine and everything necessary for the refreshment of the abbot and the prior at their order and domination.

William the priest, prior of La Grace Dieu: I was chaplain of Amelius of Bordes, prior of Saint-Antoine, and ate with him in the house of Peter of Raissac and his brothers, by his domination.

Pons of Villanova:[7] When I was vicar of Toulouse I had Peter of Raissac and his brother in my power to be punished and wanted them to give me all their goods.

They appealed to God and Saint-Pierre of Lézat and the abbot of Lézat and Amelius of Bordes, the prior, who was a great friend of mine, and they said that they and all their lands and honor and everything they had was from the abbot of Lézat and the monks and from Amelius. They also told me that they had no lords of their body other than the abbot and the prior. And while I had them in my power the abbot and Amelius, who was my friend, came to me and begged me to be merciful and release Peter and his brother to them. They insisted that the two men belonged to the abbot and monastery of Lézat and the prior of Saint-Antoine. You should know this was a serious business because I wanted their money. But because of my love for Amelius of Bordes, who was my great friend, and in answer to their repeated strenuous prayers, I handed Peter of Raissac and his brother over to them along with the little money they had with them, as the abbot and Amelius wished.

The hybrid Latin in which William the scribe recorded what these witnesses said assures us that, despite the distance in time, we are hearing their voices, unfiltered by standard formulas and rhetorical gestures, muffled only by something close to an instantaneous translation; the scribe heard Occitan and did his best to render it into some semblance of the ancient tongue he was reputed to know, but even when he scratched out his final version he could not bother—or did not know how—to classicize his diction; hearing *escazuta* (inheritance), he added a Latin case ending and hurried on; *teson* (milk-fed pig) became *tessonibus*, *encors* (confiscation) became *incurre*, *posesor* (goods) became *posse*. Speaking their familiar tongue, these voices repeat the testimony in the Escafredi case: you know who belongs to someone else by watching who gives provisions—*albergum* and *queste*—on demand, and who gets them.

Did those who belonged to another also hold their land of him? Perhaps, but not necessarily. The prior of Saint-Antoine claimed that Peter of Raissac and his brothers did, but then had to make an exception. "And all the land and all the honor that Peter and his brothers hold in the territory or tithe land of Péchabou come from the abbot of Lézat or the prior of Saint-Antoine," he said, "except for those lands that they hold of others." On this the price of certainty was self-contradiction. Land was a secondary issue; apart from those witnesses who repeated the prior's words exactly, none of them talked about it. Primary for everyone, the prior, the witnesses, the judges, and probably Peter of Raissac and his brothers as well, was the act that showed subservience to "command and domination." And that could only be a demand that was deemed in some way willful and arbitrary. What mattered was less the loads of wood, the cakes, and the milk-fed pigs than the fact that they were brought to Toulouse "for the abbot's and prior's refreshment" when ordered, the fact that the prior and his chaplain could walk into Peter's house in Raissac and command him to serve them.

Pons of Villanova goes well beyond a simple accounting of obligations, and he does so quite self-consciously. With his repetitions, his emphases and occlusions, he paints the portrait of a society. That larger context of social gesture and ritual he talks about—far more than specific demands for food and fuel—gave servility its true weight and meaning. Pons's testimony is striking precisely because on the surface it seems to have nothing to do with the prior's claim; unlike all the other witnesses, he makes no mention of the albergum, of loads of wood or pieces of lamb or pork. His story, like his repeated references to his great friendship with the prior, seems gratuitous; but it is, in fact, exquisitely relevant, for it is a story of servility in action.

Peter and his brother, in the vicar's "power" for some infraction, are subject not to some prescribed penalty but to whatever the vicar "wants." Their only recourse is to appeal to both heavenly and earthly lords. (Here then the other meaning of "lord of the body"—in contrast to the Lord on high, lord of the spirit.) In that very act they show their powerlessness and subjection, their lowliness. The prior, however, can lay claim to the "great friendship," the "love," of the vicar. The two of them are companions, and they live in a different world from Peter and his brothers, governed by very different rituals, a world in which one may "pray" a friend to show mercy, and the friend of his free will may give satisfaction. The prior's "begging" is surrounded by an aura totally lacking from Peter's appeal to his lords for succor. It is the kind of ritual performed by heroes in chivalric epics and by lovers in troubadour lyrics. It is the abasement of the saint kneeling before the throne of God, interceding for his devotee, whereas the position of Peter of Raissac and his brothers is that of the abject penitent or pilgrim beseeching the saint to intercede. In this brief tale the images of hierarchies social and divine coalesce to fix Peter and his brother in strict dependence. That was what the dispute was really about.

We must be thankful that among all the stiff-lipped, laconic documents from the twelfth century in the Lézat cartulary, this richly garrulous one survives. At the same time, we have to ask why it survives—why, for a few serfs, did the monastery of Lézat pay a scribe to scratch such a lengthy text on parchment, and then a century later, a notary to copy it into the monastery's cartulary? Why, to prove his case against them, did the prior of Saint-Antoine and the abbot of Lézat call in someone as important as the former comital vicar of Toulouse, a member of one of the great city families, to be both a witness and a member of the abbot's council called to hear the dispute? Why on this occasion did the abbot also invite Tosetus of Toulouse, scion of another important city family, to join him? These questions become more insistent when we discover that one of the witnesses to the agreement that ended the dispute two years later was none other than Bishop Fulcrand of Toulouse.[8] The fact that it was a negotiated settlement rather than one imposed from on high also seems to contradict the image of strict dependence that was at the heart of the dispute. Was there something about Peter of Raissac and his brothers that warranted calling men of this quality to keep them in dependence? How do we reconcile the language of "belonging," of being *homines proprii*, of being subject to "command

and domination," confirmed by powerful witnesses and by the abbot in council, with the intense negotiation that must have preceded the settlement of 1181, a settlement that at one and the same time recognized the dependent status of the brothers of Raissac and strictly limited their obligations to the prior?

We first run into the brothers Peter, Arnold, and Bernard Arnold of Raissac long before the dispute, in a document of 1154. Here, remarkably, they call themselves (or the scribe calls them) "lords" as they give a little patch of brushy land to Bernard Fabre and his wife to clear and plant with grain; Peter of Raissac also styles himself "cleric."[9] From all we can tell, the three brothers were peasants on the make, something like Arnold Baldriga or Peter Guitard at Pexiora, whom we encountered in the last chapter. The lands around the villages of Castanet and Péchabou, where Raissac once stood, were low marsh, bramble, and woodland stretching between the Hers brook and the main road from Toulouse to the Mediterranean; the Canal du Midi, the lowest route from the Garonne River to the Mediterranean, now flows through this little region. Late in the twelfth century it was being ditched and drained, its brush and trees supplying the firewood market of Toulouse. It was an ideal place for ambitious men to clear or get others to clear and then collect rent from them.[10] That Stephen the scribe should call the three brothers "domini" only shows how easy it was to take that title; all you had to do was collect an entry fee from the people who worked the land, a share of their crop, and a fine if they got into a dispute and you had a right to be so honored.[11] You could still be someone else's serf.

The woods and brush land around Raissac and its neighboring villages attracted some of the rich families from Toulouse as well, in particular the Villanovas and the Caramans.[12] It is possible that pressure from these families drove the brothers of Raissac into the waiting arms of the prior of Saint-Antoine and the abbot of Lézat. Might this, rather than his official duties, be the story behind Pons of Villanova's testimony that he had Peter of Raissac and his brother in his power and wanted them to give him all their goods? However that may be, as late as 1200, William Peter of Caraman and his brother Gerald of Gourdon were still claiming that the brothers of Raissac and their descendants (for all save one brother were by then dead), along with the farm of Raissac, belonged to them rather than to the prior.[13]

Happy to have the brothers' dependence confirmed in 1179 and 1181 and confirmed yet again in 1191, 1192–93, and 1200, the prior in the meantime did little to collect what they owed. The agreement of 1181 replaced the arbitrary "command and domination" by the prior with specific dues—four *quartona* of grain on the feast of Saint Julian and three solidi of Toulouse on the feast of Saint Thomas the apostle—but three years later, in 1184, even that had yet to be paid.[14] At that point the prior agreed that he would take half the brothers' fief and mortgage it to someone named Pons the scribe for fifty solidi, the value of the unpaid grain and coin; the brothers could pay off the mortgage when they had the money. Five years later, still nothing had been paid, and the prior charged them with "ill will" when they pleaded poverty. The year 1193 arrived, and the brothers still had not paid a penny. It seems hard to attribute this delay in payment to the prior's negligence, for during this same decade one or another of the brothers recognized that he held other land of the prior, and Peter on his death gave his portion of Raissac as alms to Saint-Antoine.[15]

It would seem that the brothers, at least locally, were persons of substance who, whatever their dependence, could not be pressured too hard. Even in 1192 when they were deeply in arrears in their service to the prior, Bernard Arnold of Raissac and Stephen his nephew served as witnesses when the prior agreed with Arnold of Villanova, William of Verdun, and his wife Faiana to divide some land along the Hers brook. They held land of a number of other people aside from the prior of Saint-Antoine—the agreement of 1181 lists four other lords at Péchabou alone—and others held land of them; they remained dependents to some as they remained lords to others. And when the prior first noticed they were in arrears in 1184, he did not simply demand payment and set the sum himself; he felt obliged to present the problem to local notables (*probi homines*) to evaluate the arrears; and it was only—so the text was careful to specify—after taking counsel with "men of discretion and the greatest wisdom" that he agreed to a resolution. All these negotiations point to the brothers being men of some importance in their little world of bushwhackers and woodsmen-pioneers, people who could not, in fact, be treated arbitrarily. The easy slippage from affirmation to repudiation and quickly back to affirmation, the means that the prior of Saint-Antoine vainly deployed to make the brothers meet their obligations, the way he had to mobilize a whole community: all set on edge the image of strict dependence, the image of *homines proprii*, of owned men.

The brothers of Raissac were not sports of nature in an otherwise rigid social hierarchy. Their dispute with the prior is exceptionally well lit by an exceptional collection of documents, but we do not have to look too far to find others like them.

Three serfs from the village of Douzens on the Aude River about half way between Carcassonne and Narbonne will fill out the portrait type.

Here at Douzens in 1133, Peter Raymond of Barbaira and Bernard of Canet (two powerful members of the Trencavel entourage), along with their wives and children, gave a man named Bernard Modul to the Templars. "He was our man," said Bernard of Canet and his wife Raina, "to do all our will"; he was a man whom these lords and ladies would have called their homo proprius. Why was he important enough to be "owned" by two families and the only such person to be mentioned in what might be thought of as the foundation charter of the Templar house in this village? Why should the donors specify him by name when they gave the Templars their castle and all their rights there? The charter of donation itself does not say, but Bernard Modul is mentioned in twenty-four documents: enough to allow us to gauge where he stood in his little community.[16]

In medieval conveyances, as in title deeds in the United States today, property was defined by who held the property next to it—"bounded on the north by X's field, on the south by Y's." Bernard Modul's name is mentioned in enough of these boundaries for us to know that he had land in fourteen different sections of the village's fields (the large blocks that defined separate portions of the agricultural landscape). Bernard must have had far more land than these accidental mentions reveal. Perhaps he owned as much as another serf we know, this one a serf of the cathedral chapter of Agde, who was wealthy enough to provide his sister with alods (freely held lands) in three different villages—fields, vineyards, gardens, pastureland, and a house. Presumably he still had enough left over to live on himself.[17]

For more than twenty years, Bernard Modul was a frequent witness to his lords' transactions; he was even called as a witness when Ermengard of Narbonne and members of her court arbitrated a dispute between a Lady Richa and the Templars. Bernard's brother, William Peter, was one of the major early donors to the Knights Templars on the eve of his own departure for the Holy Land. When the Templars began to develop mills on the Aude, just below the village walls, they first had to buy Bernard's riparian rights. And, like the brothers of Raissac—even though he belonged to the Templars after he was given to them by Bernard of Canet, Peter Raymond of Barbaira, and their families—Bernard Modul and his wife and sons had at least one person who belonged to them: in 1157 they sold the Templars a man named Raymond of *Carancianum* with his tenancies and services for the substantial sum of 130 sol. Melg.[18] Clearly, although Bernard belonged to the Templars "to do all their will" and held some of his property from them, the rest of his property, including Raymond, was his own to do with as he willed.

William the Fuller, whom Raymond Ugo of Aiguesvives sold to the Templars for 120 sol. Melg. in 1165, was Bernard Modul's next-door neighbor in the village. William worked the land, owing the usual dues of a quarter of his wine and a share of his wheat; his primary occupation, however, as his name tells us, was running a fulling mill on the Aude. He was one of four who joined forces and funds to build the mill in 1153, leasing the right to do so from the Templars for the substantial sum of 26 sol. Melg. per year; five years later, when one of the partners sold out to his brother in order to devote himself entirely to weaving, William the Fuller received 100 sol. Ugon. as his quarter share, plus free fulling for his wool for the rest of his life.[19] Mills were highly profitable enterprises; we have seen their importance in the city of Narbonne; they were no less in a village like Douzens, where they could be subject to a whole cascade of leases and subleases all ultimately supported by the miller and his wheel. William would have needed substantial reserves to join in his mill-building enterprise, but he and his partners had only one lessor, the Templars, to pay.[20]

The most striking of these Templar-owned men is Pons Mirabel. Garsend and her husband and Hugh Inardi and his sister Adalais gave Pons to the Templars in 1167 "for them to possess in full right." The donation contained a remarkable condition: Pons's son Peter was to marry Adalais, the Adalais who had just given his father to the Templars.[21] Pons owed the Templars 2 sol. Melg. each year at the feast of Our Lady in September as his "use and service"; about him we know nothing more, for he never again appears in Douzens's charters. But that one proviso in the donation is enough to attract our close attention. We usually assume that in the steeply hierarchical society of the Middle Ages, families practiced status endogamy (just as individuals generally do in twentieth-century industrial societies)—peasants married peasants, and between those who owned people and the people who were owned there was an unbreachable barrier. When we play the story of Pons Mirabel against this assumption, however, we hear a loud dissonance, as we heard others when we played the stories of Bernard Modul and the brothers of Raissac against similar assumptions.

The brothers of Raissac, Bernard Modul, William the Fuller, were all individuals of standing in their little communities. As witnesses their word counted. By some people in their villages, at least, they would be addressed as "my lord." Their stories (and an attentive walk through other cartularies and archives would doubtless turn up more) could, of course, be dismissed as exceptions; that way our assumptions about serfdom and medieval societies would not be bothered. But exceptions also must be explained. Only then do they truly prove—that is, test—the rule. We must allow the possibility that the rule—in this case our common image of serfdom's meaning—may not survive.

The litigation over the status of the brothers of Raissac tells us that the marker of serfdom was the obligation to give provisions on demand. Those provisions were anchored in the casal that Peter and his brothers held from the prior of Saint-Antoine. The word *casal* was one of the vernacular equivalents of the Latin word *mansus*, common as soon as one crossed the Aude River heading west. East of the river the word *masata* was commonly used.[22] In the inventory of the land of the abbey of Saint-Pons at Peyriac, which we looked at in the previous chapter, all that distinguishes those who owe such provisions from those who do not is that they hold *mansi*. Provisions for troops were due from other kinds of holdings as well—from people who held castles, from village churches, from whole towns and cities—but it is rare to find a list of services due from a mansus that does not include the albergum, the demand for provisions.

It would be nice to avoid the vexing problem of the Occitan mansus, but we cannot; the term is omnipresent in the documents.

The mansus was everywhere in early medieval Europe, in Anglo-Saxon England, in Germany, in northern France, and around the Mediterranean. Almost all modern historians have thought that the word was used to refer to a peasant family's house and associated lands, or more precisely "the land sufficient for a family."[23] In twelfth-century Occitania the term *mansus* continued to be used to speak of a house or farmstead,[24] but as we have seen, the term was also used to speak of a holding from which the lord demanded provisions for himself or his fighting men, and that in turn marked the person who provided the provisions as the property of the lord to whom he paid it, as the lord's *homo proprius*. It is time now to attend to those holdings and the obligations they imposed.

THE THEATER OF DOMINION AND HONOR

Peter of Raissac and his brothers, Bernard Modul and William the Fuller at Douzens, and other rich peasants and village entrepreneurs whose property we can trace were doubtless beneath the notice of people such as Ermengard of Narbonne and her friends, fit only for the attention of bailiffs. They were small fry in comparison with those who kept company with viscounts and bishops. But we may easily imagine them as big fish in the small ponds of their villages. Is it possible that their substantial holdings and local importance were exactly what made them valuable property to possess, worth paying substantial amounts of money to acquire, prized as a gift, worth endless litigation? If this suggestion seems bizarre on its face, it may be because of the way we usually think about serfdom.

Since the nineteenth century, if not long before, serfdom has been treated by historians as above all an economic phenomenon; it has been conceived in terms of those central concepts of classical economic theory: land, capital, and labor—the three elements required to produce economic goods. In this context, serfdom is a way to mobilize labor. Rather than controlling access to land and capital and getting people to work by offering them wages, lords of serfs used extra-economic power to force people to work or give a part of their produce. This way of thinking about serfdom has been most vigorously pursued by historians influenced by Marx, but it is hardly unique to them. Historians of all political and analytical persuasions are likely to think of corvée labor—the forced labor of peasants—when the word serfdom is mentioned. The central issues in the history of serfdom are almost always the changing ways by which lords extracted labor or a portion of their produce from their serfs. It is almost always inscribed within the history of the seignorial estate.[25]

In Occitania, however, labor services were very rare. Elisabeth Magnou-Nortier has estimated that only 6 percent of the households subject to the monastery of Gellone in the mountains north of Montpellier had to provide them, and those labor services whose exact nature we know are minimal: at Sigean in the twelfth century, subject households with two oxen owed one workday once each year at planting time and only after they had had eight days to do their own planting; those with one ox and a wagon owed the same (presumably to do carting); at Fontjoncouse the inhabitants owed ox-cart service twice a year and pack-ass service four times, but only for a distance allowing them to return no later than the following morning. Such services are typical of those across the breadth of the Occitan plain: cartage, a day's help with sowing or harvesting, messenger service, a few days of vine trimming.[26] They are hardly enough to make servitude primarily a way to mobilize labor for a seignorial estate; still less are they enough to define a person's status or the structure of an entire economy. That is why twelfth-century witnesses ignored them altogether when asked whether person A was the homo proprius of lord B.

Was serfdom then a way to mobilize revenues? Yes, of course, for the defining tags—being subject to queste and albergum—meant, as we have seen, that the dependent handed over produce to his lord. But how heavily did they weigh, these dues of domination?

Like the rare corvées, the albergum demanded for fighting men (or occasionally monks) varied widely from village to village. It was commonly defined as food for a certain number of fighting men once each year: "one provision [receptum] each year for twelve knights [caballarii], that is to say one pig sufficient for those twelve knights and their squires and two sétiers of wine by true measure of the town of Elne, and one sétier of bread wheat, and four sétiers of pinard" was the substantial levy on the mansus Eribertus (most probably a large farm), an albergum mortgaged to the church of Elne in 1101 for the nice sum of four pounds of pure silver. The two and a half sétiers of oats, four good loaves of bread, one sétier of good wine, and five chickens or a piece of meat worth five pennies, demanded as provisions for five fighting men from a subject household in Quillan in 1136, were probably closer to the usual. So were the "two good pieces of meat, good bread, and good wine and in the morning a chicken or piece of cold meat for each pair of men, and good bread and good wine" demanded in a village south of Toulouse in 1224–25. Fighting men filled their bellies with meat and alcohol, especially alcohol.[27]

That the albergum usually provided food for fighting men (milites or caballarii) suggests a linkage back through time to the taxes that supported the Carolingian army.[28] What those exact links may have been are lost to us, however, if in fact there were any; the earliest surviving mention of the albergum in the region, from 986, provided not for fighting men but for an abbot and his companions. Mentions of alberga for fighting men do not really become common until the mid-eleventh century. And whether it was fighting men or abbots who were receiving food and drink, it was not during the warring season but (on the rare occasions we get a specific time) in winter. As soon as the texts get a bit loquacious, they give an image of fighting men whiling away their hours at the hunt, waiting for their next call to arms: the lords who held Sigean from the archbishop of Narbonne were not to demand food for their dogs or falcons; at Albières, in contrast, the castellan expected legumes and bread for his dogs. (Clearly, every aspect of these dues was subject to negotiation; there was no uniformity from village to village, even when subject to the same high lord.)[29]

Furthermore, within a village the amounts could vary from household to household; the demand for provisioning could be as fragmented and individualized as the holding of plots of land, and as widely distributed among lordly beneficiaries. Let us return to Pons, the agent of Saint-Pons-de-Thomières, describing the situation in Peyriac-Minervois in 1158: Peter the Black owes provisions to the abbey for six fighting men plus two sétiers of barley; Peter of Godor and his brothers owe provisions for five fighting men and five quarters of barley; two subject households owe only for two fighting men, and only six of the sixty-nine peasants who hold land of Saint-Pons in that village owe provisions at all. Earlier in the century Archbishop Richard of Narbonne regulated the rights of one of his castellans in the village of Fontjoncouse, not far from Narbonne, by ordering, "Where the archbishop has provisions for 6 fighting men, Roland has 5; where the archbishop has 5, Roland has 4; where the archbishop has 4, Roland has 3; . . . where the archbishop has 2, Roland has the same, and breakfast." Within a decade, however, Roland had given three of the villagers "in the archbishop's right and lordship" to the abbey of Lagrasse. And at the end of the century, William of Fontjoncouse, possessor of what the scribe calls a "palace" in the village, and possibly a distant descendent of Roland, only had provisions for two fighting men from one household; his cousin Alquerius had none. Who owned the remainder of the alberga once collected by Archbishop Richard and Roland at the beginning of the century? The documents do not tell. Some were doubtless dispersed in dowries and the inevitable divisions among heirs; for others, Roland's gift to Lagrasse is symptomatic.[30] It can be matched in hundreds of gifts from one end to the other of Occitania—gifts of people "with their tenancies," gifts of "the mansus where so-and-so is seen to live"; the albergum is treated as highly valued property and, like other property, distributed as the occasion demanded.

What was the value of the provisions called albergum? Economically speaking, it was quite small. Let us take the exceptional albergum from Elne: for twelve fighting men, a pig, two sétiers of good wine, a sétier of bread wheat, and a quantity of pinard. Food prices, even in our own day, are notoriously variable; how much more so in this age long before the advent of industrial agriculture and retail distribution. We can, however, establish at least an order of magnitude: a pig was valued at 3 sol. at Narbonne in 1148, another at Sainte-Suzanne, south of Toulouse at 6 d. in 1146; between 1146 and 1154, apparently a period of severe food shortages in the Aude basin, the price of a sétier of wheat shot up from about 1 sol. 3 d. to 4 sol. 6 d.; three sétiers of wine were worth 5 sol. near Muret in the late eleventh century.[31] In normal years the provisions for these twelve fighting men would have amounted to perhaps 10 sol., depending on the price of bread grain. The more common provision for two or three fighting men would have amounted to 1 or 2 sol., a calculation confirmed by an agreement between the abbot of Saint-Pons-de-Thomières and Roger of Béziers over a new castle the abbot had built; the abbot was to give provisions for fifty fighting men each year or 50 sol. Melg., as he chose. When Pons Mirabel had his service to the Templars at Douzens fixed at 2 sol. per year, this would not have represented a reduction in what he owed but simply a stabilization.[32] For people with the holdings of Stephen Udalger or Bernard Modul or the income from a mill like that of William the Fuller, it was a very modest financial obligation; in truth, on the account books of their lords it would have been negligible.

Why then should the ownership of such people have been fought over? Why should the gift of serfs have figured so prominently in ecclesiastical endowments, in dowries, and in grants to followers? If it was not in money or goods, where did its value lie?

Might it have been the act of domination itself? That, surely, was what the language of domination said, with its talk of "doing all our will," of transferring "from our power to your power," of subjection to "force" and "requisition" and "taking," of being subject to "command and domination." At Raissac, so William the priest tells us, that domination was simply enacted: the prior of Saint-Antoine and his companion showed up at the house of Peter and his brothers and said, "We're here to be fed." It was no different at Fontjoncouse, where the archbishop, if he so chose, could receive the alberga "in the houses of the villagers," and so could his castellan. The abbot of Lézat had to give eight days notice before showing up at the house of Gerald of Saint-Marcel with eight horsemen and four foot soldiers, but he was assured he would find brill on the table "if there is one to be had in Muret."[33] The archbishop and the abbot and their military companions dining in rustic simplicity at a villager's table; not only that, but carefully regulating when, what, and how much they are to be fed: this is what the albergum seems to be about. It is an image that, like the image of a serf marrying his lord's sister, shakes our sense of the barriers between high and low, between the powerful and the weak, in medieval society. What could it have meant?

There was another occasion when people thought of providing food in quantity; it was on their deathbeds, when in their testaments they ordered food be given to the poor or to the clergy, the ritually poor.[34] These distributions of grain and wine were alms, of course, offerings freely given, conventional generosity, doubtless, but unconstrained; there seems to be no way of associating them with the required offerings of the albergum. And yet the amounts that testators stipulated bear an uncanny resemblance to the amounts laid out for the horsemen and their squires: three pigs, three sétiers of wheat, and six sétiers of wine was the provision that Archdeacon Bernard Raymond made for the clergy to celebrate the anniversary of his death; three pigs, a sétier and a half of good wheat, and a *saumata* of wine for the clergy, a half sétier of wheat, a barrel of wine, and a sheep for the poor was Peter of Saint-Hilaire's provision; a pig, two sétiers of wheat, and two of wine were the alms that Abbot Imbert of Saint-Paul of Narbonne offered for his anniversary.[35]

People can only eat so much, of course, and drink a little more, but in none of these cases was the number of people specified. All three of these testators were members of the clergy; they knew the number of clerics they would feed. But how many poor could they have numbered? Rather than a calculation of foodstuffs needed, the amounts look more like a customary sufficiency, especially when we compare them with the wealth in silver objects, in fur-lined coats, in cloth, in money, and in grain that these men meticulously apportioned among churches and hospitals and their many friends and relatives. With alms as with the albergum, the substance in the end seems less important than the act, the act of serving food.

Where alms are concerned, there can be no contention that these anniversary payments were dues or a conventional price paid for spiritual service. Like the endowments in money or land or grain, like the silver cups and plates that often went to the same clergy, they were gifts intended to carry life's fellowship of prayer across the irreversible boundary of death, to confirm beyond the need for renegotiation the place of the giver in a never-ending liturgy of remembrance. The copy of the testament, preserved in the treasury of every abbey, cathedral, parish church, and hospital that received an endowment, and in the necrologies and memory books placed on their altars, was the guarantee that memory would not dim.

The provision of food spoke of fellowship but also of service. When it was the poor who received, it therefore spoke especially of humility, of service in the most obvious manner—being below and offering up. When portrayed in images, the gesture was always the same, on bended knee with open palms lifting the offering upward, whether it was a church a patron had built, a book an author had written, or food that servants had just brought from the roasting spit. The gesture does not change from the ninth century to the fifteenth.

Here, for example, is the fourteenth-century chronicler Froissart describing the dinner of the defeated king of France in the camp of the victorious Black Prince after the battle of Poitiers in 1356:

> That evening the Prince of Wales gave a supper for the King of France and most of the captured counts and barons. The Prince seated King John and his son Philip, with Lord Jacques of Bourbon [and others] at a high table, lavishly provided, and the rest of the nobles at other tables. He himself served in all humility both at the King's table and at others. . . . He insisted that he was not yet worthy to sit at the table of so mighty a prince. . . . He constantly kneeled before him, saying, "Beloved sire, do not make such a poor meal, even though God has not been willing to heed your prayers today. . . ." At these words all those present murmured their approval. . . . It was generally agreed that in [the Prince] they would have a most chivalrous lord and master.[36]

Froissart leaves no doubt what this elaborate theater was meant to represent: not a gesture of largesse, of spreading wealth among companions, but rather an act of humility, a way to stage the proper social hierarchy, unchanged although King John was a prisoner. The height and placement of the tables, the arrangement of the guests, the kneeling at service, all were designed to display that single image.

And so we may surely read the act of offering up demanded by the albergum: as a theatrical representation of the social hierarchy, of below and above. When it was self-consciously reversed in the act of feeding the poor, it momentarily turned the hierarchy upside down at the most mysterious of limits, between life and death; otherwise it would be void of meaning. Just as a great burial, an anniversary mass, or a ritual meal for the poor proclaimed wealth and status, when a great lord or lady entered a village surrounded by a little troop of horsemen and squires (and a train of huntsmen, beaters, dog handlers, and falcon trainers) to descend on the likes of Stephen Udalger or Peter of Raissac, the act said, "I am the power here, and these men, as important as they may look to you, are my property." That was why in 1119 the archbishop's court declared that Raymond of Bages (whose son was quite wealthy, and whose later descendants kept company with the notables of Narbonne and married into the rural nobility) must "fully and honorably render his *receptum*" to the clergy of Saint-Paul of Narbonne, "that is to say, the oats and straw and stabling and beds with cushions."[37] Acts like this were meant to impress themselves year after year on the communal memories of all those who came from fields and meadows to gape.

Why else would the archbishop have insisted that at every subject mansus in Fontjoncouse he had the right to appear with one more mounted fighting man than did his castellan?[38] It was the annual occasion when the full social hierarchy made itself palpable, when it could be seen and heard, and smelled in the odors of roast pig turning on a spit. Why else choose the winter months? It was the time when warriors were not professionally occupied, to be sure, a time for hunting deer and boar and wild birds (as it is to this day), and therefore a good time to be out in the villages, but it was also a time when the villagers would be at home, slaughtering, salting, and smoking the animals that had fattened on acorns and beech mast in summer and fall, before the cycle would begin anew with trimming old vines and planting new ones. It was a time when lords (and ladies) could be there to be seen and peasants would be there to see.

There were many other occasions when lords who claimed "domination" of a place because they held a castle or were some great lord's vicar, or a castle was held of them, or simply because those rights had been granted to them, could go out and say, "I'm your lord. Give me my share." At Fontjoncouse it was the right of the castellans to demand cheese four times a year, wood on Sundays, hoofs and horns of deer and wild goats and shoulder blades of slaughtered pigs, and the archbishop's right to take a share of the kermes that fed on the scrubby oaks in the hills, those tiny insects whose bodies made a priceless vermilion dye. At Auriac it was the paws and skins of all bears and the heads and shoulders of all boars that the archbishop claimed for himself.[39]

Perhaps it was these sorts of occasional levies, some valuable, the others above all symbols of state, that were lumped together as the generic *queste*, *tolte*, and *forcie* or, in the sharply editorializing tone of the clergy of Elne, as *violencie*. When the bailiff of the count of Foix at Saint-Ybars rode into the neighboring hamlet of Padern and took whatever chickens, geese, and pigs he could find, he did it, he told the abbot of Lézat, because he had nothing else to eat, and anyway, he did the same thing in other villages around the fortified village he governed, even those belonging to other monasteries and lords. Padern belonged to the abbey, and the inhabitants quickly appealed for protection, which is how it happened to get recorded, but could this kind of behavior have been all that unusual?[40]

Some of these levies were made on mansi; like the albergum, they were a mark of owned men. Others were more generalized. As the bailiff of Saint-Ybars brazenly put it, he went out and took what he needed from the neighboring farmyards because he "ruled" and, as far as he was concerned, taking chickens for his table was part of his ruling; taking was what went with being castellan or vicar, or simply with dominating. Taking was utilitarian, but it also showed where he stood.

The grandees of this world, people like Ermengard, the Trencavels, and the counts of Toulouse, did their taking on a grander scale, for they had armies to provide for. Where the alberga due from "owned men" might be for two or three horsemen, or in exceptional cases, where the mansus or casal was a substantial farm, for ten or twelve, those levied by viscounts in their cities numbered in the hundreds. The demands for provisions was a threat that the bishop of Béziers stood ready to fight about when Viscount Bernard Ato was succeeded by his two sons. Ermengard made certain she would collect it from the inhabitants of the new suburban development that one of her followers was building just north of the city walls. Invisible in our surviving documents—because such important rights would never be given away (especially not to an episcopal rival within the city) and would therefore never wash up like so much other flotsam in an episcopal or monastic archive—equivalent quantities were doubtless levied in Agde and Nîmes, in Carcassonne and Albi.[41]

Even modest rural fortifications could face demands for provisions for hundreds of horsemen: fifty at a castle to be built at Scorcencs (probably somewhere in the Razès), a hundred horsemen and a hundred footmen at Moussoulens, two hundred horsemen and their mounts at Monthaut. Abbeys were not immune either; in 1171, Saint-Pons-de-Thomières had to add provisions for fifty fighting men to those it already owed to Viscount Roger of Béziers to settle a dispute over the construction of a new castle, and as late as 1241, Lézat owed provisions for 150 to the count of Foix. Once attuned to this practice, we can spot fleeting references to Ermengard doing the same at castles under her power.[42]

Albergum, then, covered two very different practices. For the great, for those such as Ermengard and her fellow viscounts and counts, often on the move with the men of their courts, it was a very utilitarian demand (although no less symbolic for all that), a practical way to provide for their troops when they were far from their own castles stocked with large quantities of grain and wine. (Archbishop Arnold's testament of 1149 suggests how much that could be; he gave as alms eleven modii of grain from his cellars at Narbonne [a modius being six sétiers], six and one-half modii stored at Cruscades, sixteen at Capestang, and he expected that his chickens and pigs at Salles would not only cover the expense of his funeral but leave something over for alms; we may be confident these gifts did not empty his silos, for he makes repeated reference to "the remainder.") In the villages, on the other hand, the utilitarian function of the albergum hid far behind the symbolic: it was above all a way for power to glory in itself.[43]

Yet that too had its uses, for how else would those who dominated the villages show that they did?

There in the villages a multitude could claim rights of lordship in the land, including some, at least, who were dependents of other lords. Land lordship was highly diffused. So too were the other demands that spoke of dependence, for all of them—save those that belonged to the potestativum of the great, the powers that allowed them to gather in their wealth and to field their armies—were regularly broken off piece by piece, to make a daughter's dowry, a son's inheritance, a castellan's holding, a deathbed endowment. The stack of lordships could be deep and deeply fragmented.

Those at or near the top of the hierarchy, furthermore, were busy people, with holdings in hundreds of villages, if they were Ermengard or the Trencavels, or dozens if they were a bishop or one of the inner circle of companions to the great.[44] If they were fighting men, they had their term of castle duty in one of the major cities and probably in one or more of the rural fortresses as well; politics—and thus the requirements of their own advancement—demanded that they attend upon the great, take part in campaigns that might take them anywhere from Catalonia to Provence or the Limousin; faith, as well as the demands of status, required that they at least consider the armed pilgrimage to the Holy Land, and many undoubtedly answered the call. In the villages they were not a constant presence.

The occasions when they collected their dues (or their local agents collected them) were therefore important moments to keep alive the memory of their domination, necessary to affirm the enduring truth of the social hierarchy. A document tells us that a castellan received a cheese four times a year from those subject to him. How are we to imagine this happening? Were the cheeses dropped off in a sack at the door, as a neighbor now might come drop off her oversupply of zucchini? Did an agent go from door to door followed by a boy with a cart? Is it not more likely that they were presented, along with the annual chicken, at some ceremonial occasion, a moment when dominion stood revealed?

For those who were dominated, especially those who stood in the special relationship of being owned, the status was not without its benefits as well. They were clearly expressed in one of the first documents that mentions the albergum in Occitania, in 986.

> In the name of our lord Jesus Christ. I, Sancho, priest, and I, Asnerius, for ourselves and our posterity confirm our gift of our lands and our inheritances to Saint Mary of Peyrissas and to the abbot Roger and his successors. In addition we give in perpetuity ourselves and all our posterity and all our liberty and all our honor, that is the casal of Adeilhac with all that belongs to it, in accordance with the following agreement: that once each year we shall give the abbot and all the household of his church an albergum; and the abbot and all his successors agree to defend and protect us and what belongs to us against all men to the best of his ability.[45]

The reality of that protection in the twelfth century was crucial to Peter of Raissac when he fell into the power of the vicar of Toulouse, and all that saved him was the friendship of the vicar for Peter's lord, the prior of Saint-Antoine. For men such as Peter, or Stephen Udalger, and most likely the others whose stories we have followed, with interests that spread beyond a single village, men who might fall afoul of some minor potentate in a nearby city, such access to lordly love was not to be lightly waved aside.

Meanwhile, the life of the village went its yearly round of sowing and harvesting, of vine trimming and grape pressing; olives ripened on the trees, and children were sent with sticks to knock them down; fava beans and chickpeas were gathered, and the women of the village sat by their front doors and gossiped while they shelled them; shepherds took flocks into the hills in the spring; children took oxen to pasture when the plowing was done or led pigs into the garigue or surviving patch of woods. Except at harvest time, or some other moment when extra hands had to be swiftly rounded up, except for the moment when the landlord or his agent appeared to count the sheaves of grain in the field or baskets of grapes in the vineyard and took his share,[46] except for those ceremonial occasions when the archbishop received his bear paw and the castellan his cheeses, or they brought their little troop for the annual ceremonial pig roast, and except for those moments when a fine was levied or an adulterer punished, lords and their lordships were little in evidence if there was no castle in the village—and perhaps even if there was.

In these small worlds, people such as Peter of Raissac and his brothers, Bernard Modul, and Stephen Udalger took on their importance. They were the "prudent men" (*probi homines*) who were assembled when a valuation had to be made (as happened in the dispute between the Raissac brothers and the prior of Saint-Antoine) or a boundary walked off, the people who decided on the compensation a seller was to give to a buyer when the property could not be delivered, or the repairs needed to property that was used to secure a loan; they were the people who joined in arbitrating disputes when only villagers were involved and who witnessed their eventual settlement.[47]

In the decades after 1200, as ideas drawn from Roman law began to seep into the countryside, villagers learned to think of their villages as corporations (*universitas*) and soon afterward to claim the right to elect consuls in imitation of their city betters.[48] What made that possible was that many lords might claim lordship in each village, each had his or her own revenues, and a few had the possibility on occasion to parade their dominion. But because lordship was fragmented and multiple, no single lord could dominate. The world of lordship and the world of village life—although tightly intertwined, each went its own way.

CHAPTER NINE
ERMENGARD'S ENTOURAGE

Just a few minutes walk from Ermengard's riverside palace, next door to the Greater Church of Saint-Mary (so-called to distinguish it from the other church of Saint-Mary across the river in the Bourg) stood the house of Peter Raymond of Narbonne, one of the viscountess's most trusted counselors. Artisan shops opened their cramped spaces to the narrow street in front, where Jewish men in their finest clothes hurried mornings and evenings to the Old Synagogue around the corner. Women sat by their doors, gossiping, mending stockings, shelling beans, while children ran among them playing tag. From the sober Romanesque windows of his great second-story hall, Peter Raymond could watch the passage of mules and packhorses as the cries of vendors and the shouts and laughter of men bartering by the wall drifted into the room. On the courtyard side he could check on the comings and goings of his servants as they tended the horses in his stables and stocked grain in his earthen silos and wine in his great jars. Here in his hall he dined at midday with his wife Adalais, his sons and daughters, and his squires. Here he attended to his business enterprises and the affairs of his lady the viscountess.[1]

Peter Raymond's father had bequeathed him this house. He had likewise bequeathed him his positions of power in the city and in Ermengard's court. For a few years, at least, in the early 1170s, Peter Raymond served as Ermengard's vicar, and from 1164 into the 1180s he was at her side at many of the most important moments of her political life: in 1164 when she negotiated with Raymond Trencavel the division of mining profits in the upper valley of the Orb; in 1171 when she abandoned the Aragonese camp and brought together a new Toulousain alliance, soon convincing the young Roger of Béziers to join it. He was with her at the critical moment when Sicard of Laurac capitulated to Roger of Béziers. We may surely guess that he was with her when she helped bring Alfonso of Aragon and Raymond V together at Jarnègues in 1176.[2] Throughout these tumultuous years he remained an important—perhaps the most important—member of her inner circle. And he profited.

When he died in June 1184, Peter Raymond left a dense accounting of the estate he had accumulated. The core of his holdings was urban real estate. In addition to the old family house there were others in the parish, some of which he had purchased, others that he held as security for mortgages, and one that he had inherited from his brother. He had shops on the Roman bridge connecting the City with the Bourg and four mills upriver near the village of Coursan; three of these he had bought from Viscountess Ermengard. His vineyards were spread over the rich floodplain of the Aude, north and east of the city and beyond the salt marshes on the island of Lec. He also had coin in plenty: 2,000 sol. Melg. invested in loans, enough cash on hand to leave 1,050 sol. to monasteries, the Templars, and various hospitals, and another 2,000 sol. to be given to his daughters as downpayment on their much larger cash inheritances.

Peter Raymond had married well. Whose heiress his wife was we have no way of knowing, but she brought with her an endowment of property in eighteen villages stretching across some fifty kilometers, from Ginestas and the villages around it, northwest of Narbonne, to Bessan, north of Agde; she had urban property as well—a house in Béziers and lordship rights over a mill on the Orb, all of which passed on to their children. It was to her husband rather than her relatives by birth that she left the eventual distribution of this wealth; whether common practice or not, Peter Raymond felt obliged to state that he was doing so to fulfill her last wishes.

When he distributed his estate, he favored his eldest son Berenger, who received by far the largest share of his parents' landed wealth. It was Berenger whom he declared, in the latest Roman law fashion, his "heir in both paternal and maternal estates" (*in paterna et in materna*).[3] The son who bore his own name, Peter Raymond, was destined for the clergy; he received a few houses and shops in the city, some vineyards beyond the walls, and 350 sol. worth of property held in mortgage—still a considerable inheritance. The third son, Gerald, was left with a laconic "all the rest." That did not mean he was left out in the cold; far from it. All three brothers maintained a position at court as power passed from Ermengard to her nephew and then to her grandnephew Aymeri,[4] and Gerald could easily afford the 2,000 sol. Melg. he needed to buy the vicecomital seignorial rights on the six mills he owned up the Aude, mills that long after he was buried were still known as "the mills of Gerald of Narbonne." In the 1220s, he as well as his brother Berenger proudly bore the newly imported title of knight.[5] "All the rest," although unspecified, must have been a substantial inheritance as well.

Peter Raymond's three daughters, in contrast, were endowed almost exclusively with money—on a scale, however, that befitted their father's status. Garsend, who would marry the son of one of Ermengard's other close companions,[6] received 5,500 sol. Melg. (plus the house and mill in Béziers that had belonged to her mother); Jordana received 3,300 sol. (along with a grainfield and pastureland across the river from Béziers). As for Gentiana, she had already received 3,000 sol. at the time of her marriage (to whom we do not know) and was told to be satisfied with that; her son received a mortgage valued at 940 sol.

Garsend's inheritance was more than half of the 10,000 sol. Melg. that Maria of Montpellier, the future queen of Aragon, received as dowry at the time of her second marriage to the count of Comminges in 1197. Gentiana's 3,000 sol. would have been enough to buy what was surely the most valuable piece of commercial real estate in the city—the land between the archiepiscopal palace and the Aude (along with the butcher shops just beneath the palace walls), land that in the thirteenth century would be taken to build the archbishop's new Gothic palace.[7]

The distribution that Peter Raymond made followed a pattern already common in Occitania.[8] It bespeaks a desire to keep family fortunes concentrated in a single line, yet tempered by an equally strong desire to maintain old-fashioned familial solidarity. Peter Raymond carefully set out the substitutions that were to follow if any of his heirs were to die before coming of age or without children "born of legitimate marriage." His son Peter Raymond was to succeed to Berenger's inheritance, "provided he has not been made a subdeacon," provided, that is, he had not advanced in his clerical status to the point at which he could no longer marry; next in line would be Gerald; and all the sons' portions were to remain together, with property undivided, until the full inheritances were paid to their sisters and their nephew and until Peter Raymond's three squires were given the arms of knighthood. (The use of the expression *milites faciant* here, when Peter Raymond never takes "knight" as a title either in this document or any other, demonstrates that the term still designated a professional occupation as armed warrior rather than a social status. His sons would live in a very different world.)

Peter Raymond died at a time when one social world was passing into another. His attempt to balance the new against the old, to pass his family's fortunes to one son while assuring that his other children could still live according to their station, was his way of resolving several disparate demands. He could not help but realize that around him in Narbonne vast wealth was accumulating in the hands of newcomers such as the Bistani. If the family was to retain its eminent position, it would have to rein in the traditional dispersion of its property as generation succeeded generation.

The way to do so had been shown by his betters, in particular by the lords of Montpellier. In that family the eldest had always received the lordship over the city of Montpellier and a significant portion of his father's rural strongholds, but the younger sons had also received substantial settlements or been destined for the church. As William VI of Montpellier put it in his testament of 1146, "It is not fitting that a noble man receive a beggarly inheritance."[9] To be sure, in 1172 William VII moved sharply to restrict any further dispersion of lineage resources; he left his eldest son, the future William VIII, all his rights and lands, with the charge to provide his younger brother with whatever he needed to live honorably, or, if they came to a falling out, with 1,000 sol. Melg. per year; a third son became a monk, and a fourth was supposed to become a Templar.[10] Such radical primogeniture, however, was too much for Peter Raymond; indeed it seems to have run against the grain of all the region's aristocracy. They preferred either to share the family holdings more or less equally among their sons or, at most, to favor the eldest and assure the rest enough to live nobly.[11] Peter Raymond realized that his family—and his own career—had profited from the solidity of his cousinage, that power and wealth could not be sustained unless renewing nutrients continued to flow through its many branches. The strategy he pursued on his deathbed, doubtless conceived long in advance, was crucial to the continued success of his descendants; its consequences, he knew, would echo for generations to come.

Peter Raymond left us no accounting of his ancestry equivalent to his accounting of his wealth, but by piecing together circumstantial clues we can trace the family's position back to the mid-eleventh century.

Let us begin with his son and namesake, who eventually took the surname "of Breuil," perhaps in preference to Junior, as a way to distinguish himself from his father. In taking that surname the son identified himself with another important family in the city, one that had stood high in the hierarchy of power since Guifred was archbishop, and doubtless well before. The Breuil was a sweep of floodplain formed by a wide meander of the Aude just upstream from the city, and a Gerald of Breuil was present in Ermengard's court from the 1150s into the 1180s, serving as her vicar a few years after Peter Raymond of Narbonne. If all the twelfth-century mentions of Gerald of Breuil refer to one individual and not to father and son or uncle and nephew, the youthful Laertes of the even younger Ermengard had become the Polonius of her court by the end of her career.[12] However that may be, the Gerald of Ermengard's later years had a son also named Gerald, and a grandson by the same name.

Gerald was a name the family "of Breuil" shared with those who called themselves "of Narbonne." In the 1150s, before the elder Peter Raymond appeared on the scene, a Gerald of Narbonne served in Ermengard's court; someone by that name was already affixing his name to documents in Narbonne in the 1120s; again we have no way to tell whether these were the same person or father and son. Peter Raymond in turn named his youngest son Gerald, and yet a later Gerald of Narbonne (most likely Peter Raymond's grandson) became abbot of Saint-Paul in the middle of the thirteenth century.[13] All these men, those "of Breuil" and those "of Narbonne," were surely of the same lineage. For although surnames were on the way to becoming family names in the twelfth century, they were not yet there; it was through ancestral given names that a family's aura was passed from generation to generation. And although the total number of male given names was not large, Gerald as a name was not very common in and around twelfth-century Narbonne; aside from the family "of Breuil" and that "of Narbonne," only the family "of Laredorte" used it repeatedly. When we add to this fact the decision of Peter Raymond the younger to adopt the surname "of Breuil," we have good grounds for concluding that the two families were cousins.[14]

The ancestors of these cousins were already important individuals in the city in the middle decades of the eleventh century. A great-grandfather and grandfather, Raymond Arnaldi and Berenger Raimundi (the surnames here are surely patronymic), in turn held the archbishop's vicariate in the Bourg of Narbonne, along with the archbishop's oven, some houses, a mill, and vast rights on the archbishop's lands outside the city walls (including the guard of the archbishop's vineyards in the Breuil, perhaps the origin of that later cognomen).[15] Whoever the members of the intervening generation may have been, those rights passed on in the family; in 1160, Gerald of Breuil, already active in Ermengard's entourage, was still collecting the archbishop's tax on salt in the Bourg, all the judicial fines under five solidi in the archbishop's section of the Bourg, and 10 percent of all other judicial revenues; he also held in fief a goodly share of his ancestors' other rights.[16]

FRIENDS AND COMPANIONS

Thanks to Peter Raymond's surviving testament we know more about him than about any other member of Ermengard's court, but neither the length of his lineage nor the nature of his wealth made him stand out among his colleagues. Many could—and, by the names they chose to baptize their children, did—trace their ancestry back to important lords in the city or its countryside at the beginning of the twelfth century or earlier. Doubtless only the limits on our surviving documents (and the major change in naming patterns that occurred in the mid-eleventh century) prevent us from tracing those lineages and their memories back even further.

Peter Raymond left his three sons in the guardianship of Raymond of Ouveilhan, Hugh Ermengaud, and Raymond Toll-taker (Leuderius); these must have been Peter Raymond's most trusted friends. About Hugh Ermengaud we know next to nothing; he shows up elsewhere in the surviving documents only once—a sharp reminder of their limitations. Raymond Toll-taker was a man of the same milieu as Peter Raymond, moving in the company of important people in the city of Béziers and joining the entourage of Viscount Roger of Béziers when he was in the region.[17] Raymond Toll-taker's role as guardian is one more indication of how important Peter Raymond's connections were in and around that neighboring city.

Raymond of Ouveilhan was another of Ermengard's companions. He and Peter Raymond must have been together far more than surviving documents reveal, for Raymond of Ouveilhan eventually made Peter Raymond's sons heirs to a portion of his own property; they may very well have been related by marriage.[18] He too belonged to a family whose weight had long been felt in and around Narbonne. At the beginning of the twelfth century they dominated the village of Ouveilhan from both the castle and the church next door. Soon enough they built a second castle lower down the hill on a promontory that overlooked the vast pond whose fish and salt must have provided a goodly portion of the village's income.[19] As branches of the family separated, they established themselves in other corners of the village territory. And just as other families held lordly interests in Ouveilhan, so their own interests reached as far as the Hérault River and entrenched the family in Narbonne itself.[20]

Like Gerald of Breuil, the elder Raymond of Ouveilhan and his wife Adalais held some of the archbishop's vicarial rights in the Bourg of Narbonne; they had houses and lordship rights in the City and its suburbs.[21] Their son, Peter Raymond's close friend, became an active real estate developer. What is now the shaded park of the Palace of Labor (Narbonne's community center), with its bordering boulevard and the commercial buildings beyond, were then open fields in the Ouveilhans' possession. Lying just beyond Ermengard's little suburb of Coyran, in the shadow of the city walls and the cathedral, they were ripe for development. Sometime in the mid-1150s, the youthful Raymond, still in his mother's tutelage after his father's death but graced with a well-developed eye for public relations, named these fields Belveze, "Beautiful View," and began to sell building lots. He meant his new subdivision to be an integral part of the city, with its own communal oven and an enclosure and moat that would connect with the city's wall.

Projects on this scale did not go unquestioned, however, no matter how well connected the promoter. Ermengard spotted it as a threat, for with its symbolic (and profitable) seignorial oven and its fortifications, it risked adding a new claimant to share in Narbonne's rule. She strenuously objected, and friends had to come to the rescue—in this case none other than Peter Raymond of Narbonne and his two most frequent colleagues, Hugh of Plaigne and Raymond of Salles. The matter was smoothed over. Ermengard's high power was recognized in the right to demand from the residents of the new suburb the traditional provisions for her household fighting men; the oven likewise would be hers, and there would be no enclosure between Belveze and Coyran. Raymond, however, kept his control of the land, and his "usages and justices." He was henceforth securely implanted in the city's fabric.[22]

Hugh of Plaigne, one of the arbiters in this dispute, and his nephew or grandson of the same name served Ermengard from the 1150s into the late 1180s.[23] Plaigne (or Plaine) is a common place-name in the villages all along the coast, although only the village of that name in the western Corbières is attested in the Middle Ages. Wherever they originated, they too were well established in and around Narbonne early in the century. In 1144, when the elder Hugh's brother William was given to the cathedral of Saint-Just to become a canon, his endowment consisted of half of the family's honor in the castle and village of Montredon (a few kilometers outside the city), including rights in the stone quarries, lime ovens, fisheries and salt ponds, seventeen pieces of land, four vineyards, three mansi and four men and their families, and tithes on fish and salt pans around Narbonne; in addition he received a house in the City and a house in the Bourg. With two other sons to provide for, their parents, Raymond Berenger of Plaigne and Boneta, must have had much more in reserve, property that continued to pass down the generations. When Hugh in turn gave his son Hugh to the church of Saint-Paul, the young cleric's endowment was the milling rights that Hugh the elder collected from the chapter when they ground their grain at his two mills under the Roman bridge. Here in 1179, in Hugh's shop over the mills, Pons of Olargues, one of the great barons of the upper Orb valley, gave a major gift to the abbey of Fontfroide.[24]

It was men such as these who gathered around Ermengard from the beginning to the end of her active political career. She surely had women around her as well—as Maria of Montpellier, queen of Aragon, had ladies-in-waiting and female relatives at her side, and other women of the lesser aristocracy lived in the company of their mothers, aunts, daughters, nurses, servants, and midwives[25]—but Ermengard's scribes ignored them. Only one ever appears as a witness to her acts, the otherwise unknown Esclaramunda of Saint-Felix in 1167.[26] Women held property both in their own names and as widows; their claims were treated with deference; they were executors of their husbands' wills and guardians of their children; they borrowed and lent money in their own name, held castles, and thus presumably commanded fighting men; but witnessing legal acts (other than testaments) was exclusively a male affair, and witness lists are our only access to Ermengard's court. In that court, sons succeeded fathers and nephews succeeded uncles. Gerald of Narbonne, William of Durban, William of Poitiers, and Peter of Minerve were with Ermengard in 1151 when she swore fidelity to Raymond Trencavel and received an equivalent oath in return. A later Gerald of Narbonne joined Raymond of Ouveilhan and others to witness her gift of some mills to the abbey of Fontfroide in 1191, one of her last surviving recorded acts. William of Durban was with her until 1163; his two sons Bernard and Raymond joined Peter Raymond of Narbonne, William of Poitiers, and others to witness her exchange of oaths with Viscount Roger of Béziers in 1171.[27]

They were a small world formed of friends, companions, and relations by marriage. It should not surprise us, when we walk into Hugh's shop on the Roman bridge to watch Pons of Olargues make his gift to Fontfroide, to find there William of Poitiers, Peter Raymond of Narbonne, and William of Laredorte (another frequent member of Ermengard's court in the 1160s and 1170s) serving as witnesses and bearers of Ermengard's "will and consent."[28] These and the others we have met formed a core of advisors; at the critical moments of her political life, they were the ones she insisted on having with her.

As the occasion demanded they were joined by many others, impossible at this distance to number completely, an ever-changing entourage that crowded into her chamber over the city's Water Gate, followed in her train on her pere-grinations across the countryside or to Béziers, Montpellier, and beyond, pitched their tents around hers when she was leading her army on campaign. When she rode upriver to the village of Douzens to judge a dispute between a disgruntled heiress, Richa, and the Templars, Raymond of Laredorte (probably William's cousin) and Hugh of Plaigne went with her; there they were joined by lay familiars of the Templars, such as Bernard Modul,[29] and by others who most likely were friends of Richa and her husband. When she met Raymond Trencavel deep in the wilds of the Corbières to witness the settlement of a dispute among the two brothers and sister who were heirs to the stronghold of Termes, William of Durban went with her to serve as one of the arbiters; others of her court must have been among the "many noble men who were there at the mountain pass south of Termes," but whose names Arnold of Clairan, Raymond Trencavel's favorite scribe, was too tired to write.[30] Here, as on the other occasions when she met with one of the Trencavels or with the count of Toulouse or the king of Aragon, her followers mixed with theirs.

The fortified village of Minerve. From Charles Nodier et al., *Voyages pittoresques et romantiques dans l'ancienne France. Languedoc.* By permission of the Houghton Library, Harvard University.

In some cases, perhaps in many, the followers of Ermengard and of the Trencavels were the same people. William of Durban is a case in point. Durban was a major fortress in the southern Corbières, just across a line of hills to the east of Termes. The medieval-looking castle that now dominates the village is actually a fake ruin built in the nineteenth century, but somewhere underneath must lie the foundations of this family's military and political strength. Ademar of Durban was already a person to be reckoned with in Narbonne in the last decades of the eleventh century. From then on, the successive generations can be followed without a break into the thirteenth century as castellans for both the archbishops and the viscounts in villages surrounding the city, and as persons whose word—and thus whose presence—was to be taken seriously. Somewhere in William's ancestry—perhaps his grandmother—was the Laureta who around 1116 held of Viscount Bernard Ato the castle of Ornaisons and lands that spread from Béziers to Roussillon. Although William was with Ermengard on important occasions, notably when she and the Trencavel viscounts exchanged oaths of fidelity, he made most of his career in the Trencavel camp.[31]

The lords of Minerve also moved as easily through the vicecomital palace of Carcassonne as through Ermengard's in Narbonne. These lords too we can trace through at least four generations, starting with Bernard, who in 1066 joined with the great counts and bishops of the region to arbitrate the conflict between Archbishop Guifred and Viscount Bernard Berenger (Ermengard's great-grandfather), and his brother or cousin Peter, named along with other barons and prelates of the region in the alliance of about the same time between Raymond Berenger of Narbonne (Ermengard's great-granduncle) and Raymond Bernard, viscount of Albi and Nîmes. Two generations later, another Peter of Minerve was sufficiently important for Ermengard to refrain from exiling him from her court, even though he had been a witness (and thus in all likelihood an accomplice) to her forced marriage to Alfonse Jordan in 1142; he frequented her court from the 1150s until at least 1170, at the same time frequenting the court of the Trencavels as well. When his brother William, who styled himself viscount of Minerve, handed control of the castle of Laure to his son and namesake, he was surrounded by men such as William of Durban, and William and Raymond of Laredorte, whom we have seen attending on Ermengard, and by equivalent luminaries from the court of Raymond Trencavel, including Raymond's scribe Arnold of Clairan. William the son eventually became the second husband of Ricsovendis of Termes.[32]

Lordly networks—of marriage in one generation and cousinage in the next—linked the men of Ermengard's court to others across the length and breadth of the coastal plain and the mountains that bound it to the north. So did castle guard and landholding. Between the viscounty of Narbonne and those of the Trencavels surrounding it there were no real divisions.

Already at the end of the eleventh century, when Roger son of Guilla gave an oath of fidelity to Ermengard's grandfather Aymeri for the castle of Castelmaure on the parched shoulder of Périllou Mountain in the southern Corbières, the same Roger with his brother Hugh were giving identical oaths for Carcassonne to the Viscountess Ermengard, who was the founder of the Trencavel dynasty, and her son Bernard Ato; a man who looks like the same Hugh had back in the 1060s given such an oath to Ermengard's husband Raymond and his uncle Frotarius, bishop of Nîmes, for the castle of Roquefort far away on the northern slope of the Montagne Noire.[33]

When Roger son of Guilla took that oath of fidelity to Aymeri of Narbonne, he excluded four people from what was in effect a promise to fight for the viscount—Viscountess Ermengard and Bernard Ato, Peter Olivier of Termes, and Bernard Xatmar of Laredorte. He had to refuse to fight against Ermengard and Bernard Ato because he had rendered (or was about to render) the same oath to them; but why did he also list Peter Olivier and Bernard Xatmar? The most likely reason seems to be that they were his fellow castellans at Castelmaure.[34] Peter Olivier belonged to the dynasty of Termes whose members we have already encountered disputing the division of their ancestral village in 1163; they would continue to display their might through the Albigensian Crusades and into the thirteenth century, when a distant descendant, Olivier of Termes, would become a favored companion of King Louis IX of France. Bernard Xatmar's descendent, William of Laredorte, we have already met in the shop of Hugh of Plaigne; a Raymond of Laredorte we have met in Ermengard's company at Douzens. The village from which they took their name is on the left bank of the Aude, about half way between Narbonne and Carcassonne, perfectly situating its lords to make their way in the vicecomital courts of both cities. Already in 1080, Bernard Xatmar of Laredorte and his brother Raymond were among the few "illustrious and noble men" whose presence the scribe felt obliged to record (the others, said the scribe, were "too numerous to name") at the great ceremony when Bishop Peter of Rodez, Ermengard's great-uncle, presented the cathedral church of Narbonne with some of the most important tithes in the region.[35]

The descendents of Bernard Xatmar and Raymond owned tithes and doubtless much other property in and around Narbonne. William of Laredorte, grandson of the eleventh-century Raymond, was a man of such commanding position that both the bishop of Elne in Roussillon and Viscount Roger of Béziers attended on his deathbed in 1138; for a while Raymond's great-great-grandsons, William and Peter, held the archbishop's market dues at Narbonne in mortgage for the tidy sum of 5,000 sol. Melg.; and at the end of the century, Gerald Xatmar, most likely a distant descendant of Bernard Xatmar, held the tower above the Bishop's Gate and its adjoining house. A Gerald and Raymond Mancip of Laredorte were the friends whom Ermengard's nephew Aymeri called upon in 1177 to guarantee a mortgage. All the while, other members of the family continued to cultivate their relations and their standing around the village that gave the family its name. Marriages tied the family to the lords of

Capestang and to the Pelapol family (who were both landholders in Narbonne and faithful servants of the Trencavels from the 1120s to the 1190s). We may be sure that other families also found Laredorte offspring worthy companions for their own sons and daughters.[36]

Whenever the people in Ermengard's entourage become something more than just names to us, they resemble the individuals and the families we have just met, those "of Narbonne" and "of Breuil," the Ouveilhans, Plaignes, Durbans, and Laredortes. We can spot them weaving complex webs of connection with other lordly families, asserting possession and dominance in widely separated villages, claiming rights and revenues in castles sometimes equally far apart. The pattern is general among all those of sufficient standing to take a village and its castle as their name, even those who, as far as we can tell, stayed away from the ambitions and rewards of court society and from the cabals and machinations that surely went along with them.

Here is Raymond of Portiragnes (a village near the mouth of the Orb River) surveying his possessions as he makes his testament in 1179. His horizon extends north to the priory of Saint-Mary of Cassan, where the coastal plain meets the first hills of the Massif Central; there he asks to be buried; there he places his illegitimate son to be "taught his letters" by the monks. Farther north he has property in the mountains near Pézènes, which he gives as alms to Cassan along with his personal goods at Portiragnes and the neighboring village of Servian. He has men and women in the fortified village from which he takes his name, but he has dues and property (including a residence and rights in a mill) in Servian as well as in the neighboring village of Bassan and down the coast at Valras. His religious devotion, while concentrated on Cassan, extends to the Cistercians at Valmagne, the bridge at Saint-Thibéry, the hospitals at Servian and Garrigue,[37] and the parish church at Lunas as well as those of his home villages.[38]

Here, a few years later, is Berenger of Lec dictating his testament in the house of Arnold Amalric in Narbonne. He has no children and has already sold his rights in the ancestral castle of Saint-Pierre-de-Lec (now the beach resort of Saint-Pierre-sur-Mer), perhaps to raise the large sum he now gives as alms to the Cistercians of Fontfroide; he has also sold his rights to tithes at Moujan just across the salt flats from the city, and the money he has earned is to go to his sister and her two daughters. His major holdings are in the castle of Donos and neighboring Fontjoncouse and Ripaud in the northern Corbières, where he has a house and collects crop shares from his tenants and alberga from his men. His late wife Raimunda came from a branch of the Ouveilhan family, and through her he has rights in the castle of Terral, just outside her native village. Two of his nephews, Bernard and Pons, bear the name "of Mailhac"; even before they receive their inheritance from Berenger they are firmly established in Fontjoncouse. Another nephew bears the name "of Saint-Nazaire." These names place their family origins north of the Aude River toward the Minervois.[39]

As castellans, both men would have had military obligations, Berenger to the archbishop, Raymond to the viscount. But neither appears to have coveted the honors and dangers of the heady world of court politics. If Berenger ever attended on Ermengard or on the archbishop, or Raymond on one of the Trencavels, they stayed carefully in the background, one of the crowd of notables, but not one of those so prominent or pushy as to make himself noticed by a scribe.

Numbers of their fellow village lords did push themselves forward, however. Of the thirty-five persons we can identify with strong probability belonging to Ermengard's closest circle, twenty-nine take their names from villages around the city or, like Peter Raymond of Narbonne and Gerald of Breuil, from the city itself.[40] Of the remainder, her uncle Berenger, abbot of Lagrasse, then archbishop, was one; two others bore the title of magister, one and probably both of them physicians. And a fourth, and one of the closest to her, was the seemingly mysterious William de Pictavi, a name usually translated "of Poitiers," who appears repeatedly in her company over twenty years, from 1151 to 1171.[41] His name has led to the wildest speculation. The eighteenth-century compilers of the *Histoire générale de Languedoc* opined that he might be the husband of the lady troubadour the Countess of Die, or perhaps the bastard son of William IX, count of Poitiers, fathered when the count was besieging Toulouse in 1114–15, or even the same person as the count of Valentinois in the Alps, who died in 1189.[42] Romantic notions all. The truth is much more prosaic. Where the apparent toponymic came from, we do not know, but he belonged to a local family, others of whom were known as "of Fabrezan," a strategic village and castle about half way between Narbonne and Carcassonne. Four brothers—Ermengaud, William Pons, Peter "of Fabrezan," and William "of Poitiers"—gathered at the court of Ermengard's father in 1124 to settle a dispute with the lord of Montpellier; William at the time was one of the castellans of the archbishop's village of Sigean overlooking the lagoon that served as Narbonne's port. Ermengard's companion was probably this William's son. He in turn allied himself by marriage to one of the most important families of Béziers and eventually had three sons—Ermengaud of Fabrezan, Bertrand of Béziers (named for his wife's father), and William "of Poitiers." William was clearly not one of those landless youth that some imagine populated the aristocratic courts of the twelfth century. And had we more documents we could probably identify the family origins of the two remaining unidentifiable members of Ermengard's court.[43]

INSIDERS AND OUTSIDERS

What these family histories as well as the many surviving testaments tell us is that if we view the regional nobility exclusively through the lens of Ermengard's court (or the archbishop's or the Trencavels'), we willfully distort its shape. These parts are not the whole. Nor would their summation encompass the whole. There must have been many like Berenger of Lec and Raymond of Portiragnes, castellans with interests in several villages, connected by marriage and cousinage to other village lords of the same rank or perhaps to a cadet branch of some better-placed lordly family, who doubtless fought in the wars of the greater nobility but who on the whole found hunting and falconing (and looking after their investments in land, mills, and trading ventures) more congenial to their disposition than palace politics. Given the hundreds of people who appear out of nowhere in our documents and just as suddenly disappear, people who seem to be of the same sort as Berenger and Raymond (the Lady Calva and Poncia of Coumiac, whom we met earlier in the pages of this book, are others of the same rank in female dress), they must have been numerous.

Among this regional nobility there were no borders between one viscounty and another. It is hard to imagine them even thinking of such borders (still less of a map on which Ermengard's lands would be colored red, the Trencavels' blue, and those of the counts of Toulouse yellow, in the manner of modern historical maps), for no such boundaries limited their political, religious, or marital horizons. An important family in Béziers took the name "of Narbonne," just as an important family (or families) in Narbonne took the name "of Béziers."[44] And when Ermengard and Raymond Trencavel or Roger of Béziers met, the courtiers of one would have greeted in-laws, cousins, friends, and brothers who were courtiers of the other. Those in Ermengard's entourage likely were as familiar with the council chambers or counting houses of Béziers or Carcassonne or Montpellier as they were with those of Narbonne, and (as was the case with a man named Bernard Pelapol) the closest advisors of the Trencavels might by some of their real estate holdings have been next-door neighbors to Ermengard or Peter Raymond of Narbonne.[45]

Had more of the marriage contracts and testaments of this regional nobility survived—the witnesses to those moments when families reached out to their contemporaries or strove to shape future generations to their hopes and imagination—we would be able to trace their varied connections in far greater detail. As it is, we are reduced to catching the echoes of these events in the alleys and byways of the documents collected in the treasure chests of churches and monasteries and the pitiful tattered archival remains of the great vicecomital houses. But we should not allow the constraints imposed by that long, random, and sometimes violent selection process to impose themselves on the reality we hope to reconstruct. The long list of names that appear but once in these documentary collections and then vanish again into oblivious night is the roll call of this nobility, their "family names," drawn from the region's villages, the guarantee of their local roots.

Within this regional nobility, thoroughly entwined in its complex networks, the men who gathered around Ermengard were a select group. What was the basis for their selection? Belonging to old families, surely; but how old was old? And how do we account for the apparent exclusion of some who could easily trace their ancestry back to important people in the city in the mid-eleventh century? One of our few clues is the record of an event that occurred in 1080, a half century before the birth of Ermengard.

Archbishop Guifred had died in 1079, burdened with years and papal excommunications.[46] On receiving news of his death, Pope Gregory VII was doubtless overjoyed, but he was not ready to make friends of his enemy's enemies. Ever wary of what he and his reformers called simoniacal heresy (of which Guifred had been a prize example), he named Dalmacius, abbot of Lagrasse, to the see without offering the slightest by-your-leave to the vicecomital family. The effective head of the family at this moment was Peter, bishop of Rodez, brother of the recently deceased viscount, and he was not about to let slip away the chance to undo much of Guifred's work. Although a cleric, Peter had been co-lord of the city with his brother in the manner then common among all the great families of the region.[47] To complete his control he now saw to his election as archbishop. Then on May 7, 1080, he gathered all his allies in the cathedral to witness his gift to the patron saints of the city (and the clergy who served them) of all the tithes on fish caught from Coursan to Leucate and on the salt collected in the lagoons between the city and the sea. It was the largesse expected on the occasion of ascending to such great heights and a seal on the loyalty of the local clergy to Peter's claim to the contested see. The bishops of Béziers, Carcassonne, and Agde were there "with a multitude of abbots and other clergy"; so were the count of Urgel and a host of laymen whom the scribe recording the event—a man addicted to classical allusions—carefully divided into "centurions and noble and illustrious men" (*centuriones et illustres viri ac nobiles*) and "citizens (*cives*) of Narbonne." Among the former were men whose names are now familiar to us—Laredorte, Durban, Cazouls, Sigean. Three-quarters of a century later the descendents of all but one of those here listed among the nobility would be found among Ermengard's companions.[48]

So too with the "citizens." Raymond Arnaldi, the first named, was the ancestor of the families that came to be known as Narbonne and Breuil. Bernard Peter, who took his name from the Royal Gate where the Visigothic kings once had their palace, was most likely an ancestor of the Bernard of the Royal Gate who took an oath of fidelity to Bernard of Anduze shortly after Ermengard married him; the three brothers of Villeneuve, one named Berenger Peter, were most likely ancestors of the Peter of Villeneuve who witnessed Ermengard's last public act in 1193.[49]

Ermengard depended on families who had served not just her father but her grandfather and great-grandfather, and (although invisible in the surviving documents) probably earlier generations as well. Yet in their quest for position and influence, not all old families were equally successful.

The Margalonis family, for example. Raymond Arnold Margalonis was one of the citizens recorded at that ceremony in 1080. The family seems to have flourished in the archiepiscopal milieu, and late in the twelfth century Hugh Margalonis served for at least two decades as precentor of the cathedral. As we have seen, nothing prevented families from serving both the archbishop and Ermengard as well as placing their sons in the cathedral chapter and the abbey of Saint-Paul; indeed, that seems to have been the expected road to power and wealth. Everything appeared to predict that the Margalonises would travel the same route. Arnold Margalonis was mentioned not once but twice as a witness when Raymond Berenger of Plaigne gave his son William to be a cleric of the cathedral, rubbing shoulders with Gerald of Narbonne and Gerald of Breuil; Peter Raymond of Narbonne and his brother Berenger were witnesses when the brothers Raymond, Bernard, and Peter Margalonis settled Hugh's claim to his share of their father's estate; and Peter Raymond Margalonis (along with two members of the Laredorte family) went security for Ermengard's nephew Aymeri when he bought an extravagantly expensive horse on credit.[50] Well he might be trusted to cover such a debt, for had we a twelfth-century survey of household wealth, the Margalonis family would surely have placed in the top few percent. When Peter, the son of Raymond Margalonis, died in 1218, he left each of his two daughters five thousand solidi as dowries, in total almost the same sum that Peter Raymond of Narbonne had left as dowries for his three daughters several decades earlier. He provided generously for anniversary masses for his father and himself, including a provision that a chaplain should be supported on the revenues of his house "until the end of the world," and like others of the age, he left pious donations to the hospitals and leper houses of the City and Bourg as well as to Fontfroide and other monasteries. He had property all over the city and its immediate countryside as well as farther afield at Capestang and Colombiers on the way to Béziers. How much of this he inherited and how much he acquired himself his testament does not reveal; like everyone else of his station he engaged in moneylending and invested in mills. But his standing even as a youth—and the standing of his parents—is measured by his marriage to a daughter of John Bistani, perhaps the wealthiest merchant in the city.[51] The Margalonises moved in the right circles, had the right friends. Yet only once in the surviving documents does one of them appear in Ermengard's presence.[52] They were among the excluded. So too were the families with whom we can connect them.

The Margalonises were cousins to the people who took their name from Bages, a village overlooking the great bay that formed the city's harbor; one of the Bages family, Arnold Donzel, had played a prominent role in the court of Ermengard's father, Aymeri II, at one point serving as his bailiff, yet none of the family appears in the entourage of Ermengard herself. The same was true of the Tréville family, with whom the Bages family was connected by marriage. The exclusion must have had to do with personalities or with particular political choices. If it was factional, marriage did not automatically assign a family to one or another, for the Fabrezans, who gave William of Poitiers to Ermengard's court, were also connected by marriage to the Trévilles.[53]

All of these were families of wealth and ancient lineage. Raymond of Tréville was able to lend 5,000 sol. Melg. to Archbishop Pons, taking the archbishop's rights at Fontjoncouse as security (the mortgage, in turn, became his daughter's dowry when she married Raymond of Bages; we begin to detect here the expected dowry for daughters of the wealthy nobility). Like the families with whom they were allied, the Trévilles were important landholders in the villages along the coast, at Coursan, Sigean, Peyriac, as well as the northern Corbières. The Fabrezan, for their part, could trace their lineage at least back to William, castellan at Sigean early in the eleventh century, and his son Pons, both castellan and archiepiscopal vicar. When Mabilia of Fabrezan married Raymond of Tréville, her sister Adalais married into the Trèbes family, whose members had been high in the counsels of the Trencavels since at least the 1120s; Dias, another sister, married Peter of Puylaurens, one of the great barons of the northern Pyrenees.[54] In every respect their attachments and attainments look just like those of the Narbonnes and Laredortes and Plaignes and Durbans; had there been a local Complete Peerage, they would have been in it. Yet they are all but absent from Ermengard's entourage.

Raymond of Tréville and his wife Mabilia would have been numbered among Ermengard's faithful. They took oaths of fidelity to her for their castles, as surely their ancestors had done to her ancestors. Their obligations were clear, their loyalty assumed. But they were not part of the inner circle. In fact, none of the handful of people whose oaths of fidelity to Ermengard survive ever appears otherwise in her entourage.[55] Taking such an oath went with a position, an inheritance; it did not make one an intimate. And that in a society in which connections were of utmost importance. People such as the Trévilles had their wealth, their positions of power in the countryside (or in the case of the family of the Royal Gate or that of the Capitole, their positions in the city itself). They were therefore in a position to gather others around them, to play the lord in their own backyards. We may easily imagine them collecting alberga, gathering local families around them, as we saw Guilabert of Laurac do in Pexiora and the Templars in Douzens, using their "friendship" to protect "their men" from the high-handedness of others, as the prior of Saint-Anthony did for Peter of Raissac.[56] But excluded from the inner circle, they could not broker the needs and desires of their own followers where it counted most: in the viscountess's palace, in her great hall over the Water Gate. Others kept careful guard over that sanctum.

Such exclusion implies that there were those who were "in" and those who were "out," those who had the viscountess's ear and those who waited in the outer rooms. We know the names of the former. The latter are hinted at when the chance survival of documents directs the spotlight on families such as the Margalonises and Trévilles; we cannot hope to number them, or know which side they took on what occasions. For those who for whatever reason wanted to oust the ins or undo the viscountess, the resentments of exclusion would have provided the networks and familial loyalties to be plied by the agents of the counts of Toulouse when the opportunity arose, a rich soil to work with money and promises of favor. So too in the other rich cities of the Occitan plain; we must imagine similar situations behind the ouster of William VI from Montpellier in 1141, Count Raymond's takeover of Nîmes from its youthful Trencavel heir in 1163, and the murder of Raymond Trencavel in Béziers in 1167.

Against such factional forces, the first line of defense could only be the culture of fidelity.

THE SINEWS OF POWER

THE CULTURE OF FIDELITY

CHAPTER TEN
OATHS AND OATH TAKERS

I, Bernard, son of Fida, will be true to you, Ermengard viscountess of Narbonne, daughter of the late Ermengard, by my true faith without deceit, as a man should be toward his lady to whom he has commended himself by his hands. From this moment forward I will not treacherously deprive you of your life or the limbs attached to your body, nor will any man or woman do so by my counsel or consent, nor will I deprive you of the castle of Durban or of the fortifications that are there or will be there in the future; and I will not take them from you nor will I have them taken from you, nor will any man or woman with my counsel or consent. And if any man or woman takes these from you or wants to take them from you I will come to your aid without deceit whenever you order me to do so by the terms of this oath or have me ordered to do so by your messenger, and I will neither associate nor make peace with that man or woman until I have recovered what they have taken from you and returned it to you without payment on your part and without deceiving you. And each time you order me to do so by terms of this oath or have me ordered by your messenger I will hand over the castle of Durban to you without fraud and without deceit. What is written in this charter and as one can hear and clerks can read I will hold and observe as God is my helper and these holy scriptures.[1]

Of all the oaths of fidelity that were taken to Ermengard, this is one of the few that has survived.

In the world in which we live, many of our important social and economic relationships are governed by contracts—employment contracts (individual or collective), business contracts with suppliers or customers, even prenuptial agreements. Although much of our life is lived outside the realm of contract—our relations with spouses, children, friends, colleagues—contracts nevertheless weigh heavily on the way we imagine our society, and so it has been since the time centuries ago when English philosophers imagined the beginnings of political organization in a social contract. Not so in Ermengard's world. There were, to be sure, contracts drawn up at vital moments, which filled the pages of notarial minute-books and were carefully preserved in strongboxes: contracts

for merchant ventures, for loans of money, mortgage contracts, marriage contracts, rental contracts for peasant land. Ermengard, however, and others of a
similarly exalted status would most likely have looked on contracts with a certain disdain, as the sort of business best left to her bailiffs and vicars. Her social
world and that of the men and women who surrounded her was governed not
by contracts but by oaths, especially the oath of fidelity.

POETRY, RITUAL, AND MAGIC

No English translation can simultaneously render both the sense and the ki-
netic force of the spoken Occitan, which the scribes sometimes copied down
directly (and whose presence can be detected even when they translated into
their clerical Latin). The play of powerful rhythms is perhaps best represented
graphically as a chant:

D'aquesta ora enant	From this hour forward
eu [name] non decebrai	I [name] will not deceive
te [name]	you [name]
nel ti tolrai	nor take it [i.e., the castle] from you
5 ne t'en tolrai	nor take from you anything from it[2]
ni om ne femena ab mun consel;	nor will any man or woman with my consent;
e se om o femena	and if a man or woman
od omes o femenas	or men or women
lot tollian	take it from you
10 ne t'en tollian,	or take you from it
ab aquel	with him
ne ab aquella	or with her
ne ab aquels	or with them [masc.]
ne ab aquellas	or with them [fem.]
15 fin ne societad non auria	I will have no peace or association
for per lo castel a recobrar.	except to recover the castle.
Et aitoris ten serai	And I will come to your aid
per fe e sanz engan.[3]	in good faith and without deceit.

In this text, the repeated first-person future ending of -rai (in decebrai, tolrai,
and serai) giving way to endings of -a, -as, and -an suggests a kind of proto-
poetry, whereas the stressed and unstressed syllables seem at moments to demand a versified scansion:

```
  _'_ '_ _'
  - [name] - '-'
  - [name]
  _ '_'
5 _ '_'
  _' _ '__ _ '_'
```

We are here in the presence not of legal contract but of verbal music whose
rhymes and rhythms were calculated to plant the text deep in the memory of

those who spoke and forcefully remind all who participated of the many occasions on which they had heard it before. We are in the presence of liturgy.

Already the very first words place the occasion and the ritual in another world, a world outside of normal time and place, as, without fail, the oath taker names both himself and the person to whom he swears his faith by the wombs that gave them life: Archbishop Guifred of Narbonne becomes Guifred son of Countess Guila; Raymond of Saint-Gilles becomes Raymond son of Countess Almodis; Raymond Trencavel, Raymond son of Cecilia; and, of course, Viscountess Ermengard, Ermengard daughter of Ermengard. So it was already in the earliest surviving Occitan oaths from shortly after the year 1000; so it continued at all levels of the noble hierarchy to the end of the twelfth century.[4] In contrast, in all other documents from twelfth-century Occitania we find men of high status using family names, either cognomens (Margalonis, Bistani), patronymics that have become cognomens (Benedicti, Bedocii, Sicfredi), or, most often, place-names of their major castle or property (Durban, Ouveilhan, Narbonne, Breuil). Women are named by their title of countess or viscountess, or as the wife of their husband, the daughter of their father, the mother of their sons and daughters, or often enough simply as lady such-and-such. The only exception to this practice occurs when these men and women give or receive oaths of fidelity; then they are their mother's sons and daughters.

Why this should have been so is one of the many questions about these oaths that remains an enigma, one in which we can only look for parallels in other Mediterranean cultures and guess at likelihoods. Everyone who has touched on the practice finds it a mystery.[5]

It is hard to imagine any utilitarian reason why on this one occasion, and only on this occasion, men and women—even those graced with great titles—should be named exclusively as their mother's child. To contemporaries, the names Archbishop Guifred, Count Raymond, Viscountess Ermengard would surely have been adequate, as precise a pointer as they could wish; Bernard son of William of Durban would have been far more familiar to those in his social group than Bernard son of Fida. Would society really choose this occasion to raise questions about Bernard's true paternity or Ermengard's or the archbishop's?[6]

It seems more likely that the practice comes from social habits outside our normal ken. Like the rhythms of the oath itself, it seems part of an incantation, bound up with the world of magic, love spells, maledictions, charms and countercharms. There are striking parallels to it in ancient incantatory practices from Babylonia and Egypt, adopted by Jews and spread by the Romans as far as Britain. In the early fourth century C.E., Rabbi Abaye said (reporting his mother's instructions), "All incantations . . . must contain the name of the patient's mother." The sentence was taken into the Babylonian Talmud, and the requirement—for far more than healing rites—was observed in Jewish magical spells well into the early modern period.[7] Sometime in the fifth century C.E. in upper Egypt, a lovesick Theon "to whom Proechia gave birth" buried a pair of wax dolls in sexual embrace along with an invocation of the forces of the netherworld to bring to him "with frenzied love and sexual intercourse . . . Euphemia to whom Dorothea gave birth"; a few decades earlier in Rome a heavy bettor on the races "bound" the angels and archangels to bring sickness and death on the charioteer "Cardelus, to whom Fulgentia gave birth."[8] Did such practices survive in lands in which Roman influence long remained strong, despite clerical hostility? If they did survive in an increasingly Christian Europe, they would not have been recorded. It is only for Jewish magic that we can confidently say yes. Yet the similarity between these ancient practices and the way people are named in Occitan oaths of fidelity is there to ponder. We know from the way that political references a half millennium old survive in the play songs and rhymes of children that an oral tradition can be a remarkable preservative even when the original sense of words has been totally lost. And as with those rhymes so with the oaths; the rhythms of the recitation themselves would have done much to fix the form. Is the familiar Mediterranean insult that cocks a finger at the sexual habits of an enemy's mother the last surviving remnant in our own age of this ancient usage?

Whatever may be the answer to this puzzle, by giving himself or herself a special name, one not otherwise used, the oath taker removes the occasion from the day-to-day world. Similarly, when scribes recorded these oaths for posterity, they just as strikingly left them undated, although on every other occasion they rarely failed to note at least the year in which the contract or agreement they were recording was made, and often enough the month and the day as well.[9] They seem to be saying that these are no ordinary moments or ordinary texts; like amulets and maledictions, like the Christian liturgy (which included a liturgy of malediction),[10] they connect the here and now to a higher, timeless order.

Word magic continues in the play of negatives through the oath, from the "non" in line 2 to the "sanz engan," "without treachery," at the end, a litany of promises not to harm, moving out in a sequence of synecdoches from the heart and hand, the arms and legs (the "limbs attached to your body"), to the property attached to that body and the castle for which the oath was given, and then beyond to the society—the "man and woman or men and women"—who might threaten that unity of person, body, property, and castle. It is especially negative in its most important, repeated, verbs—"non decebrai" (I will not deceive), with its full aura of possible treachery; "ne t'en tolrai" (I will not take), with its full aura of violence—which darkly mirror by antithesis the "true faith" that lies at the liturgy's heart.

Again we must ask, why? Why put fidelity in terms of what is to be avoided rather than what is to be done? To be sure, such had been the texture of oaths of fidelity since the ninth century, since the Carolingian emperors obliged all their free subjects to swear them; the tradition as it reached Ermengard and her contemporaries was already nearly a half millennium old.[11] If Bernard of Durban had been asked why these were the words he recited, he doubtless would have answered, "Because that is the way it has always been done. That is the oath my father swore and his father before him." And indeed, the oaths were formulaic in the extreme, even for an age and region in which all documents seem to be largely constructed from scribal boilerplate; this formulaic repetition so bored the eighteenth-century editors of the *Histoire générale de Languedoc* (the largest printed collection of these oaths) that, when they printed them, they regularly etceteraed all but proper names and a few indicative words. That is why we can safely reconstruct the oaths given to Ermengard, although few records survive: there are hundreds if not thousands of others that have survived, and aside from the proper names they are all but identical one to another.

To say they were formulaic and of great antiquity does not, however, answer why the pledge itself was almost entirely negative. Did they believe that acts of true faith are beyond counting, whereas acts of treachery can be precisely named and numbered? Perhaps. Or was it to recall that the Christian liturgy of malediction had made treachery the greatest of all crimes: "May he be swallowed up by the earth like Dathan and Abiron [who betrayed Moses in the desert] and burn in Hell with Judas the traitor."[12] Two centuries later, Dante would put the greatest traitors—Judas, Brutus, and Satan himself—in the lowest, frozen circle of Hell, following the intent if not the climate and clientele of this well-worn curse. To violate the oath, to betray her to whom one had sworn his faith, was to invite like punishment.

All these are possible answers. Yet they remain unsatisfying, for they do not really touch on the oaths' central conundrum. In the words "I will be faithful" (when it is included in the oaths, for in many it never appears),[13] the oath taker seems to offer trust beyond suspicion, support without stinting; yet the specifics with which the oaths are filled talk only of avoiding violence and deceit, and the few positive clauses (when they appear in the oaths of castellans) are narrow indeed, promising no more than to hand over the castle on demand and help recover it if enemies take it. They give an image of a crabbed and mean-spirited society, filled with suspicion if not with paranoia, where the best you can expect from those you count your friends is not to do you harm.

It is an image hard to pair with the loyal service of Peter Raymond of Narbonne and his family to Ermengard and her ancestors, or of the Escafredi, the Saint-Felix, and others like them to several generations of Trencavels. As common as these oaths are, it is hard to make of such bleak promises the building blocks of aristocratic society.[14]

There were, to be sure, some practical consequences especially from the promise to hand over the sworn castle on demand. This was decidedly not scribal boilerplate or mere formula. When reneged upon it could lead to serious contention, as in 1153 when Ugo Escafredi found himself caught at Roquefort-sur-Sor between his promise to render that castle to Raymond Trencavel and his oath of fidelity to his fellow castellan Jordan of Roquefort. Jordan himself was in dispute with Raymond Trencavel over some other issues, and Raymond demanded the castle; Ugo's refusal became one of the many issues that finally went to arbitration by the great barons of the region. Ugo knew that to hand Roquefort to his lord would be to betray his colleague; nevertheless, in the opinion of the arbiters, that did not excuse him from his obligation. He was bound, they said, not only to hand over the castle but to help Raymond force Jordan to "come to justice"; and so he finally agreed.[15]

This promise was what most clearly differentiated the oaths of castellans to their lords from the oaths of fidelity that joined the great aristocrats to each other—the oaths that solidified both temporary and life-long alliances and that set the final seal on every peace treaty. The former contained the promise to hand over the castle for which the oath had been sworn; the latter normally did not.[16] At one other point as well these oaths of the high aristocrats differed from those of castellans—in the promise "to be true as a man should be to his lady [lord] to whom he has commended himself by his hands," a promise that appears only in the oaths of castellans (and not always present even there). The oath of fidelity that the great aristocrats took to each other therefore did not mark subservience; it was these two special clauses that marked the particular dependence of village lords and castellans on higher lords and ladies, their free and honorable but very real subjection. And when on rare occasions we find one of these aristocrats promising another to give up castles on demand (as Viscount Bernard Ato was forced to promise Count Ramon Berenguer III of Barcelona in 1112), we know that the one has suffered a stinging defeat at the hands of the other.[17]

Yet, as important as these promises are, they occupy little place in the oaths themselves, which are so overwhelmingly preoccupied with renouncing harm, "evil deeds," and deceit. We must return again to the conundrum set by these promises—so central to the oaths that contemporaries sometimes referred to them simply as "oaths of life and limbs."[18] How is it to be resolved? The texts of the oaths by themselves will not answer. As with any liturgy or incantation or curse, to explain what is happening we must ultimately look outside it to the surrounding circumstances, to who uttered it, in whose presence, and on what occasion.

--==--

Rituals suffused all aspects of medieval life. The canonical hours set the daily round of the professional religious, of priests and monks; the liturgical succession of verses and psalms framed their year. Without our familiar clocks on the shelf and calendars on the wall, laymen likewise marked the passage of the day by the ringing of church bells and the passage of the year by the succession of holy days with their familiar processions and ceremonies; so too they marked the passages of their lives by the succession of baptism, marriage, and last rites. In much the same manner, fighting men, castellans, and aristocrats marked with their oaths of fidelity their passage into new roles and their entry into life-long communities.

Although castellans' oaths of fidelity rarely bear dates (at least not until the mid-twelfth century), internal evidence suggests they were commonly given on two kinds of occasions. The first was when an heir or heiress succeeded to a castle and to the fidelity it owed; at this moment the oath celebrated the crossing of a divide, if not from child to adult, at least from one who waits in the wings to full-fledged actor; the words bespoke a political coming of age.[19] The second was when an heir or heiress or widow succeeded to a lordship to which fidelity was due, or a new bishop mounted the episcopal throne or an abbot the abbatial chair.[20] Such a moment could not help but be one of tension, if not indeed of crisis, a time when castle holders might lay claim to new revenues or powers, when some with an eye to aggrandizement might seek allies in a neighboring lordship; it might be a time for a rival claimant to promote a rebellion, a time for negotiation, a time to bring in the "friends." We may imagine, then, the new lord or lady holding solemn court at Christmas or Easter, receiving the oaths of her faithful men and women, or, in the larger lordships (such as those of the Trencavels), her solemn peregrination from castle to castle, surrounded by a cadre of courtiers, receiving oaths and hospitality in the presence of neighbors and local notables, fixing in memory the pomp and luxury and solemnity of the occasion, making visible to all the reality of the new power.[21]

Although much of the language of gesture on these occasions is lost, there is still enough to raise in our imaginations the rich ceremony that attended on them, each participant surrounded by her or his kinsmen, followers, and dependents; the priest there with his copy of the Scriptures or with some saint's bones (evoked in the texts by an occasional "per hec sancta"); the solemn clasping of hands and lowering of eyes; the solemn chant repeated—the younger men and women coached through the lines, perhaps, by the priest or a family elder, as brides and grooms are led through traditional wedding vows today, the older ones doubtless so habituated that they know the phrases by heart; the scribe copying the oath on little slips of parchment, a text he knows so well that he cannot keep his mind on whether the words are Latin or vernacular (the scribal copies that survive are occasionally entirely in Occitan, occasionally entirely in Latin, but most often Latin with frequent slippage into the vernacular). All conspired to impress deep seriousness on the moment: the company, the visible permanence of the oath being inscribed in ink, the magic of the holy objects, the magic of the rhythmic words.

The ceremony would have been less brilliant but just as serious when the multiple castellans of a fortification took their oaths to each other, or when the *milites castri* (who did the grunt work) swore their oaths to those they served.

For just as villages had multiple lords, so castles had multiple castellans, whereas the actual task of manning the stone keeps was left in turn to their followers.[22] At the border town of Mirepoix, where the interests of the counts of Foix encountered those of the family that held Carcassonne, five men at least (three of them brothers) swore fidelity to the widowed Ermengard of the Trencavel clan in the late 1070s; some eighty years later, in 1159, eleven lords of Mirepoix swore fidelity to the count of Foix. In both of these groups were men who took the fierce cognomen Batalla, "Battle," members of a family solidly entrenched in the village. They are the first castellans we hear of there in 1063, two brothers who give their portions of the castle to the widowed countess Rangard of Carcassonne and promise their help in distraining a third brother to give his share. A William Batalla and his brother are likewise among the group who swore their oaths in 1159. But even in the late eleventh century, others who were not of the Batalla family were castellans at Mirepoix, including the high-country potentate William of Alaigne, who took the title of viscount. Along with four others who appear to be unrelated, the same Batallas who swore oaths for Mirepoix to Countess Rangard and then to her daughter Ermengard and then (at least those still alive) to Ermengard's son, Viscount Bernard Ato, also swore oaths for the same castle to William of Alaigne.[23] At other castles it was the same story. So, high in the Corbières at Niort in the 1130s, eighteen men, including six sets of brothers, gave oaths for the castle to Raymond of Niort and his brother William, some of them (that we know about, most probably there were others that we don't) at the same time giving their oaths along with Raymond and William of Niort to Viscount Bernard Ato's widow Cecilia.[24]

THE COMMUNITIES OF OATH TAKERS

Just as these men shared their castle lordship with others and at each would have sworn oaths not just to their overlords but also to their fellow castellans, so likewise the local fighting men would have sworn such oaths in turn to their own castellan. And each time a holding changed, through succession, gift, sale, confiscation, or grant, each time a dispute was negotiated and an agreement drawn up to end it, there would have been a new round of oath taking.[25] The hundreds of oaths that survive in such collections as the Trencavel cartulary, and the additional hundreds that once existed in the archives of Ermengard of Narbonne as they did in every lordly treasure chest, are thus but a tiny fraction of the thousands upon thousands that were sworn in Occitania in Ermengard's lifetime; it is a simple exercise in permutation to calculate how many are represented by the one document that records the oath of eighteen "knights of Montréal" to Raymond Trencavel and his son Roger in August 1162; if each of these knights at some moment had sworn his fidelity to each of the others, the total would have been 306.

Although some of these people may have been local toughs (like the nineteen "men of Arifat" who, "at the command" of four other "lords of Arifat," swore to guarantee the oaths of one of the lords to Viscount Bernard Ato and Cecilia), others belonged to a regional nobility at the very least; some spent their lives in the company of the great. William of Alaigne, whom we just met at Mirepoix, owed oaths for Queille, Rennes, Routier, and Taillebois in the high Corbières as well; Raymond of Niort also swore fidelity for Rennes, Routier, Tournebouix, Montaut, Castelpors, and Lastours—most of them castles in the Corbières, but the last in the mountains north of Carcassonne.[26] Two of the knights who swore oaths for Montréal in 1162 were no less personages than William of Saint-Felix, sometime vicar of Carcassonne and from the 1150s to the 1180s one of the closest advisors to Raymond Trencavel and his son Roger, and Hugh of Roumegoust, also sometime vicar, first of Carcassonne and then of Rennes, and another leading member of the Trencavel entourage from the 1160s into the 1190s.[27] They were castellans here and doubtless many other places as well; the real military duties would have been the task of their local clients. This was one of the ways in which the ultimate overlords, people of the rank of the Trencavels and Ermengard of Narbonne, would have assured the strict loyalty and subservience of the strongholds that in turn assured their dominion.

Oaths of fidelity were thus far more than individual contracts or even the markers of political and generational coming of age. They created, repaired, and remade communities.

Among the most obvious of these communities were those formed by brothers, who so often appear as joint oath-takers as well as actors in disputes and agreements concerning castles; whatever may have been the division of their father's other properties, brothers held their patrimonial castles in common, for this was the very stuff of status, and joint holding continued to travel down the generational tree to succeeding groups of cousins, keeping alive the memory of their common ancestry;[28] that (as well as donations and dowries) is the most likely explanation for the halves and quarters of castles that people held, occasionally expressed as occupancy for two, four, or eight months out of the year. Sometimes the communities included sisters as well when, whether by testament, dowry, or intestate succession, they too became castellans.[29]

No less visible was the entire community of the castle, the lords of the castle, such as those we just met at Arifat and Montréal, whose unity was assumed in all the promises to deliver and defend, a unity that in time of war was, of course, indispensable. It was a community whose loyalties one great lord could deliver to another as a dowry, as security, or as a peace offering along with the towers and stone walls its members protected.[30]

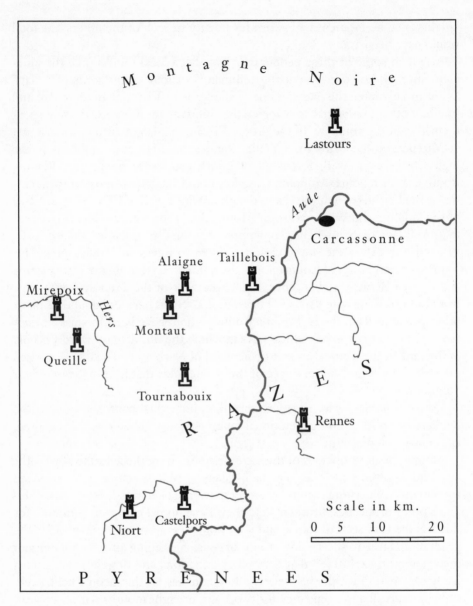

Castles for which William of Alaigne and Raymond of Niort swore oaths of fidelity

Implicit in the oaths, and perhaps the most basic of all, was the community of those who lived by their faith, whose only subjection was by their freely given oath, and whose only obligations were those of honor. Taking the oath permanently separated those who took it from those who would never take it; the oath drew a line around a consecrated elite.[31]

To be sure, there were occasions when people who were not of this elite also took oaths of fidelity. At two moments that we know about, all the heads of households in the city of Carcassonne did so, once to Count Ramon Berenguer III of Barcelona, promising to fight Viscount Bernard Ato, and once to Bernard Ato himself. Similar oaths could very well have been given in other cities as well, although they have left no trace in the archives. Neither of the Carcassonne oaths is dated, and we can only surmise when they were given; the most likely dates seem to be between 1120, when Bernard Ato was expelled from Carcassonne (probably with the connivance of the count of Barcelona), and 1124, when he recovered it. It was an exceptional time in the history of the Trencavel domains and the Barcelonese attempts to dominate them, one that called for extraordinary measures; the city's alliance was needed in warfare, and the oath was the standard means to seal such an alliance.[32] Yet within these particular oaths a difference is clearly marked that sets them off from others: although the count of Barcelona appears, as expected, as "Ramon son of the late Mahalt," the inhabitants of the city bear their common names: "Amelius of Carcassonne, Amicus Raymond of Salvaza, Peter of Vitrac, Pons his brother, Bonmacip, . . ."; their mothers are nowhere to be found. To take or receive an oath in one's mother's name seems to have been a privilege reserved for those of high status; collectively the city may for a moment have moved into the world of the great, but its individual householders stayed where they were; on these city dwellers other obligations not freely undertaken still weighed heavily.

Counts and archbishops, castellans of a quarter of a castle, long-time intimates of Viscountess Ermengard or the Trencavels, modest village lords who stayed far from dynastic politics, groups of brothers and sisters, cousins who shared the inheritance of a grandfather or great-grandfather, all took oaths of fidelity. What did they have in common? The peasants laboring in the field might think of them all as lords and ladies, and a scribe attentive to his work might remember to mark them as *dominus* or *domina*, *en* or *na*. But to a modest Raymond of Portiragnes or Berenger of Lec, the distance between themselves and Ermengard or Raymond Trencavel or the archbishop of Narbonne must have seemed as great and as untraversable as the distance between themselves and the villagers who respectfully addressed them as "my lord."[33] Some were subservient to those to whom they swore; many more exchanged oaths with those who were their equals. What did they share that made it important for them to swear not to harm someone else?

For each of them the answer is the same. Everyone who swore fidelity belonged to a community—of siblings or fellow castellans, of followers with their lords, of allies, of fellow city rulers, or of recent enemies. Most of the time, these were the people one rubbed shoulders with in camp and in court. In the political world of Occitania, these communities were fundamental. Control of territory and success in warfare depended on their stability; so, we might guess (although the documents do not reveal it), did ordinary social life beyond the household. Yet, at the same time, these communities were fundamentally fragile. Brothers and sisters, once they had shared the paternal inheritance, might be pulled in different directions by their marriage partners and their alliances; fellow castellans even more so, as the example of Hugh Escafredi at Roquefort shows; allies might in time become enemies, depending on the flow of dynastic politics; and enemies even if reconciled could (and most often did) become enemies again.

The magic of the oath and the aristocratic values it served to internalize worked, however haltingly, to counteract those threats of disintegration. The oath taker repeated "non tolrai . . . non decebrai," "I will not take, I will not harm, I will not deceive," because within those communities injury and deception were what were most feared. They were what would pull those communities asunder.

And pull apart they did, although how often there is no way to measure. At such moments all social and political pressures concentrated on one goal—to re-create the community that was lost. And in the arguments and complaints, in the bitter words and recriminations, as well as in the gestures by which friends and lords sought to heal the breach, we can see fidelity not only as sentiment but as process as well.[34] We can see the refined connections it was expected to create between emotion and cohesion, why another word for fidelity was love.

CHAPTER ELEVEN
ANGER, CONFLICT, AND
RECONCILIATION

T he contrary of love, and the joy it gave to those whom love embraced, was anger and the vengeful wrath it generated. The two emotions were constantly in dialogue, and if we attend carefully to the words of poets and disputants—for both spoke the same language—we will begin to understand something of what the oaths of fidelity meant to those who gave and received them and how those oaths gave shape to the world that Ermengard knew. Here first is Arnaut Daniel around 1200, rubbing together tears and tenderness, joy and grief:

Si be'm vau per tot a es daill,   Though I move through all backward,
mos pessamens lai vos assaill;   my thoughts leap over there to you;
q' ieu chant e vaill   I sing and am strong
pel joi que'ns fim   for the joy we had
lai on partim;   there where we parted;
mout sovens l' uoills mi muoilla   often my eyes grow wet
d' ira e de plor   with anger and tears
e de doussor,   and with tenderness
car per joi ai que'm duoilla.[1]   for through joy I have what grieves me.

Here now in the words of the participants is the story of a feud that set Polverellus and his brother against three brothers of Auriac, a feud that their friends and companions from the entourage of Raymond Trencavel attempted to resolve sometime in the 1150s.

> *Polverellus of Auriac and his brother William Peter*: We swore mutual oaths with Pons of Auriac that we would not take the castle of Auriac from him nor he from us, and that he would come to our aid if any man or woman took it from us, as we would do the same for him, until we (or he) recovered it. [Polverellus here exactly follows the words of the oath of fidelity.] Yet Pons, along with Raymond de Cuc and Isarn Ademar, captured and destroyed the castle that we had rightfully handed over to Lord Raymond Trencavel, viscount of Beziers, to whom the castle of Auriac belongs. We handed it over though Pons, Raymond, and Isarn refused to agree. Then Isarn Ademar himself built a fortification there, which his father never had. Along with their supporters, the three committed an infinite number of grievous deeds, breaking and burning churches, robbing and killing

men and women, cutting down trees and vines, and doing many other evil things to us.

Pons of Auriac, Raymond de Cuc, and Isarn Ademar, brothers: Polverellus and William Peter took the lands and rights of our brother, Bernard Pons, which Bernard had given to us. And they committed many—indeed, nearly an infinite number—of evil acts against us, breaking and burning churches, robbing and killing men and women, cutting down trees, and doing many other things to our great damage.[2]

Although the word *ira* is not used here, anger is present in nearly every phrase, anger at the deception, anger at the destruction. The long litany of evils each side had committed—the "dan" and "malfatz," which the scribe quickly Latinized as "damna" and "malefactis intolerabilibus et infinitis"—was exactly the large rhetorical gesture expected to explain and justify zealous anger; it was a figure used repeatedly in the twelfth century by chroniclers, poets, and theologians.[3] Yet it was not "mere rhetoric." The anger was itself an important fact, perhaps the most important fact for the arbiters to consider; the words expressing it were not decorations—they were essential. "Dan" and "malfatz" were both parties' primary charge against the other. And the repeated use of these words by the troubadours would have given them an even deeper resonance.[4]

Polverellus and William Peter's tales take us into the midst of a war between Raymond Trencavel and his allies and the count of Toulouse, a war whose major consequence was Raymond Trencavel's capture and imprisonment. In this conflict the events at Auriac—a major fortress in the marcher lands between Carcassonne and Toulouse—in all likelihood played an important role. Polverellus had been captured and put to ransom by Toulousain forces a decade earlier; his freedom without payment was one of the many provisions of the treaty of 1143 that dislodged Ermengard of Narbonne from the marriage bed and political clutches of Alphonse Jordan. We can understand his determined faithfulness to Raymond Trencavel. There is good reason to think, furthermore, that these castellans at Auriac were cousins.[5] And yet, although these men were presenting their charges and countercharges to a group of arbiters assembled by Raymond Trencavel, all of them familiar companions of those who were fighting, the ambient politics of dynastic warfare—the castle had been "rightfully handed over to Raymond Trencavel"—was squeezed into the narrow corner of an ablative clause. The core of the gravamens was the expectation of mutual trust and mutual help that was fundamental to the oath of fidelity, an expectation that had been deceived.

To sense the nature of the emotion involved in disputes such as this, we can turn for a moment from archival documents to the words of poets. Behind their larger-than-life portrayals we can hear an echo of our ordinary castellans whose disputes could so quickly turn to mayhem and the rituals invoked to reestablish peace and friendship.

One of the most vivid accounts of peacemaking in the epic literature of the age occurs in the poem now known by the name of its leading figure, *Raoul de Cambrai*. The second part of the poem, probably composed around 1180 using materials from a long oral tradition, relates the war that set Bernier, the vassal who had killed his lord Raoul in combat, against Raoul's nephew, Gautier. Late in the story, Bernier and Gautier and their relatives bring their feud into the king's presence, countering insult with insult and sword stroke with sword stroke as the king, the abbot of Saint-Germain, and the great men of the royal court urge that hatred be dissolved in mutual forgiveness:

> When Gautier heard this, he was beside himself. He started shouting, . . . "By God the judge of all things, you'll never see me reconciled with him—I'll cut his arms and legs off first!" Then Bernier said, "This is fool's talk I hear. You'll not live to see February, even if it means I'll never taste meat and drink again." . . . Then Gautier . . . , "You low-born bastard, you exceed all bounds! You have killed my uncle . . . , your lawful overlord, like a proven traitor!" . . . "You are altogether in the wrong," was young Bernier's reply. "As you know to your cost, I dealt you such a blow that it left a deep wound in your left side. I regret it. . . . For the love of God . . . will this war drag on forever? Do please accept compensation, noble and excellent knight." . . .
>
> Young Bernier, with his fearless countenance . . . was wearing only his breeches; he had no shirt on. He lay prostrate with arms outstretched in the form of a cross, tendering his burnished sword, and in the king's presence begged young Gautier's mercy. . . . The abbot of Saint Germain has arrived, bringing with him many precious relics. He speaks out loud. . . . "My lord Guerri [Gautier's uncle], for the love of the God of majesty, this war has gone on too long. Bernier is making you an offer in good will; if you don't accept, you'll be reproached for it." . . . "Barons," he said, "hear my suggestion. Let each of you bring forward his good, sharp sword, and yield it to your enemies so that, please God, you may be reconciled, in return for what you will hear me say: may all the sins forgiven to you be likewise forgiven to them on Judgment Day." . . .
>
> Seven hundred men take up the shout: "Oh Gautier, for the sake of him to whom all is subject, for the love of God, raise them to their feet!" "God!" said Gautier, "how it grieves me to do it!" Quickly and promptly he raises them up, and they exchange embraces like true friends and kinsmen.[6]

All here is exaggerated—language, sentiments, and numbers. Bernier and Gautier are epic figures. Their emotions must therefore be epic as well; so too the gestures—the repeated pleas for reconciliation, the outbursts of outraged honor, the invocation of divine punishment, the united voices of seven hundred men—by which the feud is calmed and the enemies transformed into friends. These gestures, however, are not pure fantasy. They are only exaggerated versions of the gestures and rituals commonly used to calm disputes such as that between Polverellus and his enemies at Auriac.

In the arbiters' judgment as in the poetic fiction there is no talk of punishment, no thought of getting even (although Raymond Trencavel commanded the court, and he—so Polverellus and William Peter implied—had likewise been deceived and betrayed), no purposing to enlarge the feud. On the contrary, the arbiters ordered Polverellus and William Peter to forgive their opponents all the injuries they had done; Pons, Raymond, and Isarn are likewise to forgive and to undo the major destruction they had caused. Fortifications were to be restored and oaths of fidelity sworn. If any further conflicts broke out between these groups, the arbiters added, "they should be reconciled with the counsel of the knights of Auriac." The arbiters' decision was a call to order and a stern reminder to the other lords of Auriac never again to give dissension its head.[7] They too, they were reminded, had responsibilities to keep the peace, to maintain the unity of the castle's little "family." Only when that proved impossible was a dispute to be brought once again to the viscount's attention.

To our modern sensibilities such sudden leaps from outraged anger to amicable embrace seem, if not fantasy (and badly imagined fantasy at that) or a pathological condition worthy of inclusion in a clinician's handbook, then an expression of the "nervous sensibility" and "uncontrolled emotionality" of a bygone age and its "perpetual oscillation . . . between cruelty and pious tenderness."[8] Commonly for us (when we indulge in explaining them), emotions and their expression are imprinted in our genetic code (if we are Darwinians), or the adult burdens of our infant socialization (if we are Freudians), or the felt expression of chemical changes in our bodies (if we are of the Prozac and Ritalin generation).[9] They are the emanations of our "inner" selves and their treatment the realm of the psychologist, psychotherapist, or pharmacist. As "feelings" they are at least in part beyond our willed control. We therefore find it very difficult to believe that a powerful emotion could so easily be turned into its polar opposite, or that anyone could be ordered by a court or urged by a crowd into doing so. Yet here they are doing just that, not only in the imagination of poets but in the drab workaday prose of a court scribe. At few moments are we more vividly aware of the distance that separates our world from that of Ermengard of Narbonne.

In Ermengard's world—the world of *Raoul* and Polverellus—the two realms we so carefully separate, the public realm of law, property, and public policy and the private realm of anger, love, hurt, and healing, were all one. It may therefore be difficult if not impossible for us to feel what she and her contemporaries felt or even to imagine those feelings, to project ourselves inside them. Although we can translate medieval terms for emotions into our modern languages, it may be the case that the medieval words do not talk about feelings in the ways we think ours do.[10]

Words for emotions are nowhere more problematic than where conflicts and their resolution are concerned. For anger, grief, shame—and love as well, as we will soon see—were intimately bound up with honor, especially the honor committed by the oath of fidelity. And honor is a public, a political value, visible only in the eyes of others, in the eyes of the community of men and women whose respect alone made honor real.[11] Anger, and the physical acts to show it, was the public display of injured honor; and it was only when that injury had been publicly recognized by the voices of the community, by the friends and neighbors called to arbitrate, that wounded honor could be soothed, combative honor calmed, and amity restored.

Again the poets are the best witnesses to the coupling of honor with the emotion of joy, as in this song by Jaufré Rudel

Er ai ieu joy e suy jauzitz,	Now I have joy and am joyful
e restauratz en ma valor,	and restored to my honor.
e non iray ja mai alhoar,	And I'll never go elsewhere
ni non querrai autruy conquistz	or seek what others have gained
. . . .	. . . .
Lonc temps ai estat en dolor,	Long I've been in distress
e de tot mon afar marritz,	and so troubled about my situation
qu'anc no fuy tan fort endurmitz	that I never went so sound asleep
que no'm rissides de paor.	that I didn't wake in fear.
. . . .	. . . .
Mout mi tenon a gran honor	They hold me in great honor,
totz selhs cuy ieu n'ey obeditz	those whom I have obeyed,
quar a mon joy suy revertitz:	for I have come back to my joy,
e laus en lieys e Dieu e lhor.[12]	and praise her and God and them for it.

Just as they sometimes witness the collision of honor and *dan* (which meant both injury and hurt), as in these words which Raimbaut de Vaqueiras addressed to the newly crowned Latin emperor of Constantinople in 1204:

E si no's meillur' en la flor,	And if the flower is not improved,
lo frugz poiri' esser malvais;	the fruit can be rotten;
e gart se q'al seu tort non bais,	let him beware lest he decline to his wrong,
qe pujatz es en grant honor,	who has risen to a great honor;
et es bels e de bon aire;	and is handsome and of noble birth;
e se vol creire mos sermos,	and if he wishes to attend to my words
ja no'i aura anta ni dan,	he will never have shame or hurt,
anz sera granz honors e pros,	but rather honor and profit,
car se pert cels c'ab lui estan,	for if he abandons those who stand with him,
tart venran de son repaire.[13]	men will be slow to serve.

Arbiters might voice their hope for concord, as they did in settling the dispute between Polverellus and his enemies. They could increase that hope by summoning the greatest people in the land to arbitrate, as Raymond Trencavel did in 1163, when he invited Ermengard and several of her close companions along with the bishop of Carcassonne, two products of the new Italian law schools (Masters Maurinus and Osbertus), and some of the most important noblemen of his court to join in settling the dispute that had set Ricsovendis of Termes and her husband against her brothers William and Raymond of Termes, when sister and brothers could not agree on their portions of the castle, the village, and command of the castle's fighting men.[14]

At the same time, they could not hide their expectation that within the community of castles or the assumed community of kinship, interest would continue to grate against interest and inevitably lead to conflict. We can see such expectations in another settlement negotiated in 1163 between the Saissacs and the Escafredi, two important families in the entourage of Raymond Trencavel. Like other lords, they shared the lordship of a number of castles, and on one occasion at the castle of Montréal, approximately twenty kilometers west of Carcassonne, their differing interests had led to a rift and then to violence. When they came to arbitration there were the usual stories of destruction and earlier agreements made under threat, the usual arguments over who held what part of the castle and the proper division of the revenues that came from its lordship. What the arbiters also had to contend with was that the wars of one family might not be the wars of the other. And so, among other things, they decided that

> Isarn Jordani [of Saissac] and his brother and nephews may use the castle of Montréal to make war against anyone they wish except for the lord of Carcassonne and Hugh Escafredi and his brothers; and the knights of the castle must support them against all persons to whom they may wish to do justice [i.e., on whom they want to revenge themselves] except for the lord of Carcassonne and Hugh Escafredi and his brothers.[15]

Most of the disputes that Ermengard and her neighbors, the Trencavel viscounts, were called upon to help settle were of this kind, disputes among heirs over the division of inheritances or disputes between fellow castellans. At least those were the settlements whose records Ermengard and the Trencavels thought worth preserving in their own archives.[16]

Within these communities fidelity did not exclude conflict. It did, however, imply that once conflict broke out and both sides had put their honor on the line that there would be negotiation and arbitration, that the "common friends" could intervene and bring about a resolution. That was incumbent even when the fidelity was not symmetrical, incumbent on Ermengard as viscountess who received the fidelity of her followers as well as on those who swore their fidelity to her. To a modern mind, the results can sometimes be surprising; where we (well trained by tough-minded modern politicians) would expect vindictiveness, a cunning vengeance, we find instead a desire to mollify, the recognition that lady and *fidelis* were condemned to live together and had better make the best of it.[17]

Here is one striking case. About twenty-five kilometers southwest of Narbonne, on the banks of a little stream called the Aussou in the first hills of the Corbières, is the village of Montséret. Just to its north stand the rough ruins of a castle. In 1153, this castle had Ermengard at loggerheads with one of the men who figured prominently in both her court and that of the Trencavels, William of Durban. Early in the century, a man named Bernard Amati and his sons controlled Montséret; they occasionally used its name as their own. Bernard Amati was a major figure in the court of the Trencavel viscount Bernard Ato and turned Montséret over to him when the viscount declared war on Ermengard's father, Aymeri II, in 1124.[18] Aymeri's response was to raze the castle ("as an act of justice," *pro justicia*, said the document from Ermengard's court recalling these events nineteen years later); it may have been one of Aymeri's last acts before departing to join the forces of the king of Aragon before the walls of Fraga. At some later date the site came into the hands of the Durban family. And when it did, William of Durban and his sons rebuilt the fortification without Ermengard's assent and to her great displeasure. It was while in the field against the count of Toulouse in Provence that the great men of her court decided it was time to negotiate a compromise. We immediately recognize their names on the witness list—William of Laredorte, William of Poitiers, Raymond of Ouveilhan, Gerald of Breuil, and others. Although the castle had been built without her consent, Ermengard agreed that William's son would hold the castle from her and swear fidelity and would do so likewise to her children "if she should have any"; to other possible heirs not even the oath would be due. Those who shared the castle with the Durbans would likewise owe Ermengard their oaths, but nothing more.[19]

We recognize here the same imperatives as those we saw in the arbitration of the dispute at Auriac: whatever else, restore a community of fidelity. The members of Ermengard's court needed no prompting to know that everyone's honor was fully engaged in whatever they negotiated. If the agreement did not satisfy the Durban's honor and Ermengard's, it would only become grounds for further feud, and they were friends with both sides. They knew instinctively as well that theirs was an on-going community, and claims of right and claims of honor would pass from generation to generation as far as they could imagine. The Durbans were not Ermengard's creatures. Castellans at numerous castles, they had numerous knights sworn to their loyalty, knights they were most likely commanding in that very campaign of 1153. They were as familiar with the court of Carcassonne as they were with Narbonne, and by their presence in both formed one of the many links of friendship in the alliance.[20] Ermengard needed them. At the same time, they needed Ermengard; for it was their easy access to her court, their position as "faithful men" of their lady, that opened the door to patronage and favor and allowed them to maintain their dominance over their own men. Everything conspired to push Ermengard, the Durbans, and the courtiers who surrounded them to heal the breach.

For Ermengard to yield was also a sign of her grace, as was her ability to bring peace out of wrath and discord. Both were gifts freely given, benevolences in the root sense, given without expectation of equivalent return, because in fact there could be no equivalent. Like God's, these gifts of grace were unaccountable; one could seek them, but only by an act of submission, by putting oneself "in her hands." For Ermengard, as for other great lords, such submission was the surest sign of her dominance, and it was unfailingly mentioned in the narrative of arbitration: "unde in manu domine Ermengardis convenerunt," "whence they agreed to put the matter in the hands of Lady Ermengard."[21]

Ermengard's hands were welcomed well beyond the limits of her viscounty. She was sometimes an arbiter of choice for those who were not her men and women, in villages and cities in which she exercised no rights of lordship, especially, it would seem, when the rights of women were in question; of the three documented disputes she was called on to arbitrate in Trencavel territory, two involved the claims of women to a share in their paternal inheritance. In one of them Ermengard demonstrated her grace with a highly unusual gesture: to resolve the dispute, she added a hundred solidi of her own to the sum the brother paid his sister to induce her to relinquish her claim.[22]

We could not be farther here from the modern ideal of disinterested judge judging by impersonal norms. This is personal lordship, desiring to assuage rather than impose, to soothe emotion and restore cohesion rather than to divide right from wrong. As such it was the necessary adjuvant to a community whose lines of fracture were held only by the promise of faith.

ARCHBISHOP RICHARD AND ERMENGARD'S FATHER

Fidelity and the oath that promised it thus lived in multiple worlds of both time and timelessness, of both particular places and groups and those which stretched outward to encompass all who lived by their sworn faith, the community of honor and grace. The group of *fideles* imitated the Christian community in linking time to eternity, the particular community to the whole body of the faithful.[23] Most often their ethos took form in what they did and when and how they did it, rather than in what they said. Occasionally, however, when a cleric of literary pretensions was involved in a dispute and shaped it around the fidelity of his adversary (as the castellan Polverellus did at Auriac), we are graced with an elaborate development of the theme. Given the circumstances that provoked such tellings, they inevitably take the form of narratives rather than abstract rules. The richest example is surely a letter that Archbishop Richard of Narbonne dictated sometime after 1117.[24] Addressing it to posterity rather than to any particular group of his contemporaries (although he surely would not have imagined anyone reading it nine hundred years later and in a tongue that did not as yet exist), he carefully unfolded his version of the events that brought him to anger.

Be it known to all faithful men of the Catholic Church both present and future, that when lord Dalmacius of holy memory, archbishop of Narbonne, died, the honors [i.e., lands and rights] of his widowed church came into the hands of Aymeri I, viscount of the city, and of his wife Mahalt. They brought them into subjection, though in accordance with the evil customs of the land these honors did not belong to them but to the count. After some time had passed, Bishop Bertrand of Nîmes was transferred to the archbishopric of Narbonne by the Roman pope, the clergy and people, and the bishops of the province of Narbonne. But because Aymeri rejected him, Bertrand was unable peacefully to possess either the see or its honors. When the viscount went to Jerusalem, Bertrand was deposed from the archbishopric by judgment of the Roman See. Meanwhile, Aymeri's wife and sons continued to hold the honors of the church and by wrongful possession confiscated whatever they could to their own use and lordship.

A short time later, the church thus stripped of its goods and honors, I, Richard, cardinal-priest of the Roman church and abbot of Saint-Victor of Marseille, was promoted to rule it by Paschal II who was then the apostolic lord, with the advice and at the request of all the clergy and people. I did not know at the time of the fraud and evil that had happened to the goods of the church. Meanwhile, Aymeri, the son of the other Aymeri who had died at Jerusalem, succeeded to the viscounty. Following the custom of his ancestors, he came with some of the barons of his land and did homage to me with his own hands [fecit mihi hominium propriis manibus] as he should have done, and he received from my hands the fiefs [fevodia] which he held from the church; these I gave him in the same way as Guifred, who was archbishop of the church before Lord Dalmacius, had given them to Berenger, Aymeri [II's] grandfather. I did this in the presence of the universal synod of the province of Narbonne.

After this, but before he made the oath to me that he ought to do, I beseeched him as my faithful friend and man that he should tell me what fiefs he held of the church and what other honors of the church his [deceased] father and his mother, who was then present, and their bailiffs held. For I knew nothing of all this. I had confidence that he—as one who ought to be faithful to the church his lord—would tell me the truth; for he had held and possessed nearly all of it for a long time and was therefore in a position to know. When he answered this question he lied to me and we began to argue. He said that certain rights within the city were divided between us in a manner other than what was written about them, that my predecessors had increased them for his ancestors, and that some which his mother had newly taken over were entirely among his rights.

From the opening sentence, this is a charged narrative, and meant to be a potent one. The archbishop leaves no doubt that he is arguing a case before the court of posterity and preparing an instrument for his successors to use to regain what he has lost. Yet although Richard was a monk as well as a cardinal and an archbishop, there is much talk of evil deeds but no explicit trace of the Evil One and his minions, no attempt to turn Aymeri into Judas or the Antichrist. Every paragraph of this complaint breathes the heated atmosphere of the great reform movement that had been shaking the Church for nearly half a century, yet there is little here to match Pope Gregory VII's thundering in his famous letter to Bishop Hermann of Metz, "All good Christians are more properly to be called kings than are evil princes; for the former, seeking the glory of God, rule themselves rigorously; but the latter . . . oppress others tyrannically. The former are the body of the true Christ; the latter, the body of the Devil."[25]

In Richard's letter the moralizing instead finds another target, one that is surely meant to rouse a lay audience and to touch Aymeri and his barons to the quick. From beginning to end the narrative is patterned on the terms of the oath of fidelity and the machinery of arbitration that allowed fidelity to be restored. Following the standard formula, Aymeri has sworn not to deprive the archbishop of his life or limbs or the church of its honors. He has promised not to deceive; yet he has lied and so has betrayed his oath. Richard directly questions his opponent's honor. In the later language of the dueling code, he "gives him the lie."

Richard, however, is not completely ingenuous himself. You would not know from reading the letter that Richard and Aymeri II were cousins, that both were descended from Viscount Berenger I, the man who decades earlier had impeached Archbishop Guifred for simony and many other crimes at a church council in Arles. In Richard's portrayal, however, Guifred is his innocent predecessor.[26] It seems likely that after the difficulties seating Bertrand, bishop of Nîmes, as archbishop (a story we know about essentially through Richard's account of it), the pope and the young viscount, Ermengard's father, settled on Richard because he was a member of the ruling family, thus returning to a centuries-old tradition of choosing the archbishop from their midst. Aymeri II clearly did not know what he was getting. Yet even if Richard had been a child-oblate at Saint-Victor, it is hard to believe that, at one moment or another, he would not have heard family stories of the relations between Guifred and the viscount his grandfather. Did he also know that at least some of the documents that he found in his archives were Guifred's forgeries? If he did, he shows no sign of caring, since the forgeries were all in his church's favor.

Aymeri II, then, has done homage and received in return the fiefs he will hold of the church "as Guifred had given them to his grandfather." There is a problem, however: those fiefs were not specified; Richard has to ask Aymeri what they were. Here, in Richard's eyes, is the first test of Aymeri's fidelity, and in his eyes the viscount fails. He lies. Although he is the archbishop's "friend and man," what he says is contradicted by the archbishop's charters. In Aymeri's eyes, in contrast, it is doubtless an issue of one man's truth against another's. From that point on, every move seems carefully choreographed.

First come the "common friends" to intervene and attempt to find a resolution:

In the end [Richard continued] he could not refute my charters and testimony [i.e., the documents that Guifred had left in the archiepiscopal archives], that of all the aforesaid rights, half belonged to the church, both now and in the future, and that his fiefs were reduced in the churches and portions of tithes that he had given to the church of Narbonne. Through common friends an agreement was negotiated between us; they asked that I increase his fiefs and that he give up to the church all the other things that at the time were in dispute between us, as was right. As an addition to his fief I gave him one-third of half of the *botaticum*; at the same time I kept as the rights of the church half of all the things that had been in contention between us, and he by his charter relinquished them.

Sometime after that certain evil persons came from him, saying he did not wish any further issues to arise between us that would provoke us to anger, pretending he wished always henceforth to behave peacefully and faithfully toward the church and me. They added that there was one right that my predecessors neither had nor claimed while his ancestors had levied it for a long time without anyone raising a quarrel about it: that is half the duty on goods, which is called *compras* in the vernacular. He wished to be specific about this and mention it by name, lest later on we should be aroused to anger over it.

I replied that (as was indeed the case) I knew nothing about this, but if he desired this so much I would put him on his soul and faith, for he was a man of the church and of me and therefore obliged to be faithful to me and to tell the truth; but if at any time I should discover by charters or witnesses that my predecessors sought or held that right, I would demand it and wish to have it. And so, keeping these rights with ill will and fraud, he took an oath "of life and limbs and fidelity" for all the honors of the church which he had or should have.

Some time later, I was leafing through the charters of the church and discovered that my predecessor Guifred had claimed this tax [i.e., the *compras*], had demanded it in a plea, and recovered it. When I discovered this I summoned Aymeri not once, not twice, but many times, both myself and through my friends and his, admonishing him by the fidelity he had sworn to me, by the homage he had done, that he not wrong the church by stealing its honor from me. Saying that if he claimed any right in the aforesaid tax, that we should go together before the good men of the land, who only wish that he and I should be in peace and concord, and that he should do what they decide.

The major questions of the reform movement are not here in dispute—the selling of prelacies and priesthoods, the granting of the symbols of episcopal office by kings and emperors, counts and viscounts. It is rather the humdrum, but ever so important, questions of whether the revenues from the city's burgeoning commerce—the compras, the botaticum, the salt taxes, the gate tolls, the tithes and revenues of churches—will flow into the treasure chests of the viscount or the archbishop. The viscount's insistence on what he claims to be his share is what Richard equates with the betrayal of his life and limbs, his castles, and the honor of his church and himself.

On the advice of the "common friends," Richard says, he has increased the viscount's fief with a portion of the botaticum, while the viscount abandons half of all the revenues he has claimed to be his alone. Then comes a second test, the issue of the compras. Here again, Aymeri is put "on his soul and faith" and takes the oath of fidelity (again in Richard's eyes) "with ill will and fraud." Here again the archbishop attempts to use the "common friends," the "good men of the land." But Aymeri resorts to force, and Richard is forced to yield. By doing so, the viscount violates an implicit part of the compact of fidelity, to allow disputes that engage the parties' honor to be negotiated to a settlement by friends, neighbors, and fellow lords. Instead he resorts to force. He places himself outside of lordly society. That is the measure of his evil ways.

This Aymeri not only refused to do but refused even to hear. Instead in a fury he put his hand on other rights and honors of the church, and whatever he could put to his own use he shamelessly seized from me, wronging me greatly and threatening worse. He ordered that no one in the territory of Narbonne should dare to take my side or the church's nor help us in word or deed. He claimed, furthermore, that I had given him those taxes (that is, the compras that I demanded) in fief: a grant I made following the deceitfulness of which you have already heard.

Hearing this I once again admonished him through his personal friends, through neighboring barons of the land, through bishops, abbots, viscounts, and knights, indeed through whomever I could, giving witness that by the oath he had given, by the many benefices that he held of the church, he should stop the evil deeds, the scandals, and the faithlessness, and either peacefully relinquish his honors to the church or come to justice. I saw that I could get nowhere with him. Nor did I have the strength to support the cruel evils he was inflicting on me. I therefore excommunicated Aymeri and all his lands, and under threat of death departed for other lands to live as I could. I was unable to go far enough away, however, and was captured, imprisoned, and treated scandalously by his friends, before at last he was willing to be corrected by justice.

The judgment of the barons of the land was of no avail to me, however, when I finally was able to reach an agreement with him. Rather, painfully and against my will, I was forced unjustly to give up the aforesaid rights—unjustly, because the laws state that a judgment in a case of spoliation is null and void unless that which has been taken is first returned, and the church had been despoiled by fraud and violence, and its rights not restored. He swore that by the faith he owed to me I would not get what I was due unless against my will I took from the church to give him what he wanted. When I did this he once again promised to be faithful to me in the future and to observe all the agreements that he had made with me.

But these promises too were too bothersome for him to keep.

[The archbishop goes on to complain of Aymeri levying duties on cochineal dye, duties at the city gates, duties on salt sales.]

In this way, as I have written, he treated me: the man who swore to be faithful to me and to the church, who did homage and swore by his oath to protect the honors of the church fully and faithfully.

All this I write to you who shall come after me to serve God and the church in my place—that you should know with what evil, what injustice, what violence this Aymeri oppressed the church and me his lord, and by taking away the justice of the church lost his own. I beseech and pray that you may recover the honor that the church lost through my negligence and weakness, because I did not have the strength to support the evil to which I was subjected. You hear the claim to justice that the church has against Aymeri and his successors. And if anyone should contradict you on this matter, you may affirm and defend it as justly to be judged yours, confident in the truth of what is written here. God is witness to the truth of what I have said and the purity of heart with which I have said it. I order you to believe it as true, putting aside all lying doubts. To all of you I can also name the witnesses to what I have said: Ato archbishop of Arles, John bishop of Nîmes, Bernard Rainardi and Adhemar archdeacons of Narbonne, Hugh abbot of Saint-Paul, Peter sacristan of Gerona, Miro of Capestang and Gaucerand his brother, Berenger Guilelmi and Raymond Guifredi, and many others both clergy and laymen, who, having seen and heard these things, know them for a certainty to be true.

We are here in the midst of a dispute not just between rulers of the same city but between cousins as well, and the feeling of kinship betrayed doubtless added to its bitterness, as it had in the fight between Berenger I and Guifred. For the call of family honor would have been to maintain the family's "honors," its lands, rights, and revenues. Richard instead answered the call of his new family, the Church Universal and the particular church that was (in the favorite metaphor of the reformers) his bride, the family for which he had abandoned his family of birth; that was the family whose patrimony he labored to protect against his own kinsmen. In this Richard showed himself every inch the child of the Gregorian Reform and the child of Saint-Victor of Marseille, the leading reform monastery in coastal Occitania, of which he himself had been abbot.[27] He also showed himself a child of the reform movement in his appeal to the truth of written documents, the truth of ink on parchment with which he sought to undermine the truth of his opponent's sworn word. Here, two ways of being in the world collided: the one was Aymeri's, built on honor emanating from the person in his actions, his bearing, and his speech, the other, the archbishop's, built on authoritative writing, just as the truths of the Faith were built upon the Book.[28] But for the archbishop, those truths as well only had meaning within the structure of fidelity.

We would not know from reading this text that over the years, Richard and Aymeri had come to agreements on a significant number of difficult questions—their claims to confiscate goods and ships shipwrecked along the coast (a claim that surely impeded the city's growth as a trading port), disputes over justice, the salt monopoly, and the control of towers on the city wall, among other things; nor would we know that the Viscountess Mahalt and young Aymeri had arbitrated a dispute between the newly installed archbishop and one of his most important castellans.[29] However long this particular dispute had gone on, Richard in his narrative distilled it to what he saw to be its essence.

Faced with restoring his church's property after a long interregnum, with castellans who had "usurped" the archbishop's dues in the countryside and monasteries that had gained a taste for independence,[30] Richard apparently believed that only through his own force of will could he reclaim the position that had once been Guifred's (eliding Dalmacius's episcopacy for reasons that he does not mention and quietly forgetting Guifred's simoniacal stains). Armed with Guifred's charters that gave him truth and right, he cast his narrative in terms that would reach the largest possible audience, in purely secular terms of fidelity and its demands.

And so Richard constructs his narrative as a reverse image of the ideal of fidelity. An essential part of that ideal is that pressures along the fault lines of lordly society, although they may be released in violence, will still eventually be abated in negotiation, compromise, and arbitration. Fidelity and community thus sustained each other. Those who shared the values of honor enforced them through suasion and shame and anger (and sometimes by fire and sword), for they all knew that as much as wealth, these values defined the hierarchy that gave meaning to their lives. As long as suasion worked, violations of fidelity, rather than subverting those values, continued in their own way to reinforce them, as arbiters called into action the rituals by which the violation would be mended and expectations reaffirmed. Both values and rituals were communal. And as long as the communities remained coherent, the culture of fidelity could survive.

Where the community was not coherent, however, at the highest levels of society, where Ermengard and her allies and enemies plotted their course, the force of the oath and what it represented became more tenuous. Its moral demands still mattered, and those demands could find voice in public opinion, the opprobrium of followers, which loudmouths such as the troubadours Bertran de Born and Raimbaut de Vaqueiras might try to arouse. But more often than not it was easily undermined by naked interests masquerading as legitimate right. Then trimming might lead to outright betrayal, and only the force of arms could restore some semblance of an ordered peace. And there in the clash of moral expectations of fidelity and the Realpolitik of power we can sense the tragedy of the many betrayals Ermengard had to suffer at the hands of those she thought to be her friends. For it was not "unruly vassals"—those mythic creatures of an older historiography that copied unthinkingly the parti pris of even older royal apologists—who were responsible for the worst violence visited upon twelfth-century Occitania but the ambitions of the great, some of whom themselves wore royal crowns, and eventually the Church as well. Doubtless the rumblings of lesser feuds most often took place in the easy darkness cast by the purposings of the powerful. In that heady world, Ermengard would learn quickly to beware of easy betrayal, and in the end it would be just such a betrayal in her own family that would lead her to her final exile.

ERMENGARD AND BERENGER OF PUISSERGUIER

Within the tightly bound world of friends and neighbors, danger to fidelity could also come from an appeal beyond, to some higher power or some higher law not subject to communal pressures or to the rituals that enacted them. Archbishop Richard in the second decade of the twelfth century—single-minded reformer though he was—could not imagine appealing to that higher realm; his vision went no further than the heirs and successors of those he knew.[31] In the early 1160s, however, Occitania suddenly became the political focus for the greatest crowned heads of Europe—the kings of England and France, the emperor, and the pope. It was a situation that a wily opportunist might hope to exploit. And so it was for Berenger of Puisserguier. Although the troubles he generated in the end came to naught, they showed the mechanisms by which the society in which he lived, a society organized by the culture of fidelity, would eventually be weakened, how with stronger ties to the northern king and his agents resident in Occitan cities it would become a society of contending rights and emerging law, the society of later Capetian France. It was a prophecy of things to come, although doubtless neither Ermengard nor those close to her were aware of it.

Puisserguier, the village from which Berenger and his family took their name, lies about twenty kilometers north of Narbonne. It does not appear among the villages divided between the sons of Amalric I in the later thirteenth century, so there is no way to tell whether Berenger rendered an oath to Ermengard for his castle, or whether he did so to the Trencavels or to the archbishop, or to no one at all.[32] Berenger's possessions stretched eastward across the plain to Florensac on the Hérault River. His richest possession, however, was surely the right he received from Raymond Trencavel to "guide" merchants on the ancient via Domitia between Narbonne and Béziers. As his pay for "keeping the road safe and secure and quiet to the best of [his] ability"—police duty or protection racket, depending on one's sense of irony—Berenger collected (according to a schedule of 1184) "from every sack of goods 13 d. Melg., from every person on horseback 13 d., from every bale 13 d., from every load of oil or fish 7 d., from every Jew 13 d." He apparently held rights of a similar sort from Ermengard, perhaps collecting his fees both in Béziers and Narbonne.[33]

The autumn of 1162 and the years that immediately followed were perilous for Ermengard. In August 1162, Count Ramon Berenguer IV of Barcelona, the linchpin of the alliance in which she had spent her adult political life, died suddenly, leaving a five-year-old boy as his successor. Raymond V of Toulouse was momentarily without a serious contender for hegemony in the region. Meanwhile, others were scouting the region for allies or advantages. In the name of his wife Eleanor, Henry II of England was making threatening gestures toward Toulouse. Pope Alexander III had just spent months in the region seeking support against his rival, the pro-Imperial Pope Victor IV. To counter Alexander, Emperor Frederick Barbarossa had been treating with the count of Barcelona. It was while on his way to meet Frederick in Turin that Ramon Berenguer died.[34]

In these circumstances, Berenger of Puisserguier decided to increase his take from his tolls. When Ermengard tried to bring him to justice he took refuge with Count Raymond V. The count and his wife Constance, sister of King Louis VII, sent him to the royal court with their letters of recommendation. The road from Narbonne to Béziers led by way of Toulouse to Paris. The correspondence with King Louis VII of France that resulted, fortuitously preserved in a manuscript copied in the Parisian monastery of Saint-Victor, takes us quickly from the silver pennies collected on merchants' packhorses into the heady reaches of regalian politics. There the plain speaking of the counting house metamorphosed into the finely spun language of deference and fidelity, loyalty and love, in which clerical latinity joined hands with troubadour lyricism.[35]

"We humbly implore Your Lordship, my revered lord," the count wrote, "that you receive kindly with your grace and love the knight Berenger,[36] bearer of these present letters, who is your liegeman and our close friend. . . . You may know that he has many enemies for our sake and that he supports us in all things to the best of his ability." To this Constance added, "You are not unmindful of the fact that this knight . . . is attentive to the interests of me and of your brother-in-law. Inasmuch as his enemies seek to do him injury, he has come to you whose name he always calls upon. . . . As his neighbors bear witness, he ought to hold his castle directly from your hand without intermediary."[37]

The scribe who composed these words had learned his craft well. Then as now, the genre demanded more gilt than truth. Berenger is introduced as the king's liegeman, holding his castle directly from the crown, although in fact that would have been impossible, because liege homage was unknown in mid-twelfth-century Occitania. Nor would Berenger ever have had the occasion to receive his castle from the king. Louis passed once through the region on his return from a pilgrimage to Santiago de Compostela in 1154, but he was then busy courting the favor of the great lords and prelates of the region and would have done nothing to offend Ermengard or Raymond Trencavel. Nor were there any royal agents in the region to receive homage in the king's place. That kind of administration would have to wait nearly a century. But facts hardly mattered. The assertion was designed to gratify the king's court, where since the days of Louis's father, vassalage and liege homage had been promoted as the vehicles to enlarge the effective range of royal rule. And in the Middle Ages as today, legitimacy derived from what people believed, not from what may in fact have been true. One way to create such belief was to assert it. Raymond and Constance were doing no more than that.

Having heard where Berenger was going, Ermengard dispatched a letter by her own messengers (a letter that incidentally pictures Ermengard in armor at the head of her troops):

> To her most excellent lord Louis by the grace of God the most strong King of the Frankish Kingdom, Ermengard, Viscountess of Narbonne, his faithful and devoted woman: may he be saved by Him who gives salvation to Kings. We have learned both from reason and from the practice of our predecessors that when we are assaulted by necessity we should seek the most certain help. Thus it is that—having been honored by you and considering myself especially yours—I should trustingly write to you as to my highest and most dear lord about the things that concern me.
>
> I inform Your Highness that a certain knight from our lands by the name of Berenger of Puisserguier will soon come to your court. As everyone in our province knows, although he ought to be subject to my jurisdiction he has been led by his levity of mind and his pride to try to wrest from me the grace of your crown and by his lies to remove himself with your help from my power, leading to the diminution and dishonor of my rights. Therefore, I earnestly entreat Your Majesty to give little faith to his deceitful tales but rather, as is right and just, let him be deluded in his lies and frustrated in his vain hopes and sent back to me who holds power over him, if it please you. If, however, you have doubts about what I say, by your letters command that he and I should come to be heard by the bishops of your land, the bishop of Maguelone and others.
>
> You have admonished me to firmly hold the peace with the count of Toulouse and to serve him. This I have done and on the fifteenth day after the Assumption of the Blessed Mary [August 30] I will march with my army against his enemies. Now and always, unless he prevents me, I will prize him with your love. Farewell my lord.[38]

These were occasions when friends were useful, and Ermengard did not hesitate to call on the pope, Alexander III, whom she had helped to welcome to Occitania when he was seeking support against his rival, Victor IV.

> Alexander, bishop, servant of the servants of God, to his most dear son in Christ, Louis, illustrious King of the Franks, greetings and apostolic benediction. We believe that word has reached the King's Highness how our sweet daughter in Christ, Ermengard of Narbonne, took special care to honor and serve us when we were in her region and to demonstrate in innumerable ways what laudable devotion she bears to us and the Church. Therefore both we and our brothers desire to show our love to her as a most dear and special daughter of the Church and to incline our spirit to her requests in so far as God and justice allow us. We there-

fore attentively commend her, whom we believe to be most devoted to you and faithful in all things, to Your Highness. And by Our Apostolic letter we ask that you—out of reverence for the Blessed Peter and us and knowing her fidelity and probity—esteem, honor, and protect her as your own faithful woman [sicut propriam fidelem tuam], and that you allow her reasonable prayers with your accustomed goodness. For this we will bear Your Highness a multitude of grace; and she, devoted, will become more devoted, and faithful, will become more faithful, and so remain for all time. Given at Sens, April 3.[39]

William of Montpellier wrote the king that Berenger was simply "denying that he holds from Ermengard the possessions which he has had from her hand and which his family has had from her ancestors"[40]—the exact contrary of the assertion that Raymond and Constance had made to their royal brother. Perhaps this had in fact been Berenger's retort when Ermengard had summoned him to her court. But on his way to Paris, at Montpellier, perhaps, or Arles, Berenger apparently encountered someone trained in Roman law who offered for a fee to help him shape a convincing argument. The lawyer told the adventurous castellan of a text just written by one of the legal masters of the region and said, "Include this in your petition." The passage ran as follows:

> The law says that neither slaves nor women can serve as arbiters. [And a few chapters later:] A judge should be one whom neither nature nor law opposes. By nature a man younger than twenty-five cannot be a judge; neither can a deaf or a blind man. By law neither a woman nor a slave nor someone of ill repute.[41]

Berenger must have congratulated himself for money well spent on that professional advice, for the king's advisors bought the argument, and when Ermengard's messengers reached the court they discovered that Berenger was already on his way home with royal letters in his favor, and he, hearing that the messengers were there, hastily wrote to the king to plead that he not reverse the decision that had been made in Berenger's favor.[42]

Then Louis or those around him weighed the profit and loss in the situation. Would their response in Berenger's favor alienate Ermengard from Raymond V, or even worse, move her in the direction of Frederick Barbarossa? Would the king gain more from supporting this minor lord as a way to make claims of high lordship in the distant south or from wooing the lady Ermengard and her allies? They quickly realized which was the prudent course. The following letter issued from the royal chancery.

> Louis by the grace of God King of the Franks to his most dear, the illustrious lady Ermengard of Narbonne, greetings. As Your Worship notified us through your dutiful messengers, the abbot of Saint-Paul of Narbonne and Peter Raymond, Roman law is used among you to decide legal issues. That law admonishes

that women should not be given the power of making legal judgments. The custom of our kingdom is much kinder. Here, if the better sex be lacking, it is allowed to women to succeed to and to administer an inheritance. Therefore remember that you are of our kingdom. We wish you to hold to the usages of our kingdom, and although you are a neighbor of the Empire, in this matter we wish that you not accede to its laws and customs. Therefore sit in judgment and examine matters with the diligent zeal of Him who created you a woman when He could have created you a man and of his great goodness gave the rule of the province of Narbonne into a woman's hands. On no account may anyone by our authority refuse to be subject to your jurisdiction because you are a woman. Farewell.[43]

This letter moved the debate onto an entirely different plane. It focused by implication on Frederick Barbarossa's diplomacy.

Barbarossa was making much of his claim to be the successor to the emperors of ancient Rome and using Roman law and the jurists of Bologna to do so. Teachers of law drew up the list of rights belonging exclusively to the emperor, which Barbarossa published at the Diet of Roncaglia in November 1158. And one of the most famous of these jurists, Rogerius, had argued successfully at the Diet of Turin in 1162 for the right of the family of les Baux to be counts of Provence.[44] Louis or his advisors must have been concerned that the spread of Roman law across Occitania might work to the emperor's advantage. He set his learned clerks to work to find an argument why it should not. The letter to Ermengard was the result. Someone in Louis's court had earned his keep, although one must wonder what Ermengard made of the phrase "Him who created you a woman when He could have created you a man." Did she think about the difference between herself and the "better sex" when she laced on her helmet and hauberk or sat in judgment surrounded by her friends?

Berenger returned to Occitania to find himself once again summoned to Ermengard's court. Possibly this very letter was read to him; certainly there were others concerning the disputed tolls. Afterward, William of Montpellier sent the king a report.

> I was among those hearing the dispute that Lady Ermengard, viscountess of Narbonne, was having with Berenger of Puisserguier. While this plea was being considered, letters arrived concerning the toll, which were presented to the said Berenger, but he treated them with contempt and would not accept them. When they were placed on his lap he contemptuously threw the letters from Your Grace on the ground, would not look at them and spurned them in the presence of bishops and barons and many others.
>
> Wherefore I humbly beseech Your Majesty with all my prayers that you not allow the said Lady Ermengard to be disinherited in this and in other matters which messengers shall speak about to Your Grace, but that the Lady Ermengard

may know your justice and piety and that my prayers have been a help to her. May it please Your Majesty to receive the Lady Ermengard's messengers kindly and to satisfy her requests for the sake of my love and prayers, if it please you.[45]

At this point the letters contained in the monastic manuscript drop the story. How long Berenger and Ermengard continued to squabble we have no way of knowing. But twelfth-century aristocratic politics rarely allowed enemies to be destroyed or even ignored for very long. Berenger and his family were too important not to be brought back within the fold. When Berenger died in 1169, the right to guide merchants from Narbonne to Béziers was still (or again) among his most important possessions.[46] Ten years later, Trencavel's son, Roger of Béziers, granted another Berenger of Puisserguier (doubtless a nephew of the first) an additional road on which to levy tolls as well as the right to collect his tolls at Béziers in pennies of Mauguio rather than in the coin of Béziers. Here is the witness list:

Alfons, by the grace of God king of Aragon, count of Barcelona and marquis of Provence
Lady Ermengard of Narbonne
Count Pedro [de Lara, Ermengard's nephew and chosen successor]
Peter Raymond of Hautpoul
Roger son of Peter, vicar of Carcassonne
Peter Raymond of Narbonne
Bertrand of Capestang
Bermund of Thézan
Raymond of Salles
Raymond Ledder[47]

We have already met many of these men, among the highest in Ermengard's and Roger's courts; among them was Peter Raymond, the very man who had been Ermengard's emissary to argue against the older Berenger in the royal court. The family of Puisserguier had reoccupied its familiar place in the neighborhood.[48] As for the proper role of women, the older Berenger on his deathbed had bequeathed all his rights and powers, including his castles (and therefore the justices belonging to them), to his mother and, after her death, to his sisters. Roman law was one thing, common familial practices another. When it came to matters of property, the latter still took precedence.

The story does not quite end there, however. Louis's help, whatever it was worth, was not totally gratuitous. Another letter reveals the king's price.

To the most honorable Louis by the grace of God most favored King of the Franks, her only lord, Ermengard, viscountess of Narbonne, his special lady, submits herself with due reverence. Your Reverence, lord, should not doubt that I and mine always obey your commands, and that all that which I have in the world is subject to your power. I ask one thing only, that Your Liberality be often mindful of me, for—after God—all my hope depends on you, my dearest lord. Therefore, every day, if I have swift messengers, I send them to you to remind you of me.

If I have not yet fulfilled your command to send you a horse, the reason is that though I have searched carefully I have not yet found one that is good enough. Therefore do not let this delay move Your Majesty against me, for I shall soon send you one that will suit Your Lordship better than any to be found in our entire land. May my lord fare well and be ever mindful of me.[49]

Narbonne was not horse country. The beast fit for a king would doubtless be found by some merchant of Narbonne across the sea in Africa, and Ermengard would pay dearly for it. A royal gift demanded a gift in return.

CHAPTER TWELVE
GIVING AND TAKING

Aymeri . . . came with some of the barons of his land and did homage to me with his own hands, . . . and he received from my hands the fiefs which he held from the church. . . .

Berenger of Puisserguier . . . is trying to deny . . . that he holds from Ermengard the possessions which he has had from her hand and which his family has had from her ancestors, and use your authority to resist her.

The time has now come for us to talk about fiefs, the grants of lands, castles, and rights whose name—most commonly *fevum* in Occitania—has one-sidedly given the name "feudalism" to the political "system" of the Middle Ages.

So familiar were these grants and so precise the social bonds they embraced that the poet Arnaut Daniel could easily turn them into allegories of love:

Ar sai ieu c'Amors m'a condug	Now I know that Love has welcomed me
el sieu plus seguran castel,	into her strongest castle,
don non dei renda ni trahug,	for which I owe neither rent nor tribute,
ans m'en ha fait don e capdel;	since she has made me its lord and captain;
non ai poder ni cor que'm vir'aillors	I have neither power nor heart to turn elsewhere
qu'Ensenhamens e Fizeutatz plevida	for Courtliness and sworn Fidelity
jai per estar, c'a bon Pretz s'i atorna.[1]	reside there and turn to good Merit.

Love in this verse is both sentiment and lady, who in the role of lord has granted the poet her castle, manned by Fidelity, Courtliness, and Merit. So far the image is transparent. Nor would anyone have been puzzled by the thought of a lady in that role; the metaphor came directly from the world in which the poet and his audience lived. But why the reference to rent and tribute not owed? Here too the answer lies in what anthropologists call "local knowledge." Arnaut is insisting that the gift is one that honors him; but to recognize this as his meaning demands that we understand the many forms the Occitan fief could take—that there could be fiefs that were less honorable, fiefs that did owe rents and tributes. (There were also, one might add, fiefs that could be considered dishonoring: the fiefs given by bad lords.)[2]

Numerous oaths of fidelity were not accompanied (as far as we know) by grants of fiefs, such as the oaths between fellow castellans. But among the great there was hardly an oath of fidelity without a grant to accompany it; every sworn castle was considered "held of" the lord to whom it was sworn, and even the pettiest grant in fief to a peasant who would work the land might demand an oath of homage and fidelity in return. In 1107, Viscount Bernard Ato of Béziers refused to do homage to Archbishop Richard of Narbonne until his claim to Capestang was satisfied. Only after long negotiations did the archbishop give him "more of his money than any archbishop gave his grandfather or any other ancestor . . . because the viscount was his cousin and a friend of long standing," and Bernard Ato in return promised not to claim that custom gave him the right to equivalent gifts from future archbishops. Then and only then did Bernard Ato give up his claim to Capestang and swear homage and fidelity.[3] Archbishop Richard seems to have had problems with just about everyone who held fiefs of him: with Olivier of Termes over the castle of Villerouge, with Bernard and Remigius of Canet over the village and fortifications of Canet, with Roland of Fontjoncouse and the castellans of Sigean over the rights each claimed in their villages, and doubtless with many others. In each case the castellans, like the viscounts, asserted their rights to collect dues or hold castles in fief while Archbishop Richard resisted until "friends" negotiated a settlement, one that inevitably involved Richard sweetening his "gift" while the castellans renounced some of their claims. Only then were the oaths sworn.[4]

Before Archbishop Richard could know enough to start any of these disputes he would have had to ask the castellans to tell him what fiefs they held of the church, as he had asked Ermengard's father, Aymeri II, to do.[5] Eventually, much later in the century, such accountings would become a formal "recognizance of fief,"[6] but from Richard's narration it would seem that the practice was not yet a formality; it had no name. Richard had to describe what he had asked from the viscount. We must imagine Ermengard not many years later asking the same of her castellans as she received their oaths of fidelity.

To the archbishop and those who "held of" him, what they received were gifts, as Richard made clear in his settlement with Bernard Ato: his additional payment to the viscount was given out of "cousinage and friendship." Yet by any measure, these were strange kinds of gifts: in most cases, apart from whatever sweetening might have been necessary to make an agreement, the people who received these gifts already had them, and Richard, when giving them, did not know what he was giving until he was told by those who received them. They were also obligatory gifts, made so by past practice. Indeed it is that past practice that is the hidden agenda in most if not all of Richard's disputes.

Although the archbishop explicitly asserts that he is battling the viscounts' and castellans' "usurpations" during the disputed bishoprics of Peter of Rodez and Bertrand of Nîmes, by constantly returning—as he does with Bernard Ato and Olivier of Termes as well as Aymeri II—to the grants of Archbishop Guifred (who died in 1079), he implicitly passes over the reign of the other archbishop who preceded him, Dalmacius.[7] Perhaps most of the usurpations were in fact his grants, or Peter's and Bertrand's as they tried to collect allies in their fights to gain the see. Richard indeed seems to have gone out of his way to efface all three predecessors from the record: even in the seventeenth-century inventory of the archiepiscopal archives, when vastly more documents were extant than now, there are numerous documents listed from Guifred, from Richard, and from his immediate successors but none from Bertrand, almost none from Peter, and very few from Dalmacius. Such differences can hardly be the result of the random ravages of time.[8]

Obligatory gifts are stock items in ethnographic literature (and indeed in myriad ways we live with them ourselves, if we want to maintain amicable familial and business relationships); they should arouse no surprise. Nevertheless, the progress of some of these gifts from hand to hand in twelfth-century Occitania is remarkable and begins to resemble the classic cowrie shells of South Asia and East Africa, or the bottles of gift sake that go from household to household in contemporary Japan. Let us pick up the trail of one "gift castle."

When Archbishop Richard sought to recover the castles he claimed that his castellans had usurped since Guifred was archbishop, this was the story he told of what happened to the castle of Villerouge in the Corbières. After the death of Guifred, he averred, Peter Olivier of Termes, joining the simoniacal bishop Peter of Rodez, "invaded" the church of Narbonne and took the castle from the cathedral's lordship. He then mortgaged it to Berenger of Peyrepertuse. Sometime later, this mortgage led to a dispute between Berenger and Peter Olivier, which was only settled when Berenger married his daughter to Peter Olivier and gave her the castle for a dowry. To get the castle back, the archbishops excommunicated both Berenger and Peter Olivier. Berenger gave up, said Richard, but not Peter Olivier, who remained excommunicated until he died. In the end only the pressures of excommunication and of the "notables of the land" ("compellente . . . omnibus probis hominibus terrae") brought Peter Olivier's son and his widow to surrender Villerouge to the church.[9] Such, at least, was Richard's version. Other documents make the story decidedly more complex. The seventeenth-century archiepiscopal inventory reveals that Richard's predecessor, Dalmacius, received oaths of fidelity for the castle from both Berenger of Peyrepertuse and from a Raymond son of Adalais, who had held the castle from Archbishop Guifred. In 1157 the castle was still in the hands of this Raymond's descendants, Rixendis daughter of Agnes and her brother Bernard.[10]

However much we would like to do so, there is no way to reconstruct a "true" story from these inventory notices and Richard's decidedly self-serving tale. The Peyrepertuse–Termes alliance went back at least to the beginning of the 1080s, when both supported Bishop Peter's move to take over the archbishopric.[11] If we assume that Richard's narrative has some grain of truth, we might imagine that Bishop Peter granted Villerouge to Peter Olivier of Termes, who mortgaged it to Berenger of Peyrepertuse, who then gave an oath of fidelity for it to Dalmacius before giving it to his daughter when she married Peter Olivier. Other scenarios are also possible. Meanwhile, Raymond of Villerouge and his descendants also held the castle of the archbishops.

Archbishop Richard cast his actions as an effort to "recover" what Berenger and Peter Olivier had "usurped," to undo the violence against his church. He was really announcing that there would be no friendship between himself and the two men. Excommunication was the final step. That was one of the reasons Berenger was included in the condemnation, although he had already alienated the castle to his daughter as a dowry. The other reason is that the archbishop was not really concerned with who had a legal claim to the castle or what bundle of rights each had taken and passed on. He was intent rather on naming the people who continued to be associated wrongfully with Villerouge because they had received it from the wrong hands—and that included everyone through whose hands the castle had passed. For Archbishop Richard, everyone's hands were soiled. The castle was not simply a place that gave the castellans power and revenues; it was also (and perhaps more importantly) a token, it was the physical embodiment of a relationship created by the act of giving and taking and reenforced by giving and taking again.

For this token to bind the giver and the taker, it did not have to be in the power or possession of either. The strange practice of one person giving what he did not have to another who did not receive it (but might be expected to help conquer it) was followed from the bottom to the top of the aristocratic hierarchy and even immortalized in the chanson de geste *The Wagon-Train of Nîmes*.[12] That nothing in fact changed hands save a promise and a token detracted in no way from the strength of the alliance that the gift solidified. Even a potential token was enough to bind.

Ermengard might have seen or been told about an example of this in her own archives: a gift of the city and county of Tarragona to her great-great-grandfather Berenger by the count of Barcelona when Tarragona was still ruled by the count's loyal Moslem tributary, the ruler of Tortosa. It would not fall under Barcelonese control for another seventy years. Archbishop Guifred likewise was not above inviting his followers to conquer the fiefs he promised but could not give, as he did with an ancestor of the Durban family. Unable to deliver a place called Berre as a fief to William Ibrinus, he offered rights in Fontjoncouse as a pledge and suggested that William take Berre by his own means if he could.[13] In the twelfth century such invitational grants of fief—invitations to conquest—would be the common coin of aristocratic alliances. In her last years, Ermengard herself would be the victim of this practice.

Real or hoped for or but imagined, something had to be given and taken in any alliance. There had to be something to embody it. To give was to honor; to give was to manifest one's love. Even in our own individualistic society an etiquette of gifts has not disappeared, although it has largely taken refuge in what we think of as the private world of family and those with whom we have close emotional ties; it speaks of intimacy. In our own days, when gifts flow into the public world of politics they quickly give off the smell of corruption, of the dirty work of "special interests"; "political friendship" looks like an oxymoron or a cover for malfeasance. Not so in the twelfth century. As Archbishop Richard makes us pointedly aware, friendship and "cousinage" were then at the very center of politics, and gifts were their vehicle. They could not be elided or abridged. And to be effective they had to be performed in the sight of all who mattered.[14]

No moment was more important for this ritual giving and giving back than when a new person entered into the lordship of a castle. Then it was required that the person who held the castle hand it over "fully and without reserve," *ad alodem* in the technical notarial language of the day, and immediately receive it back in fief. And because physical rituals embodied all significant social acts in this world—passing a stone to transfer property, throwing a stone at a tower to say, "As your lord, I forbid you to build this here"[15]—so here too the giving was turned into a ritual act. In front of witnesses the new castellan handed the keys to the castle to his lord or her agent who performed some symbolic act to signify his possession, placing a waxen seal on the keys or opening the castle gate; then, after the oath of fidelity was given, the keys were returned and those who manned the castle took their oaths in turn.[16]

The need for such a ritual can easily be surmised. Every time they brought their pennies or chickens or grain to their lord, peasants and others far down the social hierarchy recognized that their lands and revenues were held of another, recognized their subordination. In contrast, the service of those who held castles was both more limited and more inclusive. They were to hand over their castles on demand and help recover them if they were taken by an enemy, and they were to do whatever faithfulness required. But because control of castles only rarely changed hands, and as a consequence, there were few occasions to fix the relationship of lord to castellan in public memory, the ritual giving and giving back reminded all who were present and all who heard of it that the castle was indeed a gift. In the presence of witnesses and with a scribe to record the event, the castellan gave the castle completely, without restriction or reservation (probably the best translation for *ad alodem*), and only then received it as a fief, which joined the castellan anew to her lord or his lady.

Likewise, when on the losing side in a war or under some other unbearable constraint, a castellan who held his castle of one lord might be forced to receive the same castle from another lord, or one who held his castle "freely" might be compelled to give it up and receive it back from a lord. Such moments were common enough in truces or treaties when the fidelity of castles were transferred from the defeated to the victor.[17] Like most aspects of the relations between castellans and their lords, this likewise could give birth to a poetic metaphor for love.

Aissi cum cel q'a estat ses seignor	Like the man who has been without lord,
en son alo, francament et en patz,	in his alod, freely and in peace,
c'anc ren non det ni'n mes mas per amor	who has owed nothing nor paid but out of love,
ni fo destregs mas per sas voluntatz,	nor was ever distrained against his will,
et eras es par mal seignor forssatz	and now by an evil lord is violently forced—
atressi'm fui mieus mezeis longamen,	so was I myself for a long time,
qu'anc re no fi per autrui mandamen;	who did nothing by another's command;
ar ai senhor ab cui no'm val merces:	but now with my lord mercy is worth naught:
Amor, que a mon cor en tal luoc mes	Love, who has placed my heart in a place
on non aus dir ni mostrar mon talen,	where I dare not speak nor show my desire
ni per nuill plag partir no m'en puesc ges.[18]	nor will any pledge let me leave.

In Ermengard's world, gifts moved in all directions—up, down, and across the social hierarchy. Whichever way they moved, they were always an affirmation of that hierarchy.

Most often they affirmed it by the names they bore. As "forcibles," "requisitions," or simply "takings," those that moved upward from the lowest levels emphasized grasping far more than giving.[19] They could be of the most various sort. When Arnold of Lac dictated his last testament, this is how he described some of the "usages" that he and his brother possessed in the village from which they took their name:

> the wedding practice [*usaticum*] that from every man who takes a wife in the village of Lac, wherever he may come from, and from every woman of Lac who marries inside or outside the village, we have a measure of wine, a quarter of mutton, and two loaves of bread, sufficient to feed four men. If other meat is served, two *fraise* of veal [calf's mesentery] sufficient for four men. And to every woman marrying a village man we must send a saddle horse and lead her to the house she is to enter, and (whether she rides or not) she must give us a quarter of oats. And if she comes from outside the village we must send a saddle horse for her, and she must give us an émine of oats.[20]

Centuries later, dues such as this would lead mythmakers to invent the *ius primae noctis*.[21] This description, however, seems rather to evoke a rustic kermis (the wedding in *The Marriage of Figaro*, let's say, with Count Almaviva satisfied with a good meal). The village lord honors the peasant bride by sending his equipage, and he in turn is the honored guest. But there is no honor without inferior and superior, and here the subordination is expressed once again by giving food.[22]

The honorable honored others in turn, especially when about to cross from this world to the next. Then it was time to remember those terrible images of the Last Judgment shown on church porches and think of the words of the *Dies Irae*:

Judex ergo cum sedebit,	When the Judge shall take his seat
Quidquid latet, apparebit	And every hidden deed appear
Nil inultum remanebit,	And nothing unavenged remain,
Quid sum miser tunc dicturus?	What shall I, poor man, then say?
Quem patronum rogaturus,	On what patron shall I call,
Cum vix justus sit securus?	When even the just are hardly safe?

Then it was time to give to the saints whose help one would desperately need. All testaments began with gifts of land or money to saints and to those who served them in churches, monasteries, hospitals, and bridges (the last like the others under the watchful patronage of the special dead). Other great occasions, such as victory in battle or return from crusade, might likewise call for such alms giving.[23] But many more humble occasions must have done so as well, for ecclesiastical cartularies are filled with written testimony to gifts, although the texts are too grudgingly laconic to tell us much about what particular moments prompted them.

Often the gifts flowed both ways; land or rights went to the church, whereas a small quantity of coin, a few measures of grain, a horse, or some other object went to the donor *pro elemosina*. For alms were given by churches as well as to them, their modesty or form only serving to emphasize their symbolic nature.[24]

On first reading, these bilateral exchanges suggest that country scribes were bewildered as to whether they ought to be recording donations or sales. They cover all bases. "We give, hand over and sell" ("donamus . . . et laxamus et vendimus") they have the donor-seller say.[25] Were the scribes unable to distinguish a gift from a sale? In fact they regularly did. Other charters from the same period in the same collections are clearly and exclusively sales, for both great sums and little; the amounts involved had nothing to do with what the exchange was called.[26] Why then did scribes sometimes mix their genres? Possibly, in fact, because they were more attuned to the social difference between one kind of exchange and another—most particularly between a sale and a gift—than we sometimes are (as when we accept that redundant "free gift" as a marketing come-on at the supermarket).

In twelfth-century Occitania even peasants were familiar with the marketplace and what sociologists of a Marxist bent call the cash nexus. They knew there were some exchanges in which the value of what one side handed over was carefully calculated and the payment by the other was meant to match it. Already by 1170 if not before, scribes were using formulae from Roman law to take care of possible differences in value between what was sold and what was paid.[27] Likewise, then as now, people knew that sales made no further demands on either party other than to guarantee them against future challenges. No ongoing relationship was implied, even when the community of seller and buyer was small and the seller was a dependent peasant and the buyer her lord. With gifts, however, such on-going relationships were explicitly assumed. Gifts were given "for the salvation of our souls and those of our parents," salvation to be won by the repeated prayers of the priests, monks, Templars, or Hospitalers who received the gift and by the intercession of their heavenly patrons. Gifts were given to confirm and add to the gifts of parents, brothers, and sisters. Gifts were given to affirm membership in a community. The mixed genre insisted on this quality of giving even as it may have recognized the careful calculation of value expressed in "sales."[28]

⤜⬤

Gifts such as these form the larger context in which the Occitan fief must be understood. It belonged to a society in which all relations outside the family (as well, of course, as the fundamental relationship within the family, that of husband and wife) were embodied in gifts of property, gifts that did not so much transfer economic rights from one person, or group of people, to another as join them in a shared connection to that property. That is why, among the greatest at least, it sometimes did not matter who controlled the property that was "given," whether any additional economic benefit accrued from it, or even whether the gift had any real economic benefit at all.

The gifts and dues we have just been looking at, those of peasants to their lords, of serfs to those to whom they belonged, of villagers to their castellans, all moved from those who were lower to those who were higher in the social hierarchy. *Fevum*, "fief," in contrast, was the generic name for gifts and grants that moved down the hierarchical ladder or across the rung. Fiefs created clienteles and friendship networks, groups that are not always easy to distinguish, because "friendship" and "love" were the operative words to describe the attachment of followers to their lords as well as lords (and followers) to each other. The joined hands of homage and the oath of fidelity also served to make those clienteles and networks visible, but fiefs were the permanent and always present reminders of the friendship and love that held these networks together.

English-language historians have commonly restricted the term *fief* to the knight's fiefs, the land held by members of the military class in return for military and other services. The Occitan fief covered a far wider social realm. Far down the social hierarchy, even a grant of land to a share-cropping peasant—one that paid its lord the habitual quarter of grain crop or fifth of grape harvest and the common agricultural dues called the *agrarium* and *tascha*—could be called a fief. This usage, to be sure, was rare; where it appears it may merely be the result of scribal inattention.[29] Most commonly, the services owed by peasant fiefs contrast sharply with the burden of sharing the crop and paying dues in addition; for members of that lowest status they would have borne all the marks of privilege. For such fief holders might owe nothing more than the *acaptum*, a payment of a handful of pennies on receiving the fief, plus an annual rent in the form of a few pennies on All Saints' Day, or a measure of wine or two hens on Saint Michael's Day, or a salmon on the feast of Saint Peter-in-

Chains. In addition another few pennies would be due at the accession of a new lord, and a few solidi for "approval" (*laudatio* or in the vernacular, *lauzime*) when the fief was sold or mortgaged. Even the fine due if the fief holder was convicted of some infraction was fixed at a tiny sum of a few solidi.[30]

None of this was likely to bring more than a trickle of income to the lord, nor was it likely to weigh heavily on the budget of the fief holder. If weight there was, it was symbolic, the reminder on those saints' days when payments were due, of the reverence owed year round in word and deed. Yet that reverence said little about the fief holder's place in the hierarchy. Priests could hold churches and their revenues in fief from bishops and—until the Gregorian Reform put an end to the practice—from laymen as well. Even the abbot of Eaunes could feel free to accept the tithes and first fruits of a church as a fief from the abbot of Lézat, agreeing to pay not only the usual twelve pennies acaptum but an annual rent of an émine of grain as well, not much different from many a peasant fief. Seeing such practices, a peasant might indeed feel some satisfaction in calling himself his lord's *homo pagensis*, his "peasant man."[31]

And yet, although the fief was a privileged holding, accepting one and doing homage and fidelity for it implied subservience, required serving another; it was therefore an act of piety for a lord on his deathbed to release those who served him from that burden, as William Affuel of the village of Bessan near Agde did in 1176, absolving "all my men and women from their homage [ab hominisco], and freeing all they hold from dues [ab omni usatico]."[32]

William Affuel was what we might think of as a lord "of the middling sort," possessing property in several villages around Agde and anxious to spread his alms as widely as the cathedral of Maguelone, the Cistercians at Valmagne, the canons of Saint-Mary of Cassan, the Knights Hospitalers, and a number of village hospitals, in order to endow hundreds of masses for his soul. He was important enough to appear as witness on several occasions for his lord, Pons of Bessan. When he died childless he named as his heir Pons of Fenollèd, a fellow lord of the same middling sort, to whom he gave the task of founding yet more masses.[33] Peter Gaucelin, who held a fief of William Affuel, seems to have belonged to the same milieu. To distinguish people such as Peter Gaucelin from peasant fief holders, their fiefs were called "honorable," *fevum honoratum, feus francs*, and sometimes military duty was the specified service, although Peter Gaucelin, for his honorable fief, owed only six sétiers of grain.[34] Thus, neither the term *fief* nor the services rendered for it specifically marked the social place of the *fevater*, the fief holder. That too may have made the fief a privileged gift for some people—especially if they were well down the social hierarchy.

Who were these people near the bottom? We have already met some of them among the serfs and village notables. Bernard Modul of Douzens, for example, held some of his lands in fief from the couples who owned him. The fiefs went with him into the hands of the Templars. So did Peter of Raissac and his brothers. In 1181, as part of the unending search for a resolution to their dispute with the prior of Saint-Antoine, the brothers recognized that they held some of their lands in fief of the prior, owing four *quartons* of good quality wheat on the feast of Saint Julian and three solidi Tol. on the feast of Saint Thomas.[35] As might be expected from people in their position, big men among the bushwhackers and tree fellers along the Hers River, they had for years been granting fiefs from their holdings to others.[36]

Were Bernard Modul and Peter of Raissac representative of the hundreds of peasant fief holders who appear in the documents for two hundred years—most of them only names that surface once and then vanish back into obscurity? Some, at least, of these other fief holders may have been of the same status—rich peasants, small-time entrepreneurs, men with special skills whose attachment a great lord might find useful to cultivate, or men with sufficient resources of their own to undertake the arduous task of turning marsh and woodland into vineyards and grainfields that a lord could then exploit.

Although some of the fiefs recorded in Lézat's cartulary were grants of churches to priests and others were grants of tithes—the kind of revenue that by itself suggests the higher status of those who got them, especially when they owed military service in return—a handful required that the fief holder render an albergum every year (most often in this case not for knights waiting for campaign season but for the abbot and his companions on tour). This was the obligation, as we have seen, that all the witnesses took as the sign of Peter of Raissac's servitude. Yet other individuals who we discover living on the Occitan plain give an even stronger sense of that fluid social boundary where, as with Bernard Modul and Peter of Raissac, people who owed peasant dues could yet be addressed by others as "my lord" or "my lady." Such was the domina, widow of William of Genestet, who held some fields, gardens, and houses in the village of Montagnac in fief from the canons of Saint-Etienne of Agde; for these, she and her partner, Berenger of Montagnac, owed the usual agricultural tascha to the canons in addition to an albergum for three knights and a sétier of oats. The Raymond Roger who received an "honor" in fief from the abbot of Lézat sometime around 1100, paying as entry fee a horse worth twenty solidi and doing homage "with his two hands," may have been in the process of crossing the tenuous boundary separating tenant from lord; in addition to an annual albergum, he promised to lend the abbot horses "and to go with him and serve him as is right" ("et prestet equas et pergat cum eo et serviat ei sicut lex est").[37]

Other fief holders owed more backbreaking services—planting vines and cleaning ditches, clearing brush and wood, clearing fields for plowing. As urban markets expanded in the later twelfth century, there were opportunities both for landlords and for enterprising laborers. Peter of Raissac and his brothers, as we saw, were involved in clearing land along the Hers. They took their future grainfields and pastureland in fief; meanwhile, the wood they cut brought ready cash in Toulouse. At Lespinet, a village southeast of Toulouse that the twentieth-century city has now absorbed, we can follow the effects of the Toulousain demand for wine as well. There, in return for a share of the crop when the vines began to produce, village lords granted fiefs half-arpent by half-arpent, both to those who would dig and trim the vines themselves and to middlemen who were ready to take the land in fief and then lease it. Prominent among these middlemen was the prior of Saint-Antoine of Toulouse, the same prelate who fought so bitterly to have Peter of Raissac and his brothers recognize his lordship.[38]

All kinds of lands and rights could serve as fiefs—hay fields and grainfields, woods and meadows, vineyards and salt pans, mills and houses, fishing rights, churches, tithes and first fruits; men and women were held in fief;[39] so were rights of protection on the highways, tolls at city gates and sales taxes in their markets, vicarial rights,[40] rights to levy alberga, rights of justice, the right "to the archbishop's palfry when he makes his first entry into Narbonne,"[41] and, of course, at the highest levels of the social hierarchy, towers and castles.

From a practical point of view, nothing appears to distinguish fiefs from the many other ways that people held property. The peasant who received a fief could live in the house, plant the vines and harvest the grapes, sow the grain and gather in the sheaves; the entrepreneur could work the mill and collect its revenues; the priest was expected to sing his mass and collect his tithes and first fruits;[42] those who held tolls and taxes, justice, and vicarial rights could pour their profits into their treasure chests and bask in what men of a later age would call their "worship"; the castellans manned their castles and, like so many up and down the social hierarchy, imposed what they could on those subject to their power. Those who received fiefs could grant them, or parts of them, to others to hold as fiefs (as we have seen William Affuel do with the fief he held of Agde cathedral). They could sell their fiefs or mortgage them, subject only to the fief giver's "approval" (which at the bottom of the hierarchy meant nothing more than the payment of a few pennies).[43] They could bequeath them to heirs, relatives, monks or priests (the clergy sometimes paying dearly for them and for others owing only their prayers).[44] If the person who granted the fief, or his heir or successor, wished to get it back, he had to pay good money for it. So Archbishop Berenger discovered in 1160 when he negotiated to recover a quantity of his rights in the Bourg of Narbonne, including tolls, dues from sales of fiefs, and half of the vicarial oven, all of which had been in the family of Gerald of Breuil since Archbishop Guifred had granted them as a fief to Gerald's grandfather. A total of 2,000 sol. Melg. was the price the archbishop and Gerald finally settled on, and Gerald kept his share of the profits from the archbishop's justice.[45] Fiefs, in this sense, were property like any other.

Yet at the same time, those fiefs were still in some sense the property of the people who had granted them. Indeed, the services due and whatever else the person who granted the fief could claim, could themselves be granted as fiefs, or become the object of other complex transactions.[46]

In the course of the thirteenth century, professionals trained in Roman law would try to make sense of such transactions by inventing pseudo-Roman terms for what they conceived of as layers of ownership or lordship (for one word, *dominium*, served for both): "ownership of use" (*dominium utile*) for the rights of the person who profited from the revenues; "legal lordship" (*dominium directum*) for the rights of the person who collected the services from the fief, the person from whom the ownership of use was held. The notaries who drew up some conveyances for Lady Richildis and the canons of the cathedral of Agde in 1214 were struggling toward such an analysis; their words focused on the particular rights that a certain William had sold to Richildis and that a Raymond Pons would sell to the canons of Saint-Etienne—"dominatio et feudum" (superiority and fief), "consilium, dominium, et servitium" (approval, lordship, and service)—but those words still betrayed the weight of social rank and obligations. As her life approached its natural end, Richildis wanted to pledge these obligations to the cathedral canons. In return she would receive "a share in all their spiritual goods" and, after her death, a place in their book of remembrance, their "martyrology."[47] We are far here from the simple conveyance of economic goods assumed by Roman (and modern) law.

Indeed, the bipartite distinction coined by the lawyers between "ownership of use" and the higher forms of lordship could make sense of the complex relationships of fief giving and fief taking only by simplifying them and voiding them of much of their social content. The peasants who worked the land from which the fief holders drew their portions and their dues now became tenants, even if they held their land in fief. By building layer upon layer of lordships, the manipulators of rediscovered Roman law might try to describe some of the multiplicity of fief-holding and sharecropping relations that we have seen in this chapter. There was no way, however, that they could twist their new vocabulary to satisfactorily explain the story of Archbishop Richard, Berenger of Peyrepertuse, Peter Olivier of Termes, and the castle of Villerouge, where, to the archbishop, Berenger had retained sufficient interest in the castle to warrant excommunication, even after he had alienated it. Nor could they use their terms to make sense of grants such as the fief of Tarragona that the count of Barcelona gave to Ermengard's ancestor three-quarters of a century before the count had conquered the city, for he would have had no legal lordship at the time and therefore no use to grant. From the simplified image of fiefs that lawyers trained in Roman law developed and that historians have largely accepted ever since, exchanges such as these were marginalized and eventually eliminated. Occitan "feudalism" became an exception, a bizarre variant, the result of "misunderstanding."[48] The notions of "ownership of use" and "legal lordship," by focusing all attention on the "bundles of rights" associated with them, cast into deep shade or irrelevance the personal relations created by the very acts of giving and taking.[49] This is but one of the many ways in which the men of the thirteenth century and those who followed rewrote the world of Ermengard.

In Ermengard's world, these repeated exchanges and the rituals in which they were imbedded defined relations at every level of the social hierarchy, among families, between viscounts and their castellans, lords and their followers, the rich and their dependents, patrons and their clients, landlords and peasants on the make. When fissures and fractures opened wide, as affinities, passions, and ambitions tugged and strained at these manifold bonds, they were reknit with further rituals and, often enough, with giving and taking yet again. Honor had to be respected, friends had to be cherished and rewarded, lest their friendship cool and the voice of others, of enemies real or potential, sound more sweet.

Fidelity required constant cultivation; it could never be taken for granted. And it required more than giving, more than oaths. It required belief. The true genius of the aristocratic courts of Occitania, and Ermengard's chief among them, was to discover the way to cultivate that belief, to teach the virtues of fidelity as a spirited game and make mastery of its refinements the definition of who belonged, the way to turn fidelity itself into a passion. The secret was music and poetry, the songs of the troubadours.

CHAPTER THIRTEEN
LOVE AND FIDELITY

"I, Peter of Nébian, wishing to love you, William lord of Montpellier, with true love, to serve you faithfully and to dwell in your grace and protection [desiderans te . . . vero amore diligere, fideliter servire, et in gratia et sub defensione tua consistere] . . ." With these words a village castellan gave his lordship to William VII in 1160, to receive it back in fief.¹ Love helped secure the alliance of Archbishop Guifred of Narbonne with Raymond of Saint-Gilles against those of Guifred's province who were seeking to oust him as a simoniac: after swearing fidelity and promising to guard the archbishop in his share of the fortifications and tolls of Narbonne and to aid him against his enemies, the count promised *per drudariam*, "out of love," to grant Guifred in fief a third of whatever the archbishop might be able to acquire "in the county of Narbonne." Love was on the lips of Ermessend, wife of William V of Montpellier, when some decades later she gave Peter William of Pignan 500 sol. Melg. for his castle of Pignan and added 40 sol. *pro drudo*, "for [Peter William's] love." Love could be listed as part of a family's estate, like dues from peasants or lordship of castles. "They have, or should have, their men's love and support and company in deed and word in all their quarrels [an lor omes a amar et a chaptener e a rasonar e tener ab eus, o que il los aen, de totas lor naugas]," an obscure family of village lords recorded among their possessions at Millac in Périgord. We should therefore not be surprised when the epic poet of the Albigensian Crusades, William of Tudela, says of the viscount of Béziers and his followers, "Ilh eran sei ome, sei amic, et sei drut," "They were [the king of Aragon's] men, his friends, and his lovers."² In Ermengard's world, love bound lords, both male and female, to each other. The giving and re-giving of alods, fiefs, and money repeatedly renewed it; ritual oaths of fidelity repeatedly affirmed it. In land conveyances and inventories as well as poetry, the word returns like an old song.

To our modern eyes, trained to see in love only a world of private passion, a private intoxication, such talk immediately suggests the intimacy of the bedroom; depending on context it seems to advertise adultery or homosexuality, both of them incongruous when, as in these, the context is a land conveyance, a political alliance, or the description of a battle force. At few other moments can we see as clearly the distance that separates our world from Ermengard's.

Our way of construing the world, our language itself, makes of emotions a psychological or physiological state, a state "inside" rather than "outside" the individual. Love, hate, anger, joy are part of a person's character or disposition or spirit; they are frames of mind or moods, with their source in spleens, souls, genes, or hormones; they reside metaphorically in the heart or physiologically in the chemistry of the brain; they are deep, soul-stirring, rapturous, or shallow and mean-spirited. Whatever they may be, they are peculiar to our selves, as in our desires we are led to discover the truths of our inner being.[3]

Emotions may shape our social lives but not the reverse. Society can prompt us to feel anger or joy; it does not give them to us, still less impose them on us. And for some, following Rousseau, our feelings are what are most natural or genuine about us, in contrast to the disguises we present in public. For the public world, the social world, is a world of convention and, above all, of calculation; there we are guided by rational choice (so we are told) and, so we most often imagine, by self-interest. For this reason, the distinction between feeling and thought, between emotion and rationality, at times elides into the distinction between private and public. It is in private that we can express our true emotions; there we need not put on our public face; home and family, the private world, are the self enlarged.

In contrast, in the public world, competition and possessive individualism are expected. They require no explanation. Even in biology, altruism is the mystery to be decoded. Love is not a passion of the public arena; it stands outside of politics and is, for some, the very opposite of power. In this we are, of course, the children not just of Darwin but of Locke and the Enlightenment, and true to their teachings we easily project the same expectations back onto earlier societies as their true reality, just as we project them outward onto the world of nature.

Yet the language of twelfth-century land conveyances and aristocratic agreements tells us otherwise. That world may have been presented by monkish chroniclers—and therefore commonly by modern historians—as one dominated by violence, where greed was controlled only by the threat of physical force or divine retribution, but aristocratic talk was of love and anger. And they spoke in ways that tell us they did not divide "inner" from "outer" nor draw the line between "private" sentiment and "public" power where we do. Their vocabulary shaped the world differently. We may harbor the belief that talk of love in that world, when it is not a reference to sexuality, can only be an illusion. So, indeed, it may have been. But as Johan Huizinga reminds us, illusion itself is an important historical reality.[4] And if love was an illusion, it nevertheless came to the mind of William VI of Montpellier when he agreed that if Count Bernard of Mauguio could prove that William's father had sworn fidelity to the count, William would likewise swear fidelity and "along with the honor which he has, he shall come into the power and love of the count [venerit in potestate comitis vel amore]."[5]

Drut and its Latinized derivatives *drudum* and *drudaria* were often the words of choice to speak of this political love and the person who felt it. These were words of complex connotation, for in them were fused the love that joined lord and follower and the love that joined man and lady.[6] They served as signs for the shared love of political allies, of those who fought side by side, like the Viscount Raymond Roger who was the *drut* of the king of Aragon and, according to the same poet, "had love for all, / and those of his lands, over whom he was lord, / did not fear or stand in awe of him / but played with him as their companion [avia ab totz amor, / E sels de son païs, de cui era senhor, / No avian de lui ni regart ni temor, / Enans jogan am lui co li fos companhor]."[7]

At the same time, in troubadour song the word *drut* could be infused with a glow of romantic sentiment, as in these lines, which Peire Vidal addresses to his Tort-n'avetz:

De totz drutz suy ieu lo plus fis	Of all lovers I am the most faithful
qu'a midons no dic re ni man	for to my lady I neither speak nor command
ni'l quier gen fait ni bel semblan;	I ask neither kind favors nor pretty pretense;
cum qu'ilh m'estey,	however she is toward me
sos drutz suy et ab lieys dompney	I am her lover and pay court to her
totz cubertz e celatz e quetz.[8]	secretly, discreetly, quietly.

As words for friend or lover, Latin provided *amador* and *amics*. *Drut* came from Old Germanic—Frankish *druht*, Old English *dryht*, Old Norse *drótt*. In all these ancient tongues the word's primary meaning had nothing to do with erotic or sentimental relations of men and women. It was the word for "war band," and to Old High German, medieval Latin, French, and Occitan it gave the meaning "faithful friend," in the sense of one who had sworn fidelity.[9] The poetic meaning it gained as "lover" testifies to the emotion that was believed to infuse such military and political relationships.

What did such love require of its adepts? That was a question that generations of troubadours explored: the demands of a love that flourished in the ambiguous realm between sentiment and power, politics and eroticism.

⇥⇒

We think of the troubadours as singers of love. But the language of politics entered their poetry in many ways. Sometimes it was explicit and forthright, most notably in the songs of Bertran de Born, the master of warrior bravado and political invective. Sometimes it was more subtle, as in the nostalgic song that Peire Vidal addressed to Provence:

Ab l'alen tir vas me l'aire	With my breath I draw the air
qu'eu sen venir de Proensa;	I feel coming from Provence;
tot quant es de lai m'agensa	all that comes from there pleases me,

si que, quan n'aug ben retraire,
eu m'o escout en rizen
e'n deman per on mot cen;
tan m'es bel quan n'aug ben dire.

so that when I hear good things of her
I laugh when I listen
and ask a hundred more words for every one;
so pleased am I when I hear good spoken of her.

Qu'om no sap tan dous repaire
com de Rozer tro qu'a Vensa,
si com clau mars e Durensa,
ni on tan fis jois s'esclaire
per qu'entre la franca gen
ai laissat mon cor jauzen
ab leis qu fa'ls iratz rire.[10]

No one knows a more sweet home
than between the Rhone and Vence
enclosed by the sea and the Durance,
nor any where joy shines more brightly.
That is why among these noble people
I have left my joyful heart
with her who makes the angry laugh.

Because "Proensa" is a feminine noun and is referred to after it first appears by a feminine pronoun, commentaries have sometimes taken it to be a "cover name" for a lady, for the stanzas that follow could as easily be about a woman as a place. But the boundaries given at the beginning of the second stanza—"between the Rhone and Vence, enclosed by the sea and the Durance"—are explicitly political boundaries, the part of Provence ruled by the Barcelonese dynasty as defined by treaty in 1125 (although for the sake of the rhyme, Peire Vidal substitutes Vence for la Turbie). In this song the poet declares his allegiance to the Barcelonese. His beloved Proensa is very much a political lady.

Politics entered troubadour love songs most forcefully, however, through its language and metaphors. Its presence could be heard in what appear at first to be the most intimate and erotic passages. We have already seen the metaphor of castle holding and even of the *fief de reprise* used to describe the relation of the lyric "I" to the poet's lady or to Love. When we look carefully, the language of fidelity and the specific language of its oaths seem to be everywhere.

Let us recall the text of those oaths.

From this hour forward, I . . . will be faithful to you . . . by true faith without deceit as a man should be faithful to his lady [or lord] to whom he has commended himself by his hands.[11]

Here now is the troubadour Bernart de Ventadorn following lines of a most fleshly eroticism with the image of himself as the oath taker:

Ara cuit qu'e'n morrai
del dezirer que'm ve
si'lh bela lai on jai
no m'aizis pres de se,
qu'eu la manei e bai
et estrenha vas me
so cors blanc, gras e le.
. . . .
Bona domna, merce
del vostre fin aman.
Qu'e'us pliu per bona fe
c'anc re non amei tan.

Now I think that I shall die
of the desire that comes upon me
if the fair one, there where she lies,
does not welcome me next to her
to caress and kiss her
and press to me
her white body, plump and smooth.
. . . .
Good Lady, show mercy
to your true lover,
for I pledge you in good faith
that never did I so love anyone.

| Mas jonchas, ab col cle, | Hands joined, head bowed, |
| vos m'autrei e·m coman.[12] | I give and commend myself to you. |

In another poem he lifts a line directly from the oath:

Per bona fe e ses enjan	In good faith and without deceit
am la plus bel'e la melhor.	I love the fairest and the best.
Del cor suspir e dels olhs plor,	From the heart I sigh and from the eyes weep,
car tan l'am eu, perque i ai dan.[13]	for I love her so much that I am injured.

Such language, taken from the world of politics and military alliance, from the court society of great lords (male and female) and their fighting men (and women), infuses these lyrics with a troubling air. Bedroom and battlements seem incongruously joined. The world of amorous embrace slips without break into the world of political alliance and back again. Genders likewise become confused when the lady turns into a lord:

Bona domna, re no·us deman	Good lady, I ask nothing from you
mas que·m prendatz per servidor,	but that you take me as your servant
qu'e·us servirai com bo senhor.[14]	who will serve you as his good lord.

or bears as a *senhal* a name that is grammatically male—"mon Estriu," "mon Azimen," "mo Cortes," "mos Bels Vezers."[15]

A hundred years ago, the image of men kneeling before their ladies, heads bowed, hands joined, provoked French literary historians to invent the idea of courtly love to explain their behavior, so distant did it seem from normal relations between the sexes, so strange, so medieval.[16] More recent historians and literary critics have denied any reality to courtly love outside the poetry, and what is there within it they consider problematic precisely because it seems so far from what they assume to be the social realities of the age. The troubadour's lady exercises power over her lover, often expressed, as we have just seen, in the same language and gestures of fidelity that bound warriors to their lords, and this gender imagery, they argue, is paradoxical or ironic. It must be explained away. But such interpretations, whether literary or historical, assume that the world of the troubadours was one in which men alone exercised political power, in which men swore fidelity only to other men.[17] But that, as we know, was not the world of Ermengard of Narbonne.

Let us imagine a poet like Bernart de Ventadorn in Ermengard's court when a castellan like Bernard of Durban put his hands in hers and—in a decidedly unerotic setting—pledged his fidelity "by good faith and without deceit"; imagine him seeing a young man enter Ermengard's service and speak the very words that the poet then employs: "Bona domna, re no·us deman mas que·m prendatz per servidor," "Good lady, I ask nothing but that you take me as your servant." Or let us imagine the troubadour Raimon de Miraval present when a fellow castellan swears fidelity for his castle to a woman, or Raimon even doing so himself, as so many other castellans did—to Ermengard of Narbonne and Beatrice of Mauguio, to the various Trencavel widows (Ermengard at the end of the eleventh century, her daughter-in-law Cecilia and the widowed Saura and Guillelma later in the twelfth century), to the widowed Ermessend of Montpellier, or to a fellow lady castellan.[18] To the troubadours and their audience such occasions would have counted among the commonplaces of aristocratic life, ready, like the oaths of fidelity themselves, to be put to poetic use—as Raimon de Miraval does:

Mas d'una chan e d'una·m feing,	But I sing of one, and of one I have concern,
e d'aquella Miraval teing.[19]	of her I hold Miraval.

What seems to be problematic to so many historians and critics was drawn directly from life.

Lines such as these are images, however, and they exist in poetic space. That space is not a replica of reality, although it may comment on it or seek to shape it. It uses reality for its own ends, whether playful or serious or both at the same time. Troubadour lyrics are sophisticated poetry, composed for an audience of connoisseurs capable of appreciating their difficult forms and complex rhymes, capable of comparing a poet's compositions with those of his contemporaries and predecessors, capable likewise, we must imagine, of appreciating the poets' transformations of words and sentiments that they, the listeners, could remember speaking.

For this audience of aristocrats and castellans, love—that is, fidelity and service, and the expectation that service would be rewarded—was at the heart of their social being. The loyalty of village lords, of castellans and knights, without which dynastic politics would have become a masquerade and armies a sham, depended on them. Here was the substance of honor and worthiness, the actions that won praise, the source of the troubadours' "joy."

To these ideals the troubadours constantly returned, sometimes in a voice tinged with irony or anger, as in the lyrics of Bertran de Born:

Vostre reptars m'es sabors,	Your accusations I find delicious, you
ric, quar cuidatz tant valer	powerful men, you think you're worth so much
qe sens donar, per temer,	that without giving anything, simply from fear,
volriatz aver lauzors.	you would have people praise you.
. . . .	. . . .
Mas faitz vostres faitz tan gens	Act nobly
qe·us en sega digz valens.	and you will be called worthy!
. . . .	. . . .
Ric ome volh qu'ab amors	I wish rich men knew how with love
sapchan cavaliers aver	to hold knights,
e qe·ls sapchan retener	knew how to retain them
ab ben far et ab honors,	with rewards and landed honors.
e qu'ls trob om ses tort faire,	I wish one found them blameless
francs e cortes e chauzitz	open and gracious and polished,
e larcs e bos donadors.	generous and good givers.
Qu'aissi fo prez establitz:	For merit was established for this:
qu'om guerreies ab torneis	that men should fight in tournaments,
e Quaresma e Avenz	and Lent and Advent
fesson soudadiers manenz.[20]	should make mercenaries rich.

In the voice of other poets, these ideals could take on the coloration of sentimental confession or erotic hope. What should the loyal lover do if his service is not rewarded? the lyrics asked. What does a lady (lord) risk if devotion is not recognized and recompensed? Here the poet played the part, followed the troubled retainer, the man who had promised "good faith without deceit," through his waves of desire, despair, and hope.[21]

Bernart de Ventadorn was among the most accomplished at this art. In this poem, for instance, he sings the role of the *servidor* waiting for his lady (lord) to be "open, gracious, and polished, generous and a good giver," vacillating between desertion in one verse and, in the next, a fidelity that resists all ills in the hope of better things to come.

Si tot fatz de joi parvensa,	Though I make a show of joy,
mout ai dins lo cor irat.	in my heart I have great anger.
Qui vid anc mais penedensa	Whoever saw someone do penance
faire denan lo pechat?	before he had committed sin?
On plus la prec, plus m'es dura,	The more I beg her, the harder she is to me,
mas si'n breu tems no's melhura,	and if she's not better to me soon
vengut er al partimen.	the time will have come to leave.
Pero ben es qu'ela'm vensa	But it is good that she has defeated me,
a tota sa volontat,	forced me to do her will,
que s'el'a tort o bistensa,	for if she is wrong, if she hesitates,
ades n'aura pietat;	soon she will have pity;
que so mostra l'escriptura:	for thus the scriptures show
causa de bon'aventura	in matters of good fortune
val us sols jorns mais de cen.[22]	one day is worth more than a hundred.

Here only the words "dins le cor irat," "anger in the heart," recall the tough world of power, but they are enough to infuse the rest of the text with its savor and to allow the audience to hear in "forced me to do her will" an important reason for that anger.[23] In "La dousa votz ai auzida" Bernart is far more direct, and the two worlds of erotic love and the mutual love of lords and knights fuse into one. His lady is a "traïritz de mal linhatge," a "traitoress of base lineage," evoking the worst possible breach of the oath of fidelity and thus the most grievous dishonor to both the individual and (her) family.

Mout l'avia gen servida	I most nobly served her
tro ac vas mi cor volatge,	until she showed me her fickle heart;
e pus ilh no m'es cobida,	since she is not in agreement with me,
mout sui fols si mais la ser.	I am a great fool if I serve her longer.
Servirs c'om no gazardona,	Service unrewarded
et esperansa bretona	and Breton hope
fai de senhor escuder	make a squire of a lord
per costum e per uzatge.	by custom and practice.
Pois tan es vas me falhida,	Since she is so at fault toward me
aisi lais so senhoratge.	I leave her lordship.

This is the song that Bernart sends to "my lady at Narbonne . . . whose every act is so perfect that one cannot speak foolishness of her."[24] The complement is indirect, but clear: his lady at Narbonne, most likely Ermengard herself, is the exact opposite of the traitorous lady in the lyric, neither fickle nor oblivious to her obligation to reward those who serve her. In just this way, time and time again, the poets implicitly compare their patron (or hoped for patron)—the king of Aragon, the count of Saint-Gilles, the marquis of Montferrat, the viscount of Marseille—to the invented lady of the lyric, and allow their audience to play with the meanings and lessons that such comparisons might imply.

We can thus work back from the boastful and posssibly ironic dedicatory lines with which Raimon de Miraval ends his love song, "Aissi cum es genser pacors," and imagine that his twelfth-century listeners were meant to do likewise.

10 Ma domna et eu et Amors
   eram pro d'un voler tuich trei,
   tro c'aras ab lo dols aurei
   la ros'e'l chanz e la verdors
   ll'an remenbrat que sa valors
15 avia trop descendut
   car volc so q'eu ai volgut.

. . . .

20 Mas no'ill plaz que plus lo m'autrei,
   e puois midonz vol q'eu sordei.
   Be'm pot baissar car il m'a sors.
   Las, per que no'ill dol ma dolors
   puois aissi'm troba vencut?
25 q'eu ai tant son prez cregut
   q'enanzat ai sos enanz
   e destarzat toz sos danz.

   Un plait fan domnas q'es follors:
   qant troben amic qe's mercei,
30 per assai li movon esfrei
   e'l destreingnon tro's vir'aillors;
   e qant an loingnat los meillors,
   fals entendedor menut
   son per cabal receubut,
35 don se chala'l cortes chanz
   e'n sorz crims e fols mazanz.

   Eu non faz de totas clamors,

. . . .

41 mais s'ieu disia dels peiors,
   tost seria conogut
   cals deu tornar en refut.
   qe torz e pechaz es granz
45 qan domn'a prez per enianz.
   C'ab leis q'es de toz bes sabors
   ai cor c'a sa merce plaidei

. . . .

My lady and I and Love
were all three of one desire
until now, when the sweet air,
the rose, and bird song, and greening
have reminded her that her merit
had sunk too low,
when she desired what I did.

. . . .

It no longer pleases her to grant it to me.
And if my lady wants me to diminish in worth
she can easily lower me: she lifted me up.
Alas, why does my grief not make her grieve
since she finds me conquered?
For I have increased her prestige so much
that I have advanced her advantages
and turned aside all harm.

Ladies get involved in a foolish plea.
When they find a friend who asks for mercy,
to test him they make him fearful
and distrain him until he goes elsewhere.
And when they have sent the best far away,
false and petty suitors
are richly received.
Thus courtly song falls silent
and out come accusations and mad tumult.

I don't level complaints against all of them,

. . . .

but if I spoke of the worst,
soon it would be known
which should be scorned.
For wrongdoing and sin are great
when a lady gains merit through deceit.
From her who has the savor of all goodness
I have the courage to plead for mercy

. . . .

50 No'm desesper del ric socors c'ai lonjament attendut	I do not despair of the noble help so long awaited.
. . . .	. . . . . .

55 Domna, per cui me venz amors,
   cals que m'ai'enanz agut,
   a vostr'ops ai retengut
   toz faiz de druz benestanz,
   e Miraval e mos chanz.
	Lady for whom love conquers me,
	whoever may have possessed me previously,
	for you I have reserved
	all deeds befitting lovers,
	and Miraval, and my songs.

60 Al rei d'Aragon vai de cors,
   cansos, dire qe'l salut,
   e sai tant sobr'altre drut
   qe'ls paucs prez faz semblar granz
   e'ls rics faz valer dos tanz.
	To the king of Aragon go quickly,
	song, to say that I salute him
	and that I know so much more than any other lover
	how to make little merit seem great
	and great ones twice as valuable.

65 E car lai no m'a vegut,
   mos Audiartz m'a tengut,
   qe'm tira plus q'adimanz
   ab diz et ab faiz prezanz.[25]
	He has not seen me over there
	because my Audiart has held me back,
	for Audiart attracts me more than a magnet
	with distinguished words and deeds.

Like a modern-day Washington, D.C., spin doctor, Raimon (in ll. 60–68) announces he is offering his services as propagandist to the king of Aragon and is willing, if the price is right, to abandon the king's chief rival, the count of Toulouse (who is usually assumed to be hidden behind the *senhal* "Audiartz" in l. 66). But what does this have to do with the love song that Raimon is sending to the king? The listener only need remember (or in our case, as readers, look back to) the immediately preceding dedication (ll. 55–59), the one addressed to the lady within the song. "Drut" connects the two dedications verbally, but it is above all through their meaning that the two, although different, are yet the same: in both Raimon says, "I have loved others, but for you I reserve my best."

The dedication to the king of Aragon likewise picks up the theme of lines 25–27, "I have increased her prestige so much / that I have advanced her advantages / and turned aside all harm." Together with the dedications, these lines let us hear the lady of the song as a stand-in for all noble patrons, as the poet asks for his long-awaited reward (ll. 50–51). And because the patronage of poets was but a special case of the kind of patronage the great were expected to extend to all their followers, we can hear the entire song as a commentary on those lords, both men and women, who through their ill treatment "estrange the best" and receive "false and petty suitors" when the best have gone. Should this more generalized meaning be missed, Raimon draws his vocabulary directly from the world of disputes and feuds: the singer's "dol" (grief) in line 18, although he has protected her from "danz" (injury) in line 27; ladies' "plait" (plea) in line 28, in which they "destreingnon" (distrain) their "friend" in line 31, instead of granting "mercei" (mercy) in line 29; the "crims" (accusations or crimes) in line 36 and "clamors" (claim before a court) in line 37 that arise from such behavior, in which they do "torz . . . per enianz" (wrong through deceit) in line 45. Furthermore, Raimon reminds his hoped-for patron, "if I spoke of the worst / it would soon be known / who should be scorned." It is not just ladies whose fault is great

Music and words of the Comtessa de Dia

when they gain merit by deceit, and the singer of songs is there to reveal it, if only through the bittersweet indirection of springtime, ladies, and love.

Poetry and song, then, could be extensions of politics by other means—sometimes overtly so, but far more often under a cover of erotic playfulness, exploring now the theme of good lordship and now the theme of service and fidelity. To play the game, all poetic means were fair. Here, for example, is a song specifically about deceit, *engan*, the crime that every person who swore an oath of fidelity promised not to commit, and about the discord that results.

A chantar m'er de so qu'ieu non volria,	I must sing of what I'd rather not,
Tant me rancur de lui cui sui amia.	I'm so angry about him whose friend I am,
Car ieu l'am mais que nuilla ren que sia;	for I love him more than anything.
Vas lui no'm val merces ni cortesia	Mercy and courtliness don't help me
5 Ni ma beltatz ni mos pretz ni mos sens,	with him, nor does my beauty or my rank, or my mind;
C'attressi'm sui enganad' e trahïa	for I am every bit as betrayed and wronged
Com degr'esser, s'ieu fos desavinens.	as I'd deserve to be if I were ungracious.
D'aisso'm conort car anc non fi faillenssa,	It comforts me that I have done no wrong
10 Amics, vas vos per nuilla captenenssa,	to you, my friend, through any action;

Anz vos am mais non fetz Seguis Valenssa,
E platz mi mout quez eu d'amar vos venssa,
Lo mieus amics, car etz lo plus valens;
Mi faitz orguoill en ditz et en parvenssa,
15 E si etz francs vas totas autras gens.

indeed, I love you more than Seguis loved Valenssa;
it pleases me to conquer you with love,
friend, for you are the most valiant.
Yet you offer prideful words and looks to me
but are gracious to every other person.

Meravill me com vostre cors s'orguoilla,
Amics, vas me, per qu'ai razon qu'ieu'm
   duoilla;
Non es ges dreitz c'autr'amors vos mi
   tuoilla
Per nuilla ren que'us diga ni'us acouilla.

It amazes me how prideful your heart is
toward me, friend, for which I'm right to grieve;

it isn't fair that another love take you away

because of any word or welcome she might give
   you.

20 E membre vos cals fo'l comenssamens
De nostr'amor! Ja Dompnedieus non
   vuoilla
Qu'en ma colpa sia'l departimens.

And remember how it was at the beginning
of our love; may the Lord God not allow

our parting to be any fault of mine.

Proesa grans qu'el vostre cors s'aizina
E lo rics pretz qu'avetz m'en ataïna,
25 C'una non sai, loindana ni vezina,
Si vol amar, vas vos non si' aclina;
Mas vos, amics, etz ben tant conoissens
Que ben devetz conoisser la plus fina
E membre vos de nostres covinens.

The great valor that dwells in your person,
and the high rank you have, these trouble me,
for I don't know a woman, far or near,
who, if she wished to love, would not turn to you;
but you, friend, are so knowing,
you surely ought to know the truest one,
and remember what our agreement was.

30 Valer mi deu mos pretz e mos paratges
E ma beltatz e plus mos fis coratges;
Per qu'ieu vos man lai on es vostr' estatges
Esta chansson que me sia messatges.
Ieu vuoill saber, lo mieus bels amics gens,
35 Per que vos m'etz tant fers ni tant salvatges,
Non sai, si s'es orguoills o maltalens.

My rank and lineage should be of help
to me, and my beauty and, still more, my true heart.
This song, let it be my messenger.
Therefore, I send it to you, at your dwelling,
and I would like to know, my fine, fair friend,
why you are so fierce and cruel to me.
I can't tell if it's from pride or malice.

Mas aitan plus voill qu'us diga'l messatges
Qu'en trop d'orguoill ant gran dan
   maintas gens.[26]

I especially want you, messenger, to tell him
that too much pride brings harm to many persons.

In the manuscripts, this song is attributed to a woman, the Comtessa de Dia. As with a number of troubadours and trobairitz (women troubadours), she cannot be securely identified beyond her position as countess of a tiny Alpine principality (Die is a city in the Provençal Alps). She was probably a contemporary of another trobairitz, Azalais de Porcairagues, and may have frequented the court of Ermengard of Narbonne. Both appear to have belonged to a circle that included the troubadour Raimbaut d'Orange, a cousin of the lords of Montpellier.[27] As countess and familiar of the Occitan aristocracy, it is hardly astonishing that she should use the vocabulary of fidelity and dispute with the ease she shows here.

The Comtessa employs a deceptively simple poetic and musical structure to enlarge on her theme of deceit and discord. Her rhymes follow the scheme a'a'a'a'ba'b, with the feminine *a* rhymes changing for each stanza and the masculine *b* rhyme remaining the same. The melodic phrases are paired two by two in the beginning portion of the song, followed by two contrasting phrases that rise to the song's highest melodic and emotional pitch and then bring back the second and fourth phrases to close—a musical form ABABCDB. In the repeated ABAB there is a suggestion of the fundamental theme of the song: you promised fidelity, but you deceived me, the accusation returning in the once more repeated B phrase at the end.

Listening to musical phrase and rhyme scheme simultaneously, as one would in a performance, increases this sense of frustrated expectations, of deception. In the first four lines, the B musical cadence is associated with the rhyme *a*, and one might expect rhyme *a* to return with that music in the stanza's final line. Instead, the Comtessa gives us the masculine *b* sound. The melody has set up expectations that are deceived by the final rhyme sound. The net effect of rhyme and music decisively places the emotional emphasis on the last part of each stanza.

Discord is present from the beginning, in the will of the poetic first person, the "I" in the first line who is forced to sing of what she would not. Discord is announced in the second line in the reflexive verb "me rancur," the primary meaning of which was to dispute with someone: "na Florenza, la sor P. la Roca se rancurava d'en P. la Roca del mas della Britolia . . ." ("Florenza, sister of P. la Roca, disputed the farmhouse of Britolia with P. la Roca . . .").[28] At the same time, however, in this context, it carries the meaning "I am angry." Thus, from the first lines we are caught in a moment that is simultaneously legal, political, and emotional.

Discord is also present in the contrast between the singer's merit in lines 4 and 5 and her lover's treason in line 6. She loves fully. She has beauty, merit, good sense, but these are of no avail; she has not failed through any *captenensa*, here most easily translated "action" but which often has the specific meaning of military aid or protection.[29] Yet she is betrayed as she should be if she did not have those qualities or had failed her friend, and the word for that betrayal is *enganada*, the word so central to the oath of fidelity. Her lover is romantically unfaithful, and that is the same as being politically or militarily unfaithful. The two are but one.

In her charge against her lover, the lady of the song ironically reverses many of the commonplaces of troubadour lyrics. Her qualities are what the male poets claim to desire from their ladies. She has them. Why, then, is she not rewarded? The answer lies in another ironic reversal: her lover's pride, *orguoill* (ll. 14, 36, 38), linked at the end to ill will, *maltalens*. In the chansons de geste, pride is often the heroic defect of men; Roland is the prime example. In troubadour songs, however, it is most often the sin of women; it is pride that makes them haughty and distant. Here the accusation is thrown back upon her "friend."

Pride is the enemy of love because it destroys reciprocity, the reciprocity of agreement—the *covinens* of line 29—linked by remembrance to "the beginning of our love" (ll. 20–21). *Covinens, convenientia, concordia* was always the objective sought through arbitration and social pressure when disputes—*rancur*—erupted among the nobility. Agreement, the reciprocity of love, was what held society together. Here in the lyric, the lady and her lover shared equally in the making of their promise and should share in maintaining it. The one who fails to meet that obligation is guilty of breaking faith; the consequence is darkly hinted at in the final two lines. This binding of love to the social ethos of the warrior class is a final time made explicit in the messenger who takes this poem to her friend's *estatge*, often the word for the place a fighting man lives while doing guard duty, or for the period of guard duty itself.[30] The poem becomes the equivalent of the message to render a castle in accordance with an oath of fidelity.

This is the burden of the song: When the friend betrays her, he betrays the ideals by which every member of the nobility is assumed to live. He says one thing and does another. On one level the Comtessa is playing with the commonplaces of troubadour songs, holding an ironic mirror up to them, and assuming that her audience knows them well enough to recognize what she is doing when she makes the lady speak who so often in other lyrics is but a distant and silent object. At the same time, by using the language of *rancura* and *covinens*, of political agreement and military fidelity, she turns her song into a lesson in proper political behavior. Her song is an amorous song, but also a song to remind a man of his duty of fidelity and love to his lord (who may be female). Do not out of pride defraud or betray. Do not break covenants. Do not give cause for *rancura* to those to whom you are linked by *amor*. Simple lessons, to be sure, and delightfully embellished—but how essential to the proper working of society. And because women are powerful in this society, a woman as well as a man can teach this lesson.

⊷⊙

When troubadours and trobairitz visited Ermengard's court, she and those around her—the village lords we have met earlier in this book, the visitors from Catalonia and Italy, perhaps even from as far as the Orkney Islands—may have listened to songs such as this as nothing more than play, as pure theater, the way we might go to a club to hear a blues singer. To initiates, however, these songs invited far more: engagement with the complex and sometimes bravura rhyme schemes, which the poets seem occasionally to have invented to set a challenge to their fellow troubadours; attentiveness to the patterns of tension and release or the sheer playfulness in the melodies that imparted their own emotional tone to the words; remembrance of those other songs from which the troubadours sometimes borrowed or to which by indirection they occasionally referred; attentiveness above all to the ambient references these love songs made to the deepest issues of the political world in which their hearers lived.

For it was here that youth learned and their parents were reminded of their social lessons, not in preachments but in entertainments, in songs that would have been as easily and eagerly memorized as were the songs of Cole Porter and Vincent Youmens by my generation and the lyrics of rappers and rockers by the teenagers of our own day. Rhythm, rhyme, and melody would have anchored them deep in memory, indeed, as all good music, in the movements of the body itself. There they were stored as a poetical game that noble men and women might themselves feel urged to play. The man we know as the first troubadour, Count William VII of Poitou (William IX of Aquitaine), was himself one of the great aristocrats of his age. Others of that high station followed: the Comtessa de Dia, whose song we have just heard, and her fellow trobairitz, Tibors de Proensa and Countess Garsenda of Provence—of the very highest aristocracy, if the *vidas* and references in other poems may be trusted—Raimbaut d'Aurenga, a cousin of the lords of Montpellier, King Alfons of Aragon himself, and many castellans. The game was one of versifying, often in competition with fellow poets or with the great troubadours of earlier generations. It was also a game of multiple meanings, where the erotic, the social, and the political could play hide-and-seek with each other, signs and signifiers glinting and vanishing, mirroring the courtly world in a glass of make-believe, and leaving to the audience the pleasures of debating the songs' intent and the poets' purposes.

Although each song presented but a moment in the life of the lyric's "I,"

Seal of William VIII of Montpellier, who is depicted here holding a harp. By permission Archives Nationales de France.

there stretched out on either side a host of imaginable narratives (among which the later authors of the troubadour "lives" played their own fictive games), allowing ample space for the performer to shape his or her own ironic overlay. And, if nobility composed, if they "found" verses and music (for that is what *trobar*, the root of "troubadour" and "trobairitz," means), why should they not themselves have performed for the delight and instruction of their fellow noble men and women?

The narratives within the songs created their own world of amorous pain and erotic delight. But the lyric language did not let this imagined world stray far from the everyday world of its courtly audience. As the language of love was shared by those who spoke of Mars and those who spoke of Eros, we have in the lyrics not a borrowing of terms across some imaginary boundary of discourse, from outer to inner, public to private, political to emotional, but rather a continuum of language that reached from the formalized notarial at one extreme to the formalized poetic at the other, with the talk of every day spanning a broad but ill-illuminated range between.

When we see the language of power relations—of loyalty and faith, of treason and deceit—used in what are clearly erotic contexts, we have, to be sure, a projection of those relations of power and status into the world of intimacy. But by that very move we likewise have a counterreflection of the force of sexual longing back into the world of power, an eroticization of the ideology of faith and loyalty. Troubadour poetry, by eroticizing those ties, gave them a powerful reinforcement, served both to implant the proper ethos and to elaborate the code of behavior that made it visible. And how powerfully it did so. For that code continued to dominate noble life and speech for half a millennium.[31]

Did it also serve to strengthen the power of women such as Ermengard of Narbonne? Certainly we have the example of Queen Elizabeth I in England to show how amorous courtliness could be turned into a powerful tool of royal power. We have no such direct testimonies from the courts of the twelfth century. Yet troubadour poetry surely accomplished two things, both of which could only have enhanced the power of women rulers. It sharply engendered the values of faithfulness, trust, and openhandedness, of faithfulness even in adversity, even when unrewarded. At the same time, the world of manly camaraderie became an extension of that other world of courtly lover and his lady; they were not set one against the other but made a seamless whole. Both could only serve to promote the legitimacy of the *domna*. With all its playfulness, its irony and distancing, with all the seemingly formulaic quality of its sentiments, in troubadour song we are perhaps indeed hearing, directly and intimately, the beat of the courtly Occitan heart.

DYNASTIC POLITICS

1162–1196

PREFACE

To those coming of age as Ermengard approached the end of her life, she was the Princess of Love. The troubadours had done their work, and to those who took the songs as true confessions, her life began to fade into the mists of romance. To Andrew the Chaplain, writing for Marie of Champagne, she was the sweet, wise voice of a Court of Love. Those who were her companions during her fifty years of effective rule, however, would have known that the true loves of her life were not the companions of her bedchamber but of her council hall and her battle tent, the love of faithful counselors to the lady in whose court many had come of age, the love of warriors for the lady who organized the siege camp and set the order of battle.

Ermengard had passed her childhood as a plaything of urban factions vying for power and as the barely adolescent bride of a man who lusted after the power, the wealth, and the fame of her city. Freed of his political embrace she quickly came of age in the midst of wars sparked by other ambitious women or by the men who would use those women to further their own ambitions—Stephania of les Baux, Eleanor of Aquitaine, and her husband King Henry II of England. Her own ambitions were nourished by the ambitions of her city's merchants and mariners. When she was but twenty her army encamped with the Genoese and the Catalans before the walls of Tortosa. She was there with them. At the age of thirty she was one of the principals at the siege of les Baux. When the Church broke in two at the election of Pope Alexander III, she was one of his most important hosts as he negotiated for support against his rival, Pope Victor IV. From then on there would hardly be a year when she would not find herself feeling her way through the increasingly complex maze of regional politics, as the kings of Aragon, France, and England, the German emperor, and the pope all focused their attention on the lands between the Massif Central, the Alps, and the Mediterranean.

From her liberation from Alphonse Jordan in 1144 into the early 1160s, Ermengard was a faithful ally of the counts of Barcelona in all their enterprises in Occitania and Spain. Then misfortune struck. A child succeeded to the rule of Barcelona and the throne of Aragon. The count of Toulouse, Alphonse's son

Raymond V, saw in that event a door of opportunity. For thirty years Ermengard would have to deal with his ambitions, which inevitably affected her control of her city. The story of her political career is therefore intimately woven with that of her nemesis, just as it continues to be a part of the story of her traditional allies, the Trencavels, the lords of Montpellier, and the count-kings of Aragon.

Modern historians, following the lead of medieval apologists for their royal patrons, have commonly viewed the nearly constant warfare of these years as the first stages in the building of the modern state. Raymond V had no apologists, and the ultimate result of his activities was a disaster for his lineage. The story we will be following, of greed, ambition, religious fanaticism, and, finally, of treachery—human attributes all too familiar in the modern as in the medieval world—all of them unglossed with the retrospective coat of national or religious ideology, give perhaps a truer picture of Ermengard's world. It set the stage for the cataclysm that, a few decades after Ermengard's death, would destroy the society of which she had been such a vital part.

Somehow she survived, until the problem of succession to her own power finally brought her down.

CHAPTER FOURTEEN
RAYMOND V BUILDS HIS EMPIRE

In the first week of August 1162, soon after the besieging armies—including Ermengard with her troops—entered les Baux in Provence, Count Ramon Berenguer IV of Barcelona and his nephew, Count Ramon Berenguer III of Provence, started on their way across the Alps to meet Emperor Frederick Barbarossa at Turin. The emperor had promised to bring the lords of les Baux to trial for treason and had assured the Catalan rulers that he would invest them not only with the county of Provence, but likewise with the city of Arles (where the family of les Baux was entrenched) and the county of Forcalquier, north of the Durance, whose hereditary count, William II, had just died. Doubtless, in return, the Catalans would be expected to join Frederick's side in the papal schism and abandon Alexander III—who had taken refuge in the cities of Occitania—for the cause of the imperial favorite, Pope Victor IV.[1]

Suddenly, at the little village of Saint-Dalmas on the climb up to the Tende Pass, the count of Barcelona took ill. His physicians must have given him little hope, for knowing death was near, he summoned his closest advisors to his bedside—his dapifer William Raymond, Arbert of Castellvell, and his chaplain William; it was time to make his last decisions concerning his life in this world and focus his mind fully on the next. The count ordered that his remains be taken in state back to Catalonia, to be buried at the monastery of Ripoll in the Pyrenees; in return for their prayers, his executors were to give the monks the village of Molló. His nephew was to remain count of Provence, but he did not become head of the family or take over the county of Barcelona. That role was to fall to Ramon Berenguer IV's eldest son. To his second son, Peire, Ramon Berenguer left the county of Cerdagne and the overlordship of Carcassonne and Narbonne; for this he was to give oaths of homage and fidelity to his elder brother. Sanç, the youngest, was to be satisfied with nothing more than rights of reversion. The eldest, whom we know as Alfons of Aragon, would join his father's to his mother's patrimonies. His father called him Ramon, while his mother, Queen Petronilla of Aragon, called him Alfons, after her uncle, King Alfons I the Battler. In Aragon, Ramon Berenguer IV had taken no other title than that of prince. His son would be King Alfons II in Aragon and Count Alfons I in Barcelona. When he became count-king, however, he was only five years old.[2]

Quickly, the late count's advisors formed a council of regency. On its behalf the archbishop of Tarragona set off to find King Henry II of England, bearing the message that his lord had asked the king to be protector of his wife, his sons, and his lands. William of Montpellier was named the boy's guardian and agent (*curator et procurator*) for affairs in Provence. Meanwhile, in Alfons's name the council began to liquidate all possible dangers to their rule. To the west of Aragon there was a possible threat from Fernando II of Léon, who had seized control of his young nephew's kingdom of Castile; with him they immediately negotiated a treaty, sealed with the betrothal of the child Alfons to Sancha of Castile. With their Pyrenean neighbor, the king of Navarre, they concluded a thirteen-year truce.[3] Until the new king came of age, there could be no adventures.

The resources of Catalonia had always been essential to the Barcelonese alliance in Occitania and therefore to Ermengard. Nearly a century earlier, it was with bags full of Barcelonese gold that the Trencavels had won their power in Carcassonne and its region. In 1156, Ermengard had borrowed the immense sum of five thousand marcs of silver from Ramon Berenguer, giving her city as security.[4] Catalan wealth, in turn, had come from the tributary Moslem kinglets who ruled the *taïfas*, the micro-states that sprouted in al-Andalus following the collapse of the Cordoba caliphate in the early eleventh century; protection money was all that kept the Christian princes to their north at bay. So important was Moslem gold to the Barcelonese economy that resident goldsmiths produced their own imitations of dinars, combining the traditional Arabic inscriptions with their own names boldly included in Roman letters. Already by the second decade of the eleventh century, 87 percent of the known land sales in the immediate vicinity of Barcelona were for gold. When the fundamentalist Almoravids from the Maghrib reestablished control over the trans-Sahara gold routes late in the eleventh century, then conquered the petty kingdoms of al-Andalus, the supply momentarily dried up; by the 1140s, however, their power was disintegrating, petty kings were again asserting their presence in al-Andalus, and gold once again flowed north, in coins that the Christians now called *morabitani*—"Almoravids"—although the mints were as often in Murcia and Valencia as in Morocco.[5]

The Barcelonese financed the campaign against les Baux with Moslem gold, for they needed mercenaries to supplement their own and their allies' foot soldiers and siege specialists. To pay these hired cutthroats the count of Barcelona floated loans on the Montpellier money market. A few of his contracts with the moneylender William Letericus have survived: in September 1160 for 6,700 Moroccan gold pieces (*morabitanos de Barbaroia*) and the following year for another 6,000 gold pieces from Valencia, delivered at the siege of les Baux. Both were guaranteed by the count's kiss of faith and by prominent hostages from his court; there were other guarantors as well, including William of Montpellier, Raymond Trencavel, and Ermengard of Narbonne along with three of her most important followers: William of Poitiers, Peter Raymond of Narbonne, and William of Durban.[6] William Letericus carefully exacted a promise that the loans would be paid immediately from any money the count received from taïfa tribute or from the king of England; in the event of the count's demise, the loans were to be paid from his tolls and mills of Girona and his revenues of Barcelona. Other debts amounting to nearly four thousand gold pieces of Byzantium were still outstanding to the Genoese in 1167, as well as large sums in coin of Mauguio to urban lords of Provence.[7] Now with a child king across the Pyrenees, resources of this magnitude would be far more difficult to mobilize. The debts to William Letericus and others that William of Montpellier, as guardian of the king's affairs in Provence, contracted in Alfons's name during the 1160s, were still outstanding a decade later. When William of Montpellier rendered his accounts in 1171, the debts he had contracted amounted to twenty-four thousand morabitani.[8] With such debts mounting and the tribute payments halted, the Barcelonese allies in Occitania would have only their own revenues to depend on, and as rich as they were, those revenues could not match the gold promises of al-Andalus or the revenues that the count of Toulouse could wring from the traffic on the lower Rhone, which he controlled at Beaucaire, Avignon, and, above all, Saint-Gilles.

The death of Ramon Berenguer IV could not help but send a seismic shudder across the fragile landscape of Occitan dynastic politics. For nearly half a century, the rivalry between his house and the counts of Toulouse for regional hegemony had commanded the political calculations of the lords of Montpellier, the counts of Foix, the Trencavels, and Ermengard. Now, for the first time since the child Alphonse Jordan succeeded his brother as count of Toulouse early in the century, the head of one of these two great dynasties was a minor, and that gave nearly free rein to the other.

Raymond V, count of Toulouse, immediately set out to exploit his advantage.[9] If he could dismantle the Catalan alliance in Occitania and at long last bring under his sway the major lordships that separated his dominions around Toulouse and Cahors in the west from those in the Rhone valley and Provence in the east, he would have the empire across the Mediterranean coastal lands of which his grandfather Raymond IV had dreamed when he invented the title "count of Toulouse, duke of Narbonne, marquis of Provence." The political game, however, had changed greatly since his grandfather's days. There were more players, and they were far more powerful. In the early decades of the century the principals, in addition to the counts of Toulouse and Barcelona, were only the regional dynasts and their baronage. Now, that relative isolation had disappeared. The German emperor could hope to inflect the politics of Provence; the Italian cities of Genoa and Pisa had expanded their commercial and shipping privileges in the ports of Occitania, which inevitably meant military intervention as well; and, thanks in part to the artful stratagems of Count Raymond V himself, the long-standing Angevin–Capetian rivalry that for years had focused on the Norman frontier far to the north now found a reason for being in Toulouse itself, to which King Henry II of England and his wife Eleanor of Aquitaine were laying claim.

ANGEVINS AND CAPETIANS

King Henry's interest in Occitan politics had its ultimate source in events far to the east and many years earlier, during the Second Crusade. Summoned in 1147 in response to the Saljuk capture of Frankish Edessa (the modern Urfa in southeastern Turkey), the crusader armies did little more than accumulate disasters from the moment they crossed into Byzantine territory. Most of the Germans were slaughtered near Dorylaeum (the modern Eskisehir), while the French suffered severe losses during their January crossing of the wild mountains between the Meander River and Attalea on the Mediterranean coast. The crusaders' one major undertaking in the East, an ill-advised siege of Damascus in the summer of 1148, ended in a humiliating retreat after only four days of fighting. "Truly we have eaten the bread of grief and drunk the wine of sorrow," Bernard of Clairvaux (who had preached the Crusade) lamented to Pope Eugenius III.[10]

The troops who had set sail from Occitania under the leadership of Alphonse Jordan and Raymond Trencavel watched Alphonse die at Caesarea a few days after their arrival at Akko. Rumors immediately began to spread; his death was so sudden, he had to have been poisoned. Some blamed the count of Tripoli, great-grandson of the old crusader Count Raymond IV (Alphonse's father), who feared, they said, that Alphonse would himself lay claim to the county of Tripoli that his father had founded. Alphonse's bastard son Bertrand, who with his sister had accompanied their father, made the accusation public. Others suspected Queen Melisende, wife of the king of Jerusalem, the sister of the countess of Tripoli. After King Louis left, Bertrand marched north to defy his cousin. The count of Tripoli called for help from his Moslem neighbors, who fell upon Bertrand and took him and his sister captive. The strange story got back to the West that the daughter of Alphonse Jordan had become the wife of Nur ed-Din, emir of Aleppo, and the mother of his heir as-Salih.[11]

In the crusader camp, rumors were thickest around Eleanor of Aquitaine, who accompanied King Louis on the expedition. To twelfth-century monastic observers the constant bickering and outbreaks of enmity among the leaders of the Crusade and the Latin princes of the Levant could only be a sign of profound moral turpitude, and as fiasco piled on tragedy the lively and headstrong queen became the lightening rod for all suspicions. Contemporaries ascribed the youthful king's decision to take his wife with him to his infatuation, and most modern historians have followed in their wake. The king, however, may have had good political reasons as well; the court faction around her had already come into conflict with Abbot Suger of Saint-Denis, to whom Louis decided to entrust the kingdom during his absence. Whatever his reasons, his decision would have encouraged others around him to bring wives or mistresses as well. The frown of disapproval—at least among the monks—is palpable in the overwrought rhetoric of writers after the Crusade was over. "Castles [castra] are so called from the cutting off of excess [castratione luxuriae]," wrote William of Newburgh a generation later. "But our castles [that is, our crusaders] were not chaste [castra illa nostra casta non erant]. On the contrary, the brew of licentiousness among them gave forth a foam of unhappy appetites. . . . And so, with but a remnant of their forces, those two great princes escaped bitter ruin and came to Jerusalem, did nothing worthy of memory, and returned home in shame." And monks, we must recall, were the reporters and remembrancers, the media of the twelfth century.

The hardships Eleanor and her ladies endured crossing Asia Minor undoubtedly strained a marriage already made difficult by the differences in temperament between the vivacious queen, fond of courtly flirtations, and her ascetic king, who had spent his childhood being educated in the school of Notre Dame. Louis's abstemiousness in matters sexual indeed became a matter for preachers' stories. One of the favorites, told in two different works by Gerald of Wales, places Louis at a protracted siege on the borders of Burgundy. The king falls gravely ill, and his physicians diagnose the cause to be his prolonged sexual abstinence. Because Adela of Champagne, his third queen, is too far away to be brought to him, his council unanimously urge him to take an interim bedmate "to bring him remedy and restore him to life." Even the bishops and abbots at his court assure him that, given the circumstances, to do so would be no sin. To this advice, however, the king replies, "I would rather die chaste than live as an adulterer."[12] Eleanor's reputation was very different.

During the royal stay in Antioch (whose count was Eleanor's uncle, Raymond of Poitiers), scandalmongers—a troop sufficiently common in every aristocratic court to become a stock figure in troubadour poetry—were busily at work. The coziness between niece and uncle, they whispered, was somewhat more than familial. Tempers flared when Eleanor urged Louis to join her uncle in besieging Aleppo, while he insisted that his crusading vow obliged him to proceed directly to Jerusalem. She finally announced that he could go but she would stay and directly start annulment proceedings; she had had enough, she said, of "being married to a monk." To Louis, this proved the truth of the rumors of adultery; he led her off by force to Jerusalem. The break was irreparable. "The wound remained," John of Salisbury remarked fifteen years later, "hide it as best they might."[13]

When the royal couple stopped in Tusculum on their way home, Pope Eugenius tried to heal the breach. He entertained them lavishly, commanded that none henceforth should speak a word of any canonical impediment to their marriage, and tucked them into a bed decked out "with priceless hangings of his own" (again, according to John of Salisbury). For the moment, the domestic rift was covered over. It is possible that Abbot Suger, the king's principal advisor, sensed the dangers that might come from their separation and advised the king to be cautious, for should Eleanor and her rights to Aquitaine depart, the political costs would be dramatic, as they turned out to be. Suger died in January 1151, and within months Louis set in motion the ecclesiastical machinery necessary to have the marriage nullified. Monastic chroniclers harped on her scandalous life, which in time became the stuff of fantasy: at Antioch, Eleanor became the lover of a Turk, indeed of Saladin himself; in the nineteenth century Michelet would find the story too good to pass up.[14] But Louis may have been more moved by the fact that the queen had given him only daughters. Both folklore and professional medical knowledge derived from ancient Greek traditions ascribed the sex of children to the mother's physiology; even worse for Louis, his physicians would have told him that the queen would not conceive at all unless she were sexually satisfied, and it was unlikely, even if they shared a bed, that Eleanor now found any pleasure in his embrace.[15] With another wife he might yet beget a son.

Church law governing marriage was increasingly being brought to bear on aristocratic practices in the twelfth century. It had been willfully, and easily, ignored by those who undid Ermengard's marriage to Alphonse Jordan (although perhaps that marriage had never been consummated). It could no longer be easily ignored by a king of France. Fortunately for Louis, Church law proscribed marriages between persons who shared a common ancestor seven generations back. In Robert the Pious, king of France from 996 to 1031, the couple shared one five generations back on Eleanor's side, four generations on Louis's. At the time of the marriage, the bishop of Laon had calculated their consanguinity and made grumbling noises about it, although some—surprisingly for us, with our easy access to written genealogies—questioned whether it was true, and Bernard of Clairvaux, who heard of the calculation, got the degree of relationship quite wrong. Eleanor publicly recalled their consanguinity at Antioch. Now Louis told the ecclesiastical assembly that it troubled his conscience. And even though Pope Eugenius had ordered that the subject of the couple's consanguinity never again be mentioned, the prelates were happy to do the king's bidding. In March 1152, Eleanor and Louis were separated by ecclesiastical decree. Eleanor, escaping two ambushes laid for her by men who wanted to control her destiny, regained Poitiers. Eight weeks later she married the man who would become Louis's greatest enemy, Henry of Anjou.[16]

With this marriage, Henry threatened to control all the lands to the west of the Ile de France from the Channel to the Pyrenees, and he was preparing the campaign that would make him king of England. Louis's response was to refuse to recognize the marriage and to stitch together an alliance of Henry's most powerful enemies. After a few weeks of siege warfare, however, Louis agreed to a truce, leaving Henry free to launch his invasion of England. In 1153, King Stephen of England recognized Henry as his successor. In October of the following year Stephen died. Two months later in Westminster Abbey, Archbishop Theobald crowned Henry and Eleanor king and queen of England.[17]

Louis must have understood that whatever Henry's momentary problems in pacifying England, he would sooner or later return to lay claim to Eleanor's inheritance of the duchy of Aquitaine and eventually push those claims as far as the walls of Toulouse, just as Louis himself had tried to do in 1141. So Louis did what no Capetian had done before: he turned his attention toward the Pyrenees and the Mediterranean and found new allies in those who were likely to be enemies of his enemy. In quick succession he married his sister Constance to Count Raymond V of Toulouse, while he himself married the daughter of the king of Castile, who in the past had allied himself with the counts of Toulouse against the counts of Barcelona. Although Louis might have hoped for peaceful coexistence with Henry, he surely realized that Henry's ambitions, now nourished by a woman he knew all too well, would lead him south toward the Mediterranean, and he needed to have his defenses in place.[18]

We do not know who initiated the pact that brought Constance to Toulouse, but Raymond V could not have been unaware that Eleanor's marriage to Henry brought new threats to his rule and that a royal marriage could only serve his advantage. When Constance bore three sons in three years, she gave the alliance yet greater importance to her royal brother, for until at least 1159 these

Seal of Constance of Toulouse, wife of Count Raymond V of Toulouse and sister of King Louis. By permission Archives Nationales de France.

royal nephews were the only males in their generation of the Capetian dynasty; Louis VII himself would not have a son until his third wife, Adela of Champagne, gave birth to the future Philip II in 1165. Nor did Raymond have long to wait for Louis to prove his friendship.

In December 1158, King Henry II and Eleanor crossed the Channel to Cherbourg. After celebrating Christmas, they proceeded south through their dominions to meet Ramon Berenguer IV at the castle of Blaye on the Gironde. Amid the festivities, they betrothed their young children Richard (the future King Richard I) and Berengaria of Barcelona and coordinated the strike they would make on Toulouse. In early summer, Henry assembled his massive army—perhaps the largest army of his entire career—at Poitiers. Barons came with their retinues from the farthest reaches of his lands, even King Malcolm IV from Scotland, with a troop that required forty-five ships to transport across the Channel. The royal levies were heavily reinforced with mercenaries, whose wages Henry paid with "shield money" from knights who stayed home, and taxes from towns, Jews, and even the clergy. "Nothing like [it] can have been seen," writes W. L. Warren, "save on a major crusade."[19]

The army besieged Cahors, then took up its march toward Toulouse, while Raymond Trencavel, William of Montpellier, and Ermengard with their armies ravaged the countryside east of Toulouse. In early July, King Louis came to talk to Henry, and when he realized the English king could not be dissuaded, entered Raymond's city to look to its defenses in person. Rather than besiege the king, to whom he had done homage, Henry spent the rest of the summer subjugating the countryside and in early autumn decamped for Normandy, leaving Thomas Becket, his chancellor, in command at Cahors, and the Barcelonese and their Occitan allies still in the field. Eventually a truce was arranged between Louis and Henry, leaving Henry and his allies in possession of everything they had captured between Cahors and Toulouse. But Count Raymond was only indirectly included; Henry agreed to grant him a one-year truce as well and not to give aid to the Barcelonese and Raymond Trencavel if they launched attacks. But when the year was over, the threats resumed, and at Ramon Berenguer's death in 1162, the forces that Henry left behind were still playing their game of raid and besiege.[20]

In the negotiations that followed, Raymond was adamant that neither Trencavel nor the child Alfons be included in any permanent treaty. But then, quite suddenly, Raymond softened. Sometime early in 1163 he dispatched letters northward to inform King Louis that Raymond Trencavel had sworn fidelity to him and that Alfons of Aragon, desiring the king's continued friendship, was placing his lands and powers in Louis's service. What he did not mention in these letters was that high up in the Alps he had discovered a new opening for his ambitions, and peace around Toulouse was its precondition.[21]

In 1125, when Alphonse Jordan and Ramon Berenguer III first agreed to divide Provence between them, the lands south of the Durance River became Barcelonese territory, whereas those to the north fell to the house of Toulouse. To the north of Toulousain Provence lay the lands of the counts of Albon, who in the course of the eleventh century gradually extended their domination from the city of Vienne on the Rhone to Grenoble, Gap, and the Mont Genèvre Pass at the headwaters of the Durance. For Alphonse Jordan and his son and successor, the Albon's growing power as their principal Alpine neighbor must have seemed a real if distant threat. In 1162, Guigues V, dauphin of Albon, died, leaving only his child Beatrice as his successor. For Raymond the distant threat suddenly became a nearby opportunity. He negotiated her betrothal to his younger son Alberic Taillefer; then to guarantee that this prize would not escape, he took the girl with him to his own court while leaving his younger brother Alphonse in charge of the county.[22]

Raymond must have realized that this sudden move might not please his brother-in-law, the king of France. The Mont Genèvre Pass was essential to the Italian strategy of Frederick Barbarossa, for it allowed his army to move swiftly from Swabia through Vienne, Grenoble, and the Briançonnais Alps to the imperial stronghold of Turin. Guigues Dauphin had already been wooed by the emperor, who had conferred on him the title of count of Grenoble. Raymond was now in position to seek the same favor and might easily be tempted to slide into the imperial camp, as indeed he eventually did. To reassure Louis, Raymond weighed his words carefully when he wrote the king of the betrothal.

> I inform Your Highness that I have engaged my son, your nephew, to be married to the daughter of the count Dauphin, taking the fullest security to assure it, and have already taken control both of the girl and of a large part of the count's lands. As the increase which comes to us from this without doubt adds to your realm and glory, I beg Your Excellency to approve this marriage, to support it by word and deed if necessary, and to send special letters to the countess, mother of the count Dauphin, and to the great men of the country. In this way, the county of the late count Dauphin, though it belongs to the jurisdiction of the Emperor, will be for the increase of your realm both a gate and a haven.[23]

The last phrase especially must have been designed not simply to placate the monarch but to hold the illusory promise of an Italian policy to counter that of the emperor or at least a resource and a refuge in the king's continued efforts to impose his authority on the region of Forez, just to the west across the Rhone.

Yet the new acquisition must have given Raymond pause. With increasing imperial interest in Provence, why should he not give himself more room to maneuver, free himself to respond quickly to new opportunities, without worrying how his moves might sit with the king? During its decade of existence, the royal alliance had brought children and military aid, but it had also brought its share of ills. Louis had come in haste to defend Toulouse from Henry's siege; yet, as Raymond might have asked himself, would Henry so quickly have turned his attention to Eleanor's title deed to Toulouse had Constance's presence in the city not made it an especially delectable prize? There was also the possibility that Louis's third wife, Adela of Champagne, might yet give him his hoped for son, making Raymond's sons, Louis's nephews, less useful hostages to the king's diligence. Louis, on occasion, had in fact seemed surprisingly inattentive. Raymond, for example, had recently acquired the fealty of Bernard Pelet, who as the second husband of Beatrice of Mauguio had taken the title of count. Hardly had this happened when the king, at the behest of Raymond's rivals in eastern Occitania, wrote to Pope Alexander III to put Bernard's lands under the interdict; he was even pestering Raymond V to put pressure on Bernard just because of some tolls Bernard was collecting at the town of Alès. Nor was Louis known for his alacrity in coming to the defense of his subjects, despite his defense of Toulouse. Ivo, abbot of Saint-Mesmin of Châlons, had good reason to write the king petulantly, "You send us your messengers, but they do little and return home pursued by mockery. Behold, all shout, all the world says, 'Where is our lord the King? When comes the lord our King? See how we are given over to evil doers when we have no lord!' "[24] Raymond had much to think about. And those thoughts soon turned more and more to loosening the Capetian alliance.

Before long, Constance was writing to her brother:

> I inform Your Nobility, as the one in whom alone after God I place all my hope, that on the day on which our servant Simon departed from me I left my house and took refuge in the house of a knight of the town [Toulouse]. I am left without the wherewithal to find food or to give anything to my servants. The Count has no care for me, nor does he help me or give me anything from his lands for my needs. For this reason I ask you, imploring Your Highness, that if the messengers who are on the way to your court tell you that I am well do not believe them. Had I dared to write to you then, I would have told you at greater length of my distress. Farewell.[25]

More messengers followed as she made her way back to Paris. The city of Toulouse, threatened by the archbishop of Bordeaux at the head of King Henry's army camped "but a stone's throw" from its walls, also wrote despairingly.

> It has been a long time since our lord the Count was with us. We humbly pray Your Gracious Highness that you not allow Toulouse, which is yours, and us, who

are yours and of your realm, to be separated from you. If we do not have your help soon, our land will be like unto a desert. . . . We beseech Your Royal Piety that you aid our lords your nephews and defend us, who are yours, from our adversaries and send our lady, your sister, back to us.[26]

The breach, however, was final. Raymond was moving fast to completely refashion his relations with the lords of Occitania.

THE COLLAPSE OF THE CATALAN ALLIANCE

In October 1165, Raymond V and Count Ramon Berenguer III of Provence, the nephew of the late count of Barcelona, met at Beaucaire on the Rhone. Out of the meeting came an alliance against the count of Forcalquier and another momentous betrothal, this time of Raymond's eldest son, the future Count Raymond VI, to Ramon Berenguer's only child, his daughter Douce. Her dowry was to be her father's share of the yet-to-be-conquered county of Forcalquier, lands in Avignon, and half of the county of Mauguio (for Douce, of whom we will soon hear more, was the granddaughter of Beatrice of Mauguio).[27] To the great Catalan prelates, the members of Alfons I's council of regency who took part in the negotiations, this must have seemed but one more step in the difficult pacification of the wars that Alfons's father had left behind. Little did they imagine that less than a year later Douce's father would himself lie dead before the walls of Nice, with the girl, his only heiress, in the power of Raymond of Toulouse.

With the death of Count Ramon Berenguer III of Provence, only four years after his uncle, Ramon Berenguer IV of Barcelona, who would succeed to Catalan rule in Provence? Since 1112 when an earlier Douce, daughter of the Countess Gerberga, brought Provence as her inheritance into the family of Barcelona, her husband and their sons and grandson had made that territory the anchor of their trans-Pyrenean policy. Now the road seemed clear for Raymond of Toulouse to undo all that three generations had accomplished. Although Provence was not part of the young Douce's dowry when she was betrothed to the future Raymond VI, she could claim it—or her father-in-law could claim it in her name—as her inheritance. To add strength to such future claims and bring him closer to the Emperor Frederick, whose authority he could use to enforce them, Raymond V himself immediately married Douce's mother, the deceased count's widow, Richilda, who was the emperor's cousin.[28]

Alfons of Aragon, or rather the royal council in his name, was not ready to give up so easily. His father had repeatedly taken an active role in government and warfare in Provence and had often borne the title count of Provence or marquis of Provence as well. The council had been issuing privileges to Provençal churches in Alfons's name even before the siege of Nice.[29] Why should he not claim the succession? Count Raymond saw the threat to his plans and sometime in 1166 trapped Alfons inside the castle of Albaron in the Rhone delta. Only the quick action of Bertrand of les Baux—now an ally of the Catalans—rescued the child king and brought him safely to Arles.[30] By March 1167, the king was in Montpellier, taking the title marquis of Provence; over the following months, alliances were stitched together with Count Hugh of Rodez and the Genoese, while William of Montpellier was contracting further large debts in the king's name to put an army in the field.[31]

Raymond of Toulouse meanwhile continued to work out the consequences of his new freedom. To further ease his way with Frederick Barbarossa, he declared himself for the Imperial pope, now Paschal III, and ordered all ecclesiastical supporters of Alexander to leave his lands, expelling, among others, the bishop of Grenoble. Alexander responded by placing all of Raymond's lands under the interdict. Undisturbed, Raymond headed to the abbey of Grandmont in the Limousin to meet with King Henry II, who was marching south to put down rebellions in Aquitaine. Nothing apparently came of that meeting, but it was a certain sign of the direction in which Raymond now seemed to be speeding.[32]

It was soon after this, on October 15, 1167, that his fortunes took another turn upward, and the fortunes of the old Catalan alliance, of which Ermengard had been a part, reached bottom. On that day, Raymond Trencavel and some of his companions were murdered in the church of the Madeleine in Béziers. The news sent shock waves all the way to England. In the aftermath, one of the murderers, working out the penance imposed by the bishop of Maguelone, became a hermit near Saint-Omer far to the north, after his death to be declared a saint. The chief conspirator, however—at least so the Limousin chronicler Geoffrey of Vigeois was convinced—was none other than Raymond of Toulouse.[33] True or not, it was Raymond once again who profited. For two years, Trencavel's son and the Aragonese army were camped only twenty-five kilometers from Narbonne, besieging the rebellious city in vain. Meanwhile, the assassination provided yet another succession to dispute, yet another possible heiress to lay claim to her father's lands. Yet again, Raymond V was quick to see his advantage. To gain that advantage he now wooed the count of Foix and Ermengard of Narbonne.

Raymond Trencavel had one daughter by his first wife, whom he married to his distant cousin the count of Foix. This Pyrenean lineage had not forgotten that they, like the Trencavels, were descended from the eleventh-century counts of Carcassonne and had once had powerful claims to succession. In 1067, when the last count of Carcassonne died without direct descendants, they had been outmaneuvered by the count's sister and her husband, the founders of the Trencavel dynasty, and, nearly a century later, this loss still rankled. The marriage was probably meant to be but another in the long series of agreements that managed to keep the feud under control.[34] Its effect, however, was this time just the opposite.

Raymond Trencavel's second wife bore him two sons, Roger and Raymond, and a number of daughters; Roger succeeded to all his holdings.[35] For the count of Foix, however, the marriage tie was an opportunity to claim Raymond Trencavel's lands in his wife's name, and enough, as well, to prompt him to join the count of Toulouse in the hope of winning what his family had long coveted. Ermengard helped pave the way. At the beginning of December 1167, in Narbonne, in the company of Ermengard, her nephew Aymeri, and important members of her entourage, Raymond enfeoffed the count of Foix with Carcassonne, the Razès, and Albi—the entire western wing of the Trencavel lands. Even the scribe was Ermengard's clerk. She was now solidly in the camp of the count of Toulouse.[36]

What prompted the viscountess suddenly to switch sides? No document tells us directly. We can only attempt to put ourselves in her place and imagine what might have been her motivation. Her most important ally since she first came to power was now dead. She had lost the count of Barcelona who had so long helped finance her armies; his successor, the king, was still a child. Raymond's son was also young and untried and was still attempting to recover the city of Béziers. Where could she turn for support? The choices were few. Would it not be better to protect herself against aggression by attempting to pacify the region? Joining the count of Toulouse and working from the inside was perhaps the route of prudence, although, as we shall soon see, her heart was not really in it. And she had no more reason to trust Raymond V than she had had to trust his father.

Now, while Raymond V courted Emperor Frederick Barbarossa east of the Rhone to gain his support against the Catalans, to the west, with Ermengard's aid, he continued to deconstruct their system of alliances.[37] In November 1171, Ermengard arbitrated a peace between Count Raymond and Roger of Béziers, cemented by Roger's marriage to Raymond's daughter Adalais. On this occasion, Raymond might well have enfeoffed to Roger the same lands he had a few year earlier enfeoffed to the count of Foix. It was a momentous step. Only two years earlier, Roger had retaken his rebellious city of Béziers with the aid of Catalan-Aragonese troops. Now his departure from the clientele of the king of Aragon left William of Montpellier as its last major adherent in Occitania. And Raymond's next stroke of fortune put William under almost unbearable pressure.[38]

Beatrice of Mauguio had one son by her first husband, Count Berenguer Ramon of Provence. That son, Count Ramon Berenguer III, in turn had but one daughter, Douce, whom we have just seen betrothed to the future Raymond VI of Toulouse. After the death of Berenguer Ramon, Beatrice took Bernard Pelet, lord of Alès, as her second husband; by him she had a son,

Bertrand, and a daughter, Ermessend. When Bernard Pelet died in 1170, Bertrand laid claim to the county of Mauguio. Beatrice took this not just as an example of filial impropriety but as an act of defiance. Her second husband had used the title of count of Mauguio, but he had never acted in that role without Beatrice at his side. And she quite clearly thought of the title and its powers as primarily hers. Her son's pretensions looked like treachery. Bertrand threw himself into a league with William of Montpellier. Beatrice responded by disinheriting him.[39]

On April 1, 1172, she made a first disposition of her lands, dividing the castle, county, lands, and minting rights of Mauguio between her daughter Ermessend and her granddaughter, Douce. Those rights were really to be exercised, however, by Ermessend's husband, Peter Bermund of Sauve, and by Douce's future father-in-law, Raymond V of Toulouse. Peter Bermund would hold Ermessend's portion in fief of Raymond, and Beatrice would receive four thousand solidi per year as her pension. Forty years after his father, Alphonse Jordan, had been summarily excluded from controlling the child Beatrice, Count Raymond V of Toulouse became count of Mauguio. Almost immediately, William of Montpellier recognized that the principal source of his income—the mint of Mauguio—was at risk and recognized Raymond as count. And in December, when Ermessend's husband died, Beatrice and Raymond V quickly settled any possible disputed succession by marrying Ermessend instead of Douce to the future Raymond VI and giving the entire county, undivided, to the count of Toulouse. According to this new contract, Douce would only have a claim to her grandmother's county if she in turn married Raymond VI after Ermessend's death. The disinherited Bertrand of Mauguio turned to Alfons of Aragon for aid, and during the following year the royal council did its best to assemble a coalition of local castellans to unseat Raymond from his latest acquisition, but all in vain.[40]

As 1172 came to a close, Raymond V could boast that he had achieved what his ancestors could only dream of. From west of Toulouse to the high passes of the Alps, under one title or another, by his own right or in the right of his sons or daughters-in-law, he was lord. He was well placed in the court of Frederick Barbarossa. Ermengard of Narbonne and Roger of Béziers had joined him. The county of Mauguio was his. The heir to the eastern territories of the Trencavel clan, Roger's cousin Bernard Ato of Nîmes, was only eleven years old; Nîmes was under Raymond's "protection," its fighting men in Raymond's fidelity. William VII of Montpellier had died in September, leaving four sons, all of them under age.[41] Alfons of Aragon was still a minor, and it was his younger brother Peire who had been sent to Provence to take power as count under the name Ramon Berenguer IV. By carefully calculated strategic marriages and the work of a happy goddess Fortune, who brought his rivals low while their successors were still minors, Raymond of Toulouse had created a principality of unprecedented size—an "emperi fantasti," in the words of the nineteenth-century Provençal poet Frédéric Mistral.[42] Could he keep it?

For the moment, the only threat on the horizon was King Henry II. Raymond's move to take over the county of Albon, however, presented the king of England with another front on which to maneuver against him, this time in the Alps. Once again an heiress was at the center, the heiress to Savoy, but now it was Henry II's turn to play the marriage card.

East of the Rhone, between Vienne and Grenoble, the lands of the counts of Savoy marched boundary to boundary with those of the counts of Albon (which, we have seen, Raymond V acquired when he took the heiress of that family as wife for his son, Alberic Taillefer). Since the days of Amadeus III at the beginning of the century, the two families had been almost continuously at war, and neither had been able to make its own power predominate. Many of the lesser lords of the region swore fidelity to both.[43]

Humbert of Maurienne, count of Savoy since 1148, had two daughters who stood to inherit his lands. The count's castles controlled the Mont Cénis Pass over the Alps, and in 1167–68 he had forced the fleeing Emperor Frederick Barbarossa to pay dearly for his passage.[44] In 1171, in need of both money and an ally, Humbert dispatched the abbot of Cluse to seek out King Henry II in Normandy, bringing an offer the king could not help but find enticing. If Henry agreed to betroth his youngest son John to Humbert's older daughter, she would bring as her dowry a string of castles from Roussillon and Belley in the Rhone valley by way of Chambéry and the Arc and Isère Rivers to Cavour, Turin, and the valley of Aosta at the head of the Po, effectively giving John (and therefore Henry) control of the principal western passes into Lombardy. Furthermore, if Humbert had no son, John would become count of Savoy. All Humbert asked for in return was five thousand marcs of silver. Henry must have considered the price a bargain. Not only would he gain a foothold east of the Rhone, but by controlling Turin and the major passes toward it from the west he would also be in a position to put pressure on Frederick Barbarossa. Indeed, contemporary chroniclers suspected he intended to make himself or John king of Italy.[45] At the same time, he would also be able to open a multifront war against Raymond of Toulouse. When Henry arranged to meet Humbert at Montferrat in the Auvergne at the beginning of February 1173, Raymond had to head off the threat. He rushed to join them.

At Montferrat he found himself in the midst of a glittering gathering of princes. To the English chronicler Ralph of Diceto the wealth they displayed looked like the fabled treasures of Persia. Alfons of Aragon was there as well to speak with the king who had been his childhood protector. The multitude of magnates soon decamped for Limoges, where Henry arbitrated a peace between Alfons and Raymond. More astoundingly, Raymond did homage to

Henry and his son Richard for Toulouse, and promised both military service and an annual payment of a hundred marcs of silver or ten warhorses.[46]

Raymond must have hoped that this would put an end to the Angevin threats against Toulouse and its neighboring lands. By accepting Raymond's oath of homage, the king implicitly renounced Eleanor's claims and recognized him as legitimate successor to the county. Raymond also bought a momentary peace that would give him time to consolidate his recent massive gains. But the price he paid was high. Raymond had always recognized his sometime brother-in-law as his suzerain. As Louis's brother-in-law, however, he had tempered his obeisance with tones of independence; and Saint-Gilles and Provence, subject only to a distant and until recently quite phantom imperial overlordship, had strongly supported that unrestrained self-image. Now, for Toulouse at least, he was forced to recognize that the duke of Aquitaine stood between himself and the king. Even more galling, his oath could not be interpreted as one between equals—the common coin of aristocratic alliances in the twelfth century—for the promise of payment was warrant of his subservience. The days when Occitania could live by its own rhythm, stirred only by its own internal rivalries, were manifestly over.

The news that Raymond had aligned himself with Henry sent a tremor through the region. When Louis VII wrote to Ermengard in the hope of detaching her from his enemies, she replied with due reverence and undisguised exasperation:

> To the most revered King Louis, by the grace of God most high King of the Franks, Ermengard viscountess of Narbonne, his faithful and humble woman, sends greetings and the courage of Charlemagne. Most high lord! It pleased Your Highness to send Master Rudolph your messenger bearing your letter to me, your handmaiden, from which I received much pleasure and for which I send you immeasurable thanks. Concerning those things you have charged me to do—that I flee the company of your enemies and persevere in the love of you that I have shown from the beginning—I wish Your Nobility to hold as a certainty that I have neither allied myself with the enemies of your crown nor have I shown friendship toward them. In accordance with my vow to prize you with sincere affection and to strive to place myself and my forces at your command as time and place require, I desire to protect you in the affairs of Toulouse and will answer your requests when necessary. But if you would take up the arms of your right hand and the shield of your protection and raise yourself to deal a blow for the aid of Toulouse, more firmly and freely would I follow the path of your armed forces. It is not only I who mourn. All the people of our land are consumed with unspeakable sadness as we see our region, which the vigor of the kings of the Franks adorned with liberty, through your failure—should I not say through your guilt!—now fall to the lordship of another to whom it does not belong. Let not Your Highness be affronted that I dare speak thus to you, most dear lord. For the

more I am the special woman of your crown, the greater is my sadness when I see that crown fall from the height of its due state. Not only in Toulouse but in all our region from the Garonne to the Rhone, I see your adversary hurrying to accomplish his boast: that by subjecting the members of your kingdom to servitude he will more easily make its head to totter. Take on your vigor! Bring your strong arm to our region, that the audacity of your enemies may be put down and your friends may be comforted. Do what is necessary so that the prelates and princes of our region—who would want to serve you if they dared—guard Toulouse both when you are there and when you are absent. Strive to restore it to its due condition! I ask and others plead that you give no heed to the cost of doing this, for you will recover a hundred marcs for every one you spend, and your name—which is now but a shadow among us—will be exalted by all. If I pass over other things that should be said, Master Rudolph, whom you know comes from us, will tell you more. *Valete, valeant qui vos amant.* Farewell. Would that those who love you were strong.[47]

The salutation and closure were thick with irony. *Valete* meant "be strong" as well as "farewell." And it was the strength of Charlemagne—whom Narbonne's myth had made the city's liberator from the Saracens—that Ermengard thought Louis most needed. The letter may have been penned by a scribe proficient in the epistolary rhetoric of the schools, but the tone of the letter is surely Ermengard's. It sounds the despair she must now have felt. The camp of those who had once been her allies was now a school for children. Raymond Trencavel, Bernard Ato of Nîmes, William of Montpellier, Ramon Berenguer of Barcelona, Ramon Berenguer of Provence—all were dead. Their lands were in the hands of untried youngsters or weak or cautious regencies. Of all her allies from the 1140s and 1150s, she alone remained. She had tried the road of peacemaking. But now Raymond had maneuvered himself into a position of dominant power. Her only hope was in a distant and, she knew, quite feckless king. She spoke her hope. But she was not hesitant to imply her fear that it would be in vain. Meanwhile, her only choice was to follow the route of loyalty to Raymond V that the balance of forces in Occitania seemed to demand.

For Henry II, the assembly at Limoges in 1173 was a high point. Papal legates had reconciled him to the Church, accepting his oath that he had neither desired nor ordered the murder of Archbishop Becket. Through his daughters' betrothals he had allied himself with the king of Castile and the duke of Saxony.[48] Although the betrothal of his son John to Adalais of Savoy had given him an additional prospective voice in imperial politics, to some it suggested designs on the imperial crown itself.[49] And by marching to Montferrat in the heart of the Auvergne to entertain the great princes of the Rhone and the Mediterranean, Henry had forcefully shown he meant to contest that region as well with King Louis VII. His resources—especially those he could draw from England—far exceeded those of the king to whom he had sworn fidelity. The mercenaries he could muster and the allies he could buy seemed likely to block the king within the narrow confines of the royal domain, between the frontier castles of Normandy and the northern edge of the Massif Central.

Then Fortune's wheel suddenly turned, or, in the view of other contemporaries, divine justice finally struck.[50] Immediately after the meeting at Limoges, Henry quarreled with his eldest son and namesake, the courtly and spendthrift Henry that troubadours would know as "the Young King" (for he had been crowned in 1170). When Henry II promised Humbert of Maurienne that John would have three Angevin castles to bring as his portion to his marriage with Humbert's daughter, the Young King protested. Soon after, he slipped away to join his father-in-law, Louis VII, in Paris. His brothers Richard and Geoffrey followed. Queen Eleanor would have joined them as well had she not been caught by the king's men and brought back. She spent the next sixteen years in respectful but secure imprisonment. The revolt lasted a year, the war with Louis another three.[51] Meanwhile, the quarrel in the Angevin family set Count Raymond of Toulouse free to go about his business.

PEACE AT LAST

For Raymond, the task of creating and maintaining hegemony in Occitania had required that a careful campaign of acquisitions be balanced by an equal care that no well-financed outsider provide a focus for opposition. As long as Alfons of Aragon was a minor, the only serious threat came from the Angevins, and that one Raymond had adroitly finessed. But time passed; Alfons, only five when he succeeded to the throne, turned sixteen in 1173. On January 18, 1174, at a brilliant celebration in Saragossa, he received the arms of knighthood and married Sancha of Castile.[52] He was ready to shape his own policy—whether of caution, in the manner of his regency council, or of adventure in the manner of his ancestors, the coming years would tell.

Raymond lost no time in putting pressure on him. The count, as we have seen, claimed the succession to Count Ramon Berenguer III of Provence both as prospective father-in-law of the late count's heiress Douce and as husband of his widow. Yet Alfons, or his council in his name, had not renounced his own title as count and marquis of Provence: his administration and armed men remained solidly entrenched in Arles, in the forts at the mouth of the Rhone, and in the port cities of the coast. They had even captured one of Raymond's major allies, the viscount of Marseille, and put him to heavy ransom. To strengthen his hand, Raymond negotiated an offensive treaty with the Genoese. In return for the promise of sixteen galleys to help capture the major cities of the Provençal coast, Raymond promised them Marseille, Hyères, Monaco, Nice, and half of all the other ports from Arles to la Turbie. In late 1175, Alfons launched a raid on Toulouse, just before winter set in. Early the following year he crossed the Pyrenees again.[53] Would it be war or peace? To Ermengard of Narbonne, prudence seemed to dictate that she remain within Raymond's circle. Until the newly knighted king showed his hand and his ability to finance large campaigns, she could take no chances on an independent role.

In 1176 her prudence paid off. On April 18 the greatest prelates and barons from Aragon to Provence met on the little island of Jarnègues in the Rhone between Tarascon and Beaucaire to celebrate an agreement to end the conflict. It had been hammered out beforehand by a committee of seven mediators, among whom Ermengard sat as one of Raymond's representatives. Provence would again be divided along the Durance River, as it had been in 1125. Alfons would pay Raymond thirty-one hundred marcs of silver, less the three hundred marcs he was owed as ransom for the viscount of Marseille. It remained only for the two lords to take their oaths.

The banners and tents and armor must have bedazzled the eye, for the concourse of magnates equaled or surpassed the one at Montferrat three years earlier. The archbishops of Narbonne and Arles, the bishops of Vienne, Nîmes, and Saragossa, a host of abbots, the count of Foix, the viscount of Béziers, Ermengard of Narbonne, Guy Guerrejat, who ruled Montpellier in the name of his young nephew, and a mob of officials, clients, and hangers-on crowded around to watch as each of the two princes placed his hand on the Scriptures and swore to observe the treaty. The celebration went on for days. In the short time it took for the news to cross the Massif Central and be picked up by Geoffrey of Vigeois in the Limousin, the display and waste of wealth reached mythic proportions. *Potlatch* is the word that comes to the mind of the modern reader as quickly as *vanity* came to the quill of the good prior of Vigeois. The count, he reported, gave one hundred thousand solidi (two-thirds of the sum the king of Aragon had promised him) to Raymond d'Agoult, who in turn divided them among a hundred knights. Bertrand Raimbaud plowed a field and sowed it with silver pennies to the sum of thirty thousand solidi, while William Gross of Martel invited his three hundred knights to a festive dinner lit by wax candles and torchlight, and Raymond of Villademuls burned thirty horses "to show his vainglory." The countess of Urgel put a crown valued at forty thousand solidi on display. And William Mita was named "king of minstrels," "in order," said Geoffrey, "that none should be wanting." These stories have the flavor of epic exaggeration about them, and the horse sacrifice indeed may be a distant recollection of the Iliad,[54] but all the people Geoffrey named were there at Jarnègues. We should not too easily dismiss this wondrous tale of willful wastage.[55]

Did those who joined in the celebration imagine that warfare might—for a season or two at least—be kept at bay, that those who yearned for the din of battle would have to satisfy themselves in distant Spain? Or did they dream, as Bertran de Born would a decade later, of those coming days when

A Tolosa part Montagut	At Toulouse, beyond Montaigu,
fermara'l coms son gomfano	The count will unfurl his banner
el Prat Comtal costa'l Peiro;	at the Prat Comtal, beside the Place du Peyrou;
e qand aura son trap tendur	and when he's set up his tent,
e nos lur venrem de viro,	we'll take quarters around it and lie
tant que tres nuoitz i jairem nut.	for three nights on bare ground.
E serau i ab nos vengut	And with us will come
los poestatz e li baro	great men and barons,
e li plus honrat compaigno	and all the most honored
del mon, e li plus mentaugut;	and best-known companions in the world,
qe per aver, que per somo,	some for gain, some summoned,
que per precs s'i serant mogut.	some, if they're so moved, because they've been asked.
E desse que serem vengut	And when we've all arrived,
mesclar s'a'l torneis pel cambo,	the tourney in the fields will start,
e'll Catalan e'll d'Arago	and the Catalans and Aragonese
tombaran soven e menut,	will fall thick and fast;
qe no'ls sostenran lor arso,	their saddlebows won't hold them—
tant grans colps lor ferrem, nos drut!	we'll hit them hard, me and my mates!
E non pot esser remasut	And it can't be helped
contra'l cel non volon tronco,	if splintered lances fly up in the air,
e que cendat e cisclato	and if cendal, brocade,
e samit non sion romput,	and samite are torn to shreds,
cordas e tendas e paisso	along with ropes, stakes, rugs
etrap e pavaillon tendut.	tents, and pavilions.
. . . .	. . . .
Del lai pensson de garnizo,	Over there, they'd better look to their armor,
que de sai lor er atendut.	Because over here we're waiting for 'em!
Totz temps vuoill que li aut baro	I always want great barons
sion entre lor irascut!	to be fighting mad![56]

It was the likes of Bertran de Born who won. For Raymond of Toulouse soon overreached himself, and for twenty years Occitania was plunged into devastation more terrible than any it had ever seen.

What role had Ermengard actually played in the councils of Raymond of Toulouse? Documentation for the count is fragmentary, but what we have suggests an answer.[57] Between 1163 and 1176, Ermengard was present when Raymond was involved in negotiations with one of the barons of the old Catalan alliance: the count of Foix, the Trencavels, the lords of Montpellier.[58] She knew them. They probably trusted her as they did not trust Raymond V. She was the perfect go-between. In contrast, she was not a witness to such momentous acts as the betrothal of the young Raymond to Douce or later to Ermessend of Mauguio, nor was she present on any of those ceremonial occasions when Raymond made a generous gift to a church or monastery. At those moments he was surrounded by people like William of Sabran and his brother Gerald Amic, Raymond of Uzès, Raymond d'Agoult: nobles of the Rhone valley who had found in Raymond's service a high road to power and fortune.[59] Ermengard never entered that circle. Most likely she considered such a role beneath her

status. For thirteen years she was Raymond's ally but not a member of his entourage. It was as go-between and not as confidante that she helped negotiate
the treaty of 1176. It is impossible to know whether Raymond trusted her or
she trusted him. Probably they themselves were not sure, for, whatever the
solemn oaths that people took, at that level of twelfth-century politics expedi-
ency always outweighed good faith. Rather than wait for her to betray him, he
took the first possible occasion to betray her.

CHAPTER FIFTEEN
THE RAVAGING OF OCCITANIA

In 1177, just a year after the treaty of Jarnègues, Raymond at last succeeded in occupying the city of Narbonne.[1] It was a virtual repeat of his father's occupation when Ermengard was still a child. Was there a long siege, or did Raymond promote a conspiracy within the city's walls? Alas, no document tells us, and blocked by this silence we can only guess. Would an armed revolt against a ruler as prominent as Ermengard have gone unremarked by chroniclers in the north or the writers of the sparse annals of the south? News of the murder of Raymond Trencavel two decades earlier had found its way as far as England, and yet earlier in the century, local chroniclers had carefully noted the bloody uprisings in Carcassonne and Montpellier. The absence of any record suggests a bloodless coup, perhaps in Ermengard's absence. To those who heard of it, it must have seemed just another act of treachery in a world often ruled by betrayal, nothing horrific enough to be worth recording.

On Raymond's choice of this moment to engineer his coup we have more to furnish our speculations. At the end of January 1177, probably overtaken of a sudden by a fatal illness or accident, Ermengard's chosen successor, Aymeri de Lara, the younger son of her sister Ermessend, had taken the Cistercian habit of Fontfroide and died soon after.[2] Aymeri had been associated with her government since at least 1163, and his sudden disappearance brought on a crisis of anticipated succession, for there must have been some doubt whether Pedro de Lara, Aymeri's older brother, would remove himself from Castilian politics to replace Aymeri at Ermengard's side. Their father Manrique, Ermessend's husband, had died in 1164, and it was Aymeri and Pedro's uncle, Nuño Pérez, who assumed Manrique's dominant position at the court of the king of Castile; he in turn met his end at the siege of Cuenca in 1177. Although Nuño's sons quickly succeeded to their father's influence around the throne, without Pedro's continued presence in Castile the power and wealth of his branch of the family might very well be threatened, for like other great families in that kingdom, the Laras as yet had little patrimonial property of their own and depended entirely on temporary royal grants to maintain their rank and status.[3] If Pedro stayed in Castile, who would become heir apparent to Narbonne? Raymond V of

Toulouse scampered to exploit the void, making himself momentarily the duke of Narbonne in deed as well as in name.

Whatever Raymond's means, his coup provoked the old coalition to reassemble—the Trencavels, Roger of Béziers and his nephew the young Bernard Ato of Nîmes, and the lords of Montpellier, Guy Guerrejat and his nephews William and Burgundio.[4] Sometime during the winter of 1177 these chieftains met to confirm their resolve in mutual oaths:

> Never by my will or consent [they swore to each other] will Count Raymond or his son acquire Narbonne or the lands of Lady Ermengard, viscountess of Narbonne. And if by chance they do acquire it, I will do all I can with you to bring evil war upon them, until a man or woman of the lineage of Aymeri of Narbonne or the king of Aragon shall recover Narbonne and its lands.[5]

By the following autumn the young King Alfons of Aragon and his brother Peire (just given full authority in Provence and for that purpose renamed Ramon Berenguer IV) were reconstructing the alliance that had served their father so well. No apology was demanded from Ermengard for her jumping sides during the king's minority; she, after all, was the primary victim of Raymond's blunt opportunism. But Roger of Béziers was obliged to eat crow, and his words contained a barely concealed reference to Ermengard's maneuvering to put Raymond V's daughter into Roger's bed:[6]

> I, Roger viscount of Béziers, son of lady Saura, by my free will admit to you my lord Alfons, by the grace of God king of Aragon . . . , that when I was a boy and did not know how to tell the good from the bad and what is useful from what is not, I was seduced by the advice of some of my evil counselors into granting Carcassonne and other lands that I hold or ought to hold from you, and which my ancestors held from yours, to Raymond count of Toulouse, and I stirred up war against you, my lord and friend. Now, however, with more prudent counsel, I recognize that I have done wrong and I place myself in your power and beg Your Confiding Grace to forgive me my wrongdoing. . . . And to guarantee that henceforth I will observe all the agreements made between my father and yours and between me and you, and not be able to break them even if I should wish to do so, I order the men of Carcassonne and Limoux and many other prudent and great men of my lands to attend upon you with the honors and castles that they hold from me, to follow your commands as if they were your own men.[7]

Although the alliance never faltered after this, trust between Alfons and Roger would never be fully restored; it was probably at this time that a courtier in Alfons's court composed a fanciful story to explain to the young king how his family had acquired its rights over Carcassonne and other Trencavel lands—an account short on historical accuracy but long on the treacherous behavior of Roger's grandfather Bernard Ato.[8] A generation later that lack of trust would have fatal consequences for both the Trencavel family and for Barcelonese interests in Occitania. Nevertheless, as soon as roads were passable and armies could move, the war resumed. It would continue on and off from 1178 until the mid-1190s—until all the principals were dead.

By autumn 1179, Aymeri's brother, Pedro de Lara, was at Ermengard's side. As for Raymond of Toulouse, he was eventually ousted from Narbonne, but not before he profoundly reshaped the politics of Occitania and brought new plagues of violence upon its hapless population.[9] Over the following decade, sieges with their squadrons of mercenaries pillaging the countryside gave way to truces, and truces once again to renewed sieges and fresh pillaging; but neither side seemed capable—or perhaps even interested—in inflicting a decisive blow, if such a thing indeed were possible. At this distance, the events seem directionless, the motives—other than the pure joy of battle—obscure. War became an end in itself. Behind the bare chronicle of marches and treaties and mounting debts, we seem to hear a chorus singing with Bertran de Born:

Be·m plai lo gais temps de pascor,	I love the joyous days of spring
que fai fuoillas e flors venir;	that bring forth leaves and flowers;
e plai me qand auch la baudor	I love to hear the joy
dels auzels que fant retintir	of birds ringing
lo chant per lo boscatge;	their songs through the woods;
e plai me qand vei per los pratz	I love seeing the meadows
tendas e pavaillons fermatz;	clogged with tents and pavilions
et ai grand alegratge	I'm filled with joy
qan vei per campaignas rengatz	when I see lined up across the field
cavalliers e cavals armatz.	knights and horses in their armor.
. . . .	. . . .
E·us dic qe tant no m'a sabor	I tell you, nothing is as tasty,
manjar ni beure ni dormir	neither eating nor drinking nor sleeping,
cum a qand auch cridar, "A lor!"	as hearing the cry, "At 'em!"
d'amboas las partz, et auch bruir	go up from both sides, and the whinnying
cavals voitz per l'ombratge,	of riderless horses in the shadows,
et auch cridar, "Aidatz! Aidatz!"	and hearing men cry "Help! Help!"
e vei cazer per los fossatz	and seeing great and small
paucs e grans per l'erbatge,	tumble in the grassy ditches,
e vei los mortz qe pels costatz	and the dead with silk pennons waving
ant los tronchos ab los cendatz.[10]	from the lances through their ribs.

For men such as Bertran and those to whom he gave voice, a war pretext was not the same as a war aim; peace was not the norm, with war an exception. The relation was exactly the reverse. Ermengard's restoration to Narbonne did not quiet the cries of "At 'em!"; it served only as another excuse to fill the meadows with tents and horses, and ribs with pennoned lances.

Most often such occasions must have occurred deep in the historical shadows, far from the feeble light of our charters and distant chronicles: disputed successions of the far less than great, brothers unable to strike a fair division, sisters promoting claims beyond their dowries, opposing trajectories of those who shared a common castle, families convinced the demands of their over-lords violated every canon of truth and justice. Most often these disputes must have disrupted the tranquility of only a handful of parishes. Sometimes, how-ever, through ties of neighborhood, faction, or the accident of alliance, they could escalate to attract the attention of the great and be hastily registered by monastic scribes (and their modern historian successors) as the doings of a truculent and unruly baronage. Then more numerous squadrons of mercenar-ies and their camp followers took to the roads.

So it was in 1181, when Ademar of Murviel murdered Peire, the brother of King Alfons and the count of Provence. That Ademar should have been the culprit is at first glance astonishing, for, like his father before him, he had for decades been a faithful companion of the Trencavel viscounts and a major sup-port to their power around the city of Béziers. In 1149, Raymond Trencavel himself had guaranteed Ademar's marriage gift to his bride Tiburgueta, and in 1154 when Raymond was captured and imprisoned by the count of Toulouse, it was Ademar along with William Arnold of Béziers whom the viscount chose to govern the territory of Béziers until he won his release or his children grew to adulthood. But disputes over dowry rights and a complicated family succession at length brought Ademar directly into conflict with Guy Guerrejat, fifth son of William VI of Montpellier and guardian for his young nephew William VIII.[11]

Guy as successor to his brother had also taken on the responsibilities of agent for King Alfons in Provence, responsibilities that continued even after Peire (as Ramon Berenguer IV) had succeeded to the government of that terri-tory. Guy continued to contract loans for the royal government, arbitrate dis-putes, and even represent the king in the negotiations that led to the treaty of Jarnègues.[12] Were Ademar and his bullies waiting for Guy when they ambushed Peire in the delta of the Rhone? Had Peire's men gone to Guy's aid at some heated moment? Had Ademar been tempted into the fidelity of the count of Toulouse after the marriage of Roger of Béziers to Adalais? We do not know. But Peire was done in, and Ademar was held responsible. So was the count of Toulouse. King Alfons, hurrying to avenge Peire, quickly named his other brother Sanç count of Provence, rounded up allies in the region (including—in a turn as astonishing as that of Ademar, so notorious Raymond's complicity must have been—William of Sabran, one of Count Raymond's closest advisors and for two decades his constable in the Rhone valley), and in the summer of 1181 took Raymond's castle of Fourques across the Rhone from Arles; he then marched west toward Toulouse, laying waste to Murviel along the way.[13]

In the years that followed, as armies crisscrossed Occitania and Aquitaine, Raymond's empire slowly disintegrated. In the Alps the lands of the house of Albon were lost when Alberic died and his widow married the duke of Bur-gundy. He was Raymond's friend, and the wedding was celebrated at Saint-Gilles, but what would become Dauphiné was lost to the family. At the same time, in the ancient heart of the dynasty's patrimony the patricians of Toulouse, virtually free of comital control, led their militia against smaller towns and rural lords for miles around, imposing their urban lordship on the countryside; it was an Italian-style city-state in the making.[14] Raymond would keep both Mauguio and his lands in Provence, and eventually he would seize the city of Nîmes from its Trencavel viscount, but it was the heartland of his dominions rather than the borders—the lands and people around Toulouse, Albi, Saint-Gilles, and in Provence—that would now bear the devastating brunt of warfare.[15]

Bertran de Born probably spoke for all of the combatants, especially the petty cabbage-barons, when he sang

S'amdui li rei son pro ni coraios	If both kings are bold and fearless,
en brieu veirem camps joncatz de qartiers	we'll soon see fields strewn with bits
d'elms e d'escutz e de branz e d'arços	of helmets, shields, swords, and saddlebows,
e de fendutz per bustz tro als braiers,	and the trunks of men split down to their breeches,
es arage veirem anar destriers,	and we'll see horses running aimlessly,
e per costatz e per peichz manta lanza,	and lances sticking from ribs and chests,
e gaug e plor e dol e alegrança,	and joy and tears and grief and happiness,
Le perdr'er granz e'l gasainhaz er sobriers	great loss and greater gain.
Trompas, tabors, seinheras e penos	Trumpets, drums, banners, pennons,
e entreseinhs e cavals blancs e niers	standards, horses white and black,
veirem en brieu, qe'l segles sera bos,	we'll soon see, and the times will be good,
qes hom tolra l'aver als usuriers,	as we'll part usurers from their money,
e per camis non anara saumiers	and mule drivers will not dare go on roads
jorn afiçatz ni borhes ses duptansa,	in broad daylight, nor townsmen without fear,
ni mercadiers qi venga dever França;	nor merchants on their way from France.
anz sera rics qi tolra volontiers.	Those who gladly rob will be rich.

Yet the scene Bertran evokes was ultimately an illusion. Although usurers might be robbed and townsmen might fear,

Richarz metra a mueis e a sestiers	Richard will measure by hogshead and bushel
aur e argen, e ten s'a benanansa	his gold and silver, and think it happiness
metr' e donar, . . .	to spend and give, . . .
Anz vol gerra mais qe qaill' esparviers.[16]	He'll want war more than a hawk wants quail.

And where would that coin come from if not from moneylenders and from townsmen and clergy who bargained their support for charters of liberties. To maintain their forces, kings, counts, and viscounts mortgaged their castles and revenues and sold privileges in return for hard cash.[17] If anyone gained momentarily, townsmen did. In the end, however, it was probably all who lost. Valor and pride, *joi* and *pretz*, and lust for power barely concealed a landscape of desolation. Ezra Pound remarked about this particular song, "This kind of thing was much more impressive before 1914 than it has been since 1920." What would he have said had he been transported, even in imagination, back to the 1180s?[18]

Already in 1181, Abbot Stephan of Saint-Germain-des-Près, on a mission to Henry of Marcy, cardinal-bishop of Albano (who was leading an armed preaching mission against heretics in the region, about which we will read much more in the next chapter) wrote back to a friend in Paris:

> The fear of danger—from thieves, from the coterels, Basques, and Aragonese—makes the labors of travel seem light by comparison. We have been told that we would find the bishop beyond Toulouse, near Spain. We chase after him over hill and dale, through a deserted countryside, the lair of thieves and the very image of death. We see nothing but burned villages and ruined houses; we find no refuge; all threatens our safety and lays ambush for our lives. With our dear brothers I pray God and the Virgin that, if I may be useful to His Church in the future, He bring me home in safety.[19]

A few years later, writing to the bishop of Poitiers, his memories were no brighter.

> Passing there not long ago I saw the terrible fiery image of death, churches half destroyed, holy places in ashes, their foundations dug up. The houses of men had become the dwellings of beasts.[20]

Like all clerics of his age, Stephen drenched his prose in biblical language; his antipathy for the natives—in the same letter he deplored "the barbarity of the Goths, the flightiness of the Gascons, the cruel and savage habits of Septimania"—darkened the shadows and sharpened the edges of his vision. But there is no reason to think the horrors less real than those of our own century.

For decades before Stephen made his frightened journey through Occitania, monastic chroniclers had been marking the passage of mercenaries—in the Vosges, in Tuscany and Lombardy, in Normandy, England, the Limousin—marking them like a flood, a murrain, a plague, a sudden, violent, and deadly eruption. "Brabançons," "routiers," "coterels," their names were as legion as their numbers.[21] Henry II used them in his campaign against Toulouse in 1159; Frederick Barbarossa led them across the Alps in 1166; Henry employed them again in 1173 when he fought his son; and the count of Angoulême hired them when he revolted against Henry in 1176. The Brabançons were the principal troop, under the leadership of the shadowy William of Cambrai (a renegade priest, said Geoffrey of Vigeois) until he was killed in the battle of Malemort in 1177 and succeeded by the even more shadowy Lobar, "the Wolf." So bitter a memory did their passage leave behind that their name became synonymous with freebooter: a half century later, students from Brabant would discover in Paris that the name of their homeland was an insult.

By the 1180s, other troops were finding their fortunes in the employ of Henry, Richard the Lionheart, Raymond of Toulouse, Alfons of Aragon, and Roger of Béziers: Basques, Aragonese, Navarrese, companies from the Aspres and Pallars high in the Pyrenees, companies from Hainault and elsewhere in Flanders. Henry II had demonstrated how useful they could be. Disciplined infantry, experts at siege warfare—despite their baggage trains and their horde of camp followers, they could move at surprising speed for the era, covering fifteen to twenty miles a day by forced march if need be. Castles that might have held out for a year or two against traditional forces were brought down within a week or less. On the rare occasions when they were forced into pitched battle and suffered defeat, they were still sometimes the last to hold the field. Henry II had good reason to hock his crown jewels, in an emergency even his ceremonial coronation sword, to hire them.[22] But their cost went far beyond the treasure their employers had to beg, borrow, tax, or steal to pay them.

From the very first, these mercenaries had an evil reputation. Monastic chroniclers could not mention their names without adding "robbers" as dramatic epithet.[23] Wherever they appeared, in England, Germany, Italy, Aquitaine, Occitania, the litany was always the same: they plunder monasteries, burn churches, rape nuns, spare neither women nor children, kill the old and the young alike. Nor was this litany a case of one monk simply copying another; the testimony is too dispersed in place and time for that to have been possible.

For these men and their masters the clergy reserved their favorite slur: they were "heretics." In 1179, the archbishop of Narbonne, just returned from an ecumenical council in Rome, warned his suffragan bishops and abbots,

> You well know the iniquity that fills our whole province, as the hearts of our princes and fellow inhabitants grow cold to the love of God and, for our sins, how much the madness of heresy increases every day and the calamitous attacks of foreigners and the faithlessness of the people of this province.

These "heretics," he told them, were the "Brabançons, Aragonese, coterels, and Basques," and those who secretly or openly supported them, hired them, and led them, even those who sold food and drink to them or traded in their booty. The special guilty, he was careful to note, were Count Raymond of Toulouse, Roger of Béziers, Bernard Ato of Nîmes, and their most infamous captains, Lobar the Wolf and "R. of Tarazona" and his Navarrese.

> Against this gathering of evil and impiety we shall raise ourselves as a wall [the archbishop continued]. By the authority of the lord pope and the holy council and by virtue of your obedience you shall publicly excommunicate them every Sunday, ringing bells and extinguishing candles, place their lands under the interdict, prohibiting holy sacraments, except for baptism and penitence, denying even the viaticum to the dying and burial to the dead. You shall also absolve all men from their oaths of fidelity and homage, due service and agreements to these evildoers and their captains and supporters, as long as they hold fast to their iniquity.[24]

Like the archbishop of Narbonne, the English cleric Walter Map also called them "heretics" who with their mouths confess of Christ what we do, but in their actions gather bands of many thousands armed head to foot with leather, iron, clubs, and swords, who reduce monasteries, villages, and towns to ashes, rape indiscriminately, and say with all their heart, "There is no God." . . . At first some few robbers set forth and made themselves a law against law. Then men banished for sedition, false clerics, runaway monks, all those who have forsaken God, gathered around them. Now they are so numerous they cannot be counted. So strong have these phalanxes of Leviathan grown that they settle in safety or rove through whole provinces and kingdoms, hated of God and man.[25]

Walter Map was a respected courtier; he was with King Henry II at Limoges in 1173 and at Saumur when Henry's eldest son, the Young King, died at Martel. He had ample opportunity to observe the bands of hired thugs in action. Elsewhere in his writing he played the scurrilous parodist and gross liar, but this portrait, although heightened with venom, seems drawn from life.

In twelfth-century society, *noble* and *warrior* were synonymous, and men at the top lived for war and by war. Sieges and the wasting of villages were the normal stuff of military campaigns and were treated as such by monastic chroniclers; supplies of moral outrage were reserved for attacks on the possessions of their own abbeys and churches. This exceptionally heightened image of the mercenaries should therefore give us pause. Aquitaine, the Massif Central, and Occitania were being ravaged with more than normal violence. What horrified contemporaries was not that these bands fought for money; even high nobles who owed military service for their fiefs were paid when they campaigned for longer than their required term (typically forty to sixty days). It was their thirst for booty—which made them, quite literally, predatory[26]—and it was their numbers.

Henry II required thirty-seven ships to transport his army back to the Continent after a brief English campaign in 1174. If each of these carried 100 to 150 men, his troops on that occasion would have numbered 3,700 to 5,550. Armies of this size had been seen before in the Middle Ages: William the Conqueror (by one reliable estimate) mustered about seven thousand, horse and foot soldiers combined, for his conquest of England.[27] But such masses, apart from crusading armies, were exceptional—hard to muster, hard to feed. Before the campaigns of the late 1160s, a more usual army might number only a few hundred horsemen and their attendant foot soldiers. With such modest forces, it is hardly surprising that sieges of fortified towns might go on for a year or two and even then sometimes prove vain. In contrast, at a time when a large village would shelter barely a few hundred people,[28] an army of five thousand would have represented a good-sized market town on the move, producing only mayhem and feeding itself by ransacking peasant barns and silos, slaughtering cattle, and burning whatever they could not carry off. We can well understand why chroniclers (although occasionally making what seem to be reliable guesses of the numbers involved) most often saw "innumerable multitudes," or numbers that to them represented the innumerable—ten thousand, twenty thousand.[29] Poets' numbers rather than those of accountants must have seemed more real.

The chroniclers who reported Henry's campaigns lived in the Limousin, Normandy, and England; they picked up the news from knights of their locality and men in the company of King Henry and his sons. The events they heard about were therefore those in the northern and western regions of the Massif Central, in Limousin and Berry, Angoumois, Dordogne, and Quercy, and coastal Aquitaine between Bordeaux and the Pyrenees. There were no chroniclers south of Limoges, but the southern regions of Occitania were not immune from the destructive sweeps of the routiers. That is surely where Abbot Stephen saw them. The bands from the Pyrenees had to pass through coastal Occitania and the Toulousain on their way north, living off the land along the way. Some of their leaders—such as Sanç of Séranne and Curbaran—came from the area.[30] And when the archbishop of Narbonne fulminated against them and their employers in 1179, it was, as we have seen, those who were close to home that he had in mind. The Angevins may have been the most important employers of mercenaries, but they were not the only ones.

The assimilation of the Brabançons and their ilk to heretics was not the peculiar fruit of Walter Map's overheated imagination or the peculiar ire of the archbishop of Narbonne. They both merely elaborated on a canon of the Third Lateran Council, which earlier in 1179 had condemned heretics and mercenaries in the same breath, promising indulgences and the privileges of crusaders to whoever would take up the sword against them.[31] But all that Roman clamor fell on deaf ears, even among the clergy themselves. Hardly had the council concluded and the condemnation been published than the archbishop of Cologne, Philip of Heinsberg, led an army of mercenaries against Henry the Lion, duke of Saxony, his troops robbing cloisters and raping nuns along the way. A later archbishop of Narbonne was condemned for doing the same thing. And according to a contemporary chronicler, even Pope Alexander III himself, shortly after the council, took into his service "twenty thousand" Brabançons.[32]

As troops from Flanders and the Pyrenees wreaked their wrath on woeful Occitania, the world must have seemed to be moving toward the Apocalypse. Those who should have gloried in chivalry gloried instead in rape and arson. The monk Gervase of Canterbury had lauded King Henry sailing to the Continent as the King of Peace, *rex pacificus*, welcomed there like "an angel of great counsel." But what he brought in fact was blood and fire. Chroniclers on the Continent were of one mind: "after the Octave of Epiphany," wrote an anonymous monk at the northern monastery of Anchin in his account for 1182, "more knights than ever before took arms, exceeding all limits in their pillaging, burning, and killing under the banners of the Young King, his brother Richard duke of Aquitaine, the count of Flanders and Baldwin of

Hainault [and others]." On this occasion, he added, the archbishop of Rheims and Thibault of Blois tried to negotiate a truce, but the combatants "looked for war, not peace."[33] Henry II, *rex pacificus*, the King of Peace, the courtly King Henry the younger and his brothers, the gallant counts and viscounts and their barons and knights—all those men whose divine duty, so the Church taught, was to protect the poor and the weak—had turned instead into the paymasters of thieves. As the shepherds hired the wolves, the faithful could only await the hand of God.

What could be done to halt the destruction? Already before the resumption of warfare in 1177, the region's bishops had begun to recall what their predecessors had done to combat very different sorts of threats a century and more earlier. At assemblies or through circular letters to their clergy they demanded first of the princes and lords of their dioceses and then of all adult males that they swear oaths of peace, swear to observe the Truce of God. They formed armed leagues to punish those who refused. And—above all—they went after the routiers. Peace oaths, and even a tax to support enforcement of the peace by the Knights Templars, had been sporadically administered in various ecclesiastical provinces of the region since the 1140s. The bishop and count of Rodez and the bishop of Comminges recalled the old practice in 1169 and 1170. In 1177 Abbot Isembert of Saint-Martial of Limoges led a diocesan peace militia against the Brabançons. Others fought around Bourges and in the Auvergne. Sometime in the 1170s the bishop of Béziers demanded such an oath of Viscount Roger and then extended it to every male over fifteen years of age: warriors could go after each other at will, but clergy, peasants, fishermen, hunters, mourners accompanying the dead, salt porters, merchants, livestock, mills, and oil presses were to be left alone.[34] Many of these leagues had a communal war chest to finance their militias and imposed a tax on all households to pay for them. In hope—and sometimes in practice—it was a general mobilization.

If the Church's clergy could call out troops, why not the mother of God herself? Far away in the north the monk Gervase of Canterbury interrupted his chronicle of the messy squabbles between his brothers the monks of Christ Church and successive archbishops to record the miraculous story he had heard of the peace league in the city of Le-Puy-en-Velay in 1183. The only images he could find adequate to the task came directly from the Gospels:

> There was in the Auvergne in those days a certain man, faithful and just, a carpenter by trade and deeply devoted to the Virgin. One night the holy Virgin Mary appeared to him in a vision, saying, "rise up and go forth and preach peace." . . . The man rose up and went to his bishop and in a trembling voice told him what he had heard. Acting skillfully, the bishop secretly called twelve citizens of proven faith and asked them if they wished to swear to peace. They were easily won to his intention and, together with the bishop who was the thirteenth, they formed an association to preach peace and converted many to their purpose.[35]

The movement astonished all who heard of it. Down near Montpellier, a scribe dated a charter "the same year that the peace of the Virgin Mary was revealed."[36] Chroniclers again could only gasp at the "innumerable multitude" who rushed to join: rich and poor, canons regular and monks, princes, bishops, widows, and virgins. In Geoffrey of Vigeois's overheated imagination their numbers grew from an original "hundred and four or five" to fifty thousand. A canon of the cathedral in the northern city of Laon believed that the movement's treasury, to which each newcomer contributed twelve pennies, soon amounted to four million pounds. The militia became a holy order, wearing white hoods into battle (which gave them their name—Capucians from the Latin *caputium*, "hood")—while on their chests they bore a lead image of the Virgin and Child with an inscription taken from the Ordinary of the Mass: "Agnus Dei, qui tollis peccata mundi, dona nobis pacem" (Lamb of God, who takes on the sins of the world, give us peace). On the bodies of those who died besieging Mercaders, the "prince of robbers," it was reported, God miraculously left a sign of the Virgin. It was against the mercenary Curbaran that they achieved their greatest victory. Using a ruse to lure him and his troops and camp followers from the castle of Charanton in the region of Berry, the Capucians slaughtered them all and marched back to Le Puy with their surest sign of God's grace: Curbaran's head on a pole.[37]

But success on the battlefield soon turned them to other goals, of which the chroniclers give the barest hint: the peace militia, whose activities were reaching the borders of Burgundy and Berry, became in the eyes of their social betters a conspiracy against the social order, the *conjuratio* turned into a *conspiratio*, a breeding ground of social revolutionaries. "The great of the region began to tremble," wrote the canon of Laon, "and dared not claim any more than what was just from their men, neither exactions nor demands for loans." After the slaughter of Curbaran, matters got worse; "their mad fury grew, and counts, viscounts and other princes warned this ignorant and undisciplined people to behave more gently, otherwise they would feel their just anger," wrote one. "They no longer had fear nor respect for their superiors," wrote another, "but all attempted to regain the primordial liberty that our first parents had at the Creation. They forgot that servitude is the price of sin. Among them there was no distinction of great and small, but a fatal confusion that brought about the ruin of the institutions that, thanks to God, are governed by the wisdom of the great."[38] Through the noise of these uneasy clerical voices we can hear the murmurings of radical egalitarians, believers in love and brotherhood, seers of signs, perhaps, of a coming new millennium. Two hundred years later such sentiments would again find voice in the couplet made famous by the rebelling peasants of England:

When Adam delved and Eva span,
Who was then a gentleman?

In the imagination of the chronicler of Laon, writing years after the event, this ending reflected back on the truth of its beginning: the vision of the Virgin that had started it all had been a great deception worked by a canon of Le Puy; he had hired a youth to dress as the Queen of Heaven and make the ignorant carpenter believe he had seen a wonder. The chronicler of Autun was more forceful: it was all a "frightful and dangerous undertaking"; the Virgin was Satan in disguise, and even the Capucians' white penitential robe was a diabolical invention. For the bishops and abbots who had conjured up these forces, the threat of social revolt was even greater than that of the mercenaries. Quickly they closed ranks with others of the estate to which they were born.[39] With the aid of the very robbers they had tried to eradicate by proclaiming the Peace of God, bishops and abbots and their lay brothers and cousins, the great of the land, turned on the peace militias and slaughtered them. Peace might be desirable, but maintaining status and obedience and the deference of the lower to their social betters was more so. For upstarts to claim unwonted liberty was too great a price, and they paid that price with their lives. By 1185 Brabançons—by now the name was generic rather than geographical—were once again free to go their way and sell their services to the highest bidder.

CHAPTER SIXTEEN
SOWING THE SEEDS OF CRUSADE

While mercenaries ravaged Occitania, Count Raymond V of Toulouse searched yet elsewhere for aid against the enemies he had provoked. His ally would be the Church, and to entice it into the fray he conjured up the specter of heresy. His lasting contribution to Occitania would finally be a Holy War brought home to Christendom.[1]

In 1177, at the very start of the long war he began when he momentarily ousted Ermengard from Narbonne, Raymond dispatched a letter to Alexander, abbot of the monastery of Cîteaux in Burgundy.[2] Its strident tone and wild biblical images were meant to breathe the anguish of a wounded faith.

> I am shipwrecked on the shores of On High. You know that in our region the vineyards planted by the right hand of the Lord are destroyed by little foxes, the fountains have run dry, and the clouds, blown by the whirlwind, strive to suck up the waters that serve to wash clean of foul excrement and menstrual blood the house of David, and the slimy waters of flooding rivers tear out by their roots the trees that have been planted on their banks. I plead with you therefore to rise up against them and make yourself like a wall of the house of Israel, lest their words, which spread like a cancer, become strong. So far has this stinking plague of heresy spread that nearly all who believe it think they are serving God; holding as evil those who perform the mysteries of the faith, these faithless sons of iniquity turn themselves into angels of light. . . . So much has gold been tarnished . . . that priests are depraved by fetid heresy, churches lie vacant that once of old were venerated, baptism is denied, the eucharist abominated, penance held for naught, the creation of man and the resurrection of the flesh scornfully denied, and all the sacraments of the church refused, and—most sinful—they speak of two principles. . . . I who have girded on one of the two divine swords, who claim as my own the wrath of God and confess that God has made me his servant to put an end to such faithlessness, . . . find that my powers are inadequate to the task, for the more noble of my land are consumed with this heresy and with them a vast multitude of men, so that I dare not nor am I able to confront them. . . . Therefore, with a humble heart I run to seek your aid and counsel, that you extend the goodness of your prayers to crush such evil faithlessness.

For this heresy is so deeply set in their entrails that it will not be destroyed without the strong fist of God.

The monastic network carried the news all the way to England, where to the monk Gervase of Canterbury it signified that the heresy had spread not just to the ignorant rabble (*vulgus simplex*) but to priests, bishops, and princes—surely the impression that Raymond meant to convey. Against them, the count insisted, he stood steadfast. Skillfully, his secretary wove into the text of his letter the passage from the Gospel of Luke from which Saint Bernard a generation earlier had drawn so much.

> He said to them, "But now, let him who has a purse take it, and likewise a bag. And let him who has no sword sell his mantle and buy one." . . . And they said, "Look, Lord, here are two swords." And he said to them, "It is enough." And he came out, and went, as was his custom, to the Mount of Olives.[3]

Monks, lawyers, and popes had made of this difficult passage a statement of God's plan for the governance of the world: there were two swords, the spiritual and the temporal, and both were ordained of God. The second of these, Raymond now said, was his. Those who opposed him must therefore be the forces of darkness—like Judas, like all other traitors to God whose names were remembered in the solemn ritual of anathema. Heretics were Raymond's enemies. Should his enemies, whoever they might be, not be considered heretics?

Raymond called for prayers to help him against his enemies, and God's. He called as well for something far more violent:

> Because we know that such heresy cannot be crushed by the power of the spiritual sword alone, it must also be punished with the corporeal sword. For this, I am convinced, the king of France should be summoned; for I believe his presence will put an end to this evil. Should he come, I will open the cities to him, hand over towns and fortified places to his punishment, show him the heretics, and—spilling blood, if that is what the business requires—help him wipe out the armies and enemies of Christ.[4]

Given the massacres that the generation of the early 1200s was to suffer—at Béziers, Minerve, Montségur, and elsewhere—we can only shudder at the savagery of this language, for the shadow of the Albigensian Crusades to come seems to brood over all the events of the ending twelfth century. In the short run, however, Raymond's rhetoric came to little. Henry II and Louis VII agreed to march and then thought better of it. In their place an armed Cistercian mission took to the road, spent several months in western Occitania, and departed; in its wake a few heretics were condemned. But the precedent it established and the vision of Occitania it spread abroad had consequences far more vast than its immediate results. It was the advance guard of the ruin just over the horizon, when the political world this book describes would be forever destroyed.

Raymond, it must be said, did not invent this conjugation of war for the faith with war for political advantage in Occitania. Four years earlier, in 1173 when Raymond had made his pact with Henry II and Richard the Lionheart, the archbishop of Narbonne attempted to use the same tactic against the Angevins and their new ally. While Ermengard pleaded with King Louis VII to come to the aid of the monarchy's friends in their fight against an "alien lord" (Henry II), Archbishop Pons had implored King Louis to come in arms "to give peace to the Church and see to the safety of your kingdom . . . , [for] in our diocese the ship of Saint Peter is so broken with the oppression of heretics that it is in danger of sinking."[5] The archbishop's plea, however, like Ermengard's, had fallen on deaf ears in Paris. Louis did not budge, and the appeal was forgotten.

In 1177, by contrast, Raymond struck a familiar and resounding chord at the Burgundian abbey, as his letter was carefully calculated to do—his choice of Cîteaux above all. For among the Cistercians, the heretics of Toulouse and their own privileged role in combating them had for a generation been a carefully nourished memory.

The Cistercians' most heroic figure was Saint Bernard, friend of kings, tutor of popes, and the greatest preacher of his age. Among the most notable of the many pious works he performed beyond the walls of his monastery—on a par, perhaps, with his preaching of the Second Crusade—was his long campaign against the heresy of Henry of Lausanne and his supporters,[6] a crusade of exhortation that had taken him in 1145 first through the lands of Eleanor of Aquitaine, from Poitiers to Perigueux and Bordeaux, and thence to Cahors, Toulouse, and Albi.

On his way toward the Toulousain, Bernard had dispatched a letter to Count Alphonse Jordan. Its opening words may have served as the model for Raymond's letter a generation later.

> We have heard of the great evils which the heretic Henry inflicts every day on the Church. He is now busy in your territory, a ravening wolf in the guise of a sheep. . . . We can tell what sort of man he is by his fruits: churches without people, people without priests, priests without the reverence due to them, and Christians without Christ. The churches are regarded as synagogues, the holiness of God's sanctuary is denied, the sacraments are not considered sacred, and holy days are deprived of their solemnities. . . . The grace of baptism is denied, and Christian children are kept away from the life given by Christ. . . . It is shocking that he should be heard by so many and have such a large following who believe in him. Oh unhappy people!

To Bernard it was clear that the count was responsible for Henry's presence in Toulouse:

When he was chased from France for his wickedness, the only territory open to him was yours. Only under your protection co ld he ferociously ravage Christ's flock. But whether or not this is in keeping with your honor, you alone must judge.[7]

Might this monition have spurred Alphonse to take the cross and join King Louis and the Emperor Conrad on their ill-fated journey to the Holy Land? Might its memory have spurred Raymond to step forward in 1177 in the role of God's avenger? The suspicions that had been cast against his father, it seems, he now would cast against his enemies.

In this endeavor Raymond and his clerical advisors had two choice weapons at their disposal, weapons that his father had lacked: changes in the nature of heresy in the region, of which the Church leadership was thoroughly aware, and, even more important, a far-reaching change in the methods the Church proposed to use to hunt down and destroy those it considered to be the enemies of the faith.

⋗══◉

Henry of Lausanne already had behind him a long career of preaching by the time Saint Bernard caught up with him in the region of Toulouse in 1145. In 1116 or thereabouts Henry passed through Le Mans, a city to the southwest of Paris, and there a clerical enemy sketched his portrait.

> [He had] the haggard face and eyes of a shipwrecked sailor, his hair bound up, unshaven, tall and of athletic gait, walking barefoot even in the depths of winter, a young man always ready to preach, possessed of a fearful voice. His clothes were shabby, and his life eccentric: he had lodgings in the houses of the town, his home in the doorways, and his bed in the gutters. . . . Women and young boys—for he used both sexes in his lechery—who associated with him openly flaunted their excesses and added to them by caressing the soles of his feet and his buttocks and groin with tender fingers. They became so excited by the lasciviousness of the man and by the grossness of their own sins that they testified publicly to his extraordinary virility and said that his eloquence could move a heart of stone to remorse, and that all monks, hermits, and canons regular ought to imitate his pious and celibate life. They claimed that God had blessed him with the ancient and authentic spirit of the prophets, and he saw in their faces and told them of sins which were unknown to others.[8]

He could have been the model for Donatello's John the Baptist or for the hippie denizens of so many college and university towns in the 1960s.

Henry was a preacher of repentance, an athlete of God who had heard his personal revelation in Christ's words, "Leave all you have and follow me," and His admonition to His disciples at the Last Supper, "When I sent you out with no purse or bag or sandals, did you lack anything?" He was not alone in the early decades of the twelfth century to heed the call to the apostolic life in such rigorist and literal terms. For at least a century there had been many like him who wandered the roads of Europe, and especially those of northern and western France, Aquitaine, Occitania, and Italy. They learned their calling from the saints' lives that were read to visitors at famous shrines and from preachers who exhorted their listeners to "follow Christ." So, among many others, the eleventh-century Cardinal Peter Damiani insisted, "The life which our Savior led in the flesh . . . is also for us the established standard of discipline"; so in like vein an anonymous Norman cleric wrote at the end of the century: "The disciple of Christ can do nothing better than walk as Christ walked. . . . The example and form of the master should shine forth in ordering the disciple."[9] Of the vagrants who followed these urgings, Robert of Arbrissel, the founder of the order of Fontevraud, remains perhaps the most famous, seeking first in the "desert"—the woods and wasteland on the fringes of peasant villages—then in an apostolate of the open road, finally in the founding of a double abbey for men and women under the rule of an abbess, the proper consecration of a sometimes acrobatically ascetic life.[10]

Some of those who painted Robert's portrait shared the venom of Henry's clerical portraitist. "One should flee alike from elegant dress and from filthy clothing," Marbod bishop of Rennes in Brittany scolded Robert, "for the former reeks of fleshly pleasure and the latter of vainglory. . . . But with your shabby clothes so worn they show your hairshirt underneath, with your tattered cloak, bare legs, and wildly growing beard, your hair hanging around your face, as you walk barefoot among the multitude you need only a club to be taken for a madman."[11] Like Henry also, it was among women that Robert found his most devoted followers, and this too riled the good bishop, who in passing scooped some scraps from the rubbish heap of clerical misogyny to furnish his diatribe. It was a woman who brought evil into the world, he reminded the hermit-preacher, and not even David and Solomon had been able to escape their lures. The scandals that Marbod saw lurking in Robert's more lurid escapades—not just his preaching in the brothels of Normandy but his practice of sleeping chastely with young women in order to strengthen his "combat with the devil"[12]—were exactly those that the clergy of Le Mans pinned on Henry. It was bad enough that Henry, like Robert, should surround himself with prostitutes, attempting to reform them and find them husbands; as soon as his preaching went astray, this apostle of abnegation became, in the eyes of his clerical enemies, the most lascivious of men.

By the time Henry took to the road, the issue for the clergy had also become *who* was entitled to "follow Christ" in such a literal fashion, especially if the call to follow was understood as a call to preach as well. For more than a hundred years, clerical voices, especially those of monks, had been insisting on the radical division between the laity and those called to a religious life; in time that insistence had become the bedrock of the great reform movement of the eleventh century as the papacy, strongly under the influence of monastic ideologists, asserted that the Church (by which they meant the clerical order) should be "free," that is, free of interference or control by laymen and laywomen. And this radical distinction, virtually ignored in earlier ages, cut violently across both older strains of ecclesiological thought and the new calls for heightened spirituality. For where exactly was the line to be drawn? Should anointed kings, whom centuries of adulatory writing and untold images had made the very figure of Christ the King on earth, be considered laymen or not? It took over half a century of sometimes brutal conflict to resolve that question. Could women, whom the misogynist monastic mind made quintessentially "flesh," belong to the spiritual order? Some, in order to do so, were imagined as turning transvestite.[13]

It was not enough simply to distinguish those who were consecrated to the priesthood from those who were not, for a long monastic tradition had inveighed against monks taking priestly orders, and probably most monks had followed that injunction. Who then were "spiritual men"? Among the spiritual heroes of Abbot Guibert of Nogent at the beginning of the twelfth century was Count Evrard of Breteuil, who, Guibert related, left his home, his wealth, and power to "flee to foreign parts" and there "adopt a religious life . . . supporting himself by burning charcoal and hawking it through the country."[14] On the other hand, the magic lantern that other clerics were constructing to represent their world left men such as Guibert's viscount, Robert of Arbrissel, and Henry of Lausanne in a decidedly ambiguous position. "The entire company of the catholic church are either virgins or continent or married," wrote Pope Gregory VII to Bishop Otto of Constance in 1075, placing sexuality at the center of his ecclesiological vision; it was a schema used by many of his contemporaries, the three orders of the Christian people, whom some liked to think of as the gold, cedar, and stone of Solomon's Temple.[15] Because the reformers insisted that priests as well as monks should be celibate, the "married" were clearly the laity (and the reason why reformers quickly set about to bring marriage as a sacrament into the purview of the institutional Church). But the converse of this equation was not true. Some of the men and women who "renounced the flesh," leaving home and wealth behind, were either virgins or continent, and yet they were not monks or nuns or consecrated clergy. What then were they? Where did they fit? Here was a niche into which the spiritual acrobats of the open road could easily slip. When their preaching turned anticlerical, their ambiguous place in the hierarchy of sexual-social status gave the clergy ample reason to accuse them in return of every sexual excess they could imagine, and, of course, to accuse them as well of heresy.[16]

So when Henry of Lausanne first approached the city of Le Mans, southwest of Paris, on Ash Wednesday 1116, bearing a staff with a cross of wrought iron as his standard, the bishop, Hildebert of Lavardin (a friend of Robert of Arbrissel), recognized his dress, deportment, and eloquence and welcomed him into the city. Here was someone whose preaching could rouse his flock to the repentance demanded by the season. Confident that Henry would preach the gospel, Bishop Hildebert departed for Rome. The penitential guest, however, soon went beyond his appointed themes and attacked the sinfulness and corruption of the city's clergy, urging his listeners to boycott them, to treat them like "gentiles and publicans." Mob excitement soon turned to riot; the clergy's houses were sacked and destroyed. Only the rapid intervention of the count of Anjou saved their lives. Henry's oratory kept him in control of the city until Bishop Hildebert returned and chased him out of the diocese. "He fled to disturb other regions," says our chronicler, "and infected them with his poisonous breath." Where he went we do not know, but nearly twenty years later he was arrested by the archbishop of Arles and brought before a council at Pisa, where he was condemned as a heretic and ordered confined to the monastery of Cîteaux. He was soon on the road again, however, and the next we hear of him he is in Toulouse.

Henry's heresy began as anticlericalism, and in this he was likewise neither unusual nor necessarily unorthodox. Other wandering preachers of his age were equally vociferous in denouncing the failings of the clergy. In the middle of the eleventh century there had been the *pataria* in Milan, supported by the reformers in Rome, who demanded the purification of the clergy from the crime or heresy of marriage (which the reformers called nicolaitism after the mysterious Nicolaitans of Ephesus and Pergamum who were denounced in the Book of Revelations)[17] and the heresy of simony (the purchase of ecclesiastical office). Their rage at the city's archbishop and the unreformed clergy soon led to factional warfare that spread to other Lombard cities and did not abate for years. The story of another preacher of those same years, this one a Fleming, Ramihrdus by name, shows the complex responses that such denunciations might provoke. Ramihrdus was condemned by an episcopal synod at Cambrai in 1076, tied up in a hut, and burned to death by the bishop's servants. His death quickly became a cause célèbre, for Pope Gregory VII heard in the heretic's denunciations of the vices of the local clergy the very essence of his own demands for reform; he sent his legate to demand expiation for the outrageous lynching.[18] Those condemned as heretics for doubting the efficacy of the sacrament performed by a sinful priest could point to the words of Cardinal Peter Damiani himself: "No holy offering which is soiled with the crimes of impurity is received by God."[19] "Behavior which qualifies one man for prison may qualify another for sainthood," the sociologist Kai Erikson has written. Rarely has there been a place and time when this was as true as it was here in early twelfth-century Latin Christendom, when enthusiasm faced off against authority.[20]

For authority was precisely the issue. Many a wandering preacher claimed his authority from his manner of living: "Dicunt se apostolicam vitam ducere," wrote an eleventh-century monk, "They claim to lead the life of the apostles."[21] They took as a guide to living the Bible's description of the apostles and the first men and women they converted:

> And all who believed were together and had all things in common; and they sold their possessions and goods and distributed them to all, as any had need. And day by day attending the temple together and breaking bread in their homes, they partook of food with glad and generous hearts, praising God and having favor with all the people.[22]

This was, they said, their "law and discipline," and the authority they claimed thereby pushed the most extreme to denounce not just the vices of the clergy but church buildings, the hierarchy, relics, and images of saints as well; not even the crucifix was safe from their derision. To some of their clerical opponents their eloquence could only have come from magic. Against these virtuosos of voluntary poverty the monks deployed their own exclusive claim to lead the holiest of lives, to be like angels on earth in their chastity and their endless round of liturgy, while the secular clergy, whatever their mode of life, argued their unbroken apostolic succession, the consecration that empowered them to perform the miracles of the sacraments, and the demands of proper social order.

In the mid-eleventh century, when the reforming party within the Church was seeking allies wherever it could find them, the lines were not always drawn so clearly. The authority of bishops and cathedral clergy and that of the papacy or of reform-minded monasteries might be diametrically opposed, and the supporters of one might denounce those who supported the other as heretics. By 1116, however, when Henry was taking the road toward Le Mans, both clerics and monks fully recognized Rome as the disciplinary and political head of the Church, however scornfully they might denounce its venality, and they set themselves apart from the laity as a "spiritual order."

The issue of the proper life for those who vowed to follow Christ, however, had not vanished; it had only changed its valence. Bernard of Clairvaux could still write in outrage, "The bishops throw what is holy to the dogs, and cast pearls before swine, who turn upon them and tread them down. . . . The clergy fatten on the sweat of others, they devour the fruits of the earth without charge, and so 'malice is distilled from their pampered lives.' " At the Council of Etampes in 1130 he presumed to judge between the two competing claimants to the papacy not on the basis of the procedures followed by the contending factions but on the purity of Innocent II and the "singular merit of the prelates" who had elected him.[23] But what was licit for monks and clergy to say and do was not so for the laity.

Those who felt the call to preach now needed a license. Henry with due regularity received his from the bishop of Le Mans when he arrived. But denouncing the moral laxity of the clergy required something more. And when the bishop returned to Le Mans, Henry failed the crucial test. Asked to join in the recitation of the morning office, he showed he did not know the hymns or the psalms or the sequence; he was not a true cleric. And in the clergy's eyes, neither his mode of life nor the force of his preaching gave him the requisite authority to chastise them. He was duly sent packing.

Between Le Mans in 1116 and Pisa in 1135, Henry's anticlericalism developed apace. He began to attack the triumphal Church that Gregory VII's reform movement had brought into being. He rejected the need for church buildings—the parish churches, the monasteries, and the great cathedrals that were starting to rise all over Europe. He rejected the developing doctrine of purgatory and the attendant idea that gifts to the clergy and the prayers they offered in return could shorten the soul's passage through that purifying fire.[24] He rejected the baptism of children as unsupported in the New Testament. In these as in all else he rejected the clergy's preeminent role as mediators between man and God, a role that the reform movement was giving a presence and a prominence it had not known before. To his clerical interlocutors he replied by quoting Jesus, "Wherever two or three are gathered together, there shall I be." Such were the doctrines that Henry was preaching in Toulouse. In the words of a certain William the Monk, to whom we owe what knowledge we have of Henry's views, he would not "bow his presumptuous neck to the yoke of human obedience."[25]

And so to Toulouse Saint Bernard went to confront him, to expound the truth of the sacraments, to preach repentance, to work miracles. Calling upon those who followed Henry to return to the unity of the Church, Bernard left in his wake a trail of "signs and portents": the blind restored to sight, the dumb restored to speech, the maimed made straight, the clergy of Bordeaux reconciled to their archbishop. The result was a success, so at least thought Geoffrey of Auxerre, Bernard's secretary; such it may have been, although in his letter to the impatient monks of Clairvaux Geoffrey suggested guardedly that as the mission was coming to an end they had left much undone: "A land led astray by so many heretical teachings needed a great deal of preaching, but the abbot did not think that he could perform such a task and was afraid that it would be a great burden to his brothers."[26] After Bernard returned to Clairvaux, Henry was tracked down and brought to the bishop's prison in chains; there, presumably, he perished, for he is not heard from again. But the memory of the mission was kept alive both in Bernard's letters, carefully collected by Geoffrey of Auxerre, and by Geoffrey's own account. A generation later Count Raymond of Toulouse could count on it being remembered.

Among Henry's followers there was apparently no one to pick up his preacher's mantle. At least no shocked clerical voice tells us of one. Were others there in Toulouse or its environs, unrecorded, telling strange myths of creation and preaching another doctrine of salvation, precursors of the dualists on whom Raymond would call down the sword of punishment in 1177? Perhaps. Geoffrey of Auxerre in his account of Bernard's mission mentions "some of the weavers whom they call *Ariani*," who fled the city at Bernard's approach "when they heard of the portents and miracles." "Ariani," a strange reference to an ancient heresy that had disappeared by the eighth century, was one of the several names that would be used for the dualist heretics a generation later. In Flanders they would be called "weavers"; elsewhere they would be given other names. But Geoffrey says no more about them, and there is no evidence that any of these names had yet acquired what would later be their special significance.[27]

About the time of Bernard's mission, however, the dualists whom historians know as Cathars—that is, "pure ones"—had already appeared in the north.[28] They were in evidence in Perigueux around 1160 and soon after that—under the name *publicani*—in places as widespread as Arras in Flanders, England, Champagne, Burgundy, and the Rhineland. In 1165 at Lombers in the diocese of Albi, the bishop himself presided over a public debate between some of their leaders and the archbishop of Narbonne, the bishop of Nîmes, and the abbots of Cendras and Fontfroide, before an audience of other prelates and great nobles of the region. This is the first we hear of *boni homines*, "good men," as the popular Occitan name for the Cathar "Perfects." It is a striking name, expressing not only a moral accolade but a recognition of authority, for the same term, both in Latin and in Occitan, had long been used to refer to the leading men of the region's towns and villages. When the bishop of Lodève, who had questioned them about the tenets of their faith, condemned them as heretics, they replied defiantly that it was not they who were heretics but the bishop, "a ravening wolf, a hypocrite and a foe of God." Armed with a safe-conduct from the bishop of Albi, they peacefully went their way. Two years later, if a suspect document is to be trusted, the "good men" held a council at Saint-Felix-de-Caraman, east of Toulouse, where in the presence of a visiting "father" from the Balkans they elected their own bishops for Toulouse, Carcassonne, and Agen.[29]

How much of these events got onto the monastic wires to the north we do not know,[30] but the clergy of that region, and especially the Cistercians, did not need an exact report of what the "good men" had asserted at Lombers to be aware of what Count Raymond was referring to by men who "speak of two principles."

Every reasonably educated churchman of the twelfth century knew about dualism, about beliefs not only that Satan and his minions were at war with God in this world (an idea that all accepted as rigorously orthodox), or even that the body and its natural appetites, especially sexual appetites, are inherently evil (an idea deeply ingrained in much of both ancient philosophy and Christianity), but that the war of Good and Evil is inherent in the very nature of the universe, because the universe is the work of not one but two creators. Every reader of Saint Augustine's *Confessions* had learned of the doctrines of

Mani, the great third-century Mesopotamian visionary among whose followers Augustine had for a time lived. Mani had taught that the universe was a chaotic mixture of Light and Darkness, created and ruled by two powers, each absolute and eternal, and that the conflict of body and spirit within us is only a part of their cosmic battle. It was enough for learned clergy to dub "Manichee" any person who refused to eat meat or claimed that only celibates could gain salvation.[31]

In addition, the clergy of northeastern France, where Cîteaux was located, had recently been treated to a far more intimate acquaintance with dualist beliefs, and one of the images in Raymond's plea to the abbot of Cîteaux suggests that he or his secretary knew the story and meant intentionally to trigger the connection—"the vineyards of the Lord," he wrote, "are destroyed by little foxes." It was exactly this phrase from the Song of Songs that Evervin, prior of the secular canons of Steinfeld near Cologne, quoted when he appealed to Saint Bernard in 1143 or 1144 to come to his aid against the "new heretics" in his city. Saint Bernard, then preaching on the Song of Songs, was happy to comply, instructing his listeners on how to search out and question those who "preach in corners" and "lurk in darkness and in cellars," although significantly, it was apparently not their doctrine but two aspects of their behavior—their refusal to swear oaths and their practice of living with women who were neither their wives nor blood relatives—that to the saint most clearly marked them as heretics. Evervin is our first undisputable witness to the presence of Cathar heretics in the Latin world, but he knew only about their organization and rituals and nothing of their myths and theology. In 1144 Bernard apparently knew no more.[32]

By 1177, however, these new heretics had been encountered often enough in the Rhineland, Low Countries, England, and Burgundy for their doctrines and even some of their creation myths to attract the attention of the clergy. By then, as well, their neighbors had pinned on them the peculiar vernacular names by which they would thereafter be known—*piphiles, publicani*, "weavers." To their enemies they appeared to be the true heirs of Mani, and most modern historians consider them the first true dualists the Latin world had seen since antiquity. There was no longer any reason to confuse them with home-grown evangelical enthusiasts of the likes of Henry of Lausanne.[33] The audience Raymond of Toulouse addressed knew unerringly what he was talking about.

To the astonishment of the clergy who encountered them, these new heretics had both teachers and a systematic organization of bishops and other leaders, and even, so some heard, their own pope.[34] Like the ancient Manichees, they were divided into two groups, the "elect" or Perfects and the simple "hearers" or "believers." The sharp-wittedness as well as the gravity and asceticism of the Perfects and the forthright conviction with which they met their sometimes terrible earthly fate could astonish even their enemies.

The amazing thing [Evervin wrote to Bernard of Clairvaux] was that they entered and endured the torment of the flames not merely courageously, but joyfully. I wish I were with you, holy father, to hear you explain how such great fortitude comes to these tools of the devil in their heresy as is seldom found among the truly religious in the faith of Christ.[35]

Even more astonishing, on occasion, was the sex of some of their teachers: they were women, and that gave rise to the most lurid fantasies. In his early thirteenth-century chronicle the English Cistercian Ralph of Coggeshall told a story he had heard from Gervase of Tilbury. One day when Gervase was a young and sportive cleric in the household of the archbishop of Rheims, he spotted a pretty peasant girl in the fields outside the city and invited her to tumble in the hay with him. When she politely but gravely refused his entreaty, he realized from the nature of her reply—"Kind sir, if I lose my virginity nothing can save me from eternal damnation"—that she was one of "the blasphemous sect of publicani." Soon she had to answer to the archbishop of Rheims himself for her remark. To her defense she summoned another woman of the town, her "master" (*magistra*).

[This woman] perverted all the authorities which they brought forward with such subtle interpretations that it was obvious to everybody that the spirit of all error spoke through her mouth. She replied so easily, and had such a clear memory of the incidents and texts advanced against her, both from the Old and the New Testament, that she must have had great knowledge of the whole Bible, and had plenty of practice in this kind of debate: she mixed truth with falsehood and distorted the true explanation of our faith with evil intelligence.

Imprisoned and judged to be burned at the stake, she hurled at her judges, "Madmen! Do you think that you can burn me on your fire? I neither respect your judgment nor fear the fire which you have prepared."

So saying she took a ball of thread from her breast and threw it through the great window, keeping one end of the thread in her hand, calling loudly, in everybody's hearing, "Catch!" At this she was raised from the ground and flew through the window after the ball. We believe that she was taken away by the same evil spirits who once lifted Simon Magus into the air, and none of the onlookers could ever discover what became of the old witch.

The young girl, meanwhile, remained steadfast in her belief. "Many admired the way in which she let forth no sighs, no tears, no wailing, and bore the torment of the flames firmly and eagerly, like the ancient martyrs of Christ who were tortured by the pagans," Ralph reluctantly admitted.[36]

These teachers were men and women of austere life and bearing. They brought to their hearers not just a set of moral rules and a hope of salvation but also a collection of myths to explain in simple, appealing terms the source of their listeners' spiritual unease, myths that rooted the torments and troubles of individual lives in the structure of the universe itself. The ultimate source of at least some of these myths was the ancient Near East, but the fountain from which they seeped into the twelfth-century Latin world was Bulgaria, a recently conquered and evangelized outpost of the Byzantine Empire. From Bulgaria as well came preachers carrying New Testaments different from the Latin Vulgate, which local Perfects translated into the vernacular.[37]

Around the middle of the tenth century, not long after the conquest had taken place, a Bulgarian priest who took the name Bogomil—"worthy of the pity of God"—began to preach a radical vision of salvation to an audience that seems to have been composed principally of oppressed peasants. To give body to his vision he assembled the musings of Orthodox monks, among whom survived some residues of ancient Gnosis and Manichaeism, into which he stirred the beliefs of some radical Eastern sects still present on the fringes of the Byzantine world—especially the Paulicians, whose tenets harkened back to the ancient Adoptionist heresy. Exactly how he came by these texts and ideas we can only guess. Byzantine emperors had long followed the policy of deporting conquered troublemakers on one frontier to a distant one where they could put their militancy to work for the empire. Heretical Armenians had thus been planted in Macedonia in the eighth century and again in the middle of the tenth. Bogomil could have tapped the rich veins of speculation and mythology they had brought with them to this northwestern frontier. But he may have taken much as well from strictly orthodox hands, from the literature of the early Eastern church that Byzantine monks still read and copied and commented on. A complex of spiritual impulses that focused on the repression of man's sexual nature lay close to its heart. Mani himself had grown up in a Mesopotamian Christian village, and it could have been in those same profound sources of early Christianity that Bogomil discovered that the world, especially as it is manifested in our sexual desires, is the creation of Satan.[38]

To Bogomil and his followers the only proper prayer was the paternoster; their induction ceremony was a simple laying-on of hands. Like earlier dualists, they demanded of their followers a total renunciation of the world and its appetites, especially of sexuality and procreation; they renounced as well all food that came from procreation—meat, eggs, and milk. (Fish, they believed, were spontaneously generated in water, and, of course, they knew nothing of sexual reproduction in plants.) Their beliefs were based on a simple assumption: that the body and soul were radically incompatible, the one belonging to the world of Matter, the other to the world of the Spirit. To them the Orthodox priesthood were servants of "the world," and their sacraments, the veneration of saints, church buildings, liturgy, were all the work of Satan; for in their eyes, not surprisingly, the Orthodox church was but another arm of the oppressive

Byzantine conqueror and its native allies. (John the Exarch, one of the most eminent early Orthodox churchmen in Bulgaria, once contemptuously dismissed his new flock as "filthy Manichaeans and pagan Slavs.")[39] They scorned Orthodox scriptural exegesis, and to the question, How can there be evil in a world created by God or good in a world that is evil? they responded with elaborate genesis myths, at the center of which was the dominating figure of Satan.[40]

Revelation 12:7–9 was their starting point.

> Now war arose in heaven, Michael and his angels fighting against the dragon; and the dragon and his angels fought, but they were defeated and there was no longer any place for them in heaven. And the great dragon was thrown down, that ancient serpent, who is called the Devil and Satan, the deceiver of the whole world—he was thrown down to the earth, and his angels were thrown down with him.

From this the Bogomils and Cathars elaborated their own stories of paradise lost. In the homely narrative of one of these, "The Questions of John at a Secret Supper," we can almost hear the murmur of the audience of peasants on their way home from their labors in the field. Here is Satan subverting the angels of the Third Heaven,

> saying to each of them, "How much do you owe your lord?" The first answered, "A hundred barrels of oil." He said to him, "Take the bill and sit down and write fifty." And he said to another, "Now you, how much do you owe your lord?" Who said, "A hundred quarters of wheat." To him he said, "Take the bill and sit down quickly and write eighty." To the other heavens he ascended with like speech; he ascended even unto the Fifth Heaven, seducing the angels of the Father invisible.[41]

Although the text is lifted directly from Jesus's parable of the dishonest steward, it is not so much a commentary on the parable as a use of a familiar story to make heaven but another infinitely heightened version of its hearers' own lives.

A later story had Satan subvert the angels (all male) by introducing a woman into heaven. Then, having created the perishable material world, "he took the clay of the earth and made man like unto himself," imprisoning one fallen angel into the body of Adam and another into the body of Eve, and seducing her by "sating his lust with the serpent's tail." Thus, said the "Questions of John," "children are begotten of the devil and of the serpent until the consummation of the world." We are all the spirits of angels imprisoned by lust in bodies of clay. "The flesh is born of corruption," said an Occitan Cathar ritual. "The spirit is imprisoned." And if the angel did not free itself in this life by becoming a Perfect, he was immediately imprisoned in another body when he died.

Theirs was not simply a timorous avoidance of sexual activity. The Cathars planted sexuality at the heart of creation, a creation that was straitly subject to the law of decay and death. To procreate, to replicate oneself in the next generation, was only to entrap another fallen soul in this earthly clay; it was the work of the devil. Since the second century (writes Peter Brown) such rejection of the world had "flickered disquietingly along the edges of the Christian church" as holy men and women sought "to achieve the priceless transparency associated with a new creation."[42] Long centuries of theological strife had finally brought this impulse to renounce the world into a precarious balance with the humble weight of familial continuity, and therefore of the procreation needed to sustain the Christian community from generation to generation. But radicals, like the followers of Marcion and Tatian in second-century Syria and Asia Minor, continued to link the renunciation of sexual intercourse "with a regaining of the Spirit of God, and so, with man's ability to undo the power of death."[43] So in the eleventh and twelfth centuries did the Bogomils and the Cathars: it was by attaining the state of Perfect that a man or woman returned the angel inhering in the mutable body to its heavenly home.

To the modern reader, whatever our religious attachments or lack of them, there is little in these Cathar myths, as we now have them, to appeal to the imagination. None of them possesses the richness or the power of the ancient Gnostic gospels (for their audience had little in common with the somber townsmen and troubled intellectuals who listened to the "heresiarchs" of the ancient Mediterranean). To the trained Catholic theologians of the twelfth century these myths were nothing but a veil for absurd and willfully heretical doctrinal beliefs, whose contradictions and incoherence they had no trouble in demonstrating. To the surprise of those clerics, however, their own invincible demonstrations, whether at Cologne or Lombers, seemed to make little impact on either the Perfects or the believers, who happily went to the stake, if that was their fate, or returned unconcerned and unconvinced to their small towns and villages.

The reason for the failure of the orthodox in these encounters, we may suspect, was that among the twelfth-century Cathars, what the Catholic clergy saw as doctrines counted for far less than the ascetic practices of the Perfects and the proper performance of the few simple rituals the cult required: the public confession of sins (the *apparellamentum*), the hospitality that "linked them to each other by bonds of affection," the repeated chains of paternosters (the *dobla*), the breaking of bread at meals, the genuflections of the believers whenever they encountered one of the Perfects, the believer's simple plea "Pray God for me, a sinner, that he may make me a good Christian and lead me to a good end," and the laying-on of hands (*consolamentum*) that turned a believer into a Perfect.[44] Here was where they found the true undoing of the powers of the devil and of death. Evervin of Steinfeld, for example, knew that the "new heretics" condemned marriage, "but I could not discover the reason for this from them, either because they dared not tell it, or (more likely) because they did not know it." And later twelfth-century polemicists, although they drew their knowledge from people who had deserted the sect, continued to imagine it in terms of practices and sacraments. In this they were probably only following their informants. We should not be swayed by the doctrinal fixations of the Cathars' later clerical opponents to place excessive emphasis on the wild Genesis myths the heretics told. We should watch them instead as they moved from village to village and house to house, sharing their faith with those who in return would share their food before a humble hearth.[45]

In their outward demeanor—"We are the poor of Christ, wandering men," they said to their persecutors at Cologne, "leading a holy life, fasting, abstaining, working and praying by night and day"[46]—the Perfects were much like other wandering preachers of their age, much like Henry of Lausanne, some of whose followers they may have added to their fold. They were similar as well in much of what they preached, rejecting the clergy and their sacraments, rejecting infant baptism and masses for the dead. As for their peculiar insistence on sexual abstinence for all true Christians, in this they were only claiming for all the faithful what since the fourth century a priestly elite had asserted to be their own privileged state, giving them the special power to mediate between earth and heaven.

> Two ways of life were given by the Lord to His Church [Eusebius had written in his "Proof of the Gospel"]. The one is above nature and beyond common human living; it admits not marriage, child-bearing, property nor the possession of wealth. . . . Like some celestial beings, these gaze down upon human life, performing the duty of a priesthood to Almighty God for the whole race. . . . And the more humble, more human way prompts men to join in pure nuptials and to produce children.[47]

For centuries this call to priestly celibacy was laxly heard in the West. Then, around 1050, it suddenly became the trumpet blast of clerical reformers. All who were consecrated to perform the sacraments, they insisted, should bear this special stamp. To this sharp division of the virgins and the continent from the married the Cathars brought the ebullient asceticism of late-Antique Syria and Anatolia, of the "Walking Men," the "Renouncers," and the "Elect," whose enthusiasms had perhaps survived in the remote mountain villages of Asia Minor and eventually been transported from the frontier with Islam to the Balkans and from there to the West, or were perhaps rediscovered on the fringes of native spirituality. It was a very different version of Christianity, one long suppressed or forgotten, in which the cloak of leadership could fall on the shoulders of anyone capable of heroic renunciation.[48]

What this implied for the social structure of the Church and the role of its leaders within the community was potentially revolutionary. To the Cathars a Perfect's choice to avoid all sexual acts was a sign that he or she had fully renounced this created world and been rejoined to the Spirit in the other world.[49] For the eleventh-century reformers, however, celibacy as a mark of separation was also a mark of status and even more of power—a power, they were quick to claim, that caught all Creation in its net. "Does anyone doubt," Pope Gregory VII had trumpeted in a letter to the bishop of Metz justifying his deposition of the emperor, "that the priests of Christ are to be considered as fathers and masters of kings and princes and of all believers? . . . If exorcists have power over demons, how much more over those who are subject to demons and are limbs of demons! And if exorcists are superior to these, how much more are priests superior to them!" It was of the priests, he asserted, that Paul was speaking when he wrote "Do you not know that we are to judge angels? How much more, matters pertaining to this life!" Such claims were not merely the stuff of words. They were hardened in the stonework and ironwork of every major church being raised in Europe, as chancels and choirs and the mysteries performed there were veiled from the view of profane eyes by ever higher and more intricate screens. Tumultuous throngs of laity were welcome to crowd around the relics and leave their offerings, but for the holy sacraments they were only bystanders and increasingly distant bystanders at that.[50]

Such physical divisions had not yet become the commonplace of parish churches as they were of the great cathedrals, even though they too were being rebuilt on more spacious plans. Social distance, nevertheless—a distance of both birth and income—pervaded the sometimes tense dominance of the rural and small-town clergy over their flocks. The stereotype of the rural priest, of the same humble fabric as his peasant neighbors, harnessing his oxen to guide his plow through the fields, is an image that many medieval historians, even the best, find hard to resist.[51] If, however, we turn away from the chronicles written in the aftermath of the Albigensian Crusades to other less self-interested evidence, that image proves baseless.

The twelfth century was a pre-statistical age, so we cannot expect more than sparsely spaced anecdotes before 1300. Eventually, however, by the end of the thirteenth century, the need of governments for taxes brought with it a need to evaluate, however crudely, the contents of their subjects' purses. A little over a century after the period that concerns us here, the agents of the papacy were busily enumerating and assessing the ecclesiastical livings of Europe. The volumes of accounts that they brought back to Rome or Avignon open as transparent a window as we can hope for onto the economic and social niche that the rural clergy occupied in their communities.[52] They reveal that between 1300 and 1348, a century or so after the Cathars became prominent in the West, the taxable income of the rural clergy in the dioceses of Narbonne, Béziers, and Carcassonne looked like this:

Table 1. Distribution of Rural Benefices by Income, Early Fourteenth Century

Range of Assessed Income (in liv. Tourn.)	Number of Benefices per Diocese			
	Narbonne	Béziers	Carcassonne	Total
<20	22	30	18	70
21–40	84	65	59	208
41–60	55	47	48	150
61–80	27	15	20	62
>80	29	13	10	52
Total	217	170	155	542

Source: Data from *Pouillés des Provinces d'Auch, de Narbonne et de Toulouse* (ed. Perrin and Font-Reaul), 2:507–19, 545–57, 655–66. Assessment: Samaran and Mollat, *Fiscalité pontificale*, 12–22; Lunt, *Papal Revenues*, 1:73–74.

Notes: The figures given in the documents are the amount of the "tenth" (that is, the tax of 10 percent) paid by each benefice, here multiplied by 10 to get the assessed income. In principal, the assessment was based on an estimate of annual revenue from which fixed expenses were deducted. The figures for the tax, often rounded to the nearest pound or the nearest five or ten solidi, suggest that the assessments were arrived at by rough approximation and negotiation.

The numbers in the account books are surely underestimates, the end results of local negotiations and various forms of tax evasion, but they show the majority of rural clergy collecting between 20 and 60 liv. Tourn. per year, and nearly twice as many priests have incomes above that range as those who have incomes below it.

An estimated income of less than 15 liv. Tourn. exempted a benefice from paying taxes, but in 1404, even after the catastrophe of the Black Death, there were only sixteen rural churches so impoverished as to escape taxation in the diocese of Béziers, and nine in the diocese of Carcassonne. An income of between 15 and 20 liv. Tourn. must have been considered the minimum requisite endowment. In 1285, when the archbishop of Narbonne petitioned the pope for permission to build a chapel in his home village of Montbrun, Honorius IV instructed him to take no more than twenty-five pounds from the archbishopric's property for this purpose; the endowment was finally set at an income of twenty pounds.[53]

If fifteen pounds per year was considered "poverty level," two-thirds of the rural clergy had incomes two to three times that amount, and 20 percent had incomes that ranged far higher: up to 250 pounds at Villeneuve, 250 for the two benefices at Padern, 180 at Azille and Talairan—and none of these were more than peasant villages. More than a dozen rural benefices had higher incomes than those of the offices of archpriest in the cathedral chapter.

We should not, of course, exaggerate the material well-being that such wealth represented. A half century later, in a village near Toulouse, a peasant wealthy enough to bequeath dowries of twenty-four pounds to each of his daughters and more than forty to his widow (including return of her dowry)

was a man of some substance. He had twenty parcels of land (about twenty-five acres in all), two buildings, three horses, and a well-stocked storehouse, but his household furnishings were reduced to the most bare essentials of pots, plates, benches, and a table. He and his family apparently spread their bedding on straw on the floor.[54] The gap was vast between the wealth and display of these villages and that of the nearby cities, where shops on the old Roman bridge over the Aude in the heart of Narbonne were selling for 100 pounds, where merchant combines could contract with Genoese for the delivery of 10,000 sétiers of wheat from Sicily at a price of 4,750 pounds, and where the bishop of Carcassonne could be assessed for an income of 2,460 pounds, the bishop of Béziers for 3,000, and the archbishop of Narbonne for more than 6,000. Yet even a well-off rural household must have been viewed with envy by many a village neighbor. After all, ten pounds was conventionally considered the equivalent of an ounce of gold.[55]

We can, in fact, make a rough comparison of these clerical incomes with those of at least two peasant communities. Quite by chance we have a valuation made by royal commissioners in 1306 of the households in a village and a small market town in the southern Corbières, on the edge of the diocese of Narbonne. Axat with its seventy-nine households and Caramany with its thirty-five would have been similar in all ways to the villages and towns in the heart of the diocese.[56] The average valuation of real and personal property at Axat was about 14 pounds per household, at Caramany, 16 pounds 8 shillings. But medieval villages were not egalitarian societies: in these places incomes were highly inflected.

Table 2. Distribution of Households by Assessed Valuations in 1306

Range of Valuation (in liv. Tourn.)	Households in Axat	Households in Caraman
0–5	14	2
6–10	23	8
11–20	28	10
21–30	5	11
31–50	5	4
>50	4	0
Total	79	35

Source: Adapted from Maillard and Bautier, "Denombrement des feux," 318–19.

To be sure, we cannot directly compare the two tables; they measure apples and oranges. The clerical data give us an approximation of income; the royal survey gives us the estimated value of real property per household. Converting one to the other involves a large layering of assumption and guesswork, but we should at least try. In 1427, tax assessors in the great Italian city of Florence were instructed to calculate the value of agricultural land as though the rent that might be paid for it (half of its average production) was the equivalent of a 7 percent return on investment. That is far too Florentine and far too fifteenth century an accounting operation to imagine it being applied in France around 1300. The assessors of these two villages and their local informants most likely made their evaluations by the seat of their pants. Even in fifteenth-century Provence the manipulations of tax assessments were numerous and varied widely from village to village.[57] However hazardous our guess might be, even if we make the most optimistic assumption—that they calculated a quarter of annual production (a typical share-crop rental for grain land) equaled a 5 percent return on property value (the one mortgage interest rate we can calculate from a contemporary contract)—only four households in Axat and no households in Caramany would have been able to boast an income of more than 10 liv. Tourn. Even the wealthiest households in these villages would barely have earned enough to break the clerical poverty level, and on our table of clerical incomes, all the peasant households would fall into the category of less than twenty pounds. The priest at Caramany with his benefice of twenty-five pounds of taxable income and the priest at Axat with his thirty-two would truly have been cocks-of-the-walk.[58]

All this evidence, to be sure, comes from the other side of the great divide formed by the Albigensian Crusades, and it is surely possible that the Crusades and their aftermath contributed to the wealth of the Occitan clergy. Many a person, with a Dominican inquisitor breathing down his neck, may have found it prudent to give generously to the endowment of his local church, and testators everywhere regularly contributed a few solidi to their local parishes. Yet a detailed study of testaments in the region of Béziers—whose chief city the crusaders put to the torch, slaughtering all its inhabitants—shows no change of note during and after the Crusade. It was the king of France and the great ecclesiastics—bishops, cathedral chapters, and monasteries—who ultimately profited from confiscations for heresy, and they squabbled among themselves for the spoils. The stories of laymen clinging to their tithes, refusing to give them up to the clergy to whom they were due, play a large role in the explanations that post-Crusading chronicles give for Occitan anticlericalism; they seem, however, to be a reflection of mid-thirteenth-century conflicts (when the chronicles were being written) rather than an accurate memory of the pre-Crusade world.[59] The rural clergy may have been comparatively less advantaged in the second half of the twelfth century than they were around 1300, but probably not substantially so, for the great age of endowing rural churches was in fact the first half of the twelfth century, when, following the demand of the reformers that laymen "return" ecclesiastical property to the Church, the clergy of Occitania, like those of the rest of Europe, pressured the holders of tithes and other ecclesiastical dues to give them up. Their success can be measured in every church archive and cartulary of the region: nearly a third of the documents from 1077 to 1154 copied into the great Black Book of the cathedral of Béziers involve such "gifts" or "restitutions" of churches, tithes, and other dues.[60]

Along with the property must have gone, in most cases, the right to name the serving priests and chaplains. When we finally have a survey of patrons in the diocese of Carcassonne in the early fourteenth century, the priests and chaplains in fully three-quarters of the rural churches and chapels were chosen by the bishop or cathedral chapter; all the remaining had monasteries as their patrons. This again may reflect the consequences of the Albigensian Crusades, which dispossessed many of the major landholders of the diocese. The diocese of Narbonne, less touched by those wars, may better reflect the twelfth-century situation. There just under half were in the gift of the archbishop or the chapter, and another third in the gift of monasteries or the Templars or Hospitalers. The patrons of the remainder are unknown and most likely laymen.[61]

What sorts of men were these patrons likely to promote? Except in rare instances, surely not a peasant boy who had excelled in his studies. The bishops of twelfth-century Occitania came from the upper levels of the landed aristocracy; the cathedral chapters and monasteries were filled with the offspring of village lords.[62] One suspects that patrons' choices would regularly fall on the younger sons of rural lords, those they had associated with in their youthful games. What little evidence we have points in this direction: donors of tithes who specify that their clerical sons have the benefit of this income for life, and chaplains and priests whose names point to major families of rural lords.[63] The frequent proximity of the village church to the castle within these fortified settlements must likewise have pushed the local headmen to demand a trusted ally next door.[64]

The tensions that such acute disparities of wealth and status subtended in the tight little worlds of twelfth-century villages may easily be imagined. The consequences in the thirteenth century were sometimes massive indebtedness, collective conflicts that increasingly found their way into the royal courts, and riots—especially when inquisitors put a spark to the dry tinder of peasant resentment. The twelfth century, however, was not yet at that stage, at least nothing in our documents suggests so, although the speed with which the Capucians of Le Puy turned into social revolutionaries may be the first clear sign.[65] Perhaps the incessant warfare and the constant threat of mercenaries and marauders gave villagers other worries more immediate. Perhaps a lack of institutional means rendered collective action impossible (or unrecordable), and individual resentment oozed out in subtle ruses or bursts of individual anger that merely provided the local provost or bailiff with an excuse to whip the perpetrator through the streets, cut off his hand, or confiscate his pitiful household goods.[66] Whatever the tensions may have been, they provided much substance for the preaching of the Cathars.

> They claimed . . . that any who were not ordained according to Paul's instructions are not bishops and priests, but ravening wolves, hypocrites and seducers, men who want to be bowed to in the streets, to have the most prominent seats, to

sit at the head of the table at banquets; who want to be called "rabbi" and "master" . . . to wear albs and white robes, and gold and bejewelled rings on their fingers. . . . They are not good teachers but mercenaries and should not be obeyed.

It was in these terms that the "good men" condemned the Catholic prelates at Lombers in 1165. No one present could have missed the echo of Jesus condemning the scribes and Pharisees.[67] It was not avarice that the heretics condemned but pride. Did they go on to quote, "You tithe mint and dill and cumin, and have neglected the weightier matters of the law, justice, mercy, and faith"? Here was their chance to appeal to the multitude who had come to watch the confrontation. They knew the words that would echo most loudly.

In contrast, the "good men" themselves asked nothing but to be welcomed into the houses of the humble as they wandered from village to village to break bread, recite their litany of the Lord's Prayer, and bless those who humbly asked for it. Such were the preachers of two principles, the foxes in the vineyard of the lord, whom Raymond V called on the Cistercians and their friends to destroy.

CHAPTER SEVENTEEN
A WAR LIKE AN OMEN

The response to Raymond's plea to Cîteaux was immediate. The general chapter of the order met on September 13, 1177, and placed the organization of an anti-heretical campaign on the shoulders of Henry of Marcy, abbot of Clairvaux.[1] A week later, Louis VII and Henry II met at Ivry on the border of Normandy and France to sign a treaty of nonaggression that had been mediated by the good offices of the papal legate Peter of Pavia, cardinal-priest of Saint-Chrysogonus. Hearing of Raymond's plea, they decided to march to Toulouse themselves, "with strong and warlike hand."[2] Had they not, after all, just promised (under pressure from the legate) to take the Cross? But decisions were one thing, action another. Henry of Marcy planned a preaching mission on the model of his illustrious predecessor's, then thought better of it: the heretics should not be warned of the sword to come. Then the kings changed their minds as well. For a moment it must have seemed as though the south would be left to its own devices, as it had been when Ermengard and the archbishop had appealed for help in 1173.[3]

The abbot of Clairvaux, however, would not be turned aside. In early spring he wrote to the pope to request that Peter of Pavia be put in charge of an expedition. By midsummer, with the help of the two monarchs, the expedition was on its way, the legate accompanied by Henry of Marcy, Archbishop Garin of Bourges (another Cistercian), Pons d'Arsac, archbishop of Narbonne, John "of the beautiful hands," bishop of Poitiers, Bishop Reginald of Bath, and Count Raymond V of Toulouse. The fact that two of the bishops came from Angevin territory shows where Henry of Marcy and the pope thought political power in the area really lay. While passing through the Limousin on the road south, the prelates picked up a small army, including two lords—the viscount of Turenne and Raymond of Chateauneuf—whose reputation for bloodthirstiness was already well established. (The previous April, on the same day that a troop of mercenaries had been trapped and slaughtered at Malemort, the viscount helped another troop led by Lobar the Wolf to capture and sack the town of Segur. On his return from Toulouse he himself was captured and locked in a tower by a burgess of Martel who had a claim against him; no sooner did the viscount negotiate his own release than he turned on his captor and gouged his eyes out.) The viscount had strong family connections in Occitania and held a castle of the count of Toulouse; Raymond of Chateauneuf was probably a relative.[4]

To his contemporaries, Henry of Marcy must have seemed heaven-sent to be a leader of this mission against the heretics. His letters reveal a man of stony integrity; praising the cardinal of Saint-Chrysogonus to Pope Alexander, he focused on a single dazzling act—with his own eyes he had seen the legate refuse a bribe of five hundred marcs of silver to approve a rigged ecclesiastical election. Henry could be strict and irascible as a judge, a fawning courtier as a supplicant, and to his Cistercian peers a man of passionate love in the deepest Bernardine tradition.[5] But it is in his invective against the heretics that he seems to come into his own, as his imagination halts momentarily on some of the most violent images in the Old Testament. If words mark the man, Henry was ruthless, more at home in the language of violence than of compassion, every inch an aristocrat of arms in a monk's cowl.

> A new Philistine stands in our times before the ranks of Israel [he wrote in a report of his mission to Christendom], the order of heretics, an army of apostates, irreverently reviling the troops of the living God. . . . David, why do you hesitate? . . . Take up your sling and stone, and smite the brow of the blasphemer; let the evil head which he holds so imprudently high be raised by your hands on the point of his sword.[6]

In another letter, this one to Pope Alexander III, it is an image from Genesis that comes to his quill.

> There rise up from the ashes the worms of the ancient lusts of Sodom, coming forth from the rain of fire and brimstone and the lake of damnation to stain the western lands with the breath of its brood. . . . They preach like the Sodomites and, as if in Gomorrah, invite their guests to lustful sins. Can your zeal not be filled with indignation? Can they sin with impunity and you be still? The time has come for the friend of the bridegroom to avenge the injuries of the bride and raise the sword of Phinehas the priest against the lewdness of the Israelite and the Midianite woman.[7]

Into these images, but especially the image of Phinehas, Henry condensed a century of doctrinal elaboration on the theme of legitimate violence.

A century earlier, Pope Gregory VII and his colleagues had so smudged the line between monks and warriors at the command of the pope that both could be blessed with the same title: *milites Christi*, warriors of Christ. The earlier clerical suspicion of any warfare, of any bloodletting, they replaced with its glorification, provided that the warriors wielded lance and sword in the name of God. Few contributed more to this glorification of Christian militarism than

Bernard of Clairvaux himself, in whose mind the very act of killing in Christ's name was transmogrified into a penitential act. The Gregorians had performed this sanctification for the benefit of the warriors who served the papacy against the emperor; later popes and Bernard had shaped the ideology of the Holy War in the Holy Land. Bernard's "new knights" had been the Templars, a monastic warrior order. It remained for the lawyers to justify the violent suppression of heresy.[8]

Around 1140, Gratian, a Camaldolese monk writing in Bologna, completed what would become the major medieval textbook of ecclesiastical law, the *Concordance of Discordant Canons*. He posed the problem of a "just war" to his readers by imagining the following case:

> Certain bishops have fallen into heresy together with the people committed to their care. In response the pope orders the orthodox bishops of the region, who also hold civil jurisdiction from the emperor, to defend the orthodox from the heretics and to compel the heretics to return to orthodoxy. In compliance with this order, the bishops assemble an army, combat the heretics in open battles and by ambushes, killing some, despoiling others of their property, while others return to the unity of the faith through the correcting influence of incarceration.[9]

As he worked through the ways the actions of pope and bishops in this narrative might be justified, Gratian cited "revenge for injuries" as one of the several motives that could render war and other forms of violence licit, using exactly the phrase, *ulciscantur injurias*, that Henry would use in his letter to the pope.[10]

When Henry of Marcy brought to mind the story of Phinehas, however, he was surely thinking of something considerably more complex than the problem of a just war and legitimate violence, something far closer to his Cistercian heart. Faith for him, as for all the learned clergy of Latin Christendom who knew their Saint Augustine, was not a matter of individual conscience (as it was for the early Church and is for most of us); it was a part of God's plan for His Church and for humanity, a plan that the Bible, properly understood, had revealed to man. The story of Phinehas thus had to be read as both a warning and an exemplar for the Church. Henry remembered the story told in the book of Numbers:

> While Israel dwelt in Shittim the people began to play the harlot with the daughters of Moab. These invited the people to the sacrifices of their gods, and the people ate, and bowed down to their gods. So Israel yoked himself to Ba'al of Pe'or. And the anger of the Lord was kindled against Israel. . . . And behold one of the people of Israel came and brought a Midianite woman to his family, in the sight of Moses. . . . When Phinehas . . . saw it, he rose . . . and took a sword in his hand and went after the man of Israel into the inner room, and pierced both of them. Thus the plague was stayed from the people of Israel. . . . And the Lord said to Moses, "Phinehas the son of Eleazar, son of Aaron the priest, has turned

Remains of a doorway from the abbey church of Saint-Pons-de-Thomières. From Charles Nodier et al., *Voyages pittoresques et romantiques dans l'ancienne France. Languedoc.* By permission of the Houghton Library, Harvard University.

back my wrath from the people of Israel, in that he was jealous with my jealousy among them, so that I did not consume the people of Israel in my jealousy. Therefore say, 'Behold, I give to him my covenant of peace; and it shall be to him and to his descendants after him, the covenant of a perpetual priesthood.' "[11]

As the Church, to all twelfth-century theologians, was the New Israel, so the heretics must be the Israelites who bowed down to the gods of Moab. The warning embedded in this Old Testament story was clear: if this new evil was not corrected, a wrathful God would send his scourge upon the New Israel as he had threatened to send it upon the Old. On the model of Phinehas, the pope and his agents must be "jealous with God's jealousy" if they too wished to be worthy of God's perpetual priesthood. None of this had to be explained. Sender and recipient read the Bible in the same manner. The reference was all that was needed.

The Church, in Henry's mind, was more than a vague image of the people of Israel led by Moses to the Promised Land. It was shaped by seven hundred years of monastic speculation on the Christian life, as well as by the sharply hewn institutions of control that the Gregorian reform of the eleventh century had brought into being. The Church, to Henry, was a splendidly ordered social body in which all had their proper place; it was a carefully balanced hierarchy of dominance and subjection.

At the end of his life, Henry composed for the monks at Clairvaux a treatise titled "On the Pilgrimage of the City of God."[12] Meant as a work of spiritual edification, it also spelled out in detail his conception of the Church. At the very beginning he laid bare the straitness of his vision. "After the first man made from the dust of the earth filled the earthly cities of the world with people of earthly knowledge, there came the new man of celestial substance from heaven, who desired to build a celestial city on earth. By certain signs he separated its citizens, who possessed celestial wisdom, from earthly citizens: by tonsure, by the title of filiation, and by the unfailing testimony of friendship [with God]."[13] The Church may encompass the laity, but they remain "of the earth." They are driven by a "spirit of envy" against the clergy; they are Cain against Abel, Esau against Jacob, driven by jealousy of the privileges and power that the earthly citizens of heaven received at the beginning of Christian history.[14] For, like Jacob, the clergy are given by God's benediction "not only the dew of heaven, but the fat of the earth in full abundance . . . , the servitude of the people, the supplication of the crowd, and domination over their brothers."[15] Within the Church, some are assigned to create kingdoms, like the tribe of Judah, others to form the priesthood, like the tribe of Levy, "that by the two the people may be instructed and compelled to humble subjection"; the other ten tribes are the monks who are to prepare the kingdom to come.[16] Yet even Judah and Levy are not equal, for "behold how great is the glory of the power and dominion of Zion [the clergy] which rules not only over the people but over kings and emperors."[17] Henry, an ironist might judge, was determined to prove the "good men" of Lombers correct in their portrayal of the pride of the triumphant Gregorian Church.

Tonsure is the visible sign of these "celestial men," but chastity is what makes them the "sons" and "friends" of God, men of heaven on earth; for the married laity, on the other hand, there is not much hope, whatever Saint Paul and the Fathers of the Church seemed otherwise to promise. "What is more beautiful than chastity," he asked rhetorically, "which in the flesh makes men to live beyond the flesh as celestial beings, making them like the angels in heaven, where, so the Gospels testify, they neither marry nor are married; while the others, through lust, like dumb animals putrefy in their dung."[18] On this, Cistercian theologians and heretical "good men" joined hands.

Monks and heretics all responded to the same texts—"Who does not renounce all that he has cannot be my disciple," "If any man would come after me, let him deny himself and take up his cross and follow me," "Who leaves father and mother, wife and sons and fields, for my sake, will receive a hundredfold in return and possess eternal life."[19] What they renounced was the flesh.

Chastity made the true disciple. And into Christ's promise of discipleship, Henry of Marcy now read the Gregorian program—as doubtless did many other clergy of his time, for Henry was a man of action, not an original thinker, and his book was a tissue of monastic commonplaces. Discipleship, he asserted, gave them an imperium of mediation, between the seen and the unseen, earth and heaven, man and God. It gave them, in consequence, their claims to dominion over "the things of this world."

Although Augustine had taught otherwise, the force of ancient Eastern Christian wisdom—ideas once propounded by Greek writers such as Methodius of Olympus, Origen, Gregory of Nyssa, and Clement of Alexandria—now broke through the troubled consciousness of Western monks: the sin of disobedience, the sin of Adam and Eve in the Garden, was first and foremost a sexual sin. In the words of Jesus, "The angels look continually on the face of my Father who is in heaven,"[20] they heard a reference to themselves, asexual by their virginity as the angels are asexual by their nature. Through virginity they recaptured the image of God in man.[21] It was the heretics' uncanny and troubling resemblance to the monks' most cherished image of themselves, while at the same time rejecting all claims to dominance, that made them seem so sly and fearsome, "little foxes in the vineyard of the Lord."

This troubling resemblance was also what awakened the clergy's dire imaginings of unspeakable sexual depravity among the heretics. For it seemed a necessary corollary of their equation of virginity or continence with clerical dominion that all heterodoxy was a form of lust. As sexuality, the sign of the earth, and therefore of decay and death, separated man from God, the converse was also true: all who rejected submission to the hierarchy "preached like the Sodomites and invited their guests to lustful sins." And so the prelates assembled at Rheims in 1157 could completely miss the point of the heresy they imagined they were fighting; they condemned the "Manichees . . . who wishing to appear more pure, shamelessly condemn the bond of marriage which was created by God," while at the same time "they reside with women who are neither their wives nor their blood relatives." It was indeed this practice that most clearly marked them as heretics.[22]

Against such usurpations of their self-image and denunciations of their privileges the clergy were building institutional defenses from midcentury on. Bishop Hildebert of Le Mans could do nothing to the heretic Henry but send him on to the next diocese. Bernard of Clairvaux had no remedies other than preaching. Henry of Marcy and the cardinal of Saint-Chrysogonus had far more forceful weapons. The change in attitude was already marked in 1148 by a council at Rheims, presided over by Pope Eugenius III, which handed over the followers of the heretic Eon de l'Etoile to the secular power to be burned. At the same time the council declared that anyone in "Gascony and Provence" aiding, abetting, or giving shelter to "the heretics and their followers," or letting them leave for other regions, were anathema; their lands were placed under an interdict.[23] The council of 1157 ordered that the "piphiles" or "Manichees" were to be imprisoned for life; their followers, if they did not repent, were to be branded with a hot iron on their forehead, and their goods were to be confiscated; anyone who found them afterward (presumably still advocating heretical doctrines) could take them prisoner. Those publicly suspected of heresy were to purge themselves with the ordeal of hot iron or suffer the consequences.[24] Here, for the first time, suspicion of heresy alone was an *infamia*, and those thus fingered were guilty until they could prove themselves innocent. Six years later, a council at Tours demanded that the heretics "of Toulouse" be boycotted, their goods confiscated, and their gatherings punished.[25] Together with some armed cohorts, such regulations were all that Henry of Marcy and the cardinal-legate needed. They did not have to wait for the heretics to convict themselves out of their own mouths.

REHEARSAL FOR CRUSADE

In the summer of 1178 the mission arrived in Toulouse, "the mother of heresy and fountainhead of error." "We found the city so diseased," Henry reported, "that from the soles of its feet to the top of its head there was not a healthy spot in it. . . . The abomination of desolation had found a place in its streets, and serpents like those of which the prophets speak had their dwelling places in its alleys. . . . Such was the license of the heretics that as we entered the city they mocked us, . . . making signs with their fingers and calling us imposters, hypocrites and heretics."[26]

Henry and his companions began by preaching. Then they summoned the bishop, the clergy, the consuls—the chief political committee of the city—"and other faithful men who had not been touched by any rumor of heresy" and made them promise to name in writing "everyone who they knew had been or who they might in the future know to be heretics or accomplices of the heresy, and to leave out nobody at all, for love or money."[27] The net was cast. They soon had their fish—their "catalogue of an innumerable multitude." Among them was one whom Raymond V, for one, must have been delighted to see— Peter Maurandus.

Peter Maurandus was the scion of one of the new oligarchic families of the city: "great even among the ten greatest men of the city," said Henry. His father had already served around the middle of the century in the count's "chapter," the institutional predecessor of the consulate that would come to rule the city. He was, writes his biographer, a "true-blue member of the patriciate."[28] The family figured prominently among the well-to-do burghers and powerful knights who during the previous decades had slowly wrested control from the count and his officials, extracting from their preoccupied ruler a series of fiscal privileges and exemption from military service away from the city. In 1175–76 they began to nibble away at the judicial rights of the count's vicar as well.[29] The count had reasons within the city as well as on his frontiers to use the Church to trounce his enemies. And for the legate and the abbot, here was the man whose conviction would be sufficient to scare the rest to return "to the simplicity of the true gospel."

Convict him they did. Persuaded by the count to appear, Peter at first denied that he was a heretic. Asked to swear to it (for the prelates knew that the heretics always refused to swear, claiming that God had prohibited it), he suddenly found himself face to face with the full panoply of ritual magic of which twelfth-century monks had the secret. While waves of ancient chant lapped against the cathedral walls, a solemn procession of clerics and monks bore relics to the altar. We can well believe what Henry tells us: "manifest fear and paleness overcame Peter, and color of face and courage of mind alike forsook him. . . . You could see him shaken as though by some paralytic disease." He put his hand on the Gospel placed before him and swore that he would explain his beliefs on every point of faith the prelates would ask him about. But the clergy were not done playing the mage and enveloping Peter in the mists of the inscrutable. On cue, a priest lifted his eyes to heaven and, seeking an augury, opened the book on which Peter had just sworn. Then, looking at the page to which he had opened, he read out, "What have we to do with thee, Jesus, Son of God? Art thou come hither to torment us before the time?" "To us who were gathered in your name," Henry later wrote, "it gave great joy," for in those questions they heard the voice of the heretics, and they, the prelates, would be the tormentors.

But on what point of faith would they begin to question Peter? Their answer to that question shows how confused they were about the nature of the heresy they faced, in fact about all heresies, which seemed in their minds to bleed one into another like ill-fixed dyes in a bolt of cloth. As the true faith is one, they appear to have thought, so all heresies both ancient and modern must also be one, the single-minded work of Satan under different names. To Henry of Marcy, not seeing any contradiction, Peter Maurandus was both a Manichee and an Arian (a heresy named for a fourth-century Egyptian priest whose doctrines on the nature of Christ were condemned by the Council of Nicaea in 325). Yet when he and his colleagues looked in the libraries of Toulouse for a text of abjuration that they could force Peter Maurandus to swear, all they could find was the abjuration forced on Berengar of Tours—an eleventh-century monk who had questioned the real presence of Christ in the Eucharist.[30] And so the prelates asked Peter to tell what he believed about the Eucharist. To their surprise, he "betrayed the truth of his own falsity"; he replied that the consecrated bread is not the body of the Lord. That was enough. All present shouted at him, "Heretic! Criminal!" and he was led off to the count's prison.

That simple procedure was enough to convict him, and the sight of the dungeon enough to convince him that martyrdom was not to his taste. Through go-betweens he promised "to be converted so that he could be freed from the fear of imminent death and enjoy the benefits of a better life." Standing naked in the cathedral, which was crowded with his fellow townsmen, he read the confession of faith the legate handed him. The next day the action moved to the cavernous monastic church of Saint-Sernin, to which the family had connections that dated back to the very beginning of the century.[31] Here the crowd was so dense that the legate could scarcely make his way around the altar to perform the mass. Peter, naked and barefoot, was led from the great western portal to the steps of the altar as the bishop and the abbot whipped him with leather thongs. Cursing all heretics, reconciled to the Church, he heard his penance: all his goods were to be confiscated; each Sunday he was to be scourged at every church in Toulouse; he was to restore all the goods he had taken from churches, return all the interest he had earned by "usury," make amends for injury he had caused the poor; he was to pull down his tower house in the city; and within forty days he was to depart for the Holy Land, there to serve the poor for three years.[32] To both prelates and count it must have seemed a triumph.

While the legate and his associates went after lesser fish, Henry of Marcy, the bishop of Bath, and Raymond of Turenne and his forces headed off to Castres and Albi, whose bishop, William of Dourgne, had been imprisoned by the viscount, Roger of Béziers.[33] Given the destruction of the ecclesiastical archives of Albi during the religious wars of the sixteenth century, it is impossible for us to know the exact reasons why relations between bishop and viscount had reached this pass at this moment. In twelfth-century Albi as in Narbonne and Béziers, the bishops, all members of the locally entrenched seignorial class, had created their own extensive lordship within the city, developing the land that lay around the cathedral close, increasing their seignorial revenues and their taxes on trade, claiming ever broader judicial rights, and establishing their fighting men close by their palace. Thanks to the reform movement, they had largely freed themselves from the tutelage of both the counts of Toulouse and the Trencavel viscounts (who by the late twelfth century had acquired most of the comital rights in the city). Here as elsewhere in the region, bishops, cathedral chapters, and viscounts were uneasy neighbors; the city was notorious for the violence of its factional conflicts. Around 1140, the cathedral canons, who had just won their institutional independence from the bishop, carried their fight with him so far that they garrisoned the church with troops and burned down the episcopal palace.[34] It was probably another fight over the division of lordly rights that led Roger of Béziers to lock up the bishop. Henry of Marcy, however, saw heretics wherever he looked. The region was "a great cess-pit of evil, with all the scum of heresy flowing into it," and the bishop's jailers had to be heretics as well.[35]

Before this show of force, Roger of Béziers retreated, probably to Ambialet, the family stronghold up the Tarn, east of Albi.[36] At Castres, about a day's ride

Ruins of Ambialet, the principal Trencavel residence near Albi. Author photograph.

to the south of Albi, the prelates found Adalais, Roger's wife. Preaching the faith to the assembled populace, they declared Roger "a traitor, a heretic, and a perjurer for having violated the peace and the personal safety of the bishop," and "on behalf of the legate and of the kings of France and England," publicly excommunicated him.[37] With this blast of invective, Henry gave Raymond V another victory: in the minds of everyone who received his account of the mission, he permanently affixed the label "heretic" to the Trencavels. The family would never succeed in sloughing it off.

The bishop of Bath and his troops then marched north to Albi, where they encountered two of the most important Perfects of the region, one of them the Cathar bishop of Toulouse, the other probably the Cathar bishop of Agen, who willingly agreed to meet with the legate in Toulouse, provided they could go under safeguard.[38] There, to a disbelieving audience, they read a lengthy and fully orthodox profession of faith. It was painful enough for the assembled clergy to hear this, when they knew that the men had preached very different stories; a second reading was greeted with hoots of derision, and Raymond V himself offered to testify against them. It was even more painful for the legate to find himself forced to discuss the faith in the vernacular when, as he wrote afterward, "everyone knows God wrote the Bible in Latin."[39] Asked to swear to their profession of faith, they refused. Convicted by their obstinacy and by what the assembled people said about them, they were excommunicated with bell, book, and candle, and—to the legate's regret—sent on their way under the protection of the safeguard they had been issued in Albi.[40]

Henry of Marcy, meanwhile, headed back to Cîteaux.[41] He knew what had to be done. A holy war had to be launched against the likes of Peter Maurandus, and above all against the Trencavels. It was with this in mind that he circulated his account of the mission, beginning with a fiery exhortation to battle and ending with an open invitation to conquest: "It is clear from this that a fine door is open to Christian princes to avenge the wounds of Christ, to bring to the desert the garden of the Lord and to the wilderness the sweetness of paradise."[42] One of those princes, he thought, might be Henry II of England, by now reconciled to the Church for six years, absolved of complicity in the murder of Thomas Becket; to him the abbot of Clairvaux wrote immediately to thank him for the promise of lead to re-roof the church of Clairvaux. "The lands of Gascony and the noble city of Toulouse, to which we went at the behest of Your Magnanimity," he wrote, "can testify how often I spoke of the magnificent virtue of Your Majesty and how much the splendor of your faith shone forth in that dark expanse of error." As a sign of his appreciation he sent the king a finger of his predecessor Saint Bernard.[43] It was with holy war in mind that, soon afterward, he departed for the great council that Pope Alexander summoned to meet in the church of the Lateran at Rome in March 1179. He got what he wanted. In canon 27, the fathers of the council lumped together what they must have considered the two plagues of the region of Albi and Toulouse—the Cathars and the mercenaries—and not only declared them and all their protectors and supporters anathema, subject to confiscation and servitude wherever they were found, but also granted all the privileges of crusaders to those who took the field against them.[44] Henry returned to Clairvaux wearing the crimson hat of cardinal-bishop of Albano; a year later he would be Peter of Pavia's successor as papal legate.

In early summer of 1181 Henry of Marcy was back in the region with three bishops, "marching against the heretics with a large army," reported Geoffrey of Vigeois. The troops had probably been raised in the Limousin, for Geoffrey knew and thought worth recording the name of one man who was killed.[45] Henry's success this time was even greater than before. Hearing that Roger of Béziers, his wife Adalais, and the two Cathar bishops interrogated in 1179 were in the town of Lavaur, he laid siege to it. After some fighting, the gates were opened at Adalais's insistence. The Perfects revealed their true beliefs in great detail (Henry this time reporting them accurately), and Roger, according to the legate, "along with many princes promised to renounce heresy." Among the legate's other prizes was a local noblewoman, Vierna, wife of Sicard of Boisse-zon, who admitted, Henry reported ironically, that she had been "lustfully de-bauched [*stuprata*] by fifty of the more religious of the sect" and had abandoned her husband's bed and joined herself to them [*se conjunxisset*] in order to lead a more holy life." (Once again, Henry's imagination turned heretical conversion into sexual orgy.) The two Cathar bishops converted and were made canons regular at Toulouse, one at Saint-Sernin, the other at Saint-Etienne.[46] Despite such apparent success, however, Henry this time was convinced that his work was in vain. "As soon as the Catholics departed," Geoffrey of Vigeois noted with disgust, "the pigs returned to the filth of their sty." He seems to be echo-ing the legate's own assessment, perhaps his own words.[47] The stain would not be lifted from the Trencavel name.

Up to this point, Ermengard had not been touched by the storm over the Cathars. But now Henry's target became the church of Narbonne. Descending on the city, he deprived of their offices not just the archbishop, Pons of Arsac, his colleague on the mission of 1178, but also three archdeacons and the sac-ristan.[48] What could have been the reason? "Because he was ineffective and blameworthy," says a thirteenth-century chronicle of Clairvaux;[49] but that re-mark, without further detail, is so stereotyped as to be no explanation at all. In the absence of any solid evidence, once again, we can only speculate.

The archbishop of Narbonne was the only member of the expedition of 1178 who knew the politics of the region intimately, from the inside. The oth-ers had made their careers in the very different worlds of northern royal courts. If the legate and the abbot heard any word of the power politics that lay behind Raymond's appeal for help against the heretics, it would have been from the mouth of Pons d'Arsac. He was, furthermore, intensely loyal to Ermengard. While conflicts between bishops and viscounts, complete with armed revolts and assassinations, shook almost all the other cities of Occitania from the mid-twelfth century on, Narbonne remained calm (although disputes had been rife in the generations preceding Ermengard and would be again in the thirteenth century). Pons's loyalty was amply rewarded. In 1176, on the eve of Count Ray-mond's putsch against her, the act that would set all these forces of faith and vi-olence in motion, Ermengard had endowed the archbishop and his church with all her seignorial rights in a fortified village in the Narbonne countryside, in gratitude, the act said, "for the fidelity and service which I have received from you, Archbishop Pons."[50] Perhaps in conversation with his fellow prelates he raised some doubts about the real piety of Raymond V; perhaps he spoke too warmly of Ermengard's ally, Roger of Béziers. Whatever the reason, he was ousted from his archbishopric and the cathedral chapter was decapitated. The canons were required to swear that they would accept and install in their offices whomever the legate would name. For a while, it appeared as though John "of the beautiful hands," bishop of Poitiers (whose knowledge of the local language may have been as limited as Peter of Pavia's),[51] might succeed to the archbishopric, but he preferred the see of Lyons, to which he was elected at the same time. It was on this occasion that Stephen of Tournai congratulated him for escaping the "barbarity of the Goths and the cruel and savage habits of Septimania."[52] After several years of vacancy, the office was finally filled by Bernard Gaucelin, a relative of the lords of Montpellier, who had been bishop of Béziers since 1167. Henry of Marcy, the newly created cardinal of Albano, meanwhile turned his attention to other problems.

The election of Bernard Gaucelin to the archbishopric in 1184 was perhaps a sign that Occitania would once again be forgotten by the outside world, that after five years of being on the papacy's and the Cistercians' center stage it would quietly slip off into the wings.[53] It would fight with or fight off as best it could the mercenary armies that ravaged the land, and the Cathars, and soon afterward the Waldensians as well, would come and go as they pleased. Henry's pessimistic assessment of his campaign turned out, in fact, to be justified.

In Toulouse, the count and the consuls may or may not have legislated against the heretics, but Peter Maurandus and his family lost neither much wealth nor their place in society. At least one son and perhaps more joined the Cathars. Nor should we imagine that the dissidents had been driven underground and now met in secret conventicles, hidden from the light of day and the eyes of prying neighbors. Tolerance, however one might construct the reasons for it, went far beyond the circle of strict adherents. For some—both the believers in the Cathars and the believers in orthodoxy—faith was doubtless an issue of profound meaning, giving shape and purpose to life; for others, and possibly for many, it seems to have been a matter of laissez-faire. And neither the canons of the Third Lateran Council nor the eruption of the armed legatine mission in their midst seems to have changed that. Such was still the case even after the Albigensian Crusades, when people on their deathbeds might be offered a Cathar *consolamentum*, the opportunity to become one of the Perfect, and calmly reply, "No thank you, I would prefer to become a monk."[54] How much more tolerant the city must have been when repression was still far away. In 1189, eleven years after the mission of Peter of Pavia and Henry of Marcy, three brothers from a village near Toulouse could still stand before a public notary in the company of witnesses and arrange a property settlement for their mother Ava, "who has given herself over to the men who are called heretics." Like Peter Maurandus, these were men of substance, perhaps village lords, in any case owners of mills, vines, gardens, grainfields, and rights of lordship. They tried to foresee every eventuality: "If during her life," they were careful to stipulate, "there arises a scandal, and Ava cannot remain in this country, she may mortgage this property [which they had given her] for 150 sol. Tol., or 300 sol. Melg., to do with as she will."[55]

There is every reason to believe that the story Bishop William Peter of Albi recounted to the youthful William of Puylaurens was the kind of thing that could have happened, even if it was doubtless decidedly embellished in the retelling:

One night while sleeping, he said, he had a dream that he was at the bedside of his kinsman William Peter of Brens, who seemed ill. Opposite the bed there was a burning brazier, and toward it the sick man started to walk. "Where are you going," the bishop asked. "I am going to enter the flames," the sick man answered. And however much the bishop tried to stop him, he climbed into the burning brazier. Just then someone knocked on the door of the bishop's chamber and called out to those who were guarding the chamber that William Peter of Brens was very ill and the bishop should come. The bishop spent the rest of the night on the road, traveling the three leagues to where he was. When he arrived he found him gravely ill, and sat down by his bed. The sick man asked the bishop to advise him whether he should leave his inheritance undivided between his two children or whether he should divide it. The bishop advised him to divide it, for fear that one might try to cheat the other out of his share if it were given to them jointly. . . . The bishop then asked him what he wished done with his remains, whether he wanted to be buried at the monastery of Gaillac, at Candeil, or in the church of Albi. The sick man replied, "The bishop should not worry about it," because he had already made arrangements. When the bishop insisted, the sick man replied that he wanted to be taken to the "good men" [that is, the heretics]. When the bishop told him he did not have the right to do such a thing, the sick man answered, "Don't bother yourself about it, because if I can't get there any other way, I'll crawl there on all fours." When the bishop heard that he left him, as the dying man had left God, for even though he was bishop he could do nothing to stop him."[56]

Count Raymond's appeal to the Cistercians did little to help him regain control of his city or advance his war against Ermengard and the Trencavel alliance. Although there is evidence that he was forcefully playing the role of arbiter among the patricians, the wealthy businessmen, artisans and tradesmen, and the bishop, all of whom were reaching for power and privilege in the city, in 1189 he was forced to grant the bishop and consuls a substantial number of political and judicial privileges. The consuls, drawn from a group of oligarchic families of whom the Maurands were one, became the effective rulers of the city.[57] As for the holy war that Raymond hoped would destroy his enemies, it did not materialize, at least not immediately. Nevertheless, the call to Cîteaux and the missions that followed had a profound and enduring impact, one that no contemporary could possibly have measured. For when holy war did come to Occitania it would destroy not only the Trencavels and Aragonese political power in Occitania but Raymond's dynasty as well.

WHO WERE THE CATHARS?

The Cathars were first noticed in the Latin world in the Rhineland and the Low Countries. It was here that they came to be known as "weavers," "piphiles," "publicani," and eventually "Cathars." When the council of Tours referred in 1163 to the "heretics of Toulouse and Gascony," probably referring to the Cathars, the place-name had not yet become a proper name; they were the heretics "infecting those and other regions." Robert of Torigny referred to them in 1178 as "the heretics called Agenenses." But for Geoffrey of Vigeois, writing in 1182, they were the "Albigensian heretics,"[58] and although others for a short while continued to call them the "heretics of Agen" or the "heretics of Toulouse," "Albigensian heretics" was the name that stuck. Meanwhile, the bishops returning home from the Lateran council carried to all corners of the Latin Christian world the news of the spread of heresy "in the Gascon Albigeois and the region of Toulouse." The region had been permanently marked in the clerical mind, just as all those who had received the circular letter of Henry of Marcy knew that Roger of Béziers was a heretic. Although Raymond V had drawn no military or political success from calling in the Cistercians, his propaganda success was incalculable. He had lit the spark. The Cistercians would keep it alive, returning at the turn of the century with the full force of papal attention behind them. Raymond could not have known, or even imagined, that the fire he started would eventually bring down both his enemies and his own hard-won empire.

Why Occitania? Why "Albigensians"? Why, when the Cathars had flowed into the Rhineland, the Low Countries, Burgundy, and were especially thick in the cities of northern Italy and even the papal states, should they be so firmly riveted in our historical imagining to the narrow plains between Toulouse and the Mediterranean?

The primary reason, of course, is the crusades, which ultimately would turn Occitania into southern France, destroy the Trencavels, mark the end of Catalan power in the region (apart from their lordship in Montpellier), and finally with the Treaty of Paris in 1229 declare the end of the dynasty of Toulouse west of the Rhone. In this conflagration most of the other clans that played dynastic politics in the twelfth century also vanished from the stage, the most important exception being the viscounts of Narbonne. Out of the conquest and the repression of heresy eventually came the Dominican order as well as the apparatus of persecution we know as the inquisition, which profoundly shaped not just the Catholic church but all European attitudes toward the deviant and the marginal, toward those who are "not one of us."[59] The story of these crusades begins with the appeal of Raymond V and the mission of Henry of Marcy.

Is the connection of heresy and Occitania, however, merely retrospective, merely contingent on the actions of a few men, the few hundred Perfects who lived in Occitania and the men—especially the Cistercians—who eventually destroyed a society in order to suppress them? Or was it something more profound? Was there something about Occitan society that made it particularly fertile ground for the sowing of Cathar religiosity? Was there something intrinsic in the society or the mental furnishings of Occitania that allowed this "deviant" spirituality to spread with especial ease? Everyone whose curiosity has led her into the maelstrom of the Albigensian Crusades has had to confront these questions.

The polemicists and chroniclers of the twelfth and thirteenth centuries already asked these questions and gave their own answers. "Some of the knights," wrote Geoffrey of Auxerre in his account of the mission of Bernard of Clairvaux, "we found obstinate, not through error but through greed and evil will. They hated clerks and enjoyed the jokes of [the heretic] Henry, and what he told them gave them a reason and an excuse for their malice."[60] The theme has been repeated from the Middle Ages to the present. Anticlericalism and greed, greed especially for church tithes: it was the moral failure of the village nobility that allowed the Perfects their freedom to infect the people. And if it was not the animosity of the laity, then it was the weakness and ineptitude of the clergy. "At least," remarked William of Puylaurens, "they could have barked and bit."[61]

To these explanations, modern social historians of every ideological bent have added their own hypotheses: that the landholding elite were suffering in the increasingly commercialized world and were resentful of the men of new wealth elbowing their way into the ruling class; that conflict over tithes caused lords to harbor deep resentment against the clergy; that merchants through their travels and their dealings with people from distant Mediterranean shores were more open to divergent thinking, were more open-minded about religion; that those who lent money at interest found more comfort in a religion less severe in its economic morality (at least for believers in contrast to the Perfects) than the late-twelfth-century Church was becoming; that the poor and oppressed, especially those suffering from the dislocations of twelfth-century economic expansion, were prone to dissidence; that women, the other oppressed in this patriarchal society, would likewise find refuge in dissident religiosity.

About such explanations there are both general and specific remarks to be made. Some are not really explanations. Others are probably circular. Some have been, or potentially could be, empirically tested.

The twelfth-century explanation, whether in its medieval or modern presentation, is not really an explanation at all. It is a moral judgment; it attributes responsibility and guilt, and that is not an explanation in any modern sense. If it is reinterpreted as a psychological explanation, as an explanation by *mentalité*, there is no way to test or prove it other than to say that both Henry of Lausanne and the Cathars gave vent to anticlerical ideas, therefore they must have appealed to anticlerical feelings. But that, in effect, makes the phenomenon its own explanation. The argument is circular: the only evidence for the cause is the effect that is being explained. And to try to find evidence for lay anticlericalism elsewhere, in archival documents, for example, such as lay testaments,[62] is to look exactly where nothing could be found, for almost all of the archives are ecclesiastical and testaments will express only the most conventional piety. In addition, this explanation explains either too much or not enough. For, as we have seen with Henry of Lausanne, and as would be the case with later religious dissidents such as the Waldensians, anticlericalism could find an audience anywhere in Europe where clerical vigilance did not immediately suppress it. Henry of Marcy believed that all laity were envious of the clergy and harbored ill will toward them. At the end of the thirteenth century, Pope Boniface VIII, who opened a blistering invective against the kings of France and England with the words "The laity have ever been hostile to the clergy," would think the same.[63] If such were true, and not just a clerical commonplace, then anticlericalism explains neither why the Cathars took root in Occitania nor why the same attitudes elsewhere did not provide the nourishment for heresy. And finally, by the last third of the century there were alternate ways for lay piety to express itself, away from the control of the clergy yet well within the bounds of orthodoxy, in founding, endowing, and serving hospitals and other forms of social charity. Such practices were far more widespread in Occitania than was heresy.[64]

The social explanations likewise explain either too much or not enough. Taken together, they would seem to explain why any layperson would find sufficient cause for dissatisfaction with the world as it was to join a group that condemned the world as the work of the devil. And in the second quarter of the thirteenth century, when inquisitors' records begin to throw light on the structure of the Cathar community in Toulouse, such in fact was the case. Catharism had its adepts in all ranks of wealth and status in the city—the old knightly families, the new money of the twelfth century, the new men of the early thirteenth century, the artisans, women as well as men. But that exactly is the problem. We have here explanations for why the successful and the failures, the powerful and the poor, men and women, all might find solace in the society of the "good men," but no explanation for why some rather than others would do so. Furthermore, as John Mundy's analysis of the data from Toulouse amply demonstrates, there is no significant correlation between heretical beliefs and any of these social groups, except perhaps that the wealthy and the powerful were far more numerous among those condemned for heresy than they would have been in the population of the city. But this, he remarks, was most likely due to the desire of the inquisitors of the 1230s to decapitate the movement swiftly and brutally. A usurer was just as likely to be a patron of orthodoxy as he was to be a "hearer" of the Cathars; often, in fact, the division between orthodoxy and heresy ran right through a family.[65] And, of course, even if we were to find some correlation between one or more of these social groups and a penchant for associating with the "good men," it would not explain why this should have been the case here and not elsewhere. That is, none of these explanations explains why Catharism became so tightly associated with Occitania.

Before we can address that question we must first come back to asking why, in a world we imagine as an "age of faith," the faith that some people chose was heretical. Perhaps the reason had little to do with social structures and what some historians call their "tensions" and "contradictions"; perhaps the effects of place or status or gender or wealth were essentially random, affecting each individual in a different way. Perhaps it was really very simple: people listened to the Cathars and decided to become a Perfect either in midlife or on their deathbed because—for whatever their individual reasons—they found spiritual meaning in Cathar practices and teachings. It was essentially an individual choice, whether that choice was superficial or profound.[66] All that was needed was an atmosphere of tolerance sufficient to let those follow the heretics to whom that way appealed. The question then becomes not one about the appeal of Cathar practices and teachings, but rather one about why they were not repressed. Why were they so easily tolerated in Occitania?

To say that the appeal of heresy, or at least of toleration for it, was spiritual does not, of course, mean that it was divorced from matters of this world. Quite the contrary. We have seen how Henry of Marcy derived from the blessing of heaven on the celibate clergy all the very material privileges and powers that the clergy wielded over their fellow men, privileges and powers that at the same time were restricted to the members of a closed corporate body. Such beliefs, directly inherited from Pope Gregory VII and the theologian-politicians who surrounded him, were surely not confined to a few hotheads. The theologian Honorius of Autun as a jeu d'esprit could blandly derive the Latin *clericus* from *cleros*, "lot" or "heredity," because, he said, "clerics are chosen for the inheritance of the Lord."[67] Henry's long career as legate and near election as pope on the death of Urban III in 1187 would have given him many opportunities to reassure the wavering.[68] Such clerical assertions would surely not have been lost on the laity.

Popular dissent in all its manifold forms chopped away at the most fundamental premises of such beliefs. It accepted the belief that heroic self-denial was the precondition for acting as mediator between the seen and the unseen, but it denied that any institution, any hierarchy, had to authorize either that self-denial or the powers it granted. It replaced with warm human fellowship a set of distant, formalistic abstractions whose flesh and blood realities often jarred resoundingly with their ideological claims. The conversions that Bernard of Clairvaux and Henry of Marcy could work when they turned their preaching skills on the heretics and their followers suggest that such overpowering human presence was what counted most in the appeal of dissident spirituality.

At the same time, dissenters denied both in theory and practice that true spirituality had any connection with worldly power. The very way of life of the Cathar Perfects and of the Waldensians, as well as of the older preachers of popular anticlericalism, denied it. For this very reason, dissident spirituality could be an important ally in the complex battles for lordship and privilege that were being waged at every level of twelfth-century society, from village squares to the throne rooms of kings, battles that were particularly acute in Occitania. Likewise, attempts by ruling prelates to suppress dissent could easily look like opening moves in a game to destroy hard-won urban judicial and fiscal freedoms. We need not imagine that the merchant oligarchy of Arras was riddled with heresy to understand why, when Archbishop Henry of Rheims accused some of their fellow burghers of Manichaeism in 1163, they quickly offered him six hundred marks of silver to leave them alone. In thirteenth-century northern Italy, where conflicts among patricians, nobles, and prelates were intense, outside pressure on the Cathars was so weak that they could enjoy the privilege of a splintering hyperfactionalism. As R. I. Moore remarks, "Their enemy always had an enemy who would protect them for whatever reasons of his own."[69]

That the clergy should want to suppress dissident beliefs needs no explanation. The history of Christianity since Saint Paul had been one of defining the exact boundaries of what is orthodox and writing off as heretics those who crossed the line or balked at what they perceived as change, even when it masqueraded as the good old ways. But the manner of attacking such beliefs, as we have seen, underwent a profound change in the middle decades of the twelfth century. The fathers of the Third Lateran Council put it bluntly enough: "Church discipline confines itself to priestly judgment and does not inflict bloody punishment; it finds support, however, in the laws of Catholic princes, for men seek a salutary remedy once they are threatened with the death penalty."[70] The first clause represented the old order, the second clause the new. It was easy to find a body of writings stretching back to Saint Augustine to justify the change. But why did it come about?

R. I. Moore has argued that, among other things, it was the work of the new men who had flowed into the Church, men such as Henry of Marcy himself: as the offspring of a village lord he would never have found himself in the company of kings had he remained a layman, but he did as abbot of Clairvaux, papal legate, and nearly pope. There were many like him in the twelfth-century Church—men who owed their position to their intellects and their political sense rather than their birth. They would have been particularly keen on ferreting out any who might question their newly won positions.[71] They found willing allies in the great monarchs, counts, and dukes of the Latin world, in whose primitive administrations they served as workhorses—for the words they wrote, their Latinity, were the tools that could spread power over a vast land. Those rulers' power they could at the same time enlarge in a very different way, by elaborating both the rhetoric and rituals of the Christian prince. The ideology of Christian rulership, which identified the prince's sword as the sword of God, also identified the communities the princes ruled with the people of God, the biblical people of Israel, whose unity and cohesion depended on a unity of faith. The elaborators of both ideologies, that of the clergy and that of the Christian prince, were hard at work in the second half of the twelfth century, imagining the world they would like to bring into being. Religious dissidence stood in their way.

Occitania, however, was yet another world, one in which that alliance had never been created, alien to those trained in the northern courts. Raymond V, when he appealed to Cîteaux in 1177, was trying to gather the force of such an alliance; but he had to appeal to the north, to what his own letter called another country.[72] For such an alliance had never come into being in Occitan lands. In the cities of Occitania, lay rulers and bishops were most often rivals, competitors, even when the bishops came from families of the local nobility. Within the city walls they divided the rights of justice; often they shared or divided the walls themselves. And division—as in Albi and Béziers, and before and after Ermengard, in Narbonne as well—often meant conflict. In the countryside it was no different, for lordship there was but an extension of lordship in the city. All were players in the same game of dynastic politics, and although the forces deployed in the twelfth century were more vast, the rules of that game had remained essentially unchanged since the eleventh century. In Occitania the discipline of the Church could not go beyond "priestly judgment," because anything more would have required the antagonistic powers of lords and bishops to act together.

We have slowly moved from the question of why heresy appealed to its adepts to the very different question of why it was tolerated or combated. In doing so we have also narrowed our cone of vision from Europe as a whole to the peculiarities of the region I conventionally refer to as Occitania. We must now narrow the cone even further. On the eve of the Albigensian Crusades, Catharism had not spread across the entire region. The eastern regions—Nîmes, Montpellier, Agde—may have been open to the Waldensians, but there is no evidence of the Cathars making any impact there. So too in Narbonne, where the remarkably cordial relations between Ermengard and her archbishop may have forced heretics to lie low.[73]

If we take the preaching route of Dominic as a map of Cathar heresy around 1200, we can place our red pins in Béziers and the village of Servian just down the Orb River, as well as to the west at Carcassonne. The real concentration,

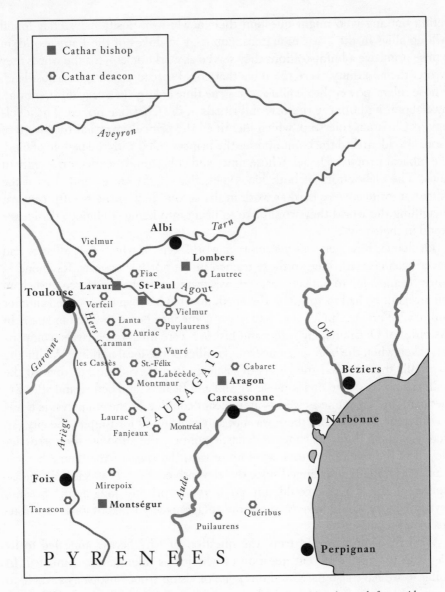

Cathar hierarchy in the early thirteenth century, according to inquisitors' records from midcentury.
Source: Brenon, *Vrai visage du catharisme*, 119.

however, is yet farther to the west, beyond the continental divide that separates the waters that flow into the Mediterranean from those that flow into the Atlantic, in the towns along the edge of the rolling plain that stretches east of Toulouse, the towns that mark the border between the Trencavel lands of Carcassonne and the Razès and the lands of the counts of Foix—Montréal, Fanjeaux, the frontier lands between Foix and Toulouse in the lower Ariège valley—and especially the triangle of the eastern Lauragais, between the westernmost spurs of the Montagne Noire on the south, Albi in the north, and Ver-feil to the west.[74] Here also were the towns and villages in which Bernard of Clairvaux chased the followers of Henry of Lausanne. Within this triangle lay Saint-Felix, site of the Cathar "council" of 1167; Lombers, where the prelates debated the "good men" two years earlier; Castres, where Henry of Marcy went to find Roger of Béziers in 1178; Lavaur, where he found the two Cathar bishops in 1181. This was the "golden triangle" of Cathar belief in the last decades of the twelfth century. Did this small region have some peculiarity that might have made it particularly tolerant of religious dissent?

At a few castles in this region the lords regularly swore fealty to the Tren-cavels—Gaillac and Brens east of Albi, Lavaur and Saint-Felix, and the string of castles that anchored their defenses on the northwestern slopes of the Mon-tagne Noire.[75] But these were truly frontier castles, outposts in a region of shaky loyalty. Two families really dominated this region, the Laurac, who held Castelnaudary and had claims to loyalties in Montréal and Fanjeaux, and the Lautrec. The Laurac family had long placed its men in the entourage of the Trencavels. But the counts of Toulouse had long-standing claims to Laurac, and the wars of the twelfth century seem to have given its lords frequent op-portunities to change sides. The lords of Lautrec, who styled themselves vis-counts, likewise constantly rode the seesaw between the two sides, dealing with the Trencavels as equals.[76] Oaths of fidelity and treaties of peace tell us nothing about conditions within this region (except that it must have been the constant tramping grounds of armed men). We may imagine it, perhaps, as an Occitan wild West, where marginals and deviants of all kinds could find toler-ance and safety. There is no proof other than geography, but the coincidence is striking.

Was late-twelfth-century Occitania the "promised land of error"?[77] The pe-culiar nature of local politics, the often tense relationships between lay lords and their ecclesiastical rivals for local power, the slowly growing organized strength of merchants within the commercial cities of the region, all made ec-clesiastical repression more difficult to impose and tolerance more likely. Yet this was probably no more true in Occitania, even in the borderlands of the Cathar golden triangle, than it was in some of the cities of northern Italy where, as we will see, Cathars were also sometimes a significant presence.

If we nevertheless instinctively connect heresy with twelfth-century Occita-nia it is surely because we are still the heirs to the Cistercian propaganda ma-chine that from the days of Bernard of Clairvaux riveted its attention on the city of Toulouse and its environs. It was to that Cistercian image that Count Raymond V appealed in 1177 in the hope of gaining new allies in the war he began by temporarily ousting Ermengard from Narbonne. The military conse-quences of that appeal were short-lived and of little import, but the names of those toward whom Raymond directed the Cistercian expedition were indelibly stained: the Trencavels and their allies in the border regions of the Lauragais, eventually touching even Ermengard's Narbonne. They would never recover. After the expedition of Henry of Marcy departed, the region slipped back into obscurity on the mental map of Church leaders. But it would take only an incident to reawaken the image of the "heretical Albigensians." And that incident would eventually come. The Cistercians would get their historical victory.

CHAPTER EIGHTEEN
IMPATIENT HEIRS

A side from members of the monastic community, how many in Occitania were aware of Henry of Marcy's expedition? Certainly those directly affected—the Trencavels, the count and citizens of Toulouse,
residents of the city of Narbonne whose church had lost its highest clergy—and
we may guess that the news traveled through the Cathar circuit as it did
through the Cistercian. To others, however, and perhaps even to those who had
to deal with the northern prelates and their band, this monastic mini-crusade
likely seemed a sideshow, especially when compared with the events that were
mobilizing mercenaries, peace militias, and eventually the militia of the Mother
of God herself: the Angevin family squabbles that had set all other ancient ha-
treds in the region vibrating in the same key. The year 1181, when Henry of
Marcy gathered his army against the Perfects and their believers, was the same
year that Ademar of Murviel assassinated Peire, count of Provence and brother
of Alfons of Aragon. It was either while Henry was laying siege to Lavaur or
not long afterward that Alfons marched through the region, laying waste the
lands of Raymond of Toulouse.

Henry's little war may have seemed to some observers a show not completely free of irony. The abbot arrived in a region already burned over by the
mercenaries in the employ of the count of Toulouse, the king of Aragon,
Richard the Lionheart, and others—the Brabançons, coterels, and routiers,
whom the Lateran council would denounce the following spring as heretics. It
was while looking for Henry of Marcy on his second mission that Stephen of
Saint-Germain-des-Près reported crossing "a deserted countryside, the lair of
thieves and the very image of death . . . nothing but burned villages and ruined
houses."[1] Under the circumstances would Henry's audience have found the
clergy's use of the same slur—heretics—to brand both Cathars and mercenaries
to be clarifying or confusing? It was not the Perfects, after all, but rather Henry
and his fellow prelates who surrounded themselves with a company of cutthroats.

We can be sure, in any case, that as soon as Henry of Marcy was out of the
region it was the warfare of the great that once again took center stage. These

wars were now provoked by heirs impatient to see the older generation out of the way. Ermengard herself would eventually succumb to them.

It was the hostile takeovers launched by the sons of King Henry II—Henry the Young King and his brothers Richard and Geoffrey—that reverberated the loudest and longest on the pages of contemporary chroniclers and provided them with ample opportunity for moralizing. "God gave Henry the chance to test himself and increase his glory in the desperate troubles he faced," wrote Gerald of Wales after the king's death, "yet once they were grown, his sons so often rebelled, and the king himself so alienated the hearts of the great men of his realm, that he could never feel safe nor rest happily." In Gerald's eyes, looking back from the safety of the early thirteenth century, it was only just retribution for the murder of Beckett and the king's adultery with Rosamond Clifford. "The more his foul actions separated him from the Lord, the more Divine Providence drove him with its whip and lured him with its favors, that he might come to his senses."[2]

Henry II's troubles began in 1173, when his eldest son, the twice-crowned Young Henry, took offense over the share of Angevin castles that Henry II wished to give to his younger son John. The argument turned into a full-scale family revolt—with Richard and Geoffrey joining the Young Henry and Queen Eleanor attempting to do the same—and then into a general revolt. Many of the great barons of Henry's island and continental possessions committed their fortunes to the younger men's side.[3] For most of the rebels, if not all, the choice was obvious. Sooner or later the son or sons would succeed to their inheritance, the Young King would become Henry III, and if he died, Richard and Geoffrey would follow in order. They would surely not forget who joined and who held back. In this world, where land, wealth, and status were synonymous, there were no offshore banks to serve as havens; in any conflict one always had to calculate the likely winner, and in a family conflict that inevitably meant the young.

In 1173–74, Henry II was victorious over his opponents north of the Loire and made a generous peace with his sons and their allies. Aquitaine, however, from Poitou to the Pyrenees—Eleanor's lands and Richard's future inheritance—continued to boil. It was Richard's job to try to put a lid on it.[4]

Then, late in the summer of 1182, the family squabbles resumed. The Young Henry demanded that his father hand over Normandy or some other territory to him to rule according to his pleasure. When Henry II refused, his son took himself off to his brother-in-law, King Philip II, in Paris. For Henry II it was a scenario he knew only too well, a repeat of the opening scene from the previous revolt. Negotiations followed, but the bickering continued unresolved. Richard finally packed his arms and trappings and, reported one English chronicler, "left behind nothing but recriminations and threats."[5] Henry II was again faced with the revolt of two sons connived in by a third and financed by the king of France. Seeing his own opportunity, Raymond of Toulouse once again sent his army to besiege the castles that Richard controlled north of Cahors. Alfons of Aragon, for his part, led his army once again through Aquitaine all the way to Perigueux to join in campaigning with the old monarch. There in his company was Ermengard herself at the head of her troops.[6] From all horizons mercenaries converged on Aquitaine. Angevin family squabbles were now an integral part of the century-long rivalry between the dynasties of Barcelona and Toulouse. In Occitania, as long since in western France and Normandy, Henry II and his three contentious sons called the tune.

When the Young King died of dysentary at Martel in the Quercy on June 11, 1183, mourned by many who had been fed and clothed by his easy ways, especially among the troubadours, a temporary peace returned to northern Aquitaine. For the mercenaries, however, it meant nothing more than changing one set of paymasters for another. North of Toulouse, around the city of Cahors, warfare between Raymond of Toulouse and Richard continued on and off into the 1190s, whenever Richard was not otherwise distracted by disputes with the barons of his duchy, his brother Geoffrey, or his father, whom he finally succeeded—with the help of Philip of France—in harrying to his death in 1189. Even Richard's departure on crusade did not stop the conflict, and on Richard's return, Raymond was suspected of conniving in his capture and imprisonment.[7] Until 1190, the forces of Alfons of Aragon likewise faced those of Count Raymond nearly every year. In the obscure narrative that we can reconstruct from alliances, truces, and the occasional mention of sieges, treachery and deceit seem the only consistency. Even King Alfons of Aragon was not spared.

In their father's will, Alfons's youngest brother Sanç had been left with nothing more than rights of reversion should his older brothers predecease him. Although Alfons, once crowned, was quick to associate his younger brothers with him (Peire received the title of viceroy and count of Provence in 1173 and Sanç began to witness royal acts in Catalonia and Provence in 1175, although usually with no title other than "brother of the king")—both were kept under close supervision.[8]

Although Sanç succeeded his older brother Peire as king's viceroy and count in Provence in 1181, he clearly harbored dark resentments. Almost as soon as he escaped his brother's oversight he signed a treaty with his family's ancient enemy Count Raymond V and the count of Forcalquier, in which they promised to do all in their power to oppose King Alfons in his war with Genoa. Alfons's response was immediate. As soon as he could muster his troops he marched on Aix. Along the way he stopped in the Rhone valley to renew the treaty of Jarnègues with Raymond V. Sanç was quickly deposed.[9]

Protected in his eastern territories by the renewed treaty with Alfons and, for a while, by the king's preoccupation with his brother's treachery, Count Raymond pursued his interests west of the Rhone against Richard and the Trencavels. At the very moment that Alfons's army was approaching Aix, Raymond expelled Viscount Bernard Ato from the city of Nîmes, putting an end to three hundred years of Trencavel control of that city. The viscount withdrew to Agde and over the next few years, under the unrelenting pressure of Raymond V, mortgaged what was left of his domains, castle by castle, to buy the services of mercenaries. For the count of Toulouse the capture of Nîmes marked a successful conclusion to a campaign he had begun in 1179. For the old Aragonese alliance in Occitania it represented a major disaster. With Mauguio and now Nîmes in the hands of the count of Toulouse, the noose was closing around Montpellier and with it the land routes that gave the Aragonese access to Provence.[10]

Farther to the west, Bernard Ato's uncle, Roger of Béziers, was faring no better. From Aix, Alfons rushed to his rescue and in April 1185 met Richard the Lionheart in Najac, where—as Alfons had just done with Roger of Béziers (perhaps at the same time and place)—the two signed an agreement to make war on Raymond of Toulouse. So much had been at risk for Roger of Béziers at this moment that in June, accompanying Alfons to the siege of Valencia, he adopted the king's son, the future Count Alfons II of Provence, as his own heir, seeming to disinherit the child his wife was then carrying (and who in fact would succeed him). "You Alfons protected and defended me from my enemies," he was made to say, "and unless you had come to bring me aid with your men and your great gifts of money to support me in my great need I would have been disinherited. You fought my wars, taking them as your own. Only through this did I keep my lands." To fix the gift in the minds of those most affected—Roger's subjects—inquests were made throughout Roger's territory to inform the king of the exact extent of his possessions and rights. Perhaps all this was merely cautionary, in case Roger's only child should be a girl or the child, girl or boy, not survive to adulthood. The king's subsequent actions, however, argue that—despite Alfons's continued attention to threats against Carcassonne—profound tensions were starting to tear the old alliance apart, the alliance to whose maintenance Ermengard had long devoted her efforts and by which, in return, she had so often been rescued from the designs of the count of Toulouse.[11]

When Alfons put down Sanç's revolt in 1185, he named as his chief administrator someone who had never been a member of the old alliance; his choice fell on Roger Bernard, count of Foix, head of a family that had always played a role on the margins of Occitan politics, but most often as an enemy of the Trencavels. Roger Bernard was the brother-in-law of Roger of Béziers, but relations between his family and the Trencavels had never been smooth. When Raymond Trencavel was assassinated in Béziers in 1167, Roger Bernard allied himself with Count Raymond V to lay claim to all the western Trencavel lands in the name of his wife, attempting to disinherit Roger of Béziers. Now, in 1185, he switched sides. Making good use of his connection to the royal dynasty (his mother was King Alfons's aunt), he turned himself into the king's major ally north of the Pyrenees. What followed would show that the counts of Foix were not to become the allies of their old enemies in the Catalan alliance so much as their powerful rivals for the favors of the king, and that the king was shedding his family's old attachments to the Trencavels, to the lords of Montpellier, and to Ermengard.[12]

In the spring of 1188, after Alfons had once again come to the aid of Roger of Béziers at Carcassonne, the third relief expedition in four years, the king gave a bloc of the Trencavel western lands—Carcassonne, the Razès to its south, and the Lauragais to its west—in fief to the new count of Foix, Roger Bernard's son and heir, Raymond Roger. This would be no mere interposition of another lord between the king and the Trencavels. The terms of the grant show a clear intention to dispossess the Trencavels entirely; they carefully divided the revenues of lordship in the Trencavel lands between the king and the count of Foix. As events turned out, Roger of Béziers was not dispossessed. In 1191, after he recovered from an illness serious enough to urge him to make his will, he gathered the greatest barons of his western lands and the fighting men of the city of Carcassonne to swear "love and fidelity" to his infant son, and in the crucible of the Albigensian Crusades these men proved true to that oath. Yet henceforth, the counts of Foix would move from the margins to the center of Occitan politics. The grant in fief to the count of Foix, although in practical terms it came to naught, shook the ground on which dynastic ambitions had been built for nearly a century. Raymond Roger of Foix became the king's point man in the west, supplanting the Catalans' old allies. And when Ermengard faced the last great crisis of her career, the ambitions of this young count and his alliance with Alfons weighed heavily on the side of those who would send the aging viscountess to end her days in exile.[13]

--✦--

Ermengard's movements during this decade we can spot only from time to time, in the company of Roger of Béziers, resolving disputes, attending to necessary business (on one occasion—a sign of the changing political scene?—with Ademar of Murviel, the murderer of the king's brother, in her court).[14] Then in March 1194 we discover her in Béziers. In her company is a group of local lords whom she had known for years but who had never been members of her entourage; two came from families that had long been associated with the Trencavels, and the others seem to be a tight group of local "friends." Only one was specifically Ermengard's friend, Ermengaud of Fabrezan, son of her faithful William of Poitiers, and it is to him she gives an astonishing gift:

> I grant you and your successors that after my death you will not be required to render any oath for your castle of Fabrezan to any of my successors or to any other person who rules over Narbonne [*urbe Narbone dominanti*].

Ermengard's grant to Ermengaud of Fabrezan, March 1194. Pergaminos Alfonso I, no. 673. By permission Archivo de la Corona de Aragón, Barcelona.

In return for this [Ermengaud of Fabrezan replies] I promise you Ermengard that I and all my successors who have lordship of the castle of Fabrezan, to the limit of our ability, will be your true and faithful supporters as long as you live in all the disputes and wars which you now have and shall have in the future. And if we are not, we are obligated to hand over our castle to you as is customary.

In all the extant documents of twelfth-century Occitania there is nothing quite like this from the hand of Ermengard or from anyone else. Why did he receive such an extraordinary favor? And above all, what were the "disputes and wars" that Ermengard of Narbonne was then engaged in?[15]

About Ermengaud of Fabrezan we know only his parentage and its long family tradition of service to Ermengard. Fabrezan, from which he took his name, stands about half way between Narbonne and Carcassonne. It guarded both the main Roman road between the two cities and the road that led up the Orbieu River to the interior of the Corbières. Ermengard clearly considered him an important ally and his aid at this moment to be worth any price. What war would have put her under such constraint?

It was not a renewal of the long-standing conflict between Aragon and

Toulouse. That conflict was at last pacified in 1190 by a new treaty negotiated on the same tiny island in the Rhone River between Beaucaire and Tarascon where fourteen years earlier Ermengard had watched the embattled dynasts temporarily come to terms. This time, however, the king and the count agreed at Jarnègues to put all their disputes—in Occitania as well as in Provence—to arbitration.

The consequences for the great families who had formed the Catalan alliance were immediate. William of Montpellier, faced with a new political reality, negotiated his peace with the man who was now count of Mauguio: the future Raymond VI of Toulouse. William recognized that he held in fief of Raymond not only a number of his most important rural castles (although without the requirement to give them up on demand) but also all the roads leading to Montpellier and his rights to profit from the coinage of Mauguio. In effect he agreed that for the most important sources of his power and wealth he was subordinate to the dynasty that he and his ancestors had battled for nearly a century.[16] After 1190, although the king of Aragon continued each year until 1194 to pass through Occitania on his way to Provence, we hear no more of sieges in the region nor of ravaged peasant villages left in his wake. Increasingly, Alfons's attention turned elsewhere, to wars against Navarre, Castile, and the Moslems. The count of Toulouse, meanwhile, embedded himself ever deeper in the Angevin–Capetian rivalry to the north.[17]

What reasons Alfons might have had for his dramatic shift in policies we can only guess. In 1180, in a move designed to separate the kingdom of Aragon from the Frankish tradition, the tradition of Charlemagne, to which the Capetians of France were increasingly appealing, a provincial council in Tarragona ordered clerical scribes no longer to date their documents by the regnal years of the kings of France, as they had always done. Henceforth in Catalonia and Aragon the date Anno Domini would suffice. Perhaps Alfons was even then beginning to think about the nature of his kingship and the difference between the lands over which he was clearly king or proprietary count—Aragon, Catalonia, Provence, and the counties of the Pyrenees his ancestors had so patiently assembled—and the lands of Occitania, where his title would have appeared more cloudy. At one point he even asked a courtier to prepare a memo on the history of his title there. So likewise in Occitania, the tradition of belonging to that slowly shaping entity, the kingdom of France, increasingly inflected both mythologies of the past and current political realities. It was, after all, to King Louis that Ermengard had appealed for succor at that moment when the Angevin threat hung heavy over western Occitania. Perhaps Alfons's meeting with King Henry II had spurred further thoughts about the demands of his title and especially about the complications, so evident in the Angevin example, that arose when a king was at the same time a count in the fidelity of the Capetians.[18] Perhaps as well his basic distrust of Roger of Béziers was now compounded by the sense that Roger was incompetent, or perhaps too incapacitated, to defend himself against the count of Toulouse and that defending him, as Alfons had had to do repeatedly in the 1180s, was an expensive as well as ultimately a losing game. Whatever the reasons, Alfons slowly but with finality turned his back on his family's traditional allies in Occitania. Thus, when trouble came, Ermengard of Narbonne would be abandoned by those on whom she had always counted.

EXILE

This time Ermengard's troubles came not from the outside, not from another dynasty attempting to wrest Ermengard's city from her grasp, but from within her most intimate circle—from her nephew Pedro de Lara, the man she had called to her side and trained as her natural heir. Ermengard now took on Henry II's role as King Lear.

Our most important clue to these tragic events comes from yet another astonishing document, the testament that Ermengard dictated on the last day of April 1196, probably the day before her death.[19] Here she adjures Pedro, "my good and dear son and sweet nephew and friend," the man who had long been associated with her rule, "for the love of God and myself" to honor her deathbed donations. If he does so, she continues,

> I will pray to the all-powerful and merciful God that He forgive him [Pedro] all the evils and wrongs and opposition and oppressions and hostilities and deprivations and misfortunes he has brought upon me and all the wickedness he has done to me, and I leave to him all my honors and all my lordships over land and sea.

Through the strenuous Latin of Berenger, the scribe who was at her bedside at this critical hour, we are surely hearing the unrestrained rancor of Ermengard herself, a woman, an aunt like a mother, a lord betrayed—enraged and unforgiving even as she expects that any moment she will breathe her last. Her spirit in the next world will pray God to forgive Pedro—if he completes her bequests—but there is no sign that even in the afterlife she intends to forgive him herself. And if this threat is not enough—even veiled as a spiritual promise—there is always a this-worldly threat: if Pedro does not heed her last wishes, she gives all her lands and powers to Count Raymond VI of Toulouse. Her anger has overwhelmed the political project of a lifetime. Behind her promise of prayer for Pedro's soul is a curse. What is the reason for this rage?

The sparse documents that remain from these tragic last three years of Ermengard's life allow us to outline the sequence of events that lead to this denouement, although they allow little more. The critical moment occurs in the summer of 1192. At the beginning of that year Ermengard (by herself) is still acting as lady of her lands in a manner that suggests no threat to her power.

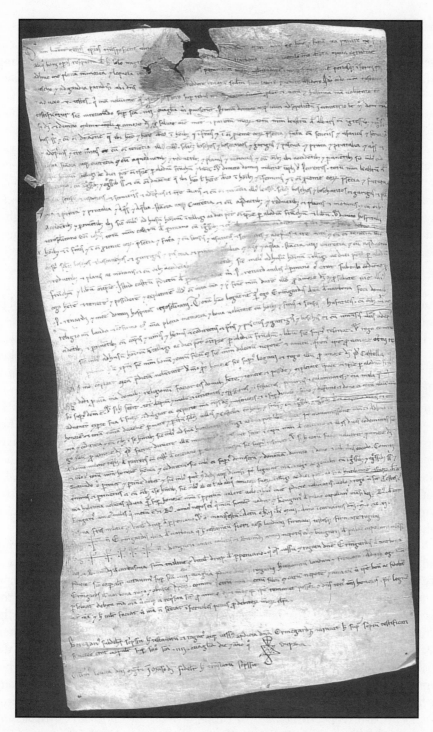

Ermengard's testament, dictated 30 April 1196. Ermengard's sign appears ten lines from the bottom. Gran Priorato de Cataluna de la Orden de San Juan de Jerusalem, arm 28, pergamino 66. By permission Archivo de la Corona de Aragón, Barcelona.

Then suddenly, in September, Pedro de Lara begins to call himself "by the grace of God viscount of Narbonne," and quickly we find him granting privileges, enfeoffing property near the city, naming arbiters in his court, selling forfeited possessions. Nowhere in the documents that record these acts is there the slightest sign of Ermengard.[20] Pedro has apparently expelled her from the city. But Ermengard has not gone quietly into retirement. Among the families who are her oldest and most faithful allies she has found supporters; Ermengaud of Fabrezan and the Trencavel allies whom we know about through the chance survival of that piece of parchment from Béziers must serve as stand-ins for an uncertain number of others. They are numerous enough for Pedro de Lara to feel unsure of the success of his coup. Early in 1193 he turns to Roger Raymond, count of Foix, for support, giving the count all the vicecomital rights and powers in Narbonne and its territories and in the foothills of the Pyrenees and taking them back in fief. The count, in turn, needs to be sure of the backing of Alfons of Aragon, so in June he travels to Huesca in Aragon to receive in fief from the king all that he has just received from Pedro de Lara. He is accompanied there by the archbishop of Narbonne, who is primarily interested in protecting his own rights in the city.

The archbishop, the king, and, one by one, those whom Ermengard might have depended on go into Pedro's camp. The one old ally who might bring her aid, Roger of Béziers (perhaps chronically ill—as we saw, he had dictated his will in 1189 and assured as best he could the loyalty of his barons to his son in 1191), dies in March 1194; his son, Raymond Roger, is only nine years old. In desperation she turns to the man who has over her long career been both her friend and her most serious enemy, to Raymond of Toulouse. To him she gives her city of Narbonne and all her powers. This alliance, however, like all her other efforts, is in vain; before the end of 1194, Raymond V himself is dead. By that time, Pedro is securely enough entrenched in Narbonne to name his son Aymeri as his heir and, in response to the call of the king of Castile, leave to fight the Moslem Almohads on the plain of Calatrava in Spain.[21]

From where does Pedro draw his strength? The first documents bearing Pedro's sign or seal leave no doubt: it is first of all the men of new wealth in the city, men who have been excluded from Ermengard's inner circle, who have joined her nephew. The names that familiarly rang through the halls of the viscountess's palace are absent—the sons of Peter Raymond of Narbonne, the families of Plaigne, Durban, Salles, Sigean, Laredorte, Ouveilhan. In their place we hear of John Bistani and his uncle William Minter, probably the wealthiest men in Narbonne (a little more than a decade later, John will become a major moneylender to the leaders of the Albigensian Crusade).[22] Along with them are others whose names betray distinctly plebeian origins: "Smith" (*Faber*), "Ox-driver" (*Boverius*), "Leather-worker" (*Pelliparius*), "Bleacher" (*Blancardus*), "Thatcher" (*Palerius*), "Quilt- (or Coat-)maker" (*Cotetus*), "from the stables" (*de Stabulo*), "from the riverbank" (*de Riparia*). Despite their mod-

Mas-Deu. Ruins of the Knights Templar house where Ermengard asked to be buried. Author photograph.

est names, these likewise are surely men of wealth, and some of them, or their descendents, will figure prominently among the "good and prudent men" of the city in the thirteenth century. They also form a network or set of interlocking networks. Although documents from the decades around 1193 are relatively sparse, a number of the persons who appear as witnesses or judges in these first official documents from Pedro's reign also turn up elsewhere, and sometimes two or three of them together. Along with these bourgeois newcomers are men from the networks of great lay families around the archbishop and cathedral chapter and urban and rural monasteries who had never found a prominent place at Ermengard's side: people from the families of Margalonis, Lac, the Royal Gate, and the Capitole.[23] Pedro has formed an alliance with those whom Ermengard kept at arm's length, with the city's new wealth and with those who gathered around the great ecclesiastical powers of the city and its rural neighborhood. Not until the second and third decades of the thirteenth century will the families of Ermengard's entourage regain what they must have thought of as their rightful place in the city and the vicecomital court.

So, deprived of her city and her power, Ermengard takes refuge in a Templar house in the first undulating foothills of the Pyrenees in Roussillon. There, on April 30, 1196, mortally ill and unable to leave her bed, she dictates her testament. Like so many others that make up this story of Ermengard's last days, this document also defies our expectations.[24] From reading other testaments we would imagine that as she prepares to step from this world into the next, Ermengard will be surrounded by those who had long been close to her: her most faithful advisors, her private chaplain, her ladies-in-waiting. But such is not the case. The witnesses who make their mark at the bottom of the parchment are two knights, Berenger Amic and his nephew Raymond, a chaplain and a friar of Mas-Deu (the Knights Templar house where she asks to be buried), and a humble Vidal, clothier of Perpignan.[25] The two Amics are not from Narbonne, nor are they members of the Trencavel entourage; most likely they are related to Gerald Amic, long one of the closest advisors of Count Raymond V. They have followed her wanderings for some time. Had Raymond dispatched them to guard her?[26] Ermengard must depend on the kindness of strangers. Those who had once surrounded her and feasted on her power have abandoned her and doubtless rushed to make their terms with the victor.

Ermengard is also impoverished. In contrast to others of her exalted position who are lavish in their testaments with cash donations to a multitude of churches and monasteries and who simply command that their executors and heirs do what is necessary to raise the cash,[27] the exiled viscountess has only vicecomital property to give and her only beneficiaries are a Hospitaler house and two Templar houses, one not far from Narbonne and the one where she has taken refuge and chosen to be buried. Rather than command, she must beg her nephew Pedro to execute these gifts, and this he never does.[28] Where are the great monastic establishments that benefited from her gifts during her long reign—the Cistercians of Fontfroide but a few miles from the gates of Narbonne, the Cistercians of Sylvanès and Valmagne, the Black Monks of Quarante and Lagrasse (where her uncle was once abbot)? Why has she not asked to be buried at Fontfroide, next to her nephew and so many familiars from her own court? Why has she forgotten the two great churches of Narbonne and its hospitals and leper houses? Having been abandoned by all, she now, so it seems, abandons all in turn, remembering only those who have comforted her in her last humiliation. She has not even a fur-lined cloak to leave to a favored maidservant, nor even, perhaps, such a maidservant with her.[29]

As a final, ironic, postmortem humiliation, the rich cartulary of Mas-Deu, which includes a list of important persons buried in its cemetery, contains not the slightest mention of Ermengard.[30] And neither of her last surviving written acts—the grant to Ermengaud of Fabrezan and her last testament—finds its way back to Narbonne; both owe their survival to their chance inclusion in the royal archives of Aragon. It is as though all conspired to hide the tragedy of her end. For a while, however, her memory will survive among the poets and among those whom their voices reach. Abandoned in the grinding world of dynastic politics by those who should have loved her, she is transformed in death into the lady of the courts of love.

Ges car estius
es bels e gens
no sui jauzens,
qu'us marrimens
mi ven de lai
don soli' aver mon cor gai.
Per que pretz pauc avril ni mai,
car cela'm torn' en non caler
qui'm sol honrar e car tener.
E s'eu pert mas bonas chansos,
los bels ditz ni'ls avinens sos
qu'eu solia per amor far,
no sai de que'm dej' alegrar.[31]

No! Summer may be
lovely and sweet,
but I'm not joyful,
for distress
comes to me from there
where my heart used to be made gay.
So I don't care if it's April or May,
for that one has turned cold to me
who used to honor me and hold me dear.
Do I lose my good songs,
the fair words and sweet melodies
I used to make for love?
What reason do I have to laugh?

EPILOGUE

CHAPTER NINETEEN
THE UNDOING OF OCCITANIA

With the death of Ermengard, the generation that dominated Occitan politics for nearly half a century passed into history. Roger of Béziers—who as a child in 1153 was placed by his father in Ermengard's "custody and service"—died in March 1194; Count Raymond of Toulouse, who had come to power in 1148, died a few months later; King Alfons of Aragon, only thirty-eight years old, died in Perpignan but a few days before Ermengard breathed her last among the Templars of Mas-Deu; only William VIII of Montpellier, who was still a child when he succeeded his father in 1172, remained. To their successors they left a world far different from the one they themselves inherited at midcentury. In their final years they questioned the old certainties and shook the old stabilities; the old alliances were gone along with the old enmities, while the new alliances were as yet untested against opponents as yet unimagined.

Of the successors, Count Raymond VI of Toulouse was probably the oldest; born in 1156, he had just turned thirty-eight when his father died. How his father trained him for his role we do not know; from time to time a chronicler notes him leading a siege or a raid in the Quercy, but until he succeeds to the county of Mauguio in 1190 he is invisible in the documents produced by his father's scribes and notaries; in fact, even after the young Raymond took the title of count of Mauguio, the elder Raymond continued to act in that capacity.[1] Given the agitation of other impatient heirs in the last decades of the century, Raymond V must have delighted in his son's discreet obedience. Peire, the son of King Alfons of Aragon, in contrast, had barely come of age when his father died. The same was probably true of Aymeri, the son of Pedro de Lara, when his father handed over Narbonne to his care and returned to Castile. Raymond Roger Trencavel, the son of Roger of Béziers, was still a child of eight when he became viscount of Béziers and Albi and lord of Carcassonne in 1194, left in the care of Bertrand of Saissac, his father's loyal companion.

All of these lords save Aymeri of Narbonne would be undone in the flaying of their lands by the crusaders from the north; Raymond Roger Trencavel and King Peire of Aragon would lose their lives—one in prison, the other in battle;

Raymond VI of Toulouse would lose his western lands, and his dynasty, like the Trencavels', would soon disappear. None escaped with his historical reputation intact. Raymond VI would be the most viciously tarred. When Peter of Castelnau, the papal legate, was murdered soon after leaving a rancorous negotiating session at Saint-Gilles, the count was assumed guilty, even if he himself did not wield the sword. It was against Raymond as a supporter of heretics that the crusade was first called. Although he was probably a man of conventional piety— and conventional aristocratic hostility to the political ambitions of the clergy— he is marked to the present day by the vituperative portrait that the Cistercian chronicler Peter of Vaux-de-Cernay painted of him: "a vicious and lecherous man" who "from the cradle always loved and cherished heretics." Historians ever since have found it easy to forget that as late as 1203 the pope could refer to the count as "our beloved son."[2] Raymond Roger Trencavel fared a little better. The worst that Peter of Vaux-de-Cernay could say against him is that "he followed his uncle's [Raymond VI's] evil example and did nothing to restrain the heretics"; about the viscount's death in prison Peter is very circumspect, for it was probably widely reported that on his deathbed he confessed and asked for communion as a good Catholic (as the poet William of Tudela relates). Not even Peter could bring himself to doubt the young viscount's faith.[3] Instead the chroniclers, and later the inquisitors, vilified those nearest to him: his sister Beatrice, one of the many wives of Raymond VI—who, says Peter of Vaux-de-Cernay, at Raymond's urging became a heretic—and above all Bertrand of Saissac, Raymond Roger's boyhood guardian.[4]

As for Ermengard's grandnephew Aymeri of Narbonne, Peter of Vaux-de-Cernay dismissed him as "the most unworthy of nobles" for his continual reluctance to fully support the crusaders.[5] Through the thirteenth century, as the counties and viscounties of the south were absorbed into a vastly enlarged royal domain, Narbonne was reduced to a minor barony, far removed from the center of power far to the north, far from the family networks of the Ile-de-France, the political axes that reached from the Paris basin to Normandy, Champagne, Vermandois, and Flanders, far removed as well from the political and theological culture of the north. It was reduced to a provincial cloth-making city that faced a Mediterranean now dominated by Genoa, Pisa, and Barcelona, a sidetrack on the major trade route that connected Italy and the eastern Mediterranean trade routes to the Low Countries. A century after Ermengard's death, another Aymeri of Narbonne, her great-great-grandnephew, would be impelled to seek his fortune and fame as a mercenary captain for the city of Florence.[6]

The force behind this undoing of Occitania was another young man who came to power in the 1190s—Lothar dei Conti from the little town of Segni in the Lazio, southeast of Rome, who took the name Innocent III when he mounted the throne of Saint Peter in 1198. At the age of only thirty-seven or thirty-eight, he was probably the youngest person ever to be elected to that office. He would reign for eighteen years and leave an indelible stamp not only on the papacy and the structure of the Church but on the entire political face of Europe.[7]

⋯⇒

Of Occitania and its heretics the new pope at first knew little.[8] His first letter on the subject, three months after his election, was addressed to the archbishop of Auch, an archdiocese in which the Cathars were hardly known. Three weeks later, when he dispatched Rainier of Ponza, his personal confessor, and a fellow Cistercian from the abbey of Fossanova to deal with important political affairs in Castile and Léon, he ordered them to investigate heresy in all the dioceses from the Alps to the Pyrenees along the way, but the language the pope used and the geography he imagined strongly suggest he knew little more about these heretics than what he found in their condemnation by the Third Lateran Council of 1179.

For the moment, Innocent had far more pressing problems closer to home. Emperor Henry VI had died just before Innocent's election. He left behind an infant son (the future Frederick II) and an alienated widow, each of them an opportunity for the new pope to exploit. He also left behind a trusted agent, his *ministerialis* Markward of Anweiler, who even after Henry's death remained firmly dedicated to his master's ambitions to join the kingdom of southern Italy and Sicily (which Henry had acquired through marriage) to the imperial lands of Lombardy and the north, all in the hands of the Hohenstaufen dynasty. Markward had troops, money, and friends at his disposal; in the cities of central Italy, which Innocent claimed as the temporal dominion of Saint Peter, he could likewise count on powerful pro-imperial, antipapal factions. There were also urban factions opposing papal control for purely local reasons, because they were excluded from the traditional institutions that controlled their cities, because of ancient enmities with those who exercised control. And among these the Cathar heresy was also spreading, right at Rome's doorstep.[9] So dangerous was it for the pope to travel far from Rome or his strongholds in the immediate countryside that Innocent waited ten years before visiting Montecassino, half way to Naples, the mother abbey of Benedictine monasticism. Breaking the weapons of Hohenstaufen ambition had to be the pope's first concern, for they made a noose around the neck of Rome. Destroying heretics was an integral part of that battle, for Cathars, "Patarines," and the imperial forces were equally "enemies of God."[10]

It was in Italy that Innocent fashioned the instruments he would soon turn on Occitania. Here, as in Occitania, religion and politics were inextricably mixed, and in the cities that Innocent claimed as papal patrimony the two made a particularly heady brew. Bishops fought with cathedral canons, papal governors played the one against the other, and in their midst the representatives of new urban wealth struggled to gain political position for themselves, while the families that had profited from their connections with the local ecclesiastics fought to keep what they had. Miracles were called on to support one faction against another, holy processions became the vehicle to assert control of the city streets, an attack on a neighboring town to gain control of a vital bridge or stretch of major road could result in a papal interdict and the cessation of all religious services for months or years on end, assassinations of bishops were not unknown, the dead then rising as saints to protect the property and power in whose cause they had died. It is not surprising that attacks on the worldly power of the clergy should have found a ready ear among the disaffected and that the asceticism of wandering preachers, Cathars and others, should shine forth as the true road to salvation. Francis of Assisi had not yet recaptured that image for orthodoxy.[11]

North of Rome toward Tuscany, in the cities of Orvieto and Viterbo, these feuds were particularly vexing. In Orvieto, long vacancies of the episcopal see combined with the concerted opposition of the cathedral canons had led to the severe dilapidation of the bishop's property. (In 1228, when the newly installed Bishop Ranerio took inventory of the moveable property belonging to the see, he found an old set of vestments, two chests, a few books, some wheat and spelt, a lame mule, and nine wine casks of which seven were empty. Part of the cathedral roof had collapsed, and grass grew between the paving stones.) Many years earlier, in 1178, when a combative man took over the bishopric and attempted to reverse the situation, he had to face not only imperial troops in the vicinity but local enemies both lay and clerical. He also had to deal with Cathar missionaries from Florence. The situation had not changed when Innocent became pope, and he had more strictly political-military interests in the area. When the Orvietan commune captured the fortified town of Aquapendente and its critical bridge on the main road from Rome to Siena, he pronounced an interdict against it, summoning the bishop to Rome and prohibiting all sacraments within the city. That gave an open field to the heretics. Nine months later, the pope thought better of his action and in response to a delegation from the city returned the bishop; along with him went a papal governor, Pietro Parenzo, whose job was to clean up the town. Both met with bitter opposition, which, on the first day of Lent, provoked an armed riot. On Parenzo's return to Orvieto after celebrating Easter in Rome, he was kidnaped and murdered. His corpse was quickly turned into a relic, buried in the cathedral, and soon performed the requisite miracles, curing the lame and the blind. Astonishingly, however, the murderers were apparently never brought to justice, and the Cathars continued to thrive in the city for another half century until in 1268 the Franciscan inquisitors supported by a Guelf commune convicted eighty-five people (eighteen of them dead). None of the living was executed, but many suffered confiscation of their goods and destruction of their houses.[12]

Toward the city of Viterbo Innocent was far more ruthless. Here he took the occasion to devise his first important new weapon against heretics. In 1199, at just the time the pope was sending Pietro Parenzo to Orvieto, the urban imperialism of the Roman city government and the opposing claims of Viterbo broke into open warfare. When the Romans sent their militia against Viterbo, Innocent refused to contribute to the Roman war chest (although his brother contributed a thousand pounds); to mollify those who controlled the city, however, he supported the Roman offensive in another way. He sent a letter to the bishop and city of Viterbo denouncing both the heretics and those who supported and protected them. All of them, he declared, were subject to the penalties that ancient Roman law imposed for high treason: capital punishment and confiscation of all their goods, both lands and chattels.

Behind Innocent's terse language in this letter and his striking equation of heresy with the ancient crime of plotting the assassination of the emperor or his chief ministers lay a firm ideological tenet: heresy is an attack on divine majesty, and the minister of that majesty on earth is the pope, "Vicar of Christ," "less than God but greater than man, who judges everything but is judged by none." Papal overlordship was not a human gift; it was a divine creation. To question papal judgment was thus also to attack God. The equation of the pope's political enemies and those who attacked clerical property and privileges with the enemies of God and heretics was therefore no mere rhetorical exaggeration. In Innocent's eyes it had legal consequences of the most terrible sort. And Innocent made certain the letter would be widely known. Eventually it would enter the standard collection of Church law and become a legislative model for secular rulers throughout Europe. Meanwhile it served a more immediate purpose: it declared that secular rulers could confiscate the goods of heretics in their territories as well as the goods of those who aided and protected them. It thus presented an open invitation for heretic hunting and eventually for the conquest of whole regions, such as Occitania, where the rulers themselves were declared protectors and supporters of heresy.[13]

Who would be the hunters? In his fight against imperial forces in southern Italy Innocent found the answer: a crusading army. The weapon that had been invented to fight the Moslems in the Holy Land would be directed against those who opposed the pope at home. Within a few months of taking office, Innocent assimilated his principal enemy in the kingdom of Sicily to those whom the Crusaders had long been fighting in the East. In the virulent letters the pope addressed to the churches of the south, Innocent labeled Markward of Anweiler, the leader of the Hohenstaufen cause, "a ruthless brigand," "the defiler of churches," "a second Saladin," "the friend of infidels," "the enemy of God." When propaganda failed to raise sufficient forces to support the papal cause, he offered those who joined battle against Markward the same remission of sins and the same legal privileges they might win as armed pilgrims to the Holy Land.

In Walter of Brienne, a nobleman from Champagne, he found a leader for this domestic crusade. Walter's family did not belong to the great aristocracy, but for a century they had been faithful crusaders; Walter's father, grandfather, and great-grandfather had all taken the cross, and none had returned alive from their adventure. The family likewise were patrons of six major monasteries, including Clairvaux itself, and Walter's uncle had been abbot of the Premonstratensian monastery of Beaulieu. The French connection, the Cistercian monastic connection, the crusading connection: all would reappear in the leadership Innocent would find for his crusade in Occitania. Innocent probably intervened to arrange the marriage of Walter with Alberia, the daughter of the illegitimate son of the last Sicilian king, and soon afterward Walter took the cross. In 1201 his small army, which included many prominent noblemen from Champagne and Burgundy, crossed the Mont Cénis Pass into Italy, and in October of that year the world witnessed the curious spectacle of a crusading army receiving remission of sins and benediction from a papal legate and invoking the name of God and Saint Peter as it advanced into battle against another army, one of whose leaders was the bishop of Troia in southern Italy. The field where they met, as it happened, was the same as the one on which Hannibal met the Romans, near the bridge of Cannae. The imperial forces were defeated, and in their own victory the papal leaders saw the hand of God. The following year Markward himself died and German resistance to the pope collapsed.[14] The pope was free to turn his attention elsewhere.

There was much on the pope's agenda—in Germany a bitterly contested election to succeed Henry VI as emperor, in Italy the continuing effort to impose papal rule on the Patrimony of Saint Peter, throughout Christendom the preparation for a new crusade to take back Jerusalem from Saladin. It is doubtful that Occitania figured high on the list. In fact, in 1202–3 Innocent was urging caution and moderation on bishops in northern Europe too eager to track down heretics in their midst.[15] Occitania might have remained no more than one among a number of minor irritations on the papal horizon had it not been for the actions of William VIII of Montpellier.

William found himself in a desperate situation, one that in origin had nothing to do with heresy or with church politics but simply with his lack of male heirs. For its nearly two hundred years of existence, the dynasty of Montpellier had produced sons to follow their fathers, and in recent generations the sense of patrilineal continuity had been reinforced by giving several sons the name of William, in case the eldest should not survive; Williams V, VI, and VII had also increasingly given preference in inheritance to the eldest son when arranging their successions. William VIII must have learned from an early age that the survival of his dynasty depended on a male successor. From his first marriage to Eudoxia, a relative of the Byzantine emperor, however, he had but one child, a daughter Maria. And so he did the only thing he could: he sent Eudoxia off to a monastery and took a new wife, Agnes of Castile, who quickly gave birth to the desired sons, one after the other.

There was only one problem with William's solution. The papacy, and especially Innocent III, had begun to pay close attention to these aristocratic marriage habits of easy wed, easy shed. In January 1200, Innocent had placed the entire kingdom of France under interdict, prohibiting all public sacraments, because the king, Philip II, had packed his wife, Ingeborg of Denmark, off to a monastery almost immediately after their marriage and then quickly found himself another bride.[16] William had every reason to fear that whatever his plans, whatever he wrote in his testament, on his death Maria, and Maria's husband, would succeed to rulership of the city; the dynasty with no other title than lord and no ancient tradition real or fictional to maintain it would vanish; the lordship that had been so carefully assembled would become some minor holdings of another house. Maria was required to renounce any claim to the family's inheritance on her marriage to the count of Comminges. But it was still imperative to carefully cultivate the pope in the hope that he would legitimate the second marriage and the children that came from it, so that his eldest son, the future William IX, would succeed to the title. For this, he must have known, the specter of heresy would be the perfect artifice.

Antiheretical polemics were being produced in the schools of Montpellier, one even dedicated to William VIII himself, but they were bookish productions without the slightest sign that the author had ever encountered a breathing, believing Cathar. Neither the trajectories of Bernard of Clairvaux or Henry of Marcy nor the archives of the thirteenth-century inquisition show any evidence of heretical presence in the city. In 1200, nevertheless, William VIII requested that Innocent send a legate to fight heresy in the region. In response the pope instructed the legate whom he was sending to deal with Philip II's marriage affair to pass through Montpellier; in his baggage the legate carried a copy of the letter Innocent had sent to Viterbo equating heresy with treason, which in turn found its way into the great cartulary that William's notary was then assembling. What the legate reported back to Rome we do not know, although the pope did order the bishop of Agde to hand over to William for execution eight heretics that he had captured. During the following two years William seems to have increased the epistolary pressure, playing on heresy with one hand while with the other he pursued his main goal of legitimating his sons and blocking the possible succession of his daughter Maria.

To the request for legitimation the pope in 1202 at last said no, just before William himself suddenly died. In his testament he named his eldest son the heir to all his lands, but in fact the question of succession was left in suspense. To William's demand that the pope concern himself directly with Occitan heresy the response came the following year. Late in 1203 Innocent summoned two monks from the abbey of Fontfroide, Peter of Castelnau and his fellow Cistercian Raoul, to begin the fight against heresy in the diocese of Narbonne. The die was cast. Increasingly, papal policy in the region would swirl around the actions of Peter of Castelnau, and it was his assassination five years later that sparked the crusade.

Innocent quickly learned from his legates how little local support he could find for his venture in Occitania. The archbishop of Narbonne scorned the legates, whose demands he found high-handed. The archbishop was a man sure of his own importance. He was the illegitimate son of Count Ramon Berenguer IV of Barcelona, and thus uncle of the reigning king of Aragon, and he had refused to relinquish his position (and income) as abbot of Monte Aragon when he became archbishop in 1191 and had fought the papacy continuously over the issue. Peter and Raoul received no better treatment from the bishop of Béziers, who likewise seems to have found the legates a threat to his own rights and privileges. The bishop refused to order the city consuls to take an oath against heretics, as the legates demanded; he refused even to lend the legates mounts or to accompany them to Toulouse. The legates must have taken their plenipotentiary powers quite literally and acted with all the seignorial hauteur of the pope himself, for soon other bishops were receiving admonitions from Rome about their comportment, and before long most of the bishops of the region were suspended or removed.

Without support in the region, without even a clergy ready to do as his legates ordered, Innocent III in May 1204 turned north, appealing to King Philip II to lead a crusade, promising him possession of the lands of the heretics and their protectors. At the same time, he asked Arnold Amaury, abbot of Cîteaux, to join the mission of Peter of Castelnau. With him the long Cistercian tradition of antiheretical campaigning in Occitania, dating back to Bernard of Clairvaux and Henry of Marcy, was once again focused on the region.

Why did Innocent turn to northern France? The question may seem beside the point to a modern reader, so used are we to thinking of the region as southern France. But as we have seen throughout this book, Capetian presence in the region was virtually nonexistent. With the exception of Louis VII's two brief forays to Toulouse early in his career, royal armies had never ventured farther south than the northern edges of the Massif Central. Ermengard may have considered Louis to be her king, but the relationship was never more than epistolary. Innocent's decision, then, was a fateful one, for its ultimate result was the absorption of Occitania into the Capetian kingdom, much of it directly into the royal domain. It was thanks to Innocent that Occitania became southern France. Why did Innocent not turn instead to the young man whom future historians would know as Peire el Catòlic, Peter the Catholic, the king of Aragon? If there had been a royal presence in the region, it was that of the king of Aragon. Peter, furthermore, was about to recognize the pope as his overlord.

Innocent left no written record to help us answer this question. His political horizons at this moment were clearly circumscribed, however, and they provide many clues.

With King Philip of France the pope's interests were twofold. First, to bring a halt to his conquest of Angevin territory on the continent. Normandy had just fallen to French armies, despite the pope's efforts to aid King John of England, who had sought the pope's intervention, and the Angevin counties along the Loire were clearly the next target.[17] At the same time, Innocent hoped to wean Philip from the Hohenstaufen side in the contest for the imperial throne. Because Otto of Brunswick, the man favored by the pope, was Angevin on his mother's side, the nephew of King John, Philip naturally supported his enemy, Philip of Swabia, the brother of the late emperor Henry VI. Perhaps the invitation was meant to distract the king, to bring peace to the north, and to bring the pope's longed-for crusade to take back Jerusalem closer to reality. The request to Philip, like all other papal attempts to intervene in royal politics, was rebuffed, but it planted a seed that would soon bear fruit.

Relations with King Peire of Aragon were more complicated. In 1202 Innocent had negotiated with Peire to have the king's younger sister marry the child Frederick II, with the Queen Mother to go along to rear her son-in-law.[18] That proposal came to naught. But two years later, in November 1204, a few months after affirming his alliance with Raymond VI of Toulouse with a marriage and a mortgage of a vast tract of land in the mountains north of Narbonne and Béziers, Peire set sail for Rome with a magnificent entourage, there to receive the sacred unction from the hands of a cardinal bishop, and the belt of a Christian warrior and the diadem of the Christian king from the pope.[19] So complex a ceremony must have been negotiated far in advance, and we might expect that Innocent would see in him the ideal instrument of his plans for Occitania. Yet it was during these same months that the pope turned instead to Philip of France. Perhaps he still thought of saving Peire for help in Sicily and southern Italy (where sporadic revolts against papal hegemony were still breaking out). Far more likely is that Innocent was repeating here a political pattern he had so often followed in his campaign in southern Italy: always protecting himself against one political ally by negotiating with another who would be the potential enemy of the first.[20] He was surely fully aware of Peire's alliances in Occitania (which now included his marriage to Maria of Montpellier, easily relinquished to him by her husband the count of Comminges) and probably did not trust him to be a pliant minister of the papal will.

Behind Innocent's choice there was surely an ideological reason as well. In the letter he wrote to William VIII of Montpellier (known by its first words, *Per venerabilem*) explaining why he could not legitimate William's sons even though he had just legitimated the children of King Philip II, the pope expounded in great detail his theory of papal jurisdiction.[21] He could not act on William's request, he said, because "you know you are subject to others, and so you cannot submit yourself to us without injuring them." William was surely puzzled by this assertion. To whom was he subject? Innocent did not say. Was it to the bishop of Maguelone to whom he had sworn fidelity for a suburb of the city? To the count of Toulouse to whom he had recently sworn fidelity for some of his rural castles? Beyond his promise not to harm these lords, in what sense was he subject to them? And why should they be concerned with the legitimacy of his heirs, a legitimacy, furthermore, that was questionable only in the eyes of the Church? In the culture of fidelity that governed twelfth-century Occitania, the pope's assertion made no sense. But political ethnography was not the pope's concern in *Per venerabilem*. His concern was to construct a vision of the political structure of the Christian world and the place of papal jurisdiction within it. The king of France, he asserted, was "emperor in his kingdom." By this he meant first of all to erect an ideological barrier to any claims an emperor might make to suzerainty over the emerging monarchies of the Christian world (claims that the late Henry VI or some intellectuals in his entourage had apparently dreamed of);[22] more importantly, he meant to imagine a world of kings who (as he wrote) "recognized no superior in the temporal realm." Over such rulers there could stand only the pope, not as temporal but as spiritual lord, to whom disputes, and therefore rights and wrongs, would go to be judged "as questions of sin." Innocent, in effect, was imaginatively constructing the Europe of sovereign states (or at least of sovereign lords ruling over many layers of subject lords) that would come into existence over the following seven centuries.

To the high pinnacle of those who, as later lawyers would say, were *sibi ipsis imperantium*, "self-commanding," William VIII could not possibly belong.[23] He had no more exalted title, after all, than lord of Montpellier; he had to be subject to someone. So must all of Occitania. In the pope's imagined geography, that someone must have been the king of France, perhaps for no other reason than that the scribes and notaries of the region (whose parchments the pope would have been familiar with) dated their documents by the regnal years of the French kings. As with southern Italy, the pope could open Occitania to conquest in the hope of bringing it into the vast hierarchical structure of which he dreamed, under the ultimate leadership of Saint Peter and his representative on earth.

Over the next four years, official preaching missions crisscrossed the roads of Occitania, menacing heretics with fire here and in the next world, chastising or suspending clergy who were guilty of living with concubines, of buying their positions, or of being too friendly with known Cathars. In 1206 they were joined by preachers of another sort, clergy, yet dressed and behaving like the adepts of "apostolic poverty" they meant to combat, among them Dominic of Osma, who would eventually become the founder of the Order of Preaching Friars, commonly known as the Dominicans. Among their converts was a man named Durand of Huesca, who founded another preaching order, the Poor Catholics.

Meanwhile, the two legates, Arnold Amaury and Peter of Castelnau, addressed themselves to the great men of the land, attempting to get them to swear to a new Peace of God. One man remained obdurate—Raymond VI of Toulouse. The demands they put to him in the pope's name must have seemed outrageous and more than a little hypocritical: among them that he swear to keep the peace with his many enemies in the Rhone valley, that he dismiss his mercenary troops (when the widespread use of mercenaries by Innocent III in southern Italy and Sicily must have been widely known in the region, as mercenaries would play their appointed role in the crusading armies to come), that he dismiss his Jewish officials (widely employed throughout the region in the lower echelons of administrations), that he stop fortifying churches (perhaps a misunderstanding on the legates' part of the fortress-churches that are still a notable architectural feature of the Occitan landscape,[24] but also ironic, given the importance of fortified churches and monasteries in the papal campaigns against Markward of Anweiler in Sicily). In January 1208, as he crossed the Rhone after a particularly fractious meeting with Count Raymond at his palace at Saint-Gilles, Peter of Castelnau was murdered.

Innocent's response was immediate. In March, probably soon after the news reached him, he addressed letters widely—to the counts and barons of France as well as the king—asking them to take arms against the count of Toulouse, who in the pope's eyes was guilty of his legate's murder (although no trial was ever held, and no one ever discovered who committed the deed) and equally guilty of supporting and protecting heretics. The count had committed treason to the divine majesty and was therefore subject to the penalties that Innocent had spelled out a decade earlier in his letter to Viterbo. The count's lands were therefore legitimate prey to all comers. Those who joined the war against him would be given all the privileges of crusaders. Arnold Amaury, abbot of Cîteaux, papal legate, and architect of the coming crusade, was ordered to present the letter to the king of France.

The king gave a procrastinating response. He was still involved in his war with King John, and to him the papal summons looked like one more interference in the internal affairs of his kingdom, especially because, the king claimed, Raymond's lands were held of him (*ad feodum nostrum pertinentem*). He allowed his barons to accept the call, however. And accept they did.[25]

By Easter 1209 the army was assembling at Lyon. It was mainly French but soon included contingents from Provence, who perhaps hoped to throw off the lordship of the count of Toulouse. But the count saw what was coming and resolved to turn it as best he could to his own advantage; he met the crusaders near Valence on the Rhone, accepted all the demands of the papal legates, handed over seven castles as security, swore the oath of peace, and himself took the cross. As one of the crusaders he could now deflect them toward his family's ancient enemy in Occitania—the Trencavels. According to the poet William of Tudela, the count had first asked the young Raymond Roger Trencavel to stand by him in defending his lands against the crusaders, but the young viscount refused. Was this story meant to put Count Raymond's actions in a better light than they deserved? Whether the story is true or not, the Trencavel lands seem, in fact, to have been the crusaders' target from the start. In the correspondence of 1204–8 there is no mention of negotiations with Raymond Roger. He does not seem to have been invited to swear the peace, and (again according to William of Tudela) when Raymond Roger tried to come to terms with the papal agents as the crusaders were approaching in 1209, the papal legate Milo "despised him and refused his request."[26] The Cistercian memories brought home by Henry of Marcy now bore their poisonous fruit.

And so the crusading army bypassed the Toulousain lands in Provence, rode by Saint-Gilles, Nîmes, Mauguio, and descended straight on Béziers. Warnings had been sent ahead that any who refused to surrender would be put to the sword "to encourage the others." And as the siege was just being put in place, to everyone's surprise the camp followers and foot soldiers managed to scale the walls of the city and open the gates to their fellows. Béziers went up in flames and all were slaughtered, men, women, and children alike. According to a later Cistercian historian, it was on this occasion that Arnold Amaury, the abbot-legate, uttered the chilling words, "Kill them all. God will recognize his own." For the clerical chroniclers, the massacre was a "miracle."[27] From Béziers the crusaders marched on Carcassonne, where Raymond Roger had decided to take his stand. The city held out until early August, when their water supply ran out, and the inhabitants and the viscount were forced to surrender. A few days later Raymond Roger died in captivity. By late summer most of the castles in the countryside had surrendered.

With the major objectives seemingly won and their crusading vows satisfied, most of the crusaders were eager to return home. Only a small contingent remained under the leadership of a minor count from the Paris region—Simon of Montfort. Had these men not been steadfast, the Albigensian Crusades might have proved as ephemeral as those first victories of the summer of 1209. Simon had been one of those who set off in 1204 to recover Jerusalem only to be turned aside by the Venetians to subdue Zara on the Dalmatian coast and then to conquer Constantinople. He was one of the few who refused to detour. Along with some relatives and vassals and his friend the Cistercian abbot of Vaux-de-Cernay, he left the siege of Zara and eventually fulfilled his crusading vow by fighting in the Holy Land. Now, again in the company of the abbot of Vaux-de-Cernay and the same men who had joined him in the East, Simon determined to finish the task of taking the entire region and destroying the heretics.[28]

When the two greatest barons of the crusading army refused to take up the Trencavel title to Béziers, Carcassonne, and Albi, Simon did so. Against the legate Arnold Amaury (who claimed the title for himself), he soon styled himself duke of Narbonne as well, and by 1212 he was ready to treat Occitania as a

The walls of Carcassonne before their "restoration" by Viollet-le-Duc. From Charles Nodier et al., *Voyages pittoresques et romantiques dans l'ancienne France. Languedoc.* By permission of the Houghton Library, Harvard University.

conquered land. In the legislation he issued at Pamiers in December of that year he set about to reorganize all that his forces controlled. The clergy received all the privileges they had long demanded and more—freedom from all taxation for both themselves and their peasants and freedom from lay justice even for those in the very lowest orders. Tithes would henceforth be strictly paid, and every household would in addition pay three pennies each year to the Pope. No markets would be held on Sunday, and all inhabitants would attend mass. And most importantly, the land law in the region would henceforth be the custom of Paris. Simon could now imagine himself ruling a land that was firmly Catholic and French. The abbot of Vaux-de-Cernay was installed as bishop in Carcassonne, the legate Arnold Amaury was archbishop of Narbonne, the monk (and former troubadour) Foulques of Marseille was bishop of Toulouse, one of Innocent's Italian legates was bishop of Agde, and other crusading prelates were installed in the remaining cities.[29] Meanwhile Simon was settling in for a long campaign of siege warfare against one stronghold after another, his armies reinforced by crusaders who came to do their forty days and then return home. The names of those strongholds are familiar: Termes, Minerve, Lavaur, and all those lesser castles whose lords had once graced the courts of Ermengard of Narbonne and her friends the Trencavel viscounts.

Year after year Simon of Montfort continued to grind away at the possessions of Raymond of Toulouse, even after Innocent III called a halt to the crusade and censured both Simon and Arnold Amaury for seizing lands of Catholics as well as those of heretics.[30] The war had now, in fact, become something other than an attack on heretics; it was an attempt by Simon of Montfort to carve out a vast barony that would stretch from the Garonne to the Rhone.

The only force that could conceivably stop him was the army of King Peire of Aragon. And in 1213, fresh from a victory over the Moslems at Las Navas de Tolosa, the king finally marched to the rescue of his ally Raymond VI. On September 13, after a fruitless attempt by the papal legates to mediate, the king's army along with forces under Raymond's leadership met Simon's forces under the walls of the little town of Muret. It was one of the few battles in open field of the entire crusade, and in the first assault the king was killed. His forces fled. The following year the counts of Foix and Comminges came to terms. Raymond VI abdicated, and with the arrival of the son of King Philip, the future Louis VIII, at the head of a fresh army of crusaders, Simon at last put his hands on the remainder of the lands of the house of Toulouse west of the Rhone.

Yet even then the conquest was not completely over. After 1214, support for Simon in the north began to dwindle, especially when Innocent at a great church council in Rome called for crusaders once again to turn their attention to Jerusalem. The dispossessed returned to Occitania. Simon was killed before the walls of Toulouse (by a rock, it was said, launched by women who were manning the mangonels on the city walls). Once again the entire crusading venture might have collapsed had the new king of France, Louis VIII, not agreed in 1226 to take up the cross. After three more years of warfare and protracted negotiations, a treaty was finally signed in Paris in 1229. Heavy burdens were placed on Count Raymond VII (who had succeeded his father in 1222), but he retained the title of count of Toulouse. He agreed that his only child, Jeanne, would marry the king's brother, Alfonse of Poitiers, and that even if the count had sons, Toulouse and all its lands would pass to Jeanne and her descendants. In the event there were no children of the marriage, Raymond's lands would become part of the royal domain. And so at last they did.

━━◉━

Nearly twenty years to conquer the land, and even then sporadic revolts continued to trouble the region until midcentury: Occitania did not slip easily into the royal orbit. As for heresy, the connection of conquest with suppression of the Cathars may very well have made sympathy for the persecuted more widespread among the old seignorial families than it had been at the beginning of the century. In a society that was being made forcibly French and Catholic, where northern prelates ruled the cathedrals and northern clergy took the places in the choir stalls once reserved for the sons of local notables, rebellion against the king may have easily slipped into rebellion against the Church. Because our knowledge of the implantation of heresy before the crusade depends on testimony given to the inquisition in the 1240s at the earliest, it is impossible to take a meaningful measure. Whatever their numbers—and despite the great auto-da-fés at Minerve, Montségur, and elsewhere—the Cathars did not slip meekly into the orthodox fold either; inquisitors were tracking down the last of them in the fastness of the Pyrenees a hundred years later.[31]

In those twenty years of unremitting warfare, however, the society that has been the subject of this book vanished beyond recall. Not even its memory survived. Occitania had never been free of marauding armies; mercenaries were a constant plague. But the objective of their paymasters had not been to destroy their enemies; it had been to gain the fidelity of those on the other side, to shift ever so slightly the balance of competing pieces in a chess game without end. The crusaders, however, came with the intention of dispossessing those who were there and taking their places. How many of them stayed and took root? In how many villages, as in Mirepoix, did a single northern lord (there, Guy of Levis, who served as Simon of Montfort's marshal) replace the multitude of castellans who had been its lords before the crusaders' arrival? As yet, we cannot say; the research remains to be done. Numbers, however, were not necessarily what counted. Although they were the enemy, the French were the conquerors and by the mere fact of that conquest their habits had prestige and were quickly emulated. The title *miles*, "knight," long common in the north but nearly unknown in Occitania before the crusade, begins to spread in the second decade of the new century.[32] The traditional oath of fidelity, nearly unchanged for two hundred years, vanished from the scene. When records of such oaths reappear, they are recognizances of fief with oaths of homage of a northern type.[33] And when thirteenth-century clergy forged early records to justify their claims to lands and powers, the titles they chose to give the men in those documents and the words they invented to have them utter were titles and words of northern origin.[34]

More importantly, the structure of twelfth-century politics vanished from memory. King Philip of France had claimed that the lands of the count of Toulouse were held of him. Innocent III had recognized that they belonged to the French kingdom. To make good his claim to the lands of the Trencavels and overlordship over Narbonne, Simon of Montfort had to assert that those lands were subject to the count of Toulouse as duke of Narbonne. When the Toulouse inheritance passed into the royal domain, that claim went with them. And so the long-standing Barcelonese–Aragonese alliance in Occitania was forgotten, and all the players in the twelfth-century political life of the region took on the figure of "unruly vassals" of the counts of Toulouse. There they have remained until the present day, characters in a morality play invented by those who conquered the region in the thirteenth century and turned it into Languedoc.

So too, as power became royal, and those who exercised power in the king's name were either knights or clergy with university training, as history was removed from familial politics and became the story of the making of the royal state, great women slowly vanished from the past as they vanished from the public places in which power was now negotiated. Ermengard the ruler, the leader of armies, was forgotten. In memory she became the mythical object of troubadours' love, with her "sisters," the countess of Champagne and Queen Eleanor of Aquitaine, a judge of erotic etiquette, removed to a higher plain where the drums and trumpets of war and the clash of arms could not be heard, where her gown could not be muddied by the rancor of deflected ambitions or the ire of frustrated appetites. And because she gave birth to no king, because the language of her poets gave birth to no national tongue but became instead a provincial "dialect" and their songs an esoteric realm of academic specialists, because she was but the ruler of a city that gradually lost its port, its industry, and its commerce, turned into a provincial backwater, her memory fragmented and finally vanished. She became but one name among many on parchments and sheets of paper dispersed from Barcelona to Paris, waiting patiently—so it seemed to me as her story took shape in my mind—waiting patiently to be rediscovered.

ABBREVIATIONS

AC	Archives communales
ACA	Archivo de la Corona de Aragón, Barcelona
AD	Archives départementales
AMN	Archives Municipales de Narbonne
AN	Archives Nationales de France
Aurell, Cat.	M. Aurell, "Le pouvoir comtal en Provence sous Alphonse Ier," vol. 2, "Catalogue des actes comtaux (1166–1196)"
BNF	Bibliothèque Nationale de France
Cart. Béziers	*Cartulaire de Béziers*
Cart. chap. cath. d'Agde	*Cartulaire du chapitre d'Agde* (ed. Terrin)
Cart. Douzens	*Cartulaires des Templiers de Douzens*
Cart. Fontjoncouse	"Cartulaire de la seigneurie de Fontjoncouse"
Cart. Lézat	*Cartulaire de l'abbaye de Lézat*
Cart. Maguelone	*Cartulaire de Maguelone*
Cart. Nîmes	*Cartulaire du chapitre de l'église cathédrale Notre-Dame de Nîmes*
Cart. Silvanès	*Cartulaire de l'abbaye de Silvanès*
Cart. St-Etienne d'Agde	*Cartulaire du chapitre cathédral St-Etienne d'Agde* (ed. Foreville)
Cart. Trencavel	"Cartulaire dit 'de Foix' alias 'Cartulaire des Trencavels' "
CD	Codice diplomatico della repubblica di Genova
GC	*Gallia Christiana*
HAC	Peter of Vaux-de-Cernay, *History of the Albigensian Crusade*
HGL	C. Devic and J. Vaissete, *Histoire générale de Languedoc*
H Malte	AD Haute-Garonne, série H, Ordre de Malte
Inv. Rocques	Bibliothèque municipale de Narbonne, MS "Inventaire Rocques"
Léonard, *Cat.*	E.-G. Léonard, ed., *Catalogue des actes des comtes de Toulouse: Raymond V (1149–1194)*
LFM	*Liber feudorum maior*
LIG	*Liber iurium reipublicae Genuensis*
LIM	*Liber instrumentorum memorialium*
MS Baluze	BNF, manuscript collection Baluze
MS Doat	BNF, manuscript collection Doat
MS Latin	BNF, manuscript Latin
MS Mél. Colb.	BNF, manuscript Mélanges Colbert
PL	J.-P. Migne, *Patrologiae cursus completus, series Latina*
Poly, Cat.	J. P. Poly, "Catalogue des actes des comtes de Provence, 945–1166"
RHGF	*Recueil des historiens des Gaules et de la France*

NOTES

INTRODUCTION

1. *Aliscans* 1 (ed. Regnier), ll. 3105–9. Regnier, like previous editors, dates the poem to the very end of the twelfth century (around the time of Ermengard's death). An abridged translation of the entire chanson de geste appears in Ferrante, *Guillaume d'Orange*.

2. *Orkeyinga Saga* (ed. Palsson and Edwards). For a discussion of this text, see Caille, "Idylle entre la vicomtesse Ermengarde de Narbonne et le prince Rognvald Kali," 229–33, and the older bibliography listed in *Poems of the Troubadour Peire Rogier* (ed. Nicholson), 164 n.

3. On the language there are two useful surveys by Pierre Bec: *Langue occitane* and, in Armengaud and Lafont, *Histoire d'Occitanie*, 256–78. *Lenga d'oc* dates from about 1290. *Occitanus*—an amalgam of *oc* and *aquitanus* (Aquitanian)—is attested around 1300. The name *provençal*, derived from *proensales*, is attested at the end of the thirteenth century and was particularly favored in the Romantic literary revival of the nineteenth. See Smith and Bergin, *Old Provençal Primer*, 1–2; Bec, *Langue occitane*, 62–65.

4. Particularly in French historiography, where the results of the Crusade used to be referred to as "la réunion du Midi à la France." Even American and English historians, such as Strayer, *Albigensian Crusades*, and Sumption, *Albigensian Crusade*, are not entirely free of the northern frame of reference, especially in their assumptions about the powers of the count of Toulouse. See my review of Strayer's work in *Speculum* 48 (1973): 411.

5. The documentation for Ermengard is widely dispersed, from the Bibliothèque Nationale de France to the Archives of the Crown of Aragon in Barcelona; a large portion, although not all, is published in *HGL* 5. The surviving documents of Raymond V are inventoried in Léonard, *Cat*. The archives of the two monasteries that must have received her benefactions—Lagrasse and Fontfroide—went up in flames during the French Revolution. What remains is only what seventeenth- and eighteenth-century scholars thought worth copying.

6. MS Doat 47 contains numerous oaths from the now vanished *Liber feudorum*, which must have been similar to the Trencavel Cartulary.

7. Martin-Chabot, *Archives de la Cour des Comptes*, vii.

8. See Débax, "Cartulaire des Trencavel," 292. There are now microfilms of this cartulary in Montpellier and Carcassonne.

9. When the manuscript for this book was nearly finished, I had the good fortune to learn of one such document in a private collection in Albi when the owner came on an Internet discussion group to ask for help in translating its contents. Somewhere out there are doubtless a few more, including perhaps even the great cartularies of the archbishops of

Narbonne, stolen sometime between the day the archives were "nationalized" during the French Revolution and crudely inventoried and the day their pitiful remains were incorporated into the public collections that are now housed in Carcassonne.

10. Quoted by Julian Barnes, "The Afterlife of Arthur Koestler," *New York Review of Books*, 10 February 2000, 23.

11. The problems of the biographer, or indeed of the historian of the Middle Ages, are in this sense hardly different from those of the biographer of a literary figure of our own day, as richly described by Leon Edel, the biographer of Henry James, in *The Age of the Archive*, but there is little possibility to explore the psychological issues Edel places at the center of the biographical quest, nor is it certain that those psychological issues would have meaning for twelfth-century people. For the same reason there is likewise little possibility of addressing the issues of women's sexuality and inner life raised by such feminist theorists of women's biography as Gutiérrez, "What Is Feminist Biography?"

12. The various references to Ermengard in troubadour poetry are discussed in *Peire Rogier* (ed. Nicholson), 160–64.

13. Translation adapted from Egan, *Vidas of the Troubadours*, 78.

14. *Peire Rogier*, 81.

15. Ibid., 88–89. The reference both to "dreit-n'avetz" and the district of Savès remains a mystery. An alternate reading replaces "en Saves" with "on ill es" (where she is); ibid., 97.

16. One of the central problems faced by students of troubadour song in the last generation has been to find an alternative to assumptions about the psychological realism of the poetry and the connection of poetry to the poet's life. On the way troubadour poetry was understood by its audiences in the thirteenth century and after, see Meneghetti, *Pubblico dei travatori*.

17. Such, at least, is implied by Orderic Vitalis's account of William on crusade: *Ecclesiastical History of Orderic Vitalis* (ed. Chibnall), 5:324–25, 342–43.

18. "Estat ai en greu cossirier," in Bruckner, Shephard, and White, *Songs of the Women Troubadours*, 10–11.

19. *Songs of Jaufré Rudel* (ed. Pickens), 164.

20. A selection of these texts in translation is available on my website, http://www.amherst.edu//flcheyet/.

21. The substantial literature on the theme is summarized and critiqued by Bynum, "Did the Twelfth-Century Discover the Individual?"

22. Moneylending: *Cart. Béziers*, no. 100; Rixendis: ibid., no. 147; Bernard of Nissan and wife: *HGL* 5:790.

CHAPTER I. THE VISCOUNTESS COMES OF AGE

1. Catel, *Mémoires*, 589; reprinted in Caille, "Ermengarde, vicomtesse de Narbonne," 38. A recently discovered document allows us to place the child Ermengard in the Vallespir (now part of Roussillon) in 1139, where she appears as a witness to a sale of land to the abbey of Arles-sur-Tech: Caille, "Ermengarde, vicomtesse de Narbonne," 12.

2. *HGL* 3:725.

3. On this family and its mythological origins, see Graboïs, " 'Roi juif' de Narbonne," and idem, "Dynastie des 'rois juifs' de Narbonne"; and in general on the Jewish community, Regné, *Juifs de Narbonne*. For the title *Nassi*, see the *Encyclopedia Judaica*.

4. Graboïs, "Étape dans l'évolution vers la désagrégation de l'Etat toulousain au XIIe siècle."

5. For the background of that title, see chap. 2.

6. Bardine Saptis: *LIG*, no. 31. Peter Monetarius: *HGL* 5:1035. A Porcellus *monetarius* appears as witness to a grant by Aymeri II in 1131: *HGL* 5:966. Is the cognomen a family name (as Caille wishes) or an occupation? I believe it is the latter, although minting could have been a family enterprise. Peter of Minerve: *HGL* 5:1024, 1025. Bernard of Minerve is one of the aristocrats who arbitrates between Archbishop Guifred of Narbonne and Viscount Bernard Berenger in 1066 (*HGL* 5:540); two years later, Peter of Minerve is one of those "excepted" from Viscount Raymond Berenger's oath of security to Raymond Bernard, viscount of Albi and Nîmes: *HGL* 5:565, I. The earliest attestation of this family's association with the Trencavels is the complex agreement between William of Minerve and Bernard Ato in 1127: *HGL* 5:941. Given the paucity of surviving charters of Alphonse Jordan, it is understandable that the remaining witnesses are unidentifiable, although others with the same names appear much later in the century: Caille, "Ermengarde, vicomtesse de Narbonne," 38–39. Peter, the scribe of the marriage contract, is called "capellanus et cancellarius meus" in Alphonse's donation to the abbey of Lézat in 1127: *Cart. Lézat*, no. 1347. See also *HGL* 5:975, 1025.

7. Witness to transactions between the abbey of Saint-Paul, the archbishop, and the viscount: MS Doat 55, fol. 152v (1117), fol. 178 (1126).

8. On the occupation of Toulouse by Philippa and William, see *HGL* 3:542, 622–25. Arnold of Levezou: *HGL* 4:649, 5:50; *GC* 6:47 and *instrum*. 37 (where Alphonse refers to the archbishop as "dominus meus"). Arnold was also descended from the vicecomital family of Narbonne through his grandmother. He succeeded his uncle as archbishop. As we shall see, the ecclesiastical members of this family had notions of familial loyalty that were quite different from those of their lay brothers and cousins.

9. Oath of 1138: *HGL* 5:1024. Castle near Albi: ibid., 1026. Treaty of 1142: ibid., 1058. For the early history of the Trencavel lands, see Cheyette, " 'Sale' of Carcassonne to the Counts of Barcelona and the Rise of the Trencavels"; for the castles, Cheyette, "Castles of the Trencavels," and Biget, "Vicomté d'Ambialet." Nearly 150 castles are represented by oaths of fidelity and other documents in the Trencavel cartulary, *HGL*, and the Doat collection, but only a few belonging to the viscounty of Nîmes are mentioned there. That eastern viscounty was administratively separated from those of the west when Bernard Ato's youngest son and namesake inherited it; late in the century it fell to the counts of Toulouse, and the few fragments that remained of its archives eventually passed from the comital archives to the royal Trésor des chartes. I have been unable to consult the unpublished thesis of Hélène Débax on the Trencavels.

10. The conflict over Beatrice of Mauguio: *HGL* 3:684–87; *LIM*, no. 65 (*HGL* 5:947); *HGL* 5:984, 988, 1007; *LIM*, nos. 80, 82; her marriage: *LIM*, nos. 72, 73 (*Cart. Maguelone*, nos. 62, 63). The revolt of Montpellier: *HGL* 3:721–23; Baumel, *Histoire d'une seigneurie du Midi de la France*, 129–38.

11. The earliest presence of a lord of Montpellier in the court of Barcelona that I have found is 1052, when William III took part in the council that resolved the conflict between Count Ramon Berenguer I and Mir Geribert: Sobrequés i Vidal, *Grans comtes de Barcelona*, 62. On the counts of Rodez, see below, chap. 6.

12. For the marriage alliances, see the genealogical tables in Aurell, *Noces du comte*. (Stasser, "Maison vicomtale de Narbonne," makes Guifred Borrel's wife Garsendis of Toulouse.) The testament of Ramon Berenguer III: *LFM*, no. 493. The grant of fief: ACA *perg. Ram. Ber. I*, no. 207, printed in Bofarull, *Condes de Barcelona vindicados*, 2:16–20. Berenger's son Raymond was a witness in 1056 to a *conveniencia* between Ramon Berenguer and the count of Besalú: ACA *perg. Ram. Ber. I*, no. 154. In 1067, Viscount Berenger II held land in Valle-Osor in Old Catalonia (*HGL* 5:546). Around 1120, Ermengard's father received the Fenouillèdes and Peyrepertusès in the southern Corbières and the valley of the

Agly as a price for his aid to Ramon Berenguer III against Viscount Bernard Ato (*LFM*, nos. 808, 809), although this may have been a renewal of long-standing rights in the area; Peter Amelius of Peyrepertuse had already rendered an oath of fidelity to Viscount Berenger before 1067: MS Doat 48, fol. 233. Aymeri II was present in Barcelona in 1131 to witness a donation by the count to the cathedral: ACA *perg. Ram. Ber. IV*, no. 5. This fragmentary record is continuous enough to indicate a constant going and coming between the two courts. The mortgage, whose text has not survived: *LFM*, nos. 810, 811.

13. Alliance: *HGL* 5:1053. Treaty: ibid., 1069. The theater of war is described in the treaty. Elements of the alignments on each side are also described in Smyrl, "Famille des Baux," and Poly, *Provence et la société féodale*, 336, who seems unaware of the connection of the warfare in Provence to the politics on the other side of the Rhone. The treaty: *HGL* 5:1069. A Bernard of Canet (most likely father and son) appears as witness to or participant in no less than fifty-five acts of the Trencavel viscounts from 1112 to 1153. Bernard of Canet was Viscount Roger's choice to broker an agreement with Alphonse Jordan concerning the election of the bishops of Albi: *HGL* 5:980. In his testament of 1154, Raymond Trencavel placed the men who were to administer Béziers and Carcassonne under Bernard's supervision.

14. The treaty specifies that Ermengard's husband was also to swear to uphold it; he is not named, and clearly Alphonse is not the husband meant (because he is mentioned separately). It is not easy to tell which Bernard of Anduze became Ermengard's husband, for there is a Bernard in that family in every generation from the early eleventh century to the beginning of the thirteenth (see the index to *HGL* 5 and 8 and to *Layettes*). Caille, "Ermengarde, vicomtesse de Narbonne," 40–41, presents a hypothetical genealogy as well as the important documentation connecting the family of Anduze to the Trencavels. In his testament of 1114, William V of Montpellier mentions an earlier testament in which he had made his brother Bernard of Anduze the guardian of his children: *HGL* 5:841. The peace treaty of 1125 dividing Provence between Alphonse Jordan and Ramon Berenguer III of Barcelona specified that Aymeri of Narbonne would hold Beaucaire and his lands in the *terre d'Argence* (part of the Rhone delta) in fief of the count of Barcelona and that Bernard of Anduze would in turn hold those of Aymeri: *HGL* 5:938. Ermengard's husband, of course, could have been this Bernard's son, although a Bernard of Anduze "senior" is a witness to the marriage of William VII of Montpellier and Matilda of Burgundy in 1157 and is mentioned in a document of 1162: *HGL* 5:1157, 1253; see also *HGL* 5:1181, III. Bernard of Anduze (junior) is thus probably the Bernard "son of Adalais" who gives an oath of fidelity to the bishop of Nîmes in 1174–75: *Layettes*, no. 257; *HGL* 8:302. There are no men of the family of Anduze identified by their oaths of fidelity as sons of Ermengard.

15. Before the fourteenth or even the fifteenth century, most medieval men and women seem to have paid little attention to their birth dates and had only an approximate sense of their own ages. No document gives Ermengard's birth year. Urban customs of Occitan cities established twenty-five as the age of majority, but women whose fathers had died could make legal contracts at age twelve, men at age fourteen. Working back from Ermengard's first marriage contract, we could therefore place her birth as late as 1130. In 1163, still childless, she associated her sister's son Aymeri with her government. If she were then in her mid-thirties, an advanced age for a childless woman, she would have been born in 1127 or 1128. Caille, on the basis of other arguments, guesses she could have been born in 1129: Caille, "Ermengarde, vicomtesse de Narbonne," 10. The Norman chronicler Orderic Vitalis composed a circumstantial account of the battle of Fraga and the events preceding and following it, probably based on reports brought back by Norman knights: *Historia ecclesiastica*, 13:8–10 (*Ecclesiastical History*, ed. Chibnall, 6:408–19). A briefer account with a very different ending is in the Castilian "Chronica Adefonsi Imperatoris," 1:55–59 (ed. Falque, Gil, and Sánchez, 176–77).

16. *HGL* 5:935.

17. See above, n. 14. Mention of his children: *HGL* 5:1013.

18. Catel, *Mémoires*, 589, gives the text of an undated oath to Bernard of Anduze by Bernard of Porta Regia and mentions the existence of a number of others (which have long since disappeared). The surviving oath "reserves" the fidelity due to Ermessend.

19. Caille shares this suspicion: "Ermengarde, vicomtesse de Narbonne," 15.

20. Ermengard's mother (for whom she was named) died sometime before 1130, perhaps giving birth to her daughter. Aymeri II remarried quickly. Ermessend bore the name of her mother. See Caille, "Ermengarde, vicomtesse de Narbonne," 10–11. Caille notes (n. 59) that the first mention of Ermessend and Manrique as husband and wife is in 1153. On the Laras, see Doubleday, *Laras*, especially for Manrique, 114–55, from which most of this paragraph is taken. For relations with Urraca, see Reilly, *Kingdom of León-Castilla under Queen Urraca*, 46–47.

21. Stasser, "Maison vicomtale de Narbonne." Placing Archbishop Aymeri in the vice-comital family depends on one's interpretation of his testament (*HGL* 5:280). There he makes pious donations for the souls of Count Pons (of Toulouse), Viscounts Odo and Mat-fred of Narbonne, and Odo's wife Richildis. Although this could be simply a recognition of his fellow rulers during his long archbishopric, it is more likely to be a recognition of kin-ship, Pons having married Garsendis of Narbonne. Of those specifically mentioned as his re-lations, his brother, "Udalgarius princeps," and one nephew, "Bernardus grammaticus," can-not be traced further; his other nephew, however, "Geiro honorabilis princeps," appears several times in connection with the vicecomital house, once in a complex transaction in-volving the mortgaging of Magrie and Cuxac by Viscountess Arsendis and her sons (for this emendation of the published document, see Regné, *Etude sur la condition des juifs de Narbonne*, 62 n), its redemption by Geiro, and conditional gift to Archbishop Ermengaud, the vis-count's brother (*HGL* 5:232, bizarrely dated "around 959" by the editors, although Ermen-gaud did not become archbishop until 977), and a second time as one of the executors of the second testament of Viscountess Adalais in 990 (*HGL* 5:320).

22. The surviving manuscripts of the epic *Aymeri de Narbonne* are from 1200 and later, but one cannot argue from silence and assert that the legends were unknown in Occitania or that there were not Occitan or Franco-Occitan versions of them. The use of the name Roland by the family of Fontjoncouse at the end of the eleventh century (Cart. Fontjon-couse, no. 9) and Olivier by the family of Termes already in the mid-eleventh century (*HGL* 5:684 [1084]; *LFM*, no. 759 [1074–1102])—both names, as far as I know, peculiar to these families and surely deriving from the Roland story—strongly argues that part of the Charle-magne cycle was current in the region, as does the importance of the Charlemagne legend in and around Narbonne. At the same time, the legends of William of Orange were alive at the abbey of Gellone and in the Rhone valley. As Amy Remensnyder remarks, "beginning in the last years of the eleventh century, many southern monasteries began to see the landscape of their origins through the frame of the *chanson de geste*" (*Remembering Kings Past*, 182). For the adoption of the name Aymeri, the argument of Rita Lejeune on this subject seems to me to be convincing, even if it has not gained wide acceptance: "Question de l'historicité du héros épique, Aimeri de Narbonne," although I would add to it by making Archbishop Aymeri one of the vicecomital family (see the previous note). For the more general issue of the Charle-magne and William of Orange legends in Occitania, see Remensnyder, *Remembering*, 190–93; also, passim, Colby-Hall, "In Search of the Lost Epics of the Lower Rhône Valley," and Saxer, "Culte et la légende hagiographique de Saint Guillaume de Gellone." Around 1300, a monk of Lagrasse, writing what he believed to be the story of the founding of his monastery, made Aymeri of Narbonne the first Christian ruler of the city, granted to him by Charlemagne after he had conquered it from the Moslems; for the monk, this mythical

Aymeri's title was count of Toulouse, duke of Narbonne, and marquis of the cities, a variation of the title that the counts of Toulouse took from Raymond IV onward; see Schneegans, *Über die Gesta Karoli Magni*, 10–13.

23. For the historical record of the earliest viscounts, see *HGL* 4:50–54, and Stasser, "Maison vicomtale."

24. On these brothers, see Caille, "Ermengarde, vicomtesse de Narbonne," 10.

25. *HGL* 5:1171; the testament, carried from Trencavel's prison in Toulouse to Béziers, was transcribed by his notary Arnold of Clairan on April 21, 1154.

26. For Ermengard's entourage, see below, chap. 9.

27. The role of monks in maintaining family memory has recently become the focus of scholarly attention, but other vehicles for memory, and the manner in which it was transformed in the days before the development of administrative records and the training of professional memory keepers is only beginning to be explored. Patrick Geary has made an important start in *Phantoms of Remembrance*.

28. "illius qui Tolosana matre natus est": Kienast, *Der Herzogstitel in Frankreich und Deutschland*, 239 n. 432.

29. Almodis: Aurell, *Noces du comte*, 257–95. Ermessend: ibid., 223–55. The creation of the Trencavel lands, Cheyette, " 'Sale' of Carcassonne." Diafronissa: *HGL* 5:1090, II (1145), and 8:585, I (1185).

30. Matfred's last surviving act is his testament, drawn up before he departed on a pilgrimage to Rome: *HGL* 5:255. The dispute settlements: *HGL* 5:259. Adalaide's last surviving act: Mouynès, "Charte d'Adalaïs, vicomtesse de Narbonne."

31. Sobrequés i Vidal, *Grans comtes*, 124, 129.

32. We know this story primarily through the partisan account dictated by Archbishop Richard sometime after 1117, translated below, in chap. 11. Mahalt and Aymeri's sons are named in a donation to the abbey of Saint-Pons: *HGL* 5:787.

33. See the remarks about the widowhoods of Catalan countesses in Aurell, *Noces du comte*, 223.

34. The earliest testimony I have found to this practice as a rule is in the customal of Saint-Antonin in the Rouergue, c. 1144: *Layettes*, no. 86. The prevalence of the practice in testaments, however, and the common appearance of halves and quarters of fiefs, castles, and other holdings make it safe to assume even in the absence of formal statements of a rule.

35. *HGL* 5:865, 867 (the relation between these testaments of 1118 is unclear and, without the originals or any way to trace the provenance of the copies that Devic and Vaissete published, cannot be resolved), 957, 961, 962. See also the brothers' succession agreement of 1132, col. 981.

36. See the division between Ermengard's descendants described below, chap. 4.

37. "Vilis enim hereditas nobilem hominem non decet": *LIM*, no. 480.

38. *Layettes*, no. 86 (c. 1144). For a detailed analysis of the exclusion of dowried daughters in Occitan customary practice around 1200, see Hilaire, *Régime des biens entre époux*, 350–55. "Et inde sit contenta": *Cart. St-Etienne d'Agde*, no. 359. See the provisions for daughters in the wills of William VI and William VII of Montpellier: *LIM*, nos. 105, 106, and the testament of Peter Raymond of Narbonne, below, chap. 9.

39. "Dono . . . omnem illam portionem hereditatis paterne que mihi ex successione communis patris Bernardi-Atonis provenit vel provenire debuit et universum jus quod in ea habeo." Only the renunciations given to Bernard survive (*Layettes*, nos. 125, 126; *HGL* 5:1148–49), but there is no reason to imagine that Raymond Trencavel did not take the same precautions. Roger's death required a complex set of negotiations and renewed oaths with everyone who had an interest in the lands he had ruled. Although Roger in his testament gave all his lands to Raymond Trencavel, Bernard immediately laid claim to some of them,

and the brothers quickly had to arrange a new division (*HGL* 5:1122). The count of Barcelona and Ermengard of Narbonne then had to be satisfied with the new division in this allied family and new oaths exchanged with them (*HGL* 5:1125, 1142).

40. Ermengard as arbiter of women's claims to inheritances: *HGL* 5:1277 (1163); *Cart. Douzens* A, no. 20 (1167); *Cart. Béziers*, no. 297 (1184), all of them taking her outside her viscounty. Daughters as equal partners in inheritance: *Cart. St-Etienne d'Agde*, nos. 142, 358, 386, 402. Compare also no. 49.

41. *LFM*, nos. 305 (misdated 1135 instead of 1136), 307; see also no. 459. On the seneschals of Barcelona, see Bonnassie, *Catalogne du milieu du Xe à la fin du XIe siècle*, 710–11, and the literature cited there.

42. For example, the dowry of Cecilia of Provence on her marriage to Viscount Bernard Ato in 1083 was five thousand solidi, of which two thousand were paid in coin and the remainder in horses, mules, cows, and oxen: *HGL* 5:682.

43. For a striking example, see the will of Berenger of Puisserguier, below, chap. 11.

44. *Cart. Maguelone*, nos. 72–74, 79, and many others.

45. For Stephania's dowry we have only her statement in 1150 after her defeat by the count of Provence: Smyrl, "Famille des Baux," 81. The donations to the count of Barcelona are printed in *LFM*, nos. 875, 876, 877.

46. Smyrl, "Famille des Baux," 36.

47. Ibid., 40–44; and Poly, *Provence*, 336–40.

48. For the early history, see Rouche, *Aquitaine, des Wisigoths aux Arabes*, especially 87–132. Philippa was sometimes called Philippia or—in the Bordelais and Poitou—Matilda, the name of her father's first wife: Richard, *Histoire des Comtes de Poitou*, 1:404 n. 2. Philippa and her husband were in control of Toulouse from 1097 to 1108 and again from 1113 until their agents were expelled by an urban revolt in 1119. After being deserted by her husband, she took refuge in the Fontevrault priory of Lespinasse, just outside Poitiers, and then at Fontevrault itself. See Mundy, *Liberty and Political Power in Toulouse*, 16–17, and the fuller treatment of Philippa's story in Richard, *Histoire*, 1:405–6, 416–23, 437–39, 467–74. Note that around 1114 it was with Philippa, not with her husband, that Viscount Bernard Ato exchanged oaths of fidelity: *HGL* 5:845.

49. See the map in Rouche, *Aquitaine*, 307. The route of northern metals via the Garonne, Toulouse, and mule back was well known in the Moslem world: Abu al-Fida', *Géographie d'Aboulféda* (trans. Reinaud and Guyard), 2:307. Warren, *Henry II*, 83–84.

50. *HGL* 5:1221.

51. See Pacaut, *Louis VII et son royaume*, chap. 7; and Warren, *Henry II*, 42–53, 82–91.

52. Tortosa: *HGL* 3:739 (see below, chap. 5); les Baux: *HGL* 3:828, 5:1264; Montpellier: *HGL* 5:1221; Homps: *HGL* 5:1268; Hauterive: *HGL* 8:270, 273; Saint-Gilles: *HGL* 8:276. For all of these events, see below, chaps. 14 and 15.

ERMENGARD'S CITY: PREFACE

1. Stendhal, *Travels in the South of France*, 166–69.

CHAPTER 2. NAMES AND TITLES, HISTORIES AND MYTHS

1. See the interesting remarks of Ghil, *Age du parage*, chap. 1.
2. See the remarks of Uitti, "Old Provençal 'Song of Saint Fides.'"
3. On such usage in the acts of Raymond V of Toulouse, see Léonard, *Cat.*, lxii. Already

in 990, the scribe serving Viscountess Adalais of Narbonne styled her "gratia Dei vicecomitissa": Mouynès, "Charte d'Adalaïs."

4. In *Raoul de Cambrai*, for example, laisse 54: "et jure Dieu qi tot a a jugier / q'il ne le feroit por l'or de Monpeslier" (ed. Kay, 70).

5. *PL* 211, col. 375.

6. On the names for this region, see Amado, "Poids de l'aristocratie d'origine wisigothique," n. 1, and the literature cited therein. An interesting late monastic use of the name Septimania is on the map from the *Beatus* manuscript of Saint-Sever (BNF Latin 8878), reproduced in Remensnyder, *Remembering Kings Past*, 85.

7. Kienast, *Herzogstitel*, 28–35, esp. n. 106, and 297–302, gives full references for the names Septimania and Gothia, and chap. 5 passim for the name Aquitania; summarized in Kaiser, *Bischofsherrschaft zwischen Königtum und Fürstenmacht*, 256. In the thirteenth century, the name Provence was momentarily favored by Pope Innocent III and some northern writers: Peter of Vaux-de-Cernay, *Petri Vallium Sarnaii Monachi Hystoria Albigensis* (ed. Guébin and Lyon), 1:3 note h. But this fared no better, doubtless because it was too solidly attached to the lands east of the Rhone.

8. The counts of Rodez (or of Rouergue) descended from Ermengaud, the younger son of Count Odo of Toulouse, who died in 918 or 919. Bertha, the wife of Count Robert of Auvergne, died around 1065. In 1032, her father Hugh guaranteed a gift of a "fisc" in Narbonne to the abbey of Saint-Paul with the clause, "quicumque de hoc transgressor fuerit . . . ab omni coetu christianorum separatus sit . . . et insuper veniat ipse comes qui erit Narbonae civitatis ipso tempore apprehendat eum usque revertere faciat eum in ipsa communia": *HGL* 5:400. For the share in selling the archbishopric, see below, chap. 6.

9. Kienast, *Herzogstitel*, 293–94, who calls this title a "Verlegenheitslösung." Around 1160, Raymond's descendant Raymond V changed the ordering of these titles, placing the most august, duke of Narbonne, first: Léonard, *Cat.*, lxii.

10. Stendhal, *Travels*, 166, 170.

11. For the ancient geography of the region, see Rivet, *Gallia Narbonensis*; the quote from Pomponius Mela is on p. 84. Clément and Peyre, *Voie domitienne*, is a popular archaeological account of that road. For classical sites and roads east of the Rhone, see Février et al., *Provence des origines à l'an mille*.

12. Février et al., *Provence*, 467.

13. *HGL* 5:147, 159. On the ancient settlement, see Laubenheimer, *Sallèles d'Aude*, 17.

14. So the story is told in the thirteenth-century *Gesta Karoli Magni ad Carcassonam et Narbonam* (ed. Schneegans); on the author and date of the text and the possible sources of the stories it tells, see Schneegans, *Über die Gesta Karoli Magni*. Scholarship on the Jewish myths is substantial. See Schatzmiller, "Politics and the Myth of Origins," especially 54–58, and the literature cited therein. Cohen, "Nasi of Narbonne," surveys the sources in the course of reviewing Arthur Zuckerman's history-fantasy *Jewish Princedom in Feudal France, 768–900* (New York, 1972). I was not able to read A. Graboïs, "Legendary Figure of Charlemagne."

15. Regné, *Juifs de Narbonne*, 13–25, and 176 n. 4, quoting from the third Thalamus, AMN AA103, fol. 130v., a text with the *incipit*, "Aysso son las antiquetatz e las noblesas antiquas de la vila de Narbona" (These are the antiquities and the ancient titles of nobility of the city of Narbonne).

16. Ibn Zenbel, a sixteenth-century compiler of earlier traditions, translated in Fagnan, *Extraits inédits relatifs au Maghreb*, 122. I have been unable to find an analysis of this text that might indicate Ibn Zenbel's source, but the description of the city's river, Roman bridge, and mills shows that the source predates the shift in the Aude to its present mouth north of the city, which occurred in the mid-fourteenth century. See also Abu al-Fida', *Géographie*, 2:262.

17. Roman, *De Narbonne à Bordeaux*; Gayraud, *Narbonne antique*, 87–102, 119–49, 498–540; Abu al-Fida', *Géographie*, 2:307.

18. For the complex and debatable history of these fortifications, little investigated in the ground, see Caïrou, *Narbonne: Vingt siècles de fortifications*. Gayraud, *Narbonne antique*, 284–90, argues for continuity between a late Antique fortification and that of the Middle Ages, contested by P.-A. Février in his review in *Provence Historique* 33 (1983): 232–35. The relation between the Roman bridge and the medieval one (of which one arch is still visible over the canal that replaced the Aude in the late Middle Ages) is also contested. The likely date for the rebuilding is the thirteenth century, when serious floods became increasingly frequent, the consequence of deforestation upstream and the construction of an ever-increasing number of mills, whose dams slowly raised the level of the river bottom. Février's skepticism about the continuity in location of the ancient bridge and its successor seems hypercritical: "Narbonne," in Gauthier and Picard, *Topographie chrétienne*, 7:19. See Gayraud, *Narbonne antique*, 304–6. For other ancient buildings that may or may not have been visible in the twelfth century, ibid., 247–81.

19. Sigal, "Contribution à l'histoire de la cathédrale," 112–32; Rey, "Cathédrale de Narbonne," 448–56; Marrou, "Dossier épigraphique de l'évêque Rusticus"; and Bonnery, "Transformations de la cathédrale de Narbonne." For a brief notice, see Bonnery, in Barral i Altet, ed., *Paysage monumental de la France*, 456–57. Bonnery's Strasbourg thesis, "Narbonne paléochrétienne," does not appear to have been published.

20. *HGL* 5:497. For more about Guifred, see below, chap. 6.

21. The pillar is now housed in the Musée des Augustins in Toulouse. The cloister in which it was placed was razed when the Gothic cathedral was built in the thirteenth century and a new cloister constructed where the old cathedral had stood. Rey, "Cathédrale de Narbonne," was the first to identify the statue as Charlemagne. It is discussed by Terpak, "Local Politics; the Charlemagne Legend in Medieval Narbonne" (with photographs). For the topography, see Esquieu, "Narbonne," in Picard, ed., *Chanoines dans la ville*.

22. Acts 13:6–13. This identification was first launched by the Roman martyrologist Ado of Vienne in the ninth century. It seems to have taken hold in Narbonne only in the eleventh: Griffe, *Histoire religieuse des anciens pays de l'Aude*, 257–58.

23. Caille, "Narbonne au moyen âge, évolution de la topographie et du paysage urbain," and idem, "Traits médiévaux du visage urbain"; Barral i Altet and Février, "Narbonne," in Gauthier and Picard, *Topographie chrétienne*, 7:20–23; Marrou, "Dossier épigraphique de Rusticus."

24. A brief account of these events is in Nadal i Farreras and Wolff, *Histoire de la Catalogne*, 249.

25. *HGL* 5:535, dated by the editors "around 1066," but the viscounts of Narbonne mentioned in the text are Raymond Berenger and his sons, and Garsendis and her sons Bernard and Peter the bishop, placing it after February 7, 1067, last known date when Viscount Berenger was still alive. It seems logical to place it as late as 1077, when he was fighting his suffragan bishops, or 1078–79, when two successive councils in Rome deposed him.

26. Acts 8:20–23.

27. The story is told in great detail by McCrank, "Restauración canonica e intento de reconquista de la sede Tarraconense, 1076–1108."

28. Cesarius of Arles had contributed one of his major works, the *Treatise on the Mystery of the Holy Trinity*, to this dispute. It finally became irrelevant in the thirteenth century when Occitania was absorbed into the kingdom of France and, at the same time, the correspondence of ecclesiastical and political boundaries was more fully recognized. On the primacy, see Vidal, "Origines de la primatie narbonnaise (XIe–XIIe siècles)."

29. McCrank, "Restauración canonica," 164–69.

30. The *vita* and the legend of Paulus Sergius are summarized by Griffe, *Histoire religieuse*, appendix iii, 252–63. These texts are set in their exact historical context by McCrank, "Restauración canonica," 164–83. The letter of pseudo-pope Stephen: *PL*, 129, cols. 818–22. A primary example of an "interpolated" Carolingian text from Guifred's atelier is *Recueil des actes de Charles II le Chauve (840–877)* (ed. Tessier), no. 49. The Carolingian documents of Lagrasse have proven over the years to be one of the most contentious collections from that period, with experts judging both ways on their authenticity. Some documents, however, appear certain to be fabrications from the tenth and eleventh centuries. See, for example, Tessier, *Actes de Charles le Chauve*, nos. 208, 341, 415, 483; and *Recueil des actes de Charles le Simple* (ed. Lot and Lauer), no. 60. The tradition continued into the thirteenth century, two of the notable examples being a pseudo-confirmation of Gelasius II (original MS Baluze 398, no. 12, published in *GC* 6:734), and a pseudo-homage of Viscount Bernard Ato in the form of a notarized *vidimus* dated 1253 (original AN J335, published in *HGL* 5:811), both fabricated to improve the abbey's claims to confiscated Trencavel lands.

31. In 1643 it formed part of the dossier prepared to fight the transfer of the diocese of Elne to the archdiocese of Tarragona: British Library MS Harley 3570, doc. 4. Like other early documents in that manuscript, it was copied from a copy dated 1154.

32. The others in western Francia that were doing so were Paris, with Saint Denis, and Limoges, with Saint Martial.

33. Jaffé and Loewenfeld, *Regesta pontificum romanorum*, no. 5420; *PL*, 151, col. 316. In the surviving documents, Raymond of Saint-Gilles takes the title for the first time in two charters to Saint-André of Avignon: *HGL* 5:707.

34. We know this above all from the individual settlements that Viscount Bernard Ato made with his castellans when he put down the major revolt of Carcassonne in 1125: *HGL* 5:917ff. *Estagium* (castle service) could last as long as four to six months each year.

35. For a detailed account, see Cheyette, " 'Sale' of Carcassonne."

CHAPTER 3. THE URBAN MARKETPLACE

1. Cros-Mayrevieille, *Histoire du comté et de la vicomté de Carcassonne*, 51–54, from a now lost original in the archives of the abbey of Lagrasse. Another copy, identical in all respects: MS Doat 40, fols. 31ff.

2. *HGL* 5:404 (dated 36th year of King Robert; did the local scribes begin counting in 987 or 996?); *Cart. Béziers*, no. 65.

3. Arab coins in Catalonia and Occitania: the older works of Botet i Sisó, *Monedes catalanes*, 1:26ff.; Monneret de Villard, "Monetazione nell'Italia barbarica," 85–111; Duplessy, "Circulation des monnaies arabes en Europe occidentale du VIIIe au XIIIe siècles"; Bonnassie, *Catalogne*, 372–84; and now above all, Balaguer, "*Parias* and the Myth of the *Mancus*"; Todesca, "Means of Exchange"; Conques: Castaing-Sicard, *Monnaies féodales*, 66–73.

4. Bonnassie, *Catalogne*, 372–84, 902–10.

5. See the reflections of Castaing-Sicard, *Monnaies féodales*, 70ff., on the disappearance of references to gold at the end of the eleventh century. Two rare exceptions, both suggesting such hoarding: Ermengard's father's mortgage of le Lac to the abbey of Lagrasse for a large quantity of silver plate and gold bullion in 1114 (*HGL* 5:838); a countergift of twenty-three ounces of "fine gold" from the monastery to a man about to depart for Santiago around 1150 (AD Pyr.-Or. B35).

6. Caille, "Traits médiévaux," 174–78. Results of archeology: Février et al., *Provence*, 468–69. Older research in literary works is summarized ibid., 471–74, and in Doehaerd, "Méditerranée et économie occidentale pendant le haut moyen âge," 586–91.

7. Caille, "Narbonne au moyen âge: évolution de la topographie," 60, and idem, "Narbonne sous l'occupation musulmane. Problèmes de topographie."

8. In the absence of serious archaeological investigations in the city, one can speak only in hazy generalities. Of the nearly century-long Moslem occupation, little trace has been found beyond what may possibly be a fragment of the mosque incorporated into the exterior wall of the archbishop's palace. The material in Lacam, *Sarrazins dans le haut moyen-âge français*, must be treated with caution. Cities that disappeared: Lugdunum Convenarum (Higounet, *Comté de Comminges de ses origines à son annexion à la couronne*, 11), Brigantio (Rivet, *Gallia Narbonensis*, 344–45); Février, *Développement urbain en Provence*, 78–85, lists other ephemeral ancient cities in the Alps. Cities reduced to farming villages: Fréjus (Février et al., *Au coeur d'une ville épiscopal: Fréjus*, 41), Nîmes (Gutherz et al., *Histoire de Nîmes*, 110–13; there is much more to be garnered from the *Cart. Nîmes*). Cimiez was abandoned for Nice: Février et al., *Provence*, 466–76.

9. Cheyette and Amado, "Organisation d'un terroir et d'un habitat concentré: Un exemple méridional," especially the map on p. 43.

10. Parish rights: in 897, a couple founding a church at Villenouvette, near Béziers, were required to compensate another church for the tithes that were being taken from it to support the new foundation. The farmlands from which the tithes were due were specified as being "in eadem parrochia consito": *Cart. Béziers*, no. 9. Other tenth-century charters mention first fruits (ibid., no. 27) and cemetery rights (ibid., no. 31), as well as tithes. On this subject, see in general, Magnou-Nortier, *Société laïque et l'église dans la province ecclésiastique de Narbonne*, 423–30. Village fortifications: Creissan, "cum ipsa turra cum cincto et vallo" (*HGL* 5:228; MS Doat 55, fol. 69 [959]); Sclatianum (a village west of Sauvian that disappeared before the twelfth century), "cum ipsa turre cum ipso pogio" (*Cart. Béziers*, no. 31); Lignan, "cum ipsa turre vel cinctos vel vallos" (*Cart. Béziers*, no. 39); at Aumes, "medietatem de ipsa turre et . . . de cincto et . . . de forticias" (*Cart. chap. cath. Agde*, no. 327).

11. MS Doat 57, fol. 3; and MS Baluze 82, fol. 144 (excerpt only in *HGL* 5:130). Aside from identifying a few of these landholders as priests, the document tells us nothing about their status, and some—or many—could themselves be peasants. Nevertheless, in the few surviving Narbonnese documents from within two decades of the Bizanet conveyance, five of the same names appear as participants or witnesses to acts involving the highest aristocracy—Alaric in 924, 925, 926, 933 (*HGL* 5:147, 150, 151, 160); Fredarius in 925 (*HGL* 5:150); Durandus in 926 (*HGL* 5:151); and Jorius in 924 and 933 (*HGL* 5:147, 160). Theodoric (and his wife), whose donation in 925 produced one of these documents (a donation also witnessed by a countess, and the viscount and the viscountess of Narbonne), may likewise have been a landholder in Bizanet: MS Doat 57, fol. 1 (*HGL* 5:150). Alaric appears in one boundary description at Bizanet, Fredarius in three, Durandus in five, Jorius in four, and Theodoric in six. As long as both Roman and Gothic names endured (until the early decades of the eleventh century), society's treasury of names was richly supplied. Individuals had only one name, yet even in long lists (such as those of the Bizanet conveyance) it is rare to find two people with the same name (in the Bizanet document, only one name out of sixty is repeated: there are two Theodorics, one of whom is identified as "the late"). The rarity of the names I have mentioned gives cautious justification to my belief that the same individuals are being named in these various contemporary documents.

12. Village moneylender: MS Mél. Colb. 414, no. 10 (995), mortgage of a vineyard at Gasparets near Narbonne for three solidi. This collection of documents taken from the archives of Saint-Paul's in Narbonne contains a number of contracts of sale of modest plots of land from one small landholder to another in villages around the city: nos. 2 (907), 3 (926), 4 (988), 9 (980?), 13 (989–96), 11 (991–1000), and 14 (1024).

13. Mills at Narbonne: MS Mél. Colb. 414, no. 5; and MS Doat 57, fol. 10 (955). Con-

ciliar action against the lord of Caraman: *HGL* 5:351. The suburbs of Béziers: *Cart. Béziers*, nos. 65, 74. Treaty between Narbonne and Montpellier: Caille, "Marchands de Montpellier et la leude de Narbonne dans le dernier quart du XIe siècle." I am not as convinced as Caille that the absence of a permanent customs collector at the port downstream from Narbonne demonstrates that this commerce was "modest." All it shows is that collecting duty at the port to be used by the merchants of Montpellier (of several that lined the lower course of the Aude) was not a full-time job. The agreement itself was important enough to require the presence of some of the most important men not just of Montpellier and Narbonne but of Béziers as well.

14. *Cart. Nîmes*, no. 102 (1007): gardens and orchards near the Maison Carré; no. 106 (1009): a field and dilapidated huts next to the bishop's garden in the shadow of the cathedral bell tower; nos. 77 (983) and 143 (1043–60): gardens, orchards, the produce of tillage (*exavo*), and a farmyard in the ancient forum. For a comparison with cities in Provence, see Poly, *Provence*, 218–23.

15. On the general role of the Jews in the ninth- and tenth-century economy, see Doehaerd, "Méditerranée et économie occidentale," 586–91; Jews in tenth-century Narbonne: Regné, *Juifs*, 51–61, who redates and identifies the participants in the early tenth-century mortgage (*HGL* 5:232) at 62 n.

16. Given the nature of the documentation, the principal basis for arguing that Christian merchants were taking an increasing role is the presence of Christian moneylenders, contemporaries of Arnold Siguini, both in the countryside (mortgage of a vineyard at Ferrals: AD Aude H36 [1019]) and in the city (loan of gold from the abbot of Saint-Paul to Viscountess Ermessind: *HGL* 5:404 [1023–32]). One can, of course, imagine them continuing to use Jews as partners or intermediaries, but there seems no necessity to do so. See also n. 12 above.

17. Cloth of gold and plate: MS Doat 57, fol. 29 (testament of Simplicius the priest, 992–93); a *sella spanesia* and a *freno spanesco*: *HGL* 5:349 (testament of archbishop Ermengaud, c. 1005); an *anaphum sclavonium* in the same testament appears to point to direct or indirect trade with Byzantium. The microscopic analysis of the clothing in the so-called sarcophagus of Guillaume Taillefer in Toulouse, dating from around 950, has cast a brilliant new light on early commerce in luxury goods. The shift the corpse was wearing, of a linen and cotton fabric, is similar to material found in upper Egypt dating from 780–950. It was most likely imported from North Africa or al-Andalus. See Crubézy and Dieulafit, eds., *Le comte de l'an mil*, 176–83. For the testament of Arnold Siguini, see note 1 above.

18. Ms Doat 48, fol. 1: market mentioned in a boundary description (not included in the extract *HGL* 5:417).

19. *Inventaire des archives de la ville de Narbonne*, II, Annexes de la série AA, 4–6. My thanks to my colleague John Servos for helping me identify the uses of some of these products. The mid-tenth century corpse in the so-called sarcophagus of Guillaume Taillefer also wore vermillion leggings woven from an early variety of merino wool and dyed with kermes, a precious cloth that probably came from Narbonne. See Crubézy and Dieulafit, eds., *Le comte de l'an mil*, 171–76.

20. "Una ciutatz fo, no sai cals," in *Poésies complètes du troubadour Peire Cardenal* (ed. Lavaud), 534.

21. House sale: MS Doat 57, fols. 77, 79. The following year, the archbishop realized another 150 solidi on the property when he sold his remaining rights in the house to the Jews: *HGL* 5:724. Tithes: MS Doat 57, fol. 65 (1080): archbishop gives abbey of Saint-Paul the tithes on fish from their own properties in the village of Peyriac-de-Mer and half of the tithes on fish sold in Narbonne or suburbs; *HGL* 5:656 (1080): he gives the cathedral canons the tithes on all fish from the Aude River "from Coursan and Fleury to Leucate"; MS Doat

57, fol. 85 (1096): Saint-Paul acquires tithes on fish from the ford at Cabrapicta (about a half mile from the city walls) from the owners of the fishery there. Saint-Paul had earlier acquired its own fishery by the mills of the bridge of Narbonne: *HGL* 5:534 (1066).

22. Bourg as a place-name: *HGL* 5:400. Acreage from Caille, "Narbonne, evolution de la topographie," 63. The suburbs under the wall of the city seem never to have been fortified in stone; at least no archaeological trace has ever been found, and it is therefore impossible to measure their acreage.

23. *HGL* 5:417. It is difficult to establish meaningful comparative prices at this early period, but Arsendis, countess of Toulouse (and a member of the vicecomital family), mortgaged three alods in the countryside for one thousand solidi sometime before 959 (*HGL* 5:232), and around 1038, half the bishopric of Albi was considered worth five thousand solidi (*HGL* 5:432).

24. Mortgage of a vineyard to the abbey of Saint-Paul for two ounces of gold, 1023–1032 (*HGL* 5:404), perhaps by a member of the vicecomital family. In 1160, the widow and executors of Raymond Udalgerii give a house to Saint-Paul as security for alms of 140 solidi, which he willed to the abbey (*HGL* 5:512; MS Latin 5211, fol. 6). Raymond was an important lord of the countryside: sixteen years earlier, he and his brothers had given Saint-Paul half of a village church, with its tithes and ecclesiastical rights (MS Doat 57, fol. 49), and in his youth he had conducted an extended and violent feud with Saint-Paul over a property near Bages (*HGL* 5:374 [1023]). The presence of the viscount and viscountess at the execution of his will recognized his local importance. There were also people willing to lend money on property that was deep in the countryside (see above, n. 12).

25. MS Doat 40, fol. 140. Six thousand solidi was the sum for which Viscount Raimond Roger that same year mortgaged all his silver mines in the mountains near Villemagne and the sum for which, three years later, he would mortgage all his rights to billet fighting men on the tenants of the bishop of Béziers and the abbey of Saint-Affrodise in Béziers: *HGL* 8:470; *Cart. Béziers*, no. 347.

26. Ermengaud of Fabrezan was the son of one of Ermengard's closest associates (William of Poitiers), and he was related by marriage to another (Peter Raymond of Narbonne); he was a faithful supporter of Viscountess Ermengard when she was exiled at the end of her life (see below, chap. 18). Berenger of Boutenac witnessed the mutual oaths of Ermengard and Roger of Béziers in 1171 (*HGL* 8:281; MS Doat 47, fol. 23) and would be an important figure in the court of Ermengard's grandnephew (MS Doat 58, fol. 154; MS Mél. Colb. 414, no. 76). On Raymond of Salles, see below, chap. 9. Trencavel knights: William Alfaric, probably descended from a man of the same name who married his son to a daughter of Viscount Bernard Ato in 1105 (*HGL* 5:794, 795); Jordan of Saint-Felix, one the knights who swore fidelity to the infant Raymond Roger in 1191 (*HGL* 8:411). Among the others mentioned in this document, Raymond Ademari may be a descendant of a man of the same name who appears in the entourage of Bernard Ato and his son Raymond Trencavel (*HGL* 5:917, 1023, 1060); Raymond Goz is probably the same as Raymond Got, who with his brother Arnold witnesses an act of Raymond of Béziers in 1173 (Cart. Trencavel, fol. 134), and a descendent of a Peter Goz, who also appears in the entourage of Bernard Ato early in the eleventh century (*HGL* 5:917).

27. He is possibly the Jacob Bistani who witnessed a land conveyance in 1177 (AMN GG1832).

28. Horse: *HGL* 5:808; ox: *Cart. Douzens* A, no. 57; house: thirty solidi, which Peter of Tournisson "ibi misit in condirectione vel levare inde suam condirectionem" (MS Doat 40, fol. 70).

29. See, for comparison, Miller, *Formation of a Medieval Church*, 87–91, 107–9; and Bourin-Derruau, *Villages médiévaux*, 276–77, 301.

30. The year 1162: MS Mél. Colb. 414, no. 42; 1177: AMN AA105, fol. 21v; 1178: MS Doat 48, fol. 28; 1196: Cart. Fontjoncouse, no. 24. William Minter, brother-in-law of John Bistani: AMN AA105, fol. 16v.

31. He appears along with Ermengard's closest associates in a document of 1170: MS Latin 5211, no. 10; in 1184 he is associated with Berenger of Boutenac, among others, in a project to build an aquaduct (or mill pond?) at Saint-Pierre-le-Clar, a few kilometers from the city: MS Doat 48, fol. 31. Endowment of son as canon of Saint-Paul: MS Doat 57, fol. 137 (1178).

32. First appearance: MS Doat 59, fol. 137; gathering of 1204: MS Doat 47, fol. 20 (among the assembled knights was William of Montcada, one of the great barons of Catalonia). Bistani as a witness: MS Doat 48, fol. 34 (1193, arbitration of an inheritance dispute between William Minter and Pedro de Lara); MS Doat 47, fol. 17 (1202); Cart. Fontjoncouse (1203); jointly with the leper house he purchases the lordship and *usaticum* on a house in the suburb of Villenueve: AN S4858, no. 14 (date missing); he holds lordship on a house in the parish of Saint-Sebastian jointly with Bertrand of Ouveilhan, Aladais of Jonquières, and Lady Nigra: AMN AA105, fol. 13v (1217); he approves sale of house by his young nephew William Minter: AMN AA105, fol. 16v (1218).

33. AD Aude H36. The villages were Roubia, Paraza, Vilarum (now a farm in the commune of Paraza), Saint-Pierre-le-Clar (commune of Montredon), and Saint-Martin-entre-Deux-Eaux (commune of Raissac).

34. In reconstructing this story I am assuming that the 1214 agreement between the archbishop and Bistani to put their claims to the arbitration of the bishop of Béziers, of which Baluze copied a fragment into what is now MS Baluze 374, no. 123, and the bull addressed by Honorius III to John Bistani (MS Baluze 380, no. 35) refer to the same issues. The papal bull does not specify which possessions "sub specie venditionis pignori obligavit," and the text of the arbitration agreement is too truncated to tell what claim Bistani had to the towers, the Capitole, and the houses; however, although nine years separate the two documents, they make a better story connected than disconnected. The sum of one thousand pounds comes from the papal bull; because no coin is mentioned, I assume this is silver bullion. I calculate the equivalent in coinage of Mauguio (in the later twelfth century, the common coin of this entire region) from the equivalents given in contemporary mortgage contracts, tabulated in Dieudonné, "Melgorien," 34. Bistani is called "probus homo" in a document of 1212: MS Doat 55, fol. 293.

35. See the will of Peter Margalonis (1218): MS Doat 40, fol. 171. A Raymond Arnold Margalonis is listed among the citizens of Narbonne who attended a great assembly in the cathedral in May 1080: HGL 5:656.

36. John, like his brother William, must have been an important donor to the city's leper house. His testament does not survive. But Peter de Armentaria, preceptor (director) of the leper house, in his own will founded a benefice for a priest to say masses for his own soul and that of John Bistani: AN S4858, no. 9.

37. In this important way, the Occitan mortgage was very different from that of Catalonia before 1050, as described by Bonnassie, *Catalogne*, 403–4. I am preparing a detailed study of these conveyances.

38. The testament of Simplicius the priest, of 992–93, for example, listed cloth of gold as well as "vascula maiora vel minora" among the objects to be disbursed: MS Doat 57, fol. 29.

39. MS Doat 40, fol. 70. Raymond Catalan is probably not the man by that name expropriated by Viscount Bernard Ato for treason in 1125: HGL 5:921; see also LFM, no. 832 (misdated, because the oath in question is to Ramon Berenguer III of Barcelona). More likely he is the Raimond Catalan who witnessed the testament of Gerard, count of Roussillon in 1172, a document probably drawn up at Fontfroide (LFM, no. 792); a few years later

he witnessed the testament of William Arnold, sacristan of Saint-Paul (MS Doat 57, fol. 139). There is no other trace of Peter de Curtibus.

40. *GC* 6, *instrum.* 38.

41. Here is a summary of some twelfth-century testaments containing bequests of mortgages, taken from a total of twenty-nine surviving testaments from the region of Narbonne, Carcassonne, and Béziers.

Name of Testator	Value of Property Held as Mortgage	Other Monetary Bequests	Source
Bernard Raimundi, archdeacon of Saint-Just	300 sol.; others have no value stated		MS Doat 55, fol. 148 (1115)
Peter of Saint-Hilaire, sacristan of Saint-Paul	800 sol. Melg., and one for which no value is stated	10 morabitani, marc of silver	MS Doat 40, fol. 70 (1148)
Gombauldus de Corneilhan	No value stated	615 sol.	*Cart. Béziers,* no. 168 (1151)
Peter of Saint-Michael	5,000 sol. Tol., plus others whose value is not stated		H Malte Puysubran 1, no. 53 (1155)
Bernard of Malespina	1,100 sol., plus others whose value is not stated		H Malte Puysubran 1, no. 69 (1164)
Raymond of Albas	16 sol. Ugon.		*Cart. Douzens* A, no. 8
Peter of Saint-Hilaire, canon of Saint-Paul	900 sol. Melg.	410 sol. Melg.	MS Mél. Colb. 414, no. 50 (1177)
Matfred, archdeacon of Saint-Nazaire, Béziers	2,600 sol. Melg.		*Cart. Béziers,* no. 259 (1177)
William Arnaldi, sacristan of Saint-Paul	300 sol. Melg.	265 sol. Melg., 30 sol. Narb, 60 morabitani	MS Doat 57, fol. 139 (1179)
Berenger of Ile-de-Lec	1,400 sol. Melg.	1,315 sol. Melg.	AD Aude G 12, no. 7 (1184)
Peter Raimond of Narbonne	1,990 sol. Melg.	3,050 sol. Melg.	H Malte Narbonne 1, no. 9 (1184)
Imbert, abbot of Saint-Paul	600 sol. Melg.	2,520 sol. Melg., plus 1,350 sol. in unsecured loans to relatives	MS Doat 57, fol. 143 (1186)

42. The division was in fact a bit more complicated. According to the *leudas vielhas*, when the goods came by land it was the fief holders (*fyvaties*) of the archbishop who collected the archbishop's share in the City and Bourg, but when the goods came by sea, the archbishop's share went directly into his coffers.

43. One-third each of wheat, oats, and fava beans: *Cart. Douzens*, xxxi and A, no. 188.

44. AMN AA103, fol. 124; printed in Narbonne. Archives communales *Inventaire 2. Annexes de la série AA*, 4–6.

45. Mills and real estate: *HGL* 5:913 (MS Mél. Colb. 414, no. 28) and *HGL* 5:966; guarding road: Inv. Rocques, *Viscomte*, no. 259.

CHAPTER 4. CITY AND COUNTRYSIDE

1. Wall of the Bourg: MS Doat 57, fol. 73 (1086); new walls of Coiran and Belveze: MS Doat 48, fol. 28 (probably around 1158); thirty-five years earlier, Coiran was already choice real estate for the city's rich and powerful: *HGL* 5:913, I (houses of Berenger of Durban and Leo magister). MS Doat 57, fol. 137 (1178), describes in detail how grain was lowered from a shop on the bridge to the mill below. Inv. Rocques, *Acquisitions*, no. 16 (1214), describes the slaughtering of pigs in a shop on the bridge. For the location of butcher shops: Inv. Rocques, *Viscomte*, no. 32 (1214); AMN AA105, fol. 18 (1216).

2. Huizinga, *Waning of the Middle Ages*, 18.

3. *Bordaria* next to the church of Saint-Sebastian (between the ancient forum and the Royal Gate): Inv. Rocques, *Acquisitions*, no. 67 (1066). It was still possible to find farmyards in the Bourg as late as 1096: MS Mél. Colb. 414, no. 25 (1096). Garden at the Porte Notre Dame: Inv. Rocques, *Archévêque seul*, no. 219 (1162–81); next to the wall: MS Doat 57, fol. 73 (1086); near Saint-Etienne-de-Villeneuve: MS Doat 59, fol. 58 (1171).

4. Saint-Georges: *HGL* 5:660 (1080), 858 (1117); *Cart. Silvanès*, no. 315 (1159). *Villa judaica*: *HGL* 5:831 (1112), 953 (1129); Inv. Rocques, *Acquisitions*, no. 32. Were the latter salt pans in Jewish hands, as the name suggests? By the twelfth century these salt pans were paying tithes to Saint-Just and Saint-Paul. Sigean: Inv. Rocques, *Sigean*, no. 1 (1181). The northern marsh: Inv. Rocques, *Fontfroide*, no. 1 (1156); *HGL* 8:390 (1188); AMN DD100 (1190).

5. MS Doat 57, fol. 85 (1096).

6. Meadow at Saint-Crescentius: Inv. Rocques, *Acquisitions*, nos. 70, 88 (1160); Inv. Rocques *Archévêque seul*, no. 218 (1178); Cazouls: Inv. Rocques, *Acquisitions*, nos. 121 (1046), 66 (1052); Champ Redon: Inv. Rocques, *Acquisitions*, nos. 86, 208 (1089); fields of Ermengard and Peter Raymond of Narbonne on the plain of Narbonne: MS Doat 59, fol. 53 (1168).

7. Grains: Inv. Rocques, *Sigean*, nos. 1, 2 (undated), and *Quillan*, nos. 98:20 (1128), 99:26 (1168); MS Baluze 81, fol. 77v (1119). Hunting: Inv. Rocques, *Albières*, no. 1 (1131); MS Doat 59, fol. 32 (1160); Cart. Fontjoncouse, no. 26 (1121–45). Irrigation: *HGL* 5:382 (1027); *Cart. Douzens* A, nos. 44 (1159), 125 (1165); more ambiguous are formulaic references to "aquae ductus et reductus" in many property conveyances and occasional references to "regum" (Occitan "rec" or "reg") as boundaries. Provisions concerning destruction by floods were regularly inserted into contracts for building or operating mills: *Cart. Douzens* A, no. 2, 118; *Cart. Béziers*, no. 312; see also the provisions prohibiting cutting wood along riverbanks, for example: *Cart. Béziers*, no. 192.

8. I have reconstructed a portion of the landscape between Béziers and the sea in Cheyette and Amado, "Organisation d'un terroir et d'un habitat concentré."

9. For references and documentation, see Sabarthès, *Dictionnaire topographique, sub*

nomine. So too around Béziers, the nearest village centers were about six kilometers from the city walls; see the map in Cheyette and Amado, "Organisation d'un terroir."

10. Cabrapicta: MS Doat 57, fol. 85; Bougna: *HGL* 5:966, 1035; MS Doat 59, fol. 135; Matepezouls: *HGL* 5:1207; Cazal de la Rocque: Inv. Rocques, *Acquisitions,* no. 123; Filou: Inv. Rocques, *Gruissan,* no. 1. See also the references in Sabarthès, *Dictionnaire géographique, sub nomine.*

11. Tithes on the salt pans were an important part of the bribe with which Peter, uncle of the viscount and archbishop elect, tried to win over the clergy of the city in 1080: *HGL* 5:656, 660; MS Baluze 82, fol. 155. Salt pans among the seignorial rights that the abbot of Saint-Paul promises to recuperate: *HGL* 5:858 (1117). Aymeri II and archbishop: *HGL* 5:831. Ermengard and archbishop: Inv. Rocques, *Viscomte,* nos. 259, 266. Ermengard and Raymond Trencavel: *HGL* 5:1264. The Genoese tariff list of 1128 (a text commonly thought to represent a considerably older state of affairs) mentions merchants of "Provence" bringing salt to the city: *LIG,* col. 32. Letter of Bernard, son of Raymond V of Toulouse to Henry II: Cayla, "Commerce languedocien de sel."

12. Cart. Fontjoncouse, no. 9 (1108). Only tiny fragments of the once rich archives of both Lagrasse and Montolieu survive. The rest went up in flames during the French Revolution. But the absence before the thirteenth century of any mention of pasturage in what does survive is remarkable. The first mention I find is AD Aude H8, no. 6 (1264). It is worth noting that there is no listing for pasturage or sheep in the index to the cartulary of the other great regional Benedictine abbey, Lézat. For the sheep *drailles* in northern and eastern Languedoc, see Clément, *Chemins à travers les âges en Cévennes et bas Languedoc.* For the early introduction of Merino sheep, see above chap. 3, n. 19.

13. Blomac: AD Aude H24 (1060), H80 (1147), H25 (1165); *Cart. Douzens* A, nos. 12, 37, 42, 54, 61, which mark a major construction campaign in the mid-twelfth century. Douzens: *Cart. Douzens* A, nos. 2, 4, 11–13, and many others (1130s on). Quillan: Inv. Rocques, *Quillan,* nos. 98:7 (1108), 98:27 (1134) *HGL* 5:675 (1082), is a crude forgery (Bernard Ato's reference to himself as viscount of Carcassonne is unlike any reference in a genuine text, and the witness list is a mix of names from the later twelfth century), but the topographical details must come from a genuine document, and they refer to a mill in the vicinity of Limoux. Esperaza: *Cart. Douzens* A, nos. 202–6. Villalier (Caumont): *Cart. Douzens* A, nos. 140–46 (1140s), misplaced on map p. 364bis. Lauquette: *Cart. Douzens* B, nos. 19, 40. Ferrals: AD Aude H65 (1111), H25 (1130). Salses: AD Pyrénées-Orientales B35 (1095, 1100). Parahou: MS Doat 59, fol. 32 (1160).

14. *Cart. Douzens* A, nos. 17, 140, D, no. 7 (at Douzens, Villalier, Blomac).

15. Except where otherwise noted, the following account is based on Berman, *Medieval Agriculture, the Southern French Countryside, and the Early Cistercians.*

16. Around Fontfroide: Saint-Martin, Quilhanet, Saint-Julien, now hamlets or ruins in the territory of Bizanet (for early references, see Sabarthès, *Dictionnarie topographique*); the equally ancient village of Joncquières was two kilometers north. The merchant road: *HGL* 5:1204 (see chap. 3). On the Cistercian myth, see Berman, *Medieval Agriculture,* 6–10; and for Fontfroide, idem, *Cistercian Evolution,* 29–32.

17. Almost all the early charters in MS Doat 59, all that remains of the archives of Fontfroide, involve grazing privileges or gifts of pasturage. Specific places mentioned in these early charters include Caunettes, Ventenac, Miraval, and Cabaret on the Montagne Noire, Parahou in the southern Corbières, and general privileges from the count-kings of Barcelona-Aragon. In general, see Grèzes-Rueff, "Abbaye de Fontfroide."

18. *Cart. Silvanès,* nos. 396, 398, 400.

19. For details, Berman, *Medieval Agriculture,* 106ff. For Silvanès, *Cart. Silvanès,* nos. 239, 241.

20. For all these men, see "Ermengard's Entourage" below, chap. 9.

21. MS Doat 47, fol. 23; *HGL* 8:281, 283 (II).

22. Even the tireless Rocques, seventeenth-century archivist to the archbishop, re-marked of a list of thirteenth-century city property holders with valuations of their holdings, a document that would make a modern social or economic historian salivate, "as this is without interest, I will say no more about it." Inv. Rocques, *Archévêque seul*, no. 217.

23. The agreement is dated March 24, 1271: *HGL* 8:1728. It provided that doubts and complications were to be arbitrated by Gerald of Narbonne, abbot of Saint-Paul, and Berenger of Puisserguier; but those complications were in the end put to the arbitration of Guy de Levis: AD Hérault G274 (February 6, 1272 n.s.). Further complications arising from the interpretation of this first arbitral agreement were again put to Guy de Levis a decade later: MS Doat 48, fols. 163–82. The testament mentioned in both the first agreement and the second arbitration looks like legal boilerplate rather than a reference to an actual document: "quitavit . . . totum quidquid juris et rationis habebat . . . seu petebat . . . ratione . . . testamenti seu ultime voluntatis dicti domini Amalrici quondam patris sui et ratione etiam donationis facte sibi inter vivos vel ante nuptias seu propter nuptias . . . seu quocumque alio modo." No further mention is made of the provisions of the testament, and the agreement between the brothers specifies how all the questions normally dealt with in a testament would be taken care of: their father's debts, their mother's dowry and rights to her portion of the inheritance, their sisters' dowries. Would they have done this had there been a testament?

24. The recognizance: *HGL* 8:1735. A comparison of the two lists—one of which is secondhand (from MS Latin 9996), the other of which (AD Herault G274) is a copy made in 1663 from a medieval copy of the original—makes it possible to resolve all but three of the problematic place-names.

25. There were major disputes between Simon and the new archbishop, Arnold Amaury, but they mainly concerned property rights within Narbonne itself: MS Mél. Colb. 414, nos. 69 (1213), 80 (1232); MS Doat 55, fol. 299 (1214). By midcentury, the interminable conflicts between viscounts and archbishops had settled down to a kind of trench warfare over jurisdiction of particular kinds on particular streets or even in particular shops. Papal protection for Aymeri: MS Baluze 392, no. 583 (1215).

26. Which became the subject of a complaint by the archbishop: Inv. Rocques, *Viscomte*, no. 259.

27. As Peyriac and Marmorières were in 1232: Inv. Rocques, *Viscomte*, no. 269.

28. Compare Ermengard's donations to the abbey of Quarante, discussed below. Barely a handful of documents survives from this abbey (in MS Doat 58), yet in those few the vice-comital house of Narbonne and its closest companions figure prominently.

29. Lagrasse is named as a beneficiary of Viscount Matfred's will: *HGL* 5:255 (966). The mortgage of le Lac: *HGL* 5:838. It is listed among the castles of Lagrasse in the pancarte of Pope Calixtus II in 1119: Robert, *Bullaire du pape Calixte II*, no. 39. It also appears in the pancarte of Gelasius II (MS Baluze 398, no. 12, published in *GC* 6, col. 434), but this list, which purports to be from just a year before that of Calixtus, is far more extensive and includes many places that Lagrasse did not acquire until the thirteenth century; it is most probably a thirteenth-century forgery.

30. For the early history, see Bonnassie, *Catalogne*, 149–52, map p. 151, and genealogy p. 163. For eleventh-century holdings, *LFM*, nos. 496, 497, 500. Donations to Lagrasse: *HGL* 5:215 (953), 776 (1103); *GC* 6, *instrum.* 23 (1073); AD Aude H161 (1111).

31. *LFM*, nos. 506, 508, 808. On the warfare of 1112–13, see Cheyette, " 'Sale' of Carcassonne," 857–59. In the *LFM*, the grant immediately precedes an act of alliance in the form of an oath of fidelity (also undated) directed against Bernard Ato, almost certainly from this period.

32. Catel, *Mémoires*, 589. King Louis VIII claimed the overlordship of the Fenouillèdes and Peyrepertusès during the Albigensian Crusades and in 1226 granted them in fief to Count Nuño of Roussillon: MS Latin 11826, no. 19; MS Baluze 392, no. 574.

33. *HGL* 8:1729.

34. *HGL* 5:1289. For a full discussion of this text, see Amado, "Seigneurie des mines en pays de Béziers," from whom I depart mainly in not seeing here a distinction between public and private powers but only different forms of lordship. Villemagne: *HGL* 5:255, 276, 287, and many others. Early possessions of the vicecomital family: Dotz, Poujol, Saint-Gervais, Caussiniojouls, Villemagne in the joint testament of Viscount Matfred and his wife Adalaide in 966 (*HGL* 5:255); Dotz and Colombiers and "the alod between the Jaur and the Sérou" (near Saint-Pons) in Adelaide's first testament of 978 (*HGL* 5:284). We might be able to identify more had these documents survived in the original (rather than second- or third-hand) and had we as complete a topographic dictionary for the Hérault département as we do for the Aude.

35. Mourcairolles: *HGL* 5:316. See also *HGL* 5:425 (oath of security c. 1036) and col. 494 (oath of security c. 1059). Boussagues is first mentioned in 1117, in a donation that implies it had previously been held of the predecessors of Viscount Bernard Ato of the Trencavel family: *HGL* 5:853; Cart. Trencavel, fol. 162. (For comparison, see the document of 1116, *HGL* 5:852.) Brusque and Boissezon: *HGL* 5:568 (1069). Lunas: *HGL* 5:865 (testament of Bernard Ato, 1118).

36. Three major rivers have their headwaters in this region: the Tarn (Albi's river), the Orb (Bézier's river), and the Hérault (Agde's river).

37. MS Doat 40, fol. 114. On the area's political importance, see my discussion of the treaty of 1112 between Ramon Berenguer III and Viscount Bernard Ato in Cheyette, " 'Sale' of Carcassonne," 857–59.

38. See the articles by Rancoule and Solier, Gourdiole, and Bonami in *Mines et mineurs en Languedoc-Roussillon;* for a more general overview, see Labrousse, "Exploitation d'or et d'argent dans le Rouergue."

CHAPTER 5. CITIES OF MAMMON, CITIES OF MARS

1. At Douzens, between Narbonne and Carcassonne, the price of wheat was 2 sol. Ugon. per sétier in 1150 (*Cart. Douzens* A, nos. 177, 178) and 4 sol. 6 d. Melg. in 1154 (ibid., A, no. 48). In 1163, the exchange ratio of the coinage of Carcassonne to that of Mauguio was 3:2.2 (AD Aude G76); assuming the same ratio held a decade earlier, the price in 1150 would have been 1 sol. 6 d. Melg. And yet four sales of vineyards to Douzens on April 7, 1150, for quantities of grain rather than coin make one suspicious that it may have been a bad year for winter crops and some families faced grim shortages.

2. For maps and photographs of Roman roads in Languedoc, see Clément, *Chemins à travers les âges*, 130–36, 105–8, and for an archaeological stratigraphy of the Domitia, 112.

3. *HGL* 5:1204.

4. We can follow one from the gate of Fontfroide to near Ornaisons, linking Ermengard's Roussillon road to the Aquitaine road from Narbonne to Carcassonne and Toulouse. The map of the Institut Géographique National names this the "vieux chemin de Fontfroide." Was this also her project? Or was it built by the monks themselves?

5. Berman, *Medieval Agriculture*, 121–24. See *Cart. Silvanès*, no. 314, in which Ermengard puts her name to such a privilege: the monks may pass the road under the walls of Cazouls (Hérault) without paying toll. The donor, Bernard Raimond of Cazouls, was a member of her court.

6. A sign of their growing importance: in 1123 the militia of Toulouse rescued the young Alphonse Jordan from a siege in Orange on the Rhone and brought him in triumph back to his city: "Chronicle of Saint-Sernin of Toulouse," *HGL* 5:50.

7. The brief account of the Balearic expedition in Abulafia, *Mediterranean Emporium*, 3–6, does not, however, mention the participation of Narbonne and Montpellier.

8. On the party kings, see Wasserstein, *Rise and Fall of the Party-Kings;* on Barcelonese ambitions, see Bonnassie, *Catalogne*, 866.

9. On these relations see Bonnassie, *Catalogne*, 351–54, 866. I am less convinced than Bonnassie that the last bit of folklore has any basis in fact. For other evidence of cooperation across the religious divide and a convincing interpretation of the nature of those relationships, see Fletcher, "Reconquest and Crusade in Spain."

10. Al-Idrisi, *Description de l'Afrique et de l'Espagne par Edrisi* (trans. Dozy and De Goeje), 231.

11. See Fletcher, "Reconquest and Crusade," and idem, *Quest for El Cid.*

12. Bonnassie, *Catalogne*, 866, 868; O'Callaghan, *History of Medieval Spain*, 218–22.

13. See above, chap. 1.

14. Fenoullèdes and Peyrepertusès: *LFM*, nos. 808, 809, on whose circumstances see Cheyette, " 'Sale' of Carcassonne," 857–59. Beaucaire and the *terre d'Argence: HGL* 5:938 (misread by Devic and Vaissete, *HGL* 3:662), which specifies that Bernard of Anduze is to hold these in turn of Aymeri; also the mutual oaths of fidelity, ACA *perg. Ram. Ber. III*, no. 270 (now missing, but copied in the nineteenth-century inventory), where Alfonse Jordan and Ramon Berenguer promise mutual aid against all except Aymeri, William of Montpellier, Bernard of Anduze, and the count of Fourcalquier. Ramon Berenguer's testament: *LFM*, no. 493; supplemented by his gift to his daughter Mahalt, *LFM*, no. 738, also witnessed by Aymeri; the following day he witnessed a major gift to the cathedral of Barcelona: ACA *perg. Ram. Ber. IV*, no. 5.

15. Richildis, wife of Viscount Odo, appears as a witness or presiding over a court in a number of documents from 924 to 977. She is identified as daughter of Count Borrel and Countess Garsendis in 936: *HGL* 5:147, 153, 161, 222, 256, 281, 1510. For activities of Viscountess Richildis of Narbonne in Ampurias: Simó Rodríguez, "Aportación a la documentación condal catalana." In 1056, Raymond Berenger, the son of the viscount, was one of the witnesses to a *conveniencia* between the count of Urgel and Ramon Berenguer I: ACA *perg. Ram. Ber. I*, no. 154. In 1067, Viscount Berenger and his wife mortgaged two of their Catalan fiefs—the castle of Solterra on the plain of Vich and property at Osor, between Vich and Gerona—back to Ramon Berenguer I: *HGL* 5:546. At the same time, the Barcelonese held lands, not precisely identified, in the viscounty of Narbonne: see, for example, the testament of Ramon Berenguer I, *LFM*, no. 492. See also the testamentary gift of Countess Ermessendis (1058), to Berenger of Narbonne, *LFM*, no. 491. There were other Narbonnese as well in high places in Catalonia; a William Miro of Narbonne and a Roger Pons of Narbonne were among the witnesses to the sale by the aging Countess Ermessend to her grandson Ramon Berenguer I and his wife Almodis of her powers and rights in Barcelona, Gerona, and Ausona: *LFM*, no. 214.

16. The *conveniencia* ACA *perg. sin fecha Ram. Ber. I*, no. 207, now partly illegible (published in Bofarull y Mascaró, *Condes de Barcelona*, 2:17–20). Devic and Vaissete date the agreement to 1050: *HGL* 3:312. On the conquest of Tarragona, see McCrank, "Restauración canonica," and more briefly, Sobrequés i Vidal, *Grans comtes*, 190ff.

17. Archives communales de Narbonne, *Inventaire 2. Annexes de la série AA*, doc. 1. *Bagneria* is most likely the "montana loca nomine Bagnare" close to the walls of Tortosa mentioned by the Genoese chronicler Caffaro, "Ystoria captionis Almerie et Turtuose," in *Annali Genovesi*, 86.

18. Texts printed in Ruiz Domenec, "En torno a un tratado comercial entre las ciudades de Genova y Barcelona en la primera mitad del siglo XII," 159–60, who believes that the primary (although not exclusive) commodity in this trade was slaves.

19. Cited in Constable, "Genoa and Spain in the Twelfth and Thirteenth Centuries," 637.

20. In the Middle Ages the term *spices* covered a vast array of items that would not be included in this category in the aisles of our grocery stores today. Most of these goods came from far to the south and east of Egypt. Those distant roads were still closed to Christian merchants in the twelfth century, although not, of course, to Jews, whether from Genoa, Narbonne, or Catalonia. For the Jews' possible role in the early commercial activities of Genoa, see Airaldi, "Groping in the Dark."

21. Kedar, "Mercanti Genovesi in Alessandria d'Egitto," 24–26.

22. Maragone, *Gli annales Pisani, sub anno* (in Pisan dating practice); CD 1:9; Caffaro, *Annali*, 13; Krueger, "Genoese Trade with Northwest Africa in the Twelfth Century," 377–78. It is not certain that Genoese took part in all these raids.

23. Al-Bakri, *Description de l'Afrique septentrionale* (trans. Slane), 67, 85, 117, 121. *Rum* was the generic name for the Christian world in Moslem geographical writings.

24. On all these early naval activities, see Marçais, "Villes de la côte algérienne et la piraterie au moyen âge," 124, 128; Krueger, "Genoese Trade," 378.

25. Caffaro, *Annali*, 16.

26. Bribe: ibid., 20–21, notes. Innocent II and promotion to archbishop: CD 1:75–80; Cafaro, *Annali*, 26–27; Maragone, *Annales, sub anno* 1134. Treaty of 1149, CD 1:243.

27. Krueger, "Genoese Trade," 378.

28. Caffaro, *Annali*, 5–9; for a discussion of the first consulate and the meaning of *compagna*, see Day, *Genoa's Response to Byzantium*, 72–73.

29. CD 1:11–12. See, on all this, Favreau-Lilie, *Italiener*, 43–48. Our knowledge of the extent of Genoese gains during their eastern adventures is complicated by the probability that the most important document, the grant by King Baldwin I at the siege of Akko in 1104, is a later Genoese fabrication. See the painstaking discussion in *Italiener*, 79–111.

30. *LIG* 1:16, 18, 19; CD 1:28–33. Narrative of these events in Runciman, *History of the Crusades*, 2:64–70, from whom I take the identification of Gibelletum and Castrum Rogerii; further discussion in Favreau-Lilie, *Italiener*, 116–25. It is possible that the abbey was in real control of Saint-Gilles: Poly, *Provence*, 279–80. According to Runciman, the Genoese only received a trading quarter in Tripoli and two-thirds of Jebail, which became the hereditary fief of the Genoese Ugo Embriaco.

31. *LIG* 1:39–40, correctly re-dated by Caille, "Consulat de Narbonne," 243. The Narbonnese decree on shipwrecks: *HGL* 5:829.

32. *LIG* 1:54–56. Their attention in the mountains behind the city was directed mainly at securing control of the route to Pavia and to Monferrato; CD 1:72, 87, 90, 124, and others.

33. *LIG* 1:87–88.

34. Ibid., 89–90; treaty of Genoa, Pisa, and Montpellier to make war on Alphonse Jordan along with the count of Rodez and the three Trencavel brothers, 1143.

35. CD 1:149–52. Alphonse Jordan promised that the merchants would be safe and secure in Saint-Gilles and in his portion of Lunel, and "in Narbona et de Narbona in antea vos non offendam nec offendere in aliquo loco faciam" (nor will I injure you in Narbonne or have you injured in any place). Some sense of the value of the sum the two maritime powers received can be derived from contemporaneous contracts; in 1146, Viscount Bernard Ato of Nîmes mortgaged to his nephew Rostang de Posquières all rights of justice over the Posquières family's men, women, and property in the diocese of Nîmes as well as the overlordship of three castles for a mere eighty marcs of silver by weight of Saint-Gilles (*HGL*

5:1092); in 1156, Raymond Trencavel mortgaged the tolls of Saint-Thibéry—where the bridge of the via Domitia over the Hérault River met a major road north—to William of Montpellier for 13,000 sol. Melg. (*HGL* 5:1181). It is then hardly surprising that the treaty stipulated a drawn-out schedule of payments spanning more than ten years.

36. Caffaro, *Annali*, 33–35. The smaller ships (*golabrii*), according to Krueger, *Navi e proprietà navale a Genova*, 24–26, had a charge of approximately 37.5 nautical tons, in comparison to that of the *navis*, which was 100 to 150 tons. Both of these types of vessels were sail propelled. The galleys, in contrast, were oared vessels and more of a war or pirate ship than a merchant vessel.

37. On this crusading turn, see Fletcher, "Reconquest and Crusade," especially 39–41; on the papal crusading privileges and the role of crusaders in the wars of 1147–48, see O'Callaghan, *Medieval Spain*, 230–32.

38. *LIG* 1:123–27.

39. *LFM*, nos. 462–64.

40. CD 1:228, 265–68; *LFM*, no. 463.

41. See Krueger, "Post-War Collapse and Rehabilitation in Genoa," corrected by Day, *Genoa's Response*, 74–79.

42. *LIG* 1:16, 19, and others. Favreau-Lilie argues persuasively that the privileges Bohemond granted in Tripoli in 1098 were granted to a group of individual Genoese rather than to the city itself; likewise the oaths of aid and fidelity these individuals took lay only on themselves and not on the city as a whole: *Italiener*, 46–48. Even if the grant of Baldwin I of 1104 is a later forgery, as Favreau-Lilie argues, it could have been constructed on a genuine text (as was the case with most medieval forgeries); what was important for the forger was to add the rights (in this case, in the city of Akko) that did not appear in the original. The Genoese must have received some privileges to purchase their participation in the siege of Akko. It is noteworthy that the document we have is cast in the same terms as the genuine text from Bertrand of Saint-Gilles in 1109—one argument in favor of its being at least modeled on a genuine grant from 1104.

43. For subtle analysis of this practice, see White, *Custom, Kinship, and Gifts to Saints*, and Rosenwein, *To Be a Neighbor of Saint Peter*.

44. Day, *Genoa's Response*, 71–73. See also the careful analysis of the complex relationship between Archbishop Daimbert of Pisa and the Pisan fleet in Palestine in 1099–1100, and of the Genoese interest in assuring that Daimbert be deposed from the patriarchate of Jerusalem, which he briefly claimed, in Favreau-Lilie, *Italiener*, 55–61, 84–86.

45. Day, *Genoa's Response*, 48.

46. Ibid., 48–51. For examples of oaths see CD 1:90 (Ponzone), 107 (Lavagna), 119 (Portovenere), and others in this volume.

47. Day, *Genoa's Response*, 94–95.

48. "[A]dvenerunt ianuam legati . . . ex parte domni arnaldi narbonensis archiepiscopi . . . et ex parte Aimerici narbonensis vicecomitis atque aliorum consulum narbonensium et totius populi pro discordiis et forisfactis . . . cum ianuensibus . . . requirentes pacem.": *LIG* 1:39. "[S]it notum omnibus quod discordia et lis que erat inter ianuenses et pisanos et comitem ildefossum sic pacificata est. concordia talis est quod nos burgenses sancti egidii pro rebus ianuensium et pisanorum quas comes cepit reddemus vobis.": *LIG* 1:82.

49. "[U]nus de concivibus vestris perpetuo ero": *LIG* 1:87.

50. *LIG* 1:123, 125.

51. *LFM*, no. 464 (dated by the editor as 1154–62): "Comes se nichil Ianuensibus dedisse, sed ipsi per se ipsam suam partem expugnasse et excepisse, . . . ac propterea se de eorum porcione non teneri dicebat."

52. Caffaro, *Annali*, 1:85–88.

53. "[P]ro sumptibus machinarum": *LIG* 1:123. On the importance of the Genoese artisans to the siege work of the First Crusade, see Favreau-Lilie, *Italiener*, 44, 50, and elsewhere.

54. One thinks, for example, of the almost exactly contemporary *Deeds of Louis the Fat* by Abbot Suger of Saint-Denis.

55. Caffaro, *Annali*, 1:85–89.

56. Because the notary did not have Mommsen or Pauly-Wissowa at his elbow, there is no reason to enlarge on his historical confusion; as correspondents on the Ancien-l Internet discussion group have pointed out to me, the ancient Roman censors had nothing to do with the triumph. I think my translation is what the crabbed Latin of the grant means, but I give it here so the reader may judge: "Constitucionibus quidem sacris sanctitum esse quatinus viris contra Mauros ac barbaros ceterosque catholice fidei contrarios contendentibus meritorum beneficia irrogentur, necnon potestatibus quarum obsequio sese crebris inextimandisque minime recusant subjacere periculis sedulo decorentur seu censitorum ordine triumphatores scribantur quo tam posteris quam presentibus perpetim memorie obtineantur." Archives communales de Narbonne, *Inventaire 2. Annexes de la série AA*, doc. 1. The office of censor was taken over by the Emperor Domitian in C.E. 84–85 and thereafter disappeared: Jolowicz, *Historical Introduction to the Study of Roman Law*, 336.

57. The *Usatici Barchinone*, the "Usages of Barcelona," were probably redacted during the same period of time as the conquest of Tortosa, although their core goes back to the eleventh century; see Bonnassie, *Catalogne*, 2:711–28.

58. For William Raymond, seneschal or dapifer, and Bernard of Bel-lloc, see the index to the *LFM;* for Peter Raymond of Narbonne, see below, chap. 9; the witness Peter of Fossat is probably to be identified with the man of the same name who witnessed a grant by the canons of Saint-Paul in 1136 (MS Mél. Colb. 414, no. 31). Perhaps the composition of the witness list made certain that there would be one witness from the *civitas* of Narbonne and one from the *burgum* across the river.

59. Mundy, *Liberty and Political Power*, chaps. 5, 7, 8, 10.

60. The thirteenth- and fourteenth-century cartularies of Narbonne (AMN AA99, AA101–AA106) are replete with records of protests, recognitions, arbitrations, and litigation over these boundaries.

61. Rhone treaties: CD 1:316–22; treaty with William I of Sicily: CD 1:338–42, 344–49. See, in general, Day, *Genoa's Response*, 23ff., 81ff.

62. The editor of the CD (at 1:317) placed the undated treaty in 1155, whereas the editor of the *LIG* placed it in 1143 (at 1:87). The manner in which Montpellerian commerce with Genoa is described in an agreement actually dated 1155 (CD 1:320)—"quod homines loci vestri [i.e., from Montpellier] veniens secus terram a Montepesulano vel qui temporis sevitia . . . pelagus ingressi fuerint, dummodo bona fide quam citius poterint inde mercium transmutacione contracta pelagus exeant et Ianuam . . . revertantur, . . . tuti erunt atque securi"—suggests a continuation of an already existing arrangement: the one agreed to in 1143. It seems unlikely that this agreement and the one printed in CD 1:317–20 would have been negotiated at the same time. I therefore favor the date in the edition of the *LIG*. Lanfranco Pevere, mentioned in the text as receiving the oath from William of Montpellier, was consul in 1143 and in 1154. Because it is possible that the oath was taken before the document was drawn up, this is not an overwhelming argument.

63. *HGL* 8:163; CD 2:50–52.

64. CD 2:127–31. For a narrative of these wars, see below, chap. 14.

65. Ibid., 275–77. A brief account of these events can be found in Michaud and Cabanis, *Histoire de Narbonne*, 152–53.

66. Caille, "Consulat de Narbonne," correcting Emery, *Heresy and Inquisition in Nar-*

bonne, 25, and Gouron, "Diffusion des consulats méridionaux," 33–34. My interpretation of events differs somewhat from Caille's, who sees the earlier use of the term *consul* as a mere verbal imitation of Italian practice in documents drawn up overseas (246). The fact that the documents come from the siege of Tortosa as well as the cities of Genoa and Pisa seems to me to argue against this. If *probi homines* or *boni homines* is what they were called at home, neither term would have been foreign to the notary of Count Ramon Berenguer who drafted that document.

67. AMN AA105, fol. 21v (1177). Such *probi homines* are also mentioned in an act of 1200: AN S4858, no. 21. That "prudent man" is not a personal honorific but an official title is indicated by the fact that Arnold Amalric elsewhere appears without it: AN S4858, no. 22 (also AMN AA104, fol. 192) (1192). The same is true of those who appear in the act of 1200. Both acts concern special obligations of the city's leper house: in the earlier document, selling property that had been donated to the house with the "counsel" of the "prudent men"; in the later one, witnessing the entrance of someone "as a brother" into the leper house on condition that he receive "victum et vestum honorifice . . . sicut unum de melioribus et venerabilioribus fratribus ibi manentibus." Perhaps the *probi homines* in this case had, among other duties, that of being the official city overseers of the leper house.

68. AMN AA99, fol. 1. The full title given to Raymond, count of Toulouse, duke of Narbonne, marquis of Provence, shows that the viscount had been presented with a written text and not just with a memory of an event.

69. See below, chap. 15.

70. On this, Caille's judgment, in "Consulat de Narbonne," seems to me convincing.

71. See the index in Giovanni scriba, *Cartolare*. A mint could attract mercantile activity in various ways: one document in this notarial notebook shows Ingo della Volta, one of the most powerful merchants in Genoa, arranging in 1163 to liquidate in Melgorian coin at Montpellier a partnership initially contracted in Genoese pounds in Genoa: ibid., no. 1060.

72. Caille, "Métropole des deux versants," 153–55.

73. Money changers: *Layettes* 1:119.

CHAPTER 6. THE BISHOP IN THE CITY

1. The urban archaeology needed to document all this has unfortunately not been done in Occitania, but a certain amount can be reconstructed from standing structures and archival documentation. For Narbonne: Caille, "Traits médiévaux," 180–84, especially the plan of the cathedral complex on 177; Mortet, "Notes historiques et archéologiques sur la cathédrale de Narbonne"; and the thirteenth-century plan in Esquieu, "Narbonne," 320. Where pre-Gothic structures have disappeared, as at Béziers, we know of them from the many references to the *opera* in the cartularies. Topographical indications also occasionally appear in early documents at Béziers, Agde, and Nîmes. For comparative archaeology elsewhere in the Midi, see Février, *Développement urbain*, 55–60; Esquieu, *Autour de nos cathédrales*; Février et al., *Fréjus*, 43–46; Guild, *Cathédrale d'Aix-en-Provence;* and for late-Antique buildings, "Narbonne," in Gauthier and Picard, *Topographie chrétienne*, vol. 7.

2. Among many examples of testamentary gift: *HGL* 5:316 (990); of bridal gift: *HGL* 5:428 (1037) (Pons of Toulouse to his bride Majora); *HGL* 5:738 (1095) (Bertrand, son of Raymond IV of Toulouse, to Electa of Burgundy). Magnou-Nortier's interpretation of this second document, in *Société laïque*, 551, speculating that its language shows the effects of the Gregorian Reform in Albi, seems to me untenable, given the explicit terms of the agreement between Alphonse of Toulouse and Viscount Roger in 1132, which recognizes to the latter the exclusive right to the *episcopatus* as well as the *episcopi electionem cum ipso episcopo* (*HGL*

5:980). Mortgage: *HGL* 5:404; and Cart. Trencavel, fol. 32 (c. 1038), completed by *HGL* 5:452 (c. 1045). Abbeys as well as bishoprics were possessions of great lay lords: *HGL* 5:415. For the archbishops of Narbonne, see the episcopal list in *HGL* 4:247–48. For the bishops Frotarius: *HGL* 5:190–92 (942); the episcopal lists in *HGL* 4; and the genealogical table in Cheyette, " 'Sale' of Carcassonne," 829. In general for Occitania, Magnou-Nortier, *Société laïque*, 344–49; completed by Biget, "Épiscopat du Rouergue et de l'Albigeois," 182, 184–87, especially n. 37; and for Provence, Poly, *Provence*, 254–57.

3. See the pertinent remarks of Moore, *First European Revolution*, 13.

4. Albi: Biget, "Épiscopat du Rouergue," 182, and idem, "Récits d'une histoire oubliée," 35–36. William of Gelone: see Calmette, "Famille de Saint Guilhem"; Levillain, "Alliances des Nibelungen"; Amado, "Poids de l'aristocratie," and idem, "Pouvoirs et noblesse dans la Gothie." Carolingians: Biget, "Récits," 39–40; Saltet, "Origine méridionale des fausses généalogies carolingiennes." Gerald of Aurillac: Lewis, "Count Gerald of Aurillac and Feudalism in South Central France in the Early Tenth Century," 57–58; and the somewhat more sanguine and legalistic assessment of Magnou-Nortier, *Société laïque*, 353–56.

5. *HGL* 5:522; Mundy, *Liberty and Political Power*, 14–17; Lacger, *Gaillac en Albigeois*, 12–13; Biget, "Récits," 51; *HGL* 5:517, 519. For comparison, see Venarde, "Réforme à Apt."

6. The common stuff of what Occitan charters call *dominicatura* or *domingadura* or, in the later twelfth century, *dominatio*. Two examples of such lists: *Cart. Béziers*, no. 65 (c. 1050), a grant in fief; and MS Doat 57, fol. 68 (1080), gift by the archbishop of Narbonne to the monastery of Saint-Paul.

7. Mundy, *Liberty and Political Power*, 234 n. 27.

8. *HGL* 5:685.

9. Narbonne: *HGL* 5:496; Caille, "Origine et développement de la seigneurie temporelle de l'archevêque," 20–28; Albi: *HGL* 5:980. Raymond's title is in a charter for Saint-Pons-de-Thomières: *HGL* 5:697. Kaiser, *Bischofsherrschaft*, 256–338, reviews all the data.

10. Tarragona: see above, chap. 5; division of Carcassonne: see Cheyette, " 'Sale' of Carcassonne."

11. *HGL* 5:980.

12. *HGL* 5:860. See Caille, "Seigneurie temporelle," 28–30.

13. Béziers: *HGL* 5:685; Carcassonne: Mahul, *Cartulaire et archives de Carcassonne*, 5:404–5; Albi: *HGL* 5:1063, 1333; Narbonne: MS Baluze 82, fol. 41; confirmation by Pope Adrian IV, MS Baluze, fol. 40. This *ius spolii* included the right to confiscate the moveables of the deceased bishop.

14. Inv. Rocques, *Archévêque seul*, 112. The original, like most of the archives of the medieval archbishops, has disappeared.

15. For details and documentation, see Cheyette " 'Sale' of Carcassonne," 841–43.

16. One such treasure chest has survived and is displayed in the episcopal museum of La Seo d'Urgel.

17. *Recueil des actes de Charles II le Chauve* (ed. Tessier), no. 49.

18. *HGL* 5:496. Etienne Baluze dated it 1056 and was followed in this by Mansi, but Devic and Vaissete demonstrated that the accusations must have been read at a council in Arles in 1059 or in Toulouse in 1060: *HGL* 4, n. xxxv.

19. Mansi, *Sacrorum conciliorum nova et amplissima collectio*, 19:843–44; Bishop Frotarius of Nîmes and his nephew Viscount Raymond excommunicated for simony: *HGL* 5:519; Bernard, count of Besalú, "eager to expel the heresy of simony from [his] land," gives Saint-Martin-Lys to Saint-Pons-de-Thomières for reform: *HGL* 5:571. See, in general, Magnou-Nortier, *Société laïque*, 461–63.

20. Guifred was excommunicated at the Council of Florence in 1055, possibly, however, for his involvement in the dispute between Count Ramon Berenguer and Countess Almodis

of Barcelona and Ramon Berenguer's grandmother Ermessend. Bofarull y Mascaró, *Condes de Barcelona*, 2:6. The story is passably obscure: see Magnou-Nortier, *Société laïque*, 469. By the viscount's account, both Narbonne and Urgel were bought for one hundred thousand solidi. This similarity and the round number suggest that we should read this amount as a poet's rather than an accountant's figure. As bishop of Urgell, Guillem Guifred was the very model of a warrior prelate. He probably killed Viscount Folc of Cardona with his own hands and was later himself assassinated: Bonnassie, *Catalogne*, 550–51.

21. *HGL* 5:498–9. My account of Guifred's career follows that of Caille, "Seigneurie temporelle," 22–28.

22. Oath of Bernard, count of Besalú to Guifred (after 1068): Inv. Rocques, *Archévêque seul*, 116; papal confirmation of archiepiscopal lands in 1107: *HGL* 5:805. The two lists do not correspond exactly: Conilhac, Canet, and Villedaigne, as well as a number of sites in the southern Corbières and Roussillon appear on the earlier list but not the later. Many of these castles had doubtless been built on ancient archiepiscopal estates. Sigean was given to the archbishop in 926 (*HGL* 5:151), Fontjoncouse in 963 (*HGL* 5:251). Villerouge, given by Charles the Bald to his *fidelis* Stephen in 849 (*Recueil des actes de Charles II le Chauve*, 1:318), came to the archbishop along with other property of this "Spanish" refugee. When Archbishop Richard came to the see, his first concern was to establish his rights within the city (see his fight with Ermengard's grandfather: *HGL* 5:831, 860) and to regain control of his castles: Fontjoncouse (Cart. Fontjoncouse, no. 9), Villerouge (*GC* 6, *instrum.* 32), Capestang (*HGL* 5:801), and Canet, whose construction he was planning (MS Doat 55, fol. 130). For all this, see below. It is noteworthy that Creissan "cum ipsa turra cum cincto et vallo," purchased in 959 (*HGL* 5:228), is not included in later lists of fortifications. It was off the main routes and was probably not kept in repair. In the papal list of 1107 and later confirmations of 1153 and 1156, the one problematic fortification is Auriac. From the early eleventh century on, Auriac was sworn to the fidelity of the Trencavels (Cart. Trencavel, fols. 8–9, 57v–58, 104; *HGL* 5:387). Were there two castles in this tiny village of the upper Corbières?

23. At Cruscades there still stands a magnificent seventeenth-century bridge built when the road was reconstructed under Louis XIV. Capestang: see the map in Cheyette, "Castles of the Trencavels"; also Bautier, "Recherches sur les routes de l'Europe médiéval: II. Le grand axe routier est-ouest du midi de la France," 299–300; and plates in Perez, *Cadastres antiques en narbonnaise occidentale*. Richard's claims: *HGL* 5:801.

24. Cart. Fontjoncouse, no. 7 (original AD Aude G7, no. 1). See n. 22 above for disputes at Villerouge, Fontjoncouse, and Canet. In the last, it is "ut eosdem milites in sua fidelitate retineret" that the archbishop grants them as a fief the castles and towers and fortifications that will be built there. The only oaths of fidelity to survive from such retainers are from Fontjoncouse: Cart. Fontjoncouse, nos. 8 and 10.

25. *HGL* 5:538, 541. I follow Caille in identifying the Raymond in the first act with the Raymond in the second and in seeing the two separate texts as one complex act. It was commonplace in this area for *convenientiae* to be confirmed by oaths of fidelity.

26. Toulouges: *LFM*, no. 708. Besalú: Bonnassie, *Catalogne*, 702–3; Magnou-Nortier, *Société laïque*, 470–71.

27. The dating of these events cannot be resolved. Raymond Berenger I was still alive in March 1067, for he and his wife contracted a mortgage in February 1067, to which his sons Raymond, Bernard, and Peter were witnesses (*HGL* 5:546), and he witnessed the marriage of Adelais to William Raymond of Cerdagne in March (*LFM*, no. 814). Yet the arbitral document in which Bernard Berenger is named viscount is dated October 6, 1066. None of the originals exist; we are dependent on copies made by Baluze and Petrus de Marca in the seventeenth century and the editors of the *HGL* in the eighteenth. The complex elements of the dating clause of the 1067 documents are all in agreement, although one dates the begin-

ning of the reign of King Philip to 1059 and the other to 1060. The easiest copying error would be in the date of the arbitral agreement, dropping an "I" to make 1066 rather than 1067. It is also possible that the scribe of this document was dating by the Pisan style, whereas the others used the more common Florentine style.

The convenientia between Raymond Berenger II and Raymond Bernard viscount and Ermengard viscountess of Béziers (*HGL* 5:563–66) is the clearest evidence for a disputed succession, in which Bernard Berenger and the third brother Peter, bishop of Rodez, were the victors. The convenientia must have been negotiated between the death of Viscount Raymond Berenger I and the resolution of the succession to the county of Carcassonne in March 1068, because a count of Carcassonne, unnamed, is mentioned in the two oaths of fidelity that join the agreement: *HGL* 5:563, 565, 566. Several documents suggest that Raymond Berenger II was his father's chosen successor: ACA *perg. Ram. Ber. I*, no. 154 (1050–54), where he appears as a witness to a convenientia between the counts of Barcelona and Besalú, and is named as "vicecomitis filius de Narbone"; also *HGL* 5:432 (no. 272, III), where in 1066 he is the only one named with his mother and father in a donation to the monastery of Saint-Paul.

My account of these events differs in some respects from that of Caille, "Seigneurie temporelle."

28. *HGL* 5:540. In this text, taken from Baluze, the name of the count of Besalú appears erroneously as Raymond. Baluze apparently here suffered from a common copyist's error and let his eyes stray to the Raymond who appears just before. This error, like the unfortunate truncating of the text, follows Baluze's own manuscript copy, MS Baluze 374, p. 414. It makes a simple error in transcribing the date more believable.

29. *HGL* 5:535, 536. Recall that the count of Rodez had shared the payment when Guifred became archbishop. On the death of Bertha, the last heiress in the line descending from Ermengaud (died between 936 and 940), Raymond of Saint-Gilles fought her husband, Robert II of Auvergne, for the succession. In the convenientia with Guifred, Raymond pointedly calls himself count of Rodez.

30. *HGL* 5:538, 541 (no. 275, III) (original MS Baluze 392, no. 586). Bernard's oath has not survived. It was perhaps among those that Baluze saw and dismissed with the remark, "Il y a quantité d'hommages semblables à celuicy fait en divers temps aux archevesques de Narbone par les vicomtes de cete ville": MS Baluze 374, p. 352. In 1119, Archbishop Richard referred to the *fevodia* that Guifred gave to Raymond Berenger I, and his oath of fidelity and homage: *HGL* 5:860. See my remarks on *HGL* 5:540 above, n. 28; it cannot be used as Caille does in "Seigneurie temporelle," 27. Magnou-Nortier's portrait of Guifred (*Société laïque*, 472–74) is an apologia colored in the rosiest tones of a Sunday school picture.

31. Wiederhold, *Papsturkunden in Frankreich*, 794–95: confirmation by Eugenius III of possessions of the archbishopric. The new castles are Montels and Poilhes (on the western side of the Capestang marsh), Ventenac and a rebuilt Canet (opposite each other on the lower Aude), Quillan (where the Aude emerges from its narrow canyon through the plateau of the Pays de Sault), and Gruissan (commanding the principal entrance into the lagoon that served as the port of Narbonne). All the castles mentioned in the confirmation of 1107 remained, but, apart from Canet, the others mentioned only in the oath of 1068 had disappeared, most likely fallen into disrepair, or become outdated and not thought worth rebuilding.

32. In his fight with Ermengard's father (c. 1119), Richard made a major point of the documents he found in his archives, especially those from Guifred's reign: *HGL* 5:860 (original MS Baluze 392, no. 579). On writing and "the truth" in Gregorian political thought, see Cheyette, "Invention of the State."

33. My account of these events follows R. Bousquet, "Civilisation romane," 92–93; and

Kaiser, *Bischoffsherrschaft*, 266–71. Bousquet's thesis on the Rouergue in the eleventh and twelfth centuries was never published; so despite the abundance of published cartularies from the region, its history remains obscure. See also Biget, "Épiscopat du Rouergue," n. 32.

34. Here is a description of le Lévezou, half way between Rodez and Millau, in the 1955 edition of the *Guide Bleu Cévennes-Languedoc*: "c'est un haut plateau désert, nu, triste et froid, couvert de landes de bruyères, de fougères et d'ajoncs, dominé de mamelons dénudés; terres froides où ne s'acclimatent que de maigres cultures de seigle et de sarrasin, sans autre beauté que l'immensité mêmes de ses horizons." The unusual patronymic of Raymond Frotardi (bishop c. 1095) suggests a link to the men by the name of Frotard who controlled the area between le Lévezou and the Tarn, just downriver from Millau (see Bousquet, "Civilisation romane," 93). Adhemar, bishop from c. 1099 to c. 1144, was Raymond's cousin: Dufour, *Evêques d'Albi*, 85. Other identifications have been with the family of Cantobre (east across the Larzac from Millau) or with that of Belcastel, down the Aveyron from Rodez: Biget, "Épiscopat du Rouergue," n. 168. Bishop Hugh: Wiederhold, *Papsturkunden*, 874–75.

35. Kaiser, *Bischofsherrschaft*, 317. Luchaire, *Etudes sur les actes de Louis VII*, no. 367.

36. MS Doat 57, fol. 24 (988–89).

37. *HGL* 5:399 (MS Doat 57, fol. 46) (1032). Other examples from the charters of Saint-Paul are MS Latin 5211 D, no. 5 (1036); *HGL* 5:534 (MS Doat 57, fol. 56) (1066); MS Doat 57, fol. 68 (a donation by the bishop himself) (1080); MS Doat 57, fol. 85 (lumping together archbishop, abbot, clergy, count, and viscount) (1096). The dangers of alienation continued to be real, even in the thirteenth century. In the 1220s, Peter Amiel, archbishop of Narbonne and stalwart supporter of King Louis VIII, gave his sister Maria all the honors and rights he had received as camerarius of the cathedral of Béziers from Simon de Montfort, leader of the Albigensian Crusade: MS Doat 55, fol. 340.

38. *Cart. Béziers*, nos. 70, 71 (1057–61), completed by no. 58. Ibid., no. 66 (1053).

39. Teudaldus reports the clergy saying, "We have this *judicium veritatis* that Isimbert held the horn with the ink with which that testament was written when Pons called the Black, canon of Saint-Nazaire, departed to visit the Holy Sepulchre" (*Cart. Béziers*, no. 77); and in response to Bishop Arnold, "We have a *cartam et judicium veritatis* that Bishop Stephan gave that gift to the canons of Saint-Nazaire" (*Cart. Béziers*, no. 85). In the Carolingian texts he was reading, the term *judicium veritatis* referred to court judgments; in Teutaldus's mind, however, "judgment of truth" referred to any written document, a charter of gift or a testament. None of those Carolingian texts as they existed in the Saint-Nazaire archives have survived, but there is a series from the monastery of Montoliou, on the Montagne Noire east of Carcassonne, that thanks to seventeenth- and eighteenth-century copyists escaped the ravages of time and revolutionary bonfires. The following textual comparison serves as evidence for my hypothesis about the model of these three documents in the Béziers cartulary. *Cart. Béziers*, no. 66: "Ubi venerunt clerici Sancti Nazarii Sedis Biterrensis in villa que vocant Aspirano Bernardus claviger et prepositus . . . ante Ermengaudo de Casalis et filio [s]uo Matfredo . . . et ceterorum bonorum hominum. Et querelaverunt et proclamaverunt se de Odone Bernardo et de . . . de ipsa ecclesia que est sita in villa Bitignano. . . . Quod ut audierunt seniores . . . interrogaverunt ipsos clericos de ipsa interpellatione si haberent cartam aut ullum judicium veritatis. Et ipsi clerici respondentes dixerunt: Nos habemus talem judicium veritatis, quod Isimbertus . . . tenuit cornu cum tincta de quo fuit scriptus illud testamentum. . . . Ast vero dicti seniores ut audierunt clericis talem rationem fatentes, sciscitaverunt Odonem et fratres suos qui de hoc responderunt. Et illi dixerunt: nos non habemus aliam scripturam. Sed avus noster et pater noster tenuerunt ipsam ecclesiasm . . . per alodem. Et illi seniores . . . judicaverunt inter eos bataliam cum scuto et baculo et prolongaverunt placitum usque ad aliud placitum. . . . In eorum presentia venerunt supradicti clerici et querelaverunt se sicuti soliti erant proclamare, de Odone . . . et

de suis fratribus . . . quod tollunt Domino deo et Sancto Nazario supradictaum ecclesiam et tenent malum ordinem. Et illi e contrario respondentes: Nos non tollimus vobis ipsam ecclesiam . . . sed vidimus eam tenere ad patrem nostrum omnibus diebus vite sue." *HGL* 5:137 (918): "Cum in Dei nomine resideret Aridemandus episcopus sedis Tolosae civitatis, cum viro venerabili Bernardo, qui est missus advocatus Raymundo comite Tolosae civitatis et marchio . . . una cum abbatibus, presbyteris, judices, scaphinos, et regimburgos . . . qui jussis causam audire, dirimere, et legibus definire, id est . . . et aliorum plurimorum bonorum hominum qui cum eos residebant in mallo publico in castro Ausona in die sabbato. Ibique in eorum praesentia veniens homo nomine Adalbertus . . . dicebat: Domne episcope et vos judices, jubete me audire et facite mihi justitiam de iste Arifonso, abbate S. Johannis Baptistae Castri Malaste. . . . Iste . . . abbas et ipsa congregatio . . . retinent vilare cujus vocabulum est Villa-Fedosi . . . injuste et malum ordine. . . . Tunc interrogaverunt ipsi judices . . . jam dicto abbate, qui respondere vellis de ac causa. . . . Et Soniarius [advocatus] stetit et dixit: Non retinet iste abbas . . . cui ego vocem prosequor, ipsum villarem. . . . injuste et malum ordine, sed legibus eum acquisierunt antecessores sui per scriptura emtionis [*sic*] legalibus factus. . . . Cum autem ipse episcopus . . . et ipse judices audissent Soniario mandatarium . . . sic respondentem . . . ordinaverunt Soniario mandatarium ut aramiret suas scriptura et litteras dominicas quod ille ibidem postulavit. . . . Iterum ad ipsum placitum . . . venit Arifonsus abba et advocatus Soniarius . . . in praesentia jam dicto ep[iscopo] . . . et sic praesentavit ipsos praeceptos. . . . Rursum vero nos episcopus et judices . . . interrogavimus Adalberto . . . si potebat habere scripturas aut testes aut ullum judicium veritatis ut possit approbare quod beneficius debet esse de seniore suo." See also *HGL* 2:331, 5:97, 160. Such Carolingian-style judgments survived in a somewhat decayed form in the counties of the Pyrenees into the early eleventh century. See *HGL* 5:337 (Elne, 1000), 356 (Cerdagne, 1010), 366 (Besalú, 1018). Compare *HGL* 5:359 (Béziers, 1013) and 374 (Narbonne, 1023).

40. "[S]icut sonat in praeceptis regum": *HGL* 5:536.

41. Compare the story told King Alfons of Aragon concerning his family's acquisition of Carcassonne, in Cheyette, " 'Sale' of Carcassonne," 831–32.

42. Guifred: *HGL* 5:540; Richard and Aymeri II: ibid., 831; Ermengard: Inv. Rocques, *Viscomte*, nos. 259, 266.

43. For details, see Biget, "Épiscopat du Rouergue," 196–98; his reading of this change as class conflict within the nobility must surely be taken with a grain of salt.

44. Auriac, *Histoire de l'ancienne cathédrale d'Alby*, 51–53, 184–96; Kaiser, *Bischofsherrschaft*, 282–84; Dufour, *Evêques d'Albi*, 35–40; *HGL* 5:1333. Castaldo, *Eglise d'Agde*, 35–41.

45. Béziers: *Cart. Béziers*, nos. 166, 187, 188. Narbonne: Wiederhold, *Papsturkunden*, 720–22 nn. Others: Wiederhold, *Papsturkunden*, 840 (the monks of Aniane occupy the church of Cresel "per violentiam"), 838–39, 842–43 (reform of nunnery of Saint-Félix-de-Montseau by the bishop of Maguelone); British Library, MS Harley 3570, first document (unnumbered): letter of Urban III on complaint of the archbishop of Narbonne that the abbot of Saint-Pons "ecclesias . . . secularibus potestatibus fultus invadat" (Wiederhold, *Papsturkunden*, 722 n. 4).

46. The text is printed and commented on in Bisson, "Organized Peace in Southern France and Catalonia." The date of the promulgation is uncertain. It is known only by a confirmation of 1155 (and later reconfirmations). Bisson (apparently unaware of the particulars of local politics at the time), dates it on other grounds to 1145–47.

47. See the next chapter.

48. Comminges: Bisson, "Organized Peace," 221. Toulouse: probably as part of a peace treaty, Raymond V granted the men of the Trencavels forty days to make amends for breach of his peace before he would take action: *HGL* 5:1270. The other surviving documents of the

treaty are *HGL* 5:1267–69. Rodez and other cities: Bisson, "Organized Peace," 221–22. The taxes were called *compensum* in the clerical Latin of Uzès, *communia pacis* in that of Rodez: (Hoffmann, *Gottesfriede und Treuga Dei*, 117, 119; Kaiser, *Bischofsherrschaft*, 268, 317; *GC* 1, *instrum.* 50; *HGL* 5:1201). Béziers: *Cart. Béziers*, no. 232. Taxes at Albi: *GC* 1, *instrum.* 6 (1191).

49. Kaiser, *Bischofsherrschaft*, 283–84; Compayré, *Etudes sur l'Albigeois*, 141. Kaiser gives a full account of the building of episcopal lordships in the other Trencavel cities and, for Agde, his work may be supplemented with Castaldo, *Eglise d'Agde*.

50. Confirmation by Paschal II: *GC* 6, *instrum.* 433. The printed evidence is summarized in Kaiser, *Bischofsherrschaft*, 288–90; the handful of unpublished charters in AD Aude add nothing substantial.

51. See Mundy, *Liberty and Political Power*, 19–20. In 1077 Bishop Isarn referred to Count William as "senior mei": *GC* 13, *instrum.* 9. That same year, William granted the canons of Saint-Etienne of Toulouse the right to freely elect their bishop: *HGL* 5:629. It was only in 1105 or 1106, after the death of Isarn, however, that they finally had a chance to exercise this right. After Alphonse Jordan's return, writes Mundy, "episcopal synodal justice in criminal matters is never heard of again."

52. Guillaume de Puylaurens, *Chronique* (ed. Duvernoy), 40–41.

53. Arnold Amaury, the papal legatine leader of the Crusades, Cistercian though he was, tried after the defeat of Count Raymond VI to claim for himself as archbishop of Narbonne the title of duke of Narbonne: Emery, *Heresy and Inquisition*, 60–62. The bishops of Agde battled into the fourteenth century to be recognized as viscounts of their city: see Cheyette, "Sovereign and the Pirates." The bishops of Mende fought long to be recognized as counts of the Gévaudan: Strayer, *Reign of Philip the Fair*, 192.

54. The year 1112: *HGL* 5:827. For the later events, see below, chaps. 16 and 17.

CHAPTER 7. LORDSHIP

1. "[D]ominationibus, mero et mixto imperio, jurisdictio, exercitu et cavalcata, feudis, feudalibus, albergis, censis, usaticis, quistis, taschis, agrariis et fructum omnium portionibus, venationibus, piscationibus, pascuis, herbagiis, nemoribus, silvis, ripariis, lapidicinis, aurifo-dinis, argentifodinis quae vulgariter minaria nuncupantur, terris et vineis possessionibus cultis et incultis, molendinis, furnis proprietatibus et iuribus aliis": AD Hérault G274.

2. The term comes from Justinian's *Digest*, bk. 2, I (*De Jurisdictione*), 3, quoting Ulpian: "simple (*merum*) *imperium*" is defined as being "in possession of the power of the sword for the purpose of punishing evildoers," and "mixed *imperium*" is "that which is evinced in granting *bonorum possessio*" (*Digest of Justinian* [trans. Monro], 1:66). For the use of this distinction but without the Roman terminology, see the dispute discussed at the end of this chapter. During much of Ermengard's lifetime it was not the only or even the predominant way of distinguishing one kind of justice from another.

3. Inv. Rocques, *Niort*, no. 43, where the lord of Niort surrenders to the archbishop the "forciis et justiciis" he has, except for justice of homicide and adultery in Niort. Compare, e.g., Inv. Rocques, *Gruissan*, no. 1 (1084); *HGL* 5:831 (1112); and other twelfth-century documents that describe grants of justices or disputes over them.

4. Southern, *Making of the Middle Ages*, 86.

5. In the scholarship of the last generation, this practice has been stimulated largely by the work of Georges Duby, first in his pathbreaking *La société dans la région mâconnaise*, and then in works of popularization such as *The Early Growth of the European Economy*. It appears

in almost all the literature inspired by these works. For a recent defense of the view that violence was the root of seignorial power after the year 1000, see Bisson, "Feudal Revolution."

6. This historiographic story has never been fully told and is much in need of telling. It is a repeatedly recurring theme in Boureau, *Droit de cuissage: Histoire de la fabrication d'un mythe (XIIe–XXe siècle)*, especially chap. 7.

7. The bibliography is now immense. The most important titles are mentioned in the notes to Bisson, "Feudal Revolution." For extended treatment, see Fossier, *Enfance de l'Europe, Xe–XIIe siècles;* and Poly and Bournazel, *Mutation féodale, Xe–XIIe siècles* (trans. Higgitt, *Feudal Transformation, 900–1200*). Barthélemy began a rapidly growing critique in "Mutation féodale a-t-elle eu lieu?" and now extended in *Mutation de l'an mil a-t-elle eu lieu*, and idem, *An mil et la paix de Dieu*. See also White, "Repenser la violence"; and the debate in *Past and Present* following the appearance of Bisson's article.

8. *HGL* 5:831 (1112); and Inv. Rocques, *Viscomte*, no. 259 (undated).

9. See above, chap. 4.

10. The year 1163: "excepto corpore ipsius castri, retento mihi . . . in praedicta medietate potestativo et alberga . . . et retentis similiter justitiis quae ad potestatem pertinent et similiter retenta . . . expeditione seu cavalgada in toto castro et omnium hominum ibidem commorantium": *HGL* 5:1273. In 1177 she likewise confirmed Gausbert of Coumiac's testamentary donation in the same castle "salvo potestativo meo": MS Doat 58, fol. 140. In 1182: "de meo iure et dominio in vestrum transfero omnes feodos et quidquid iure dominii in eis . . . habeo quoscumque in omnia terra mea et potestativo meo . . . acquirere poteritis": MS Doat 58, fol. 142. In 1215: "quam honorem jure potestativi sine certo usatico et servicio et foriscapio a me tenebat" is the description of Calva's holding: MS Doat 58, fol. 154. The confirmation of Ermengard's 1182 grant does not mention adultery among the reserved crimes. (Coumiac is now a farm in the commune of Cessenon.)

11. "[S]cilicet potestativum, albergam, cavalgadam, justitias, firmantias et omnino quae ad vicecomitem Narbonensis in eodem castro . . . ac districtu pertinere solebant": MS Doat 55, fol. 241.

12. MS Doat 58, fols. 140 (1179), 144 (1184).

13. MS Doat 58, fols. 130, 148, 154, 165; AD Hérault G274; *HGL* 8:1735. Only in this way can we understand how Roger of Béziers could give the *guidagium* on the *camino Francigena* to the lords (plural) of Rieux (*HGL* 8:322), or how Ouveilhan, from which an important family took its name and on whose territory it possessed not one but several castles (see below, chap. 9), could also appear in the testament of Peter Raymond of Béziers (Cart. Trencavel, fol. 179; MS Doat 40, fol. 98).

14. Because some of the lordship rights were shared with the viscount of Béziers, a copy was apparently transmitted to him and eventually found its way into the Cart. Trencavel, fols. 124v–27v. The document is titled "scriptum commemorationis de censis et usibus honoris que sancti Poncii habet unumquemque annum in castro Perriaci et de indominicatura"; at the end, Pons of Auriac calls himself the abbey's "ministralis." There is no indication in the text itself that Pons was reading from his own written records or that the sacristan's scribe was copying such records, although, of course, such a possibility cannot be excluded. Field names or section names of the village territory are only rarely given, but the nature of the holdings as they follow each other in the account—vineyards, a few grainfields, gardens, more grainfields, more vines, and so forth—suggest strongly that he is surveying the village section by section; in conveyances of individual pieces of agricultural land, vineyards are most often bounded by other vineyards, gardens by gardens, grainfields by grainfields, indicating that each section of the Occitan village territory was devoted to a particular type of crop within a general system of polyculture. For a detailed description of this Mediterranean

polyculture and its distribution in an Italian setting, see Toubert, *Structures du Latium médié-val*, 199–294.

15. The *tascha* on grain and the malt render (*bracaticum*) must have been fixed amounts or fixed percentages, like the fourths or occasional fifths, for some fields paid only halves or quarters of these renders. The lands of Saint-Pons *indominicato* amounted to eight *quartairada* and six *medallata* of vine, two "fields," a terraced field, twenty *sestairada* of grainfields, some otherwise unspecified "land," a "great garden," and another vineyard and an olive orchard that Pons of Auriac himself holds as a mortgage for the modest sum of three solidi. These were located in more than ten different sections of the village territory. There is no indication of labor services being used to work this land, and the renders of food for eight men twice a day suggests day laborers hired when necessary during the season and fed by the four households subject to this render.

16. For more on these forms of holding, see the next chapter.

17. Mentioned in an undated agreement concerning rights in Peyriac negotiated by Roger of Béziers and Peter of Minerve; the parties involved place it between 1142 and 1163: *Cart. Trencavel*, fol. 109. *Cart. Douzens* A, no. 29.

18. For example, *Cart. Béziers*, no. 153 (1142): the cathedral chapter leases land on the bank of the Orb River to a tenant who holds neighboring riverbank land from Pons of Thézan.

19. The use of mortgage contracts (*pignoratio*) in Occitania is extraordinarily complex. I have completed a study of the phenomenon, which will be published elsewhere.

20. See Cheyette, " 'Sale' of Carcassonne."

21. MS Mél. Colb. 414, nos. 4 (944?), 11 (991?), 13 (989–96), 12 (1010), and a number of others, all from the tiny village of Escales on the Aude River, about half way between Narbonne and Carcassonne; sales are of dwellings in the village, plots of land, vineyards, all for very small sums of money. There is no mention in any of them of lordship dues. *Cart. Béziers*, no. 61 (1026): sale of two pieces of land at Lieuran (about ten kilometers north of Béziers) *ad laborandum*, under no lordship, for fifty solidi.

22. One of the earliest examples is *Cart. Béziers*, no. 24 (955): the vinedresser is to have the first four harvests for himself and afterward to pay a fourth of the harvest as rent to the church of Béziers. Grapevines take at least three years to mature. For a general discussion, see Bourin-Derruau, *Villages médiévaux*, 1:96–101.

23. The earliest example I have found is *Cart. Douzens* A, no. 58 (1143); the earliest from Pexiora follow soon after: H Malte Puysubran (Pexiora), 1, nos. 54, 55, 63; 17, no. 2. Compare AMN GG1931 (1152): lease of a grainfield to the hospital of Saint-Just for an entrance fee of twenty-five solidi, reserving a fourth of harvest and all transfer dues.

24. The rarity of charters of leasehold in ecclesiastical cartularies should not surprise us. They had no use in establishing rights to land and therefore were hardly worth copying. Those that did get copied involved leases granted by those who held land of the cathedral chapter and therefore owed seignorial dues or some other recognition of its rights at the time of transfer: *Cart. Béziers*, nos. 75 (1067) lease of a house, 83 (1080) of a tavern at the market gate, 103 (1097) of a building lot. In 1107, when the canons of Saint-Nazaire give a pasture by the river's edge to be turned into a grainfield, without demanding an entrance fee, the laborer who receives it has to supply his own seed and use his own animals to carry the canon's share of the crop to their granary; he is not pennyless either: *Cart. Béziers*, no. 109. The absence of an entrance fee here, or in a later grant of a field to be put to agricultural use at the river's edge (no. 153), is probably to be explained by the amount of clearing to be done and the delay expected before that work would produce a profitable crop. Compare AD Pyrénées-Orientales B35 (1146): the camerarius of the abbey of Lagrasse leases a spring near Salses to be dammed and made into a pond; the abbey and their fellow lords will provide the

animals and equipment to do the work and the food for the family who are doing it; the lessees pay an entrance fee of 52 sol. Roussillon.

25. For the role of Cistercian administrators in developing secular fiscal administrations in the following century, see Schneider, *Vom Klosterhaushalt zum Stadt- und Staatshaushalt*, who mentions in passing a Cistercian *conversus* who rescued the finances of the archbishop of Cologne in the 1160s (26–27). Berman, *Medieval Agriculture*, does not have anything to say directly about record keeping, but her description of the organization of Cistercian granges, especially their ability to respond to market demand, presumes some kind of centralized administration and record keeping to go along with it. I have not been able to locate any detailed study of Templar and Hospitaler financial administration, but the heavy obligations placed on European commanderies to supply money, horses, and transportation for their members in the Latin kingdoms of the east also suggest well-organized record keeping and administration. There are a few words on this subject in Barber, *New Knighthood*, 251–54; and Selwood, *Knights of the Cloister*, 169–80.

26. H Malte Douzens 37, nos. 10a and 10b, and a defective copy no. 4. For Roger's departure on crusade, see *Cart. Douzens* D, no. 4.

27. H Malte Douzens 37, nos. 9 and 10c; five witnesses are listed "qui istam honorem monstraverunt."

28. At least one inventory of a Trencavel vicecomital honor has survived in writing, however: in a recognizance of fief in the village of Mèze, the description of the fief (oven, fields of forage crops and grain, *dominationes*) is followed by a list of vicecomital landholdings that is similar in all ways to those we have seen. It is a list of fields, vines, and other holdings defined by their boundaries, which are mainly the names of the holders of neighboring fields, vines, and so forth. Cart. Trencavel, fol. 160 (1175).

29. The following discussion is based on the documents in H Malte Puysubran (Pexiora), 1.

30. Fortunately, the archives of the military orders in coastal Occitania somehow escaped the burning and pillaging of the wars of religion in the sixteenth century and the revolution at the end of the eighteenth, but it would be sheer fantasy to imagine that the bundles of parchment are still as thick now as they were, let us say, in 1200.

31. Calculated from the names of boundary landholders in a donation by Archbishop Arnust to the abbey of Saint-Paul: MS Doat 57, fol. 3; MS Baluze 82, fol. 144 (published in fragmentary form in *HGL* 5:130). One could argue that some of these landholders are peasants, and so it might be, but some of the same names (and thus the same persons?) appear as witnesses to early tenth-century archiepiscopal charters, and some of the landholders are priests; at the very least, we seem to be looking at freeholders, whether they pushed the plow themselves or not.

32. H Malte Puysubran, 13, no. 2: a *memoria* sworn by the village consuls, undated, but in a late thirteenth- or early fourteenth-century hand; a hole has eliminated the figure for households valued at between 100 and 200 liv. Tourn. For a discussion of these tax evaluations, see below, chap. 16.

33. Bernard Miro of Laurac, for example, who holds a tithe as security on a loan of seventy solidi in H Malte Puysubran, 1, no. 31, and who appears as a donor in ibid., no. 5. Probably the same as the Bernard Miro of Laurac who witnessed the testament of Viscount Bernard Ato in 1118: *HGL* 5:865.

34. In addition to Bernard Miro (previous note), Peter William of Roquefort, one of the Carcassonne rebels of 1120, and Roger de la Tor, one of those who guaranteed the repentent rebels in 1125: *HGL* 5:917.

35. "[P]ropter necessitatem atque penuriam quam nos habuimus": H Malte Puysubran, 1, no. 9. The donation of 1118 is at no. 3; its text ambiguously suggests that the Hospitalers

had loaned money to Pons and another relative, Arnold Guitard, and taken these plots of land as security.

36. Guilabert of Laurac: *HGL* 5:738, 824, 837 (and Cart. Trencavel, fol. 139), 849, 867, 868, 908. Missing from the published edition of the mutual oaths of Bernard Ato and Philippa (*HGL* 5:845), he is included among the witnesses in Cart. Trencavel, fol. 33. Although his prominence in the village is unmistakable, I have found only one direct gift from Guilabert to the Hospitalers of Pexiora—a man and his family and holding in the village of Laurabuc in 1122: H Malte Puysubran, 24, no. 1. Gifts on Guilabert's death: H Malte Puysubran, 1, no. 5. Peter William: *HGL* 5:917.

37. One striking example: H Malte Puysubran, 14, no. 6.

38. Ibid., 14, nos. 6, 11; ibid., 18, nos. 6, 7. Arnold's rights eventually came into the Hospitalers' possession, and with them all his parchments.

39. *HGL* 5:923–25. The value of the mortgages granted in these few surviving documents amounts to more than twenty-four hundred solidi.

40. Cart. Trencavel, fols. 218–19 (undated).

41. H Malte Puysubran, 30, nos. 1, 2. The names place the property involved to the east of Villefranche-de-Lauragais, about half way between Pexiora and Toulouse.

42. See the beginning of this chapter.

43. Detailed account in Cheyette, " 'Sale' of Carcassonne." Another nearly contemporary example: the agreement between Count Roger and his cousin, the count of Foix, in 1063: "et de ipsas justicias de comitatu . . . ego . . . [tibi] medietatem de ipsas justicias no t'en tolre ne no las devedare" (*HGL* 5:524).

44. See *HGL* 5:831 (1112); and the lengthy tale Richard told of his conflicts with Aymeri II, below, chap. 11.

45. *HGL* 5:831.

46. *Cart. Béziers*, nos. 139, 140 (whose text is less corrupt than that in *HGL* 5:975): "quistam et firmancias, placita et justicias, et manleitis [*sic*] . . . in villa Biterrensi habeat sicut Arnaldus . . . cum esset episcopus habuit"; Roger and Raymond "deinceps non accipiant fidejussores vel aliquas aliquo modo justicias." That their widowed mother the Viscountess Cecilia took part (in fact is named first) in the mortgage suggests that Raymond and Roger were still under age.

47. Ermengard: *HGL* 5:1273 (1163). Trencavels: *HGL* 5:1018: a grant of a castle in fief by Roger of Béziers "salva mea fidelitate et meo seniorivo et mea justitia." *HGL* 5:1142: Raymond Trencavel grants the monastery and inhabitants of Saint-Thibéry freedom from military service (*cavalgadam*) "et totas justitias . . . et placitare per meam curiam praeter homicidium et esguogozamentum [*sic*, adultery]". Other examples: *HGL* 5:1105, 1134; and Cart. Trencavel, fol. 160. In 1190, Viscount Roger went so far as to give the Hospitalers of Campagnoles "adultery and theft," but there is no mention of homicide: *HGL* 8:403. Justices as part of a dowry: *HGL* 5:1092 (1146, confirming a gift of the previous generation).

48. As might be expected, the earliest thirteenth-century documents record disputes over who has the right to exercise jurisdiction over particular criminals rather than actual trials or convictions, for example, AC Narbonne AA109, fols. 25 (1253), 28 (1254); AA469 (1261). To the best of my knowledge the earliest records of actual criminal cases in this region date only from the fourteenth century: for example, AC Miraval-Lauragais S1.

49. Sabarthès, *Dictionnaire topographique*, s.v. Fourches, Fourques.

50. For an example, see the dispute over justices at Alzonne, below.

51. Béziers: *HGL* 5:840. Narbonne: Inv. Rocques, *Acquisitions*, no. 110.

52. Formula: Inv. Rocques, *Gruissan*, no. 1 (1084): grant of the castle of Gruissan and its "domination"; *HGL* 5:858 (1117): promise by the newly "reformed" abbot of Saint-Paul, Narbonne, to recover the property he had alienated to his friends; two examples among

many. Mines: *HGL* 8:412 (1191): agreement between Roger of Béziers and the family of Termes concerning lordship over the mines of Palairac and elsewhere in the Termenès. Markets: *HGL* 5:1130 (1152): Raymond Trencavel complains that his "minister" in Limoux has turned to his own use "omnes justitias et mensuram ipsam que vocatur emina et mejeiram olei et omnes fallos et putatorias et retrodecimum de annona de mercato."

53. The dispute: *HGL* 5:1134, X (1153). On the Escafredi, see Cheyette, " 'Sale' of Carcassonne," nn. 128, 145.

54. A unique appearance for this bishop, Raymond of Lautrec. His predecessor, Amelius Raymond of Le Puy, was one of the clerics who arbitrated a dispute between Viscount Bernard Ato and Archbishop Richard of Narbonne around 1107 (*HGL* 5:801), witnessed the oath of fidelity that Count Alphonse Jordan swore to Bernard Ato around 1123 (*HGL* 5:907), and arbitrated the dispute between the count and Viscount Roger over control of the bishopric of Albi (*HGL* 5:980), all occasions when the appearance of this prelate is not surprising. Bishop Raymond's presence in 1153 is perhaps better understood as a familial connection with the Escafredi, whose roots were in the region between Albi and Lautrec.

55. "[Q]uia facta erant ad communem utilitatem tam eorum quam aliorum qui aliquid juris habent."

56. The distinction is of sufficient importance to quote the Latin at length: "Si homines qui sunt proprii juris eorum eandem villam habitantes vel eorum militum qui in eadem habent homines habuerint aliquas lites vel causes de terris vel de vineis vel de debitis aut etiam de aliis rebus propter quas non desideratur corporalis vindicta, tunc dominus Raymundus Trencavellus non exigat ab eis fidanciam neque justitiam. Si autem homines habuerint conflictum . . . veluti de furto vel de homicidio seu de sacrilegio vel de perjurio vel de sanguinis effusione aut de fascinatione seu de adulterio et de fractione viarum publicarum et omnino . . . in qua est desideranda corporalis poena, in his . . . accipiat dominus Raymundus fidancias et justitiam tam ab hominibus eorum quam ab aliis omnibus hominibus qui habitant in eadem villa cujuscumque sint." *HGL* 5:1134. It is a resolution that does not easily fit into the paradigm I sketched out years ago in Cheyette, "Suum cuique tribuere."

CHAPTER 8. SERFDOM AND THE DUES OF DOMINATION

1. "Bodily lord": *Cart. Lézat*, no. 1495 (1179); "homo indominicatus": *Cart. Trencavel*, fol. 124v. *Cart. Douzens* A, no. 1, à propos of Bernard Modul: "quia ipse homo noster erat ad faciendum nostram voluntatem"; no. 31: "ad omnem vestram voluntatem faciendam pro vestro proprio alodio ac jure plenario in perpetuum possideatis"; other quotes from nos. 33, 51. Such donations are frequent in the charter collections of the military orders, but they show up as well in dowries, grants of fief, and other transactions. Three examples of manumissions from the region of Agde are discussed in Bourin-Derreau, *Villages médiévaux*, 1:210ff.; more generally the problem of serfdom and of "les hommes donnés" are discussed in *Villages médiévaux*, 131–32, 210–17. See also Magnou-Nortier, *Société laïque*, 539–46. Neither resolves all of the problems that the peculiarities of Occitan serfdom present. There seems no harm in looking once again at these people and at the issues their status raises.

2. One of the best recent discussions, placing a detailed portrait of one region's serfdom in a European-wide comparative context, is Freedman, *Origins of Peasant Servitude in Medieval Catalonia*. Barthélemy presents a vigorously polemical view of the problem for the period that concerns us here in "Qu'est-ce que le servage, en France, au XIe siècle?" with references to earlier French scholarship. Many of the phenomena I discuss here were described a half century ago by Duby in the Mâconnais but little attended to since then: see Duby, *Société aux XIe et XIIe siècles dans la région mâconnaise*, 47, 123, 257, among many pages where

the subject is mentioned. Because freedom is the other side of any definition of serfdom, there is much to be drawn from the articles in Fried, *Abendländische Freiheit*.

3. One of the rare occurrences: *Cart. St-Etienne d'Agde*, no. 300 (1140), discussed later in this chapter.

4. For numerous examples of the use of this term for peasant services, see the index rerum of *Cart. Douzens*, s.v. They appear along with other property rights: salt pans, mills, queste, forced payments (*forcie*), justices. What may be referred to are corvées such as the ox-cartage or pack-ass rights granted to the castellans of Fontjoncouse in 1108: Cart. Fontjoncouse, no. 9. In a document of 1144, *servitium* is explicitly defined as bringing food at Christmas for three fighting men—a quarter of pork, three little barrels of wine, and a sétier of barley "and other services which peasants [*villani*] do for their lords": MS Doat 55, fol. 212. It can also weigh on urban houses and their inhabitants and refer to military service, watch duty, and taxes: MS Doat 59, fol. 142. More generically it was used to speak of the duties of someone who holds a castle, "ad meum servitium vel veram fidelitatem": *HGL* 5:1037 (an 1139 copy of a charter drawn up between 1067 and 1077). Archbishop Richard could speak of the "servitium [et] fidelitatem" he would receive from Viscount Bernard Ato: *HGL* 5:801 (1107). For other examples, see Brunel, *Plus anciennes chartes*, Glossaire, s.v. servizi. What appears to be the earliest Occitan document using *servitus* is an Agde testament of 1147, which uses a strikingly Roman vocabulary: Gouron, "Liber und libertas," 200, the best discussion of the language of freedom and servitude in the region. On the various meanings of serfdom, Devroey makes some useful distinctions in "Men and Women in Early Medieval Serfdom."

5. *HGL* 5:1134. Each side was to appear with oath takers, and each was then to select two or three from the opponent's group who would then collectively swear to the truth.

6. *Cart. Lézat*, no. 1495 (1179).

7. On whom see Mundy, *Repression of Catharism at Toulouse*, 292–94, and idem, *Liberty and Political Power*, 52–53.

8. On Tosetus, see Mundy, *Repression of Catharism*, 270–76; final compromise: *Cart. Lézat*, no. 1498 (1181).

9. *Cart. Lézat*, no. 1489. The land, described as a "trossiculum de barta ad trahendum," is given in fief. On these peasant fiefs, see the classic articles of Richardot, "Fief roturier," and Ourliac, "Hommage servile."

10. *Cart. Lézat*, nos. 1462–1500.

11. "[R]eddant inde eis agrarium de labore terre in eadem terra vel in area ubi blatum teretur ad electionem dominorum et reacapte quando evenerit VI. d., si clamorem habent domini de eis per hoc fevum fidantias inde habeant, et IIII.^{or} d. justiciam si inculpantur favatarii," all of it scribal boilerplate found in dozens of grants of peasant fiefs in the Lézat cartulary: no. 1489. They collected equivalent dues and exercised *dominatio* over other people in the area as well: no. 1490 (1171–72). As the land came into Lézat's hands, so did the Raissac brothers' archives, and thanks to the lack of discrimination of the hired notaries who put the cartulary together, finally into our hands as well.

12. Mundy assumes that Arnold of Villanova, a landholder in the area (*Cart. Lézat*, nos. 1079, 1462, 1465, 1466, 1488), is related to the family from which Pons of Villanova comes: *Repression of Catharism*, 300. William Peter of Caraman: ibid., 197 n. 1.; Mundy, *Men and Women at Toulouse*, 137.

13. *Cart. Lézat*, no. 1079.

14. At Toulouse, a *quarton* was three *émines*, but the value of the latter in modern measures is not known; in the region, it varied from twenty-six liters at Montpellier to eighty at Agde (Zupko, *French Weights and Measures*, 63). There are six saints by the name of Julian in the ecclesiastical calendar, and their feast days spread from January to August; that of Saint Thomas is December 21.

15. *Cart. Lézat*, nos. 1080, 1462–68, 1479–90, 1494–1501.

16. *Cart. Douzens* A, no. 1. On the three individuals discussed in the following paragraphs, see the introduction to *Cart. Douzens*, xxxv–xxxvi. For Bernard Modul or Modol, see ibid., index nominum.

17. *Cart. St-Etienne d'Agde*, no. 300.

18. Ermengard's arbitration: *Cart. Douzens*, no. 20 (1167). William Peter's gifts: nos. 4, 25, 41. Mills on the Aude: no. 13. Sale of Raymond of *Carancianum*: no. 33.

19. In 1163, 30 sol. Ugon. equaled 22 sol. Melg.: AD Aude G76 (1163); 100 sol. Ugon. would therefore equal 73 s. 4 d. Melg. or about 1.5 marcs of silver.

20. *Cart. Douzens* A, nos. 14, 17, 19; D, nos. 7, 18, 23. A "cascade" of leases is laid out, ibid., A, no. 2, and discussed in the introduction to the cartulary, xxxi.

21. *Cart. Douzens* A, nos. 27, 64.

22. Stephen Udalger, a wealthy peasant who died in 1110, held two *masatae* from the lord of Caussiniojuls. He had another lord as well, Peter Rainardi, one of the powerful nobles of Béziers. (On them, see Amado, "Famille aristocratique," 2:8–18.) Stephen's holdings lay scattered east and south of Béziers, from Aureilhan and Cabrials all the way to Fleury, half way to Narbonne. Many of the holdings were alods; some were peasant fiefs. Some he "bought to work"; others were worked by his "men and women." He was therefore a lord as well as a peasant. *Cart. Béziers*, no. 114.

23. Durliat summarizes the earlier views in *Finances publiques* before offering his own contrarian views: 195–203.

24. Examples: sale of a mansus in Narbonne, with the purchaser allowed to raise the walls as high as he wishes (MS Doat 57, fol. 77 [1091]); a mansus forms a boundary with a *domus*, and the two terms are used interchangeably (Cart. Fontjoncouse, no. 17 [1162]); a mansus is a farmstead (*Cart. Béziers*, no. 31 [969]). The examples could be multiplied beyond the reader's patience. I do not agree with the account of Magnou-Nortier, "Terre, la rente et le pouvoir dans les pays de Languedoc," 42ff., especially as it concerns the late tenth and eleventh centuries, but it would take a re-analysis of all her texts to demonstrate why, and this book is no place for such an exercise.

25. For a nuanced account of the French historiography on this question, see Barthélemy, "Qu'est-ce que le servage," 234–38.

26. Sigean: Inv. Rocques, *Sigean*, no. 2 (undated); in the French of the inventory, these are due from each *maison*; because the language of the inventory follows the Latin closely, this surely stands for *mansus*. Fontjoncouse: Cart. Fontjoncouse, no. 9 (1108); due "in omnibus mansis amasatis"—another striking attempt to disambiguate the term, using as a modifier the same word that Stephen Udalger does in his testament. Other examples in *Cart. St-Etienne d'Agde*, no. 355 (village of Mermian): one mansus owes two solidi and two sétiers of barley, two days of oxen work at planting, an ass and a man to bring in grain and at wine harvest, a man to beat grain, and an ass and man to bring it to the silo. See other examples in Magnou-Nortier, *Société laïque*, 136–47.

27. Elne: *HGL* 5:768. Pinard, the cheap, low-quality house wine you find in village cafes in Languedoc, seems the most likely equivalent for "IV sextarios currentes vilanos." Quillan: Inv. Rocques, *Quillan*, no. 98:28. Neither Magnou-Nortier, *Société laïque*, nor Bourin-Derruau, *Villages médiévaux*, gives anything as explicit as these texts.

28. On which, see Durliat, *Finances publiques*, 222–29, with references to earlier literature.

29. Earliest example: *Cart. Lézat*, no. 372. The next mentions of alberga do not appear in this cartulary until the third quarter of the eleventh century (no. 1577). For other areas of Occitania, see the discussions in Magnou-Nortier, *Société laïque*, 137, and Bourin-Derruau, *Villages médiévaux*, 1:131–32. Albergum to be rendered "between Christmas and Lent" (Inv.

Rocques, *Peyriac*, no. 17 [1200]) is but one example among many. Dogs: Inv. Rocques, *Sigean*, no. 1 (undated); *Albières*, no. 1 (1131).

30. Peyriac-Minervois: Cart. Trencavel, fols. 124v–27v. Meals for "men of the abbey" that were part of the dues of several peasants were not called albergum (for this document, see chap. 7). Fontjoncouse: Cart. Fontjoncouse, nos. 9, 26 (1121–45, since the archbishop is Arnold), 27 (datable c. 1185 on the basis of other documents mentioning the same village lords). Division among heirs and dowry: *Cart. Lézat*, nos. 140, 1152.

31. Pig: MS Doat 40, fol. 70 (1148); *Cart. Lézat*, no. 882. Wheat: *Cart. Douzens* A, no. 184 (1146) (approximating on the basis of the relation of the price of barley and wheat given in the following documents from 1150, and calculating the ratio of the solidus Ugon. of Carcassonne to the solidus Melg. at 65:50, as given by a mortgage contract of 1165 [MS Mél. Colb. 414, no. 46]); The prices in *Cart. Douzens* A, no. 48 (1154) seem to mark the height of the grain crisis. A whole series of land sales to the Templars in 1150 for quantities of grain, all of them in the spring, suggests its seriousness, even though the price of a sétier of wheat had only reached 2 sol. Ugon. (or 1 sol. 7 d. Melg.): *Cart. Douzens* A, nos. 177–80. Wine: *Cart. Lézat*, no. 1577.

32. Saint-Pons: Cart. Trencavel, fol. 35 (1171); Pons Mirabel: *Cart. Douzens*, no. 64.

33. Raissac, see above, this chapter, n. 6. Fontjoncouse: Cart. Fontjoncouse, no. 9, "Et si archiepiscopus voluerit accipere arberga in domibus rusticorum." Lézat: *Cart. Lézat*, no. 1597.

34. This practice seems to be primarily clerical; such provisions appear specifically only in their testaments: Archdeacon Bernard Rainardi, 1115 (MS Doat 55, fol. 148), Peter of Saint-Hilaire, 1148 (MS Doat 40, fol. 7), Archbishop Arnold of Lèvezou (*GC* 6, *instrum.* col. 38, no. 45), although some clergy did not specifically provide for them (Rainard of Maureilhan, 1154: *Cart. Béziers*, no. 182; Archdeacon Matfred, 1177: *Cart. Béziers*, no. 259), and some lay testaments appear to allow them as a possibility (Peter of Saint-Michael, 1155: H Malte Puysubran 1, no. 53; Berenger of Puisserguier: 1168, *Cart. Béziers*, no. 225; Alamanda, 1170: *Cart. Béziers*, no. 233). Later in the century such gifts seem to be institutionalized (and distanced?) through the office of the almoner (William Arnold, sacristan of Saint-Paul, 1179: MS Doat 57, fol. 139).

35. MS Doat 55, fol. 148 (1115); MS Doat 40, fol. 70 (1149); MS Doat 57, fol. 143 (1186). *Saumata* is not listed as a measure of quantity in Zupko, *French Weights and Measures*; the Old Occitan equivalent means "the quantity a pack animal can carry."

36. Froissart, *Chronicles* (trans. G. Brereton), 143–44.

37. MS Baluze 81, fol. 77; receptum seems here to be a synomym for albergum. Peter Raimundi's testament: Inv. Rocques, *Fontfroide*, no. 12; gift of a later Raymond of Bages to the hospital of Saint-Just in the presence of men such as Peter Raymond of Narbonne, Ugo of Plaigne, Peter Raymond Margalonis, and Jacob Bistani: AMN GG1832 (1177); his marriage to Englesa of Fontjoncouse (1182): Cart. Fontjoncouse, no. 21.

38. One of the issues Archbishop Richard thought he had settled with Roland of Fontjoncouse in 1109, it returned to exasperate his successor Arnold of Lèvezou: Cart. Fontjoncouse, nos. 9, 26.

39. Ibid.; Inv. Rocques, *Albières*, no. 1.

40. "Violencie": *HGL* 5:768. Saint-Ybars: *Cart. Lézat*, no. 1045 (1246), very late for our purposes, but it is hard to believe that much had changed in this regard since the twelfth century except for the institutional procedures that left documentation in their wake.

41. Béziers: *HGL* 5:978, *Cart. Béziers*, no. 139; Narbonne: MS Doat 48, fol. 28.

42. Scorcencs [the reading of this name is uncertain]: Cart. Trencavel, fol. 32 (1186); Moussoulens: ibid., fol. 156 (1175); Monthaut: *HGL* 5:957 (1137); Lézat: *Cart. Lézat*, no. 920; Saint-Pons: Cart. Trencavel, fol. 35 (1171). Ermengard demanded an albergum for ten

fighting men each year at *Coemeracum* (which I have not been able to identify) when it was given to Quarante: *HGL* 5:1273; it is listed immediately after her potestativum and before her right to justice and military service, which she also reserved. Albergum is listed in the company of the same in her gift to Archbishop Pons d'Arsac in 1176: MS Doat 55, fol. 241.

43. Raymond Trencavel's grant of the castle of Verdalle in the Tarn to Isarn of Puylaurent includes the provision "si ego ad partes illas applicuero, tu per te vel villicum tuum albergum quem habere . . . ut fiat disponas": *HGL* 5:1140. Archbishop Arnold's testament: *GC* 6, *instrum.* col. 38, no. 14.

44. See the next chapter.

45. *Cart. Lézat*, no. 372.

46. Lease contracts for a share of the crop often specify that the lord may count out his share in the field (in which case he presumably transports it himself) or that the tenant brings it to the lord's barn (in which case there is probably no check on whether it really is a quarter or a fifth of the produce).

47. All examples given by Bourin-Derruau, *Villages médiévaux*, 1:315–26, in her detailed account of the emergence of *probi homines* in Occitan villages during the twelfth century.

48. Ibid., 325–26.

CHAPTER 9. ERMENGARD'S ENTOURAGE

1. Much in the following paragraphs is based on Peter Raymond's testament: H Malte Narbonne, 1, no. 9.

2. Peter Raymond as vicar: *HGL* 8:281, 283 (II). The other occasions: *HGL* 8:278, 281, 283 (II), 353 (V). No one from Ermengard's entourage is listed among the witnesses to the treaty of Jarnègues, but it is hard to believe that at such a momentous gathering she would have been alone. For all these events, see chaps. 16 and 17 below.

3. On the spread of Roman testamentary forms in Occitania, the most significant of which appear in Peter Raymond's testament, see Gouron, "Plus anciens testaments français."

4. In 1204 they joined in witnessing the oath of fidelity rendered by Dalmad de Crexel, one of the major figures in the court of Alfonso I of Aragon, for the castle of Fenouillet (MS Doat 47, fol. 20; for Dalmad in Alfonso's court, see *LFM*, index, *sub nomine*).

5. MS Doat 48, fol. 42 (1220). On the name see Sabarthès, *Dictionnaire topographique*, 262. The two brothers use the title when Berenger and his wife emancipate their son Peter Raymond in view of his marriage to the daughter of Bernard of Béziers; MS Doat 57, fol. 168 (1227). See also AMN AA105, fol. 27 (1228), where property given as dowry is in Gerald's *seniorivum*.

6. She is named wife of Berenger of Béziers in *Cart. Béziers*, no. 303 (1185), whom Amado ("Famille aristocratique," 2:19) identifies as one of the sons of William of Poitiers (on whom see below, n. 43). She holds land of Raymond Vassadel in the rich fields of Divisanum across the river from Béziers (*Cart. Béziers*, no. 320).

7. Maria's dowry: *LIM*, no. 204. The property next to the archbishop's palace: Inv. Rocques, *Acquisitions*, no. 104 (1159).

8. See especially in the matter of dowries, Hilaire, *Régime des biens entre époux*.

9. "Vilis enim hereditas nobilem hominem non decet": *LIM*, no. 180.

10. *LIM*, nos. 94–96. Vidal, "Mariages dans la famille des Guillems," 235–37. The second son apparently died young, the third became bishop of Agde, and the fourth eventually married but received little property.

11. See above, chap. 1.

12. The earliest reference to Gerald serving as a witness, and thus presumably at least

twenty-five years old, is in 1144 (MS Mél. Colb. 414, no. 57); the last is in 1197 (MS Doat 55, fol. 206). It seems more likely that these were father and son or at least two succeeding generations.

13. MS Doat 57, fol. 190 (1256).

14. The most thorough discussion of naming practices is found in Amado, "Famille aristocratique," 1:104–17. Compare a similar practice in the twentieth-century Kybalie: Bourdieu, *Outline of a Theory of Practice*, 36–37.

15. It is unclear whether these two were father and son or belonged to the same generation. Inv. Rocques, *Acquisitions*, no. 3, states that they were grandfather and great-grandfather of Bertrand and Raymond of the Woods; no. 110 states that they were both grandfathers of Gerald of Breuil; rights to the same property are involved in these two documents, so they are surely the same two men. Because all that survive are inventory summaries, there is no way of judging which is correct. Raymond Arnaldi, however, was active in 1066 and 1080, Berenger Raimundi in 1096–97. The second name in both cases is probably a patrinymic, which would make the latter the son of the former. I have found nothing more about Bernard and Raymond of the Woods; the surname comes from another section of Narbonne's rural territory. For Guifred's grant of extensive rights in fief to Raymond Arnaldi, see Inv. Rocques, *Acquisitions*, no. 67; for Berenger Raimundi as vicar, see MS Mél. Colb. 414, no. 25. Raymond Arnaldi is called *civis* in *HGL* 5:656; is the Berenger Raimundi "de Civitate" (MS Doat 57, fol. 85; *HGL* 5:752) the same as the archbishop's vicar in the Bourg, or did that cognomen serve to distinguish the two?

16. Gerald of Breuil first appears as witness in one of Ermengard's acts in 1153: *HGL* 5:1152.

17. Hugh Ermengaud: *HGL* 8:322, where he serves as a witness for Viscount Roger of Béziers. Raymond Toll-taker witnessed a gift of Peter of Magalas to Saint-Nazaire of Béziers in 1172 (*Cart. Béziers*, no. 240), the oath of Assalit of Vieussan to Viscount Roger for the castle of Vieussan in 1176 (Cart. Trencavel, fol. 159), and Roger's grant in fief to Peter's brother-in-law, Bernard of Puisserguier, of tolls on the road between Saint-Thibéry and Marseillan in 1179 (*HGL* 8:337, I). See the genealogy in Amado, "Famille aristocratique," 2:306.

18. Raymond and Peter Raymond appear together in the surviving documents only once, when the latter helps arbitrate a dispute between the former and Viscountess Ermengard in the mid-1150s (MS Doat 48, fol. 28). The inheritance of Peter Raymond's grandson and namesake (the son of Berenger of Narbonne) included an oven, a part of a house, and lordship rights in Narbonne and a portion of the castle of Ouveilhan that came from Raymond: MS Doat 57, fol. 168 (1227).

19. The site of the lower castle is now marked only by some stone rubble. When I visited the village in the 1970s, the name was still alive in the memory of older village residents. "But," said one of them, "it's long been gone. You should go and visit our Cathar castle up next to the church." Television had worked its way. Imagine the historian fifty years hence reconstructing local history from native lore.

20. It is impossible to reconstruct the exact genealogy of this family during the twelfth century. William of Ouveilhan and his brother Berenger of Fontcalvi seem to be a branch; William witnesses acts of Raymond Berenger of Ouveilhan and vice versa. The portion of land at Fontcalvi that the brothers received as a *fevum honoratum* from the archbishop in 1184 is shared with the lords of le Terral (MS Doat 59, fol. 101); the document looks like a division of family holdings under the lordship of the archbishop. Lordship at Murviel near Ouveilhan: MS Baluze 82, fol. 169 (1124). For the relation of village church and castle: MS Doat 55, fol. 157 (1119); and MS Baluze 82, fol. 169. For the pond and the lower castle and the pond's economic exploitation: *HGL* 8:390. Lordships of other persons at Ouveilhan:

family of le Villar (MS Doat 55, fol. 203); Berenger Bonet and William of Moujan (*HGL* 8:390); Berenger of Narbonne (MS Doat 57, fol. 68); Peter Raymond of Béziers (Cart. Trencavel, fol. 179; MS Doat 40, fol. 98). Raymond of Ouveilhan's holdings at Gruissan: Inv. Rocques, *Gruissan*, no. 2; at Coumiac: MS Doat 58, fol. 144; Raymond witnessed a family settlement in the Pézenas family in 1152: *Cart. chap. cath. d'Agde*, no. 191.

21. Inv. Rocques, *Acquisitions*, nos. 101, 119; and the grant of Berenger of Narbonne to his son Peter Raymond mentioned in n. 5 above.

22. MS Doat 48, fol. 28; the Doat copy is dated 1158, although the text itself bears no date. Raymond agreed to the arbitration "with the consent and at the will of" his mother. The oven eventually returned to Raymond (by purchase? gift?), for it is one of the pieces of property that passes to Peter Raymond's son and grandson (see n. 18 above). For other Ouveilhan family holdings in Narbonne, see AMN AA105, fol. 13v; MS Doat 57, fol. 168.

23. Either the elder or the younger served as her vicar in the 1170s: MS Doat 55, fol. 241.

24. Hugh appears for the last time in 1188: MS Doat 59, fol. 118; *HGL* 8:390. William's endowment: MS Doat 55, fol. 206. Young Hugh's endowment: MS Doat 57, fol. 137. Hugh's shop (*operatorium*): MS Doat 59, fol. 89.

25. Maria of Montpellier: *HGL* 8:533 (1205). See, in general, Amado, "Femmes entre elles."

26. Esclaramunda: *HGL* 8:273.

27. Oaths of fealty (1151): *HGL* 5:1142. Gift to Fontfroide (1191): MS Doat 59, fol. 135. Oaths (1171): MS Doat 47, fol. 23.

28. MS Doat 59, fol. 89. On the Laredorte family, see further on in this chapter.

29. Richa and the Templars at Douzens: *Cart. Douzens* A, no. 20. Termes: *HGL* 5:1277. On Bernard Modul, see chap. 8.

30. *HGL* 5:1277 (1163).

31. Ademar of Durban (*HGL* 5:656; MS Baluze 82, fol. 155) served as judge in 1097 (*HGL* 5:752). Members of the family appeared as witnesses or participants in no fewer than twenty-one documents from the Narbonne region between 1080 and 1229. William of Durban appears in an additional nineteen documents between 1139 and 1163 in the company of the Trencavels; in addition to those in *HGL* 5 (see the index), Cart. Trencavel, fols. 31, 59, 160. Sometime between 1146 and 1161, William of Saint-Felix, vicar of Carcassonne, gave a copy of Laureta's recognizance and oath to William of Durban, presumably because he was heir to her rights: Cart. Trencavel, fol. 104.

32. Bernard in 1066: Inv. Rocques, *Viscomte*, no. 264; Peter in 1066–67: *HGL* 5:565–66. The Peter of midcentury is witness to six of Ermengard's surviving documents, apart from her marriage contract (on which, see chap. 1); during the same period he is witness to six Trencavel documents. William "viscount": *HGL* 5:1239, III (1161). The complex relationships among these men and their sons is given in *HGL* 8:317, I; MS Doat 59, fol. 79. William and Ricsovendis of Termes: *HGL* 8:412 (1191).

33. Oath for Castelmaure: *HGL* 5:694, II (dated by the editors "around 1084"). For Carcassonne: *HGL* 5:692, II. For Roquefort on the Sor (probably the ruins upstream from the Malemort falls, near the village of Cammazes): Cart. Trencavel, fol. 66; *HGL* 5:521. Later castellans of Roquefort were a succession of Hugh Escafredis; this Hugh "son of Guilla" could very well be the Hugh Escafredi who witnessed acts in 1068 and 1071: *HGL* 5:558, 588.

34. Such exceptions to oaths of fidelity and security were common among the very highest aristocracy, counts and viscounts, but extremely rare in the oaths of castellans. The nearest parallel is an undated oath of Guilabert of Laurac and his sons to Viscount Bernard Ato "against all men and women except for those of Laurac": Cart. Trencavel, fol. 139v.

35. Tithes on all the salt collected between the city and the village of Sigean at the river's mouth and on all the fish caught between Coursan and Leucate—essentially the whole Narbonnese coast: *HGL* 5:656. On this ceremony and the people present, see below.

36. Grant by Bishop Peter of Rodez: *HGL* 5:656, completed in MS Baluze 82, fol. 155 (1080). Tithes: MS Doat 58, fol. 8 (1114); MS Doat 57, fols. 106 (1120) and 120 (1138), which mentions William's last will. Market tolls—mortgaged to Peter and William by Alfaric of Saint-Nazaire, descendant and namesake of one or the other "illustrious and noble men" of 1080, who held the tolls in fief of the archbishop: Inv. Rocques, *Acquisitions*, no. 105. Tower over the Episcopal Gate: Inv. Rocques, *Acquisitions*, nos. 112 (1170), 113 (1195), 9 (1198), 8 (1199). Aymeri's mortgage: *HGL* 8:318, III. Raymond of Laredorte witnesses his neighbor, Peter Raymond of Puychéric, becoming a monk of Lagrasse: AD Aude H25 (1165); Raymond "Catalanus" of Laredorte gives oath of fidelity to the abbey of Caunes for the castle of Azille and many other (unnamed) fiefs: MS Doat 58, fol. 288 (1171); his uncle had taken the name William of Azille (Azille is the next village to the north of Laredorte). The exact relation of these individuals to others who took the same family name cannot be known. I suspect that the surnames served to distinguish the various contemporary Geralds, Raymonds, and Williams. Gaucerand of Capestang, who appears in the Trencavel entourage from 1162 to 1184 and, along with Peter Raymond of Narbonne and Raymond of Salles, swears on behalf of Ermengard to keep an agreement with Roger of Béziers in 1172 (*HGL* 5:283, III), is the brother of Pons and Gerald Xatmar of Laredorte: H Malte Narbonne, 1, no. 11 (1190). Gerald Xatmar's daughter Raimunda marries Amblard Pelapol: Inv. Rocques, *Acquisitions*, no. 113. Other Pelapols hold land in the immediate vicinity of Narbonne, bounded by property of Ermengard and Peter Raymond of Narbonne: MS Doat 59, fol. 53. In the surviving documents, members of this family appear 112 times in the Trencavel entourage during the twelfth century. Amblard and his brother Bernard are witnesses to the settlement between Hugh Escafredi and Raymond Trencavel discussed in chap. 7. For other appearances of Amblard, see his name in *HGL* 5, index, and Cart. Trencavel, fols. 54, 95.

37. Identified by Amado ("Famille aristocratique," 2:687) as Sainte-Marie-la-Garrigue, far up the Hérault River near Montpeyroux. See also Thomas, *Dictionnaire topographique de l'Hérault, sub nomine*.

38. *Cart. Béziers*, no. 270. I have read "Lanaz" as Lunas and "Laviranum" as Lavania or Lavenaria, now Laval-de-Nèze in the commune of Lunas. Although no one with the name of Portiragnes appears in Trencavel documentation, Raymond's attachment to Cassan, one of the favored churches of that vicecomital family, suggests that he was part of their network.

39. AD Aude G12, no. 7 (1184). Other documents concerning Berenger at Fontjoncouse: Cart. Fontjoncouse, nos. 22, 29. Bernard and Pons: Cart. Fontjoncouse, nos. 23, 27. Arnold Amalric appears as one of the *probi homines* of the city in 1177 (AMN AA105, fol. 21v) and elsewhere in the company of people such as Peter Raymond's son Berenger of Narbonne, Hugh of Plaigne, and William Bistani (AMN AA104, fol. 192; AN S4585, no. 22; Cart. Fontjoncouse, no. 24).

40. I have identified these thirty-five in the following way. Beginning with a list of all persons who witness documents in which Ermengard appears as a participant or a witness herself, I have first eliminated all those who can be positively identified as belonging to the entourages of the king of Aragon, the count of Toulouse, or the Trencavels when one or more of those persons are also present. Then I have eliminated clergy who witness gifts to churches or settlements of disputes over church lands. From those who remain I include only those who appear as witnesses at least twice. Given that we probably have considerably less than one percent of all the documents that once existed for Ermengard's activities (averaged out over the years of her effective rule, they amount to just about one per year, although the distribution is uneven), this last step may appear overly cautious. It seems the

only way to eliminate those who may be present because they are friends, allies, or neighbors of other people involved in the transaction being documented, even though it clearly risks eliminating people who should be included in the count. Many of those who appear only once can also be identified as belonging to prominent families of the region. They do not seem, therefore, to detract from the conclusions I have reached.

41. William appears twelve times in surviving documents as a witness to Ermengard's acts—as frequently as does Peter Raymond of Narbonne—between 1151 (*HGL* 5:1142) and 1171 (MS Doat 47, fol. 23).

42. *HGL* 3:799–800. See also Pattison, *Raimbaut d'Orange*, 29–30.

43. The early-twelfth-century generation: *LIM* 183; *HGL* 5:1084 (truncated) completed by Inv. Rocques, *Sigean*, no. 8. Marriage into the family "of Béziers": Amado, "Famille aristocratique," 2:16 and genealogy, 19 (who mysteriously identifies William as belonging to the family of Hautpoul). Sons: *Cart. Béziers*, no. 320. For this last Ermengaud, see also below, chap. 18.

44. Narbonne: most visible in the career of Bernard of Narbonne in the cathedral chapter of Béziers: *Cart. Béziers*, nos. 219, 238, 243, 244, and many others. A Raymond of Narbonne, who seems to be a resident of Montpellier, lends money against the security of tolls at the port of Lattes in 1170; he must have been connected to the "Narbonne" family at Béziers, for the mortgage document (as well as others involving the same moneylender) wound up in the archives of that city's cathedral: *Cart. Béziers*, no. 231 (1170), also no. 224 (1168). Béziers: Rainard Salomonis of Béziers, a major landholder in Béziers itself (*Cart. Béziers*, nos. 65, 67, 75; Amado, "Famille aristocratique," 2:11–12, 19); his son held fiefs of the archbishop of Narbonne in 1089: Inv. Rocques, *Acquisitions*, no. 86. A William of Béziers was active in the last decades of the eleventh and beginning of the twelfth century: AD Bouches-du-Rhone 1H60, no. 290; *HGL* 5:953. A Berenger of Béziers was active late in the twelfth century: *HGL* 5:1267; MS Doat 59, fol. 91; AN S4858, no. 21.

45. See n. 36 above.

46. See chap. 6.

47. Peter both archbishop and viscount: *HGL* 5:656, 660, and others; takes oath to Guifred: ibid., col. 541; see also ibid., cols. 546, 634, and others. For the practice of co-lordship, see Cheyette, " 'Sale'of Carcassonne."

48. The one exception is Rainard Amati, *vir magni testimonii*, whose father (?) Raymond is mentioned as a witness in 1060 (MS Doat 57, fol. 51). The cognomen Amati appears to die out after 1134; Bernard Amati of Montseret (a village about five kilometers from the city's gates) is the last example I find: *HGL* 5:1000. The other noble names are Saint-Nazaire, Coursan, Peyrepertuse. An Ermengaud of Cazouls holds the "Great Tower" of the city in 1066 (Inv. Rocques, *Viscomte*, no. 264), while a Raymond and William of Cazouls witness Ermengard's next-to-last surviving act (ACA *perg. Alfonso I*, no. 673, on which see below, chap. 18). Bertrand of Coursan, probably a grandson of the Coursan of 1080, is a witness to one of Ermengard's acts in 1152 (MS Doat 48, fol. 19). Bertrand of Saint-Nazaire is a witness to the same act and to two others in the 1150s (*Cart. Silvanès*, no. 313; MS Baluze 82, fol. 41). Berenger of Peyrepertuse probably came in the company of the count of Urgel; he and his sons are active in Narbonne in the decades before and after 1100, but family members do not reappear in the city until 1193 (MS Doat 59, fol. 139; Inv. Rocques, *Acquisitions*, no. 14.

49. For Raymond Arnold, see above, n. 15. Oath of Bernard of the Royal Gate: Catel, *Mémoires*, 589. Peter of Villeneuve: ACA *perg. Alfonso I*, no. 673.

50. Raymond Arnold Margalonis reappears with many of the same witnesses in Archbishop Peter's donation to the cathedral canons in 1089 (MS Doat 55, fol. 123). Hugh Margalonis is already a canon in 1157 (MS Doat 55, fol. 235); he is precentor by 1176 (ibid., fol. 241) and still holds that office in 1196 (Cart. Fontjoncouse, no. 24). Arnold Margalonis as

witness: MS Doat 55, fol. 206. Peter Raymond as guarantor for Aymeri: *HGL* 8:318, III; the horse cost 1,100 sol. Melg. Peter Raymond was a cousin of the four brothers, Peter, Raymond, Bernard, and Hugh (MS Doat 40, fol. 171).

51. MS Doat 40, fol. 171. For the Bistani family, see chap. 3.

52. MS Doat 58, fol. 140 (1177), when Gausbert of Coumiac gave some property to the abbey of Quarante. A single appearance such as this tells us nothing about a person's usual associations. The Margalonis family could have had a close relationship with Quarante or could have been an important local landowner: Peter Raymond Margalonis witnessed the mutual oaths of Lady Calva and the abbot for the castle of Argeliers in 1193 (MS Doat 58, fol. 148).

53. The relationship of cousinage is implied by Raymond and Peter Raymond Margalonis appearing along with Vidianus of Bages as beneficiaries in the testament of Raymond of Bages in 1156 (known only through the inventory summary: Inv. Rocques, *Fontfroide*, no. 12). Arnold Donzel is identified as the brother of Raymond of Bages in MS Baluze 81, fol. 77v; he witnesses various acts of Aymeri II and his wife: MS Mél. Colb. 414, no. 28; MS Doat 55, fol. 177; and *HGL* 5: 966, where he appears as the viscount's *bajulus*. Marriage of Raymond of Bages with Englesa of Tréville: Cart. Fontjoncouse, no. 21. Englesa's mother Mabilia was a daughter of Ermengaud of Fabrezan: Inv. Rocques, *Peyriac*, no. 7. Mabilia's sister was known as Adalais "of Trèbes": Inv. Rocques, *Peyriac*, no. 30. Englesa's sister Raimonda married John Benedicti, member of another important city family: Inv. Rocques, *Peyriac*, no. 11; Inv. Rocques, *Acquisitions*, nos. 8, 113.

54. Mortgage of Fontjoncouse: Cart. Fontjoncouse, no. 24. The Fabrezan at Sigean: Inv. Rocques, *Sigean*, nos. 62, 64. The family names Bages, Fabrezan, and Tréville appear with some frequency in Inv. Rocques under the heading of these villages, as well as in the Cart. Fontjoncouse and the documents from Fontfroide in MS Doat 59. By the end of the twelfth century, if not well before, they and the family that took Fontjoncouse as their name were all related. Adalais of Trèbes was Mabilia's sister (see previous note). Bernard of Trèbes served as vicar of Carcassonne in the 1140s: *HGL* 5:1047, 1060. Dias and Peter of Puylaurens: *HGL* 5:1150. Ermengaud of Fabrezan's confirmation of a donation to Fontfroide by the children of Berenger of Peyrepertuse, a donation made in the castle of Fabrezan, suggests a family relation there as well: MS Doat 59, fol. 138.

55. Catel, *Mémoires*, 589, who does not indicate which castle or castles were named in their oath. The others given by Catel are from Bernard of the Royal Gate (for Narbonne), Udalgarius and Peter Arnold of Fenouillet (for Peyrepertuse), Peter Roger (for Castelmaure), William "son of Casta" (for Fraisse), and Bohemond of Sigean (for Roquefort).

56. For all these examples, see chaps. 10 and 11.

CHAPTER 10. OATH AND OATH TAKERS

1. *HGL* 5:1204, II. The text follows a standard formulary, with the exception of the last clause, which only appears occasionally. For a full discussion of the clauses in these oaths, see Magnou-Nortier, "Fidélité et féodalité méridionales."

2. The translation here is passably problematic, depending on whether one interprets the "ti" ("t' ") as being in the dative or accusative case. The alternate translation would be "or take you from it." My thanks to my colleague Margaret Switten for clarifying this.

3. Brunel, *Plus anciennes chartes*, no. 25: oath of Raines, son of Rocia, to his brother William Rainon, c. 1128.

4. Guifred and Raymond of Saint-Gilles: *HGL* 5:535, among many others. Raymond

Trencavel and Ermengard: *HGL* 5:1142, also among many, many others. Frotarius, Sicard, and Isarn for the castle of Lautrec: *HGL* 5:301, 312; Cart. Trencavel, fols. 30v, 115v (dated by the editors of *HGL* as c. 989 for unknown reasons, but surely eleventh century: see Débax, "Serments de Lautrec"). There are numerous oaths to Viscount Ato "son of Gauciane," including one for the castle of Lombers by the same Isarn "son of Rangard," who took the oath to Frotarius for Lautrec: Cart. Trencavel, fol. 16; see also fols. 12 (Roquefort-sur-Sor), 19–20 (Lavaur), 47 (Salvagnac); *HGL* 5:388 (Dourgne-sur-Taur); and, securely datable to 1028, Cart. Trencavel, fols. 8, 58; and *HGL* 5:387 (Auriac). The family passion for hoarding parchment seems to have begun with Viscount Ato and his brother, Bishop Frotarius of Nîmes. The absence of earlier surviving oaths does not prove they were not given. On the contrary, the oath of Count Roger to Archbishop Ermengaud of Narbonne (summarized Inv. Rocques, *Peyriac de Mer*, no. 1) for half of Peyriac "which Viscount Raynard held" implies continuity from the mid-tenth century at least; Count Roger is most likely "Roger II," grandson of Roger "the Old," count of Carcassonne; this would place the oath in Inv. Rocques around 1010, the approximate date of the death of Roger's uncle, Count Raymond, and represent Roger's succession to part of the lands of Count Raymond's wife, Garsend, viscountess of Béziers. Raynard, viscount of Béziers, died in 969.

5. See Magnou-Nortier, "Fidélité et féodalité méridionales," 121; and Aurell, "Détérioration du statut de la femme aristocratique," 14–17.

6. Compare *HGL* 5:1152 and 1204, II, the first a *compositio*, the second an oath of fidelity involving both the family of Durban and Ermengard. The argument that identification through the mother is more exact—*mater certus, pater incertus*, or in Shakespeare's words " 'Tis a wise man who knows his own father"—has been cautiously suggested by Magnou-Nortier, whereas Aurell suggests that the mother's name was used "only when there was danger of confusion between several persons" with the given name, the "stock of female names" being much richer than the stock of male names. (For references, see previous note.) To the first one can respond that the supposed "uncertainty of paternity" would seem to be far more important in inheritance claims; but in those cases, identification as a mother's child appears only when the mother's estate is at issue. To the second, the response must be that the use of the mother's name is far more universal in Occitania than Aurell finds it to be in Provence and that the stock of female names among the aristocracy is no more adventurous than that of male names. Mothers' names are used in oaths even by those men with highly unusual names limited in use to a single or only a few family lines, as in the Sicard and Isarn (of Lautrec) of the very earliest oath.

7. Shabbat 66b, quoted in Gager, *Curse Tablets and Binding Spells*, 14. See his discussion of the practice, which starts to appear in the Roman world in the second century C.E. See also Trachtenberg, *Jewish Magic and Superstition*, 115, 140. My thanks to Shaye J. D. Cohen for bringing the latter work to my attention. There is no reason to hypothesize a link back to some ancient matrilineal practice, for which there is not a shred of evidence. For the medieval Christian world as for the Jewish, we can follow the remark of Cohen: "Relics . . . which surface miraculously . . . a millennium after the period of their [supposed] origins are remarkable relics indeed" ("Matrilineal Principle," 13).

8. Gager, *Curse Tablets*, 101–6, 67–71. See also the curse tablets reproduced in Kondoleon, *Antioch: The Lost Ancient City*.

9. This practice begins to change in the second half of the twelfth century when written copies of oaths start to include both witness lists and dates, bringing them closer to the form of other notarial documents.

10. Little, *Benedictine Maledictions*.

11. Magnou-Nortier, "Fidélité et féodalité méridionales," 116–19.

12. See Little, *Benedictine Maledictions*.

13. Almost none of the Occitan oaths in Brunel, *Plus anciennes chartes*, contain the phrase; they go straight to the promise not to deceive.

14. A tradition that seems to begin with A. Germain, editor of the *LIM*: see notes on 506, 608, 612, among many others.

15. *HGL* 5:1136.

16. *HGL* 5:427 (c. 1036), 524 (c. 1063), 803 (1107), 1024 (1138), among many others.

17. See Cheyette, " 'Sale' of Carcassonne," 857–59.

18. See, for example, the narrative of Archbishop Richard of Narbonne, below, chap. 11.

19. Clearest when the succession is mentioned, for example, *HGL* 5:852. See also the coming of age of Raymond Ato of Murviel: *HGL* 8:389, II.

20. We can see this in the large collection of Trencavel oaths in those sworn first to the widowed Ermengard (with or without her son Bernard Ato) after the death of Viscount Raymond, then to Bernard Ato, then to his widow Cecilia and her two sons, then to each of the sons, and so forth, through the century. For a few castles the record is complete enough to present the same person taking the oath to successive lords, for example, Peter son of Imperia to Viscount Bernard Ato (*HGL* 5:364; Cart. Trencavel, fol. 55) and then to his widow and two sons (Cart. Trencavel, fol. 53) for Niort; Roger son of Belissendis to Ermengard and then to her son Bernard Ato and his two sons for Mirepoix (Cart. Trencavel, fols. 50, 51).

21. The witness lists to some of the later oaths, or to the agreements to which the oaths were appended, especially the numerous examples in the Trencavel cartulary, bespeak a mobile court joined by local adherents as it moved from place to place.

22. *HGL* 5:1288, III (1165): dispute between Raymond Trencavel and the castellans of Saint-Juery, near Albi, over Raymond's construction of a new castle on the site, resolved by agreeing that the castellans will give oaths to Raymond for the castle and that *milites castri* will in turn "save" the fidelity of Raymond and of the abbot of Castres when they take their oaths to the castellans.

23. *HGL* 5:516 (1063) (from Cart. Trencavel, fols. 107, 115); for what may be taking place here, see Cheyette, "On the *fief de reprise*." Cart. Trencavel, fols. 50, 51 (undated oaths to Ermengard and Bernard Ato, last quarter of the eleventh century). A Batalla was among those who engaged in the Carcassonne revolt of 1120: *HGL* 5:917. Cart. Trencavel, fol. 49v (undated oaths to William of Alaigne by some of those giving oaths to Ermengard); *HGL* 5:956 ("circa 1129") and 1227 (1159). William's successors take the title of viscount right through the twelfth century: Cart. Trencavel, fols. 135, 68, 69.

24. Cart. Trencavel, fols. 53, 54, 67, 68.

25. In 1192, Lady Calva and her husband "by command of [her] mother Adalais" exchanged oaths of fidelity with the abbot and cellarer of the abbey of Quarante for the castle of Argeliers; she had possibly received her share of the castle as a dowry (for her mother was still alive and her father was nowhere mentioned). Quarante had received its portion of the castle as a pious gift in 1154. The confirmation of that gift and a 1214 confirmation of Calva's testamentary donation to Quarante make explicit that the viscountess of Narbonne and her successors exercised *seniorivum* and *potestativum* over the castle. We may assume, therefore, that oaths of fidelity were rendered to her as well (MS Doat 58, fols. 130, 148, 154). This is a particularly striking example of a castle held jointly by an Augustinian monastery and a woman, which nevertheless still owed military service (explicitly reserved by Viscount Aymeri in his confirmation of 1214). In 1145, Fides daughter of Maria and Pons of Vintrou exchanged oaths with Jordan of Prohencoux for the castle of Boussagues, following an agreement that Jordan would hold the castle for four months (February, March, April, and July) and Fides and Pons for the other eight: Cart. Trencavel, fol. 162v (also MS Doat 167, fols. 18, 20; incompletely published *HGL* 5:1065). The castle had been held of the

Trencavels at least since Viscount Bernard Ato, and the presence of Raymond Trencavel as a witness to the oaths of 1145 demonstrate his interest. See also the dispute between joint holders of Auriac: *HGL* 5:1131.

26. Arifat: *HGL* 5:836 (from Cart. Trencavel, fol. 43v.); William of Alaigne at Queille (Cart. Trencavel, fol. 71), Rennes (fol. 64), Routier (fol. 63), and Taillebois (fol. 75); Raymond of Niort at Niort and Castelpor (fols. 54, 67), and at the other castles (*HGL* 5:965).

27. *HGL* 5:1252 (from Cart. Trencavel, fol. 135v.). For William and Hugh, see the name indexes to vols. 5 and 8 of the *HGL*, s.v. S. Felice (Guillelmus de) and Romegos (Ugo de).

28. Two examples among many—the complex agreement between three brothers and the son of a deceased fourth brother concerning their shares in castles in the modern department of the Tarn: *HGL* 5:1306, V; the oaths of two brothers and their brother-in-law on behalf of his wife to Raymond V for the castles of Montclar[-de-Comminges] and Montpézat: *HGL* 5:1283, VII.

29. Division by month: Cart. Trencavel, fol. 162v (see the more full discussion above, n. 25); *HGL* 8:319 (Berenger of Caux holds castle of Vailhan from September to November); Brunel, *Plus anciennes chartes*, no. 29 (oath for January and February at the castle of Moriès and February, March, and April at Marchastel in the Gévaudan). Sisters: the example in n. 25 above of Argelières suggests such a division, perhaps at the mother's generation; more explicit examples are Ricsovendis and her brothers at Termes (*HGL* 5:1277, 8:412) and the castles held by Arnold of Fenouillet, which by his first testament of 1173 passed jointly to his four sisters, for which they were to give oaths of fidelity to Ermengard of Narbonne (H Malte Homps 5, no. 4; the terms modified by second testament a few months later, MS Doat 59, fol. 72). Testaments were often the occasion for arranging such complex divisions and the passage of divided fragments should one or another line fail to produce heirs. By his testament of 1145, for example, Imbert of Montady passed the castle from which he took his name to his son Raymond, whereas his daughter Saurina received his half of an honor in the castle of Tersan (a place that has disappeared; perhaps it was on the bank of the Aude near Moussan; see Sabarthès, *Dictionnaire topographique*, s.v. Saint-Etienne-de-Tersan): AD Hérault, G694.

30. Marriage contract of Ermessendis with Rostagnus of Posquières (*HGL* 5:894): "sic habeant seniores ejusdem castri illud castrum ... per te et per manum tuam, sicut modo habent per nos." Treaty of 1143 between Alphonse Jordan and the Trencavel allies (*HGL* 5:1069): a castellan "debet solvere sacramenta et reddere ipsa sacramentalia." Oath of knights of Albi, whom Roger "has as security [*pignus*]": *HGL* 8:351.

31. I follow here the perceptive analysis (of very different rites of passage) by Bourdieu, "Rites as Acts of Institution."

32. *HGL* 5:804; *LFM*, no. 832. See my discussion of the date of these oaths in Cheyette, " 'Sale' of Carcassonne," 859–60.

33. For these two men, see the previous chapter.

34. For a discussion of the way oaths were used rhetorically in disputes, see White, "Stratégie rhétorique dans la *Conventio* de Hughes de Lusignan."

CHAPTER 11. ANGER, CONFLICT, AND RECONCILIATION

1. Arnaut Daniel, "Chanson do˙ ill mot son plan e prim," in *Poetry of Arnaut Daniel* (ed. Wilhelm), 8–9. The language of the first line is obscure; see Wilhelm's comments, 86–87.

2. *HGL* 5:1131 (and Cart. Trencavel, fol. 215), dated by the editors "around 1152," but it could be any time between 1150, when Raymond Trencavel succeeded his brother Roger, and the death of Bishop Pons of Carcassonne, one of the arbitrators, in 1159. All the other

arbiters appear elsewhere in the company of Raymond Trencavel during the 1150s and early 1160s.

3. The literature has been surveyed in detail by White, "Politics of Anger"; and zealous anger explored by Barton, " 'Zealous Anger' and the Renegotiation of Aristocratic Relationships."

4. The ARTFL database of Provençal poetry (www.lib.uchicago.edu/efts/ARTFL/databases/PROV/) lists 281 occurrences of *dan* and 83 of *maltraire* or some variant in the corpus of troubadour songs. For *dan*, see also Cropp, *Vocabulaire courtois*, 277. On the complex judgments that arise in the perception of violence and therefore on its use in accusations, see Miller, *Humiliation*, especially chap. 2, "Getting a Fix on Violence."

5. Treaty of 1143: *HGL* 5:1069. The brothers Raymond "Polverels" and William Peter gave oaths of fidelity for Auriac to Raymond Trencavel's older brother, Roger, probably in the late 1130s. At the same time, Pons "son of Ermengard Polverella" likewise rendered his fidelity. These could have been the same men as those involved in the dispute of the 1150s or their immediate ancestors. The unique names Polverellus, Polverella surely mark a family connection. Cart. Trencavel, fol. 9.

6. *Raoul de Cambrai* (trans. Kay), 307–19, with substantial elisions. See also White's comparison of this passage with the feuding settlements he studies, in "Feuding and Peace-Making in the Touraine."

7. Four other unrelated men gave oaths of fidelity to Raymond's elder brother Roger for Auriac: Cart. Trencavel, fols. 57v–58v.

8. All of them the expressions of great twentieth-century medievalists: Marc Bloch, J. E. A. Jolliffe, and Johan Huizinga, quoted in White, "Politics of Anger," 128–29.

9. Barbara Rosenwein explores the various modern "paradigms" for explaining emotions in her concluding summary to *Anger's Past*.

10. As suggested by White, "Politics of Anger," 129–31, following the extensive anthropological writing on the social construction of emotion.

11. Of the vast literature, both historical and anthropological, see especially Stewart, *Honor*; Peristiany and Pitt-Rivers, *Honor and Grace in Anthropology*; and the classic, Peristiany, *Honour and Shame: The Values of Mediterranean Society*.

12. Jaufré Rudel, "Belhs m'es," in *Poetry of Cercamon and Jaufré Rudel* (ed. and trans. Wolf and Rosenstein), 130–31.

13. Raimbaut de Vaqueiras, "Conseil don a l'emperador," in *Poems of the Troubadour Raimbaut de Vaqueiras* (ed. Linskill), 225–28. On the multiple and complex meanings associated with "de bon aire" and *debonereté*, see Hyams, "What Did King Henry III of England Think in Bed," 113–24.

14. *HGL* 5:1277, II. Among the arbiters is Hugh Escafredi, whom we meet elsewhere in this chapter as a disputant.

15. *HGL* 5:1275. We have met Hugh Escafredi before in chap. 7. Isarn Jordani was one of the lords of Saissac (where the Escafredi were likewise castellans), from which he and his family took their family name. According to the settlement, the Escafredi and the Saissacs were also partners at the castle of Villalégut (on what is now the territory of Montréal and already razed in 1163).

16. Most of the surviving arbitrations of these two vicecomital houses were found by the eighteenth-century authors of the *HGL* either in cartularies in the royal archives in the castle of Foix or in the archives of the Chambre des Comptes in Montpellier, to which they had found their way from the original vicecomital treasuries. Both of these royal archives were destroyed by fire in the eighteenth century. Ermengard as arbiter: MS Doat 48, fol. 19; *HGL* 5:1271; *HGL* 8:309 (II), 390, and the case below. The Trencavels: *HGL* 5:789, 1063, 1131, 1134, 1138, 1271, 1275, 1287; Cart. Trencavel, fols. 19, 35, 109. Conflicts be-

tween churches and monasteries and lay claimants to their property seem most often to be settled in Occitania by "friends" or ecclesiastical arbiters. If more ecclesiastical archives had survived—particularly those of Fontfroide, the house favored by Ermengard and her predecessors, or Saint-Mary of Cassan, a house patronized by the Trencavels—our conclusions might be different. The two exceptional disputes involving clerical property in which Ermengard was called upon to intervene have both been preserved in Fontfroide's fragmentary archives. They are at the same time symptomatic of the way ecclesiastical cases were handled. The most revealing is a case of 1176 involving a deathbed donation to Fontfroide disputed by the donor's daughter, Agnes, and her husband. Originally arbitrated by the canons of Saint-Paul "with the counsel and authority" of the archbishop and Ermengard, the resulting division of the property was then reversed by Ermengard and the "common friends," the part attributed to the monastery going to Agnes and Agnes's to the monastery; MS Doat 59, fol. 89.

17. A classic statement of the sociology of dispute settlement in this period is in Davies and Fouracre, "Conclusion," in *Settlement of Disputes in Early Medieval Europe*, 228–40, whose interpretations differ somewhat from those presented here.

18. Bernard Amati was one of the barons who helped make peace between Bernard Ato and the count of Barcelona in 1112 (*HGL* 5:827); he witnessed no less than eleven of the surviving acts of the viscount between 1116 (ibid., col. 852) and 1127 (ibid., col. 941).

19. *HGL* 5:1152, IV. The presence of the bishop of Fréjus among the witnesses suggests that the agreement was made in Provence.

20. It was at the end of the campaign of 1153 that Raymond Trencavel, captured and imprisoned by the count of Toulouse, left his young son Roger "in God's custody and in Ermengard's and in her service" (*HGL* 5:1171).

21. *Cart. Douzens*, no. 20. The "hands" are those of the high lord—Ermengard, the Trencavels—although the actual work of arbitration was most often done by members of their courts. In the standard formula, the alternative to "in manu" is "in potestate." Thus although this *manus* is clearly not the same as the one exercised by a husband over his wife and household in classical Roman law, the equivalence of "hand" and "power" most likely derives from that distant source. For a suggestive analysis of the mediative role of grace in societies of honor, see Pitt-Rivers, "Place of Grace in Anthropology." His remark is pertinent here: "It would appear that there are in Western civilization two opposed—and ultimately complementary—registers: the first associated with honor, competition, triumph, the male sex, possession, and the profane world, and the other with peace, amity, grace, purity, renunciation, the female sex, dispossession in favor of others, and the sacred" (242).

22. *HGL* 5:1271 (1163) at Carcassonne, involving property at Villarzel and Ladern; *Cart. Douzens*, no. 20 (1167) at Douzens. The third arbitration outside the viscounty is *Cart. Béziers*, no. 297.

23. To the poet of *Song of Sainte Foy*, the most forceful manner in which this child martyr could express her faith in God was as his *fidelis*; see Clark, trans., "Song of Sainte Foy," 278–80.

24. Dated 1117 by Devic and Vaisette in *HGL* 3:631 and as "around 1119" where they edit the text in *HGL* 5:860. The critical element for dating is the presence of the archbishop of Arles and the bishop of Nîmes among the witnesses Richard records. The archbishop of Arles and several other bishops were present when Richard's dispute with the abbot of Saint-Paul was terminated in 1117; *HGL* 5:858.

25. Gregory VII, *Correspondence of Pope Gregory VII*, trans. Emerton, 171–72.

26. For a detailed account of these earlier events, see chap. 6.

27. Saint-Victor had developed important reform connections with the churches of Nar-

bonne in the last decades of the eleventh century, when Archbishop Dalmacius gave both the churches of Saint-Mary in the bourg (now called Lamourguier, where the great collection of Roman inscriptions is stored) and Saint-Crescentius outside the walls to the abbey: AD Bouches-du-Rhone 1 H59, nos. 282, 284, 290; MS Doat 58, fol. 1.

28. I have developed this theme of orality and writing in the Gregorian Reform in my essay, Cheyette, "Invention of the State."

29. *HGL* 5:829, 831 (1112); Cart. Fontjoncouse, no. 9 (1108).

30. MS Doat 55, fols. 120, 154, 159; AD Aude G9, no. 1; *GC* 6, *instrum.* 32.

31. In his reference to "judgments in cases of spoliation" he was recalling a provision of Roman law that was incorporated into the law of the Church.

32. No oaths are recorded in the Trencavel cartulary, and the village does not appear in the inventory of the archiepiscopal archives. The archbishop had a castle in the neighboring village of Capestang and interests elsewhere in the immediate vicinity. So did the viscounts of Narbonne. Berenger and his brothers appear in the 1170s and 1180s in the entourage of the viscount of Béziers, and his major testamentary donation to Saint-Mary of Cassan suggests a close Trencavel association.

33. For Berenger's possessions, see his testament, *Cart. Béziers*, no. 225 (1169), and the enfeoffment of the same rights to his brother in 1184, *HGL* 8:377. See also *HGL* 8:338. For the same kinds of rights on the *caminum qui dicitur Francigena*, the lords of Rieux were willing to promise Viscount Roger of Béziers an albergum for fifty horsemen and their mounts every year: *HGL* 8:322. Our only information on the reasons for Berenger's conflict with Ermengard comes from oblique references in the correspondence with King Louis VII. They are not very explicit, and much must be surmised.

34. See below, chap. 14.

35. The dates of these letters were omitted by the copyist, but the presence of Alexander III at Sens, mentioned in one of the letters, dates them securely between late 1163 and the first months of 1165. I have changed their order from that in *RHGF* to bring them into a more logical narrative sequence.

36. The text reads "your grace and our love," but this is most likely a copyist's error: latin *nos* and *vos* in their various forms are easy to confuse in medieval manuscripts.

37. *RHGF* 16:90, letters no. 277, 278.

38. Ibid., 90, no. 275.

39. Ibid., 89, no. 273.

40. Ibid., 90, no. 276.

41. *Lo Codi*, II, 18 and III, 1; in the Fitting edition, see pp. 32, 38, summarizing Paulus at *Digest of Justinian* V, 1, 12: "By custom women and slaves [do not have the capacity to be judges], not because they are wanting in judgment, but because it is an established rule that they are not to discharge civil offices" (trans. Munro, 1:304). On the date and place of composition of *Lo Codi*, see Gouron, "Du nouveau sur *lo Codi*, and idem, "Lo Codi, source de la Somme au Code de Rogerius."

42. *RHGF* 16:91, no. 279.

43. Ibid., no. 280.

44. Gouron, "Du nouveau," 273.

45. *RHGF* 16:89, no. 274. Another letter from the bishop of Maguelonne accompanied this, telling the same story: ibid., no. 272.

46. *Cart. Béziers*, no. 225.

47. *HGL* 8:337, 338. Raymond Ledder is probably Raymond Toll-taker, the friend of Peter Raymond of Narbonne mentioned in chap. 9.

48. Capestang, Thézan, and Salles are neighboring villages to Puisserguier. Peter Raymond of Hautpoul and Bernard Peter of Olargues were two important counselors of Vis-

count Roger. Peter son of Roger was the Viscount's vicar. Here, yet once again, we have two courts meeting together.

49. *RHGF* 16:91, no. 281.

CHAPTER 12. GIVING AND TAKING

1. *Lanquan vei fuell' e flor frug*, in *Canzoni* (ed. Toja), 221–23. Kay reads the final line differently: *Subjectivity in Troubadour Poetry*, 54.

2. As White points out in his as yet unpublished paper, "Giving Fiefs and Honor," which I thank him for sharing with me.

3. "[A]rchiepiscopus, qui consanguineus et antiquus amicus erat, donavit ei plusquam alii archiepiscopi non dederant avo et aliis antecessoribus ejus de pecunia sua. . . . conventum est inter eos ut ecclesiae et successoribus archiepiscopi per consuetudinem non quereretur hoc quod archiepiscopus propter amicitiam fecerat, sed semper vicecomes et successores ejus facerent hominium . . . propter fevum et propter talen pecuniam quam dedit Guifredus Petro Raimundi avo ejus": *HGL* 5:801.

4. *GC* 6, *instrum.* 32; MS Doat 55, fol. 130; Inv. Rocques, *Sigean*, no. 5; Cart. Fontjoncouse, no. 9 (AD Aude G9, no. 1). The last asserts, "Ricardo in episcopatu consecrato facta est magna dissensio inter eum et castellanos atque vicarios honoris ecclesie quod multa que sui juris erant in proprios usus redegissent et nova usatica adjecissent."

5. See the previous chapter.

6. *Cart. Béziers*, no. 222 (1167), and MS Doat 58, fol. 288 (1177), are the earliest surviving recognizances I have found, although controversies all through the century imply that claims to holdings in fief were constantly made (and rejected), as in the dispute between Aymeri II and Archbishop Richard.

7. And so, when Richard granted Sigean to Raymond William of Fabrezan, it was again "as his grandfather held it from Archbishop Guifred": Inv. Rocques, *Sigean*, no. 5.

8. See Geary, *Phantoms of Remembrance*, for comments on the shaping of the past by the cartulary makers of the eleventh century. That work continued apace in the twelfth and thirteenth centuries.

9. *GC* 6, *instrum.* 32.

10. Bernard Raimondi of Villerouge and his wife Agnes held land at Villerouge in fief of Archbishop Richard in 1117; the name Raymond is here most likely a patronymic, and Rixendis and Bernard the couple's children: Inv. Rocques, *Villerouge*, nos. 1–4, 7–9. In 1229 yet another Raymond of Villerouge, possibly a descendent, is one of the knights of Narbonne who swears fidelity to Louis VIII: MS Mél. Colb. 414, no. 76.

11. Both shared the friendship of the count of Roussillon as well: *HGL* 5:656, 660, 694; *LFM*, no. 759.

12. "William laughed aloud. . . . 'I ask for the kingdom of Spain, and Tortolouse, and Portpaillart on the coast, and the city of Nîmes, and Orange. . . . No-one ever bore a shield for you in those parts nor did you ever have a knight in your pay there and your estate will not be impoverished thereby.' . . .

"Said noble Louis . . . , 'Noble knight, come forward. I will do what you wish. Have Spain as your fief. Take this glove in token. I give it to you on this understanding, that if toil and hardship mount up for you, I shall have no responsibility for you.'" *Wagon-Train*, laisses 18, 24 (*William, Count of Orange* [ed. Price], 70, 72).

13. On this practice, and especially the gift of Tarragona, see Cheyette, " 'Sale' of Carcassonne," 863–64. Guifred and William Ibrinus: Cart. Fontjoncouse, no. 7. The rare name "Ibrinus" surfaces in the Durban family at the end of the twelfth century.

14. Kay's analysis of gift giving in twelfth-century chansons de geste adds pertinent literary evidence to this: *Chansons de Geste in the Age of Romance*, 25–48.

15. A stone to make a transfer: *Cart. Béziers*, no. 88; throwing a stone: *Cart. Maguelone*, no. 179.

16. Ritual narrated: *Cart. Maguelone*, no. 270 (1203), at the castle of Teyran, northeast of Montpellier. How long such a ritual existed there is no way of knowing. For a detailed analysis, see Cheyette, "On the *fief de reprise*," written before I stumbled on the Maguelone document.

17. For a number of examples, see Cheyette, " 'Sale' of Carcassonne."

18. Monk of Montaudon, *Poésies du moine de Montaudon* (ed. Routledge), 24–25.

19. See above, chap. 8.

20. MS Doat 40, fol. 185 (1222). I assume that "frastra" in the text is a mistaken reading for *frassa*, the wonderful French dish *fraise de veau*.

21. Boureau, *Droit de cuissage*, is devoted to the development of the myth.

22. Note the similarity in so many ways to the albergum described in chap. 8.

23. A particularly famous example is the gift by Count Roger the Old of Carcassonne to the monastery of Saint-Hilaire of several villages and churches in the Razès to give thanks for his victory over Count Oliba of Cerdagne in 981: *HGL* 5:293. Elaborate literary narratives such as this are rare in Occitania after the year 1000. At its consecration in 1115, Saint-Mary of Cassan was enriched with relics "brought from overseas," including a cross presented by William the Englishman containing wood from the Cross, stone from the Holy Sepulcher, from the site of the Nativity, Calvary, the "stone that was rolled away," the Virgin's sepulcher and Mount Sinai: *HGL* 5:850. In Cheyette, " 'Sale' of Carcassonne," I erroneously made Cassan a Trencavel foundation; it was in fact founded by an otherwise unidentifiable William Alcherius of Béziers (*HGL* 5:654), but Raymond Trencavel chose to be buried there (*HGL* 5:1171), and if the monastery's archives had not all but disappeared we might know more of its role in the Trencavel entourage. On gifts to saints, see in general, White, *Custom, Kinship*. On the pattern of testamentary donations in Occitania, see Bourin-Derruau, *Villages médiévaux*, 1:277ff.

24. Examples could be taken from almost any cartulary. I take these from *Cart. Douzens* A: coin and grain *pro elemosina*, no. 220 (1167); coin, no. 25 (1146); a horse *pro compra*, no. 21 (1135).

25. *Cart. Douzens* A, no. 22.

26. As, for example, 103 sol. Melg. *mittibiles et percurribiles* for three "pieces" of land: *Cart. Douzens* A, no. 22, when the "alms" given in countergift are more often in the neighborhood of 30 to 40 sol. "Sales" for very modest sums: *Cart. Douzens* A, nos. 32 (9 sol.), 34 (10 sol.), 43 (15 sol.).

27. *Cart. Douzens* B, no. 51 (1170). Four years earlier, the phrase appears in a donation (*Cart. Douzens* A, no. 44). It is one of the earliest signs of what will be the progressive Romanization of notarial documents. The mixed formula "we sell and give" appears as late as 1158 in the same village (B, no. 17).

28. For a general discussion, see (in addition to White, *Custom, Kinship*), Rosenwein, *Neighbor of Saint Peter*, and Bouchard, *Sword, Miter, and Cloister*. Two striking examples of such continuity are in the *Cart. St-Etienne d'Agde*: no. 257 (canons give in fief to Pons Carbonel the honor that his uncle gave to the canons twelve years earlier when he became a *conversus* at Saint-Etienne); and nos. 258, 261, 262 (grant in fief to Peter of Mèze of property quitclaimed fifty years earlier by an earlier Peter of Mèze and probably given by a yet earlier ancestor). Sometimes the prices in sales may have had more to do with the social position or relationships involved than with the value of the property sold; see, for example, the striking difference in payment that the canons of Agde made to two different fief holders for their shares in the identical tithes: *Cart. St-Etienne d'Agde*, nos. 267, 270.

29. *Cart. Lézat*, nos. 837 (1187), 1469 (1191), 1031 (1194). The vast majority of such

sharecropping grants to peasants, of which perhaps a hundred or more survive in the archives of the Templar and Hospitaler houses from the twelfth and thirteenth centuries, are in the form of donations *ad acaptum*, with no mention of fief or homage.

30. There are literally hundreds of examples of such grants in the Lézat cartulary: see the index rerum s.v. *feudum, fevum*. Nos. 1356–92 are a series of investitures of arable land or vineyards to peasants, all from the last half of the twelfth century.

31. Priests: *Cart. Lézat*, no. 1597 (1061–90), layman and wife granting a church with portion of tithes and first fruits to a priest; no. 1209 (1130–40), abbot grants church as fief; no. 712 (1171), granting tithes. Bishop of Agde gives church in fief to the abbot of Gellone (1190): MS Latin 9999, no. 110. Abbot of Eaunes: *Cart. Lézat*, no. 491 (1192). *Homo pagensis*: *Cart. Lézat*, no. 850 (1246); the expression may be a late development, but it conforms to long-established practice.

32. *Cart. St-Etienne d'Agde*, nos. 82, 100.

33. Pons's testament, in which he endows those masses, is *Cart. St-Etienne d'Agde*, no. 93 (1187). The two men appear twice together as witnesses: nos. 176, 215.

34. The fief of Peter Gaucelin's was so labeled: *Cart. St-Etienne d'Agde*, no. 100. For other examples, see *Cart. Lézat*, index s.v. *feudum honoratum* (a significantly incomplete list); and *Cartulaire de la Selve* (Ourliac and Magnou), no. 124. Military service: *Cart. Lézat*, nos. 1714 (1061–1108), 1211 (1197), 111 (1246). It is difficult to locate Peter Gaucelin exactly; although there are three contemporary men by that name in the Agde cartulary, only occasionally are they distinguished from each other by the village from which they came.

35. For Bernard Modul and Peter of Raissac and his brothers, see above, chap. 8. *Cart. Douzens* A, no. 1; *Cart. Lézat*, no. 1498.

36. *Cart. Lézat*, no. 1489 (1154), with the usual dues of agrarium (when the land is planted with grain), reacaptum, fidantias, justicia, and laudatio.

37. Priests as fief holders: *Cart. Lézat*, nos. 239 (cf. no. 242), 1209, 1597. Tithes: nos. 569 (in which the fief holder is assumed to have a *nuncius* who collects them), 1197. Military service: nos. 1211, 1215. For Peter of Raissac and his brothers, see above, chap. 8. The widow of William of Genestet: *Cart. St-Etienne d'Agde*, no. 133 (1167). Berenger of Montagnac is listed among the tenants of the canons in an estate inventory from Montagnac around the same time: no. 130. Raymond Roger: *Cart. Lézat*, no. 1715 (1061–1108).

38. Thanks to the prior's involvement, the documents illuminating the process at Lespinet have washed up in the cartulary of Lézat: nos. 1356–1406, with some interruptions. Woods: nos. 1478ff.

39. *Cart. Lézat*, no. 48.

40. Inv. Rocques, *Inféodations*, no. 1; ibid., *Sigean*, no. 64; ibid., *Acquisitions*, nos. 109, 110, and others; MS Doat 50, fol. 51 (1228).

41. Inv. Rocques, *Antugnac*, no. 3.

42. Explicitly so in *Cart. Lézat*, no. 1597 (1061–90).

43. These fees are a standard provision in most of the grants of fief in the Lézat cartulary.

44. In 1154 Ermengard—after a dispute decided in her court—allowed the abbey of Quarantes to keep the half of a tower and rights of lordship that Raymond Gaucelin held of her at Argelliers, the monks paying the substantial sum of fifteen hundred solidi. In 1182, "as a pure gift" ("titulo mere liberalitatis") she gave "whatever fiefs and rights of lordship" the same abbey might acquire "in my lands and potestativum": MS Doat 58, fols. 130, 142.

45. Inv. Rocques, *Acquisitions*, no. 110.

46. Among the fiefs that Raymond of Treville sold back to Archbishop Berenger in 1203 was the albergum due from one-sixth of a fief that two men held of the archbishop, which the archbishop had given Raymond in fief. For this, the archbishop paid 650 sol. Melg.: Inv. Rocques, *Acquisitions*, no. 15. See also the next note.

47. "[F]acimus te . . . participem omnium bonorum spiritualium; et promittimus . . . quod faciemus obitum tuum scribere [*sic*] in martyrologio Beati Stephani": *Cart. St-Etienne d'Agde*, no. 407. The other documents in this transaction are nos. 406 and 408 (1202–14). On the development of this distinction between the two forms of dominium in the work of medieval teachers of Roman law, see Meynial, "Note sur la formation de la théorie du domaine divisé."

48. "The truth is that the legal concepts [of fief] . . . had been imperfectly understood by a regional society familiar with quite different practices": Bloch, *Feudal Society*, 176.

49. The attempt to find such bundles of rights is the starting point, most notably, of Reynolds, *Fiefs and Vassals*, leading her to dismiss as unimportant most of the concerns of this chapter.

CHAPTER 13. LOVE AND FIDELITY

1. He received 850 sol. Melg. as well. *LIM*, no. 538, followed by oath of fidelity, no. 539 (1060). For a discussion of this ritual giving and receiving, see Cheyette, "On the *fief de reprise*."

2. Raimond IV: *HGL* 5:535. William of Pignan: *LIM*, no. 404. The sense of *drudaria* given in Niermeyer, *Mediae latinitatis lexicon minus*, taken from Du Cange—a share of revenue belonging to a lord's wife—is clearly inapplicable to both of these examples, although it appears in another document from Montpellier: AN P1353. Milac: Brunel, *Plus anciennes chartes*, no. 225. William of Tudela, *Chanson de la croisade* (ed. Martin-Chabot), 1:70. For a wider view of the sentiment of love as political and social phenomenon, see Jaeger, "Amour des rois," and his more recent *Ennobling Love*, especially 11–24, 36–53, 104–6; Clanchy, "Law and Love in the Middle Ages"; White, "*Pactum . . . Legem Vincit et Amor Judicium*." Compare with anger, grief, and hatred as political phenomena: Rosenwein, *Anger's Past*.

3. See Lutz, *Unnatural Emotions*, 53–80.

4. "History pays too little attention to the influence of these dreams of sublime life on civilization itself and on the forms of social life" (Huizinga, *Waning of the Middle Ages*, 29).

5. *LIM*, no. 106.

6. See Cropp, *Vocabulaire courtois*, 52–66.

7. William of Tudela, *Chanson de la croisade albigeoise*, 1:44.

8. Peire Rogier, "Per far exbaudir mos vezis," in *Peire Rogier* (ed. Nicholson), 61.

9. See Du Cange, *Glossarium mediae et infimae latinitatis*, s.v. Cropp, *Vocabulaire courtois*, 59 n. 37, refers only to W. von Wartburg, *Französisches etymologisches Wörterbuch*, and W. Meyer-Lübke, *Romanisches etymologisches Wörterbuch*, but there is an immense literature on the semantic field of this word in old Germanic languages, where its primary meaning is associated with the war band, from which, by the time of Otfrid, it had gained the meaning of "friend." Other recent work has proposed an early meaning of "festive band" or a link to Germanic "growth magic." Enright, *Lady with a Mead Cup*, 71–74, attempts to reconcile these versions of the word's etymology, with full references at 71 n. 8. The fullest account is in Green, *Carolingian Lord*, 270–357 and passim.

10. *Poésies de Peire Vidal*, 60.

11. See above, chap. 10.

12. Bernart de Ventadorn, "Pois preyatz me, senhor," in *Songs of Bernart de Ventadorn* (ed. Nichols, Galm, and Giamatti), 145–46.

13. "Non es mervelha s'eu chan," ibid., 132–33. Bernart's choice of "dan" as rhyme word here, whose meaning ranges from emotional "hurt" to "damage to rights," adds force to the political language of the first line. See Cropp, *Vocabulaire courtois*, 277–80.

14. "Non es meravelha s'eu chan," in *Bernart de Ventadorn*, 132–33.

15. The first was used by Raimon de Miraval, the other three by Bernart de Ventadorn.

16. For the story of this invention, see Paden, "Troubadour's Lady as Seen through Thick History."

17. For a brief critical survey of such theories, see Cheyette and Switten, "Women in Troubadour Song."

18. Ermengard, wife of Raimond Bernard, and one of the founders of the Trencavel family fortunes (see Cheyette, " 'Sale' of Carcassonne," 853–56); Cecilia, wife of Ermengard's son Bernard Ato and mother of viscounts Raimond Trencavel, Roger of Béziers, and Bernard Ato of Nîmes; Saura, wife of Raimond Trencavel; Guillelma, wife of Bernard Ato of Nîmes. All ruled as widows, and oaths of fidelity survive to all of them. Ermessendis, the widow of William V, would have received them as well. In the dynasty of Montpellier there were other important women overlords of castles as well: Tiburgis, daughter of William of Omelas, and Adalais, widow of Burgundio. Among the castles held of the lords of Montpellier, we know of six that had a woman castellan at some time during the twelfth century.

19. Raimon de Miraval, "Cel que no vol auzir chanssos," in *Cansos of Raimon de Miraval* (ed. Switten), 183.

20. Bertran de Born, "S'Abrils e fuolhas e flors," in *Poems of the Troubadour Bertran de Born* (ed. Paden, Sankovitch, and Stäblin), 256–65.

21. For an interesting, if often obscure, discussion of the song as fictional theater, see Warning, "Moi lyrique et société chez les troubadours."

22. "Le tems vai e ven e vire," in *Bernart de Ventadorn*, 129–30.

23. For a discussion of such crucial emotional/political words in these songs as *ira* and *dolor*, see White, "Politics of Anger," and Barton, " 'Zealous Anger' and the Renegotiation of Aristocratic Relationships in Eleventh- and Twelfth-Century France."

24. "La dousa votz," in *Bernart de Ventadorn*, 104–5.

25. "Aissi cum es genser pascors," in *Raimon de Miraval*, 144–45.

26. Text and translation (amended) from Bruckner, Shepard, and White, *Women Troubadours*, 6–9. In l. 19 I prefer to read the verbs as third person, as the Bruckner et al. edition allows, although they choose in their translation to make the verbs first person. The music was transcribed by Margaret Switten. In the manuscripts, both music and words are attributed to the Comtessa. For a detailed discussion of the music, see Pollina, "Melodic Continuity and Discontinuity in *A chantar m'er*," and Cheyette and Switten, "Women in Troubadour Song," 32–33.

27. Bruckner et al., *Women Troubadours*, 143, and Rieger, *Trobairitz*, 608–14.

28. Brunel, *Plus anciennes chartes*, no. 298 l. 58.

29. Ibid., no. 225 l. 27.

30. For example, ibid., no. 34 l. 1: "E la tor Blanca .vii. mes d'estatga."

31. See the comments of Martines, "Ritual Language in Renaissance Italy."

CHAPTER 14. RAYMOND V BUILDS HIS EMPIRE

1. Aurell, Cat., nos. 363bis, 364. For the Forcalquier genealogy, Poly, *Provence et la société féodale*, 34.

2. Testament: *LFM*, no. 494. When Petronilla formally handed over Aragon and Barcelona to her son in 1164, she called him "filio meo Ildefonso, . . . qui in testamento . . . viri mei vocaris Raimundus" (my son Alfons, who is called Ramon in my husband's testament): *LFM*, no. 17. "Prince of Aragon": William of Newburgh, *Chronicles*, 1:124–25.

3. Caruana, "Itinerario," 76, 78. William of Montpellier styles himself *procurator* in two

debt contracts of 1167: ACA *perg. Alfonso I*, nos. 48, 55; he rendered his accounts in 1171: ibid., no. 105.

4. *LFM*, no. 810. The text of the mortgage, unfortunately, does not survive.

5. James Todesca gives a brief survey of this monetary history as well as photographs of the Catalan imitations in "Islamic Coinage in Christian Spain." On the flow of gold to Barcelona, see Bonnassie, *Catalogne*, 1:372–99, 417–25, especially the tables and graphs, 374–75. For the *taïfas*, see Wasserstein, *Party-Kings*.

6. ACA *perg. Ram. Ber. IV, apendice* no. 8: "Morabitinos aiadinos et lupinos," the former named for Ibn Yyad, king of Valencia, the latter for his successor Ibn Mardanish, known to Christians as el Rey Lobo. See Ubieto Artur, "Morabedis ayadinos," who does not include these contracts in her list of documents mentioning this coinage.

7. Debts to William Letericus: ACA *perg. Ram. Ber. IV, apendices* nos. 8, 9; to Genoese and Bertrand Porcellet of Arles: Aurell, *Cat.*, nos. 7, 24.

8. The loan of 1160, ACA *perg. Ram. Ber. IV, apendice* no. 8, bears an endorsement dated 1174 by which the hostages and the scribe recognized the truth of the document, sworn before Guy Guerrejat, uncle and tutor of the young William VIII. The account of 1171 is ACA *perg. Alfonso I*, no. 105. A few of the documents he must have deposited at that time are still in the archives: ibid., nos. 48, 55 (both 1167), 56 (1168). The parade of debt continued: ibid., nos. 162, 171 (1174), 207 (1176), both contracted by Guy Guerrejat. Their presence in the royal archives can only mean that they were contracted in the king's name.

9. For what follows, see the judicious remarks of Léonard, *Cat.*, xxvii–xxxii.

10. Bernard of Clairvaux, *Letters*, no. 399 (older editions, no. 256). See also Robert of Torigny in *Chronicles* (ed. Howlett), 4:154. In English, the classic account of these events remains Runciman, *History of the Crusades*, 2:247–88.

11. Runciman, *History*, 2:280; and *HGL* 3:754–55, 758. The last story is told by Robert of Torigny, in *Chronicles*, 4:266.

12. Gerald of Wales, "Gemma ecclesiastica," in *Opera*, 2:216–17, and "Liber de principis instructione," in *Opera*, 8:132.

13. William of Newburgh, "Historia" in *Chronicles* (ed. Howlett), 1:66–67; Pacaut, *Louis VII*, 59–60; John of Salisbury, *Historia pontificalis*, 53.

14. *RHGF* 12:229, 286: two anonymous later-medieval "brief histories of France." The legend about Saladin began with an anonymous minstrel of Rheims less than a century after Eleanor's death. For this and later stories, see Chambers, "Some Legends concerning Eleanor of Aquitaine." See also Vacandard, "Divorce de Louis le Jeune," 414.

15. See the remarks of Gillingham, "Love, Marriage," 251–52; Cadden, *Meanings of Sex Difference*, 93–97, 246–48. Examples of the medical literature that Louis's physicians would have followed are in Barkai, *History of Jewish Gynaecological Texts*.

16. John of Salisbury, *Historia pontificalis*, 53, who also tells the story of the couple's passage through Italy on their way home. Bernard gave them a common ancestor three generations back: *Letters*, 371. Audiard, Eleanor's great-grandmother, was King Robert's granddaughter. Through King Henry I's grandmother Adela, King Robert's daughter, Eleanor, was as closely related to her next husband, the future Henry II. For contemporaries the problem would have been lost information about descent on the female side, because Louis's direct descent from Robert was undisputed. Surprisingly, even Vacandard at the end of the nineteenth century does not give the correct genealogy: "Divorce de Louis le Jeune," 417. See Warren, *Henry II*, 42–45; and Pacaut, *Louis VII*, 60–65.

17. Pacaut, *Louis VII*, 63–65; Warren, *Henry II*, 45–53.

18. Pacaut, *Louis VII*, 187, 191–94; Boussard, *Gouvernement d'Henri II*, 417ff.; Warren, *Henry II*, 82ff.

19. Benjamin, "Forty-Years War," 271; Warren, *Henry II*, 85–88; Boussard, *Gouverne-*

ment d'Henri II, 417–23. The primary narratives are the "Continuatio Beccensis," in *Chronicles* (ed. Howlett), 4:321–23; Robert of Torigny, ibid., 4:200–203, 205; and William of Newburgh, ibid., 1:121–26.

20. *RHGF* 16:21–23. At an uncertain date, perhaps in the spring of 1161, when forces were mustering on the Norman and Angevin frontier (William of Newburgh, in *Chronicles*, [ed. Howlett], 1:130–31), the city government of Toulouse heard rumors that they were about to be attacked and asked Louis to keep them informed of Henry's movements: *RHGF* 16:68–69. Further details in Benjamin, "Forty-Years War," 171–72.

21. *RHGF* 16:70–72.

22. Previté-Orton, *Early History of the House of Savoy*, 329.

23. *RHGF* 16:70.

24. Alès: ibid., 83–85. The letter writers also called on Louis to ask Alexander III to place all the offender's lands under interdict. Ivo's letter: ibid., 87.

25. Ibid., 126.

26. Ibid., 109, 127–28.

27. *LFM*, no. 898. On Beatrice of Mauguio, see above, chap. 1.

28. *HGL* 6:21, 68. *LFM*, no. 899. Her marriage to Ramon Berenguer had helped ease the way to the prospective Catalan–Imperial alliance in 1162: Fried, "Friedrich Barbarossas Krönung in Arles," 356.

29. Aurell, Cat., nos. 1–3.

30. *Gesta comitum barcinonensium*, 379.

31. Aurell, Cat., nos. 7, 7bis, 7ter; Caruana, "Itinerario," 94–97; ACA *perg. Alfonso I*, nos. 48, 55. The Genoese demanded assurances that the royal debts to them would be paid and their maritime rivals excluded from ports under Barcelonese control.

32. Raymond and Alexander: *HGL* 6:19–20. Through the intervention of King Louis, the city of Toulouse managed to have the interdict lifted for itself, as long as the count was not present there. Meeting with Henry II: Benjamin, "Forty-Years War," 273–74.

33. *HGL* 6:28–29; William of Newburgh, in *Chronicles* (ed. Howlett), 1:126–30. By the time the story reached this chronicler, the victim's name had become William Trencavel and the place of the murder the cathedral. On the saint, see Sigal, "Bernard le Pénitent."

34. See Cheyette, " 'Sale' of Carcassonne." In each generation, border conflicts as well as mortgages and other *convenientia* that repaired relations, kept the memories alive: for example, *HGL* 5:734–38 (and Cart. Trencavel, fol. 84), 926, 961, 963–64, 1071, 1118, among many others.

35. A false or partially falsified codicil to Raymond Trencavel's will, bearing an erroneous date, formalizes Roger's succession: *HGL* 8:266. For a discussion of this curious document, most likely concocted after the Albigensian Crusade, see chap. 17. The conjunction in this text of a brief statement making Roger of Béziers his heir and a much longer text (the part that is certainly a forgery) concerning the seneschal of Albi makes it conceivable that the forger expanded on a genuine original.

36. *HGL* 8:273. Among the witnesses was one of the few women to be mentioned as members of Ermengard's court, the otherwise unidentifiable Esclaramond of Saint-Félix.

37. During Frederick's stay in Burgundy in 1170, Raymond joined him at Givors, where he found himself in the company of such imperial dignitaries as Bishop Ludwig of Basel and Berthold von Zähringen: Georgi, *Friedrich Barbarossa und die auswärtingen Mächte*, 276–77. On the complexities of imperial politics in Provence in the 1170s, see Fried, "Friedrich Barbarossas Krönung in Arles."

38. *HGL* 8:276–79. With the exception of William of Sabran, all the witnesses to the marriage were from the entourage of Roger and Ermengard, including William of Poitiers, Raymond of Salles, Peter Raymond of Narbonne, and Gaucerand of Capestang. The oath

from Raymond to Roger that survives was doubtless the counterpart of an oath of fidelity made in the other direction, accompanied—according to Roger's own statement in 1178—by a grant of lands in fief.

39. *HGL* 6:44–45.

40. The first division of Mauguio: *Cart. Maguelone*, 1, no. 155. The mint: ibid., no. 156. The settlement with Raymond: *HGL* 8:293. Bertrand and Alfons: *LFM*, nos. 870, 871. Unfortunately, of the *conveniencia* with the lords of Lunel and Bernis concerning Mauguio, dated October 1173, only the title remains: *LFM*, no. 872.

41. Nîmes: *HGL* 5:1265. William VII: *LIM*, no. 184.

42. Quoted by Léonard, *Cat.*, xxxi.

43. On this traditional rivalry, see Guichonnet, *Histoire de la Savoie*, 141, and Previté-Orton, *House of Savoy*, chaps. 3 and 4.

44. Georgi, *Friedrich Barbarossa*, 182; Previté-Orton, *House of Savoy*, 332–37.

45. Roger of Hoveden, not one to mince words, says the king "bought" (*comparavit*) the girl for his son: *Gesta regis*, 1:36. On Henry's suspected Italian ambitions: Georgi, *Friedrich Barbarossa*, 285 and n. 233; Gerald of Wales, *Opera*, 8:157.

46. Ralph of Diceto's remark: *Opera Historica*, 1:353. On the treaty and Raymond's homage: Roger of Hoveden, *Gesta regis*, 1:36; Robert of Torigny, in *Chronicles* (ed. Howlett), 4:255. The details in Roger of Hoveden's text make one suspect he saw the oath of homage. The chroniclers do not give the text of the peace between Raymond and Alfons. It is possible that it is the undated document now housed in the departmental archives of the Bouches-du-Rhone, B 286, in which Raymond promises Alfons a ten-year truce in that part of Provence traditionally under Catalan lordship. On the basis of the names mentioned in the document, Léonard dates it 1167–73: *Cat.*, no. 66. In 1170 the two Alfonsos—of Castile and of Aragon—signed a peace treaty in which they referred to Henry as "like our father," "quem pro patre habemus": *LFM*, no. 32. Alfonso of Castile had just been betrothed to Henry's daughter.

47. *RHGF* 16:158–59.

48. See Warren, *Henry II*, 530–34, 117.

49. Gerald of Wales, *Opera*, 8:157.

50. Ibid., 159.

51. See Warren, *Henry II*, chap. 3, and Gillingham, *Richard I*, 41–51.

52. Caruana, "Itinerario," 145–46. The marriage contract has not been published, and the knighting ceremony is known only from a chance mention in the dating clause of a private contract.

53. The evidence for Catalan activity in the years of Alfons's minority has been assembled in Aurell, *Cat.*, nos. 1–19. The ransoming of the viscount of Marseille is mentioned in the treaty of Jarnègues of 1176 (see below). Raymond's treaty with the Genoese: Léonard, *Cat.*, 66bis, 66ter. Alfons was in Perpignan in November and December 1174 and in Limoux in December 1175: Caruana, "Itinerario," 79, 86. The evidence for the raid in 1175 is presented by Altisent, "A propos de l'expédition d'Alphonse le Chaste."

54. Which Geoffrey most likely would have known through the first-century compendium *Ilias Latina*. My thanks to my colleague Rebecca Sinos for this suggestion.

55. The treaty is printed in *LFM*, no. 899, and summarized in Léonard, *Cat.*, no. 81. Hugh Gaufredus, master of the Knights Templars, presided over the arbitration. Ermengard and Raymond's closest advisor, his constable William of Sabran, along with (an otherwise unknown) Ismido de Pauta, represented Raymond; Guy Guerrejat and two of Alphons's closest advisors and companions, Arnold of Vilademuls and Raymond of Montcada, represented the king. Geoffrey of Vigeois's account: "Chronicle," in *RHGF* 12:444. What one should make of it is hard to say. Apart from the countess, the persons he mentions—if we ac-

cept that Ramnous de Venoul, or de Meullo, is Raimond of Villademuls, and that William de Mita is really William de Mota—are all named as witnesses to the treaty. (These transformations could be the work of manuscript copyists.) He clearly had some accurate information, to which, as usual, he added his own hyperbole.

56. Bertran de Born, "Lo coms m'a mandat e mogut," in *Bertran de Born* (ed. Paden et al.), 104–11. Translation from Bonner, *Songs of the Troubadours*, 144–45, with some modifications.

57. The archives of the counts of Toulouse passed with all their lands into the hands of the Capetians. At the end of the fourteenth century they still numbered 497 parchments plus six registers. But the principal body of documents remained in the south, in the Court of Accounts of Montpellier, and were burned there in 1793. Léonard, *Cat.*, lists 158 documents for a reign of forty-five years, or a little more than three documents per year. Compare this, for example, with Caruana's "Itinerario," which includes only documents mentioning and dating that king's presence (and does not include, therefore, the vast number of administrative documents issued in his name or undated documents, such as oaths of fidelity) and which averages about eighteen documents per year.

58. See Léonard, *Cat.*, index s.v. Ermengarde.

59. The career of one of these, Gerald Amic, can be followed in some detail through thirty-four documents in the J series of the Archives Nationales: see *Layettes du trésor des Chartes* (ed. Teulet), 1, index s.v. Amicus, Geraldus.

CHAPTER 15. RAVAGING OF OCCITANIA

1. In the absence of chronicles, only two meager documents tell us of the coup: a grant to the Knights Templars dated December 21, 1177, at Narbonne (*HGL* 8:328) and the mutual oaths of Raymond's enemies described below.

2. Aymeri first appears at Ermengard's side when she makes a gift to the tiny monastery of Sainte-Eugenia in 1163 (document in collection A. Combes, Albi; mentioned in *HGL* 3:837). The date of his disappearance is problematic: the charter giving himself as a monk to Fontfroide is dated January 23, 1176 (that is, 1177 in the Gregorian calendar: MS Doat 59, fol. 70), yet by a document dated June 1177 he buys a horse worth eleven hundred solidi on credit from a couple in Salses, giving three important members of Ermengard's court as hostages (*HGL* 8:319). The most likely resolution to this conundrum is to assume that this second document is dated "Pisan style" (thus beginning the year at the Annunciation [March 25] that precedes January 1, when our year begins—a form of dating frequently used in the region) that is, June 1176 in the Gregorian calendar. In January 1177 (Gregorian calendar) he went with King Alfons to negotiate and sign a treaty with Pisa at Tarascon on the Rhone (ACA *perg. Alfonso I*, no. 214; Caruana, "Itinerario," 165; Aurel, Cat., no. 34). He then accompanied the king back to Perpignan. According to the charter, he gave himself to Fontfroide in the king's presence "in a vineyard outside of Perpignan," suggesting a sudden decision rapidly executed rather than a long-contemplated retreat from the world.

3. For Manrique's death, see Doubleday, "Laras," 148; the *Crónica geral de Espanha de 1344*, 4:275–76, gives a colorful (but probably imaginary) account of his death in single combat with his archenemy from the Castro family. In 1167, when Ermessend gave property to the monastery of Santa Maria de Huerta, Pedro was there to confirm, but not Aymeri (*Cartulario del Monasterio de Santa Maria de Huerta*, no. 7); in a gift of 1172 he styles himself "dux Narbone" (ibid., no. 16). Doubleday's "Laras" is largely devoted to an account of the family's property holdings; for those of Manrique, see "Laras," 125, and for Nuño and his sons, 149–216.

4. These two Occitan families were now also allied by marriage; Bernard Ato of Nîmes was the son of Guillelma of Montpellier and, in 1177, still under the tutelage of his maternal uncle Guy Guerrejat: *HGL* 8:327–28.

5. Ibid., 325.

6. See above, chap. 14.

7. *LFM*, no. 854. A host of oaths and agreements accompanied this avowal in November: ibid., nos. 855–65; *Layettes du trésor des Chartes*, nos. 297, 298. Alfons had been with Roger and Ermengard at least since October, when Bernard Ato of Nîmes had also reaffirmed his alliance: *HGL* 8:337–39; *LFM*, nos. 867–68. The alliance with Peire (alias Ramon Berenguer IV) was sealed with a gift *en reprise* of three castles in the mountains of the Albigeois: *HGL* 8:339–40; *LFM*, nos. 863, 864.

8. For the text of this account, see Cheyette, " 'Sale' of Carcassonne," 831–32, where my summary of the politics of this moment in n. 13 is likewise short on accuracy.

9. Pedro is first in evidence at Ermengard's side in October 1179: *HGL* 8:337. The "Petrus comes" who appears frequently in the charters of Santa Maria de Huerta in Castile (see above, n. 3) is absent there from 1179 to 1189 and then only appears again in 1195 and 1199–1200; he seems most likely to be our Pedro de Lara: *Cartulario del Monasterio de Santa Maria de Huerta*, passim. Ermengard was fully back in control of Narbonne by 1182 when she negotiated a treaty with Genoa: *LIG*, no. 337. It is possible that Raymond of Toulouse reentered Narbonne again in 1184, when Raymond Vassadeli of Puisserguier, taking in fief the right to "protect" traffic (that is, collect tolls) on the road from Béziers to Narbonne, promised to support Roger of Béziers against "the lord of Toulouse and the lord [masculine] of Narbonne": *HGL* 8:377–78; the most likely interpretation of this phrase is that it is a reference to Raymond's title of count of Toulouse and duke of Narbonne; it is certainly not a mistranscription for "lady," for just a month earlier Ermengard along with some of the members of Roger's court arbitrated Raymond Vassadeli's dispute with another Biterrois lord over land in the village of Baissan: *Cart. Béziers*, no. 287.

10. Bertran de Born, "Be·m plai lo gais temps de pascor," stanzas 1 and 5, in *Bertran de Born* (ed. Paden et al.), 339, 343.

11. For the story, see Amado, "Famille aristocratique," 2:97–102, 416–20, and genealogy, 426.

12. Debts: ACA *perg. Alfonso I*, nos. 162, 171, 207; arbitration: Aurell, Cat., no. 40. For treaty of Jarnègues, see above, chap. 14.

13. Aurell i Cardona, "Expansion catalane en Provence," 103, gives a brief account of the murder and its aftermath. For Alfons's allies: ACA *perg. Alfonso I*, no. 337 (Aurell, Cat., no. 120), where William of Sabran receives the oath of Bernard of Anduze against Raymond on behalf of King Alfons in the presence of a number of other great lords of the region. Caruana in "Itinerario" says Alfons met with Henry II in July 1183, but this is impossible because Henry was then in England. Siege of Fourques: Aurell, Cat., no. 60.

14. Albon: Fournier, *Royaume d'Arles et de Vienne*, 72 n. 3; *HGL* 4:225–26, 6:106. Toulouse: Mundy, *Liberty and Political Power*, 68.

15. Acquisition of Nîmes: *HGL* 8:335. References to specific destructive moments are rare yet revealing: for example, the charter of reparations that Alfons of Aragon granted the abbey of Franquevaux "for the damages which I inflicted on the monks in the Argence [a region on the Rhone just south of Arles that was part of the lordship of Saint-Gilles] when I was laying siege to Fourques": *HGL* 8:382.

16. Bertran de Born, "Miei serventes vuolh far dels reis amdos," in *Bertran de Born* (ed. Paden et al.), 396–401. The two kings are Richard the Lionheart and Alfonso of Castile, and the poem probably dates to the 1190s, but its sentiments are surely not restricted to that decade.

17. It was in April 1184, perhaps just after King Alfons had rescued the city for him, that Roger of Béziers granted a major charter of privileges and liberties to the inhabitants of Carcassonne. The text does not mention the quid pro quo, but it is hard to imagine that there was none. *HGL* 8:374–76. See likewise the privileges Alfons granted to Tarascon, Arles, and Nice during the 1180s (Aurell, Cat., nos. 76bis, 84, 87) and his 1185 recognizance of the debts both his grandfather and father owed the bishop of Avignon (ibid., no. 77).

18. Quoted in Bonner, *Songs of the Troubadours*, 282.

19. Stephan, bishop of Tournai, epistola 73: *PL* 211:371–72.

20. Epistola 75: ibid., 375.

21. Many were known simply by their place of origin, the most famous—or infamous— being those from Brabant. The vernacular names, *rota / ruta / route* and *coterel* have given rise to endless etymological conjectures. The first seems to have meant simply a band or following, before it took on the special meaning of a band of freebooters. The second may have come from *cultellus* (knife) or from *coterel* (a small coat of mail). (See Contamine, *War in the Middle Ages*, 243–44, to be corrected by Grundmann, "Rotten und Brabanzonen," 424–36. Much of the account that follows comes from Grundmann's work, which includes in the notes extensive quotations from twelfth-century writers.) Even contemporaries played with folk etymologies. The Limousin monastic chronicler Geoffrey of Vigeois heard the name "pailler," which in its context seems to refer to the Pyrenees county of Pallars, but which Geoffrey derived from *palearii*, "strawmen." Contamine has a learned footnote speculating on this etymology (*War in the Middle Ages*, 244).

22. On this "revolution" in warfare, see Boussard, "Mercenaires au XIIe siècle," and the brief remarks in Warren, *Henry II*, 232–34, who is so royalist in his attitude toward King Henry that he almost succeeds in turning these cutthroats into London bobbies.

23. "Rex Angliae ruptores, imo raptores, . . . exacrabiliter investivit," wrote a chronicler of Angers: Grundmann, "Rotten und Brabanzonen," 437 n. 1. Grundmann's assertion that the word does not mean "robber" in this context is not convincing. The word play here and elsewhere would lose its force if the expression were not derogatory. The remainder of this paragraph uses material from Grundmann's article.

24. *HGL* 8:341.

25. Walter Map, *De nugis curialium*, 118–19, translation revised.

26. Payment for military service: see the discussion in Contamine, *War in the Middle Ages*, 90ff. Booty: *praeda* in medieval Latin meant both robbery and booty; see Grundmann, "Rotten und Brabanzonen," 437 n. 1, and any dictionary of medieval Latin.

27. Boussard, "Mercenaires," 218–20; Contamine, *War in the Middle Ages*, 52.

28. There are almost no direct means for making such estimates, but one can make a very rough approximation by projecting forward from the manorial data in Domesday Book, for example, or backward from tax assessments of the early fourteenth century.

29. Vincent of Prague speaks of 1,500 Brabançons led to Rome by Philip of Heinsberg in 1166 (Grundmann, "Rotten und Brabanzonen," 442 n. 3); William of Newburgh speaks with remarkable precision of 800 horse soldiers and 4,000 foot soldiers in the service of the king's enemies in 1173, whereas others number them 10,000 or 17,000 (as quoted in Grundmann, "Rotten und Brabanzonen," 454 n. 1); Geoffrey of Vigeois puts 20,000 in the service of the Young King in 1183, with 1,500 prostitutes in their company (ibid., 466 n. 4 and 469 n. 3), and in 1184 places Lobar and Sanç and their "innumerabili hoste Exandonensem quasi ab anxietate appellatam" at Saint-Gerold d' Aurillac: *RHGF* 18:223; it was one of Geoffrey's favorite descriptors (as, for another example, the "innumerable force" that the "Young King" and his brother Geoffrey brought to Limoges in preparation for an attack on their brother Richard in 1183; ibid., 213). The number of dead at the battle of Dun-le-Roi that year

is variously given as 10,525, 7,000, and 17,000 (Grundmann, "Rotten und Brabanzonen," 469 n. 2).

30. Séranne is a mountainous area in the Hérault: Norgate, *Richard the Lion Heart*, 53. Geoffrey of Vigeois gives Sanç's name as "of Savannac" (which could be a village by that name in the Hérault): *RHGF* 18:214. One manuscript of Geoffrey of Vigeois gives Milhau (in the Aveyron) as Curbaran's home: ibid., 219.

31. Alberigo et al., *Conciliorum oecumenicorum decreta*, Lateran III, canon 27.

32. Grundmann, "Rotten und Brabanzonen," 436–39.

33. Gervase of Canterbury, *Historical Works*, 1:300; "Ex annalibus aquicinctensis monasterii," *RHGF* 18:535.

34. Hoffmann, *Gottesfriede und Treuga Dei*, 112ff.; and the more recent rapid survey by Bisson, "Organized Peace." The sworn peace of Béziers is in *HGL* 8:275, dated by the editors "around 1170."

35. Gervase of Canterbury, *Historical Works*, 1:300–301. Geoffrey of Vigeois, closer to the events in time and place, gives "104 or 5" as the number of his original adherents, does not mention the vision, and says of the bishop, "He was astonished at the man's lowliness and scorned his common speech": *RHGF* 18:219. Gervase and Geoffrey give the two most detailed contemporary accounts of the events.

36. *HGL* 8:355.

37. Geoffrey of Vigeois, *RHGF* 18:219; Robert of Autun, canon of Saint-Mary's, ibid., 251; anonymous of Laon, ibid., 705–6.

38. *RHGF* 18:706, 729; see also Géraud, "Routiers au douzième siècle," 145–47. Geoffrey of Vigeois stopped writing his chronicle before these events, in 1183. Gervase of Canterbury was interested only in their miraculous appearance and early achievements.

39. *RHGF* 18:705, 729–30. On the continuity of the "culture of rebellion" in the Middle Ages, with specific discussion of the Capucians, see Oexle, "Kultur der Rebellion."

CHAPTER 16. SOWING THE SEEDS OF CRUSADE

1. To my pleasure, the article of Jean-Louis Biget, "Les Albigeois," published long after this and the following chapter were first written, presents in brief the same narrative as I do here.

2. On the dating of this letter (1177 in Gervase, but 1175 in Léonard, *Cat.*, no. 55), see Congar, "Henri de Marcy," 10 n. 31.

3. Luke 22:36–39. Bernard of Clairvaux, *Five Books on Consideration*, 118 (iv, 7), and idem, *Letters*, no. 399 (older editions, no. 256). See Kennan, "The *de Consideratione* of St. Bernard of Clairvaux."

4. Gervase, *Historical Works*, 1:269–71. Chroniclers much closer to Toulouse, such as Geoffrey of Vigeois and Robert of Auxerre, are utterly silent on the letter and the Cistercian mission, although they are well aware of the later mission *manu militari*. The monastic telephone did not make connections everywhere.

5. *RHGF* 16:159–60. See Ermengard's letter above, chap. 14.

6. Fichtenau, *Heretics and Scholars*, 59, asserts that this usual toponymic—Henry of Lausanne—is a mistake but shows that the alternate name of Henry the Monk is likewise probably a misnomer.

7. Bernard of Clairvaux, *Letters*, no. 317 (older editions, no. 241).

8. Moore, *Birth of Popular Heresy*, 34.

9. Quoted in Constable, *Three Studies in Medieval Religious and Social Thought*, 180, who in part 2 lays out the many versions of "imitating Christ" that coexisted in the first fifteen

hundred years of Christian history but insists that in the eleventh century, imitation "deepened . . . into a passionate devotion to His humanity, which increasingly excluded other models" (179).

10. Manteuffel, *Naissance d'une hérésie*, chaps. 1–3; Landes, "Vie apostolique en Aquitaine en l'an mil"; Leyser, *Hermits and the New Monasticism*. For Robert of Arbrissel, see Bienvenu, *Etonnant fondateur de Fontevraud, Robert d'Arbrissel*; Smith, "Robert of Arbrissel's Relations with Women."

11. Marbod, bishop of Rennes, epistola 6, in *PL* 171:1483.

12. Bienvenu, *Robert d'Arbrissel*, 65–68.

13. Pauline Stafford makes some cogent remarks on the inconsistencies and tensions within tenth- and eleventh-century "reform" ideas, especially with reference to gender, in "Queens, Nunneries and Reforming Churchmen," 6–15; for Saint Eugenia and Saint Eufrasia, see ibid.

14. Guibert, abbot of Nogent, *A Monk's Confession* (ed. Archambault), 25–28; idem, *Self and Society in Medieval France* (ed. Benton), 55.

15. Constable, *Three Studies*, 305–12.

16. On the complex story of celibacy in the Church, see the essays in Frassetto, *Medieval Purity and Piety*.

17. Revelations 2:6, 15.

18. Pataria: brief narration in Manteuffel, *Naissance d'une hérésie*, 15–23; further bibliography in Blumenthal, *Investiture Controversy*, 103. Ramihrdus: Moore, *Origins of European Dissent*, 62–63.

19. In his invective against clerical homosexuality and masturbation, in *Book of Gomorrah*, 76.

20. Erikson, *Wayward Puritans*, 5.

21. For this and what follows, see Lobrichon, "Chiaroscuro of Heresy," and Landes, "Vie apostolique," 581–87.

22. Acts of the Apostles 2:44–47.

23. Bernard of Clairvaux, *Letters*, no. 158 (in older editions, no. 152). See the discussion in White, "Gregorian Ideal and Saint Bernard of Clairvaux," 335–41.

24. On the growth of this idea in the eleventh and twelfth centuries, see Le Goff, *Birth of Purgatory*.

25. See Moore, *Origins*, 92–101.

26. Moore, *Popular Heresy*, 43.

27. See Moore, *Origins*, 199–200; Lambert, *Cathars*, chap. 1; Fichtenau, *Heretics and Scholars*, chap. 2.

28. On this name see Fichtenau, *Heretics and Scholars*, 87, who believes the name came not from Greek but from a German vernacular term (it first appears in a sermon of Ekbert of Schönau), which Ekbert confused with the ancient Novatians who called themselves Katharoi; Ekbert would have known of them from reading Augustine. If it is really a Greek term, it is puzzling that the Bogomils never used it.

29. Early Cathars: Lambert, *Cathars*, chap. 2; Fichtenau, *Heretics and Scholars*, chap. 3. The so-called council of Lombers: Moore, *Popular Heresy*, 94–98 (in abridged form). Meeting at Saint-Félix-de-Caraman: Moore, *Popular Heresy*, chap. 3, and Wakefield and Evans, *Heresies of the High Middle Ages*, 126–41, 189–200. Brief discussion of the literature in Moore, *Origins*, 212–15; see also Hamilton, "Cathar Council of St. Félix de Caraman Reconsidered."

30. That incurable collector and compiler Roger of Hoveden included an abbreviated version of the record of Lombers in *Chronica* (2:105–17), but he dates it to 1176 and probably learned about it—and got his copy of the record—from the bishop of Bath or someone in his company after the mission of 1177. He did not know of Raymond's letter to the abbot

of Cîteaux and probably ascribed the kings' momentary plan to fight the heretics to the meeting at Lombers.

31. Ancient Manichaeism: Lieu, *Manichaeism in the Later Roman Empire*, and idem, *Manichaeism in Mesopotamia*. Medieval use of the name: Wakefield and Evans, *Heresies*, see index s.v. Manichaeans, and Moore, *Origins*, 9 and passim; detailed comparison of Cathars and Manichees in Hagman, "Catharisme: Un néo-Manicheisme?"

32. Song of Songs 2:15. This text was already interpreted in this manner by Origen (see Kolmar, *Ad capiendas vulpes*, 9, and the references he cites), and by Saint Augustine. Revived in the eleventh century, the symbol was widely used in the twelfth: Congar, "Henri de Marcy," 13 n. 37. It seems likely, however, that whoever composed Raymond's letter had learned the topos from Saint Bernard. Evervin's appeal is translated in Wakefield and Evans, *Heresies*, 127–32, and Moore, *Popular Heresy*, 74–78. Bernard's sermon on "the little foxes" in reply is also found in Wakefield and Evans, 132–38. Analysis of both texts in Brenon, "Lettre d'Evervin de Steinfeld," and Kienzle, "Tending the Lord's Vineyard," pt. 1; a more fragmented version is in Fichtenau, *Heretics and Scholars*, 63–65, 79–80, 99–100.

33. Although some twelfth-century authors did, for example, Ekbert of Schönau: Moore, *Popular Heresy*, 88–94. Fichtenau insists on the differences: *Heretics and Scholars*, chaps. 2 and 3.

34. On this curious issue of the Cathar "pope," doubtless a Western misunderstanding of the Byzantine word for "father," see Brenon, "Lettre d'Evervin de Steinfeld," 26.

35. Moore, *Popular Heresy*, 75.

36. Ralph of Coggeshall, *Chronicon Anglicanum*, 122–24; the translation is from Moore, *Popular Heresy*, 87. The incident took place some time after 1176. Gervase of Tilbury was the author of the *Otio imperialia*, an encyclopedic collection of geographic and scientific information and stories of marvels of nature. Ralph's description of Gervase's encounter with the girl (which could be Gervase's himself) sounds as though it came straight from a troubadour pastorela: "Quam salutans, et unde et cujus esset filia, et quidnam ibidem sola ageret, diligenter inquirens, cum ejus pulchritudinem diutius attendisset, hanc tandem de amore lascivo curialiter affatur. Cui illi simplici gesta et cum quadam verborum gravitate respondit."

37. Bernard Hamilton surveys the passage of Bogomil texts to the west in "Wisdom from the East." Anne Brenon believes that the surviving vernacular New Testament of Cathar origin (in a Lyon MS) derives from a pre-Vulgate version, most likely of Greek origin (Brenon, *Vrai visage du catharisme*, 28–29), but the comparison with Vulgate manuscript variants has not yet been done.

38. Brief accounts of Bogomil and Bogomilism in Lambert, *Medieval Heresy*, 13–23, and idem, *Cathars*, 23–37, and in Moore, *Origins*, 139–67; more detailed treatment in Angelov, "Bogomilisme." What follows in the next several paragraphs is largely a summary recasting of my article "Cathars" in the *Dictionary of the Middle Ages*, 3:182–86, which gives further bibliography. (In that article, alas, Bulgaria became transmuted into Bosnia, where Bogomilism became a kind of "state church" in the thirteenth century and endured until the Ottoman conquest. See Rakova, "Bogomilisme et l'église bosniaque." Like medieval heretics before the inquisitors, I hereby renounce my errors on this and other matters. My apologies to my readers.)

39. Lambert, *Medieval Heresy*, 13.

40. Myths rather than a myth; on this multiplicity, see Fichtenau, *Heretics and Scholars*, chap. 6.

41. Wakefield and Evans, *Heresies*, 459.

42. Brown, *Body and Society*, 53.

43. Ibid., 86. I do not wish to claim, of course, that the Bogomils and Cathars were in any way the theological heirs of these earlier teachers, only that such impulses inhered in that

great and varied body that we call the Christian tradition and were always ready at a propitious moment to inspire a reading or hearing of the Scripture.

44. Quote from James Capelli, a thirteenth-century Franciscan who was the most sympathetic of all medieval enemies of the Cathars: Wakefield and Evans, *Heresies*, 303. On rituals, succinct description in Brenon, *Vrai visage*, 78–88; for *consolamentum*: Brenon, "Fonctions sacramentelles du consolament."

45. Evervin: Moore, *Popular Heresy*, 76. Description of practices and sacraments: Ekbert of Schönau, in ibid., 88–94; or the questions put to the "good men" at Lombers in 1165, ibid., 94–96. On the diversity of Cathar beliefs in Italy, see Lansing, *Power and Purity*, 10–19, 81–134; on the difficulty contemporaries had distinguishing heretics from the orthodox, Dossat, "Cathars dans les documents de l'inquisition"; and for the astonishing story of Armanno Pungilupo, a thirteenth-century Cathar of Ferrara who nearly became a saint, Merlo, *Eretici ed eresie medievali*, 107–11, and Zanella, *Hereticalia*, 3–14.

46. Moore, *Popular Heresy*, 76.

47. Quoted in Brown, *Body and Society*, 205.

48. See ibid., especially 203; for a detailed consideration of the reformers campaign for clerical celibacy, Frassetto, *Medieval Purity and Piety*.

49. Although no texts tell us so specifically, this must have been the reason why the sexual lapses of the Perfects caused such chaos among believers, and especially among those to whom they had given the *consolamentum*—the laying-on of hands that made a Perfect. The power of the Perfect to perform this important sacrament came from the belief that he was already joined to the world of the Spirit. A sexual lapse was not simply a sin, it was a sign that the joining had not taken place, that the Perfect was still attached to this world and his powers nonexistent. Abstinence was not simply a heroic act of self-denial, it was a symbolic proof that one had successfully abandoned the world of the devil. Such lapses and their fissiparous consequences were gleefully and unsympathetically reported by the Dominican historian of the Cathars, Anselm of Alessandria (Wakefield and Evans, *Heresies*, 361–73), for whom they were but one more sign of the falsity of the sect.

50. Gregory VII, *Correspondence* (trans. Emerton), 166–75. Rood screens: Gamber, *Sancta Sanctorum*, 109–10.

51. For example, Duby, *History of Medieval Art*, 1:91. Even Lambert finds the image, taken from the chronicle of William of Puylaurens, to his liking: *Cathars*, 67.

52. See the remarks of Lunt, *Papal Revenues*, 1:73–74.

53. Tax exemption: *Pouillés des Provinces d'Auch, de Narbonne et de Toulouse* (ed. Perrin and Font-Réaulx), 2:554. Montbrun: Griffe, *Anciens pays de l'Aude*, 91.

54. Wolff, "Fortunes et genres de vie dans les villages du Toulousain aux XIVe et XVe siècles," 331–32. The text of this and other peasant testaments is in Wolff, "Inventaires villageois du Toulousain."

55. Shop in Narbonne: MS Doat 57, fol. 223 (1285). Wheat contract: MS Doat 51, fol. 358 (1311). Episcopal assessments: *Pouillés des Provinces d'Auch, de Narbonne et de Toulouse* (ed. Perrin and Font-Réaulx), 2:507, 545, 655. Pound equivalent in gold: AMN AA110, fol. 141v (1313).

56. Maillard and Bautier, "Dénombrement des feux." For a comparison of these populations to those of Provence, see Baratier, *Démographie provençale*.

57. Herlihy and Klapisch-Zuber, *Tuscans and Their Families*, 13–15. Provençal assessments: Zerner, *Cadastre, le pouvoir et la terre*, 112–18.

58. Revenues of Caramany and Axat: *Pouillés des Provinces d'Auch, de Narbonne et de Toulouse* (ed. Perrin and Font-Réaulx), 2:535–36. Interest rate: MS Mél. Colb. 414, nos. 87 and 88 (1251–52). A field at Escales mortgaged for a year for 135 sol. Melg.; after the end of the year, the borrowers were to pay 6 d. per month as penalty. Fourteen months later, the

mortgage was sold to a third party for 144 sol. Melg. Using the Florentine formula and calculating the rent at the more typical Occitan share-cropping rate of one-quarter of production, capitalized at 5 percent, we find that land producing 10 liv. Tourn. annually would be valued at 50 liv. Tourn.; at a rent of one-third of production, land producing 7 liv. 10 sol. annually would be valued at 50 liv. Tourn. Capitalized at 7 percent, land would require annual production worth, respectively, 14 liv. Tourn. and 10 liv. 10 sol. to reach a valuation of 50 liv. Tourn. Or to put it another way, calculating rent as one-quarter of income, capitalized at 5 percent, we find that the poverty-level clerical benefice of 15 liv. Tourn. per annum would be valued at 75 liv. Tourn.; capitalized at 7 percent, it would be valued at 54 liv. Tourn. Larger "rental portions" would, of course, give larger valuations. Using the same Florentine formula, with rent calculated at one-quarter and a 7 percent return, it would have taken property worth 89 liv. Tourn. to produce the revenues of the benefice at Caramany, and more than 114 liv. Tourn. to produce those at Axat.

59. Bourin-Derruau, *Villages médiévaux*, 1:298–300 and 1:187 n. 40.

60. Ibid., 1:275–77, 284–89. A regionwide history of the postwar settlement, with its redistribution of property and lordships (and the massive recomposition of the collective memory to justify the results), remains to be written. Important but partial survey on a village level: ibid., 2:115–44. James Given, in *State and Society*, gives only the briefest suggestion. Gifts of tithes and other dues: Béziers: *Cart. Béziers*, nos. 82–183. Of the seventeen grants of tithes to the abbey of Lagrasse that remained in its fragmentary archives, only three are post-Crusade, and eleven are pre-1150.

61. Griffe, *Anciens pays de l'Aude*, chaps. 5 (Narbonne) and 6 (Carcassonne).

62. See the few remarks in Bourin-Derruau, *Villages médiévaux*, 1:282ff. Far more may be gleaned from the lists of names in Barthès, *Documents nécrologiques du diocèse de Béziers*. The few pages that Magnou-Nortier devotes to the subject of the social class of the clergy, in *Société laïque*, 432–35, concern the tenth century and are not relevant here.

63. *Cart. Béziers*, nos. 168, 182; MS Doat 55, fols. 142, 144; and notably MS Baluze 82, fol. 169 (1125), probably the last example of an inherited village priesthood in the diocese of Narbonne, agreed to by the reforming Archbishop Richard only for the life of the brother whom the village lord placed in the local church. Afterward the benefice was to be in the gift of the cathedral chapter "ut sic illud abominabile destrueretur ne amplius praefata Ovelliani ecclesia haereditaria successione daretur." Among the rural chaplains to be found in the Black Book of Béziers are members of the families of Thézan and Bassan and Bernard Moriceno, later *caput scole* and precentor of the cathedral chapter: *Cart. Béziers*, nos. 116, 119, 124. When the abbot of Montolieu made Arnold of Brugairolles rector of the church of that village, he did not follow the newly established canon law on "presentation" but simply "gave and commended" it "for life," in return for a promise to lodge and feed the abbot and six knights (*equitantibus*) once each year. Possession of the village surname at this date suggests that Arnold was from a seignorial family of that village. MS Doat 69, fol. 139 (1188). Arnold's successor was William of Rieux, who, with his brother, was given license to become a monk whenever he wished, again a sure sign of status: MS Doat 69, fol. 151.

64. See the agreement specifically on this issue at Ouveillan: MS Doat 55, fol. 157.

65. Only the briefest of references, surprisingly, in Bourin-Derruau, *Villages médiévaux*, 2:187; see also 1:299. For indebtedness, a striking example from the Corbières, southwest of Narbonne: in 1257, fourteen men of Malvies were forced to borrow 225 liv. Tourn. from Regina and her son Astruc, Jews of Lagrasse, to pay their tithes (AD Aude H41). In 1292, 109 towns and villages collectively sued the prelates and churches within the sénéschausée of Carcassonne in protest against their claim to a monopoly of drawing up wills and marriage contracts (MS Baluze 388, no. 333). (This is three-quarters of a century earlier than a similar case I described in Cheyette, "Procurations by Large-Scale Communities.") Almost as

soon as the institutional means were available—the creation of syndics to represent the corporate body (*universitas*) of the village in court—suits against the clergy began: AD Aude H201 (1284), suit of Cambieure (with a population of thirty households) against the monastery of Saint-Hilaire over quest and tallages; AC Fabrezan (Aude), doc. 1 (1311), dispute between the village of Villerouge (Aude) and the rector of the parish church over tithes and first fruits. These disputes are hard to distinguish from disputes over seignorial rights and probably were not distinguished by the participants.

66. AD Aude H166 (1273).

67. Moore, *Popular Heresy*, 96, referring to Matthew 23:6–8. The great eleventh-century reformer Peter Damiani had already castigated the clergy in this way; it could well have been a preacher's commonplace. *Opusculum* 22, cited in Fichtenau, *Living in the Tenth Century*, 7.

CHAPTER 17. A WAR LIKE AN OMEN

1. Much of the narrative that follows is based on Congar, "Henri de Marcy," and idem, "Eglise et cité de Dieu chez quelques auteurs Cisterciens."

2. Roger of Hoveden, *Chronica*, 2:144–51, and idem, *Gesta Regis*, 1:191–94, 198–99. Gervase of Canterbury, surprisingly, knew nothing about the kings' plans. He apparently never received the letter from Peter of Pavia describing the mission.

3. See above, chaps. 14 and 16.

4. Geoffrey of Vigeois, in *RHGF* 12:446–47. Léonard, *Cat.*, no. 108.

5. Thirty-two surviving letters are printed in *PL* 204:215–52. See especially letter 5, to Henry II; letter 30, a judgment in a dispute between the abbot of Saint-Sever and the monastery of Sainte-Croix in Bordeaux; letter 13, to the bishop of Cavaillon congratulating him on his election; and letter 25, to an unnamed friend. The letter to Pope Alexander is letter 11, col. 221.

6. Translated in Moore, *Popular Heresy*, 117.

7. *PL* 204:220–21, epistola 11.

8. A striking example of that early abhorrence of violence was the decision of the newly appointed Norman prelates of England immediately after the Conquest to impose penance on those who had fought in the battle of Hastings: *English Historical Documents* (ed. Douglas and Greenaway), 2:606–7. For the antique and Carolingian background, see Russell, *The Just War in the Middle Ages*, 11, 30–33; for the Gregorian reform and holy war, Erdmann, *Origin of the Idea of Crusade*, chaps. 7 and 8; Bernard of Clairvaux, "Liber ad milites templi. De laude novae militiae," in *Opere*, 1:425–84, especially 444–49.

9. Causa 23 of Gratian's *Decretum*, fully discussed in Chodorow, *Christian Political Theory and Church Politics*, 228–46; see also Russell, *Just War*, 64–68.

10. Henry is just as likely to have found the phrase in Saint Augustine, where Gratian found it, as in Gratian's work.

11. Numbers 25:1–13.

12. *PL* 204:251–402 (hereafter cited by *tractatus* and column no.). For an analysis of Henry's ecclesiology see Congar, "Henri de Marcy," 72–77, on which my account is largely based.

13. Tract. 2, col. 263.

14. Tract. 10, col. 326ff.

15. Tract. 12, col. 342.

16. Tract. 4, col. 286.

17. Tract. 7, col. 309.

18. Tract. 4, col. 288.

19. Henry cited them all as speaking of the "new man": tract. 2, col. 264.

20. Matthew 18:10.

21. See, especially, Bugge, *Virginitas*, 5–35, 42–43.

22. Mansi, *Sacrorum conciliorum*, 21:843, canon 1.

23. Ibid., 718. For what follows, see the discussion in Moore, *Formation of a Persecuting Society*, 24–27.

24. Mansi, *Sacrorum conciliorum*, 21:843, canon 1.

25. Ibid., 1177, canon 4.

26. *PL* 204:236; translation from Moore, *Popular Heresy*, 117–18, slightly revised.

27. *PL* 204:237; translation from Moore, *Popular Heresy*, 118–19, slightly revised.

28. Mundy, *Repression of Catharism at Toulouse*, 13.

29. Mundy, *Liberty and Political Power*, 43–58.

30. Mundy has systematically compared the text of Peter Maurandus's abjuration to that of Berengar of Tours in the appendix to his "Noblesse et hérésie. Une famille cathare: Les Maurand," 1222–23. This text, which was included by Gratian in his textbook of canon law, was included in many other twelfth-century anthologies.

31. Mundy, *Repression of Catharism*, 229 n. 1.

32. Moore, *Popular Heresy*, 121. Peter did in fact relinquish his rights to tithes to Saint-Sernin. We can assume that Raymond V saw to it that Peter's tower house was destroyed. Whether the poor ever benefited or whether he ever went to the Holy Land can only be a matter of conjecture. See Mundy, "Noblesse et hérésie. Une famille cathare," 1213.

33. William III, bishop from 1157 to 1185, was from the family of the lords of Dourgne: Dufour, *Evêques d'Albi*, 38–39. The castle of Dourgne had been held in fidelity to the ancestors of the Trencavels at the end of the tenth and beginning of the eleventh centuries (Cart. Trencavel, fols. 7 and 8; *HGL* 5:412), but by the mid-twelfth their lords had joined other lords of border towns in playing the Trencavels against the counts of Toulouse. In his capitulations of 1142 and 1143, for example, the count of Toulouse promised to have the lords of Dourgne swear fidelity to Raymond Trencavel. There is no documentary evidence, however, that they ever did (*HGL* 5:1058, 1069).

34. MS Doat 110, fol. 70; *HGL* 5:1333.

35. In March 1193, Roger and a new bishop finally came to an agreement on their respective rights: MS Doat 105, fol. 117. For a detailed summary of all the surviving material concerning lordships in Albi, see Kaiser, *Bischofsherrschaft*, 277–84, and more briefly, Biget, "Récits," 54–55. In Italy those who opposed episcopal political claims or disputed episcopal property rights were regularly labeled heretics: Lansing, *Power and Purity*, 30.

36. Henry says only that Roger retreated to "the most remote and inaccessible part of his land," not a bad description for Ambialet, set high above a horseshoe bend in the wild gorge of the upper Tarn.

37. Moore, *Popular Heresy*, 121–22.

38. Wakefield and Evans, *Heresies*, 706 n. 18.

39. "[Q]uia evangelia et epistolae, quibus tantummodo fidem suam volebant confirmare, Latino eloquio noscuntur esse conscripta." Roger of Hovedon, *Gesta Regis*, 1:203.

40. The account of Peter of Pavia is included ibid., 202–6; translated in Moore, *Popular Heresy*, 113–16.

41. The two accounts of this mission, one by Peter of Pavia, the other by Henry of Marcy, had two quite different purposes and thus cover two different moments in the encounter with the heretics. The legate's was a warning to all Christians to be on the lookout for the two Perfects who had been sent to him from Albi and who he had been forced to release unharmed because they had traveled to Toulouse under safeguard. It therefore con-

cerns only his examination of those two men. In contrast, Henry's, as I point out below, was a broad appeal for holy war.

42. Moore, *Popular Heresy*, 122.

43. *PL* 204:219–20, epistolae 5 and 6.

44. Mansi, *Sacrorum conciliorum*, 22:231–33. See also Foreville, *Latran I, II, III et Latran IV*, 134–58, 210–23. Elie Griffe, in an effort to portray both the expedition of 1178 and the Third Lateran Council as essentially pacific and pastoral in their attitudes toward the Cathars, has argued that the portion of canon 27 granting crusader status applied only to those who took the field against the mercenaries: *Débuts de l'aventure cathare*, 118–19; but the text of the canon itself refuses such interpretation. Not only is it titled *De haereticis*, assimilating the mercenaries throughout to heretics, but its very first sentence is, "According to the word of Saint Leo, the discipline of the Church is satisfied with the judgment of the priest alone and does not inflict corporal punishment; it finds support, however, in the laws of catholic princes, for men seek a salutary remedy when they are threatened with physical punishment [*supplicium*]." The Church threatened the heretics with excommunication and refused to bury the guilty in consecrated ground. It was up to warriors to do the rest, and that is what the council demanded.

45. Again Griffe tries to tone down the military side of Henry's expedition, but Geoffrey of Vigeois is categorical: "Legatus . . . tunc multo cum exercitu perrexit contra haereticos Albigenses": *RHGF* 12:448.

46. Sicard of Boissezon was a lord in the Trencavel clientele. In 1190 he and his brother and a third man received a newly built castle, the *podium de Caslon*, from Roger: Cart. Trencavel, fols. 232v, 245. He appears once as a witness in Roger's charters: *HGL* 8:453. For the Perfects' conversion, see Griffe, *Débuts de l'aventure cathare*, 128–30.

47. Geoffrey includes in his account portions of a letter from Henry of Marcy that has not otherwise survived. And although Geoffrey occasionally shows a fondness for obscure diction, the vocabulary and grammar of this whole passage are more redolent of Henry's Latinity: *RHGF* 12:449. Parts of his account also suggest he was copying a document whose writing he could not clearly interpret—"Vienna" for the more common Occitan woman's name Vierna, and "Boissa" for the place-name Boissezon (Boissedon or Boissedunum in medieval documents)—but these errors could just as likely have developed in the manuscript tradition; "multis in locis ab amanuensibus deformata" said the eighteenth-century editor: *RHGF* 18:211. Robert of Auxerre, who must have worked from the same source, likewise thought the campaign was fruitless: Robert of Auxerre, "Chronicon," in *Monumenta Germaniae Historia, Scriptores*, 26:245.

48. There is some uncertainty about whether the deposition took place in 1180 or 1181. See the discussion in Congar, "Henri de Marcy," 33–35, and nn. 108, 109. The papal letter cited in n. 109 leaves no doubt that Pons d'Arsac was deposed.

49. Cited in Griffe, *Débuts de l'aventure cathare*, 133.

50. MS Doat 55, fol. 241.

51. See above, note 39.

52. *PL* 211:375, epistola 75. Griffe, *Débuts de l'aventure cathare*, 134–35; Congar, "Henri de Marcy," 40.

53. Bernard was the son of Gaucelin of Lunel and Guillelma of Montpellier, thus from a family closely allied with both Ermengard and the Trencavels. The exact date of his election is unclear, because he retained the administration of the bishopric of Béziers until 1184: *HGL* 4:250.

54. Mundy, *Repression of Catharism*, 16 nn. 30 and 31, 229–41, and 69 n. 14, citing an Inquisition record of 1246 recounting events approximately fifteen years earlier.

55. *Layettes du trésor des Chartes*, 1, no. 353.

56. Guillaume de Puylaurens, *Chronique*, chap. 3, 30–33. William IV, elected bishop in 1185, was forced to resign in 1227: Dufour, *Evêques*, 39. William Peter of Brens had an interesting fictional posthumous history, in the creation of a fake codicil to Raymond Trencavel's will: *HGL* 8:266. Here William Peter is made "seneschal" of Raymond Trencavel, an official never otherwise attested in the Trencavel documents. Although Brens was a castle sworn to Trencavel fidelity and many oaths survive, there is no sign in them or anywhere else of a William Peter.

57. Mundy, *Liberty and Political Power*, 63–67.

58. Robert of Torigny, "Chronica," 279. For the council of Tours, see Wakefield and Evans, *Heresies*, 720, who point out (n. 1) that the title, "Ut cuncti Albigensiu haereticorum consortium fugiant," was a later addition. See also Biget, "Albigeois," 225–26. Geoffrey of Vigeois: *RHGF* 12:448.

59. Moore, *Formation of a Persecuting Society*, especially chaps. 3 and 4.

60. Moore, *Popular Heresy*, 43; see also Guillaume de Puylaurens, *Chronique*, 24–27.

61. Guillaume de Puylaurens, *Chronique*, 42. For a twentieth-century version of both these explanations, see Griffe, "Catharisme dans le diocèse de Carcassonne"; and for a critique of these traditional views, Dossat, "Clergé méridionale."

62. As Monique Bourin-Derruau, for example, has attempted, in *Villages médiévaux*, 289–300.

63. The bull "Clericis laicos," printed in Dupuy, *Histoire du différend*, 14–15.

64. Mundy, "Charity and Social Work in Toulouse, 1100–1250"; Bourin-Derruau, *Villages médiévaux*, 273–310.

65. Mundy, *Repression of Catharism*, 54–64.

66. Yves Dossat has some pertinent remarks on how difficult it might have seemed for a person in the twelfth or thirteenth century to distinguish very well between certain aspects of the heresy and similar attitudes in contemporary orthodoxy. For them, he remarks, the distinctions may not have been as clear as they are for us (or, we might add, as they were for the polemicists and inquisitors of the thirteenth century), for even among the clergy there were those who were sympathetic to the "good men" and their followers: Dossat, "Cathares dans les documents de l'Inquisition." For the same thing in Italy, see Lansing, *Power and Purity*, 92–96.

67. Quoted in Constable, *Three Studies*, 314.

68. Congar, "Henri de Marcy," 43.

69. Moore, *Origins of European Dissent*, 182–84, 237. For Italy, see the lucid remarks of Lansing, *Power and Purity*, 8–11. Zambon, "Hérésie cathare dans la marche de Trévise," is largely concerned with doctrine.

70. Mansi, *Sacrorum conciliorum*, 22:231–32.

71. Moore, *Persecuting Society*, chap. 4. My brief summary is, alas, a necessarily crude reduction of his complex and finely balanced argument.

72. His appeal was for help "ex vestris partibus." See chap. 16.

73. They were certainly present in Narbonne in the thirteenth century when renewed conflict between archbishops and viscounts and the advent of an increasingly powerful consulate gave them some breathing room. Emery, *Heresy and Inquisition*.

74. Vicaire, *Saint Dominic and His Times*, 93–94, 98–112, although the reader should be warned that Father Vicaire gets his information about heretics in these regions mainly from the hardly unbiased *Hystoria albigensis* of Peter of Vaux-de-Cernay. The geography, however, is confirmed by the location of the Cathar bishoprics and deaconates in the decades after 1200: Brenon, *Vrai visage du catharisme*, 116–20, from which my map is drawn.

75. Brens and Gaillac along with Cahuzac and Montaigu: Cart. Trencavel, fols. 1–4, 11, 39v, 217v; *HGL* 5:411, 412, 438, 521, 1066, 1220. Lavaur and Saint-Felix: Cart. Trencavel,

fols. 19–21; *HGL* 5:412, 1019, 1066; MS Doat 166, fols. 235, 254, 256. For maps and full references to other castles, see Biget, "Vicomté d'Ambialet."

76. Laurac: Cart. Trencavel, fols. 66v–67, 100, 110, 133, 139v; *HGL* 5:588, 1220. The oaths of fidelity for Lautrec are among the earliest to survive: Cart. Trencavel, fols. 30v, 115v; *HGL* 5:301, 312. For the various members of this family in the twelfth century, see the indexes of *HGL* 5 and 8, s.v. Lautrico, and for Sicard, viscount, Léonard, *Cat.*, nos. 1, 2, 10, 54.

77. The subtitle of the English translation of Le Roy Ladurie's *Montaillou*.

CHAPTER 18. IMPATIENT HEIRS

1. See above, chap. 15.

2. Gerald of Wales, "Liber de principis instructione," in *Opera*, 8:163 and 172, the latter a propos of 1183. For more, see 180–81, 187–88, 212.

3. See above, chap. 14.

4. Warren, *Henry II*, 136–49, 564–80.

5. Roger of Hoveden, *Gesta Regis*, 1:292. For this and what follows: Warren, *Henry II*, 584–601; Benjamin, "Forty-Years War," 276–77; Gillingham, *Richard I*, 52–74; Caruana, "Itinerario," 213–14.

6. *RHGF* 12:392.

7. For details: Warren, *Henry II*, 610–26; Benjamin, "Forty-Years War," 277–81. Gillingham, *Richard I*, 74–75; Roger of Hoveden, *Chronica*, 3:431. Roger of Wendover, *Flores Historiarum*, 2:39–40.

8. Peire: Aurell, *Cat.*, no. 18. Sanç: ibid., nos. 25, 29–31, and others; Caruana, "Itinerario," 83 ("Sancii comitis Cerritanie frater regis," the only surviving exception), 89, 118. When Alfons delegated all his authority in Provence to his brother Peire, he established a council whose consent Peire required before he could take any important action: Aurell, *Cat.*, no. 46. Surely such would have also been the case when Sanç succeeded Peire. Only in 1183 was Sanç given the tiny counties of Carladès and Gévaudan as his own to rule: ibid., no. 72bis.

9. On their side the Genoese promised to supply ten thousand men to besiege and destroy the city of Marseille, *LIG* 1:313; Léonard, *Cat.*, no. 116. Sanç had but a few month's earlier promised the viscounts of Marseille not to attack them: Aurell, *Cat.*, no. 74 (AC Marseille, AA3, no. 4). Renewal of Jarnègues: *LFM*, no. 900. Deposition: Aurell, *Cat.*, no. 81. Sometime in 1184, Sanç also traitorously handed over the important castle of Ariza on the Aragonese–Castilian border to Alfonso VIII of Castile; Alfons of Aragon regained it by treaty in 1186: Benjamin, "Forty-Years War," 278, citing Rodericus Ximenius de Rada, "Historiae de rebus Hispanie." Sanç reappears years later in the shadow of the king: Aurell, *Cat.*, no. 96 (1190).

10. War in Quercy: Benjamin, "Forty-Years War," 276. Nîmes: *HGL* 8:335 (alliance with lords in the neighborhood of Nîmes), 380 (confirmation of the privileges of the citizens of Nîmes, most likely the first important act the count would make on taking over the city). Bernard Ato at Agde: *LIM*, nos. 470–77. The last act recorded in Cart. Trencavel (in a different hand from all the others) is Bernard Ato's "gift" of Nîmes and Agde to Simon of Montfort. During the Albigensian Crusades the bishop and chapter of Agde concocted a series of documents purporting to be Bernard Ato's gift of the city and viscounty to them when he became a canon of the cathedral. On these forgeries, see my review of Cart. Agde, in *Speculum* (1998).

11. Treaty of Najac: Benjamin, "Forty-Years War," 283–85; Benjamin's hypothesis that

the proper date is 1186 is impossible given Alfsons's itinerary for that year as given by Caruana, "Itinerario," 155–60. Roger's treaty: ACA *perg. Alfonso I*, no. 366 (dated April 1184, which seems to be a copyist's mistake; the name of where the treaty was made has been scratched out). Roger's adoption of the king's son: *HGL* 8:383. The witness list tells us the act was made in the king's presence; he was then besieging Valencia: Caruana, "Itinerario," 152. Following Devic and Vaissete (*HGL* 6:114–16), this act has been seen as nothing more than a *fief de reprise*, a ritual gift and countergift made when a lord or follower succeeded to an inheritance (see Cheyette, "On the *fief de reprise*"). This adoption, however, in which Roger reserves the use of his lands and dominions for life, has no relation to the normal *fief de reprise*, in which the gift is immediately returned (sometimes with additional lands and powers) in fief. Nor would the *fief de reprise* involve the inquests that followed this act, of which one survives: *GC* 6, col. 142, no. 19.

12. Caruana, "Itinerario," 150; *Gallia Christiana Novissima*, 1 (diocese of Aix), *instrum.*: 15–16; for the events of 1167, see above, chap. 14.

13. Grant in fief: Baudon de Mony, *Relations politiques des comtes de Foix avec la Catalogne*, 2:32, no. 19. The terms of this grant suggest that Alfons and his advisors closely read the agreements made in 1067 between his distant ancestors, Count Ramon Berenguer I and Almodis, and those of Roger of Béziers, Ermengard (of Carcassonne), and her husband Raymond Bernard. It was perhaps at this moment (rather than twenty years later, as I once hypothesized) that the copies through which we know of those agreements were made: ACA *perg. Ram. Ber. I*, nos. 392 and 393, and *perg. Alfonso I*, no. 275; for description, see Cheyette, " 'Sale' of Carcassonne," 833 and n. 19. Roger of Béziers's testament: MS Doat 40, fols. 114, 116. Baronial oath: *HGL* 8:411.

14. *HGL* 8:353, V (with Roger of Béziers); MS Doat 59, fol. 118 (with Ademar of Murviel).

15. For the story that follows I am indebted to Jacqueline Caille, who has reconstructed the most likely narrative to be drawn from the last documents of Ermengard's reign and was kind enough to share her ideas with me before her article (which includes texts of the Fabrezan donation [ACA *perg. Alfonso I*, no. 673] and Ermengard's testament) appeared in print: "Ermengarde, vicomtesse de Narbonne." For Ermengaud and his family, see chap. 9.

16. New treaty of Jarnègues: Léonard, *Cat.*, no. 135; and Aurell, *Cat.*, no. 91. Recognizance of fief by William of Montpellier: *LIM*, no. 87.

17. In 1193, Emperor Frederick Barbarossa gave the kingdom of Arles (that is, Provence) to King Richard the Lionheart, including the homage of the count of Saint-Gilles/Toulouse: Roger of Hoveden, *Chronica*, 3:225.

18. Dating of documents in Aragon: Bisson, *Medieval Crown of Aragon*, 37. Problematic title to Carcassonne: Cheyette, " 'Sale' of Carcassonne," 831–32.

19. Miret y Sans, "Testamento de la vizcondesa Ermengarda de Narbona," re-edited by Caille, "Ermengarde, vicomtesse de Narbonne," 43–46, followed by French translation. On the problem of dating Ermengard's death, see ibid., 22–23; of the various dates given in medieval necrologies I opt here for the one that conforms to the usual practice of deathbed testament.

20. Caille, "Ermengarde, vicomtesse de Narbonne," 21–22.

21. Birth of Raymond Roger Trencavel: *HGL* 5:33; death of Roger of Béziers: ibid., 33, 36. Pedro's alliance with the count of Foix and the king of Aragon: *HGL* 8:425. Ermengard's with Raymond of Toulouse implied by her testament: Caille, "Ermengarde, vicomtesse de Narbonne," 44–46. Raymond's death: Léonard, *Cat.*, xi (none of the narrative sources give an exact date). Aymeri named Pedro's successor: Catel, *Mémoires*, 594; Caille, "Ermengarde, vicomtesse de Narbonne," 24.

22. On the Bistani family, see chap. 3.

23. The names mentioned are those of witnesses or vicecomital judges; they appear in

the first three documents in which Pedro acts as viscount: MS Doat 58, fol. 148; 59, fol. 137; 48, fol. 34. John Bistani and Peter Cotetus are witnesses to two of these. Of the men appearing in these documents, John Bonus senior and Bernard Blancardus appear nowhere else. In 1229, Bernard Lunesius (probably a descendent of the Stephan Lunesius of 1193) is consul, while John Bistani and his brother Raymond, John Monetarius the son of William, Peter of Quillan, Pedro's vicar in 1193, and Peter Boverius (probably a descendent of Raymond Boverius of 1193) are all "good men" (*probi homini*) of the city (MS Mél. Colb. 414, no. 76). William Pelliparius witnesses a sale to the city's leper house in 1177 (AMN AA104, fol. 179). Peter Cotetus sells his consent to a bequest to the leper house in 1192 (AN S4858, no. 22), and with Peter Raymond Faber (brother of the William who is one of Pedro's judges in 1193) witnesses a transaction with the abbey of Saint-Paul, of which Arnold of Lac is a canon. William of Lac is cellarer (originally the wine keeper but here the official in charge of landed property) of the abbey of Quarante in 1193, when Lady Calva gives her oath of fidelity to the abbey at the house of Peter of Lac in Narbonne, with Raymond of Lac and Arnold among the witnesses and Pedro de Lara giving his consent as viscount (MS Doat 58, fol. 148); master Peter Arnold of Lac is a vicecomital judge at the same time. Master Peter, a witness in 1193, is abbot of Saint-Paul. The families of the Royal Gate (*Porta Regia*) and the Capitole (*Capitolium*) appear frequently in episcopal and cathedral documents of the twelfth century but very rarely in those of Ermengard. We begin to see here the familial links among the higher clergy and their lay brothers and cousins that Pedro is using to engineer his coup. William Faber appears with Berenger Palerius, a witness to Lady Calva's oath, as early as 1177 (AMN AA105, fol. 21v). William's brother Peter Raymond appears along with John Bistani and William Monetarius as a witness to an act of Pedro's son Aymeri in 1204 (MS Doat 47, fol. 20). A William Faber (son?) along with two other Fabers is a "good man" in 1229. When Berenger Palerius receives an inheritance in 1209, two witnesses are a cousin, Ermengaud Gausberti (relative of William Gausberti, a judge in 1193?), and Peter Raymond de Riparia (relative of Arnold, a witness in 1193?) (MS Mél. Colb. 414, no. 64). Berenger's son, Aymeri Palerius, is also a "good man" of Narbonne in 1229.

24. A necrology from the church of Saint-Paul, Narbonne, notes her death "apud Port," a common name for Pyrenean passes, but gives 1197 as the date: *HGL* 5:39. The testament itself mentions no place, only that Ermengard is "iacens in lectulo meo diruta nimia egritudine"; see above, n. 19. The Templar house of Mas-Deu in which she asked to be buried was near Trouillas in Roussillon. The buildings of the commandery remained until the end of the Second World War, when the Germans, who were using it as a munitions dump, blew it up.

25. I take his name to be his occupation.

26. See the index to Léonard, *Cat.*, s.v. Geraldus Amici. In contrast, this cognomen does not appear anywhere in twelfth-century Narbonnese documents or in the substantial Trencavel documentation. Ermengard says of one, "qui mecum est," and of the other "qui mecum similiter vadit."

27. In his testament of 1189, Roger of Béziers left 8,700 sol. Melg. to eleven monasteries, chalices worth 100 sol. each to seven others, and 1,500 sol. to feed and clothe the poor: MS Doat 40, fol. 114.

28. Caille notes that the three fortified villages that form her bequests are still vicecomital property in the mid-thirteenth century: "Ermengarde, vicomtesse de Narbonne," 27; see AD Hérault G274 and *HGL* 8:1735.

29. Compare, for example, the third (and last) testament of Maria of Montpellier in 1213: d'Achery, *Spicilegium*, 3:576.

30. Caille, "Ermengarde, vicomtesse de Narbonne," n. 123. I have been unable to consult the two manuscript theses she cites here.

31. *Poésies de Peire Vidal*, 92.

1. Léonard, *Cat.*, no. 142.

2. *HAC*, 24, 22; this account by Peter of Vaux-de-Cernay of the heretical propensities of Raymond and other Occitan nobles has been taken seriously even by scholars such as Fichtenau (*Heretics and Scholars*, 150–51) and Lambert (*Cathars*, 63). *PL* 214: 273 no. 29 (on which see Zerner, "Question sur la naissance," 441–42).

3. *HAC*, 49, 69; William of Tudela, *Song of the Cathar Wars*, 18–19, 29; Guillaume de Puylaurens, *Chronique*, 63.

4. *HAC*, 23–24, 13. See also the testimony concerning Bertrand's presence at gatherings of Cathars given to inquisitors in the 1240s, recounted by Roquebert, *Épopée cathare*, 114–15; other families closely associated with the Trencavels also appear in these records, although testimony of such precision given in the 1240s about events occurring shortly after 1200 is surely subject to extreme caution. Many of these same families had been dispossessed by the crusaders and were implicated in the revolts of the 1220s and 1240s; testimony may have been sought to justify the confiscation of their property for reason of heresy.

5. *HAC*, 134.

6. Oerter, "Campaldino, 1289," 432. Aymeri's *baile* at the battle of Campaldino was a man from another old Occitan family, William Bernard of Durfort.

7. In contrast, Innocent's immediate predecessor, Celestine III, was eighty-five when he was elected and over ninety when he died. Thanks to his maternal uncle, Pope Clement III, Lothar had been introduced to curial affairs when barely out of his teens. He was named cardinal deacon of Saints Sergius and Bacchus at age twenty-nine. For more information, see Sayers, *Innocent III*, and Tillmann, *Pope Innocent III*.

8. I owe much of what follows to Zerner, "Question sur la naissance," and to her unpublished essay, "L'Affaire albigeoise." My thanks to Prof. Zerner for sharing this manuscript with me.

9. Lansing, *Power and Purity*.

10. For Innocent's ambitions in central Italy, see Maccarrone, "Papato e regno di Sicilia," and Bolton, " 'Except the Lord Keep the City,' " and the works cited therein; for Montecassino, Bolton, "For the See of Simon Peter," 12. Van Cleve, *Markward of Anweiler and the Sicilian Regency*, despite its age, remains fundamental. For Innocent's frequently vituperative language in his letters to cities, see also Webb, "Pope and the Cities."

11. For a list of cities that Innocent chided at one moment or another for harboring "enemies of God" and heretics—even electing them to positions of power, see Webb, "Pope and the Cities."

12. The story of Orvieto is told in exemplary fashion by Lansing, *Power and Purity*. For more details see Maccaronne, "Orvieto e la predicazione della crociata," especially 9–48.

13. On Innocent's letter to Viterbo, *Vergentis in senium*, see Ullmann, "Significance of Innocent III's decretal 'Vergentis.' " On the political circumstances (commonly ignored in commentaries on this letter), see Partner, *Lands of St. Peter*, 238–39 (who does not mention *Vergentis*). See also Webb, "Pope and the Cities."

14. On the crusade against Markward, see Van Cleve, *Markward of Anweiler*, especially 97, 106, 142, 147, 175, and 186. On Walter of Brienne, see Arbois de Jubainville, "Catalogue d'actes des comtes de Brienne."

15. Zerner, "Question sur la naissance," 632–33.

16. Baldwin, *Government of Philip Augustus*, 82–87.

17. For a detailed account of papal negotiations, see Bolton, "Philip Augustus and John," 117–23.

18. Van Cleve, *Markward of Anweiler*, 198–99.

19. Ceremony described in Sayers, *Innocent III*, 83–84. Negotiations between Pere and Raymond VI: Ventura, *Pere el Catòlic*, 62–63.

20. Numerous examples are chronicled by Van Cleve, *Markward of Anweiler*; see especially the account of the negotiations with Walter of Brienne to become count of Lecce (141ff.).

21. On this decretal, see Tierney, "Tria quippe distinguit judicia."

22. See Folz, *Concept of Empire*, 110–11.

23. The expression is from the fourteenth-century Italian lawyer Baldus de Ubaldis. The full citation is in Cheyette, "Sovereign and the Pirates," 63 n. 67.

24. Bonde, *Fortress-Churches of Languedoc*.

25. Philip's response is translated in *HAC*, 305–6. There are many narratives of the war. Two in English are Sumption, *Albigensian Crusade*, and Strayer, *Albigensian Crusades*, neither of which shows an adequate understanding either of Occitan society or of the political circumstances surrounding the Crusades. In French, Roquebert, *Épopée cathare*, is immensely detailed and based (although sometimes uncritically) on manuscript as well as printed sources.

26. William of Tudela, *Song of the Cathar Wars*, 15–16.

27. See the extended discussion by the translators of *HAC*, Appendix B, 289–93. Also Berlioz, "Tuez-les tous."

28. *HAC*, 58–59; Zerner and Piéchon-Palloc, "Croisade albigeoise, une revanche."

29. The statutes of Pamiers are translated in *HAC*, Appendix H. For episcopal lists, see *HGL* 4.

30. Translated in *HAC*, 309–10.

31. Le Roy Ladurie, *Montaillou*; Fournier, *Registre d'inquisition de Jacques Fournier* (ed. Duvernoy).

32. The earliest example I have noted of a local lord using the title is 1213, when Arnold of Saint-Valière witnesses an arbitration between the viscount of Narbonne and Arnold Amaury, the new archbishop: MS Mél. Colb. 414, no. 69.

33. The last oath in the old form that I have discovered is dated December 1209 (Peter of Fenouillet to Viscount Aymeri, MS Doat 59, fol. 345). The earliest of the new form, again by Peter of Fenouillet (perhaps the son), is dated 1242 (ibid., fol. 341v). Viscount Amalric is here surrounded by a group of men identified as "his knights."

34. Two striking examples are the supposed homage of Viscount Bernard Ato to the abbot of Lagrasse in 1110 (*HGL* 5:811) and the supposed testament of Raymond Trencavel in 1160 (*HGL* 8:266), both of them manifest forgeries of the mid-thirteenth century. In the former, the text is a recognizance in the thirteenth-century form, the witnesses are drawn from much later documents, and the king has the wrong name. In the second, apart from a faulty date, Raymond's agent in Albi is called "seneschal," a northern office unknown in Occitania in the twelfth century; the name of this "seneschal," otherwise unrecorded in the rich Trencavel archives, is taken from a heretic story in the chronicle of William of Puylaurens (*Chronica*, 31–33).

BIBLIOGRAPHY

MANUSCRIPTS CONSULTED

The archives of both ecclesiastical bodies and noble families were dispersed into various public and private holdings in the course of the seventeenth and eighteenth centuries and particularly at the time of the French Revolution; the following list attempts to reassemble many of these fragments. The listing is, in so far as possible, by the originating archives, with ecclesiastical archives first, followed by archives of secular lords and cities. I list under "Miscellaneous" those collections too varied to restore in this manner.

Archbishop of Narbonne and Saint-Just Cathedral

AD Aude, série G
Bibliothèque Municipale de Narbonne, MS 1639 "Inventaire des archives de l'archevesque de Narbonne" called "Inventaire Rocques"
British Museum, MS Harley 3570
MS Baluze 59, 82, 374, 378, 380, 381
MS Doat, 55, 56
MS Latin 11015

Church of Saint-Paul, Narbonne

MS Baluze 81, 82, 392
MS Doat 57
MS Latin 5211D
MS Mélanges Colbert 414

Church of Notre-Dame du Bourg (Lamourgier), Narbonne

MS Doat 58
AD Bouche-du-Rhone 1H59

Bishop of Agde

MS Latin 9999

Bishop of Béziers and Saint-Nazaire Cathedral

AD Hérault, série G
MS Doat 60, 61, 62
MS Latin 12773

Bishop of Carcassonne and Saint-Nazaire Cathedral

AD Aude, série G, 76
MS Latin 12773

Caunes Abbey

MS Doat 58
Archives Nationales (Paris), L997, no. 3

Fontfroide Abbey

AD Aude, série H, 206, 211, 212, 458, 595
MS Doat 59

Lagrasse Abbey

AD Aude série H (many cartons)
MS Doat 66, 67
MS Latin 5455

Montolieu Abbey

AD Aude série H, 192, 193
MS Doat 69

Quarante Abbey

MS Doat 58

Valmagne Abbey

AD Hérault, microfilm 260–61bis: "Cartulaire de Valmagne"

Templars and Hospitalers

AD Haute-Garonne, série H, ordre de Malte: Douzens, Homps, Narbonne, Puysubran (Pexiora)

Viscounts and Viscountess of Narbonne

AD Hérault, série G 274
MS Baluze 374
MS Doat 47–49, 51, 55, 57, 59
MS Mélanges Colbert 414
BNF MS nouvelle acquisition française 3601, no. 2
Private collection of A. Combes, Albi

Trencavel Family

Société Archéologique de Montpellier, MS 10: "Cartulaire des Trencavel"

Counts of Barcelona and Kings of Aragon

ACA pergaminos

City of Narbonne (including Bourg)

AMN. Note: at the time I worked in this archive it still had not been reorganized after its hasty packing on the eve of World War II. Apart from its substantial cartularies ("Thalamus"), AA 99, 101, 103–6, 109, most of the remainder no longer had shelf numbers or had not been matched up with the prewar manuscript inventory.
Archives Nationales (Paris), S4858 (leper houses and hospitals)
MS Mélange Colbert 414

City of Béziers

AC. Note: at the time I worked in this archive it likewise had not been catalogued. The manuscripts had no shelf numbers.
Archives Nationales (Paris), K1176, nos. 31–33.

Miscellaneous

AD Pyrénées-Orientales, série B
Archives Nationales (Paris), P 1353
MS Baluze 81, 392
MS Doat 38 (marriage contracts)
MS Doat 40, 41 (testaments)
MS Doat 50, 128, 248
MS Latin 11016, 11017, 11826
MS Mélange Colbert 413

WORKS CITED

Abu al-Fida'. *Taqwim al-buldan. Géographie d'Aboulféda*. Trans. Joseph T. Reinaud and S. Stanislas Guyard. Paris: Imprimerie Nationale, 1848.
Abulafia, David. *A Mediterranean Emporium*. Cambridge: Cambridge University Press, 1994.
Abu-Lughod, Lila, and Catherine Lutz. "Emotion, Discourse, and the Politics of Everyday Life." In *Language and the Politics of Emotion*, ed. Lila Abu-Lughod and Catherine Lutz. Cambridge: Cambridge University Press, 1990.
d'Achery, Luc. *Spicilegium: Sive collectio veterum aliquot scriptorum*. Ed. Stephanus Baluze and Edmundus Martene. Paris: Montalant, 1723.
Airaldi, Gabriella. "Groping in the Dark: The Emergence of Genoa in the Early Middle Ages." In *Miscellanea di studi storici*, 2:9–17. Collana storica di fonti e studi 38. Genoa, 1983.
Alberigo, Joseph, Joseph Dossetti, Perikle Jeannou, Claudio Leonardi, and Paolo Prodi, eds. *Conciliorum oecumenicorum decreta*. Bologna: Istituto per le Scienze Religose, 1973.
Aliscans. Ed. Claude Regnier. Les classiques français du Moyen Age 110–111. Paris: Champion, 1990.
Altisent, Agustí. "A propos de l'expédition d'Alphonse le Chaste à Toulouse en 1175." *Annales du Midi* 79 (1976): 429–31.
Amado, Claudie Duhamel. "La famille aristocratique Languedocienne: Parenté et patrimoine dans les vicomtés de Béziers et d'Agde." Thèse de doctorat, Université de Paris IV (Sorbonne), 2 parts in 5 vols., 1994.
——."Femmes entre elles: Filles et épouses languedociennes (XIe–XIIe siècles)." In *Femmes–mariages–lignages: Mélanges offerts à Georges Duby*, 125–55. Brussels: De Boeck Université, 1992.
——. "Poids de l'aristocratie d'origine wisigothique et genèse de la noblesse septimanienne." In *L'Europe héritière de l'Espagne wisigothique*, ed. Jacques Fontaine and Christine Pellistrandi. Rencontres de la Casa de Valázquez 35. Madrid: Casa de Valázquez, 1992.
——. "Pouvoirs et noblesse dans la Gothie: Formation du réseau aristocratique biterrois au Xe siècle." In *Catalunya i França meridional a l'entorn de l'any mil*, ed. Xavier Barral i Altet et al., 160–73. Barcelona: Generalitat de Catalunya, Departament de Cultura, 1991.

——. "La seigneurie des mines en pays de Béziers et en Razès." In *Mines et mineurs en Languedoc-Roussillon*, 125–44.

Andreas Capellanus [Andrew the chaplain]. *Andreas Capellanus on Love (De amore et amoris remedio)*. Ed. P. G. Walsh. London: Duckworth, 1982.

Angelov, Dimitar. "Le Bogomilisme: Envergure bulgare et européenne." *Heresis* 19 (1992): 1–19.

Arbois de Jubainville, Henry d'. "Catalogue d'actes des comtes de Brienne." *Bibliothèque de l'Ecole des Chartes* 33 (1872): 1–48.

Archives Communales de Narbonne. *Inventaire des archives communales antérieures à 1790*. Ed. Germain Mouynès. Narbonne: E. Caillard, 1871.

Armangaud, André, and Robert Lafont, eds. *Histoire d'Occitanie*. Paris: Hachette, 1979.

Arnaut Daniel. *Canzoni*. Ed. Gianluigi Toja. Florence: Sansoni, 1961.

——. *The Poetry of Arnaut Daniel*. Ed. James J. Wilhelm. Garland Library of Medieval Literature, Series A3. New York: Garland, 1981.

Arnold, Benjamin. *Princes and Territories in Medieval Germany*. New York: Cambridge University Press, 1991.

Aurell, Martin. "La détérioration du statut de la femme aristocratique en Provence (Xe–XIIIe siècles)." *Moyen Age* 40 (1985): 5–32.

——. *Les noces du comte: Mariage et pouvoir en Catalogne (785–1213)*. Histoire Ancienne et Médiévale 32. Paris: Publications de la Sorbonne, 1995.

——. "Le pouvoir comtal en Provence sous Alphonse Ier." Vol. 2, "Catalogue des actes comtaux (1166–1196)." Thèse de doctorat, Université de Provence, 1980.

Aurell i Cardona, Martin. "L'expansion catalane en Provence au XIIe siècle." In *La formació i expansió del feudalisme català: Homenatge a Santiago Sobrequés i Vidal*, ed. Jaume Portella i Comas, 175–97. Girona: Estudi general, revista del Collegi Universitari de Girona, 1985.

Auriac, Eugène d'. *Histoire de l'ancien cathédral et des évêques d'Alby*. Paris: Imprimerie Nationale, 1858.

Averkorn, Raphaela. "Die Cistercienserabteien Berdoues und Gimont in ihren Beziehungen zum laikalen Umfeld." In *Vinculum Societatis: Joachim Wollasch zum 60. Geburtstag*, ed. Franz Neiske, Dietrich Poeck, and Mechthild Sandmann, 1–35. Sigmaringendorf: Glock und Lutz, 1991.

Bachrach, Bernard S. "Henry II and the Angevin Tradition of Family Hostility." *Albion* 16 (1984): 111–30.

——. "Some Observations on the Origins of the Countess Gerberga of the Angevins." In Bachrach, *State-Building in Medieval France*, no. 2. Collected Studies 486. Aldershot, Hampshire: Variorum, 1995.

al-Bakri, Abu 'Ubayd 'Abd Allah ibn 'Abd al-'Aziz. *Déscription de l'Afrqiue septentrionale*. Trans. William MacGuckin, baron de Slane. Algiers: A. Jourdan, 1913.

Balaguer, Anna M. "*Parias* and the Myth of the *mancus*." In *Problems of Medieval Coinage in the Iberian Area*, ed. Mário Gomes Marques and D. M. Metcalf, 3:499–545. Santarém: Sociedade Numismatica Scalabitana, Instituto de Sintra, 1988.

Baldwin, John. *The Government of Philip Augustus*. Berkeley and Los Angeles: University of California Press, 1986.

——. "The Image of the Jongleur in Northern France around 1200." *Speculum* 72 (1997): 635–63.

Baratier, Edouard. *La démographie provençale du XIIIe au XVIe siècle, avec chiffres de comparaison pour le XVIIIe siècle*. Paris: S.E.V.P.E.N., 1961.

Barber, Malcolm. *The New Knighthood: A History of the Order of the Temple*. Cambridge: Cambridge University Press, 1994.

Barkai, Rom. *A History of Jewish Gynaecological Texts in the Middle Ages*. Brill's Series in Jewish Studies 20. Leiden: Brill, 1998.

Barral i Altet, Xavier. "Monuments et espace urbain dans le Midi de la France et en Catalogne." In *Catalunya i França meridional a l'entorn de l'any mil*, ed. Xavier Barral i Altet et al. Barcelona: Generalitat de Catalunya, Departament de Cultura, 1991.

——, ed. *Le paysage monumental de la France autour de l'an mil*. Paris: Picard, 1987.

Barthélemy, Dominique. *L'an mil et la paix de Dieu: La France chrétienne et féodale*. Paris: Fayard, 1999.

——. "Les auto-déditions en servage à Marmoutier (Touraine) au XIe siècle." In *Commerce, finances et société (XIe–XVIe siècles): Recueil de travaux d'histoire médiévale offert à M. le Professeur Henri Dubois*, ed.

Philippe Contamine, Thierry Dutour, and Bertrand Schnerb, 397–415. Cultures et civilisations médiévales 9. Paris: Université de Paris–Sorbonne, 1993.

——. *La mutation de l'an mil a-t-elle eu lieu: Servage et chevalerie dans la France des Xe et XIe siècles*. Paris: Fayard, 1997.

——. "La mutation féodale a-t-elle eu lieu? (Note critique)." *Annales, E.S.C.* 47 (1992): 767–77.

——. "Qu'est-ce que le servage, en France, au XIe siècle?" *Revue Historique* 582 (1992): 223–84.

Barthès, Henri. *Les documents nécrologiques du diocèse de Béziers*. Saint-Genies-de-Fontedit: H. Barthès, 1988.

Barton, Richard E. " 'Zealous Anger' and the Renegotiation of Aristocratic Relationships in Eleventh- and Twelfth-Century France." In *Anger's Past*, ed. Barbara H. Rosenwein, 153–70.

Baudon de Mony, Charles. *Les relations politiques des comtes de Foix avec la Catalogne*. Paris: Picard, 1896.

Baumel, Jean. *Histoire d'une seigneurie du midi de la France*. Montpellier: Causse, 1969.

Bautier, Robert Henri. "Recherches sur les routes de l'Europe médiévale: II. Le grand axe routier est-ouest du midi de la France d'Avignon à Toulouse." *Bulletin philologique et historique (jusqu'à 1610)*. 86e Congrès des Sociétés Savantes (1961). Comité des travaux historiques et scientifiques. Paris, 1963.

Bec, Pierre. *La langue occitane*. Paris: Presses Universitaires, 1986.

Belperron, Pierre. *La croisade contre les Albigeois et l'union du Languedoc à la France (1209–1249)*. Paris: Plon, 1942.

Benjamin, Richard. "A Forty-Years War: Toulouse and the Plantagenets, 1156–96." *Historical Research: Bulletin of the Institute of Historical Research* 61 (1988): 270–85.

Berlioz, Jacques. *"Tuez-les tous. Dieu reconnaîtra les siens." Le massacre de Béziers (22 juillet 1209) et la croisade contre les albigeois vus par Césaire de Heisterbach*. Portet-sur-Garonne, France: Loubatières, 1994.

Berman, Constance Hoffman. *The Cistercian Evolution: The Invention of a Religious Order in Twelfth-Century Europe*. Philadelphia: University of Pennsylvania Press, 2000.

——. *Medieval Agriculture, the Southern French Countryside, and the Early Cistercians: A Study of Forty-three Monasteries*. Transactions of the American Philosophical Society 76, part 5. Philadelphia: American Philosophical Society, 1986.

Bernard of Clairvaux. *Five Books on Consideration*. Trans. John Anderson and Elizabeth Kennan. Cistercian Fathers 37. Kalamazoo, Mich.: Cistercian Publications, 1976.

——. *Letters*. Trans. Bruno Scott James. London: Burns Oates, 1953.

——. "Trattati." In *Opere*, vol. 1, ed. Ferruccio Gastaldelli. Milan: Scriptorium Claravallense, 1984.

Bernart de Ventadorn. *The Songs of Bernart de Ventadorn*. Trans. Stephen G. Nichols Jr., John A. Galm, and A. Bartlett Giamatti. Studies in Romance Languages and Literature 39. Chapel Hill: University of North Carolina Press, 1965.

Bertran de Born. *L'amour et la guerre: L'ouevre de Bertran de Born*. Ed. and trans. Gérard Gouiran. Aix-en-Provence: Université de Provence, 1985.

——. *The Poems of the Troubadour Bertran de Born*. Ed. and trans. William D. Paden Jr., Tilde Sankovitch, and Patricia Stäblin. Berkeley and Los Angeles: University of California Press, 1986.

Bienvenu, Jean Marc. *L'étonnant fondateur de Fontevraud, Robert d'Arbrissel*. Paris: Nouvelles Editions Latines, 1981.

Biget, Jean Louis. " 'Les Albigeois': Remarques sur une dénomination." In *Inventer l'hérésie? Discours polémiques et pouvoirs avant l'Inquisition*, ed. Monique Zerner, 219–56. Nice: Centre d'Etudes Médiévales, Faculté des Lettres, Université de Nice Sophia-Antipolis, 1998.

——. "L'épiscopat du Rouergue et de l'Albigeois (Xe–XIe siècle)." In *Catalunya i França meridional a l'entorn de l'any mil*, ed. Xavier Barral i Altet et al., 181–201. Barcelona: Gerealitat de Catalunya, Departament de Cultura, 1991.

——. "Récits d'une histoire oubliée." In *Histoire d'Albi*, ed. J. L. Biget, 33–56. Toulouse: E. Privat, 1983.

——. "La vicomté d'Ambialet de ses origines à la fin du XIVe siècle." *Bulletin des Sciences, Arts et Belles-Lettres du Tarn*, 3me sér., 36 (1978): 3–29.

Bisson, Thomas N. "The 'Feudal Revolution.' " *Past and Present* 142 (1994): 6–42.

——. *The Medieval Crown of Aragon : A Short History*. New York: Oxford University Press, 1986.

——. *Medieval France and Her Pyrenean Neighbours: Studies in Early Instituional History*. Studies presented to the International Commission for the History of Representative and Parliamentary Institutions 70. London: Hambledon, 1989.

——. "The Organized Peace in Southern France and Catalonia, ca. 1140–ca. 1233." In *Medieval France and Her Pyrenean Neighbours*, 215–36.

——. "The Problem of Feudal Monarchy: Aragon, Catalonia, and France." In *Medieval France and Her Pyrenean Neighbours*, 237–56.

——, ed. *Cultures of Power: Lordship, Status and Process in Twelfth-Century Europe*. Philadelphia: University of Pennsylvania Press, 1995.

Bloch, Marc. *Feudal Society*. Trans. L. A. Manyon. Chicago: University of Chicago Press, 1961.

Bloch, R. Howard. *Medieval Misogyny and the Invention of Western Romantic Love*. Chicago: Chicago University Press, 1991.

Blumenthal, Uta Renate. *The Investiture Controversy: Church and Monarchy from the Ninth to the Twelfth Century*. Philadelphia: University of Pennsylvania Press, 1988.

Bofarull y Mascaró, Prospero de. *Los condes de Barcelona vindicados*. Barcelona: J. Oliveres y Monmany, 1836.

Bolton, Brenda, "Except the Lord Keep the City: Towns in the Papal States at the Turn of the Twelfth Century." In *Innocent III*, article no. 3.

——. "For the See of Simon Peter." In *Innocent III*, article no. 2.

——. *Innocent III: Studies on Papal Authority and Pastoral Care*. Collected Studies 490. Aldershot, Hampshire: Variorum, 1995.

——. "Philip Augustus and John: Two Sons in Innocent III's Vineyard." In *Innocent III*, article no. 5.

Bonde, Sheila, *Fortress-Churches of Languedoc : Architecture, Religion, and Conflict in the High Middle Ages*. New York: Cambridge University Press, 1994.

Bonnassie, Pierre. *La Catalogne du milieu du Xe à la fin du XIe siècle*. : Publications de l'Université de Toulouse–Le Mirail, série A, 23, 29. Toulouse: Université de Toulouse–Le Mirail, 1975.

Bonner, Anthony, trans. *Songs of the Troubadours*. London: George Allen and Unwin, 1973.

Bonnery, André. "Les transformations de la cathédrale de Narbonne au IXe siècle." *Annales du Midi* 102 (1990): 635–42.

Bordeaux, Michèle. *Aspects économiques de la vie de l'Eglise aux XIVe et XVe siècles*. Paris: Librairie Générale de Droit et de Jurisprudence, 1969.

Botet i Sisó, J. *Les monedes catalanes*. Barcelona, 1905.

Bouchard, Constance. *Sword, Miter, and Cloister: Nobility and the Church in Burgundy*. Ithaca: Cornell University Press, 1987.

——. *"Those of My Blood": Constructuing Noble Families in the Middle Ages*. Philadelphia: University of Pennsylvania, forthcoming.

Bourdieu, Pierre. *Outline of a Theory of Practice*. Trans. Richard Nice. New York: Cambridge University Press, 1977.

——. "Rites as Acts of Institution." In *Honor and Grace in Anthropology*, ed. J. G. Peristiany and Julian Pitt-Rivers, 79–89. Cambridge Studies in Social and Cultural Anthropology 76. New York: Cambridge University Press, 1992.

Boureau, Alain. *Le droit de cuissage: Histoire de la fabrication d'un mythe (XIIe–XXe siècle)*. Paris: Albin Michel, 1994.

Bourin-Derruau, Monique. *Villages médiévaux en bas-Languedoc: Genèse d'une sociabilité (Xe–XIVe siècle*. Chemins de la mémoire. Paris: L'Harmattan, 1987.

Bousquet, R. "Civilization romane." In *Histoire du Rouergue*, ed. Henri Enjalbert, 83–112. Toulouse: E. Privat, 1979.

Boussard, Jacques. *Le gouvernement d'Henri II Plantegenêt*. Paris: Librarie d'Argences, 1956.

——. "Les mercenaires au XIIe siècle: Henri II Plantagenet et les origines de l'armée de métier." *Bibliothèque de l'Ecole des Chartes* 106 (1945): 189–224.

Brenon, Anne. "Les fonctions sacramentelles du consolament." *Heresis* 20 (1993): 33–50.

——."La lettre d'Evervin de Steinfeld à Bernard de Clairvaux de 1143: Un document essentiel et méconnu." *Heresis* 25 (1995): 7–28.

——. *Le vrai visage du catharisme*. Portet-sur-Garonne: Loubatières, 1990.

Brown, Peter. *The Body and Society: Men, Women and Sexual Renunciation in Early Christianity*. New York: Columbia University Press, 1988.

Bruckner, Matilda, Laurie Shepard, and Sarah White, trans. *Songs of the Women Troubadours*. Garland Library of Medieval Literature 97A. New York: Garland, 1995.

Brunel, Clovis, ed. *Les plus anciennes chartes en langue provençale*. Geneva: Slatkine Reprints, 1973.

Brunel-Lobrichon, Geneviève, and Claudie Duhamel Amado. *Au temps des troubadours*. Paris: Hachette, 1997.

Bugge, John. *Virginitas: An Essay in the History of a Medieval Ideal*. International Archives of the History of Ideas. Series Minor 17. The Hague: Martinus Nijhoff, 1975.

Burns, E. Jane. "The Man behind the Lady in Troubadour Lyric." *Romance Notes* 25 (1985): 254–70.

Bynum, Caroline. "Did the Twelfth Century Discover the Individual?" In Bynum, *Jesus as Mother: Studies in the Spirituality of the High Middle Ages*, 82–109. Publications of the Center for Medieval and Renaissance Studies, UCLA, 16. Berkeley and Los Angeles: University of California Press, 1982.

Cadden, Joan. *The Meanings of Sex Difference in the Middle Ages: Medicine, Science, and Culture*. New York: Cambridge University Press, 1993.

Caffaro. *Annali Genovesi di Caffaro e de'suoi continuatori*. Ed. Luigi Tommaso Belgrano. Fonti per la storia d'Italia. Rome: Istututo Storico Italiano, 1890.

Caille, Jacqueline. "Le consulat de Narbonne." In *Les origines des libertés urbaines: Actes du XVIe Congrès des historiens médiévistes de l'enseignement supérieur*, 243–63. Publications de l'Université de Rouen 157. Rouen: Université de Rouen, 1990.

——. "Ermengarde, vicomtesse de Narbonne (1127/29–1196/97): Une grande figure féminine du Midi aristocratique." In *La femme dans l'histoire et la société méridionales (IXe–XIXe s.)*, 9–50. Fédération Historique du Languedoc Méditerranéen et du Roussillon. Actes du 66e congrès. Montpellier: Arceaux, 1995.

——. "Une idylle entre la vicomtesse Ermengarde de Narbonne et le prince Rognvald Kali des Orcades au milieu du XIIe siècle?" In *Hommage à Robert Saint-Jean*, ed. Guy Romestan, 229–33. Mémoires de la Société Archéologique de Montpellier 21. Montpellier: Société Archéologique de Montpellier, 1993.

——. "Les marchands de Montpellier et la leude de Narbonne dans le dernier quart du XIe siècle." *Bulletin Historique de la Ville de Montpellier* 5 (1985): 3–4.

——. "La métropole des deux versants (461–1091)." In *Histoire de Narbonne*, ed. J. Michaud and A. Cabanis, 93–118.

——. "Narbonne au moyen âge: Évolution de la topographie et du paysage urbain." In *110e Congrès national des sociétés savantes. Section d'histoire médiévale*, 57–96. Paris: Comité des Travaux Historiques et Scientifiques, 1986.

——. "Narbonne sous l'occupation musulmane (première moitié du VIIIe siècle). Problèmes de topographie." *Annales du Midi* 87 (1975): 97–103.

——. "Origine et développement de la seigneurie temporelle de l'archevêque dans la ville et le terroir de Narbonne (IXe–XIIe siècles)." In *Narbonne: Archéologie et histoire*, 2:9–36.

——. "Les seigneurs de Narbonne dans le conflit Toulouse–Barcelone au XIIe siècle." *Annales du Midi* 97 (1985): 227–44.

——. "Seigneurs et 'peuple' de Narbonne (XI–XVe siècles)." In *Histoire de Narbonne*, ed. Jacques Michaud and André Cabanis, 119–140.

——. "Les traits médiévaux du visage urbain (Ve–XVe siècles)." In *Histoire de Narbonne*, ed. Jacques Michaud and André Cabanis, 173–200.

Caïrou, René. *Narbonne: Vingt siècles de fortifications*. Connaisance de Narbonne 1. Narbonne: Commission Archéologique de Narbonne, 1979.

Calmette, Joseph. "La famille de Saint Guilhem." *Annales du Midi* 18 (1906): 145–65.

Cardenal, Peire. *Poésies complètes du troubadour Peire Cardenal (1180–1278)*. Ed. and trans. René Lavaud. Toulouse: E. Privat, 1957.

Cartulaire de Béziers (Livre noir). Ed. J. Rouquette. Paris: Picard, 1918.

Cartulaire de l'abbaye de Lézat. Ed. Paul Ourliac and Anne Marie Magnou. Collection de documents inédits sur l'histoire de France, série in-8 17. Paris: C.T.H.S, 1984.

Cartulaire de l'abbaye de Silvanès. Ed. P. A. Verlaguet. Archives Historiques de Rouergue 1. Rodez: Carrère, 1910.

"Cartulaire de la seigneurie de Fontjoncouse." *Bulletin de la Commission Archéologique et Littéeraire de Narbonne* 1 (1877): 107–341.

Cartulaire de Maguelone. Ed. J. Rouquette and A. Villemagne. Montpellier: Louis Valat, 1912.

Cartulaire du chapitre cathédrale St-Etienne d'Agde. Ed. Raymonde Foreville. Paris: CNRS, 1995.

Cartulaire du chapitre d'Agde. Ed. Odile Terrin. Publications de la Société d'Histoire du Droit et des Institutions des Anciens Pays de Droit Ecrit 1. Nîmes: Privately printed, 1969.

Cartulaire du chapitre de l'église cathédrale Notre-Dame de Nîmes. Ed. Eugene Germer-Durand. Nîmes: Catélan, 1874.

Cartulaires des Templiers de Douzens. Ed. Pierre Gérard and Elisabeth Magnou. Collection de documents inédits sur l'histoire de France, série in-8 3. Paris: Bibliothèque Nationale, 1965.

Cartulario del Monasterio de Santa Maria de Huerta. Ed. Jose Antonio Garcia Lujan. Biblioteca hortense. Serie A, documenta 1. Huerta: El Monasterio, 1981.

Caruana, J. "Itinerario de Alfonso II de Aragón." In *Estudios de edad media de la Corona de Aragon*, 7:73–298. Zaragoza: Consejo Superior de Investigaciones Cientificas, seccion de Zaragoza, Escuela de Estudios Medievales, 1962.

Castaing-Sicard, Mireille. *Monnaies féodales et circulation monétaire en Languedoc (Xe–XIIIe siècles)*. Cahiers de l'Association Marc Bloch de Toulouse. Etudes d'histoire méridionale 4. Toulouse: Association Marc Bloch, 1961.

Castaldo, André. *L'eglise d'Agde (Xe–XIIIe siècle)*. Travaux et recherches de la Faculté de Droit et des Sciences Economiques de Paris, série Sciences Historiques 20. Paris: Presses Universitaires de France, 1970.

Catel, Guillaume. *Mémoires de l'histoire du Languedoc*. Toulouse: Arnoud Colomiez, 1633.

Cauvet, Emile. "Etude sur l'établissement des Espagnols dans la Septimanie aux VIIIe et IXe siècles et sur la fondation de Fontjoncouse." *Bulletin de la Commission Archéologique et Littéraire de Narbonne* 1 (1876): 345–520.

Cayla. "Le commerce languedocien de sel au XIIe siècle." *Bulletin de la Commission Archéologique de Narbonne* 25 (1959): 81–85.

Chambers, Frank M. "Some Legends concerning Eleanor of Aquitaine." *Speculum* 16 (1941): 459–68.

La chanson de la croisade albigeoise. Ed. Eugène Martin-Chabot. Les classiques de l'histoire de France au moyen âge. Paris: Les Belles Lettres, 1960.

Cherchi, Paolo. *Andreas and the Ambiguity of Courtly Love*. Toronto: University of Toronto Press, 1994.

Cheyette, Fredric L. "The Castles of the Trencavels: A Preliminary Aerial Survey." In *Order and Innovation in the Middle Ages: Essays in Honor of Joseph R. Strayer*, ed. William C. Jordan, Bruce McNab, and Theofilo F. Ruiz, 255–72. Princeton: Princeton University Press, 1970.

——. "The Invention of the State." In *Essays on Medieval Civilization*, ed. Bede K. Lackner and Kenneth R. Philp, 143–71. Austin: University of Texas Press, 1978.

——. "On the *fief de reprise*," *Les sociétés méridionales à l'âge féodal: Espagne, Italie et sud de la France, Xe–XIIIe s. Hommage à Pierre Bonnassie*. Ed. Hélène Débax. 319–24. Toulouse: CNRS, Université de Toulouse-Le Mirail, 1999.

——. "Procurations by Large-Scale Communities in Fourteenth-Century France." *Speculum* 37 (1962): 18–31.

——. "The 'Sale' of Carcassonne to the Counts of Barcelona (1067–1070) and the Rise of the Trencavels." *Speculum* 63 (1988): 826–64.

——. "The Sovereign and the Pirates, 1332." *Speculum* 45 (1970): 40–68.

——. "Suum cuique tribuere." *French Historical Studies* 6 (1970): 287–99.

Cheyette, Fredric L., and Claudie Amado. "Organisation d'un terroir et d'un habitat concentré: Un exemple méridional." In *Habitats fortifiés et organisation de l'espace en Méditerranée médiévale*, ed. A. Bazzana, P. Guichard, and J. M. Poisson, 35–44. Lyons: Travaux de la Maison de l'Orient 4, 1983.

Cheyette, Fredric L., and Margaret L. Switten. "Women in Troubadour Song: Of the Contessa and the Vilana." *Women and Music* 2 (1998): 26–45.

Chodorow, Stanley. *Christian Political Theory and Church Politics in the Mid-Twelfth Century: The Ecclesiology of Gratian's Decretum*. Publications of the Center for Medieval and Renaissance Studies, UCLA, 5. Berkeley and Los Angeles: University of California Press, 1972.

Cholakian, Rouben C. *The Troubadour Lyric: A Psychocritical Reading*. New York: Manchester University Press, 1990.

"Chronica Adefonsi Imperatoris." In *Chronica hispana saeculi XII*, ed. Emma Falque, Juan Gil, and Antonio Maya Sánchez, 1:147–248. Corpus Christianorum; Continuatio Medievalis 71–72. Turnhout: Brepols, 1990.

Chronicles of the Reigns of Stephen, Henry II, and Richard. 4 vols. Ed. Richard Howlett. Rolls Series. London: Longman, 1884–89.

Clanchy, Michael. "Law and Love in the Middle Ages." In *Disputes and Settlements: Law and Human Relations in the West*, ed. John Bossy, 47–68. Cambridge: Cambridge University Press, 1983.

Clark, Robert L. A., trans. "The Song of Sainte Foy." In *The Book of Sainte Foy*, trans. Pamela Sheingorn, 275–84. Philadelphia: University of Pennsylvania Press, 1995.

Clément, Pierre A. *Les chemins à travers les âges en Cévennes et bas Languedoc*. Montpellier: Presses du Languedoc, 1983.

Clément, Pierre A., and Alain Peyre. *La voie domitienne: De la via domitia aux routes de l'an 2000*. Montpellier: Presses du Languedoc/Max Chaleil, 1991.

Codice diplomatico della repubblica di Genova. Ed. Cesare Imperiale di Sant'Angelo. Fonti per la Storia d'Italia, Carte e Scrittori 77, 79, 89. Rome: R. Istituto Storico Italiano per il Medio Evo, 1936.

Codrington, Oliver. *A Manual of Musalman Numismatics*. Asiatic Society Monographs 7. London: Royal Asiatic Society, 1904.

Cohen, Jeremy. "The Nasi of Narbonne: A Problem in Medieval Historiography." *Association for Jewish Studies Review* 2 (1977): 45–76.

Cohen, Shaye J. D. "The Matrilineal Principle in Historical Perspective." *Judaism* 34 (1985): 9–17.

Colby-Hall, Alice. "In Search of the Lost Epics of the Lower Rhone Valley." In *Romance Epic: Essays on a Medieval Literary Genre*, ed. Hans Erich Keller, 115–28. Studies in Medieval Culture 24. Kalamazoo, Mich.: Medieval Institute, 1987.

Compayré, Claude. *Etudes historiques et documents inédits sur l'Albigeois, le Castrais et l'ancien diocèse de Lavaur*. Albi: M. Papailhian, 1841.

Le comte de l'an mil. Ed. E. Crubézy and C. Dieulafit. *Aquitania*, supplément 8. Toulouse: Direction Régional des Affaires Culturelles Midi-Pyrénées, 1996.

Congar, Yves M.-J. "Eglise et cité de Dieu chez quelques auteurs Cisterciens à l'époque des Croisades, en particulier dans le *De Peregrinante civitate Dei* d'Henri d'Albano." In *Etudes d'ecclésiologie médiévale*, article no. 8. London: Variorum, 1983.

——. "Henri de Marcy, abbé de Clairvaux, cardinal-évêque d'Albano, et légat pontifical." In *Analecta monastica. Textes et études sur la vie des moines au moyen âge, 5e série*, 43:1–90. Studia Anselmiana. Rome: Pontificium Institutum S. Anselmi, 1958.

Constable, Giles. *Three Studies in Medieval Religious and Social Thought*. Cambridge: Cambridge University Press, 1995.

Constable, Olivia Remie. "Genoa and Spain in the Twelfth and Thirteenth Centuries: Notarial Evidence for a Shift in Patterns of Trade." *Journal of European Economic History* 19 (1990): 635–57.

Contamine, Philippe. *War in the Middle Ages*. Trans. Michael Jones. Oxford: Blackwell, 1984.

Crónica geral de Espanha de 1344. Ed. Luis Filipe Lindley Cintra. Fontes narrativas da historia portuguesa 2. Lisbon: Imprensa Nacional, 1983.

Cropp, Glynnis M. *Le vocabulaire courtois des troubadours de l'époque classique*. Geneva: Droz, 1975.

Cros-Mayrevieille, J. P. *Histoire du comté et de la vicomté de Carcassonne*. Carcassonne, 1846.

Damian, Peter. *Book of Gomorrah: An Eleventh-Century Treatise against Clerical Homosexual Practices*. Trans. Pierre J. Payer. Waterloo, Ont.: Wilfrid Laurier University Press, 1982.

Davies, Wendy, and Paul Fouracre, eds. *The Settlement of Disputes in Early Medieval Europe*. Cambridge: Cambridge University Press, 1986.

Day, Gerald W. *Genoa's Response to Byzantium, 1155–1204: Commercial Expansion and Factionalism in a Medieval City*. Urbana: University of Illinois Press, 1988.

Débax, Hélène. "Le cartulaire des Trencavel." In *Les cartularies*, ed. Olivier Guyotjeannin, Laurent Morelle, and Michel Parisse. Paris: Ecole des Chartes, 1993.

——. "Les serments de Lautrec: Redatation et reconsidérations." *Annales du Midi* 109 (1997): 407–80.

Devic, Claude, and Joseph Vaissete. *Histoire générale de Languedoc*. Toulouse: E. Privat, 1872–93.

Devroey, Jean Pierre. "Men and Women in Early Medieval Serfdom: The Ninth-Century Frankish Evidence." *Past and Present* 166 (February 2000): 3–30.

Dieudonné, A. "Le melgorien: Exemple de variations de monnaie médiévale." *Revue Numismatique*, ser. 4, 35 (1932): 31–35.

The Digest of Justinian. Trans. Charles H. Munro. Cambridge: Cambridge University Press, 1904.

Doehard, René. "Méditerranée et économie occidentale pendant le haut moyen âge." *Journal of World History* 1 (1954): 571–91.

Dossat, Yves. "Les cathares dans les documents de l'inquisition." In *Cathares en Languedoc*, 71–106. Cahiers de Fanjeaux 3. Toulouse: E. Privat, 1968.

——."Le clergé méridionale à la veille de la croisade Albigeoise." *Revue Historique et Littéraire du Languedoc* 1 (1944): 263–78.

Doubleday, Simon R. "The Laras: An Aristocratic Family in the Kingdoms of Castile and Leon, 1075–1361." Ph.D. diss., UMI Dissertation Services, Harvard University, 1996.

Duby, Georges. "Dans la France du Nord-Ouest au XIIe siècle: Les 'jeunes' dans la société aristocratique." *Annales, E.S.C.* 19 (1964): 835–46.

——. *The Early Growth of the European Economy: Warriors and Peasants from the Seventh to the Twelfth Century*. Ithaca: Cornell University Press, 1978.

——. *History of Medieval Art, 980–1440*. Geneva: Editions d'Art Albert Skira, 1986.

——. *Love and Marriage in the Middle Ages*. Trans. Jane Dunnett. Chicago: University of Chicago Press, 1994.

——. *Medieval Marriage: Two Models from Twelfth-Century France*. Trans. Elborg Forster. Baltimore: Johns Hopkins University Press, 1978.

——. *La société aux XIe et XIIe siècles dans la région mâconnaise*. Bibliothèque Générale de l'Ecole des Hautes Études en Sciences Sociales. Paris: Armand Colin, 1953.

——. "Women and Power." In *Cultures of Power*, ed. Thomas N. Bisson, 69–89. Philadelphia: University of Pennsylvania Press, 1995.

Dufour, Jean. *Les évêques d'Albi, de Cahors et de Rodez des origines à la fin du XIIe siècle*. Mémoires et documents d'histoire médiévale et de philologie 3. Paris: C.T.H.S., 1989.

Duplessy, J. "La circulation des monnaies arabes en Europe occidentale du VIIIe au XIIIe siècle." *Revue Numismatique* 5me sér., 18 (1956): 101–63.

Dupuy, Pierre. *Histoire du différend d'entre le pape Boniface VIII et Philippe le Bel*. Paris: Cramoisy, 1655.

Durliat, Jean. *Les finances publiques de Dioclétien aux Carolingiens (284–889)*. Sigmaringen: Thorbecke, 1990.

Edel, Leon. *The Age of the Archive*. Monday Evening Papers 7. Middletown, Conn.: Center for Advanced Studies, Wesleyan University, 1966.

Egan, Margarita, trans. *The Vidas of the Troubadours*. Garland Library of Medieval Literature 6B. New York: Garland, 1984.

Emery, Richard W. *Heresy and Inquisition in Narbonne*. Studies in History, Economics, and Public Law 480. New York: Columbia University Press, 1941.

English Historical Documents. Vol. 2. Ed. David C. Douglas and G. W. Greenaway. London: Eyre & Spottiswoode, 1953.

Enright, Michael J. *Lady with a Mead Cup: Ritual, Prophecy and Lordship in the European Warband from La Tène to the Viking Age*. Portland, Ore.: Four Courts Press, 1996.

Erdmann, Carl. *The Origin of the Idea of Crusade*. Trans. Marshall W. Baldwin and Walter Goffart. Princeton: Princeton University Press, 1977.

Erikson, Kai T. *Wayward Puritans: A Study in the Sociology of Deviance*. New York: John Wiley and Sons, 1966.

Esquieu, Yves. *Autour de nos cathédrales: Quartiers canoniaux du sillon rhodanien et du littoral méditerranéen*. Monographie du Centre de Recherches Archéologiques 8. Paris: CNRS, 1992.

——. "Narbonne." In *Les chanoines dans la ville: Recherches sur la topographie des quartiers canoniaux en France*, ed. Jean Charles Picard, 317–28. De l'archéologie à l'histoire. Paris: De Boccard, 1994.

Fagnan, Edmond. *Extraits inédits relatifs au Maghreb*. Algiers: J. Carbonel, 1924.

Favreau-Lilie, Marie Luise. *Die Italiener im Heiligen Land vom ersten Kreuzzug bis zum Tode Heinrichs von Champagne (1098–1197)*. Amsterdam: Adolf M. Hakkert, 1989.

Ferrante, Joan. *Women as Image in Medieval Literature*. New York: Columbia University Press, 1975.

——, ed. *Guillaume d'Orange: Four Twelfth-Century Epics*. New York: Columbia University Press, 1974.

Février, Paul Albert. *Le développement urbain en Provence de l'époque romaine à la fin du XIVe siècle*. Bibliothèque des Ecoles Françaises d'Athènes et de Rome 202. Paris: Boccard, 1964.

Février, Paul Albert, et al. *Au coeur d'une ville épiscopal: Fréjus*. Fréjus: Comité d'Animation Culturelle, 1988.

——. *La Provence des origines à l'an mil: Histoire et archéologie*. Rennes: Editions Ouest-France, 1989.

Fichtenau, Heinrich. *Heretics and Scholars in the High Middle Ages, 1000–1200*. Trans. Denise A. Kaiser. University Park: Pennsylvania State University Press, 1998.

——. *Living in the Tenth Century: Mentalities and Social Orders*. Trans. Patrick J. Geary. Chicago: University of Chicago Press, 1991.

Fitting, Hermann, ed. *Lo Codi, in der lateinischen Übersetzung des Ricardus Pisanus*. Aalen, Germany: Scientia Verlag, 1968.

Fletcher, R. A. "Reconquest and Crusade in Spain c. 1050–1150." *Transactions of the Royal Historical Society*, ser. 5, 37 (1987): 31–47.

Fletcher, Richard. *The Quest for El Cid*. New York: Knopf, 1990.

Folz, Robert. *The Concept of Empire in Western Europe from the Fifth to the Fourteenth Century*. Trans. Sheila Ann Ogilvie. London: Edward Arnold, 1969.

Foreville, Raymonde. *Latran I, II, III, et Latran IV*. Histoire des conciles oecuménique 6. Paris: L'Orante, 1965.

Fossier, Robert. *Enfance de l'Europe, Xe–XIIe siècles: Apects économiques et sociaux*. Nouvelle Clio 17. Paris: Presses Universitaires, 1982.

Fournier, Jacques. *Le registre d'inquisition de Jacques Fournier, évêque de Pamiers (1318–1325)*. Ed. Jean Duvernoy. Toulouse: E. Privat, 1965.

Fournier, Paul. *Le royaume d'Arles et de Vienne (1138–1378)*. Paris: Picard, 1891.

Frassetto, Michael, ed. *Medieval Purity and Piety: Essays on Medieval Clerical Celibacy and Religious Reform*. New York: Garland, 1998.

Freedman, Paul. *The Origins of Peasant Servitude in Medieval Catalonia*. Cambridge: Cambridge University Press, 1991.

Fried, Johannes. "Friedrich Barbarossas Krönung in Arles (1178)." *Historisches Jahrbuch* 103 (1983): 347–71.

——, ed. *Die abendländische Freiheit vom 10. zum 14. Jahrhundert: Der Wirkungszusammenhang von Idee und Wirklichkeit im europäischen Vergleich*. Vorträge und Forschungen. Sigmaringen: Thorbecke, 1991.

Froissart. *Chronicles*. Trans. Geoffrey Brereton. Harmondsworth: Penguin, 1978.

Gager, John G., ed. *Curse Tablets and Binding Spells from the Ancient World*. New York: Oxford University Press, 1992.

Gallia Christiana in provincias ecclesiasticas distributa. 16 vols. Ed. Dionysius Sammarthanus and Paulus Piolin. Paris and Rome: Victor Palme, 1870.

Gallia Christiana novissima. Histoire des archévêchés, évêchés et abbayes de France. 7 vols. Ed. J. H. Albanes. Montebéliard, 1899–1920.

Gamber, Klaus. *Sancta Sanctorum: Studien zur liturgischen Ausstattung der Kirche, vor allem des Altarraums*. Studia Patristica et Liturgica 10. Regensburg: Friedrich Pustet, 1981.

Gaunt, Simon. *Gender and Genre in Medieval French Literature*. Cambridge: Cambridge University Press, 1995.

Gauthier, Nancy, and Jean Charles Picard, eds. *La topographie chrétienne des cités de la Gaule, des origines au milieu du VIIIe siècle*. Vol. 7. Paris: De Boccard, 1987.

Gayraud, Michel. *Narbonne antique des origines à la fin du IIIe siècle*. Revue Archéologique de Narbonnaise, supplément 8. Paris: De Boccard, 1981.

Geary, Patrick J. *Phantoms of Remembrance: Memory and Oblivion at the End of the First Millennium*. Princeton: Princeton University Press, 1994.

——. "Vivre en conflit dans un France sans état: Typologie des mécanismes de reglement des conflits (1050–1200)." *Annales, E.S.C.* 41 (1986): 1107–33.

Georgi, Wolfgang. *Friedrich Barbarossa und die auswärtingen Mächte: Studien zur Aussenpolitik 1159–1180*. Europäische Hochschulschriften, III 442. New York: Peter Lang, 1990.

Gerald of Wales. *Opera*. 8 vols. Ed. J. S. Brewer, J. F. Dimock, and G. F. Warner. Rolls Series. London: Eyre and Spottiswood, 1861.

Géraud, H. "Les routiers au douzième siècle." *Bibliothèque de l'Ecole des Chartes* 3 (1841): 125–47.

Gervase of Canterbury. *Historical Works*. Ed. William Stubbs. Rolls Series. London: Longman, 1879.

Gesta comitum barcinonensium. Ed. L. Barrau Dihigo and J. Masso Torrents. Barcelona: Casa de Caritat, 1919.

Ghil, Eliza Miruna. *l'age du Parage: Essai sur le poétique et le politique en Occitanie au XIIIe siècle*. University Studies in Medieval and Renaissance Literature 4. New York: Peter Lang, 1989.

Gillingham, John. "Love, Marriage and Politics in the Twelfth Century." In *Richard Coeur de Lion*, 243–55. London: Hambledon, 1994.

——. *Richard I*. New Haven: Yale University Press, 2000.

Giovanni scriba. *Il cartolare di Giovanni Scriba*. Ed. Mario Chiaudano and Mattia Moresco. Regesta chartarum Italiae 19. Rome: R. Istituto Storico Italiano per il Medio Evo, 1935.

Given, James. *State and Society in Medieval Europe: Gwynedd and Languedoc under Outside Rule*. Ithaca: Cornell University Press, 1990.

Goldin, Frederick. "The Array of Perspectives in the Early Courtly Love Lyric." In *In Pursuit of Perfection: Courtly Love in Medieval Literature*, ed. George Economou and Joan Ferrante. Port Washington, N.Y.: Kennikat Press, 1975.

Goody, Jack. "Religion and Ritual, the Definitional Problem." *British Journal of Sociology* 12 (1961): 142–64.

Gouron, André. "Diffusion des consulats méridionaux et expansion du droit romain aux XIIe et XIIIe siècles." In *La science du droit dans le Midi de la France au Moyen Age*, article no. 1.

——. *Droit et coutume en France aux XIIe et XIIIe siècles*. Collected Studies 422. Aldershot, Hampshire: Variorum, 1993.

——. *Etudes sur la diffusion des doctrines juridiques médiévales*. Collected Studies 264. London: Variorum, 1987.

——. "Liber und libertas in Südfrankreichs Praxis und Statutenrecht (XII. und XIII. Jahrhundert)." In *Droit et coutume en France aux XIIe et XIIIe siècles*, article no. 22.

——. "*Lo Codi*, source de la Somme au Code de Rogerius." In *Etudes sur la diffusion des doctrines juridiques médiévales*, article no. 11.

——. "Du nouveau sur *lo Codi*." In *La science du droit dans le Midi de la France au Moyen Age*, article no. 8.

——. "Les plus anciens testaments français." In *Droit et coutume en France aux XIIe et XIIIe siècles*, article no. 3.

——. *La science du droit dans le Midi de la France au Moyen Age*. Collected Studies 196. London: Variorum, 1984.

——. "La science juridique française aux XIe et XIIe siècles." In *Etudes sur la diffusion des doctrines juridiques médiévales*, article no. 2.

Graboïs, Aryeh. "La dynastie des 'rois Juifs' de Narbonne (IXe–XIIIe siècles)." In *Narbonne: Archéologie et histoire*, 2:49–54.

——. "Une étape dans l'évolution vers la désagrégation de l'Etat toulousain au XIIe siècle: L'intervention d'Alphonse-Jourdain à Narbonne (1134–1143)." *Annales du Midi* 78 (1966): 23–36.

——. "The Legendary Figure of Charlemagne in Medieval Hebrew Sources" [in Hebrew]. *Tarbiz* 36 (1996): 31–38.

——. "Le 'Roi Juif' de Narbonne." *Annales du Midi* 109 (1997): 165–88.

Green, D. H. *The Carolingian Lord: Semantic Studies on Four Old High German Words*. Cambridge: Cambridge University Press, 1965.

Gregory VII, Pope. *The Correspondence of Pope Gregory VII: Selected Letters from the Registrum*. Trans. Ephraim Emerton. Records of Civilization. New York: Columbia University Press, 1932.

Grèzes-Rueff, François. "L'abbaye de Fontfroide et son domaine foncier au XIIe–XIIIe siècles." *Annales du Midi* 89 (1977): 253–80.

Grierson, Philip. "Carolingian Europe and the Arabs: The Myth of the Mancus." *Revue Belge de Philologie et d'Histoire* 32 (1954): 1059–74.

Griffe, Elie. *Les anciens pays de l'Aude dans l'antiquité et au moyen âge*. Carcassonne: Imprimeries Gabelle, 1974.

——. "Le catharisme dans le diocèse de Carcassonne et le Lauragais au XIIe siècle." In *Cathares en Languedoc*. Cahiers de Fanjeaux 3. Toulouse: E. Privat, 1968.

——. *Les débuts de l'aventure cathare in Languedoc (1140–1190)*. Paris: Letouzey et Ané, 1969.

——. *Histoire religieuse des anciens pays de l'Aude*. Paris: Picard, 1933.

Gruber, Jörn. *Die Dialektik des Trobar: Untersuchungen zur Struktur und Entwicklung des occitanischen and französischen Minnesangs des 12. Jahrhunderts*. Beihefte zur Zeitschrift für romanische Philologie 194. Tübingen: Niemeyer, 1983.

Grundmann, Herbert. "Rotten und Brabanzonen." *Deutsches Archiv für Geschichte des Mittelalters* 5 (1942): 419–92.

Guibert, abbot of Nogent. *A Monk's Confession: The Memoirs of Guibert of Nogent.* Trans. Paul J. Archambault. University Park: Pennsylvania State University Press, 1996.

——. *Self and Society in Medieval France: The Memoirs of Abbot Guibert of Nogent.* Trans. John F. Benton. New York: Harper and Row, 1970.

Guichonnet, Paul, ed. *Histoire de la Savoie.* Toulouse: E. Privat, 1988.

Guild, Rollins, Jr. *La cathédrale d'Aix-en-Provence.* Paris: CNRS, 1987.

Guillaume de Puylaurens. *Chronique.* Ed. and trans. Jean Duvernoy. Sources d'Histoire Médiévale. Paris: CNRS, 1976.

Gutherz, Xavier, et al. *Histoire de Nîmes.* Aix-en-Provence: Edisud, 1982.

Gutiérrez, Rachel. "What Is Feminist Biography?" In *All Sides of the Subject: Women and Biography,* ed. Teresa Iles. New York: Teachers College Press, 1992.

Hagman, Ylva. "Le catharisme: Un néo-Manichéisme?" *Heresis* 21 (1993): 47–59.

Hallam, Elizabeth M. *Capetian France, 987–1328.* New York: Longman, 1980.

Hamilton, Bernard. "The Cathar Council of St. Félix de Caraman Reconsidered." *Arhivum Fratrum Praedicatorum* 48 (1978): 23–53.

——. "Wisdom from the East: The Reception by the Cathars of Eastern Dualist Texts." In *Heresy and Literacy, 1000–1530,* ed. Peter Biller and Anne Hudson. Cambridge: Cambridge University Press, 1994.

Herlihy, David, and Christiane Klapisch-Zuber. *Tuscans and Their Families: A Study of the Florentine Catasto of 1427.* New Haven: Yale University Press, 1983.

Higounet, Charles. *Le comté de Comminges de ses origines à son annexion à la couronne.* Saint-Gaudens: L'Adret, 1984.

Hilaire, Jean. *Le régime des biens entre époux dans la région de Montpellier du début du XIIIe siècle à la fin du XVIe siècle.* Paris: Editions Montchrestien, 1957.

Hoffmann, Hartmut. *Gottesfriede und Treuga Dei.* Schriften der Monumenta Germaniae Historica 20. Stuttgart: Hiersemann, 1964.

Huchet, Jean Charles. "Les femmes troubadours ou la voix critique." *Littérature* 51 (1983): 59–90.

Huizinga, Johan. *The Waning of the Middle Ages.* London: Edward Arnold, 1924.

Hyams, Paul. "What Did King Henry III of England Think in Bed and in French about Kingship and Anger." In *Anger's Past,* ed. Barbara H. Rosenwein, 92–124.

al-Idrisi. *Description de l'Afrique et de l'Espagne par Edrisi.* Trans. R. Dozy and M. J. De Goeje. Leiden: Brill, 1968.

Jaeger, C. Stephen. "L'amour des rois: Structure sociale d'une forme de sensibilité aristocratique." *Annales, E.S.C.* 46 (1991): 547–71.

——. *Ennobling Love: In Search of a Lost Sensibility.* Philadelphia: University of Pennsylvania Press, 1999.

Jaffé, Philippe, ed. *Regesta pontificum romanorum.* Rev. ed. by S. Loewenfeld, F. Kaltenbrunner, P. Ewald, and G. Wattenbach. Leipzig: Veit, 1885.

Jaufré Rudel. *The Poetry of Cercamon and Jaufré Rudel.* Ed. and trans. George Wolf and Roy Rosenstein. Garland Library of Medieval Literature, series A5. New York: Garland, 1983.

——. *The Songs of Jaufré Rudel.* Ed. and trans. Rupert T. Pickens. Studies and Texts 41. Toronto: Pontifical Institute, 1978.

John of Salisbury. *Historia pontificalis.* Ed. Marjorie Chibnall. Oxford Medieval Texts. Oxford: Clarendon Press, 1986.

Jolowicz, H. F. *Historical Introduction to the Study of Roman Law.* Cambridge: Cambridge University Press, 1954.

Kaiser, Reinhold. *Bischofsherrschaft zwischen Königtum und Fürstenmacht. Studien zur bischöflichen Stadtherrschaft im westfränkisch-französischen Reich im frühen und hohen Mittelalter.* Pariser historische Studien 17. Bonn: Ludwig Röhrscheid, 1981.

Kan, Sergei. "The Nineteenth-Century Tlingit Potlatch." *American Ethnologist* 13 (1986): 191–212.

Kay, Sarah. *The Chansons de Geste in the Age of Romance: Political Fictions.* Oxford: Clarendon Press, 1995.

——. *Subjectivity in Troubadour Poetry.* Cambridge Studies in French. Cambridge: Cambridge University Press, 1990.

Kedar, Benjamin. "Mercanti Genovesi in Alessandria d'Egitto negli anni sessanta del secolo XI." In *Miscellanea di studi storici,* 2:19–30. Collana storica di fonti e studi 38. Genoa, 1983.

Kennan, Elizabeth. "The *de Consideratione* of St. Bernard of Clairvaux and the Papacy in the Mid-Twelfth Century: A Review of Scholarship." *Traditio* 23 (1967): 73–115.

Kienast, Walter. *Der Herzogstitel in Frankreich und Deutschland (9. bis 12. Jahrhundert).* Munich: R. Oldenbourg, 1968.

Kienzle, Beverly M. "Tending the Lord's Vineyard: Cistercian Rhetoric and Heresy, 1143–1229. Part I: Bernard of Clairvaux, the 1143 Sermons and the 1145 Preaching Mission." *Heresis* 25 (1995): 29–61.

Köhler, Erich. *Trobadorlyrik und höfischer Roman; Aufsätze zur französischen und provenzalischen Literatur des Mittelalters.* Neue Beiträge zur Literaturwissenschaft 15. Berlin: Rutten and Loening, 1962.

Köhn, Rolf. "Freiheit als Forderung und Ziel bäurlichen Widerstandes (Mittel- und Westeuropa, 11.–13. Jahrhundert)." In *Die abendländische Freiheit vom 10. zum 14. Jahrhundert,* ed. Johannes Fried, 325–88.

Kolmer, Lothar. *Ad capiendas vulpes: Die ketzerbekämpfung in Südfrankreich in der ersten Hälfte des 13. Jahrhunderts und die Ausbildung des Inquisitionsverfahrens.* Pariser historische Studien 19. Bonn: Ludwig Röhrscheid Verlag, 1982.

Kondoleon, Christine, ed. *Antioch: The Lost Ancient City.* Princeton: Princeton University Press and Worcester Art Museum, 2000.

Krueger, Hilmar C. "Genoese Trade with Northwest Africa in the Twelfth Century." *Speculum* 8 (1933): 377–95.

——. *Navi e proprietà navale a Genova; seconda metà del sec. XII.* Atti della Società Ligure di Storia Patria, nuova serie 25:1. Genoa: Società Ligure di Storia Patria, 1985.

——. "Post-War Collapse and Rehabilitation in Genoa (1140–1162)." In *Studi in onore di Gino Luzzatto.* 2 vols., 1:117–28. Milan: A. Giuffrè, 1949.

Kuttner, Stephan. "The Revival of Jurisprudence." In *Renaissance and Renewal in the Twelfth Century,* ed. Robert L. Benson and Giles Constable, 299–323. Cambridge: Harvard University Press, 1982.

Labrousse, Michel. "Exploitation d'or et d'argent dans le Rouergue et l'Albigeois." In *Rouergue et confines,* 91–108. Fédération Historique du Languedoc Méditerranéen et du Roussillon. Rodez: Société des Lettres, Sciences et Arts de l'Aveyron, 1958.

Lacam, Jean. *Les Sarrazins dans le haut moyen-age français.* Paris: Maisonneuve, 1965.

Lacger, Louis de. *Gaillac en Albigeois, son évolution historique.* Textes et mémoires relatifs a l'histoire des anciens diocèses du Tarn 3. Paris: Picard, 1924.

Ladner, Gerhart B. "Two Gregorian Letters on the Sources and Nature of Gregory VII's Reform Ideology." *Studi Gregoriani* 5 (1956): 221–42.

Lambert, Malcolm. *The Cathars.* Oxford: Blackwell, 1998.

——. *Medieval Heresy: Popular Movements from Bogomil to Hus.* New York: Holmes and Meier, 1976.

Landes, Richard. "La vie apostoloque en Aquitaine en l'an mil. Paix de Dieu, culte des reliques, et communautés hérétiques." *Annales, E.S.C.* 46 (1991): 573–93.

Lansing, Carol. *Power and Purity: Cathar Heresy in Medieval Italy.* New York and Oxford: Oxford University Press, 1998.

Laubenheimer, Fanette. *Sallèles d'Aude. Un complese de potiers gallo-romain: Le quartier artisanal.* Documents d'archéologie française 26. Paris: Maison des Sciences de l'Homme, 1990.

Layettes du trésor des Chartes. Ed. Alexandre Teulet. Archives de l'Empire. Inventaires et documents. Paris: H. Plon, 1863.

Le Goff, Jacques. *The Birth of Purgatory.* Trans. Arthur Goldhammer. Chicago: University of Chicago Press, 1984.

Lejeune, Rita. "La question de l'historicité du héros épique, Aimeri de Narbonne." In *Economies et sociétés au moyen âge: Mélanges offerts à Edouard Perroy,* 50–62. Etudes 5. Paris: Publications de la Sorbonne, 1973.

Léonard, Emile-G, ed. *Catalogue des actes des comtes de Toulouse: Raymond V (1149–1194).* Paris: Picard, 1932.

Le Patourel, John. *Feudal Empires, Norman and Plantagenet.* London: Hambledon, 1984.

Le Roy Ladurie, Emmanuel. *Montaillou: The Promised Land of Error.* Ed. Barbara Bray. New York: George Braziller, 1978.

——. *Les paysans de Languedoc.* Paris: S.E.V.P.E.N, 1966.

Levillain, Léon. "Les alliances des Nibelungen: La famille de saint Guilhem et celle des Gérold." *Annales du Midi* 50 (1938): 5–66.

Lewis, Archibald R. "Count Gerald of Aurillac and Feudalism in South Central France in the Early Tenth Century." *Traditio* 20 (1964): 41–58.

Leyser, Henrietta. *Hermits and the New Monasticism: A Study of Religious Communities in Western Europe, 1000–1150.* New York: St. Martin's Press, 1984.

Liber feudorum maior. Ed. Francisco Miquel Rosell. Barcelona: Consejo Superior de Investigaciones Científicas, 1945.

Liber instrumentorum memorialium: Cartulaire des Guillems de Montpellier. Ed. A. Germain. Montpellier: Société Archéologique de Montpellier, 1884.

Liber iurium reipublicae Genuensis. Ed. Ercole Ricotti. Historiae patriae monumenta, vol. 7, pt. 1. Turin, 1854.

Lieu, Samuel N. C. *Manichaeism in Mesopotamia and the Roman East.* Leiden and New York: Brill, 1994.

———. *Manichaeism in the Later Roman Empire and Medieval China.* Tübingen: J. C. B. Mohr, 1992.

Little, Lester K. *Benedictine Maledictions: Liturgical Cursing in Romanesque France.* Ithaca: Cornell University Press, 1993.

Lobrichon, Guy. "The Chiaroscuro of Heresy: Early Eleventh-Century Aquitaine as seen from Auxerre." In *The Peace of God: Social Violence and Religious Response in France around the Year 1000,* ed. Thomas Head and Richard Landes, 80–103. Ithaca: Cornell University Press, 1992.

Lopez, Robert S. "An Aristocracy of Money in the Early Middle Aes." *Speculum* 28 (1953): 1–43.

Luchaire, Achille. *Etudes sur les actes de Louis VII.* Brussels: Culture et Civilisation, 1964.

Lunt, William E., ed. and trans. *Papal Revenues in the Middle Ages.* 2 vols. New York: Columbia University Press, 1934.

Lutz, Catherine A. *Unnatural Emotions: Everyday Sentiments on a Micronesian Atoll and Their Challenge to Western Theory.* Chicago: University of Chicago Press, 1988.

Maccaronne, Michele. "Orvieto e la predicazione della crociata." In *Studi su Innocenzo III,* 3–163. Padua: Antenore, 1972.

———. "Papato e regno di Sicilia nel primo anno di pontificato di Innocenzo III." In *Nuovi studi su Innocenzo III,* 137–170. Rome: Istituto Storico Italiano per il Medio Evo, 1995.

Magnou-Nortier, Elisabeth. "Fidélité et féodalité méridionales d'après les serments de fidélité (Xe–début XIIe siècle)." In *Les structures sociales de l'Aquitaine, du Languedoc et de l'Espagne au premier âge féodal,* 115–42. Paris: CNRS, 1969.

———. *La société laïque et l'église dans la province ecclésiastique de Narbonne (zone cispyrénéenne) de la fin du VIIIe à la fin du XIe siècle.* Publications de l'Université de Toulouse–Le Mirail, série A 20. Toulouse: Université de Toulouse–Le Mirail, 1974.

———. "La terre, la rente et le pouvoir dans les pays de Languedoc pendant le haut moyen âge, II: La question du manse et de la fiscalité foncière en Languedoc pendant le haut moyen âge." *Francia* 10 (1982): 21–65.

Mahul, M., ed. *Cartulaire et archives des communes de l'ancien diocèse de Carcassonne.* 6 vols. Paris: Didron et Dumoulin, 1857–1882.

Maillard, François, and Robert Henri Bautier. "Un dénombrement des feux, des individus et des fortunes dans deux villages du Fenouillèdes en 1306."In *Bulletin philologique et historique jusqu'à 1610 (1965),* 309–28. Paris: Comité des travaux historiques et scientifiques, 1968.

Mansi, Joannes Dominicus. *Sacrorum conciliorum nova et amplissima collectio.* Graz: Akademische Druck-u. Verlagsanstalt, 1961.

Manteuffel, Tadeusz. *Naissance d'une hérésie: Les adeptes de la pauvreté volontaire au moyen âge.* Trans. Anna Posner. Civlisations et Sociétés 6. The Hague: Mouton, 1970.

Maragone, Bernardo. *Gli annales pisani.* Ed. Michele Lupo Gentile. Rerum Italicarum Scriptores, nuova ed. 6:2. Bologna: N. Zanichelli, 1930.

Marçais, G. "Les villes de la côte algérienne et la piraterie au moyen âge." *Annales, Institut d'Etudes Orientales, Univerisité d'Alger* 13 (1955): 118–42.

Marrou, Henri Irénée. "Le dossier épigraphique de l'évêque Rusticus de Narbonne." *Rivista di Archeologia Cristiana* 46 (1970): 331–49.

Martin-Chabot, Eugène, ed. *Les archives de la Cour des Comptes, Aides et Finances de Montpellier, avec un essai de restitution des premiers registres de sénéchaussée.* Université de Paris. Bibliothèque de la Faculté des Lettres 22. Paris: Felix Alcan, 1907.

Martines, Lauro. "Ritual Language in Renaissance Italy." In *Riti e rituali nelle società medievali,* ed.

Jacques Chiffoleau, Lauro Martines, and Agostino Bagliani, 59–76. Collectanea 5. Spoleto: Centro Italiano di Studi sull'Alto Medioeve, 1994.

McCrank, Lawrence J. "Restauración canonica e intento de reconquista de la sede Tarraconense, 1076–1108." *Cuadernos de Historia de España* 61–62 (1977): 145–245.

Meneghetti, Maria Luisa. *Il pubblico dei travatori: Ricezione e riuso dei testi lirici cortesi fino al XIV secolo.* Modena: Mucchi, 1984.

Merlo, Grado Giovanni. *Eretici ed eresie medievali.* Bologna: Il Mulino, 1989.

Meynial, Edouard. "Notes sur la formation de la théorie du domaine divisé (domaine direct et domaine utile) du XIIe au XIV siècle dans les Romanistes." In *Mélanges Fitting,* 2:409–61. Montpellier: Imprimerie Générale du Midi, 1907.

Michaud, J., and A. Cabanis, eds. *Histoire de Narbonne.* Toulouse: E. Privat, 1981.

Migne, J. P., compiler. *Patrologiae cursus completus, series Latina.* Paris: J. P. Migne, 1844.

Miller, Maureen. *The Formation of a Medieval Church: Ecclesiastical Change in Verona, 950–1150.* Ithaca: Cornell University Press, 1993.

Miller, William Ian. *Humiliation, and Other Essays on Honor, Social Discomfort, and Violence.* Ithaca: Cornell University Press, 1993.

Mines et mineurs en Languedoc-Roussillon et régions voisines de l'Antiquité à nos jours (Actes du XLIX congrès). 1976. Fédération Historique du Languedoc Méditerranéen et du Roussillon. Montpellier: University Paul-Valéry, 1977.

Miret y Sans, Joaquín. "El testamento de la vizcondesa Ermengarda de Narbona." *Boletín de la Real Academia de Buenas Letras de Barcelona* 1 (1901): 41–46.

Monneret de Villard, U. "La monetazione nell'Italia barbarica." *Rivista Italiana di Numismatica,* 2d ser., 2 (1919): 65–138.

Monson, Don A. "The Troubadour's Lady Reconsidered Again." *Speculum* 70 (1995): 255–74.

Montaudon, monk of. *Les poésies du moine de Montaudon.* Ed. Michael J. Routledge. Montpellier: Centre d'Études Occitanes de l'Université Paul-Valéry, 1977.

Moore, R. I. *The Birth of Popular Heresy.* New York: St. Martin's Press, 1975.

——. *The First European Revolution.* Oxford: Blackwell, 2000.

——. *The Formation of a Persecuting Society: Power and Deviance in Western Europe, 950–1250.* Oxford: Blackwell, 1987.

——. *The Origins of European Dissent.* Oxford: Blackwell, 1985.

Mortet, Victor. "Notes historiques et archéologiques sur la cathédrale, la cloître, et le palais archiépiscopal de Narbonne." *Annales du Midi* (1888): 401–14; (1889): 274–87, 439–57.

Mouynès, G. "Une charte d'Adalaïs viscomtesse de Narbonne (990)." *Mémoires de la Société archéologique et scientifique de Carcassonne* 4 (1878): 97–102.

Mundy, John Hine. "Charity and Social Work in Toulouse, 1100–1250." *Traditio* 22 (1966): 203–87.

——. *Liberty and Political Power in Toulouse, 1050–1230.* New York: Columbia University Press, 1954.

——. *Men and Women at Toulouse in the Age of the Cathars.* Studies and Texts 101. Toronto: Pontifical Institute, 1990.

——. "Noblesse et hérésie. Une famille cathare: Les Maurand." *Annales, E.S.C.* 29 (1974): 1211–23.

——. *The Repression of Catharism at Toulouse: The Royal Diploma of 1279.* Studies and Texts 74. Toronto: Pontifical Institute of Mediaeval Studies, 1985.

Müssigbrod, Axel. "Das Necrolog von Saint-Pons de Thomières." In *Vinculum Societatis: Joachim Wollasch zum 60. Geburtstag,* ed. Franz Neiske, Dietrich Poeck, and Mechthild Sandmann, 83–117. Sigmaringendorf: Glock und Lutz, 1991.

Nadal i Farreras, Joaquim, and Philippe Wolff. *Histoire de la Catalogne.* Toulouse: E. Privat, 1982.

Narbonne: Archéologie et histoire (Actes du XLVe congrès). Fédération Historique du Languedoc Méditerranéen et du Roussillon. Montpellier: F.H.L.M.R.–Université Paul-Valéry, 1973.

Newman, Martha G. *The Boundaries of Charity: Cistercian Culture and Ecclesiastical Reform, 1098–1180.* Stanford: Stanford University Press, 1996.

Norgate, Kate. *Richard the Lion Heart.* London: Macmillan, 1924.

Oberto scriba. *Oberto scriba de mercato (1190).* Ed. Mario Chiaudano and Raimundo Morozzo della Rocca. Documenti e studi per la storia del commercio e del diritto commerciale italiano 11. Turin: Bottega d'Erasmo, 1971.

O'Callaghan, Joseph F. *A History of Medieval Spain.* Ithaca: Cornell University Press, 1975.

Oerter, Herbert L. "Campaldino, 1289." *Speculum* 43 (1968): 429–50.

Oexle, Otto Gerhard. "Die Kultur der Rebellion: Schwureinung und Verschwörung im früh- und hochmittelalterliche Okzident." In *Ordnung und Aufruhr im Mittelalter*, ed. Marie Theres Fögen, 119–37. Frankfurt-am-Main: Klostermann, 1995.

Orderic Vitalis. *The Ecclesiastical History of Orderic Vitalis*. Ed. and trans. Marjorie Chibnall. Oxford: Clarenden Press, 1969.

Orkneyinga Saga: The History of the Earls of Orkney. Trans. Hermann Palsson and Paul Edwards. London: Hogarth Press, 1978.

Ourliac, Paul. "L'hommage servile dans la région toulousaine." In *Mélanges d'histoire du moyen âge dédiés à la mémoire de Louis Halphen*. Paris, 1951.

Ourliac, Paul, and Anne Marie Magnou. *Le cartulaire de la Selve: La terre, les hommes, et le pouvoir en Rouergue au XIIe siècle*. Paris: CNRS, 1985.

Pacaut, Marcel. *Alexandre III; étude sur la conception du pouvoir pontifical dans sa pensée et dans son oeuvre*. L'Eglise et l'état au moyen âge 11. Paris: J. Vrin, 1956.

———. *Frederick Barbarossa*. Trans. A. J. Pomerans. New York: Scribner's, 1970.

———. *Louis VII et son royaume*. Paris: S.E.V.P.E.N., 1964.

Paden, William D. "The Troubadour's Lady as Seen through Thick History." *Exemplaria* 11 (1999): 221–44.

Partner, Peter. *The Lands of St. Peter*. Berkeley and Los Angeles: University of California Press, 1972.

Pattison, Walter T. *The Life and Works of the Troubadour Raimbaut d'Orange*. Minneapolis: University of Minnesota Press, 1952.

Peire Rogier. *The Poems of the Troubadour Peire Rogier*. Ed. Derek E. T. Nicholson. Manchester: Manchester University Press, 1976.

Peire Vidal. *Les poésies de Peire Vidal*. Ed. Joseph Anglade. Les classiques français du moyen âge. Paris: Champion, 1923.

Perez, Antoine. *Les cadastres antiques en narbonnaise occidentale*. Revue archéologique de narbonnaise, supplément 29. Paris: CNRS, 1995.

Peristiany, J. G., ed. *Honour and Shame: The Values of a Mediterranean Society*. Chicago: University of Chicago Press, 1966.

Peristiany, J. G., and Julian Pitt-Rivers, eds. *Honor and Grace in Anthropology*. Cambridge Studies in Social and Cultural Anthropology 76. New York: Cambridge University Press, 1992.

Peter of Vaux-de-Cernay. *The History of the Albigensian Crusade*. Trans. W. A. Sibly and M. D. Sibly. Woodbridge, Suffolk: Boydell, 1998.

———. *Petri Vallium Sarnaii Monachi Hystoria Albigensis*. Ed. and trans. Pascal Guébin and Ernest Lyon. Société de l'Histoire de France. Paris: Honoré Champion, 1926.

Pistarino, Geo. "Genova medievale tra Oriente e Occidente." *Rivista Storica Italiana* 81 (1969): 44–73.

Pitt-Rivers, Julian. "Postscript: The Place of Grace in Anthropology." In *Honor and Grace in Anthropology*, ed. J. G. Peristiany and Julian Pitt-Rivers, 215–44.

Pollina, Vincent. "Melodic Continuity and Discontinuity in *A chantar m'er* of the Comtessa de Dia." In *Miscellanea di studi romanzi offerta a Giuliano Gasca-Quierazza*, 2:887–96. Alessandria: Edizioni dell'Orso, 1988.

Poly, Jean Pierre. "Catalogue des actes des comtes de Provence, 945–1166." Ph.D. diss., Université de Paris II, 1972.

———. *La Provence et la société féodale (879–1176): Contribution à l'étude des structures dites féodales dans le Midi*. Paris: Bordas, 1976.

Poly, Jean Pierre, and Eric Bournazel. *La mutation féodale, Xe–XIIe siècles*. Nouvelle Clio 16. Paris: Presses Universitares, 1980.

Pouillés des Provinces d'Auch, de Narbonne et de Toulouse. Ed. Charles Edmond Perrin, Jacques de Font-Réaulx, and assisted by Odon de Lingua de Saint-Blancat. Recueil des historiens de la France publié par l'Académie des Inscriptions et Belles-Lettres. Paris: Imprimerie Nationale/C. Klincksieck, 1972.

Previté-Orton, C. W. *The Early History of the House of Savoy (1000–1233)*. Cambridge: Cambridge University Press, 1912.

Radding, Charles N. *The Origins of Medieval Jurisprudence: Pavia and Bologna, 850–1150*. New Haven: Yale University Press, 1988.

Raimbaut de Vaqueiras. *The Poems of the Troubadour Raimbaut de Vaqueiras*. Ed. and trans. Joseph Linskill. The Hague: Mouton, 1964.

Raimon de Miraval. *The Cansos of Raimon de Miraval: A Study of Poems and Melodies*. Ed. and trans. Margaret Louise Switten. Cambridge, Mass.: Medieval Academy of America, 1985.

Rakova, Smejana. "Le bogomilisme et l'église bosniaque." *Heresis*, no. 19 (1992): 19–30.

Ralph of Coggeshall. *Chronicon Anglicanum*. Ed. Joseph Stevenson. Rolls Series. London: Longman, 1875.

Ralph of Diceto. *Radulfi de Diceto decani Lundoniensis opera historica*. Ed. William Stubbs. Rolls Series. London: Longman, 1876.

Raoul de Cambrai. Ed. and trans. Sarah Kay. Oxford: Clarendon Press, 1992.

Recueil des actes de Charles II le Chauve (840–877), roi de France. Ed. Georges Tessier, Arthur Giry, and Maurice Prou. Chartes et diplomes relatifs à l'histoire de France 8. Paris: Imprimerie Nationale, 1943.

Recueil des actes de Charles II le Simple, roi de France. Ed. Ferdinand Lot and Philippe Lauer. Paris: Imprimerie Nationale, 1940.

Recueil des historiens des Gaules et de la France. 24 vols. Paris: Aux dépens des libraires associés, 1738–1904.

Regné, Jean. *Etude sur la condition des Juifs de Narbonne du Ve au XIVe siècle*. Narbonne: Caillard, 1912.

Reilly, Bernard F. *The Kingdom of Leon-Castilla under Queen Urraca, 1109–1126*. Princeton: Princeton University Press, 1982.

Remensnyder, Amy G. *Remembering Kings Past: Monastic Foundation Legends in Medieval Southern France*. Ithaca: Cornell University Press, 1995.

Rey, Raymond. "La cathédrale de Narbonne." *Société Française d'Archéologie. Congrès Archéologique de France* 112 (1954): 446–75.

Reynolds, Susan. *Fiefs and Vassals : The Medieval Evidence Reinterpreted*. New York: Oxford University Press, 1994.

Richard, Alfred. *Histoire des comtes de Poitou, 778–1204*. Paris: Picard, 1903.

Richardot, H. "Le fief roturier à Toulouse." *Revue historique de droit français et étranger*, ser. 4, 14 (1935): 307–59, 495–569.

Rieger, Angelica, ed. *Trobairitz: Der Beitrag der Frau in der altokzitanischen höfischen Lyrik; Edition des Gesamtkorpus*. Beihefte zur Zeitschrift für romanische Philologie 233. Tübingen: Niermeyer, 1991.

Rivet, A. L. F. *Gallia Narbonensis: Southern France in Roman Times*. London: Batsford, 1988.

Robert, Ulysse, ed. *Bullaire du pape Calixte II*. Paris: Imprimerie Nationale, 1891.

Robert of Auxerre. "Roberti canonici S. Mariani Autissiodorensis Chronicon." *Monumenta Germaniae Historia, Scriptores*, 26:226–76.

Robert of Torigny. "Chronica." In *Chronicles of Stephen, Henry II, and Richard I*, vol. 4, ed. Richard Howlett. Rolls Series. London: Longman, 1884.

Rodriguez, María Isabel Simó. "Aportación a la documentación condal catalana (siglo X)." In *Miscelánea de estudios dedicados al Profesor Antonio Marín Ocete*, 2:1011–36. Granada: Universidad de Granada and Caja de ahorros y monte de piedad de Granada, 1974.

Roger of Hoveden. *Chronica*. Ed. William Stubbs. Rolls Series. London: Longmans, Green, Reader, and Dyer, 1868.

———. *Gesta Regis Henrici Secundi Benedicti Abbati*. Ed. William Stubbs. Rolls Series. London: Longmans, Green, Reader, and Dyer, 1867.

Roger of Wendover. *Flores historiarum*. Ed. Henry G. Howlett. 3 vols. London: Longman, 1886–89.

Roman, Yves. *De Narbonne à Bordeaux: Un axe économique au Ier siècle avant J.-C.* Lyon: Presses Universitaires, 1983.

Roquebert, Michel. *L'épopée cathare*. 3 vols. Toulouse: E. Privat, 1970–98.

Rosenwein, Barbara. *To Be the Neighbor of Saint Peter: The Social Meaning of Cluny's Property, 909–1049*. Ithaca: Cornell University Press, 1989.

———, ed. *Anger's Past: The Social Uses of an Emotion in the Middle Ages*. Ithaca: Cornell University Press, 1998.

Rouche, Michel. *L'Aquitaine, des Wisigoths aux Arabes, 418–781*. Paris: Ecole des Hautes Études en Sciences Sociales, 1979.

Ruiz Domenec, José Enrique. "En torno a un tratado comercial entre las ciudades de Genova y

Barcelona en la primera mitad del siglo XII." In *Atti del Io Congresso Storico Liguria-Catalogna, Oct. 1969*. Bordighera: Istituto Internazionale di Studi Liguri, 1974.

Runciman, Steven. *A History of the Crusades*. New York: Harper and Row, 1965.

Russell, Frederick H. *The Just War in the Middle Ages*. Cambridge Studies in Medieval Life and Thought, 3d series 8. Cambridge: Cambridge University Press, 1975.

Sabarthès. *Dictionnaire topographique du département de l'Aude*. Paris: Imprimerie Nationale, 1912.

Saltet, Louis. "L'origine méridionale des fausses généalogies caroligiennes." In *Etudes d'histoire méridionale dédiées à la mémoire de Léonce Couture*, 77–96. Toulouse: E. Privat, 1902.

Samaran, Charles, and Guillaume Mollat. *La fiscalité pontificale en France au XIVe siècle*. Bibliothèque des Ecoles Française d'Athènes et de Rome 96. Paris: Albert Fontemoing, 1905.

Saxer, Victor. "Le culte et la légende hagiographique de Saint Guillaume de Gellone." In *La chanson de geste et le mythe carolingien: Mélanges René Louis*, 565–89. Saint-Père-sous-Vézelay: Musée Archéologique, 1982.

Sayers, Jane. *Innocent III, Leader of Europe 1198–1216*. London: Longman, 1994.

Schatzmiller, Joseph. "Politics and the Myth of Origins: The Case of the Medieval Jews." In *Les Juifs au regard de l'histoire: Mélanges en l'honneur de Bernhard Blumenkranz*, ed. Gilbert Dahan. Paris: Picard, 1985.

Schneegans, Friedrich, ed. *Gesta Karoli Magni ad Carcassonam et Narbonam*. Halle: E. Karras, 1898.

——. *Über die Gesta Karoli Magni ad Carcassonam et Narbonam; ein Beitrag zur Geschichte des altfranzöschen Epos*. Halle: E. Karras, 1897.

Schneider, Reinhard. *Vom Klosterhaushalt zum Stadt- und Staatshaushalt: Der zisterziensische Beitrag*. Monographien zur Geschichte des Mittelalters 38. Stuttgart: Hiersmann, 1994.

Selwood, Dominic. *Knights of the Cloister; Templars and Hospitallers in Central-Southern Occitania, 1100–1300*. Woodbridge, Suffolk: Boydell, 1999.

Sigal, Louis. "Contribution à l'histoire de la cathédrale Saint-Just de Narbonne." *Bulletin de la Commission archéologique de Narbonne* 14 (1921): 11–153.

Sigal, Pierre André. "Bernard le Pénitent et la révolte de Béziers de 1167." *Annales du Midi* 101 (1989): 275–77.

Smith, Jacqueline. "Robert of Arbrissel's Relations with Women." In *Medieval Women*, ed. Derek Baker. Studies in Church History. Subsidia 1. Oxford: Blackwell, 1978.

Smith, Nathaniel B., and Thomas G. Bergin. *An Old Provençal Primer*. New York: Garland Publishing, 1984.

Smyrl, Edwin. "La famille des Baux." In *Cahiers du Centre d'Études des Sociétés Méditerranéennes*, 2:7–107. Publication de la Faculté des Lettres et Sciences Humaines, nouv. sér. 59. Aix-en-Provence: Faculté des Lettres et Sciences Humaines, 1968.

Sobrequés i Vidal, S. *Els grans comtes de Barcelona*. Barcelona: Editorial Vicens-Vives, 1970.

Solier, Yves. *Narbonne (Aude): Les monuments antiques et médiévaux*. Guides Archéologique de la France. Paris: Ministère de la Culture et de la Communication/Imprimerie Nationale, 1986.

Southern, Richard W. *The Making of the Middle Ages*. New Haven: Yale University Press, 1953.

Stafford, Pauline. "Queens, Nunneries and Reforming Churchmen." *Past and Present* 163 (May 1999): 3–35.

Stasser, Thierry. "La maison vicomtale de Narbonne aux Xe et XIe siècles." *Annales du Midi* 105 (1993): 489–507.

Stendhal. *Travels in the South of France*. Trans. Elisabeth Abbot. New York: Orion, 1970.

Stewart, Frank H. *Honor*. Chicago: University of Chicago Press, 1994.

Strayer, Joseph R. *The Albigensian Crusades*. New York: Dial, 1971.

——. *The Reign of Philip the Fair*. Princeton: Princeton University Press, 1980.

Structures féodales et féodalisme dans l'Occident méditerranéen, Xe–XIIe siècles: Bilan et perspectives de recherches. Collection de l'Ecole Française de Rome. Rome: Ecole Française de Rome, 1980.

Sumption, Jonathan. *The Albigensian Crusade*. London: Faber, 1978.

Switten, Margaret, and Howell Chickering, eds. *The Medieval Lyric: Anthologies and Cassettes for Teaching. A Project Supported by the National Endowment for the Humanities and Mount Holyoke College*. South Hadley, Mass., 1988.

Terpak, Rances. "Local Politics; the Charlemagne Legend in Medieval Narbonne." *Res* 25 (1994): 97–110.

Thomas, Eugène. *Dictionnaire topographique du Département de l'Hérault*. Paris: Imprimerie Impériale, 1865.

Tierney, Brian. "Tria quippe distinguit iudicia. A note on Innocent III's decretal 'Per venerabilem.'" *Speculum* 38 (1962): 48–59.

Tillmann, Helene. *Pope Innocent III*. Trans. Walter Sax. Europe in the Middle Ages: Selected Studies 12. Amsterdam: North-Holland, 1980.

Timbal, Pierre. *Un conflit d'annexion au moyen âge: L'application de la coutume de Paris au pays d'albigeois.* Bibliothèque Méridionale, 2e série 33. Toulouse/Paris: E. Privat/Marcel Didier, 1950.

——, ed. *La Guerre de Cent Ans vue à travers les registres du Parlement (1337–1369)*. Paris: CNRS, 1961.

Todesca, James J. "Means of Exchange: Islamic Coinage in Christian Spain, 1000–1200." In *Iberia and the Mediterranean World of the Middle Ages: Studies in Honor of Robert I. Burns S. J.*, ed. Larry J. Simon, 1:232–58. Leiden: Brill, 1995.

Toubert, Pierre. *Les structures du Latium médiéval; le Latium méridional et la Sabine du IXe siècle à la fin du XIIe siècle*. Bibliotheque des Ecoles Francaises d'Athenes et de Rome 221. Rome: Ecole Française de Rome, 1973.

Trachtenberg, Joshua. *Jewish Magic and Superstition*. New York: Atheneum, 1974.

Ubieto Artur, Maria Isabel. "Los morabedis ayadinos, circulación y cambio en el Reino de Aragón según la documentación coetánea." *Numisma* (Madrid) 34 (1984): 209–25.

Uitti, Karl D. "The Old Provençal 'Song of Saint Fides' and the Occitanian Concept of Poetic Space." *L'Esprit Créateur* 19 (1979): 17–36.

Ullmann, Walter. "The Significance of Innocent III's Decretal 'Vergentis.'" In *Etudes d'histoire du droit canonique dédiées à Gabriel Le Bras*, 1:729–41. Paris: Sirey, 1965.

Vacandard, E. "Le divorce de Louis le Jeune." *Revue des Questions Historiques* 24 (1890): 408–32.

Van Cleve, Thomas C. *Markward of Anweiler and the Sicilian Regency*. Princeton: Princeton University Press, 1937.

Venarde, Bruce L. "La réforme à Apt (Xe–XIIe siècles): Patrimoine, patronage et famille." *Provence Historique* 152 (1988): 131–47.

Ventura, Jordi. *Pere el Catòlic e Simó de Montfort*. Barcelona: Aedos, 1960.

Vicaire, Marie Humbert. *Saint Dominic and His Times*. Trans. Kathleen Pond. New York: McGraw-Hill, 1964.

Vidal, Henri. "Les mariages dans la famille des Guillems, seigneurs de Montpellier." *Revue Historique de Droit Français et Étranger*, ser. 4, 62 (1984): 231–45.

——. "Les origines de la primatie narbonnaise (XIe–XIIe siècles)." In *Narbonne: Archéologie et histoire*, 2:121–128.

"Vita Benedicti Aniacensis." *Monumenta Germaniae Historica, Scriptores* 15:200–222.

Wakefield, Walter L., and Austin P. Evans, eds. and trans. *Heresies of the High Middle Ages*. Records of Civilization, Sources and Studies 81. New York: Columbia University Press, 1969.

Walter Map. *De nugis curialium (Courtiers trifles)*. Ed. and trans. M. R. James. New York: Oxford University Press, 1983.

Warning, Rainer. "Moi lyrique et société chez les troubadours." In *Archéologie du signe*, ed. Lucie Brind'Amour and Eugene Vance, 63–100. Papers in Medieval Studies 3. Toronto: Pontifical Institute of Medieval Studies, 1983.

Warren, W. L. *Henry II*. Berkeley and Los Angeles: University of California Press, 1973.

Wasserstein, David. *The Rise and Fall of the Party-Kings: Politics and Society in Islamic Spain, 1002–1086*. Princeton: Princeton University Press, 1985.

Webb, Diana M. "The Pope and the Cities: Anticlericalism and Heresy in Innocent III's Italy." In *The Church and Sovereignty*, ed. Diana Wood, 135–52. Oxford: Blackwell, 1991.

White, Hayden V. "The Gregorian Ideal and Saint Bernard of Clairvaux." *Journal of the History of Ideas* 21 (1960): 321–48.

White, Stephen D. *Custom, Kinship, and Gifts to Saints: The Laudatio Parentum in Western France, 1050–1150*. Chapel Hill: University of North Carolina Press, 1988.

——. "Feuding and Peace-Making in the Touraine around the Year 1100." *Traditio* 42 (1986): 195–263.

——. "Giving Fiefs and Honor: Largesse, Avarice, and the Problem of 'Feudalism' in Alexander's Testament." Unpublished manuscript.

——. "Pactum . . . Legem Vincit et Amor Judicium: The Settlement of Disputes by Compromise in Eleventh-Century France." *American Journal of Legal History* 22 (1978): 281–308.

——. "The Politics of Anger." In *Anger's Past*, ed. Barbara H. Rosenwein, 129–52.

——. "Repenser la violence: De 2000 à 1000." *Médiévales* 37 (1999): 99–113.

——. "Stratégie rhétorique dans la *Conventio* de Hugues de Lusignan." In *Mélanges offerts à Georges Duby*, 2:147–57. Aix-en-Provence: Publications de l'Université de Provence, 1992.

Wiederhold, Wilhelm, ed. *Papsturkunden in Frankreich: Reiseberichte zur Gallia Pontificia*. Acta Romanorum Pontificum 7–8. Vatican City: Biblioteca Apostolica Vaticana, 1985.

William, Count of Orange: Four Old French Epics. Ed. Glanville Price. Totowa, N.J.: Rowman and Littlefield, 1975.

William of Malmesbury. *De gestis regum Anglorum*. Ed. William Stubbs. Rolls Series. London: Eyre and Spottiswoode, 1887.

William of Newburgh. "Historia rerum anglicarum." In *Chronicles of the Reigns of Stephen, Henry II and Richard I*, vol. 1, ed. Richard Howlett. Rolls Series. London: Longman, 1884.

William of Tudela. *La chanson de la Croisade Albigeoise*, vol. 1, ed. Eugène Martin-Chabot. Les classiques de l'histoire de France au moyen âge. Paris: Les Belles Lettres, 1960.

——. *The Song of the Cathar Wars: A History of the Albigensian Crusade*. Trans. Janet Shirley. Brookfield, Vt.: Ashgate, 1996.

Wolff, Philippe. "Fortunes et genres de vie dans les villages du Toulousain aux XIVe et XVe siècles." In *Miscellanea Mediaevalia in Memoriam Jan Frederik Niermeyer*, 325–332. Groningen: J. B. Wolters, 1967.

——. "Inventaires villageois du Toulousain." In *Bulletin philologique et historique jusqu'à 1610 (1965)*, 481–544. Paris: Comité des travaux historiques et scientifiques, 1968.

Wolter, Heinz. "Friedrich Barbarossa und die Synode zu Pavia im Jahre 1160." In *Köln: Stadt und Bistum in Kirche und Reich des Mittelalters. Festschrift für Odilo Engels zum 65. Geburtstag*, ed. Hanna Vollrath and Stefan Weinfurter, 415–53. Cologne, Weimar, Vienna: Böhlau, 1993.

Zambaur, Eduard von. *Die Münzprägung des Islams, zeitlich und örtlich geordnet*. Ed. Peter Jaeckel. Wiesbaden: Fritz Steiner, 1968.

Zambon, Francesco. "L'hérésie cathare dans la marche de Trévise." *Heresis* 18 (1991): 21–41.

Zanella, Gabriele. *Hereticalia: Temi e discussioni*. Spoleto: Centro Italiano di Studi sull'Alto Medioevo, 1995.

Zerner, Monique. "L'Affaire albigeoise." Unpublished manuscript.

——. *Le cadastre, le pouvoir et la terre: Le comtat venaissin pontifical au début du XVe siècle*. Collection de l'Ecole Française de Rome 174. Rome: Ecole Française de Rome, 1993.

——. "Question sur la naissance de l'affaire albigeoise." In *Georges Duby: L'écriture de l'histoire*, ed. Claudie Duhamel-Amado and Guy Lobrichon, 427–44. Bibliothèque du Moyen Age 6. Brussels: De-Boeck Université, 1996.

Zerner, Monique, and Hélène Piéchon-Palloc. "La croisade albigeoise, une revanche." *Revue Historique* 267 (1982): 3–18.

Zupko, Ronald Edward. *French Weights and Measures before the Revolution: A Dictionary of Provincial and Local Units*. Bloomington: Indiana University Press, 1978.

INDEX

Note: Page numbers with an *f* indicate figures. Abbreviations: abp., archbishop; bp., bishop; ct., count; cts., countess; k., king; q., queen; vct., viscount; vcts., viscountess

Abraham ben David of Toledo, 16
Adalaide, vcts. Narbonne, 27
Adalais of Toulouse, 26f, 265, 317, 319
Adela of Champagne, 260, 262
Ademar of Durban, 176
Ademar of Murviel, 277, 331, 335
Adultery
    jurisdiction over, 131, 133, 145
    Louis VII on, 257
    punishment for, 107, 146
    in troubadour poetry, 10, 233
Agde, 2f, 4, 19
Agnes of Castile, 352
Aicfred of Levezou, 15f
Albergum, 151, 161, 166
    alms and, 162
    disputes about, 164-65
    for fighting men, 159-60
    as marker of serfdom, 157, 159, 164
    ritual of, 163
    types of, 165
    value of, 160
Alberic Taillefer, 261, 277
Albi, 2f
    bishops of, 105-6, 120-21, 316, 321
    heresy in, 121, 122, 316
    viscounts of, 4, 26f, 78, 176
Albigensian Crusades, 3-4, 122, 347-60
    Cisterians and, 287-88, 322
    financing of, 62
    heresy and, 356-57
    Innocent III and, 353-57, 360
    Narbonne and, 75
    Simon of Montfort and, 75, 358-60
    Walter of Brienne and, 351-52
Alexander III, pope, 97, 214-16, 251, 253, 262
    Henry of Marcy and, 309, 318
    mercenaries of, 282, 357

Alfons I, k. Aragon (the Battler), 20f, 21-22, 246, 253
Alfons II, k. Aragon, 20f, 253-54, 260, 266-67, 277, 279
    changing alliances of, 334-35, 337-38, 340
    death of, 347
    Raymond V and, 263-64, 270-71, 333
    regency for, 254-55, 263-64
    Roger of Béziers and, 275-76, 334
    Sanç and, 333
    Sancha of Castile, wife of, 254, 270
Alfons II, ct. Provence, 334
Alfonso VI, k. Castile, 85
Alfonso VII, k. Castile, 22, 91, 94-95
Alfons of Poitiers, 360
Ali 'ibn Mochehid, 85
Allegory, 220
Almeria, 91, 95
Almodis of la Marche, 18f, 27, 85
Alphonse Jordan, ct. Toulouse, 17-18, 18f, 21-24, 42, 122
    Bernard of Clairvaux and, 288-89
    Bremund of Béziers and, 145-46
    death of, 256
    as Ermengard's husband, 14, 16-21, 24, 200
    Genoa and, 89
    Gerberga, cts. Provence and, 25
    Pedro Gonzalez and, 22
    Narbonne and, 20-21, 52, 90, 100, 120
    natural children of, 256
    Trencavels and, 18-19, 256
    William of Montpellier and, 19, 30, 90-91
Amalric, Arnold, 100
Amalric I, vct. Narbonne, 73, 129
Amaury de Montfort, 62
Ambialet, 2f, 316, 317f
Amelius of Bordes, 151-52
Andrew Chaplain, 1, 251

Anger, 200–202, 206–8
  honor and, 203
  in troubadour poetry, 199–202, 244
  violence and, 309–10
Angevin-Capetian rivalry, 256–60, 262, 268,
    288, 331, 337–38, 355
Anticlericalism, 292–94, 301, 305, 323–24.
    See also Clergy
Apulia, 27
Aquitaine, 33, 42
  dukes of, 33, 268 (*see also specific dukes*)
  Richard the Lionheart and, 332–34
Aragon
  dating of documents in, 337
  kings of, 15–16, 20f, 33, 85, 251–52
    Innocent III and, 354–55
    mercenaries of, 279–81, 331
    in troubadour poetry, 4–5
    See also specific kings
Argens, 111, 112f
Arles, 2f, 216, 253
Arnaut Daniel, 199, 220
Arnold Baldriga, 141, 154
Arnold of Clairan, 175, 176
Arnold of Levezou, 15f, 17
Arsendis, cts. Carcassonne, 26f
Aude River, 2f, 3, 39, 46–48, 57, 68f, 157
Augustine (saint), 295–96, 313, 326
Auriac, 199–201
Axat, 304–5
Aymeri, as family name, 1, 15f, 23
Aymeri I, vct. Narbonne, 15f, 108, 207
Aymeri II, vct. Narbonne, 15f, 100, 108–9
  Bernard Ato and, 205
  death of, 21, 85
  Ramon Berenguer III and, 77, 85–86
  Richard, abp. Narbonne and, 206–12,
    221–22
Aymeri III, vct. Narbonne, 100–101, 133, 348
Aymeri de Lara, 15f, 23, 174, 177
Azalais de Porcairagues, 6

Bages family, 182–83
Baldwin of Jerusalem, 89, 92, 114
Balearic Islands, 83–85, 90, 91
Barcelona, 83, 85–87, 96–97, 322
  counts of, 4, 16–21, 20f, 251–54 (*see also
    specific counts*)
  Genoa and, 87, 93, 94
  Provence and, 17–18, 236, 337
  Pyrenee lands and, 77
  Toulouse and, 17–18, 97
Bardine Saptis, 14, 17
Basques, 254, 279–80
Batalla family, 194
les Baux, 2f, 31f, 253–56
Beatrice, cts. Mauguio, 20f, 30, 262, 265–66
Benedict of Aniane, 106

Berenger, abp. Narbonne, 15f
Berenger, vct. Narbonne, 15f, 86, 207, 208
Berenger of Lec, 178, 180, 197
Berenger of Peyrepertuse, 222–23
Berenger of Puisserguier, 213–19
Berenguer Ramon I, ct. Provence, 20f, 30, 265
Bernard Amati, 205
Bernard Ato I (Trencavel) (d. 1129), 26f, 27,
    176
  Aymeri II and, 205
  as moneylender, 142
  oaths to, 194, 195
  Ramon Berenguer III and, 77, 85, 192
  Richard, abp. Narbonne and, 221
  succession of, at Béziers, 145–46
  will of, 29
Bernard Ato II, vct. Nîmes (d. 1159), 18–19,
    26f
Bernard Ato III, vct. Nîmes (d. 1214), 26f,
    266, 275, 334
Bernard Berenger, vct. Narbonne, 15f, 176
Bernard Gaucelin, abp. Narbonne, 320
Bernard Gerardi, 142–43
Bernard Modul, 149, 155–58, 161, 166–67
  fiefs of, 228–29
  Templars and, 175
Bernard of Anduze, 16, 21–22, 181
Bernard of Canet, 21, 155
Bernard of Carcassonne, 14, 17
Bernard of Clairvaux, 256, 258, 287, 293, 326
  Alphonse Jordan and, 288–89
  Evervin of Steinfeld and, 296–97
  Henry of Lausanne and, 288–89, 294, 323
  Knights Templars and, 310
  militarism of, 309–10
  on Song of Songs, 296
Bernard of Durban, 187, 191
Bernard Pelet, lord of Alès and ct. Mauguio,
    234, 262, 265–66
Bernard Xatmar of Laredorte, 177
Bernart de Ventadorn, 6, 8
  fidelity oaths and, 236–37, 239–40
Bertrand, bp. Nîmes, 28, 207, 208
Bertran de Born, 212, 271–72
  politics of, 235, 238
  on war, 276, 278
Bertrand of les Baux, 264
Bertrand of Maugio, 266
Bertrand of Saissac, 347, 348
Besalú family, 77
Beuraticum, 131
Béziers, 2f, 56
  bishops of, 145–46, 354
  clerical income of, 303
  sacking of, 358
  Trencavel viscounts of, 4, 18–19, 25–26,
    26f, 27, 78, 85–86, 120, 136
  See also specific viscounts

Bishops
  authority of, 105–17, 293–94, 354
  Bernard of Clairvaux on, 293
  family of, 105–9
  reform movement and, 51, 53, 114–18,
    209, 228
  See also Clergy
Bistani family, 60–64
Bogomils, 298–300. See also Cathars
Bologna, 217
Boniface VIII, pope, 324
Brabançons, 279–83, 285, 331
Bremund, bp. Béziers, 145–46
Breuil family, 171–72, 181
Bulgaria, 298–99
Bureaucracy, 139
Burgundy, kingdom of, 32, 277
Bynum, Caroline, 12

Caffaro, 88, 89, 94–95
Calva, lady of Argeliers, 133, 135, 180
Canet, 111, 112f
Capestang, 111, 112f, 221
  lords of, 177–78
Capital punishment, 146
Capucians, 283–85, 306
Caraman, 304–5
Carcassonne, 2f, 53, 275, 359f
  bishops of, 122, 359
  clerical income in diocese of, 303
  counts of, 4, 14, 17, 26f, 27, 253
  revolt of, 197, 274
  Trencavels and, 27, 53, 264–65, 334–35
Castelmaure, 176–77
Castile
  kings of, 4–5, 15–16, 85 (see also specific
    kings)
  queens of, 22, 254, 270, 352
Catalonia, 3, 41, 55, 337
  See also Barcelona
Cathars, 122, 295–97, 322–30
  Albigensians and, 322–23, 327–30
  Cistercians and, 287–88, 308–30
  consolamentum of, 320
  diet of, 298
  hierarchy of, 328f
  Innocent III and, 349–51
  myths of, 299–301
  in Orvieto, 350
  Perfects of, 295, 301, 331
  prayers of, 298, 300
  priests and, 306–7
  Raymond V and, 286–87, 295, 314
  Raymond VI and, 357
  rituals of, 300
  sexuality and, 297, 299–302, 319
  women teachers of, 297–98
  See also Heresy

Celibacy, 291, 301–2, 312–13
Cerdagne, 15f, 27, 51, 105, 114, 253
Chansons de geste. See Epic poetry
Charlemagne, 1, 23, 33, 118, 337
  Narbonne and, 44, 49–50, 110
Chrétien de Troyes, 1
Cid, El, 85, 114
Cistercians, 83, 307
  Bernard of Clairvaux and, 288, 323
  Cathar heresy and, 287–88, 308–30, 322,
    323, 329
  and deserted places, 71–72
  sheep herding by, 70–74
  See also individual monasteries and abbots
Cîteaux, 286, 308, 354
Clergy, 305–6, 312
  Cathars and, 306–7
  celibacy and, 291, 301–2, 312–13
  criticism of, 292–94, 301, 305, 323–24
  income of, 302–5
  See also Bishops
Cluny, abbey of, 106, 108
Cognomens, 189
Comminges, 120
  counts of, 26f, 353, 360
Compagnia, 89, 93
Compras, 209, 210
Comtessa de Dia, 10, 179, 242f, 243–46
Conilhac, 17, 111, 112f
Conrad III, Holy Roman Emperor, 32
Constance, cts. Toulouse, 18f, 214–16,
    259–60, 262
Contracts
  leasehold, 137–39
  mortgage, 137
Corporations, 167
Corsica, 88, 92
Corvées, 158
Coumiac, 132–35, 180
Courtly love, 8–11
  See also Love; Troubadour poetry
Crusade
  First, 89, 92
  as just war, 310
  Second, 91, 256–57, 289
  See also Albigensian Crusades
Cruscades, 111, 112f
Cupidity, 58

Dalmace de Creisello, 62
Dalmacius, abp. Narbonne, 207, 212, 222
Dan, 200, 203
Dante Alighieri, 3, 41, 191
Denia, king of, 83–85
Desiderii-Salvii family, 106
Devic, Claude, 15–16
Diafronissa, 26f, 27
Dies Irae, 225–26

Divorces, 29, 257–58
Dominicans, 305
Dominic of Osma, 327, 328f, 356
Douce, daughter of Ramon Berenguer III, ct. Provence, 263, 265, 266
Douce, wife of Ramon Berenguer III, ct. Barcelona, 17, 19, 20f, 25, 86
Douzens, 2f, 136, 155–57
Dowries, 183
 inheritances and, 28–29
 mortgages as, 63
 peasant, 303
Drut, 233, 235, 241
Dualism, 295–96. *See also* Manichaeism
Durance River, 2f, 17–18, 31, 236, 261
Durand of Huesca, 356
Dye, vermilion, 163–64, 210

Eleanor, duchess of Aquitaine, 1, 4, 18f, 33–34, 251, 362
 divorce of, 257–58
 Henry II and, 214, 256–60, 270
 Louis VII and, 34, 256–58
 Raymond V and, 268
 Toulouse and, 4, 33–34
Eon de l'Etoile, 313
Epic poetry, 1, 49, 113, 114, 200–202
 conflict resolution in, 201–2
 fiefs in, 223
 lordship in, 153
 pride in, 244–45
 the name Aymeri in, 23
Ermengard (mother of Ermengard of Narbonne), 15f, 187
Ermengard (Trencavel), 26f, 27, 194
Ermengaud, Hugh, 172
Ermengaud of Fabrezan, 335–37, 336f, 340
Ermessend, sister of Ermengard of Narbonne, 15f, 22, 274
Ermessend, widow of Ramon Borrel, 26f, 27
Ermessend, wife of William V of Montpellier, 233, 238
Escafredi family, 147, 198, 204
 serfs of, 150–51
Esclaramunda of Saint-Felix, 174
Etampes, Council of, 293
Eugenius III, pope, 256–58, 313
Eusebius of Caesarea, 301
Evervin of Steinfeld, 296–97, 300–301
Evrard of Breteuil, 291

Fabrezan family, 179, 183, 336–37
Faydida of Uzès, 18f, 21
Fernando II, k. Léon, 254
Feudalism, 13
 Absolutism and, 130
 bourgeoisie and, 53

fiefs and, 220
 the State and, 130–31, 144, 356
 See also Lordship
Fidelity oaths, 86, 177–78, 183, 187–98
 castellan, 224–25
 changes in, 361
 community and, 194–98, 205, 206, 210, 212
 conflict resolution and, 199–200, 203, 205, 208
 drut in, 235
 enforcement of, 212–13
 eroticism and, 236–37
 fiefs and, 220–21, 361
 formulaics of, 188–92, 208
 inheritance and, 145
 language of, 193
 lordship and, 194–98
 mother's names in, 189–90, 197
 northern, 361
 rituals with, 192–94, 212
 texts of, 187, 188
 in troubadour poetry, 236–38
 See also Oaths
Fiefs
 alliances and, 223–24
 fidelity oaths and, 220–21, 361
 giving of, 224–28
 recognizance of, 221
 services for, 227–29
 social hierarchy and, 227–32
 types of, 230
 See also Feudalism
Foix, 2f
 counts of, 26f, 194, 264–65, 334–35, 340, 360
Fontfroide, 2f, 71–72, 91–92, 178, 342
Fontjoncouse, 111, 160, 163, 221, 223
Food prices, 80, 160–61
Forcalquier, 253, 263
Forcia, 150, 164, 225
Frederick I, Holy Roman Emperor, 32, 97, 261
 Ermengard and, 216–17
 Henry II and, 267
 Ramon Berenguer III and, 253
 Raymond V and, 263–66
Frederick II, Holy Roman Emperor, 348
Froissart, Jean, 162–63
Frotarius of Albi, 105
Frotarius of Nîmes, 26f, 107
Fulcrand of Toulouse, 153

Garonne River, 2f, 46
Garsend, cts. Béziers, 25, 26f, 78
Garsenda, cts. Provence, trobairitz, 246
Genoa, 87–95, 333
 alliances of, 83, 96–97

consulate of, 89, 91–92
Narbonne and, 90, 93–101, 99f
Pisa and, 88–93, 97
Raymond V and, 270
Geoffrey of Auxerre, 294–95, 323
Geoffrey of Vigeois, 264, 319, 322
Gerald Amic, 272, 342
Gerald of Breuil, 171–72, 230
Gerald of Wales, 257
Gerberga, cts. Provence, 20f, 25, 31, 263
Gervase of Canterbury, 283, 284, 287
Gervase of Tilbury, 297
Gifts, 220–32
  bribes and, 224
  church, 305–6
  etiquette of, 224
  fiefs and, 224–28
  of grace, 205–6
  for king's justice, 218–19
  obligatory, 221, 222
  rituals with, 224–25, 232
  to saints, 92, 106–7
  sales and, 226–27
  social hierarchy and, 225, 227, 232
Giraut de Bornelh, 6
Gnosticism, 298, 300
Graboïs, Aryeh, 16
Gregory VII, pope, 108, 181, 292
  on monks, 290–91, 294
  on priests, 302
  on princes, 208
  reforms of, 51, 53, 114–18, 209, 228
Guibert of Nogent, 291
Guifred, abp. Narbonne, 109–14, 118, 208,
    212, 233
  castles of, 109–12, 112f
  death of, 181
  excommunication of, 110, 113, 181
  mother of, 189
  Raymond Berenger, vct. Narbonne, and,
    110–14
Guifred Borrell, ct. Barcelona, 20
Guifred of Cerdagne, 15f, 51, 105
Guifred the Hairy, ct. Besalú, 77
Guigues, ct. Albon, 261
Guilabert of Laurac, 140–41, 183
Guy de Levis, lord of Mirepoix, 72, 129,
    143–44
Guy Guerrejat, 271, 275, 277

Heiresses, 25–30, 170, 216–18
Henry II, k. England, 30, 251, 270–71
  Albigensian Crusades and, 287, 332
  Alfons II and, 254, 337–38
  Thomas Becket and, 260, 269, 318
  chroniclers of, 282
  death of, 333
  Eleanor of Aquitaine and, 256–60, 270

Frederick Barbarossa and, 267
  Henry of Marcy and, 318
  Louis VII and, 258–60, 262, 269, 308
  Walter Map and, 281
  mercenaries of, 279–83
  Raymond V and, 267–70, 288
  Savoy and, 267
  sons' revolt against, 332–33
  Toulouse and, 4, 34, 214, 256–60
Henry VI, Holy Roman Emperor, 348, 352,
    355
Henry of Lausanne, 288–96, 301, 324
  Bernard of Clairvaux on, 288–89, 294, 323
Henry of Marcy, 308–14, 325–27, 331
  Alexander III and, 309
  on celibacy, 312–13
  Henry II and, 318
Henry the Young King, 332–33
Heresy, 286–307, 325–26
  Adoptionist, 50, 298
  Albi and, 121, 122, 316
  Arian, 295, 315
  Armenian, 298
  Bogomil, 298–300
  dissent and, 325–27
  of Henry of Lausanne, 288–96, 301
  Innocent III and, 348, 351
  mercenaries and, 280–82, 285
  in Montpellier, 353
  nicolaitism, 292
  Paulician, 298
  punishments for, 313–14
  of Ramihrdus, 292
  Raymond V on, 286–87
  sexuality and, 233, 292, 319
  simoniacal, 51, 106, 181, 292
  suspicion of, 314
  as treason, 351
  trials for, 314–16, 319
  Waldensian, 122, 326, 327
  "weavers," 295, 296, 322
  witches and, 297
  See also Cathars
Hildebert of Lavardin, 291–92
Hohenstaufens, 349, 351, 355
Homines proprii, 150, 153, 155, 158
Honor
  anger and, 203, 244
  dominion and, 158–67
  fidelity and, 231
  giving and, 223–24
  oath taking and, 196–97
  questioning of, 208
  in troubadour poetry, 203
Hugh, ct. Rodez, 116, 120, 264
Hugh Escafredi, 147, 191–92, 204
Hugh of Plaigne, 61, 64, 173–75
Huizinga, Johan, 66, 234

Humbert of Maurienne, ct. Savoy, 267
Hyères, 270

Ingeborg of Denmark, 353
Innocent II, pope, 119, 293
    Pisa-Genoa conflict and, 88, 92
Innocent III, pope, 3, 348–57
    Peire, k. Aragon, and, 355
    Philip II and, 353–55, 361
    Raymond VI and, 357
    William VIII and, 353, 355–57
Inquisition, 305, 327–29, 328f, 348
Interest. See Usury
Isarn Ademar, 199–200, 202
Isarn Jordani of Saissac, 204

Jarnègues, 270–71, 274, 337
Jaufré Rudel, 10, 203
Jews
    as merchants, 56
    in Narbonne, 16, 45, 46f
    tolls for, 213
John, k. England, 270, 350
John Bistani, 60–64, 182, 340
John of Salisbury, 257–58
John XIII, pope, 50
Justices, lordship and, 131, 143–47

Knights Hospitalers, 74, 119
    Ermengard and, 342
    of Pexiora, 139–43
    record keeping and, 139
Knights Templars, 74, 91
    Bernard of Clairvaux and, 310
    Ermengard and, 341–42
    mills of, 156
    and Peace of God, 110, 283
    privileges of, 120
    serfs of, 149, 155–57

Lagrasse, abbey of, 2f, 62, 76–77, 342
Language
    Catalan, 3, 41
    emotional, 200, 202–3, 234, 244
    legal, 214, 244
    of oaths, 193
    of troubadour songs, 247
    vernacular, 3, 193, 318
    violent, 309–10
Languedoc. See Occitania
Lara family, 15f, 22–23, 274. See also specific
    persons
Laredorte family, 171–72, 177–78, 182, 340
Lateran Council of 1179, 318, 320, 326, 331,
    349
Lautrec, 329
Leasehold contracts, 137–39
Lézat, abbey of, 2f, 151–54, 161, 166

Liege homage, 214–15. See also Lordship
Loans
    gold and, 54
    pledges for, 141
    security for, 60
    usury and, 62
    See also Mortgages; Usury
Lobar the Wolf, 279, 280, 308
Lordship, 129–48
    "banal," 130
    bodily, 149, 151, 153
    domina/dominus and, 127, 154
    drut and, 233, 235, 241
    fidelity oaths and, 194–98
    honor and, 158–67
    humility and, 162–63
    justices of, 131, 143–47
    "legal," 231
    meanings of, 127–28
    military obligations and, 179
    mortgages and, 141
    multiplicities of, 139–43
    networks of, 176–84
    papal, 351
    personal, 206
    potestativum and, 131–34, 138
    powers of, 107, 113–14, 144
    rights belonging to, 129–30, 133
    suzerainty and, 355
    tenants and, 229
    use of force and, 144, 210
    See also Fiefs; Serfdom
Louis VII, k. France, 1, 214
    on adultery, 257
    Albigensian Crusades and, 287
    Alexander III and, 215–16
    Berenger of Puisserguier and, 214–18
    Eleanor of Aquitaine and, 33–34, 256–58
    Ermengard of Narbonne and, 214–19,
        268–69, 288
    Henry II and, 258–60, 262, 269, 308
    Ramon Berenguer III and, 261–62
    Toulouse and, 4, 261–63
Louis VIII, k. France, 360
Louis IX, k. France, 73, 77, 177
Love
    allegories of, 220
    conception and, 258
    drut and, 233, 235, 241
    fidelity and, 225, 233–47
    language of, 247
    pride and, 244–45
    property and, 233
    See also Courtly love

Magnou-Nortier, Elisabeth, 158–59
Magrie, 138–39
Maguelone, 2f, 103–5, 117, 355

Mahalt (Ermengard's grandmother), 15f, 27–28, 207
Malcolm IV of Scotland, 260
Malfatz, 200
Manichaeism, 296, 298, 313, 315, 326
   See also Cathars
Manrique de Lara, 22–23, 274
Mansus, 135, 157–58, 163, 164
Marbod of Rennes, 290
Marcabru, 8
Margalonis family, 182–84, 341
Maria of Montpellier, 20f, 174, 355
Marie of Champagne, 1, 247, 362
Markward of Anweiler, 349, 351, 357
Marriage
   dowries and, 28
   Ermengard's contract of, 14–15
   heiresses and, 25–30
   tax on, 225
Marseille, 2f, 90, 101, 270
Mas-Deu, 2f, 341f, 342
Matfred, vct. Narbonne, 27
Matilda (Henry I's daughter), 30
Mauguio, 2f, 19, 266, 337, 347
Maurandus, Peter, 314–16, 318, 320
Military service, 130, 133, 179, 361
   billeting and, 135
   Capucians and, 283–85
   citizens and, 83–87, 145
   commerce and, 80–102
   fiefs and, 227
   mercenaries, 279–83, 285, 308, 331–34, 357, 361
Millau, 2f, 115
   counts of, 15f, 115, 118
Mills, 80, 169
   Templar, 156
   textile, 70, 71f, 156
Minerve
   castle of, 2f, 175f
   lords of, 176
Mining, 72f, 78–79, 131
Minnesingers, 3. *See also* Troubadours
Mints, 54, 116
Miracles of Saint Gilles, 87
Mirepoix, 194, 196f, 361
Moissac, abbey of, 106
Monaco, 270
Moneylenders, 54, 56–57, 60, 62
   clergy as, 63–64
   See also Loans
Monopolies, 131, 145
Montaudon, Monk of, 225
Montferrat, 267–68
Montpellier, 2f, 105, 216, 264, 284
   alliances of, 83, 96–97
   Alphonse Jordan and, 19
   Court of Accounts of, 5

Genoa and, 90–91
heresy in, 327, 353
lords of, 4–5, 28, 243, 252, 320, 322
   See also specific persons
Moore, R. I., 326
Morabitani, 87, 95, 254
Mortgages, 60
   contracts for, 137
   justices and, 144
   loans and, 141
   lordship rights and, 141
   as negotiable instruments, 63
   tenant, 141, 143
   See also Loans
Mundy, John, 324–25
Muret, battle of, 360

Names
   family, 171–72, 189
   in oaths, 189–90, 197
   regional, 42
   titles and, 41–45
   in troubadour poetry, 9, 23
Narbonne
   archbishop of, 15f, 17, 50–52, 62, 103–23
      deposition of, 108, 319–20, 354
      disputes of, 206–12
      and papal legates, 354
      See also specific archbishops
   Bourg of, 46f, 55–58, 230
   Capitole of, 48, 57, 62
      family of, 61, 62, 183, 341
   castles around, 44, 72f–73f
      archbishop's, 109–12, 112f
   Charlemagne and, 44, 49–50, 110
   churches of, 46f, 48–50
   city life of, 57–60, 66
   clerical income in diocese of, 303
   Consuls of, 100
   duke of, 4, 16–17, 43, 52
   economy of, 54–61
   environs of, 66–69, 68f, 72f, 73f, 74–79, 109–12, 112f
   Ermengard's exile from, 338–42
   as family name, 171–72, 180, 181
   Genoa and, 90, 93–101, 99f
   Jewish community of, 16, 45, 46f
   Laras and, 22–23
   maps of, 2f, 46f, 68f, 71f, 72f, 112f
   merchants of, 60–64
   militia of, 83–87
   mining in region of, 72f, 78–79, 131
   Pisa and, 97–100, 98f
   Roman past of, 43–48, 55
   Royal Gate of, 46f, 47f, 57, 61, 62, 181
      family of, 181, 183, 341
   tax table of, 64
   Tortosa and, 83–87, 84f, 95

Narbonne (*continued*)
    Toulouse and, 52
    viscounts of, 4–5, 15f, 20, 27 (*see also specific viscounts*)
Navarre, 254, 279–80
Nice, 263, 270
Nîmes, 2f, 56, 223
    Alphonse Jordan and, 19
    bishops of, 26f, 28, 107, 207, 208
    viscounts of, 4, 19, 26f, 78, 176
Nuño Pérez, 274

Oaths
    Cathars and, 329
    of peace, 120
    of security, 134
    See also Fidelity oaths
Occitania, 2f, 4–5, 28–30
    corvées in, 158–59
    dialects of, 41
    economy of, 54–57, 66–72, 77–80, 96–101, 160–61
    fiefs in, 220, 227
    France and, 41–42
    heresies in, 286–307 (*see also* Albigensian Crusades)
    names for, 42
    as part of France, 360–62
    Raymond V and, 253–73, 276
    Roman law in, 216–17
    Sicily and, 97
    See also Provence
Odo, vct. Narbonne, 20
Orb River, 2f, 77–78
Orkeyinga Saga, 2–3
Orvieto, 350
Otto of Brunswick, 355

Paris, Treaty of (1229), 322
Paschal III, pope, 264
Paulus Sergius, bp. of Narbonne, 49–52
Peace and Truce of God, 120–21, 283–85
Pedro de Lara, vct. Narbonne, 15f, 23, 218, 274
    John Bistani and, 61–62
    entourage of, 340–41
    Ermengard and, 338–40, 342
Pedro Gonzalez, 22
Peire, brother of K. Alfons II, 20f, 253, 266, 277, 331, 333
    renamed Ramon Berenguer IV, 275
Peire, k. Aragon, 20f, 347, 355, 360
Peire Cardenal, 58
Peire d'Alvernhe, 6
Peire Rogier, 6–10
Peire Vidal, 235–36, 342–43
Pelapol family, 178, 180
Per venerabilem, 355–56

Peter, bp. of Rodez, 177
Peter Belhomme, 24
Peter Berenger, 14
Peter Bermund of Sauve, 266
Peter Damiani, 290, 292
Peter Guitard, 140, 154
Peter Margalonis, 62, 182
Peter Mint-master, 14, 17
Peter of Anduze, 21
Peter of Castelnau, 348, 353–54, 357
Peter of Minerve, 14, 17, 21, 24, 174
Peter of Montbrun, 14, 17
Peter of Nebian, 233
Peter of Pavia, 308, 318, 320
Peter of Raissac, 151–58, 161, 166–67, 183
    fiefs of, 228–29
Peter of Vaux-de-Cernay, 348
Peter of Villeneuve, 181
Peter Olivier of Termes, 177, 222–23
Peter Raymond of Narbonne, 73, 96, 174, 216, 218, 255
    children of, 169–70
    inheritance of, 168
    wife of, 168–69
    will of, 168–72
Peter William of Mauremont, 140, 142
Peter William of Pignan, 233
Petrarch, 3, 42
Petronilla, q. Aragon, 253
Pexiora, 139–43
Peyriac-Minervois, 135–38
Philip II, k. France, 260, 332, 333, 360
    Innocent III and, 353–55, 361
Philip of Swabia, 355
Philippa, heiress of Toulouse, 4, 18f, 25, 33
Pignan, 233
Piphiles, 296, 314, 322. *See also* Cathars
Pisa
    alliances of, 83
    Genoa and, 88–93, 97
    Narbonne and, 97–100, 98f
Poitiers, 33, 258, 260, 288
    Alphonse Jordan and, 33
    bishop of, 279, 308, 320
    See also William IX, duke of Aquitaine; Philippa
Polverellus of Auriac, 199–204
Poncia of Coumiac, 132–35, 180
Pons d'Arsac, abp. Narbonne, 308, 319–20
    Ermengard and, 133, 319
Pons of Auriac, 135–39, 199–200, 202
Pons of Olargues, 174
Pons of Villanova, 151–53
Posquières family, 115–16, 118
Potestativum, 131–34, 138. *See also* Lordship
Primogeniture, 170–71, 352
    Occitan wills and, 28–29
    shared inheritance vs., 73

Private life, 12, 202, 234–35
Property rights, 129–31, 134
    love and, 233
    multiple lordships and, 139–43
    over people, 147–50
    tenants and, 136–38, 143
    title deeds and, 156
    of women, 174
    See also Lordship
Provence
    Barcelona and, 4, 17–18, 236, 261, 337
    counts of, 4, 20f, 30
    Kingdom of Burgundy and, 32
    major ports of, 90
    Peire Vidal on, 235–36
    Toulouse and, 18f
    See also Occitania
Provisions. *See Albergum*
Publicani, 295–97, 322. *See also* Cathars
Puisserguier, 213

Quarante, abbey of, 132–35, 342
Queille, 195, 196f
"Questions of John at a Secret Supper," 299
Quista, 150, 151, 159, 164, 225

Raimbaut de Vaqueiras, 203, 212
Raimbaut d'Orange, 242
Raimon de Miraval, 238, 240–41
Rainier of Ponza, 349
Ralph of Coggeshall, 297
Ralph of Diceto, 267
Ramihrdus, 292
Ramon Berenguer I, ct. Barcelona, 20f, 85, 86
Ramon Berenguer II, ct. Barcelona, 15f, 20f, 85
    See also Mahalt
Ramon Berenguer III, ct. Barcelona, 17, 20f, 85
    Alphonse Jordan and, 261–62
    Bernard Ato and, 192, 197
    marriage to Douce of Provence, 25, 31–32
    See also Mahalt
Ramon Berenguer IV, ct. Barcelona, 20f, 274, 277
    advisors of, 253
    death of, 213, 214, 253–55
Ramon Berenguer III, ct. Provence, 253, 263, 270
Ramon Borrell, ct. Barcelona, 26f, 27
    Genoese and, 85, 87, 94
Rangard of La Marche, 26f, 27, 194
Raoul de Cambrai, 201–2
Raymond, ct. Carcassonne, 25–26
Raymond IV, ct. Toulouse (Raymond of Saint-Gilles), 4, 16–17, 17, 18f, 115, 189
    Narbonne and, 40, 42–43, 50–51
    Philippa and, 33

Raymond V, ct. Toulouse, 18f, 213–14, 252
    Alexander of Cîteaux and, 286, 308
    Alfons II and, 263–64, 270–71, 333
    Catalan alliance and, 263–70
    Cathar heresy and, 286–87, 296, 308, 317–18, 322–23
    death of, 340, 347
    documents from, 5
    empire of, 253–73
        decline of, 277–78, 322
    Ermengard and, 34, 100, 214–16, 265, 272–73, 276, 329–30
    Frederick Barbarossa and, 263–66
    Genoa and, 270
    Henry II and, 267–70, 288
    Louis VII and, 260
    mercenaries of, 279–80, 334
    Narbonne claim by, 52
    occupation of Narbonne, 274–75
    Peter Maurandus and, 314–15
    Pons d'Arsac and, 319–20
    Richard the Lionheart and, 333–34
    Trencavels and, 23–24, 266, 333–34
    in troubadour poetry, 4–5
Raymond VI, ct. Toulouse, 18f, 26f, 347, 348
    abdication of, 360
    betrothal of, 263, 265
    Ermengard's will and, 338
    Innocent III and, 357
    in troubadour poetry, 4–5
    wife of, 266
    William of Montpellier and, 337
Raymond VII, ct. Toulouse, 360
Raymond Arnaldi, 181
Raymond Berenger, vct. of Narbonne, 15f, 176
    Archbishop Guifred and, 110–14
    death of, 113
Raymond Gaucelin, 134
Raymond Leolder. *See* Raymond Toll-taker
Raymond of Chateauneuf, 308–9
Raymond of Laredorte, 176
Raymond of Niort, 194, 195, 196f. *See also* Bernard Ato II and III
Raymond of Ouveilhan, 172–74, 178
Raymond of Poitiers, ct. Antioch, 257
Raymond of Saint-Gilles. *See* Raymond IV, ct. Toulouse
Raymond of Salles, 173, 218
Raymond of Tréville, 183
Raymond of Turenne, 316
Raymond Pons, ct. of Toulouse, 27
Raymond Roger, ct. of Foix, 335, 340
Raymond Toll-taker, 172, 414n. 47
Razès, 4
Reconciliation, 199–219
    in epics, 201–2
    use of force and, 210

Reginald, bp. of Bath, 308, 316, 318
Requisitions, 150, 151, 159, 164, 225
Rhone River valley, 2f, 86
  Genoa and, 97
  Toulouse and, 17–18
Richard, abp. Narbonne, 15f, 114–15,
    144–46, 213
  alberga and, 160
  Aymeri II and, 206–12
  Bernard Ato, vct. of Béziers and, 221
  fiefs of, 221–23
Richard the Lionheart, 1, 268, 270, 331
  Aquitaine and, 332–34
  genealogy of, 18f
  Raymond V and, 268–70, 288, 333–34
  in troubadour poetry, 4–5
Ricsovendis of Termes, 176
Rituals
  for *albergum*, 163
  of conflict resolution, 201–2, 212
  to detect heretics, 315
  with fiefs, 224–25, 232
  oath taking, 192–94
Rixendis de Perez, 13
Roanvaldr, earl of Orkneys, 2–3
Robert Guiscard, 15f, 27
Robert of Arbrissel, 290–92
Robert of Torigny, 322
Rodez, 2f, 43, 115, 116, 120
Roger, vct. Béziers, 18–19, 161, 164, 168, 177
  accused of heresy, 316–17, 319, 322
  Adelais, wife of, 265
  Alfons II and, 275–76, 334
  death of, 340, 347
  Ermengard and, 174, 265, 266, 320, 335
  excommunication of, 317
  gift of Magrie to Knights Hospitalers,
    138–39
  son of, 347
Roger Bernard, ct. Foix, 26f, 334–35
Roger Raymond, ct. Foix, 340
Roman law
  categories of lordship and, 230–31
  common good in, 147
  differences of sale value in, 226
  Italian schools of, 203, 217
  villages as corporations in, 167
  women in, 216–18

Saint-Antoine of Toulouse, 151–55
Saint-Gilles, 2f, 101
  counts of, 4, 18f, 43, 115
  Genoa and, 89–91, 97
  See also Toulouse, counts of
Saint-Mary-of-Cassan, 178
Saint-Pierre-de-Lec, 178
Saint-Pons-de-Thomières, 135–39, 161,
  164

Saints
  family, 106–7
  gifts to, 92, 106–7
  Last Judgment and, 225–26
  oath taking rituals and, 193
  relics of, 113
Saissac family, 204
Salles, 111, 112f
Salt-making, 69–70
Salt taxes, 69, 110, 145, 208. *See also* Taxes
Salvius (saint), 106, 107
Sanç, brother of K. Alfons II, 20f, 253, 333
Sancha of Castile, 254, 270
Sancho Ramirez, k. Aragon, 33
San Lorenzo of Genoa, 92
Saptis, Bardine, 14, 17
Saragossa, 85
Savoy, counts of, 267, 269
Senhals, 9
Serfdom, 149–84
  corvées and, 158–59
  honor and, 158–67
  markers of, 157, 159, 164
  recognition of, 150–58
  tenants and, 136–38, 143
  See also Lordship
Sexuality, 233
  Cathars and, 297, 299–302, 319
  Christian clergy and, 312–13
Sheep herding, 70–72
Shipbuilding, 85
Sicily, 97, 101, 351, 357
Sigean, 111, 112f, 179, 181, 183, 221
Simon of Montfort, 75, 358–61
Simony, 208, 297
  heresy of, 51, 106, 181, 292
Slavery, 149. *See also* Serfdom
Song of Roland, 49
Southern, R. W., 129
Stephania of les Baux, 30–33, 251
Stephen of Tournai, 320
Stephen Udalger, 161, 166–67
Suger, abbot of Saint-Denis, 257, 258

Tarn River valley, 2f, 19
Tarragona, 50–52, 85, 223
Tascha, 135, 147, 227
Taxes
  agrarium, 227
  beuraticum, 131
  botaticum, 208–9
  on clerics, 302–5
  compras, 209, 210
  on draft animals, 120–21
  salt, 69, 110, 145, 208
  tascha, 135, 147, 227
  wedding, 225
  See also Tolls

Termes family, 177, 203–4, 221–23, 359
Textiles, 57, 70, 71f, 156
Thomas Becket, 260, 269, 318
Tibors de Proensa, 246
Tolls, 82, 87, 107, 131, 145, 209, 230
  dispute with Berenger of Puisserguier over,
    213–18
  table of tolls (1153), 57–58, 64
  on via Domitia, 213
  See also Taxes
Tòlta, 150, 164, 225
Tortosa, 83–87, 91–97, 223
  sieges of, 85–87, 91, 97, 251
Tosetus of Toulouse, 153
Toulouse, 18f
  Cathars of, 318
  consulate of, 314
  counts of, 16–25, 322
    Barcelona and, 17–18, 97, 251–52, 255
    bishops and, 118
    Genoa and, 91
    Narbonne and, 52
    in Rhone valley, 17–18, 18f
    Trencavels and, 27
    See also specific counts
  Eleanor of Aquitaine and, 4, 30–34
  Henry II and, 4, 34, 214, 256–60
  heretics of, 288, 320, 322, 324–25
  Poitiers and, 4, 33
  Roman roads of, 33
  as Visigoth capital, 42
Trèbes family, 183
Trencavel family, 26f
  Albigensian Crusades and, 75, 357–59
  Alfons II and, 275–76
  Alphonse Jordan and, 17–19
  archives of, 5–6
  Bremund, bp. Béziers, and, 145–46
  Carcassonne and, 53, 197
  counts of Barcelona and, 53, 197
  counts of Foix and, 264–65, 334–35
  Ermengard and, 19, 176, 180, 252
  fidelity oaths to, 194–97
  as heretics, 317–19, 322, 329
  justices of, 145–46
  matriarchs of, 25–27
  mines of, 78–79
  origins of, 27
  Raymond V and, 23–24, 266, 333–34
  Raymond VI and, 357–58
  in troubadour poetry, 4–5
  See also names of individual family members
Trencavel, Raymond, 18–21
  Ademar of Murviel and, 277
  assassination of, 264
  Berenger of Puisserguier and, 213
  Ermengard and, 69–70, 78–79, 131, 174,
    252

Escafredi family and, 147, 192
  imprisonment of, 23–24
  oaths to, 194–95
  Polverellus of Auriac and, 199–204
  salt tax and, 69–70
  Second Crusade and, 256
  serfs of, 150–51
Trencavel, Raymond Roger, 347, 348, 357–58
Tréville family, 183–84
Trobairitz, 10, 179, 242f, 242–46
Troubadour poetry
  adultery in, 10
  allegories in, 220
  anger in, 199–202, 244
  fidelity in, 212, 236–38
  formulaics of, 24, 247
  honor in, 203
  joy in, 199, 203, 238, 278
  language of, 247
  legal Latin and, 214
  lordship in, 153
  music and, 242f
  names in, 9, 23
  politics in, 235–36, 242, 246–47
  pride in, 244–45
  razos of, 9
  realism of, 8–11
  rhyme schemes of, 243–44
  scandalmongers in, 257
  themes in, 8–11
Troubadours, 3
  Ermengard and, 6–8, 342–43, 362
  "I" of, 8–10, 244–47
  language of, 41
  patrons of, 4–5, 240, 241, 333
  vidas of, 4–5, 9–10
  women, 10, 179, 242f, 242–46
  See also specific ones, e.g., Marcabru
Trouvères, 3
Turin, 261, 267

Universitas, 167
Urban II, pope, 51, 52
Urban III, pope, 325
Urgel
  bishopric of, 110
Urraca, q. Castile, 22
Usury, 316, 325
  Church campaign against, 62
  mortgages and, 60
  See also Loans
Uzès, 21
  lords of, 18f, 115–16

Vaissete, Joseph, 15–16
Vernacular languages, 3, 193, 318
Via Domitia, 43, 48, 57, 68f, 81, 114
  tolls on, 213

Victor IV, pope, 214, 215, 251, 253
Villedaigne, 111, 112f
Villemagne, abbey of, 78
Villeneuve family, 181
Villerouge, 222
Visigoths, 42, 48
Viterbo, 350–51, 357
Volta family, 97

Wagon-Train of Nîmes (poem), 223
Waldensians, 122, 326, 327. *See also* Heresy
Walter Map, 280–82
Walter of Brienne, 351–52
"Weavers," 295, 296, 322. *See also* Cathars
Wedding tax, 225
Widows, 25–30, 170, 216–18
Will(s), 28–29
  Arnold Siguini's, 54, 56–57
  Bernard Ato's, 28–29
  dowries and, 28
  Ermengard's, 338, 339f, 341–42
  food provisions in, 161–62
  heiresses and, 25–30, 170, 216–18
  Occitan, 28–29
  Peter Raymond's, 168–72
  primogeniture and, 28–29
  William VI's, 28, 170, 352
William, vct. Alaigne, 194, 195, 196f
William IV, ct. Toulouse, 4, 18f, 33
William V, lord of Montpellier, 233, 352
William VI, lord of Montpellier, 18–19, 30,
    32, 96, 234–35, 277
  Genoese and, 90, 94–97
  revolt of Montpellier agains, 19, 90, 274
  will of, 28, 170, 352
William VII, lord of Montpellier, 170, 233,
    352
  agent of Alfons II, 254–55, 264

death of, 266
Raymond V and, 260, 265–66
William VIII, lord of Montpellier, 170, 271,
    275, 277, 334, 335, 347
  Innocent III and, 352–53, 355–56
  Raymond VI and, 337
  seal of, 246f
William IX, lord of Montpellier, 353
William IX, duke of Aquitaine, 4, 25, 141,
    246
  poetry of, 8, 10, 41
William X, duke of Aquitaine, 4, 18f, 25
William Arnold of Béziers, 277
William Bistani, 60–64
William Fuller, 156–58, 161
William Letericus, 254–55
William Minter, 61–62, 64, 340
William of Dourgne, 316
William of Durban, 174–76, 189, 255
  Ermengard's conflict with, 205–6
William of Firminum, 151–52
William of La Grace Dieu, 151–52
William of Laredorte, 174–77
William of Minerve, 21
William of Newburgh, 257
William of Niort, 194
William of Poitiers, 4, 174, 179, 183, 205,
    246, 255, 335
William of Puylaurens, 321, 323
William of Sabran, 277
William of Tudela, 233, 357–58
William Peter of Albi, 321
William Raymond, 29, 87, 94, 253
William Raymond, *dapifer*, 87, 91, 94, 96,
    253
William the Shortnose, 114
William Tudela, 348
Witches, 297. *See also* Heresy

VOLUMES IN THE SERIES
Conjunctions of Religion and Power in the Medieval Past
edited by Barbara H. Rosenwein

Medieval Cruelty: Varieties of Perception from Late Antiquity to the Early Modern Period
by Daniel Baraz

Unjust Seizure: Conflict, Interest, and Authority in an Early Medieval Society
by Warren Brown

Ermengard of Narbonne and the World of the Troubadours
by Fredric L. Cheyette

Speaking of Slavery: Color, Ethnicity, and Human Bondage in Italy
by Steven A. Epstein

Surviving Poverty in Medieval Paris: Gender, Ideology, and the Daily Lives of the Poor
by Sharon Farmer

The Bishop's Palace: Architecture and Authority in Medieval Italy
by Maureen C. Miller